John

VOLUME 2

Reformed Expository Commentary

A Series

Series Editors

Richard D. Phillips
Philip Graham Ryken

Testament Editors

Iain M. Duguid, Old Testament
Daniel M. Doriani, New Testament

John

RICHARD D. PHILLIPS

VOLUME 2

JOHN 11–21

P U B L I S H I N G
P.O. BOX 817 • PHILLIPSBURG • NEW JERSEY 08865-0817

Unless otherwise indicated, Scripture quotations are from The Holy Bible, English Standard Version, copyright © 2007 by Crossway, a publishing ministry of Good News Publishers. Used by permission. All rights reserved.

Scripture quotations marked (NIV) are from the HOLY BIBLE, NEW INTERNATIONAL VERSION®. NIV®. Copyright © 1973, 1978, 1984 by International Bible Society. Used by permission of Zondervan Publishing House. All rights reserved.

Italics within Scripture quotations indicate emphasis added.

ISBN: 978-1-59638-180-3 (cloth)
ISBN: 978-1-62995-093-8 (ePub)
ISBN: 978-1-62995-094-5 (Mobi)

Printed in the United States of America

Library of Congress Cataloging-in-Publication Data

Phillips, Richard D. (Richard Davis), 1960-
  John / Richard D. Phillips. -- 1st ed.
      volumes cm. -- (Reformed expository commentary)
  Includes bibliographical references and index.
  ISBN 978-1-59638-180-3 (cloth)
  1. Bible. John--Commentaries. I. Title.
  BS2615.53.P54 2013
  226.5'077--dc23
                          2013031308

To Sharon
In loving gratitude for companionship in life and partnership in ministry

and to Christ the Word
"In him was life, and the life was the light of men" (John 1:4).

CONTENTS

Part 4: Witness and Ministry among Believers

71. Love Delayed (John 11:1–6)   5

72. A Timely Lesson (John 11:7–16)   14

73. I Am the Resurrection and the Life (John 11:17–26)   24

74. Two Portraits of Faith (John 11:27–32)   33

75. Jesus Wept (John 11:33–37)   43

76. Lazarus Raised (John 11:38–44)   52

77. One Man to Die (John 11:45–57)   61

78. Fragrant Devotion (John 12:1–11)   71

79. Behold, Your King Is Coming! (John 12:12–19)   80

80. The Hour of Glory (John 12:20–26)   91

81. Lifted Up (John 12:27–34)   101

82. Darkness and Light (John 12:35–43)   111

83. Christ Vindicated (John 12:44–50)   121

Part 5: Jesus' Parting Ministry to the Disciples

84. Love to the End (John 13:1)   133

85. Washing the Disciples' Feet (John 13:2–11)   143

86. Blessed Servanthood (John 13:12–17)   153

87. One to Betray (John 13:18–30)   163

88. A New Commandment (John 13:31–35)   173

89. Before the Rooster Crows (John 13:36–38)   183

Contents

90. In My Father's House (John 14:1–3)   193

91. I Am the Way, the Truth, and the Life (John 14:4–6)   202

92. Whoever Has Seen Me (John 14:7–11)   212

93. Greater Works Than These (John 14:12)   222

94. Ask in My Name (John 14:13–14)   232

95. If You Love Me (John 14:15)   241

96. The Other Helper (John 14:16–17)   251

97. Because I Live (John 14:18–24)   261

98. My Peace I Give (John 14:25–31)   271

99. I Am the True Vine (John 15:1–5)   281

100. Abiding in Christ (John 15:6–11)   291

101. No Greater Love (John 15:12–17)   301

102. Hated without a Cause (John 15:18–25)   311

103. Witness to the World (John 15:26–16:4)   322

104. The Spirit's Ministry to the World (John 16:4–11)   333

105. The Spirit's Ministry to the Church (John 16:12–15)   343

106. In a Little While (John 16:16–22)   353

107. Praying to the Father (John 16:23–27)   363

108. Christ Overcoming the World (John 16:28–33)   373

Part 6: Jesus' High Priestly Prayer

109. The Hour of Glory (John 17:1–2)   385

110. Eternal Life (John 17:3)   395

111. Mission Accomplished (John 17:4–5)   405

112. The People of Christ (John 17:6–8)   416

113. The High Priestly Prayer (John 17:9–13)   426

114. Sanctified in the Truth (John 17:14–17)   436

115. Sent into the World (John 17:18–19)   446

116. Christian Unity (John 17:20–23)   456

117. To See My Glory (John 17:24)   466

118. God's Love in Us (John 17:25–26)   477

Part 7: Crisis and Conquest through the Cross

119. The Arrest of Jesus (John 18:1–11)   489

120. Before the Rooster Crowed (John 18:12–27)   499

121. Kingdoms in Conflict (John 18:28–38)   510

122. Behold the Man! (John 18:38–19:6)   521

123. Authority to Judge (John 19:6–12)   531

124. King of the Jews (John 19:13–22)   541

125. Beneath the Cross (John 19:23–27)   552

126. The Death of the Savior (John 19:28–30)   563

127. Why Did Jesus Die? (John 19:30)   573

128. Finished! (John 19:30)   584

129. On Him Whom They Pierced (John 19:31–37)   594

130. Secret Disciples (John 19:38–39)   604

131. A Garden Burial (John 19:38–42)   614

132. Inside the Empty Tomb (John 20:1–10)   624

133. To My Father and Your Father (John 20:11–18)   635

134. The Greatest News Ever Heard (John 20:18)   645

135. The Crucified Christ Preaching (John 20:19–21)   655

136. Power and Authority (John 20:22–23)   665

137. Thomas Believing (John 20:24–29)   675

138. That You May Believe (John 20:30–31)   684

139. Back to Galilee (John 21:1–14)   693

140. Peter Restored (John 21:15–17)   703

141. The Original and Eternal Call (John 21:18–25)   714

Contents

Select Bibliography of Commentaries Cited or Consulted   725

Index of Scripture   729

Index of Subjects and Names   753

John

THE PASSION OF CHRIST

PART 4

Witness and Ministry among Believers

71

Love Delayed

John 11:1—6

When Jesus heard it he said, "This illness does not lead to death.
It is for the glory of God, so that the Son of God may be glorified
through it." (John 11:4)

One of the chief blessings of life is close friends. The ancient Roman statesman Cicero wrote, "With the exception of wisdom, I am inclined to think nothing better than [friendship] has been given to man by the immortal gods."[1] A true friendship is not spoiled by the changing of seasons or the turning of fortunes. The Bible says, "A friend loves at all times" (Prov. 17:17). Especially in times of trouble, friends are close by, comforting with their presence, strengthening with their words, and sympathizing with their hearts.

We might wonder whether the Son of God would need friends or whether his being the Messiah would keep Jesus from human intimacy. But Jesus seems to have enjoyed friendship very much. Perhaps his closest friends, whose company he most enjoyed and whose home was most comfortable to him, were the three siblings who lived together in the town of Bethany: Mary, Martha, and Lazarus.

1. Quoted in George Selde, *The Great Thoughts* (New York: Ballantine, 1985), 79–80.

5

John 11 begins the last section of John's Gospel before Jesus' final entry into Jerusalem. It was an interlude from his public affairs and from his increasing conflict with the religious leaders. It was also a time of ministry to those closest to him, as Jesus sought to strengthen the faith of his friends and disciples before taking up the cross.

MARY, MARTHA, AND LAZARUS

Since we will be spending time with this family from Bethany, it is a good idea for us to get to know them. This family is mentioned in all four Gospels, and they seem to have been personally close to Jesus. We don't know how they met him or how long they had known him. What we do learn is the difference that Jesus made in their lives.

First, we might consider Lazarus, whose name is made famous by the miracle recorded in this chapter. Lazarus might have been a quiet man; not one of the Gospels quotes him as saying anything. Quiet people sometimes think they make little difference, but Lazarus shows us how wrong they are. Each of us should know how to tell others about Jesus. But Lazarus shows us what a difference we can make simply by showing the power of Christ in our lives.

During the time span of this chapter, Lazarus dies and is raised from the dead. Afterward, his family held a banquet in Jesus' honor. Lazarus was seated with Jesus, and John tells us that a large crowd came to see them both—perhaps hundreds or even thousands of people. So powerful was Lazarus's witness that the hostile authorities decided to kill not only Jesus, but Lazarus, too, "because on account of him many of the Jews were going away and believing in Jesus" (John 12:11). Like him, you may not be a great speaker for Jesus, but, as James Montgomery Boice reminds us, "You should be especially careful that your life demonstrates the reality of that [spiritual] resurrection that Jesus has performed in you so that others might turn to him and believe in him because of what they see."[2]

Another family member was Martha, who was made famous by Luke's record of an earlier meeting at their house. Jesus was there, and Martha was working hard to take care of things. But her sister, Mary, was sitting

2. James Montgomery Boice, *The Gospel of John*, 5 vols. (Grand Rapids: Baker, 1999), 3:810.

at Jesus' feet and listening to his teaching. Martha complained, "Lord, do you not care that my sister has left me to serve alone? Tell her then to help me" (Luke 10:40). Martha was a classic example of someone who serves but is caught up in herself. "My . . . me . . . me," she complained, just as many people do today. Jesus reproved Martha, pointing out that Mary was doing the more important thing by spending time with him.

If Lazarus's witness was transformed by his resurrection, it seems that Martha's attitude was also changed. I say this because in the next chapter we see her serving again while Jesus and others recline at the table. But this time there is no complaining! The resurrection of her brother seems to have turned her mind away from her petty problems and directed her service as a joyful gift to the Lord.

Lazarus gave his witness to Jesus, and Martha gave her service. But the third family member, Mary, gave herself to Jesus. Practically every time we see Mary, she is sitting at Jesus' feet, which in that day was the proper posture of a disciple. This probably indicates an awareness of his deity, as well as the wholehearted submission of her life. In Luke 10, Mary is seated at Jesus' feet. In John 11, when Jesus arrives at their home, Mary falls at his feet (John 11:32). And in the banquet that occurs afterward, she washes his feet with her hair. Mary loved Jesus as her Lord and Savior, and she gave him the gift of her complete devotion.

Mary teaches us another important point. The first time we find her sitting at Jesus' feet, Luke says that she was listening to his teaching (Luke 10:39). It is because she opened her mind to his Word that Mary more than anyone else seems to have understood Jesus. She was the quickest to learn the lesson of his miracles and the most fervent to worship him. Learning the truth from Jesus' teaching, she surrendered her life to him and poured out her most costly gifts at his feet.

OUR PRIVILEGE IN PRAYER

John 11 starts Jesus off where chapter 10 left him—across the Jordan where John the Baptist had begun his ministry. While he was there, Lazarus became ill. So Mary and Martha sent word to Jesus: "Lord, he whom you love is ill" (John 11:3).

The sisters might have been surprised that this could happen, since they use the word *behold*. Some English translations leave this out, but the Greek text reads, "Lord, behold, he whom you love is ill." If this indicates surprise on their part, it should not have, since even those who are very close to Jesus will suffer the trials of this life. People sometimes conclude that an illness or other affliction indicates a separation from God's affection. But the sisters specifically identify Lazarus as one who was loved by Jesus and yet was ill. Charles Spurgeon comments, "The love of Jesus does not separate us from the common necessities and infirmities of human life. Men of God are still men. The covenant of grace is not a charter of exemption from consumption, or rheumatism, or asthma."[3]

But this does not mean that Christians are just like everyone else, because we have the privilege of prayer. Praying involves more than making petitions of the Lord; it rightly includes adoration, confession, and thanksgiving as well. But when it comes to asking of the Lord, Mary's and Martha's example shows three important points about prayer.

First, they made their need known to the Lord. They simply brought the matter to Jesus, as we should do in our prayers. John Calvin states: "We are not forbidden a longer form of prayer; but the chief thing is to cast our cares and whatever troubles us into the bosom of God, that He may supply the remedy. This is how those women act towards Christ. They explain their trouble to Him intimately and look for relief from Him."[4] This is the great comfort that any believer can and should seek in times of anxiety, since, as the psalm says, "God is our refuge and strength, a very present help in trouble" (Ps. 46:1).

We are not told by John, but sending this message to Jesus must have brought a great peace to Martha's and Mary's souls. No doubt they were doing everything they could for their brother. A physician would be there, with the sisters close at hand. But we are not doing all we can until we pray to the Lord. Christians should make use of every good and natural means available: in sickness, we should secure the best medical care; when needing a job, we should look through the advertisements or see a job counselor; in legal trouble, we should hire the best attorney. But as J. C. Ryle writes:

3. Charles H. Spurgeon, *Metropolitan Tabernacle Pulpit* (London: Banner of Truth, 1971), 26:73.
4. John Calvin, *New Testament Commentaries*, trans. T. H. L. Parker, 12 vols. (Grand Rapids: Eerdmans, 1959), 5:2.

In all our doing, we must never forget that the best and ablest and wisest Helper is in heaven, at God's right hand. Like afflicted Job, our first action must be to fall on our knees and worship. Like Hezekiah, we must spread our matters before the Lord. Like the holy sisters at Bethany, we must send up a prayer to Christ. Let us not forget, in the hurry and excitement of our feelings, that none can help like Him, and that He is merciful, loving, and gracious.[5]

Second, we should note the basis on which the sisters sent their prayer: "He whom you love." They did not appeal to Jesus on the basis of their love or Lazarus's love for him, but on the basis of his love for them. Not that they did not love Jesus. "They did love him," Boice writes, "but they knew that their love for Jesus would never in a million years be an adequate basis for their appeal. . . . [This] is the only grounds that any of us can ever have in approaching the Almighty."[6]

This principle holds in every area of salvation. God did not send his Son because the world loved him. For the world does not love God. But the Bible proclaims, "God so loved the world, that he gave his only Son" (John 3:16). "In this is love," John says, "not that we have loved God but that he loved us and sent his Son to be the propitiation for our sins" (1 John 4:10). Even our love for God stems from his love for us. John adds, "We love because he first loved us" (1 John 4:19). Therefore, Matthew Henry says, "Our love to him is not worth speaking of, but his to us can never be enough spoken of."[7]

Knowing this will provide a great encouragement to our prayers. We feel distant from God because of our cool hearts and mixed performance. But our prayers are offered not in our own name but in Jesus' name, that is, on the basis of his perfect life and saving work. Our prayers are accepted because God loves us, a love that he has proved once for all by offering his Son for our sins on the cross.

Third, having made their need known to the Lord, Lazarus's sisters seem to have left the manner of his reply up to Jesus. I do not deny that what they wanted was implied: they wanted Jesus to come immediately. But what they said was simply, "Lord, he whom you love is ill" (John 11:3). The women knew

---

5. J. C. Ryle, *Expository Thoughts on the Gospels: John*, 3 vols. (Edinburgh: Banner of Truth, 1999), 2:258.

6. Boice, *John*, 3:816.

7. Matthew Henry, *Commentary on the Whole Bible*, 6 vols. (Peabody, MA: Hendrickson, 2009), 5:842.

enough about Jesus that they did not weary him with advice or complaints, but simply placed the matter into his loving hands and left it to him.

The better we know God—in his holiness, power, wisdom, and love—the more we will do the same. The God who has already sent us his very best in his Son is certain to work all things for the good of those who love him (Rom. 8:28).

The Love That Waits

Jesus' response to this message is one of the best examples of God's approach to answering our prayers. The first thing it shows is *his perspective* on our trials. "When Jesus heard it he said, 'This illness does not lead to death'" (John 11:4).

At first glance, this statement might seem odd and might seem to call Jesus' competence into question, for the simple reason that Lazarus's illness did lead to death. After all, just two days later, Jesus informed his disciples that Lazarus had died. How, then, could Jesus say that Lazarus's illness "does not lead to death"?

The answer is that Jesus knew both his ability and his intention to travel to Bethany and raise Lazarus from the grave, just as he has pledged the resurrection of every believer. Whatever affliction the Lord may be pleased to allow us to endure, Jesus knows that it leads not to death but to eternal life. There is a resurrection awaiting every believer. Even our bodies will be raised in glory. Whenever a Christian dies, fellow believers can and should respond, "This will not lead to death!" "He will be raised!" This is what Paul said: "What is sown is perishable; what is raised is imperishable. It is sown in dishonor; it is raised in glory. It is sown in weakness; it is raised in power. It is sown a natural body; it is raised a spiritual body" (1 Cor. 15:42–44). The great doctrine taught in this chapter—the Christian doctrine of the resurrection—is a wonderful source of comfort in affliction and especially in the face of death.

The same might be said of other trials. We might be subject to injustice now, but in the end believers will be justified by God. We might suffer humiliation, but it leads to glorification. We might struggle in poverty, but out of this come heavenly riches. We might be lonely and sorrowful, but by trusting in Jesus—who secured every spiritual blessing for us through his death and resurrection—we will have fellowship with God and with other believers and be filled with joy. Jesus' words might be engraved on every Christian tombstone and emblazoned on every Christian trial: "This does not lead to death."

Jesus' response to Lazarus's illness shows not only his perspective on our trials, but also *his plan* for delivering us from trouble. It is a plan that troubles many believers and causes some to doubt his love. But John 11:5–6 tells us Jesus' plan for responding to this plea: "Now Jesus loved Martha and her sister and Lazarus. So, when he heard that Lazarus was ill, he stayed two days longer in the place where he was."

What a remarkable combination this is: Jesus loved them, *so* he waited for Lazarus to die! Jesus did not wait because he was indifferent to these friends or because he was still trying to figure out how he felt about them. He loved them, so he waited.

This reminds us that the Lord works in our lives according to his timetable and his purposes. He is loving enough not to do what we want him to do but what we need him to do (whether we are aware of it or not!). We see this principle at work throughout the Bible. Faithful Joseph was tossed into a dark prison for refusing to commit a sin. There, he prayed for God's deliverance and waited. And waited. He waited for over two years. Then, according to God's own timetable—based on his wonderful plans for Joseph and the way he intended to use Joseph for his larger plans—God delivered him in a marvelous way. It was only afterward that Joseph could explain to his brothers who had betrayed him: "You meant evil against me, but God meant it for good" (Gen. 50:20). What Joseph saw by sight looking backward, we are called to see in the present by faith in God and his Word.

But this is often not easy. Kent Hughes eloquently writes:

> When a child dies in his mother's arms as she cried to God for help and the ambulance lies stalled two blocks away, we wonder if God cares. When a Christian is falsely accused and pleads with God to bring the evidence to clear him, and it is only after his reputation is ruined that the evidence comes, we wonder if God cares. When we plan some great event for God and the whole thing falls through, we wonder if God cares.[8]

8. R. Kent Hughes, *John: That You May Believe* (Wheaton, IL: Crossway, 1999), 282.

Such thoughts might have gone through Martha's and Mary's minds as they frequently looked out their window or went to stand in the doorway, expecting to see Jesus racing to their aid. "He will come," they would have assured each other. But all the while, Jesus was waiting for the thing they most feared to happen. Why the delay for those he loved?

The answer is seen in the changes that we have already noted about each of these three. Jesus intended for Lazarus to be a witness of his divine glory, and this required Lazarus to be raised from the dead. Jesus intended to transform Martha's attitude. Is there much doubt that she would have been complaining about him and how he had let her down? So Jesus wanted to change her heart. And Jesus wanted to continue teaching Mary, for there were great things about his kingdom that she barely guessed until Lazarus came walking out of the tomb. Jesus also has plans to change, transform, and enlighten us, and those plans inform his timetable in answering our prayers.

In other words, Jesus knows that there are more important things than that we should be delivered from sickness, provided with a good job, or helped out of any number of other trials. Our faith, for instance, is more important, and Jesus puts it ahead of our other needs. Our witness is more important. Our attitude is more important. Ultimately, Jesus thinks it is most important that we do what Mary did after his power was fully revealed: he wants us to lay our most costly gifts at his feet, and especially to offer the gift of our very selves.

We see, therefore, Jesus' perspective on this situation, and his plan for responding. But finally, he told his disciples *his highest purpose* in the affairs of our lives: "It is for the glory of God, so that the Son of God may be glorified through it" (John 11:4).

It is the chief end of man to glorify God. This is what truly is highest and best in all things, that the perfections of the excellencies of the glories of God should be displayed in the affairs of earth. It would have been good for Jesus to have come to Bethany in time to heal Lazarus. But the time was short for Israel; the cross lay just days ahead. Others had been healed, and the people did not believe. So Jesus did something even better: he waited for Lazarus to die, and after he had been buried in the tomb, Jesus raised him to life. John tells us the result: "Many of the Jews therefore, who had come with Mary and had seen what he did, believed in him" (John 11:45).

Are you willing for God to use your life for his glory and the salvation of others? Or do you hold lesser agendas more dear? If we resent God's glorifying himself through our trials and affliction, we will miss out on the joy and wonder that ought to be ours. God *will* glorify himself in our lives, for his glory is his chief end as well as ours. How much better for us to rejoice in all situations, knowing that God's glory is going forth through his sovereign grace for and through us.

THE DEATH THAT LEADS TO LIFE

If you find it difficult to set aside your own will for the will of God, remember that Jesus is not asking anything of you that he did not accept for himself. Jesus himself experienced this in a way that none of us ever will. Jesus was maliciously accused, unjustly convicted, and cruelly put to death. Where was his Father in all this? Did not the heavenly Father love his Son? How could God delay as the crown of thorns was placed on Jesus' head, as the nails were beaten through his hands and feet, and as Jesus suffered such torment on the cross?

The Bible answers that God had a perspective on the death of Jesus, seeing the open tomb beyond the cross. God had a plan that was higher than merely preserving Jesus from harm—a plan to save sinners such as you and me through the blood of Christ. And God had a purpose: that his own glory would be displayed in his Son, crucified as the Lamb of God for the sins of the world.

Yet even Jesus cried, "My God, my God, why have you forsaken me?" (Matt. 27:46). But he persevered in faith, knowing that his was a death that leads to life, not only for him but for all who trust in him. So he prayed, "Father, into your hands I commit my spirit!" (Luke 23:46).

Because of that life-giving death, the same will be true for us. To be a Christian means to die to sin, to worldly pleasures, and to our own agenda for our lives, and ultimately means the death of our bodies. But with Jesus, who conquered death, as our Savior, all of these will lead to life. And then the love of Jesus, our dearest Friend, which was once delayed, will be near at hand forever.

72

A Timely Lesson

John 11:7–16

Jesus answered, "Are there not twelve hours in the day? If anyone walks in the day, he does not stumble, because he sees the light of this world. But if anyone walks in the night, he stumbles, because the light is not in him." (John 11:9–10)

Many of Benjamin Franklin's sagest bits of advice dealt with time. He said, "Early to bed, early to rise, makes a man healthy, wealthy, and wise." "Remember," he added, "that time is money." Franklin also asked, "Dost thou love Life? Then do not squander Time; for that's the stuff Life is made of."[1]

The Bible also takes a keen interest in time. Paul wrote, "Look carefully then how you walk, not as unwise but as wise, making the best use of the time, because the days are evil" (Eph. 5:15–16). Jesus also spoke about time: about his own time, about our time, and about the need to define our times through faith in God.

The Time of Death

In keeping with this practicality, the Bible insists that in order to understand the time of life rightly, we must also understand the time of death.

1. George Selde, *The Great Thoughts* (New York: Ballantine, 1985), 142.

Unlike the philosophies, which either ignore death or offer only fanciful explanations, the Bible gives us definitive teaching regarding death. The French existentialist Albert Camus once said that death is philosophy's only problem. But that is quite a problem! Ravi Zacharias notes, "Anyone who has watched a loved one die understands that philosophical problem well."[2] So people wonder about death. What is it? To what does it lead? Some of the Bible's most important teaching is in answer to such questions.

In fact, the difference between Christians and non-Christians is seldom seen more clearly than in the face of death. This was certainly true in the time of the Bible. Leon Morris comments:

> For the ancient world, death was a horror, the end of everything. . . . The inscriptions on the tombs of antiquity may be impressive in their use of costly materials, but, rich as they are, they are full of hopelessness. By contrast, the roughly scratched inscriptions in the catacombs where Christians were buried abound in hope, the sure and certain hope of resurrection in Christ.[3]

The same could be said today. For most people, a funeral is only a mournful, dreadful affair. But Christians sing songs of joy and hope, rejoicing amid tears for the eternal life we have in Christ.

John 11 takes place in the context of death, the death of Lazarus, and provides some of the Bible's most elevated teaching on the Christian hope in death. Jesus presents this hope in memorable words centered on himself: "I am the resurrection and the life. Whoever believes in me, though he die, yet shall he live" (John 11:25). But earlier, while still making his way to the scene of death in Bethany, Jesus spoke other words about death that are also important. Speaking of the recently deceased Lazarus, Jesus said, "Our friend Lazarus has fallen asleep, but I go to awaken him" (11:11).

This is one of several places where the Bible describes death for believers as *sleep*. The Old Testament often speaks of "going to rest with your fathers" (Deut. 31:16 NIV). Luke says that when the martyr Stephen died, "he fell asleep" (Acts 7:60). Paul describes Christians who have died as those "who have fallen asleep in Christ" (1 Cor. 15:18). By the use of this term, the Bible distinguishes between the death that truly is death and the death that is not.

2. Ravi Zacharias, *Can Man Live without God?* (Dallas: Word, 1994), 158.
3. Leon Morris, *Reflections on the Gospel of John* (Peabody, MA: Hendrickson, 1986), 407.

Thus Jesus said, when a family summoned him to help their daughter who just had died, "The girl is not dead but sleeping" (Matt. 9:24).

What does this term *sleep* tell us about Christian death? For one thing, sleep does us no harm, and this can also be said about death in Christ. Although death is our great enemy, and although dying involves a difficult process for everyone involved, the Bible is clear that no harm comes to the Christian in death. This is why the believer in Psalm 23 speaks of walking through the valley of the "shadow" of death. Matthew Henry writes, "There is no substantial evil in it; the shadow of a serpent will not sting nor the shadow of a sword kill."[4] To be sure, it is dreadful to stand in the shadow of so fearsome an enemy as death, but Christians know that Christ has removed its sting. "He underwent the full horror that is death and in doing so transformed death, so that for his followers it is no more than sleep."[5]

But not only is sleep not harmful, it is actually beneficial. The same is true of death for the Christian. "Death," says A. W. Pink, "is simply the portal through which he passes from this scene of sin and turmoil to the paradise of bliss."[6] When Jesus told his disciples that Lazarus was sleeping, they thought only in natural terms. But what they said about sleep is true of death as well: "Lord, if he has fallen asleep, he will recover" (John 11:12). The Bible echoes this: "'Blessed are the dead who die in the Lord from now on.' 'Blessed indeed,' says the Spirit, 'that they may rest from their labors, for their deeds follow them!'" (Rev. 14:13).

Sleep is often the best prescription for those who ail from sickness or fatigue. Sleep restores the body, and the sleep of death does even more. It transforms us into glory, removing every vestige of sin and sorrow. John Owen explains:

> When, at death, the soul departs from the body, it is immediately freed from all weakness, disability, darkness, doubts and fears. The image of the first Adam will then be abolished. All physical weaknesses and infirmities will have gone for ever. . . . It is by virtue of the death of Christ alone that the souls of believers are freed by death from the presence of sin and all the effects

---

4. Matthew Henry, *Commentary on the Whole Bible*, 6 vols. (Peabody, MA: Hendrickson, 1992), 3:259.

5. Morris, *Reflections*, 407.

6. Arthur W. Pink, *Exposition of the Gospel of John* (Grand Rapids: Zondervan, 1975), 583.

that sin had wrought on their bodies, and being freed their souls flourish and expand to their fullest extent.[7]

Like sleep, the death of a Christian is also temporary. Winston Churchill expressed this conviction through his own funeral. It was a sad occasion for Britain, the end of an era. Many eyes were weeping at St. Paul's Cathedral in London as the bugler sounded the slow, mournful notes of taps. But no sooner had the last note drifted away than the bugler played again. The tune was reveille, the notes with which soldiers are called to a new day. Churchill thus reminded his mourners that death leads to a new morning. Christians likewise can know that the sleep of our own deaths will end when a trumpet call summons us to the new day of unending glory.

Paul writes of the body that awaits us: "It is sown in dishonor; it is raised in glory. It is sown in weakness; it is raised in power. It is sown a natural body; it is raised a spiritual body" (1 Cor. 15:43–44). And in these glorified bodies, God's people will engage not only in joyful worship but also in joyful work forever. James Montgomery Boice rightly comments: "Heaven will not be restful in the sense that there will be no work to do. But it will be restful in the sense that what we do will be done without toil; that is, without the strain, labor, and sorrow that work involves in this life because of sin's curse."[8] The book of Revelation's picture of heaven thus concludes, "They will need no light of lamp or sun, for the Lord God will be their light, and they will reign forever and ever" (Rev. 22:5).

When we compare death to sleep, we do not mean that the believer's conscious self is asleep between death and the final resurrection. When the apostle Paul expressed his conviction, "For to me to live is Christ, and to die is gain," he explained: "My desire is to depart and be with Christ" (Phil. 1:21, 23). Thus we believe that in death our spirits are with Christ. As Jesus said to the believing thief on the cross: "today you will be with me in Paradise" (Luke 23:43). Paul explained that for our spirits to be "away from the body" is for us to be "at home with the Lord" (2 Cor. 5:8). The Westminster Confession of Faith summarizes the whole of the Bible's teaching on our experience immediately following death: "the souls of the righteous,

---

7. John Owen, *The Glory of Christ*, abr. R. J. K. Law (Edinburgh, Banner of Truth, 1987), 124.
8. James Montgomery Boice, *The Gospel of John*, 5 vols. (Grand Rapids: Baker, 1999), 3:840.

being then made perfect in holiness, are received into the highest heavens, where they behold the face of God, in light and glory, waiting for the full redemption of their bodies" (32.1).

These are all reasons why Christians experience joy in the face of their own death, and why our grief is lifted by hope when another believer dies. Jesus, too, rejoiced in death. He said to his disciples: "Lazarus has died, and . . . I am glad" (John 11:14–15).

There are two evident reasons why Jesus was glad, the first of which is his knowledge of the resurrection. Jesus knew that Lazarus would not remain long in the grave; he was on his way to raise him. This is something that only Jesus can do. When a patient dies, doctors are helpless. But Jesus' ministry practically begins with death. He said, "Our friend Lazarus has fallen asleep, but I go to awaken him" (John 11:11).

Jesus rejoiced in Lazarus's death for a second reason: he explains, "For your sake I am glad that I was not there, so that you may believe" (John 11:15). Had Lazarus not died, Jesus "would have been deprived of this opportunity . . . to give the mightiest display of His power that He ever made prior to His own death."[9] Likewise, Christians facing death should capitalize on this once-in-a-lifetime opportunity to give their most powerful witness. We should plan our funerals to testify to our hope and give glory to the God of eternal life. Thus wrote the famous mathematician John Venn to a friend: "I have some of the best news to impart. One beloved by you has accomplished her warfare, has received an answer to her prayers, and everlasting joy rests upon her head. My dear wife, the source of my best earthly comfort for twenty years, departed on Tuesday."[10]

But it needs to be emphasized that this is true only of the believer. For those who die apart from Christ, nothing that we have said about death is true. Death is not beneficial; it is not temporary; and it leads not to a new morning of everlasting light, but to an endless night of wrathful darkness. Why is this? Jesus said, "Unless you believe [in me] you will die in your sins" (John 8:24). "Whoever believes in the Son has eternal life," Jesus promised. But "whoever does not obey the Son shall not see life, but the wrath of God remains on him" (3:36).

9. Pink, *John*, 587.
10. Quoted in J. C. Ryle, *Holiness* (Durham, UK: Evangelical Press, 1979), 190.

THE TIME OF LIFE

If we understand the time of death, we will be equipped to understand the time of life. Another Christian mathematician, Blaise Pascal, understood this, saying that he had learned to define life backward and live it forward. He meant that he first defined death and arranged his life accordingly. This is probably why Jesus gives instruction about both life and death in this passage from John 11.

Jesus had departed Jerusalem to minister beyond the Jordan, when news came that his friend Lazarus was deathly ill. But instead of racing to his side, Jesus waited for two days. Only then did he say, "Let us go to Judea again" (John 11:7). It is noteworthy that he spoke of returning to the country, Judea, instead of the town, Bethany. It seems that Jesus was testing his disciples, since it was the national leaders who sought his life. The disciples replied, "Rabbi, the Jews were just now seeking to stone you, and are you going there again?" (11:8). They had yet to understand fully who their Master was, so they feared the danger against him and, of course, themselves. Christians are similarly tested when the Lord calls us to follow paths that seem hazardous to our self-interest. But if we realize who it is who sends us, and what wisdom guides his commands, we will set off down the path without fear.

In reply, Jesus instructed them about his own perspective about the time of life. His response took the form of a rhetorical question: "Are there not twelve hours in the day?" (John 11:9). The ancient Jews divided the day up into halves, corresponding to day and night. Therefore, by saying, "Are there not twelve hours in the day?" Jesus reminded them that there is an allotted time for life and work.

This prompts at least two reflections, the first of which is that the times of our lives are granted to us by God. This point was made by the apostle Paul when he told the Athenians that God not only created all of mankind, but "determined allotted periods and the boundaries of their dwelling place" (Acts 17:26). It is God who has determined when we should live and when we should die. The great Confederate general and fervent Christian, Stonewall Jackson, also made this point after the First Battle of Manassas, when one of his aides commented on his lack of fear amid the flying bullets. Jackson replied, "My religious belief teaches me to feel as safe in battle as in bed. God has fixed the time for my death."[11]

And this was Jesus' very point in speaking to his disciples. How are we to avoid being driven from our course by the fear of human enemies and worldly threats? The answer is to realize God's sovereignty over all our affairs. We must surely exercise prudence and care, but we should never avoid doing what is necessary or right out of fear. The writer of Hebrews made this point as well to the early church as it faced Nero's deadly persecution: "For he has said, 'I will never leave you nor forsake you.' So we can confidently say, 'The Lord is my helper; I will not fear; what can man do to me?'" (Heb. 13:5–6).

But there is a corollary to this principle, namely, that we have *only* the time that God has allotted. For this reason, Christians should be diligent and bold, wasting neither time nor opportunity. This was another point that Jesus was making. His cross was fast approaching, and there was work to be done. He must do it!

We, too, have a brief time to live for God. If we are to tell others the soul-saving gospel, now is the time. If we are to display the power of Christ in our marriages, in our families, or at work, we need to do it now. If we plan to raise godly children, now are the years of their upbringing. The great French conqueror Napoleon is said to have remarked: "It may be that I will lose a battle. But I will never lose a minute!" Christians should not be frantic about life, but understanding the time of our lives, we should approach all the work that God has given us with godly urgency.

Jesus amplified this statement, adding, "If anyone walks in the day, he does not stumble, because he sees the light of this world" (John 11:9). Christians should be fearless, he means, not only because God has appointed our times, but because we live in the light of his presence.

In Jesus' time, as in much of the world today, people did not go out at night. There were no streetlights to guide them, so walking at night risked stumbling or falling. This principle remains true when it comes to living in light of God's will. When we seek our own way, we often stumble. God has revealed his Word, and if we make up our own rules, it is like walking blindly in the night. But if we take God's Word as our guide, our steps will

11. Quoted in Burke Davis, *They Called Him Stonewall: A Life of Lt. General T. J. Jackson, C.S.A.* (New York: Fairfax Press, 1988), 13.

be sure. Psalm 119:105 wisely says, "Your word is a lamp to my feet and a light to my path."

The same can be said when it comes to God's calling on our lives. Many Christians have a real sense of what God is calling them to do. They see a need and they can meet it. They see an opportunity for the gospel and they can fill it. Yet how many do not! They have their own plans, their own dreams, their own path. But when they follow them they stumble, because the path of blessing for a Christian is always the path of obedience to God's Word and of faithfulness to God's clear calling.

Jesus said, "If anyone walks in the day, he does not stumble, because he sees the light of this world." On a spiritual level, the truest meaning is found in our need to see, believe, and follow him. Do we have reasons to fear in this life? We certainly do, just as the disciples feared to return to Judea. They would have been foolish not to recognize the real threat to Jesus and themselves, just as only fools ignore the real threats to their well-being in this life. The only true answer is to walk in faith with Jesus Christ.

If we walk in the light of Christ, we find God's blessing for all the times of our life. We look to the past and our record of sins against God. What can preserve us from God's judgment? The answer is our *justification*, that is, our righteous acceptance with God through faith in Christ. Romans 3:24 instructs us that we "are justified by his grace as a gift, through the redemption that is in Christ Jesus." Our sins are forgiven through the blood of his cross, so that we look upon the time of our past and know that "in him we have redemption through his blood, the forgiveness of our trespasses, according to the riches of his grace" (Eph. 1:7). Knowing that we are justified in Christ, Christians can face life without fear.

The time of our present lives also finds meaning through faith in Jesus. What is life all about? The Bible answers with our *sanctification*. This means the process by which God is growing us in holiness. People want to know God's plan for their present lives, and the Bible tells us the first thing we need to know: "This is the will of God, your sanctification" (1 Thess. 4:3). Realizing this, the disciples would have known that if Jesus called them to Judea, any trials there would be for the sake of their perfection and growth as Christians.

Jesus also provides the answer for the time of our future. What does the future hold? Christians ask. The Bible answers with our *glorification*.

21

Whatever path we tread in this life and whatever trials or dangers we might face, if we walk with Jesus we travel into an eternal life of glory. Paul commented, "For this light momentary affliction is preparing for us an eternal weight of glory beyond all comparison" (2 Cor. 4:17).

If we will really live in the light of Christ, delighting in his presence, following wherever he leads, knowing and trusting our justification, sanctification, and glorification in him, it will transform our approach to life. The disciples preferred to remain at ease, to use the time for their own benefit and enjoyment. They wanted to shrink from hardship and danger. But Jesus would have us approach life with a holy zeal, not fearing man or wasting our lives in selfish, vain pursuits, but living and sharing his gospel, serving his kingdom, and seeking his glory.

THE TIME OF CHRIST

Jesus knew his times. He knew that when he arrived in Bethany, Lazarus would be found dead. But he planned to raise Lazarus as a display of his saving power. He also knew what would then result. While many would believe and be saved, his enemies would harden their resolve against him. The next stop was Jerusalem and the cross. Jesus was moving toward *his* death, yet that was his most fervent desire. Death for him would not be the blissful rest of peace; his death involved anguished torment, as the holy Son of God took upon himself the righteous wrath of God for the sins of all his people. But he would do it for our sakes, as the Good Shepherd who lays down his life for his sheep. And through the cross, Jesus knew he would receive the crown of eternal glory and a kingdom that would never fail.

The disciples did not yet understand. But at least one of them, Thomas, knew enough to say that even if it meant death, he wanted to be with Jesus: "So Thomas, called the Twin, said to his fellow disciples, 'Let us also go, that we may die with him'" (John 11:16). Little did Thomas appreciate that he could not share in the unique death that Jesus would suffer for his disciples' salvation. Yet his heart was that of a true disciple, wanting to share in his Master's woe as well as receiving his blessings.

In time, Thomas would get his wish. For while Jesus would take up the cross alone, it remains true that everyone who trusts in him must take up his or her own cross and follow. To be a Christian requires us to die to many things we have loved. We must die to self-righteousness, to sinful pleasure, to worldly esteem, comfort, and our own cherished plans for life.

Why would anyone do this? Because we know that God not only has allotted us our times in this life, but has also willed that everyone who lives and dies with Jesus, trusting in his blood and living by his light, will be saved. He said when he got to Bethany: "I am the resurrection and the life. Whoever believes in me, though he die, yet shall he live" (John 11:25). And then he asked the question that above all else will define the time of our death and the time of our life: "Do you believe this?" (11:26).

73

I Am the Resurrection and the Life

John 11:17–26

Jesus said to her, "I am the resurrection and the life. Whoever believes in me, though he die, yet shall he live, and everyone who lives and believes in me shall never die. Do you believe this?"
(John 11:25–26)

*I*n addition to being a book of divine revelation and astonishing theological depth, the Gospel of John is also a work of great literary art. And as is true of the Bible generally, John's craftsmanship is not at the expense of truth. Instead, it is in part through John's craftsmanship that God's message about Jesus is conveyed.

Such is the case as John records Jesus' arrival at Bethany, where the family of Lazarus was deep in mourning. John writes: "Now when Jesus came, he found that Lazarus had already been in the tomb four days. Bethany was near Jerusalem, about two miles off, and many of the Jews had come to Martha and Mary to console them concerning their brother" (John 11:17–19). There could hardly be a more potent setting for the message that Jesus came to reveal, a message about himself as the giver of resurrection life. There was Jesus' friend Lazarus, dead and buried for four days. There were the sisters, who had trusted Jesus to come and save their brother, but now mourned in bitter grief. But this was not just a private affair, for a multitude of Jews had come from nearby Jerusalem to participate in the mourning rites.

If any of them had known what Jesus intended to do, they would have agreed that this was a perfect setting. But Jesus knew that there was one more feature of this scene, for in a few days he would enter Jerusalem for his last time, beginning a week that would end with his own death on a cross, which in turn would lead to his own resurrection from the grave.

MARTHA'S ANGUISHED PLEA

Jesus traveled to Bethany at the urging of Martha and Mary to come and heal their brother. They put all their trust in Jesus, and during the desperate hours of their vigil their eyes must often have wandered to the road, looking for Jesus' appearance. Finally Jesus came, but too late. For Lazarus was dead.

When Jesus arrived, the two sisters each responded in accordance with their character: "So when Martha heard that Jesus was coming, she went and met him, but Mary remained seated in the house" (John 11:20). This matches the picture given in Luke 10:38–42, where Mary sat quietly at Jesus' feet while Martha busied herself with chores. On that occasion, Jesus applauded Mary for her quiet devotion. Here, however, it is Martha's passionate activity that is rewarded by Jesus' revelation. There is a time for quiet reflection, but there is also a time for action; by failing to go to Jesus, Mary missed out on the glorious declaration that Martha received.

Martha greeted Jesus with words that many commentators have taken as a rebuke, but that more likely simply reflect the frustration of her grieving heart: "Martha said to Jesus, 'Lord, if you had been here, my brother would not have died'" (John 11:21). Surely this statement repeated words that Martha and Mary had said to each other many times in the previous days. "When will Jesus get here?" they asked as Lazarus declined. "If only Jesus had been here," they must have wept over his dead body. It was with this in her heart that Martha raced down the road to meet Jesus: "Lord, if you had been here, my brother would not have died." William Barclay writes: "When Martha met Jesus, her heart spoke through her lips. . . . Martha would have liked to say: 'When you got our message, why didn't you come at once?'"[1]

Christians sometimes think it wrong for a believer to speak so frankly with the Lord. But God invites us to pour our hearts out to him. "[Cast] all your anxieties on him, because he cares for you," the Bible urges (1 Peter 5:7). This includes our burdens and our griefs, our questions and our frustrations. The Psalms are filled with such expressions, and many a faithful prophet cried out, "How long, O Lord, how long!" God's willingness to receive the grieving complaints of our hearts is proved by Jesus' tender ministry to Martha on the road into Bethany.

One thing I have discovered about grieving Christians is that they often lose hold of truths that they ought to know about the Lord. As believers, their broken hearts reach out to the Lord, but their grieving minds grope in shadows. We see this phenomenon in Martha's words: "if you had been here." When she cried that if only Jesus had been present Lazarus might live, she was forgetting that Jesus' divine power is not limited by space. Earlier in John's Gospel, an official asked Jesus to come and heal his ailing child. But Jesus did not even bother to make the trip: "Jesus said to him, 'Go; your son will live'" (John 4:50). When the official returned, he learned that his son had recovered at the very time Jesus had spoken. Martha might have known that, but her anguished mind lost hold of this truth. Understanding this helps us to minister to those who grieve. When eyes that are clouded by tears fail to see, and when trembling hands lose their grip on faith, our calling is not to rebuke them for unbelief but to gently remind them of the grace and truth of the Lord.

Martha displays another tendency of unbelief, namely, that of presuming on God's promises. When Martha said, "Lord, if you had been here, my brother would not have died," she assumed that the Lord willed that her brother recover. But John has informed us that this was not Jesus' intention. John wrote that "when [Jesus] heard that Lazarus was ill, he stayed two days longer in the place where he was" (John 11:6). Jesus arrived exactly when he intended to, on the fourth day of mourning. The significance of this may be revealed by an ancient Jewish tradition that the soul lingered near the body

1. William Barclay, *The Gospel of John*, 2 vols. (Philadelphia: Westminster, 1975), 2:105–6.

until after the third day, when the body began to decay. By arriving on the fourth day, Jesus intended "that there might be no doubt that Lazarus was dead and that there might therefore be no cause for doubting the miracle"[2] that he intended to perform.

In a similar way, Christians sometimes think that God has failed them when a loved one dies, or when some other grievous event takes place. But God has not promised to preserve us from death or any other trial. "It is appointed for man to die once, and after that comes judgment," states Hebrews 9:27. So until Jesus returns, it is God's will for each of us to die, suffering the curse of our race for Adam's sin (see Gen. 2:17; Rom. 5:12). The same is true for sickness, poverty, injustice, and sorrow. Jesus assured us, "In the world you will have tribulation" (John 16:33). Our faith will stand up better to grief if we remember what God has and has not promised, resting our faith where it belongs, on the teaching and promises of God's Word.

What we can be sure of is that all our trials are apportioned by the hand of a holy, good, and loving God. Paul writes, "We know that for those who love God all things work together for good, for those who are called according to his purpose" (Rom. 8:28). Precisely because we do not always feel that this is true, we need to know that it is true.

We know that Martha had not lost her faith in Jesus, not only from our insight into grief but also because of what she went on to say: "even now I know that whatever you ask from God, God will give you" (John 11:22). It is unlikely that Martha was specifically thinking of a resurrection, because later, when Jesus approaches the tomb, she tries to stop him: "Lord, by this time there will be an odor, for he has been dead four days" (11:39).

So what did Martha mean when she blurted out that God will give Jesus anything he asks? I think Martha's grieving heart simply reaches out with the faith that she can still lay hold of. She simply asks him to help as only he can do. D. A. Carson states it well: "Even now, in her bereavement, she has not lost her confidence in Jesus, and still recognizes the peculiar intimacy he enjoys with his Father, an intimacy that ensures unprecedented fruitfulness to his prayers."[3]

2. James Montgomery Boice, *The Gospel of John*, 5 vols. (Grand Rapids: Baker, 1999), 3:851.
3. D. A. Carson, *The Gospel of John* (Grand Rapids: Eerdmans, 1991), 412.

The Best Kind of Comfort

It is always good to turn to the Lord, and Jesus ministered to Martha's grief with the best kind of comfort, a promise of salvation for Lazarus: "Jesus said to her, 'Your brother will rise again' " (John 11:23).

We always want to give comfort to those who grieve, though our mouths often stumble over what to say. But Jesus has true comfort to give. We offer the important comfort of sympathy, fellowship, and love. But Jesus offers something better. He offers the comfort of a solution for that which grieves our souls: Lazarus will rise again. Mark Johnston writes, "The immediacy and the seeming finality of death are such that comfort of a unique order is needed to begin to banish its shadow."[4] This is the comfort that Jesus, and only Jesus, can give.

This means that the highest form of Christian comfort is to direct the suffering heart to Jesus. This is what Paul did in one of his letters: "We do not want you to be uninformed, brothers, about those who are asleep, that you may not grieve as others do who have no hope. For since we believe that Jesus died and rose again, even so, through Jesus, God will bring with him those who have fallen asleep" (1 Thess. 4:13–14). The best ministry to those who grieve is the ministry of God's Word, and his promises of a resurrection for those who believe in Christ. Our knowledge of life beyond the grave does not remove the grief from death, but it does restore the hope to grief.

Martha was struggling through this, and she replied, "I know that he will rise again in the resurrection on the last day" (John 11:24). This shows that she, along with many other Jews in that day, believed in a final resurrection. This was the main distinction between the Pharisees, who believed in a life to come, and the Sadducees, who did not.

You will sometimes hear it said that the Old Testament faith did not include a hope of life after death. William Barclay states this, writing: "One of the strangest things in scripture is the fact that the saints of the Old Testament had practically no belief in any real life after death. . . . In the early days, the Hebrews believed that the soul of every man, good and bad alike, went to Sheol . . . [where] they lived a vague, shadowy, strengthless, joyless life, like spectres or ghosts."[5]

---

4. Mark G. Johnston, *Let's Study John* (Edinburgh: Banner of Truth, 2003), 157.
5. Barclay, *John*, 2:106.

It is hard to imagine any hope from a faith like that! And how wrong is this view, for the Old Testament frequently reveals a hope of life with God in the end. One of the earliest of all books, Job, includes this triumphant hope in the resurrection: "I know that my Redeemer lives, and at the last he will stand upon the earth. And after my skin has been thus destroyed, yet in my flesh I shall see God" (Job 19:25–26). David likewise expressed a fervent hope of glory and joy after death: "You will not abandon my soul to Sheol, or let your holy one see corruption. You make known to me the path of life; in your presence there is fullness of joy; at your right hand are pleasures forevermore" (Ps. 16:10–11). In Psalm 73, Asaph expressed the same hope: "I am continually with you; you hold my right hand. You guide me with your counsel, and afterward you will receive me to glory" (Ps. 73:23–24). The thought of glory with the Lord has always been the hope of God's people, and the comfort of this hope is given to sustain us amid all the griefs of life.

JESUS' STAGGERING REVELATION

Jesus is the master minister, and his purpose all along had been to strengthen the faith of his disciples through Lazarus's death. The first to benefit was Martha, who wisely raced to meet him as he arrived. With this in mind, Jesus continued with the fifth of the seven "I am" statements of the Gospel of John. Seven times, Jesus uses the great "I am" name of the Lord to reveal the greatest truths of his salvation. "I am the bread of life," he told the hungry crowd in John 6. "I am the light of the world," he cried to the revelers at the Feast of Tabernacles (John 8:12). When those false shepherds, the Pharisees, cast one of Christ's sheep out from the synagogue, Jesus replied, "I am the door. If anyone enters by me, he will be saved" (10:9), and "I am the good shepherd. The good shepherd lays down his life for the sheep" (10:11). Now, at the scene of Lazarus's death, he gives this staggering revelation to grieving Martha: "I am the resurrection and the life. Whoever believes in me, though he die, yet shall he live, and everyone who lives and believes in me shall never die" (11:25–26).

These are among the most precious and important words ever to fall from Jesus' lips. J. C. Ryle comments that Jesus "tells [Martha] that He is not merely a human teacher of the resurrection, but the Divine Author of all resurrection, whether spiritual or physical, and the Root and Fountain of all life."[6]

There are questions about how to take Jesus' statement, especially since in verse 25 he asserts that those who believe in him will live, even though they die, while verse 26 says that believers will never die. The best way to understand this is that Jesus first identifies himself as the source of resurrection and life. He next explains his resurrection, following death, and then he treats the eternal life that follows the resurrection. We might say that Jesus lays out resurrection life at the beginning in himself; in the middle, after death; and then at the end, in a life that will never again experience death, forever and ever.

First, Jesus reveals himself as the source of "the resurrection and the life." We may hope in the resurrection because Jesus himself has entered into death and risen from the grave. "The whole human race is plunged in death," writes John Calvin. "Therefore, no man will possess life unless he is first risen from the dead. Hence Christ teaches that He is the beginning of life."[7] "In him was life," John said in chapter 1, "and the life was the light of men" (John 1:4). Therefore, "All who face the recurrent death situations of life and wrestle with questions of death and life can find an answer only through faith in him."[8] To believe in Jesus is to receive the benefit not only of his life and death, but also of his resurrection; from him through faith, Christians are entered into glory through the light of his open tomb. "Because I live," Jesus said, "you also will live" (14:19).

If the resurrection's beginning and source rests with Jesus himself—with his divine person and saving work—then the middle of Christ's resurrection promise deals with his answer to death: "Whoever believes in me, though he die, yet shall he live" (John 11:25). Here is the answer—the only true answer—to the problem of death. By trusting in Jesus, we gain the promise of resurrection life. "Your brother will rise again" (11:23), he told Martha, and so he says of all who believe.

Some argue that Jesus is speaking here of spiritual death, not physical death, an analogy that the New Testament certainly makes. But Jesus speaks

6. J. C. Ryle, *Expository Thoughts on the Gospels: John*, 3 vols. (Edinburgh: Banner of Truth, 1999), 2:297.

7. John Calvin, *New Testament Commentaries*, trans. T. H. L. Parker, 12 vols. (Grand Rapids: Eerdmans, 1959), 5:8.

8. Herman Ridderbos, *John: A Theological Commentary* (Grand Rapids: Zondervan, 1997), 396.

of believers who die, and the context strongly favors a reference to physical death. J. C. Ryle therefore explains his meaning: "As surely as I, the Head, have life, and cannot be kept a prisoner by the grave, so surely all my members, believing in Me, shall live also."[9]

Jesus' second statement elaborates on the resurrection he gives, and the third statement refers to the life that believers gain from him: "Everyone who lives and believes in me shall never die" (John 11:26). This is the end awaiting all who trust in Jesus Christ, a life that will never end: Jesus adds, literally, that we "will never die forever." Benjamin B. Warfield therefore writes, "Whatever Death is, and all that Death is . . . that is what we shall be saved from in this salvation. And whatever Life is, and all that Life is . . . that is what we shall be saved to in this salvation."[10]

Resurrection Life

The Gospel of John is sometimes called the Gospel of Belief. And if there is one place above all where this Gospel most powerfully summons us to faith in Jesus Christ, it might be here. Can there be a greater reason to believe on Jesus than his claim to hold the key to the problem of death? Jesus promises life: abundant life, and eternal life. And within a handful of days after this promise, he himself would prove his claims and seal his promises by rising from the grave in resurrection power. Jesus proclaims, "I am the resurrection and the life" (John 11:25). This means that Jesus gives the meaning of life and the answer to death. He promises, "Whoever believes in me" will live even though he dies. And "everyone who lives and believes in me shall never die" (11:26).

No wonder, then, that Jesus concluded the encounter with Martha by asking the all-important question: "Do you believe this?" It is still the all-important question, the great question confronting everyone who hears his words even today. How you answer this one question determines nothing less than the great question of life and the unavoidable question of death.

Indeed, to believe in Jesus is to start living this resurrection life even now. We do not have to wait until we die to receive new life from Christ; his

9. Ryle, *John*, 2:298.
10. Benjamin B. Warfield, *The Saviour of the World* (1916; repr., Edinburgh: Banner of Truth, 1991), 47.

resurrection begins in us the moment we believe. This was Paul's explanation of what it means to enter into new life through faith in Christ: "You were dead in . . . trespasses and sins . . . . But God, being rich in mercy, because of the great love with which he loved us, even when we were dead in our trespasses, made us alive [that is, resurrected us] together with Christ" (Eph. 2:1, 4–5). This is the gift that God offers to anyone who will come in faith to Jesus. Those who believe in him are freed from the power of death even before they die, and they receive his never-ending life even now, to live in this world as those who have everything to gain and nothing to lose.

This is what Tokichi Ishii learned after two women came to his prison cell to talk about Jesus Christ. He had an almost unparalleled criminal record, having murdered men, women, and children in the most brutal way, and was awaiting his just execution. As the Christian women spoke, Tokichi glowered at them like a savage animal. Eventually, they gave up trying to talk with him, but they left a Bible in his cell. He picked it up and began to read. And he kept reading. He could not put it down. Finally, he came to the point in the Gospel where Jesus, hanging on the cross, spoke aloud: "Father, forgive them, for they know not what they do" (Luke 23:34). Tokichi later recalled, "I stopped. I was stabbed to the heart, as if pierced by a five-inch nail. Shall I call it the love of Christ? Shall I call it His compassion? I do not know what to call it. I only know that I believed, and my hardness of heart was changed."[11]

Believing in Jesus, through the Word of his Gospel, Tokichi Ishii received the beginning of resurrection life. Later, the jailer came to lead him to the scaffold. "He found, not the hardened, surly brute he had expected, but a smiling radiant man, for the murderer had been born again. Literally, Christ brought Tokichi Ishii to life."[12] And by believing in Jesus, though he died, yet will he forever live.

In every kind of prison cell that sin can devise, whether pleasure or pain, pride or despair, and with the threat of death facing every man, woman, and child, Jesus offers the same to everyone who believes. "I am the resurrection and the life," he declares. And he asks, "Do you believe this?"

11. Barclay, *John*, 2:109.
12. Ibid.

74

Two Portraits of Faith

John 11:27–32

She said to him, "Yes, Lord; I believe that you are the Christ, the
Son of God, who is coming into the world." (John 11:27)

*I*n the Sermon on the Mount, Jesus made an extraordinary claim about the Bible: "Truly, I say to you, until heaven and earth pass away, not an iota, not a dot, will pass from the Law until all is accomplished" (Matt. 5:18). This reminds us that every word in Holy Scripture—even every syllable—is placed there by God's will and purpose. This should teach us to pay careful attention to every verse and, indeed, every word in the Bible.

An example of this principle can be seen in John chapter 11, an account filled with mighty words and deeds. For that very reason we might overlook verses that seem incidental, such as these presenting Jesus' interaction with the sisters Martha and Mary. But John is careful to insert them, perhaps to honor these women who were so dearly loved by the Lord. But when we remember that the primary Author of Scripture is the Holy Spirit, we should also realize that these verses are recorded for our spiritual benefit. In particular, Martha and Mary present to us two portraits of a living and saving faith.

Martha's Faith: "Lord, I Believe"

Martha was first to encounter Jesus when he arrived at Bethany. She and her sister, Mary, had sent for Jesus when their brother became ill. But Jesus had not arrived in time to save Lazarus—so it seemed, at least—and a grieving Martha went out to meet him. Martha came seeking answers, saying, "Lord, if you had been here, my brother would not have died" (John 11:21). As she saw things, the problem was Jesus' delay in coming, though her faith was strong enough to hope that Jesus could still do something: "Even now I know that whatever you ask from God, God will give you" (11:22).

The Christian faith does in fact give answers to the great questions of life and death. Jesus did not rebuke Martha; instead, he declared his resurrection power: "I am the resurrection and the life. Whoever believes in me, though he die, yet shall he live" (John 11:25). But having given this answer, Jesus pressed Martha to receive it: "Do you believe this?" he concluded.

Martha's reply is a good example of saving faith: "She said to him, 'Yes, Lord; I believe that you are the Christ, the Son of God, who is coming into the world'" (John 11:27). This is so important a statement of Christian faith—equal in value to Peter's Great Confession in Matthew 16:16—that we should carefully consider each element.

Perhaps most important are Martha's opening words: "Yes, Lord; I believe." This shows the attitude of faith. Martha does not quarrel with Jesus. She does not dissect his words with the scalpel of her preconceived ideas. Instead, she receives and believes Jesus' teaching because she knows who Jesus is. Martha says "Yes" to Jesus because she knows him as "Lord": she knows that he is the divine Sovereign whose word is absolute.

This is where true faith begins, by turning our ears and opening our minds to the Word of God. James Montgomery Boice comments that Martha "gives the basis of her understanding. The basis is the word of Christic. . . . This does not mean that she understands everything he has been saying—in fact, she does not—but rather that she accepts it, whatever it is, because she knows that his words are trustworthy."[1]

The only way to come to faith, and the only way to grow in faith, is to listen humbly when the Bible speaks. Donald Grey Barnhouse writes: "What is the food that makes our faith strong? The written Word of God.

1. James Montgomery Boice, *The Gospel of John*, 5 vols. (Grand Rapids: Baker, 1999), 3:856.

What is the foundation of our hope? The written Word of God. What is the cause of our obedience, and the directive of our action? The written Word of God."[2]

Where the Bible speaks, faith says, "Yes, Lord." Job learned this lesson in the midst of his intense suffering. For his own purposes, and ultimately for Job's blessing, God permitted Satan to visit Job with great trials. Not surprisingly, Job complained to God, questioning the fairness of his treatment as a more or less righteous person. One of Job's dialogue partners described him: "Job opens his mouth in empty talk" (Job 35:16). Finally God revealed himself, presenting Job with a display of his divine majesty. Confronted with true deity, Job understood his error in disputing with God. He said, "I lay my hand on my mouth" (40:4). This is the attitude of faith. Job stopped talking and started listening. This does not mean that Job stopped asking the Lord for answers, but rather that he ceased quarreling with God about the answers he received: "I will question you," he said, "and you make it known to me" (42:4).

Martha had seen the same divine majesty in Jesus, and when he answered her sincere question, she replied, "Yes, Lord; I believe." It is with this attitude that faith begins.

Martha's reply also reminds us that Christian faith includes content. There are truths that Christians must believe. John's main purpose in writing this Gospel was to commend these truths to our faith: "These are written so that you may believe that Jesus is the Christ, the Son of God, and that by believing you may have life in his name" (John 20:31). This is the very faith that Martha confesses, and that we must also know and believe if we are to be Christians.

First, Martha believed that Jesus is "the Christ." The Hebrew word for this is *Messiah*, from the word that means "to anoint." Jesus is "the Anointed One." In its fullest sense, this refers to the three divinely appointed offices of the Old Testament: prophet, priest, and king. These anointed offices served to reveal God's truth, offer sacrifices for sin, and establish God's sovereign reign. To believe that Jesus is the Christ is therefore to believe that he is the true and final Prophet, the true and final Priest, and the true and final King over God's people.

2. Donald Grey Barnhouse, *Exposition of Bible Doctrines, Taking the Epistle to the Romans as a Point of Departure*, 10 vols. (Grand Rapids: Eerdmans, 1954), 3:366.

It is doubtful that Martha could have articulated all this at this point. But she lived in a time of heightened messianic expectation. The Jews were looking for a conqueror to oust the Roman occupiers and a political leader to restore peace and prosperity. Behind this hope was the general belief that "one day God would send a specially anointed individual who would be the herald of salvation."[3] Martha believed that Jesus was this Messiah, just as we must believe, for Jesus alone is the One who brings God's salvation to earth.

Second, Martha declared her faith in Jesus as "the Son of God." This, too, could have a generic meaning, signifying someone as being especially godly in character. But Martha clearly meant far more than this. Did she understand that in Jesus' virgin birth, the eternal, divine Son had taken up human flesh? Did she grasp that Jesus possesses all the attributes of deity, "the same in substance," and "equal in power and glory" with God the Father?[4] Probably she did not. But she must have been present on one of the many occasions when Jesus identified himself as the Son of God, and she believed in his unique deity in some vital sense.

Belief in Jesus as the Son of God is essential to Christianity; one simply is not a Christian without this confession. Many people are attracted to Jesus' teaching, yet they deny his full deity. But to do so is to reject the heart of the Christian faith. Jesus' teaching is not uniquely true unless he is the Son of God; indeed, in this case, his teaching is not true at all, since Jesus taught that he is God's Son. The same can be said of Jesus' mighty works, and especially of his death on the cross. The reason that Jesus could perform miracles is that he is God's Son. Most significantly, the reason why Jesus' death has any importance to us is that since he is the Son of God, his blood is precious enough to make an atonement for the sins of all who believe.

There was a third element of Martha's confession of faith. She believed that Jesus is "the Christ, the Son of God, who is coming into the world" (John 11:27). This means that Jesus is the One promised in the Old Testament who would bring the salvation of which it spoke. Jesus is the child promised to Adam and Eve to crush the Serpent's head (Gen. 3:15); the Passover Lamb slain to redeem God's people from sin (Ex. 12:13); the great Prophet whom

---

3. Boice, *John*, 3:858.
4. Westminster Shorter Catechism 6.

Moses foretold (Deut. 18:18); the Servant of the Lord who was crushed for our iniquities and by whose wounds we are healed (Isa. 53:5); and the King of the line of David whose throne will last forever (2 Sam. 7:16).

Jesus asked Martha, "Do you believe this?" (John 11:26), and now the question must be put to you. Do you believe that Jesus of Nazareth, revealed in the pages of Holy Scripture, is the Messiah—the Savior that God has sent to a sinful, dying world? Do you believe that Jesus is God's very Son, the second person of the eternal Trinity, "very God of very God,"[5] manifested in the flesh? And do you look upon him as the promised Deliverer that God has sent not only to a fallen, sinful world, but to save you from God's just wrath against your sins?

Notice, finally, that the content of Martha's faith was wholly centered on Jesus himself. Being a Christian means far more than embracing traditional values or admiring the Sermon on the Mount. It means coming to Jesus as Martha did, perhaps with questions of your own, looking to God's Word to hear what he says, and replying, "Yes, Lord; I believe." "I believe in you, Jesus. I believe what the Bible says about you. And I rest my hope for eternal life on you." If you believe this, then Jesus promises you salvation. "Whoever hears my word and believes him who sent me has eternal life," Jesus said. "He does not come into judgment, but has passed from death to life" (John 5:24).

MARY'S FAITH: "LORD, I COME"

Martha and Mary are quite similar, as one might expect of sisters. They were both deeply involved—physically, emotionally, and spiritually—in the recent death of their brother, Lazarus. They had together sent a summons to Jesus, and together they anguished in waiting for his arrival. Together they mourned the death, and they even said the same thing to Jesus when he finally came to Bethany. But what makes them so interesting is the way in which they were so very different. They experienced their shared grief in different ways, and they expressed their shared faith differently, too.

While Jesus met with Martha, Mary remained in the house with the mourners. So Jesus sent Martha to summon Mary. John recounts: "When [Martha] had said this, she went and called her sister Mary, saying in private,

5. Nicene Creed, 325 A.D.

'The Teacher is here and is calling for you.' And when she heard it, she rose quickly and went to him" (John 11:28–29).

Mary displays a portrait of faith that is different from Martha's. Martha's faith said, "Yes, Lord; I believe." Mary speaks less, but if we could put words in her mouth, her faith would say, "Yes, Lord; I come." John makes a point of how quickly Mary answered Jesus' call: "She rose quickly and went to him." Just as with Martha, Jesus had appealed to Mary's faith. Jesus appealed to Martha's faith by asking whether she believed. But he appealed to Mary's faith by waiting outside the town and calling her to come. Jesus always seeks to exercise and strengthen our faith, especially in times of trial and loss.

Just as Jesus taught Martha, he summons each of us to receive his Word. And just as Jesus summoned Mary to come, Jesus also calls each of us to himself. Matthew Henry comments: "When Christ our Master comes, he calls for us. He comes in his word and ordinances, calls us to them, calls us by them, calls us to himself."[6] Martha whispered Jesus' summons to Mary in private, perhaps fearing the reaction of the visitors from Jerusalem; likewise, the Holy Spirit delivers Jesus' call to us in the quiet of our hearts.

If we are to contrast Martha's faith with Mary's, we might say that Martha's faith was of the head, whereas Mary's faith was of the heart. That can be an unhelpful distinction, since the head and the heart are never truly separate. But in all the Gospel accounts, Mary is presented as a more emotional figure and Martha as a thinker and doer. Martha came to Jesus seeking answers, but Mary came for love.

John's description of Mary's meeting with Jesus highlights three features of her faith. The first is her personal devotion to Jesus. Mary was grieving bitterly, following the established rites for mourning. The grieving in her house would not have been the "gentle, restrained, shedding of tears. It would be unrestrained wailing and shrieking almost hysterically,"[7] in accordance with the Jewish custom. But when she learned of Jesus' coming, Mary left all that and went straight to him. As George Hutcheson observes, "Such as have the opportunity of comfort from Christ will prefer him to all the

---

6. Matthew Henry, *Commentary on the Whole Bible*, 6 vols. (Peabody, MA: Hendrickson, 2009), 5:849.

7. William Barclay, *The Gospel of John*, 2 vols. (Philadelphia: Westminster, 1975), 2:112.

comforts they can receive from friends."[8] Mary was such a person, and her faith expresses itself in her instant attraction to his presence.

Moreover, Mary was not influenced by the opinions of other people. It was neither popular nor safe to identify with Jesus, particularly among people from nearby Jerusalem, where the leaders were openly seeking to take Jesus' life. Many people are kept from Jesus today for fear of what people will say. But Mary's heart was devoted to Jesus, so when he called, she immediately came. We must do the same.

Mary's faith is further revealed by what she did when she came to Jesus: "Now when Mary came to where Jesus was and saw him, she fell at his feet" (John 11:32). There are three major accounts of Mary in the New Testament: in Luke 10, here, and in John 12. In each passage, Mary is found at Jesus' feet. This was her way of expressing her faith to Jesus, by worshiping him. And there can hardly be a better way! The book of Revelation opens up a window into heaven, and what we see there is the worship of the exalted Lord Jesus Christ. "Worthy are you," the four living creatures and twenty-four elders sing, "for you were slain, and by your blood you ransomed people for God" (Rev. 5:9).

This raises a question for us. Why do we come to church? True faith in Jesus comes primarily to worship him, that is, to exalt his name, celebrate his saving work, and gather at his feet to hear his Word.

Finally, Mary reveals a faith that relies completely on Jesus to meet her every need. In this case, Mary's great need was for comfort, so she cried to Jesus, "Lord, if you had been here, my brother would not have died" (John 11:32). These are the very same words Martha spoke; only a minor alteration is seen in the Greek original. But there is an obvious difference in purpose. Mary shows none of the quarreling that Martha may have shown. She comes reverently, humbly, and pours out her heart at Jesus' feet. With the greatest spiritual intimacy, she is free to share her deepest feelings with her Lord.

This is the kind of faith to which we are all invited. Jesus responded to Mary with the most compassionate love. John writes, "When Jesus saw her weeping, and the Jews who had come with her also weeping, he was deeply moved in his spirit" (John 11:33). If we know Jesus, love Jesus, and trust Jesus

---

8. George Hutcheson, *Exposition of the Gospel of John* (Lafayette, IN: Sovereign Grace Publishers, 2001), 230.

with the ardent faith of Mary, we will experience a compassion in him that will overwhelm our hearts.

A FULL AND BALANCED FAITH

A comparison such as this between Martha's and Mary's faith invites some questions: Which is right? Which is better? The best answer is to realize that together these sisters portray a full and balanced faith. A mature and full faith is neither that of the head nor of the heart only, but that with mind and heart joined in faith in Christ.

Some of us are more like Mary. In this case, John's narrative offers suggestions for how such a faith can grow. There are many Christians for whom faith is a far more emotional matter than one of knowledge. It is not that they do not believe the essential truths about Jesus. After all, Mary called Jesus "Lord," just as Martha did. And she would not have fallen at his feet and worshiped him if she did not believe what Martha perhaps better understood. But Mary's faith is especially manifested in her feelings.

Mary displays some of the weaknesses of a faith that is driven by the emotions. She seems, for instance, to have been more captured by grief than her sister. The thought of "what might have been" seems to have overwhelmed her. She was overcome by the thought of Jesus' absence when in fact he was close at hand. Therefore, while Martha, helped by her knowledge of Jesus, kept looking for his coming, Mary gave herself over to the grief that he had not yet come. The wails of the mourners, many of whom were likely professionals at sorrow, captured more of Mary's attention and penetrated her heart more deeply.

If yours is a Mary kind of faith, then it is likely that you can grow by devoting more effort to knowing God's Word, which the Bible greatly stresses (Rom. 12:2; 2 Peter 3:18). Far too many Marys gravitate to more emotional settings—in this case, in the house of loud mourning, and today in worship that is driven largely by the passions—when their faith would deepen in places of reverent study. Growth in a Mary's faith will often take the form of greater steadiness under affliction and a better-informed understanding of Christ's saving work.

Martha's faith could also grow. She was helped in her grief by her stronger grasp of truth; the circumstances did not afflict her as they did her sister, and she was better prepared for Jesus' coming. For her, Jesus is "the Teacher"

(John 11:28), and what she had learned from Jesus helped her greatly. But Martha should also learn to know Jesus as Mary did: as her loving Master and the Minister of her heart.

Like Martha, many biblically astute Christians busy themselves with God's work. As Mary is always seen at Jesus' feet, Martha is generally found serving (Luke 10:40; John 12:2). But service without a heart connection to Jesus leads to anxiety, frustration, and bitterness. The way to grow such a faith is to nurture a closer personal devotion to Jesus. When our service is rendered not merely out of convictions of the mind but also from a heart devoted to Christ, his presence sweetens every hardship, and the mere privilege of serving the One we love brings joy to all our work.

What should a Martha do to grow his or her faith? The best answer is an increased attention to prayer. Prayer is the garden where love for Christ grows. Our knowledge of truth should bring us to come and kneel at Jesus' feet. Our desire to serve must be focused through our personal relationship with Jesus. If the Marthas among us will nurture this heart devotion, their faith not only will say, "Yes, Lord; I believe," but will add a fervent love for Jesus, saying, "Yes, Lord; I come."

A FAITH FOR YOU

Jesus came to Bethany to minister to the faith of his disciples, each according to his or her need. But Jesus had others in mind who were not yet his disciples. For by waiting on the road, Jesus not only called Mary to come to him, but also arranged for the visiting mourners to follow: "they followed [Mary]," John writes, "supposing that she was going to the tomb to weep there" (John 11:31). These mourners would be well repaid for their ministry of comfort to these sisters whom Jesus loved. They would be present to witness the greatest miracle Jesus ever performed before his own resurrection. Something similar happens today when non-Christians come to church, perhaps to show kindness to their Christian neighbors, perhaps out of curiosity, or perhaps out of a need that they can hardly express. But Jesus blesses their attendance, causing his gospel to be preached, the good news that is "the power of God for salvation to everyone who believes" (Rom. 1:16).

Perhaps you have come, not yet believing in the way that Martha did. Jesus offers to teach you, and by his Holy Spirit he would reveal his divine majesty to your mind and heart. What can you do in order to receive Jesus and be saved? Jesus calls you to echo Martha's confession of faith: "Yes, Lord; I believe that you are the Christ, the Son of God, who is coming into the world" (John 11:27).

And perhaps you have come, still lacking Mary's worshiping love for Jesus. Jesus calls you all the same. Like Mary, your heart can rise up, answering, "Yes, Lord; I come." If you do—if you believe and if you come to Jesus with mind and heart—it will be the beginning of something truly wonderful. Jesus said, "Whoever believes in the Son has eternal life" (John 3:36). That eternal life will grow in you, and you will grow forever in the knowledge of the truth of God and the experience of God's love through Jesus Christ.

75

JESUS WEPT

John 11:33—37

When Jesus saw her weeping, and the Jews who had come with her also weeping, he was deeply moved in his spirit and greatly troubled. (John 11:33)

*I*t is not easy for us to know God. This is partly because God is so different from everything else in our experience. This is the primary meaning of God's *holiness*: God is wholly other from us. He says, "For as the heavens are higher than the earth, so are my ways higher than your ways and my thoughts than your thoughts" (Isa. 55:9). Our knowledge of God is also impaired by the effects of sin within us. We are prone to folly and rebellion, and our thoughts about God are therefore often warped.

Difficult though it is to know God, however, it is vitally important that our thoughts about God are true. This is why the Bible is so valuable, since in the Bible God reveals saving truth about himself. This is also why Jesus is so important to the Bible. Jesus is the fullest revelation of God, "the image of the invisible God," Paul says (Col. 1:15). Jesus is the divine Son who manifests the person of the Father: he said, "Whoever has seen me has seen the Father" (John 14:9).

Considering Jesus, then, is the best way to come to know God. For instance, some people in our overly tolerant age do not think God is really bothered by sin. But watching the violence with which Jesus cleansed the temple (John 2:13–16) or listening to him speak about hell (Matt. 5:22; 18:8–9) will correct this opinion. Some people think of God almost as a feeble bystander. But watching Jesus still the wind and the waves upon the lake (Matt. 8:23–26) or seeing him call dead Lazarus out from the grave will show us the truth about God's mighty power. Still others think of God as an unfeeling tyrant. Ours is a cruel world, and in the midst of suffering, people can think that God simply doesn't care. If you have been tempted to think of God this way, I know of no other passage to show you otherwise than when Jesus wept before Lazarus's tomb. John 11:35 might be the shortest verse in the English Bible. But for those who want to know the heart of God, the words "Jesus wept" are among the greatest.

GOD CARES

Lazarus was a member of a family that was greatly loved by Jesus. So when Jesus arrived at the scene of mourning for Lazarus's death, the sisters Martha and Mary brought their grief to him. Mary, especially, fell at Jesus' feet, weeping. John records, "When Jesus saw her weeping, and the Jews who had come with her also weeping, he was deeply moved in his spirit and greatly troubled" (John 11:33).

Jesus' reaction shows us that God cares about our sorrows. He did not look on disinterestedly as Mary grieved, but his heart was pierced. William Barclay comments, "So deeply did Jesus enter into the wounded hearts and the sorrows of people that His heart was wrung with anguish."[1] In this Jesus manifested God in the flesh, who cares about his people. We see this in the Psalms, where David states, "The LORD has heard the sound of my weeping" (Ps. 6:8), and "He does not forget the cry of the afflicted" (9:12).

Does it matter that God cares about us? It matters very much and should draw us to him. Many people struggle with truths about God that they find hard to accept, especially his sovereignty and his wrath against sin. But what a difference it makes when we realize that this sovereign, holy God cares

---

1. William Barclay, *The Gospel of John*, 2 vols. (Philadelphia: Westminster, 1975), 2:113.

about us. I have learned as a pastor that there are people who pay little attention to your teaching until they realize how much you care for them. This realization changes everything! The God who calls you to kneel before his Word is a God whose ears are attentive to your cry and who is close to the broken in heart (Ps. 34:15, 18). It is because they think Jesus needs prompting to care about our griefs that some people wrongly pray to dead saints or to Mary. But how wrong this is! Jesus does not need to be made to care about us. Christ's groaning at this scene of sorrow in Bethany ought to draw us near to Jesus and to God the Father in prayer, realizing how much they care.

Questions are raised about what it was that aroused Jesus' emotions. This issue is complicated by the fact that the word describing Jesus' feelings is generally used to express sternness and even anger. It is not just that Jesus was troubled but that he was indignant. Jesus was not merely saddened but outraged at the scene before him.

Some commentators argue that Jesus was appalled by the hypocritical mourning of the visitors from Jerusalem. After all, they represented people who hated Jesus and all that he stood for; what were they doing with Jesus' friends at a time like this? Alternatively, some state that Jesus was unhappy with the unbelief implied by Mary's tears.

Our best guide to understanding Jesus' attitude is his own statement of what was on his mind. Jesus did not demand, "What are you doing here?" or "What is wrong with you?" Instead, he asked, "Where have you laid him?" (John 11:34). This shows that it was the fact of Lazarus's death that burdened his soul. It is death itself that rouses Jesus' anger. Herman Ridderbos writes that Jesus' emotion "is the revulsion of everything that is in him against the power of death."[2]

We often see Jesus depicted in artwork as almost passive and aloof. But as Jesus approaches the grave of his friend to wage warfare against death, he comes with a passionate zeal. No warrior ever waded into his enemy's ranks with greater ferocity than Jesus did in warring with death. When Jesus looks on death, he sees the wreckage caused by sin and he sees the fingerprints of his hated enemy, the devil. Benjamin B. Warfield notes:

> Jesus approached the grave of Lazarus in a state, not of uncontrollable grief but of inexpressible anger. . . . The emotion which tore his breast and clamoured

2. Herman Ridderbos, *John: A Theological Commentary* (Grand Rapids: Zondervan, 1997), 402.

for utterance was just rage. . . . It is death that is the object of his wrath, and behind death him who has the power of death, and whom he had come into the world to destroy. Tears of sympathy may fill his eyes, but . . . his soul is held by rage, and he advances to the tomb, in Calvin's words, "as a champion who prepares for conflict."[3]

This reminds us that even though Christians possess a glorious hope of resurrection, we are not therefore indifferent to the outrage that is death. Jesus was not unaffected by Lazarus's death. Christians should feel no differently: when we fight against death with our serving hands, with our tearful prayers, and with our gospel witness, we are waging holy warfare under the banner of Christ.

GOD FEELS

When Jesus asked to be shown Lazarus's grave, they told him, "Lord, come and see" (John 11:34). Arriving at the tomb, "Jesus wept" (11:35). Charles Spurgeon comments: "There is infinitely more in these two words than any sermonizer, or any student of the Word, will ever be able to bring out of them, even though he should apply the microscope of the utmost attentive consideration."[4]

One thing we should observe is how clearly this verse contradicts a common mistake about God. When the ancient Greeks thought about God, they described him with the word *apatheia*. It is the word from which we get *apathy*. They meant that by definition it is not possible for God to feel emotion. God cannot feel love, anger, disappointment, hope, or any other emotion. They reasoned that if God can be made to feel joy or sorrow, then someone else has had an effect on him. That person has therefore held power over God, and it is not possible for God to be in anyone's power. This being the case, "it must mean that God cannot have feelings. He must be lonely, isolated, compassionless."[5] But these two words, "Jesus wept," destroy this reasoning by showing us that God does feel. Some reply that Jesus wept in his human nature only, forgetting that the reason he became man was to

---

3. Benjamin B. Warfield, *The Person and Work of Christ* (Philadelphia: Presbyterian and Reformed, 1950), 115–16.

4. Charles H. Spurgeon, *Metropolitan Tabernacle Pulpit* (London: Banner of Truth, 1970), 35:338.

5. James Montgomery Boice, *The Gospel of John*, 5 vols. (Grand Rapids: Baker, 1999), 3:874.

reveal God to us. James Montgomery Boice comments, "Jesus wept and thus revealed a God who enters into the anguish of his people and grieves with them in their afflictions."[6]

It is true that God feels in a way that is different from the way that we feel. For one thing, God's feelings are never mixed with sin as ours are. Moreover, it is true that God's feelings do not indicate a change in God. The Bible states that in him "there is no variation or shadow due to change" (James 1:17). So when we say that God feels, we do not mean that God has been surprised or that his nature has altered. What we mean is that things that happen on this earth are real and that the God who is also real has feelings about them. It is true that by weeping, Jesus proves his true humanity. But as God in the flesh, Jesus shows us that God feels with his people because "Jesus wept."

This also makes an important point about tears. Since Jesus possesses a true humanity—indeed, a perfect humanity—and since Jesus wept, we should not be ashamed to do likewise. Some Christians seem to think that by virtue of their salvation they have been lifted out of the human condition. But being a Christian makes us not less human but more human. And there are things in this world for which Christians should weep. Christians are not stoics, and the stiff upper lip is not a sign of grace.

Death is certainly a cause for sorrow. It is not wrong to weep over the death of a loved one. Jesus knew that he was about to raise Lazarus back to life, yet still he wept. Let this thought sanctify every mournful tear you have cried for a loved one who has died. J. C. Ryle said, "There is nothing unworthy of a child of God in tears. Even the Son of God could weep. It shows us, above all, that the Saviour in whom believers trust is a most tender and feeling Saviour. . . . He knows what we go through, and can pity."[7] How impoverished we would be if the Bible did not contain this shortest of verses: "Jesus wept." Christians have rightly derived blessing from God in their own tears and an unspeakable comfort from knowing that Christ weeps with us in our grief over death.

The word used to describe Jesus' weeping (*dakryo*) is found only here in the New Testament; it does not describe uncontrolled sobbing, but

---

6. Ibid.

7. J. C. Ryle, *Expository Thoughts on the Gospels: John*, 3 vols. (Edinburgh: Banner of Truth, 1999), 2:304.

rather states that tears poured down his face. And in a world like ours, there is something wrong if Christ's people seldom shed tears. We are rightly busy trying to do good and advance the cause of Christ's kingdom. But here we see that tears are part of the way in which we represent his grace. Many Christians are zealous to share the gospel with sinners. But does the sin and the misery of sin lead us to weep for them and with them? Christians rightly rally against the sin of abortion. But do we shed tears for the babies, the mothers, and even the abortion doctors? We should. Christians are disturbed by the promotion of homosexuality in our society, but shouldn't we weep for the homosexuals themselves? Lazarus's grave spoke to Jesus of the whole ruinous complex of sin in our world, and he wept. If we have his heart for the world, we will weep for and with the world as well.

Years ago a Christian woman traveled to North Africa as a missionary among the Muslims in Tunisia. She persisted through years of difficult labor in that hardened land. Her approach was simply to show Christ's love to people and seek opportunities to tell them about Jesus. One young Muslim man took English classes with her, and every week as she taught him, she spoke about Jesus. The man listened but remained unmoved. This went on for months, until the time drew near for him to go away to college. Just before he was leaving, he dropped by to say good-bye and thank the Christian woman. They had tea, and she took this final opportunity to appeal to him about his salvation. But he once again politely refused to consider the gospel. After a while, he got up and said his farewell, walked out the door, and headed down the path. But then he stopped, and looking back he saw his teacher standing in the door with tears streaming down her face. Overwhelmed by her great love for him, he resisted no longer. Returning to her living room, he soon had his heart opened to receive Jesus as his Lord and Savior.[8]

Could it be that Christ's love for the lost—a brokenhearted love that feels and weeps—is the missing ingredient in our witness of Christ's gospel? Weeping itself is not the answer. But possessing the heart of Jesus—a heart that is able to shed tears—is essential to our ministry of his grace to the world, to our neighbors, and to our own children.

8. Boice, *John*, 3:890.

GOD LOVES

John notes that the Jewish onlookers were impressed by what they saw in Jesus. They exclaimed, "See how he loved him!" (John 11:36). This is another reason why Jesus was angry at Lazarus's death, and why he wept at the tomb: because he loved him.

Jesus' tears show us that God cares and God feels, and also that God loves. God loves his people. This is why he cared about Martha's and Mary's anguish: he loved them. And Jesus' love for Lazarus was not ended by death. As George Hutcheson writes, "Christ's love to his own will follow them even to their graves."[9]

When you love someone, you rejoice at that person's joy and you grieve for his or her grief. Love always shares and participates in feelings. This should encourage us in our ministry to one another. But how much better is the ministry of God's love. Too many people—even Christians—are angry with God when troubles come. But God is not the problem behind our grief; God in his love is the answer to which we should turn. Jesus did not begin to love Martha and Mary when he grieved with them, and his love for Lazarus did not start with his tears. But it was when he grieved and wept that the people saw how much he loved them.

Yet even in such a scene, there were some who criticized Jesus. You will find that even when your actions are most pure and loving, there will always be someone to malign you and impugn your motives. This is especially true of those who represent Jesus in this world. Some of those looking on said, "Could he who opened the eyes of the blind man also have kept this man from dying?" (John 11:37).

These Jews remembered the miracle of John 9, in which Jesus had given sight to the man born blind, which happened in Jerusalem. And their question raises an important matter: does Jesus' love enable him only to weep along with the others? If he possesses the power that he earlier displayed, isn't there something more that he could do?

Let us admit that if this account ended in John 11:35 with the words "Jesus wept," then Jesus would not be much of a Savior. What if Jesus had wept at the tomb and then gone away? We might admire him and we might even love him. But we would not be able to entrust our destiny into his hands.

9. George Hutcheson, *Exposition of the Gospel of John* (Lafayette, IN: Sovereign Grace Publishers, 2001), 233.

Yet Jesus was not finished, and he did not leave. This reminds us that we should do more than sympathize with the weak and afflicted; we should do what we can to help them in their need. But while our help eventually fails, Jesus' help does not. He had not arrived too late to help dead Lazarus. And his tears were not the end of his ministry but the beginning. He came to the tomb not merely to exercise his heart but to extend his saving power. In the most dramatic fashion possible, Jesus silenced his critics by raising Lazarus from the grave.

Even Lazarus's resurrection was not his fullest answer to the criticism. For within days Jesus would enter Jerusalem and do a greater work for his people. He had spoken of this in his parable of the good shepherd: "I am the good shepherd," he said. "The good shepherd lays down his life for the sheep" (John 10:11). And as he later said, "Greater love has no one than this, that someone lay down his life for his friends" (15:13).

Years later, when the apostle John wrote his first epistle, he named the cross as the greatest proof of God's love: "In this the love of God was made manifest among us, that God sent his only Son into the world, so that we might live through him. In this is love, not that we have loved God but that he loved us and sent his Son to be the propitiation for our sins" (1 John 4:9–10). It is there at the cross that we can echo the words spoken of Jesus at Lazarus's tomb, only now saying, "See how he loved us!" and "See how he loved me!" We remember God's words through the angel, when Abraham had been willing to offer his son Isaac: "now I know that you fear God, seeing you have not withheld your son, your only son, from me" (Gen. 22:12). If Abraham had been present when Jesus died on the cross, he would have spoken in return to God: "Now I know that you love me, seeing you have not withheld your Son, your only Son, from me!"

Even at the cross, Jesus was not finished. For three days after he died, he did something greater even than raising Lazarus from the grave. Jesus himself rose from the dead, our sin having been conquered by his blood and death now conquered by the resurrection life he gives to us. This means that we have an even better reason to believe in Christ's love for us than Martha and Mary did. We have seen him shed for us not only his tears but also his blood for our sins on the cross. If you have held yourself back from Jesus because you doubted God's love, let both the tears and the blood of Jesus show you the depth of his love. And let them draw you to him in saving faith.

LOVE'S CONQUEST

It has now been almost two thousand years since Christ died and rose again, and people are dying and weeping still. But Jesus is not finished yet. Even now, ascended into heaven, he looks down with sympathetic eyes, sharing our sorrows, and upholding us by his love. Hebrews 4:15 cites this as a mighty reason to pray: "For we do not have a high priest who is unable to sympathize with our weaknesses," since Jesus has lived and wept and died in this very world.

But the day is coming when Jesus' victory will be complete. For when history has served its purpose by gathering all of Christ's purchased flock, Jesus will return in power and glory. The Bible ends with a world made new in the final coming of its King: "Behold, the dwelling place of God is with man. He will dwell with them, and they will be his people, and God himself will be with them as their God. He will wipe away every tear from their eyes, and death shall be no more, neither shall there be mourning, nor crying, nor pain anymore" (Rev. 21:3–4).

This is our salvation as the Bible tells it, and it is a complete salvation that meets our every need. God's Word promises that "those who sow in tears shall reap with shouts of joy!" (Ps. 126:5). And every one of Christ's redeemed will say to our caring, feeling, and loving God, "You have delivered my soul from death, my eyes from tears" (116:8).

Will you be there? That is the great question. The question is not whether or not you will weep or die in this world. We all will. But if you see in Jesus the loving eyes of God bent toward you, and if you believe on him for your salvation, then even death will lead you into life, and the tears you shed now will all be wiped away by the loving hand of God.

76

LAZARUS RAISED

John 11:38–44

*He cried out with a loud voice, "Lazarus, come out." The man
who had died came out, his hands and feet bound with linen
strips, and his face wrapped with a cloth.* (John 11:43–44)

The raising of Lazarus from the grave is arguably Jesus' greatest miracle before his own resurrection. Here, Jesus conquers not just sickness but death itself. And unlike earlier instances when Jesus raised someone who had just died, here we have the raising of a man who had been lying in the grave for four days and whose body was suffering decomposition.

The raising of Lazarus concludes the first half of John's Gospel, often called *The Book of Signs*. These chapters center on seven miracles that are signs of Jesus' deity. The Bible uses the number seven to represent completion, and this miracle fittingly completes John's record of signs. The first miracle, in which Jesus turned water into wine, symbolized Jesus' power to give life. "This seventh, climactic sign demonstrates Jesus' power over death, thus foreshadowing his own resurrection."[1] Alexander Maclaren writes that

1. Andreas J. Kostenberger, *John* (Grand Rapids: Baker, 2004), 343.

this miracle "crowns the whole, whether we regard the greatness of the fact, the manner of our Lord's working . . . , the revelation of our Lord's heart, the consolations which it suggests to sorrowing spirits, or the immortal hope which it kindles."[2]

CHRIST'S LESSON IN FAITH

Lazarus had become ill, and his sisters, Martha and Mary, had summoned Jesus. When Jesus arrived, his friend was already dead. Drawing near to the tomb, he had shared the sorrows of those he loved. John 11:35 records that "Jesus wept."

Once at the tomb, Jesus was "deeply moved again" (John 11:38). This shows that he enters into our sorrow and feels the pain of our suffering. Yet like a warrior come to the battle, Jesus immediately acts: "Take away the stone," he says (11:39). With these words, his tension is released into action. Herman Ridderbos writes: "Enough now of tears and wailing! Enough honor has been bestowed on death! Against the power of death God's glory will now enter the arena!"[3]

If we think about the setting, we will not be surprised at Martha's reaction to Jesus' command to unseal the tomb. "Lord," she objected, "by this time there will be an odor, for he has been dead four days" (John 11:39). This provides an important confirmation of this resurrection. We cannot object, as some have tried to do, that Lazarus was prematurely buried or was merely near to death, since Martha warns about his decomposition.

It is easy to criticize Martha's unbelief, as some have done. But Jesus was acting to expose a decomposing body, which would be a horror especially to those who loved him. It is true that Martha had forgotten what Jesus had earlier told her. When she met him on the way into town, Jesus promised, "Your brother will rise again" (John 11:23). But anyone who has buried a loved one will not be quick to criticize Martha's alarm. She shows how easily our faith breaks down under trial and how often we need encouragement to remember what we believe.

For this reason, I do not think Jesus' answer was a rebuke. Instead, he took the occasion to offer a lesson in faith. A study of the New Testament will show that at the scenes of his miracles, Jesus is always concerned for the faith of his disciples. Earlier, when the disciples' boat was sinking and

2. Alexander Maclaren, *Expositions of Holy Scripture*, 17 vols. (Grand Rapids: Baker, 1982), 10:98.
3. Herman Ridderbos, *John: A Theological Commentary* (Grand Rapids: Zondervan, 1997), 403–4.

Jesus quieted the winds and the waves, he first said to them, "Why are you afraid, O you of little faith?" (Matt. 8:26). On his way to Bethany to raise Lazarus, he told the disciples, "Lazarus has died, and for your sake I am glad that I was not there, so that you may believe" (John 11:14–15). Now, standing before the tomb, Jesus instructs Martha, "Did I not tell you that if you believed you would see the glory of God?" (11:40). Earlier, Jesus had said to her, "I am the resurrection and the life" (11:25). Having said this, Jesus now reminds Martha that if her faith will persist for a few minutes longer, she will see this glorious reality unveiled before her eyes.

Jesus' instruction to Martha overturns a widely held opinion. People say that "seeing is believing." But Jesus tells Martha that if she believes, she then will see. It is true that when it comes to men and women, we often can only trust their word when we see the results. Someone applies for a job and tells us that he is capable of doing it. We may hire him, but we also watch his performance. Only when we see what he can do can we really believe what he has said. But when it comes to God, his Word is enough for us to believe. And if we believe God, taking him at his Word, then we will see and receive our salvation.

Christians are just as challenged today to believe and see the glory of God. Donald Grey Barnhouse writes:

> It makes all the difference in the world, if you lose your job and say, "This catastrophe is not for my dishonor and my hurt, but it's for the glory of God that Christ may be magnified." The doctor comes and says to you, "I'm sorry to tell you that as far as I know, medical science can do absolutely nothing for you. Your case, from our point of view, . . . is incurable." It's a wonderful thing to say, "My Father measured this. He it is that put the spoon to my lips. The medicine may be a little bitter, but He knows what He's doing. He's the Great Physician. And He's the Great Resurrector. He's the One who's constantly able to bring life out of death. And out of the death of my circumstances, He is able to bring the life of joy and victory and triumph."[4]

In all circumstances, and especially in every trial, if we believe, we will see God's glory in the way he provides for us, the way he strengthens us, and the way he saves us. And many others will see his glory through our faith.

---

4. Donald Grey Barnhouse, *Illustrating the Gospel of John* (Grand Rapids: Revell, 1973), 149.

Christ's Example of Faith

It seems that Jesus' words were enough for Martha. She believed and the stone was removed. So now, having given a lesson in faith, Jesus offered an example of faith: "Jesus lifted up his eyes and said, 'Father, I thank you that you have heard me. I knew that you always hear me, but I said this on account of the people standing around, that they may believe that you sent me'" (John 11:41–42).

The first example that Jesus provides is that our faith must look upward to God: "Jesus lifted up his eyes." Martha's problem was that her eyes were looking down at the difficulties and saw only the obstacles to salvation. There was Lazarus's grave; what could possibly be done? Her eyes were filled with her circumstances when her faith should have been filled with God. This is what our faith should gain from our study of Scripture: an awareness of the power and grace of God. This is the lesson of Psalm 121, which begins, "I lift up my eyes to the hills. From where does my help come? My help comes from the LORD, who made heaven and earth" (Ps. 121:1–2). God is the Creator. When we look upward to him, we see the power that made all things and therefore is mighty to save.

Second, Jesus' faith displays bold confidence in God. He prayed, "Father, I thank you that you have heard me. I knew that you always hear me" (John 11:41–42). Apparently, Jesus had already prayed for Lazarus's resurrection, so he approaches the grave with a bold confidence in God's power. Our faith should act the same way: we should boldly believe in God's power and thank him even in advance for the blessings that he will provide. "I will never leave you nor forsake you," God has said (Heb. 13:5). "My God will supply every need of yours according to his riches in glory in Christ Jesus," Paul assures us (Phil. 4:19). Ours should be like Jesus' faith standing before Lazarus's tomb, thanking God and knowing that he will show his mighty power.

If anything should embolden our confidence in God, it is Jesus' raising of Lazarus and his own resurrection from the grave. Here, we find that God is not resigned to the status quo of death, sin, misery, and corruption. Those who trust in him will find that the Lord is faithful to deliver us, not from the presence of trials, but from the power of evil, death, and sin. We are not Christ, and God has not given us power to raise the dead. But God has promised us power to persevere with joy in every trial. There is unbreakable hope for those who know the resurrection power of God, the result of which is a holy boldness in prayer.

Third, Jesus reminds us that our faith is to give a witness to the world about God. He concluded his prayer, "I said this on account of the people standing around, that they may believe that you sent me" (John 11:42). Jesus was praying aloud, not to draw attention to himself but to point to God. He wanted all who heard—and there were many Jews who had gathered around—to believe that it was God who had sent him and was at work in him. Our faith should have a similar effect, encouraging others to seek their own relationship with God through Christ. William Barclay comments, "So much that we do is attempted in our own power and designed for our own prestige. . . . It may be that there would be more wonders in our life, too, if we ceased to act by ourselves and for ourselves and set God in the central place."[5]

CHRIST AS THE OBJECT OF FAITH

The episode at Lazarus's tomb tells us much about faith. Yet its main purpose is to reveal Jesus not merely as an example of faith, but as the great object of our faith. For this reason Jesus prayed that we "may believe that [God] sent me" (John 11:42).

It must have been dramatic to see Jesus walking up to Lazarus's tomb, calling for the stone to be removed, and, when it was removed, praying as he did to his Father in heaven. These were bold claims—to declare that God always hears him and that God had sent him. The onlookers might have been opening their mouths to object. This was, after all, an open challenge to their unbelief. But before anyone else could act, Jesus spoke again: "When he had said these things, he cried out with a loud voice, 'Lazarus come out'" (John 11:43). And at the call of Christ, to the amazement of all and the glory of God, as John relates, "the man who had died came out" (11:44).

John emphasizes that Jesus cried in a loud voice. The reason was not that he needed to shout loudly. But Christ was speaking in his divine authority. His was the voice that had called the cosmos into being (see John 1:1–3), and now that same voice calls the dead back to life. Even the grave does not withstand his power. A. W. Pink writes, "Here was public proof that the

5. William Barclay, *The Gospel of John*, 2 vols. (Philadelphia: Westminster, 1975), 2:116.

Lord Jesus had absolute power over the material world and over the realm of spirits. At His bidding a soul that had left its earthly tenement was called back from the unseen to dwell once more in the body."[6]

Because of this, Jesus is a Savior whom we can wholly trust. In the face of death, we look to him and find death's Conqueror. Gary Burge tells of a woman named Barbara, whose faith encouraged him early in his Christian life. One day she called to say that the doctors had discovered an inoperable brain tumor. Over the next two months, Barbara physically wasted away before his eyes. At their last meeting, she held his hand and spoke with confidence. "Don't worry about me," she said. "I'm about to go on the greatest adventure of my life." Soon afterward, she died.

Many people speak this way because they are avoiding the reality of death. But Barbara was not. Burge writes, "Her confidence was grounded in the strength of her knowledge of Jesus Christ. She knew him. She knew who he was. She knew his power and his ability. And she knew that he was waiting for her the moment she died. . . . Jesus overpowered death at the tomb of Lazarus. Jesus likewise overpowered the dread of death for Barbara."[7]

Jesus raised Lazarus back to a mortal life, which means that Lazarus later died again. But imagine his thoughts as he lay on his deathbed the second time. No doubt he still had uneasiness about the experience of dying. But imagine his confidence. "He knew that Jesus had a relationship with death like no other. Jesus was 'resurrection and life,' and so he was not going to the grave alone."[8] We know the same thing about Jesus, not because we have returned from the dead, but because of the witness of God's Word. Therefore, by trusting in Jesus, we may lie down on our deathbeds, confident of rising again.

John places a distinct emphasis on Jesus' voice. Jesus called to Lazarus, and by the word of Christ, the dead man rose. This resurrection is a picture of how every conversion takes place: by the call of Christ in the gospel as it is preached, witnessed, or read. Earlier, Jesus had taught, "My sheep hear my voice, and I know them, and they follow me" (John 10:27). Peter wrote, "You have been born again . . . , through the living and abiding word of God" (1 Peter 1:23).

6. Arthur W. Pink, *Exposition of the Gospel of John* (Grand Rapids: Zondervan, 1975), 614.
7. Gary M. Burge, *John*, NIV Application Commentary (Grand Rapids: Zondervan, 2000), 329.
8. Ibid.

The call of Christ has power to raise the dead and convert the sinner. It is often remarked that this is why Jesus spoke the name *Lazarus*: otherwise, all the tombs would have opened! Likewise, Jesus calls sinners to saving faith by name. We refer to this as the effectual call, that mighty work by which Christ calls us personally in his gospel and draws us with power so that we believe and follow him.

This means that by the power of Christ, even our poor preaching and stammering witnessing have power to save those who hear. I experienced this dramatically while witnessing the gospel to a group of Muslims in Uganda. I spoke of our need for forgiveness and of God's provision of his own Son to die on the cross to pay for our sins. This led to questions, which I tried to answer with God's Word. Other questions came, and after some time I had presented the gospel plainly. So, thinking I had found a good opportunity, I asked whether my Muslim hearers wanted to profess their faith in Jesus. One of them replied, "Mguzu [that is, white man], we already have believed. We were just waiting for you to stop talking so we could tell you!" It was not I but Christ who converted them through his Word.

What makes it possible for a white American, speaking through an interpreter, to lead a group of African Muslims to profess their faith in Christ? At the beginning of our conversation, they were openly hostile to Christianity, and thirty minutes later they had prayed as Christians and were meeting members of the local Christian church. What causes this? It is not the persuasive power of man, but the saving power of Christ calling in his Word. Therefore, let us preach God's Word. Let us speak the gospel of Jesus, because it is, the Bible says, "the power of God for salvation to everyone who believes" (Rom. 1:16). The voice of Christ that raised Lazarus from the grave still speaks in the Word so that those dead in sin come to spiritual life.

If Jesus' cry before Lazarus's tomb speaks of the power of his Word, then Lazarus's resurrection depicts the experience of everyone who believes. Paul states as much in Ephesians 2 when he describes our conversion as a spiritual resurrection. Before coming to Christ, Paul teaches, we are "dead in . . . trespasses and sins" (Eph. 2:1). This means that we are spiritually dead, unable to lift a finger to assist our own salvation. We are dead to God. We care nothing for God's Word. We have no interest in worship or the things of heaven. But when the call of Christ penetrates our hearts, we are raised to spiritual life. Paul says, "But God, being rich in mercy, because of the great love with which he loved us, even when we were dead in our trespasses, made us alive together with Christ" (2:4–5). As a result of spiritual rebirth, brought about by the power of Christ in his Word, we are changed. Our hearts are open to God. Our minds hunger for his teaching of truth. Our hearts are warmed to Christian fellowship. And our souls yearn to worship the God of grace. This is the spiritual resurrection, the new birth experienced by everyone who believes.

Notice what Jesus said after Lazarus had come forth: "The man who had died came out, his hands and feet bound with linen strips, and his face wrapped with a cloth. Jesus said to them, 'Unbind him, and let him go'" (John 11:44). This shows that, having been raised to life with Christ, we are no longer to go on wearing graveclothes. Like Lazarus fresh from the grave, the newborn Christian still bears the marks of death and sin. If he is to experience the new life to which he is called, the old life must be left behind, and the clothes of death exchanged for garments of holiness. "Put off your old self," Paul writes, "which belongs to your former manner of life and is corrupt through deceitful desires, and . . . put on the new self, created after the likeness of God in true righteousness and holiness" (Eph. 4:22–24).

Have you embraced Jesus' call to live in a new and holy way? Or are you still wrapped in the graveclothes of your former existence? If you are, then realize not only that Jesus calls you to a new life, but that he has power to transform you in holiness. Just as Lazarus experienced his resurrection by hearing Christ's voice, you will be transformed by the power of God's Word. But you must come to church and hear it. You must study the Bible for yourself. Then you will be "transformed by the renewal of your mind" (Rom. 12:2).

And know that on a great day to come, the voice of Christ will be heard throughout creation. For Christ will return according to the promise of his gospel. The Bible proclaims, "The Lord himself will descend from heaven with a cry of command, with the voice of an archangel, and with the sound of the trumpet of God. And the dead in Christ will rise" (1 Thess. 4:16). Jesus cried, "Lazarus, come out" (John 11:43), and the man who was dead came back to life. This is the Savior that we need, the saving Lord whom we must trust. He is the Savior whose power conquered death by his resurrection. And on that great day to come, when Christ cries out once more, it will be the voice of our loving Savior that we hear, a voice we recognize as our own Good Shepherd, and he will lead us into eternal resurrection life in the house of the Lord forever.

CHRIST'S POWER, OUR PRIVILEGE

The account of the raising of Lazarus concludes with a final wonderful detail. Notice that when Lazarus came forth, Jesus told others—undoubtedly Martha, Mary, and the other disciples—to "unbind him, and let him go" (John 11:44). This shows that Jesus delights to have us participate in his saving work of life. Earlier, he had called for others to remove the stone; now others are called to remove Lazarus's graveclothes. This shows that there is work for us to do. The power is Christ's, but ours is the privilege to play a part in the salvation of others. James Montgomery Boice comments:

> We cannot bring the dead back to life. But we can bring the word of Christ to them. We can do preparatory work, and we can do work afterward. We can help remove stones—stones of ignorance, error, prejudice, and despair. After the miracle we can help the new Christian by unwinding the graveclothes of doubt, fear, introspection, and discouragement.[9]

Are you willing to play such a role in the saving work of Christ? Have you prepared yourself to witness, encourage, instruct, and serve? A. W. Pink writes, "There is no higher privilege this side of Heaven than for us to be used of the Lord in rolling away gravestones and removing graveclothes."[10]

---

9. James Montgomery Boice, *The Gospel of John*, 5 vols. (Grand Rapids: Baker, 1999), 3:896.
10. Pink, *John*, 209.

77

ONE MAN TO DIE

John 11:45–57

But one of them, Caiaphas, who was high priest that year, said
to them, "You know nothing at all. Nor do you understand that
it is better for you that one man should die for the people, not
that the whole nation should perish." (John 11:49–50)

Great events usually produce differing reactions among different people. When the hijacked airliners brought down the Twin Towers on September 11, 2001, Americans grieved while others, far away, danced in the streets. The reactions depended on the people's relationship to those involved and their attitude toward what had happened. Presidential elections also produce differing reactions. One side wins and begins planning its agenda, while the losers lament and begin planning to derail the new administration.

Jesus' miracle of raising Lazarus from the dead was this kind of polarizing event. At a time of already heightened tension, Lazarus's resurrection raised the stakes; the Jews must either receive Jesus as the Savior or harden their opposition. John reports that some of both took place: "Many of the Jews therefore, who had come with Mary and had seen what he did, believed in him, but some of them went to the Pharisees and told them what Jesus had done" (John 11:45–46).

A Cynical Council

When we consider the actions of those who did not believe, we gain a stark portrait of unbelief. We sometimes wonder how people we know who have heard the gospel can continue in unbelief. But as John relates to us a meeting of the Sanhedrin, the Jewish ruling council, to deliberate what to do about Jesus, we see how deeply seated the sin of unbelief can be. It is a condition that can be overcome only by the saving grace of God.

Some who had observed the raising of Lazarus went to the religious leaders: "So the chief priests and the Pharisees gathered the Council and said, 'What are we to do? For this man performs many signs. If we let him go on like this, everyone will believe in him'" (John 11:47–48). Here were the best men of the nation—at least those elevated to the highest religious and political office—the chief priests, the Sadducees, and the Pharisees, the men most devoted to holiness. No doubt they opened their meeting in prayer. Yet the purpose of their meeting was to oppose the growing popularity of Jesus. No charge was made against his actions, and none denied the miracles that he had displayed. We might expect them to consider how to support his work and encourage people to follow him. But instead we find a most cynical council determined to thwart Jesus' mission.

The Sanhedrin saw the fact of Jesus' miracles as a great problem: "What are we to do? For this man performs many signs" (John 11:47). Earlier, they might have questioned the authenticity of Jesus' miracles. But now they no longer doubt. One would not think it a problem for a holy man who could heal the sick and raise the dead to appear. The reason it was a problem was that Jesus' manifest spiritual authority unmasked their own illegitimacy as spiritual leaders. These men were mainly interested in maintaining their own privileged positions. "If we let him go on like this," they reasoned, "everyone will believe in him" (11:48). The implication was that the people would no longer look to them for spiritual leadership.

There was also an implicit threat that they saw darkening the situation. Jesus' arrival might cause a religious uproar, and their Roman masters disliked uproars of all kinds. Therefore, they worried, "the Romans will come and take away both our place and our nation" (John 11:48). By "place," they might have meant the temple, although they might also have meant their own privileged positions, which were granted by the Roman governor. By "our nation," they meant the limited self-government they enjoyed. Bruce Milne explains: "Jesus clearly had much support among the masses, and that was likely to grow rather than diminish. The outcome could well be an abortive popular rising which the Romans would speedily and ruthlessly put down, and in the process impose direct rule, with possible further desecration, if not destruction, of the temple."[1]

How should we evaluate this cynical council of the Sanhedrin? First, they had come to rely on worldly powers rather than on God's power. These men were the guardians of the ancient Jewish faith, which looked back on God's deliverance in parting the Red Sea, fondly remembered David slaying Goliath, and applauded Elijah for his victories in God's power, including the raising of the dead. They were happy to teach these things, but when it came to their own situation, they thought differently. Jesus had come, displaying the power of God, yet they opposed him for fear of Roman swords. Gordon Keddie says of them: "God and Scripture did not figure at all in [their] reasoning. There was no appeal to truth, no evidence of spiritual commitment to the God of their fathers, but only policy and politics, power and position. . . . There was, in fact, no place for truth."[2]

They further show that religious people are sometimes Jesus' most bitter opponents. The Sadducees and Pharisees were enemies, yet they banded together against Jesus. They represent the kind of religion that is interested in erecting financial and political empires but little concerned with real saving power. Jesus is always a threat to such religion. Jesus demands a radical commitment to the Word and power of God. He calls us to risk losing everything in this world for the sake of his kingdom; indeed, he calls us to take up the cross, die to sin and self, and follow him. That is a very different kind of religion from that with which most people are comfortable. This same kind of opposition that Jesus received is encountered whenever sin and the cross are preached, as well as the radical calling of Christian

1. Bruce Milne, *The Message of John: Here Is Your King!* (Downers Grove, IL: InterVarsity Press, 1993), 173.

2. Gordon J. Keddie, *A Study Commentary on John*, 2 vols. (Darlington, UK: Evangelical Press, 2001), 1:441.

discipleship, which relies on God's power alone. If we want earthly ease from our religion, we will likely take the view of the Sanhedrin. But if we crave for the salvation that God gives, we will look on Jesus as a Messiah, rather than a threat to our lifestyle.

How do we preserve ourselves from this cynical pragmatism of the Jewish leaders? One way is to resolve always to obey the commands of God's Word. If we find ourselves rationalizing sin or compromising, as these men did, we can be sure that we have gone astray. Another way is always to have in mind God's saving mission in the world. In the time of the Sanhedrin, they knew that God had promised to send the Messiah; their first concern, then, should have been to recognize and support him when he came. In our time, God has promised to send forth his gospel and draw many to salvation. Whatever else we are seeking to promote, our first passion should be that we uphold and preach the good news of Jesus for the saving of souls.

If the attitude of the Sanhedrin is a challenge to religious unbelievers, it is no less a challenge to irreligious unbelievers. Many people avoid the gospel not because they expect that it is false but, like the Sanhedrin, because they suspect that it is true. James Montgomery Boice tells of a woman who was invited to attend a gospel meeting. She answered, "I am afraid to go for fear I will get converted." On another occasion, a minister asked a wife why her husband had been absent from church. "Well," she said, "he is afraid to come; for when he comes and hears the Word, it takes him nearly two weeks to get over it."[3] But the thing for us to get over is unbelief! The gospel offers to make us right with God and enter us into a changed life of holiness and blessing. If you fear to lose your unbelief, then you are as cynical and foolish as these Jewish leaders.

A CHILLING PROPHECY

Every group of this sort has a key leader who will either confront or reinforce its unbelief. The Sanhedrin's leader was the high priest, whose name was Caiaphas. He rebuked the others for their panicked thinking. "You know nothing at all," he stated. "Nor do you understand that it is better for you that one man should die for the people, not that the whole

3. James Montgomery Boice, *The Gospel of John*, 5 vols. (Grand Rapids: Baker, 1999), 3:900.

nation should perish" (John 11:49–50). There it was, the chilling conclusion to their cynical reasoning.

Caiaphas was a clear-eyed pragmatist. He knew that "sometimes one has to put up with a lesser evil to prevent a larger one, here the death of one for the sake of the nation as a whole."[4] In those days, the high priest was expected to collaborate with the Romans, since it was the Roman governor who had put him into office. But perhaps Caiaphas was sincerely concerned that the temple not be desecrated, not knowing that the temple was a picture of Jesus, God incarnate, and not realizing that the greatest desecration was the one that he was about to commit. John provides the chilling conclusion of his reasoning: "So from that day on they made plans to put [Jesus] to death" (John 11:53).

Even if we put the best possible construction on Caiaphas's motives, his method was entirely wrong. His calling was to fear God rather than the Romans. His duty was to uphold justice, not to sacrifice it on the altar of politics. For these very reasons, he failed miserably. By putting Jesus to death, Caiaphas did not secure Jerusalem's safety but ensured its destruction. Having rejected the true Messiah, the Jews went on to follow false messiahs who led them in revolt against Rome, with the result of Jerusalem's bloody destruction in A.D. 70. William Barclay writes, "The very steps they took to save their nation destroyed their nation."[5]

The history lesson provided by Caiaphas is that it never pays to oppose God. Boice comments: "You cannot frustrate God. You can oppose him, but only you will pay the consequences, as did these men. You may oppose him, but Christianity will spread. The Bible says, 'Many are the plans in the mind of a man, but it is the purpose of the Lord that will be established' (Prov. 19:21 RSV)."[6]

That God's power was at work to overturn the evil counsel of these false leaders is evident in what John goes on to say: "He did not say this of his own accord, but being high priest that year he prophesied that Jesus would die for the nation" (John 11:51). In the greatest irony, Caiaphas had spoken the truth, although with a meaning that he neither intended nor understood.

Caiaphas spoke, by the overruling providence of God, a great answer to the greatest question: Why did Jesus Christ die? Answers to this question

4. Herman Ridderbos, *John: A Theological Commentary* (Grand Rapids: Zondervan, 1997), 409.
5. William Barclay, *The Gospel of John*, 2 vols. (Philadelphia: Westminster, 1975), 2:122.
6. Boice, *John*, 3:901.

are found all through the Bible, since the purpose of the Bible is to point to Jesus' life, death, and resurrection. One answer is given by the Old Testament sacrificial system, which called for spotless lambs to be sacrificed for human sin. An answer was given in the Passover Feast, which Caiaphas and the Jews were even then preparing to observe. This remembered the night of Israel's deliverance from Egypt. The angel of death came to slay all the firstborn sons. But God's people spread the blood of a sacrificed lamb over their doors; seeing this, the angel of the Lord's wrath "passed over" and spared them. Other answers were given by the prophets, and in the New Testament there are doctrinal explanations. But there are few short explanations of the cross as accurate as that spoken by the high priest Caiaphas: "One man should die for the people" (John 11:50).

With these words, Caiaphas prophesied the nature of Jesus' atoning death: it was a vicarious sacrifice. The word *vicarious* signifies that Jesus died in the place of others. The word *sacrifice* means that he gave himself in payment for their sins. James Montgomery Boice writes: "It was Christ taking their place, dying in their stead, taking upon himself the guilt and punishment of their sins, in order that there might be nothing left for them but God's heaven."[7] Isaiah had explained, "He was wounded for our transgressions; he was crushed for our iniquities; upon him was the chastisement that brought us peace, and with his stripes we are healed. All we like sheep have gone astray; we have turned—every one—to his own way; and the LORD has laid on him the iniquity of us all" (Isa. 53:5–6).

This is a teaching that many find offensive; they object to being told that they can be made right with God only by Jesus' dying on the cross in their place. But their objection fails to realize the true gravity of sin. This is the true reason why "one man should die for the people"—not to spare them the vengeance of the Romans but to spare them the righteous wrath of God. Most of us treat sin lightly, but it is not possible for God to do so, because God is holy and his justice is perfect. I have been told by many who reject the cross, "My God is a God of love, not of judgment." But it is precisely the God of love who takes such offense at our hating, lying, stealing, and betraying. God is love. And it is also true that "God is light, and in him is no darkness at all" (1 John 1:5). Whether we take our sin seriously or not,

7. Ibid., 3:905.

the Bible is clear in stating that "the wrath of God is revealed from heaven against all ungodliness and unrighteousness of men" (Rom. 1:18).

There are others who call the idea that Jesus died to pay for our sins an immoral teaching, since God thus punishes his innocent Son. But this objection fails to realize just who Jesus is. Jesus is God the Son. J. Gresham Machen observed, "It is perfectly true that no mere man can pay the penalty of another man's sin. But it does not follow that Jesus could not do it; for Jesus was not mere man but the eternal Son of God. . . . The Christian doctrine of the atonement, therefore, is altogether rooted in the Christian doctrine of the deity of Christ."[8] In the mystery of the Godhead, not only did God the Father give his only Son, but God the Trinity suffered self-sacrifice to redeem lost sinners. In the perfect unity of wills between Jesus the Son and God the Father was a loving resolve to free us from our sins. Therefore, one writer states:

> [Jesus] offered himself as a sacrifice in our stead, bearing our sin in his own body on the tree. He suffered, not only awful physical anguish, but also the unthinkable spiritual horror of becoming identified with the sin to which he was infinitely opposed. He thereby came under the curse of sin, so that for a time even his perfect fellowship with his Father was broken. Thus God proclaimed his infinite abhorrence of sin by being willing himself to suffer all that, in place of the guilty ones, in order that he might justly forgive. Thus the love of God found its perfect fulfillment, because he did not hold back from even that uttermost sacrifice, in order that we might be saved from eternal death through what he endured.[9]

Caiaphas's prophecy further shows that Christ's death was a definite atonement. Jesus died not just to make salvation possible for all—although the value of his death is sufficient for all—but actually to redeem "the people" of God. The definite article shows that it was a definite group of people for whom Jesus died. He died, John says, "to gather into one the children of God who are scattered abroad" (John 11:52). Notice how John puts this. He does not say that whoever believes becomes a child of God wherever that person lives, though this is true. But in keeping with the strong emphasis on the doctrine of election in this Gospel, John tells us that scattered throughout

8. J. Gresham Machen, *Christianity and Liberalism* (1923; repr., Grand Rapids: Eerdmans, 1996), 126.
9. H. E. Guillebaud, *Why the Cross?* (Chicago: InterVarsity Press, 1947), 185.

this world and through the ages of this world are "the children of God." They are the ones whom Jesus earlier identified as those whom "the Father has given me" (6:37, 39), for whom he therefore died, and who thus are brought to faith by the regenerating work of the Holy Spirit.

The glorious consequences of Jesus' death were far beyond Caiaphas's imagining. To the high priest, this was a sordid, though sadly necessary, affair. But God reveals it as an act of amazing grace. By his death, Jesus not only redeems but gathers his flock throughout the world. This is why the atoning sacrifice of Christ is the chief and most beloved doctrine of all true Christians. Whereas Caiaphas sought to preserve the temple as the holy gathering place for the Jews, Jesus has erected his cross as the great gathering point where God's children from every tribe and tongue come to meet with God, worship, and receive his saving blessings.

A Crowd Divided

The final verses of John 11 bring to a conclusion the first half of this Gospel, which as we have noted is often named *The Book of Signs* for its focus on Jesus' miracles. It is a fitting conclusion, for it shows the three parties on whom its message focuses: Jesus and his disciples, the uncommitted crowd, and the hostile religious leaders.

First, we see Jesus. John says that he "therefore no longer walked openly among the Jews, but went from there to the region near the wilderness, to a town called Ephraim, and there he stayed with the disciples" (John 11:54). Jesus was preparing himself and his disciples for what he knew was soon to come. He knew what was being plotted against him; he is, as always, master of the situation, never surprised by the works of man. Jesus provides the exact contrast to his ungodly opponents. While they were willing to break God's command to avoid difficulty, Jesus embraces the most fearful trial in obedience to God's will. Trusting in God, he courageously faces what lies before him, unwilling to leave his calling and duty undone.

Then we have the undecided crowds. John says, "Now the Passover of the Jews was at hand, and many went up from the country to Jerusalem before the Passover to purify themselves. They were looking for Jesus and saying to one another as they stood in the temple, 'What do you think? That he will not come to the feast at all?'" (John 11:55–56). While performing their ritual purification, they failed to appreciate the defilement that was about to happen. Boice writes, "They were content merely to observe the outcome, which they knew well meant the execution of a perfectly innocent man."[10]

Finally, we observe the religious leaders, of whom John writes: "Now the chief priests and the Pharisees had given orders that if anyone knew where he was, he should let them know, so that they might arrest him" (John 11:57). Their plans were laid, and they merely awaited Jesus' arrival to spring into action.

A History Lesson

All of this presents a vital question for us. The crowds asked, "What do you think?" and the question now comes to us. The religious leaders, noting Jesus' mighty signs, asked, "What are we to do?" (John 11:47), and this question comes now to us as well.

There really are only three options, illustrated by these groups. First, like the crowd, you can avoid taking a position on Jesus, as many people do today. But the problem now is the same as the problem then: the evidence for Jesus is simply too strong. Any honest assessment of the facts of Jesus' life will yield proof that he is the Son of God, just as the facts of his death and resurrection prove him as the Savior of the world. You can ignore him and maintain the status quo of your life, but the facts of Jesus will not go away. Especially in death, you will face your disinterest in Jesus. He said, "Unless you believe that I am he you will die in your sins" (John 8:24). And how will you ignore Jesus on that great day to come, of which the Bible speaks, when every knee will bow "and every tongue confess that Jesus Christ is Lord, to the glory of God the Father" (Phil. 2:11)?

Second, you can oppose Jesus, as Caiaphas and the Sanhedrin did. But in doing so, you will join the ranks of history's great losers. History is filled with the record of those who opposed Jesus and his gospel. All of them are gone, but his church and gospel remain. You can oppose Jesus, but can you really hope to be successful? By opposing Jesus and his gospel, you will only join the lamentable company of those condemned in God's Word, who "take counsel together, against the LORD and against his Anointed."

10. Boice, John, 3:910.

The Bible says, "He who sits in the heavens laughs; the Lord holds them in derision" (Ps. 2:2–4).

If we understand who Jesus really is, as the rulers did, or if we have heard the Bible's report of him, as did the crowds in that day, there is only one sensible option—the third one: to believe on Jesus and follow him. But you object, "This will mean surrendering my lifestyle to Jesus!" Indeed it will, for Jesus is Savior only to those who take him as Lord. He will summon you to the cross, and by losing your life, you will gain it in resurrection triumph. You will be neither a victim of history, as the crowds were, nor an enemy to history, as were the religious leaders. Instead, you will be a beneficiary of God's saving plan for history through the life and death of his only Son. Your life will gain a real significance, and in the end Jesus will receive you into everlasting glory.

78

FRAGRANT DEVOTION

John 12:1–11

Mary therefore took a pound of expensive ointment made from pure nard, and anointed the feet of Jesus and wiped his feet with her hair. The house was filled with the fragrance of the perfume.
(John 12:3)

ohn 12:1 marks a major transition in John's Gospel, beginning his account of Jesus' final week that concludes with the cross. The seven-day period that begins here is the greatest week in history. The seven days of creation were, of course, of great significance. John also takes care in recording the first seven days of Jesus' ministry (see John 1:19–51). But the surpassing importance of Jesus' final week can be seen in the fact that John devotes almost half his Gospel to it, an emphasis that we see reflected in the other Gospels.

Combining the Gospels, we can arrange a rough chronology of Jesus' last days. On Saturday, he dined with Lazarus and his sisters. On Sunday, Jesus entered triumphantly into Jerusalem. He returned to Jerusalem on Monday, cursing the barren fig tree on the way. Tuesday saw his last public preaching in Jerusalem, concluding with Jesus' retirement to the Mount of Olives, giving the Olivet Discourse to his disciples. On Wednesday, he stayed again in Bethany, returning to the city on Thursday to observe the Passover with his disciples, after which he was arrested. That night and morning Jesus was tried, and on Friday he was crucified.[1]

I find it interesting to observe the difference between what John records as compared with the content of the other Gospels. While Matthew, Mark, and Luke focus mainly on Jesus' public events, John writes of the private fellowship that Jesus enjoyed with his close circle of disciples. John seems to have enjoyed Jesus' intimate affection (see John 13:23), and his Gospel dwells on the theme of fellowship with Christ.

DEVOTION MODELED

Jesus had been staying away from Jerusalem until the time had come for his dramatic entry. But now as that time drew near, he returned to Bethany. His coming was greeted with joy and thanksgiving for the recent event of Lazarus's resurrection. To celebrate Jesus' return, "they gave a dinner for him there. Martha served, and Lazarus was one of those reclining with him at table" (John 12:2).

This banquet provides a lovely portrait of different believers' offering different kinds of ministry to the Lord. Martha's gift was service, and she offered it gladly. Risen Lazarus served as a witness of Jesus' saving power, so he sat next to him at the feast. Mary was known for her deep devotion to Jesus. John recounts: "Mary therefore took a pound of expensive ointment made from pure nard, and anointed the feet of Jesus and wiped his feet with her hair. The house was filled with the fragrance of the perfume" (John 12:3).

This verse records one of the most beautiful scenes from the life of Jesus. Mary stands out for her portrait of loving devotion, displaying four features of devotion to Christ that all of us should emulate.

First, Mary's devotion was *courageous*. Chapter 11 concluded with ominous news from the religious leaders, who broadcast that anyone who knew where Jesus was "should let them know, so that they might arrest him" (John 11:57). One who failed to do this would likely be accused as an accessory alongside Jesus. Yet Mary and the others openly hosted Jesus for this meal.

---

1. It is possible, however, based on parallels between John 12:1–11 and Mark 14:1–9, that Jesus' feast with Martha, Mary, and Lazarus took place on Wednesday but was placed earlier by John for thematic reasons.

As we learn, Lazarus was in particular danger, since the rulers sought to eliminate him as the evidence of Jesus' miracle. Nonetheless, these courageous disciples placed their devotion to Christ ahead of their own safety.

Second, Mary exhibited a *costly* devotion. She "took a pound of expensive ointment made from pure nard" to anoint Jesus. This would have been a bottle of perfumed oil of the highest quality. Judas claimed that its value was "three hundred denarii," roughly a year's wages for a working man, or tens of thousands of dollars in today's money. This was expensive oil of the very highest quality.

Some commentators conclude from this that Mary, Martha, and Lazarus must have been wealthy. If this is the case, they set a good example for those with great financial means today. One of the dangers of wealth is that it creates an appetite for pleasure and valuable things. Statistics show that rich people tend to give away a smaller portion of their money than poorer people do. But Mary was not this way. If she could afford valuable things, she also did not hesitate to give them lovingly to Jesus.

But it is quite possible that Mary was not a wealthy person. This jar of oil might have been a family legacy or a unique treasure that she had acquired. Whatever the case, her devotion was such that she delighted to offer the very best she had to show her love for the Master. Thinking nothing of herself, she found her great delight in giving her very best for Jesus' blessing.

Mary's gift challenges us regarding the price that we are willing to pay as disciples of Jesus. What is your most treasured possession? Is it your stock portfolio? If so, then one way you can place Jesus first is to give sacrificially from your treasured assets out of love for him. Is it your lifestyle? Then you should consider giving up recreation to do service in the church or share the gospel with others. Is it the standard of living you provide for your family, which you would not give up to go into full-time Christian work? Is it the self-image that worldly acceptance provides you, so that you will not boldly identify yourself as a Christian? If so, you should examine your heart and recalculate the value of the Lord Jesus Christ, drawing near to him to cultivate the costly devotion of Mary.

F. B. Meyer tells of an occasion when a preacher suggested that his hearers make a love offering to Jesus of something that was especially precious. We love to give costly gifts to each other, so why not make a costly gift to Jesus? As the offering plate was passed, jewels and other valuable items filled the trays. But among them was something especially precious. An older woman had given a note stating that her daughter had long wanted to go to far lands as a missionary, but that this mother had stood in her way, not wanting to part with her. Now, out of her love for Christ, she would stand in the way no longer, but would give her daughter up to Jesus to spread his gospel in the world.[2]

What a blessing it is when our awareness of the priceless love of Christ has set us free from our need to possess people and things. If we have Jesus, we have everything that we could ever really want or need. But sometimes we have to let go of other things we love to recognize the preciousness of Christ.

Third, Mary's was a *humble* devotion. The use of perfume was customary for special events. This was a time when bathing was infrequent, and the hot climate produced body odors. A host would place a daub of oil on the head or face of a guest, but Mary's devotion was such that she did far more for Jesus. With Jesus reclined at the low table and his legs extended outward, Mary proceeded to anoint not only Jesus' head but also his feet.

This is noteworthy because it was considered beneath people to wash the feet of others. Even slaves had rights, and one of their rights was that they did not have to touch their master's dirty and unpleasant feet. But Mary did not hesitate to wash and anoint Jesus' feet. Skip Ryan comments: "Mary is giving up her rights before the Lord. There is nothing He cannot ask of her. Touching his feet becomes her pledge of unconditional service."[3]

Undoubtedly, Mary's humility before Jesus arose from her awareness of who he was. If she had previously known, his raising of her brother proved his deity as the very Son of God. So for Mary, any service to Jesus was an honor and pleasure, an occasion to worship him and show thanks for what he had done. She was like John the Baptist, who said, "He who is mightier than I is coming, the strap of whose sandals I am not worthy to untie" (Luke 3:16). John meant that the most menial thing he might do for Jesus is not beneath him but is actually above him, so glorious and great is the Lord Jesus Christ. In contrast, those who hold back from service to Christ, especially humble service, can only be those who have not comprehended the grace and glory of God in the face of Christ.

Mary's devotion to Christ was more than humble; it must also, fourth, be described as *extravagant*. If the disciples who looked on were amazed

2. F. B. Meyer, *The Life of Love* (Old Tappan, NJ: Revell, 1987), 190.
3. Joseph "Skip" Ryan, *That You May Believe* (Wheaton, IL: Crossway, 2003), 249.

when she anointed Jesus' feet, they were shocked when she "wiped his feet with her hair." It was scandalous for a woman to unbind her hair in public. A married woman could be divorced by her husband for this, and a single woman could be stoned. For a woman to let down her hair expressed intimacy, openness, and fervent love, and it was done only in the privacy of the home amid close family members. So by not only unbinding her hair but using it to wipe Jesus' feet, Mary expressed a completely surrendered devotion in which nothing was held back. She knew she was completely safe in his holy presence, and seeing him as her divine Lord, she desired that nothing stand between her devotion and him.

Where did Mary get this devotion? The answer is found in every Gospel account in which she is often seen sitting at Jesus' feet. Mary had turned her attention to Jesus, had noted how different he was from everyone else, had listened to his teaching, and had given him her heart. Everyone who draws near to Jesus this way will also feel the kind of devotion for him that Mary displayed.

A similar example was a man who wanted to be a preacher but lacked the needed gifts. He became a successful businessman and earned a great deal of money. But he always wanted to do something for Jesus, so he helped to open up a mission hall in the center of a major city. After the mission closed each Friday, he would arrive in working clothes with a bucket of water and a brush. On his knees he scrubbed the floor and washed the chairs. For quite a while, no one knew of this service. But on Saturday some men from his company went into the mission and found him scrubbing. "You shouldn't be doing this!" they cried. "We will do it ourselves, or pay someone else to do it." But he objected. "No," he said, "please let me do it. I want to do it for Jesus' sake." That is precisely the point: "for Jesus' sake." Whatever we can do we also should do out of hearts surrendered to him.[4]

DEVOTION CHALLENGED

It is sometimes quipped that no good deed goes unpunished. Whether that is true or not, it is true that genuine devotion to Christ seldom goes unchallenged. So it was for Mary: "Judas Iscariot, one of his disciples (he who

4. James Montgomery Boice, *The Gospel of John*, 5 vols. (Grand Rapids: Baker, 1999), 3:920.

was about to betray him), said, 'Why was this ointment not sold for three hundred denarii and given to the poor?'" (John 12:4–5). Here is a challenge that is frequently made against the passionate devotion to Jesus displayed by Mary. It is better, many would argue, to do practical good works instead of spending time with the Lord.

This spirit is very much alive today. Preachers hear people complain that sermons focus on the glories of Christ rather than the practical needs of their own lives. Whenever time or treasures are offered up simply to exalt the glory of Jesus, some will complain that they could have been better used for the interests of man. Many people echo Judas's opinion today, little realizing whom they are quoting. William Hendriksen writes, "Judas is the type of man who has money on his mind all the while. He views everything from the aspect of pecuniary value."[5] What a contrast he presents to Mary, who viewed everything from the aspect of the glory of Christ.

But there is a second objection to Mary's devotion to Jesus, one that the former is often employed to mask. John writes, "[Judas] said this, not because he cared about the poor, but because he was a thief, and having charge of the moneybag he used to help himself to what was put into it" (John 12:6).

Judas proves how persuasively a hypocrite can play the role of a disciple, even one entrusted with high privileges. It is interesting that Jesus, who surely knew that Judas was a thief if John did, should nonetheless place Judas in charge of the money donated to support the disciples. Jesus was evidently no more afraid of what Judas might do by stealing than by what Judas would do by betraying him.

Mary's devotion offended Judas because his focus in religion was on gaining for himself. All he could think of when Mary poured her oil on Jesus was the money that he might have taken for himself if it had been sold. Mary broke her bottle to give all that she had to Jesus, while Judas wanted to break into the money pouch to take from Jesus. We should be warned if there are signs of Judas's thinking in our hearts, coming to church without any devotion to Jesus, seeking only business contacts or social benefits. Judas's greed led him to betray Jesus, making his among the most reviled names in all of history and ultimately costing him his very soul.

5. William Hendriksen, *Exposition of the Gospel according to John*, 2 vols., New Testament Commentary (Grand Rapids: Baker, 1953), 2:177.

Jesus spoke out to defend Mary: "Leave her alone, so that she may keep it for the day of my burial. For the poor you always have with you, but you do not always have me" (John 12:7–8). Jesus was not speaking callously about the poor; all through the Gospels, his concern for mercy is obvious. Rather, he argues that our concern for the problems of this world should not displace our worship of the Savior from heaven. Gorden Keddie explains: "At that moment . . . , they stood at the hinge of history. Jesus would not always be with them. . . . Salvation itself was about to be secured for the world that Jesus had come to save."[6] Since Jesus was about to die on the cross, the very best use of the oil was the anointing of his body. Indeed, it is probable that through all the events to come—Jesus' arrest, his unjust trial, his cruel murder, and his burial in the tomb—the fragrance of Mary's devotion still clung to his body.

DEVOTION THREATENED

This account of Jesus' anointing provides a model of devotion and answers a challenge to devotion to him. But devotion to Jesus is also threatened with deadly violence: "So the chief priests made plans to put Lazarus to death as well, because on account of him many of the Jews were going away and believing in Jesus" (John 12:10–11).

If devoted Mary threatened Judas's conscience, resurrected Lazarus threatened the hostile Jewish leaders far more. Her devotion offered a lasting memorial to the divine glory of Christ, but Lazarus's witness offered a memorial to the divine power of Christ. Indeed, as people learned that Jesus had returned to Bethany, they were just as fascinated to see Lazarus as they were to see the Lord. John states: "When the large crowd of the Jews learned that Jesus was there, they came, not only on account of him but also to see Lazarus, whom he had raised from the dead" (John 12:9).

Lazarus was an unlikely "star witness" for Jesus as the Messiah. Nothing outstanding about him is ever recorded in the Gospels, and he never says anything worth recording. So what is it about Lazarus that makes his witness so powerful? "The answer is not in what Lazarus did for Jesus," writes Kent Hughes. "It is in what Jesus did for Lazarus." The same is true

6. Gordon J. Keddie, *A Study Commentary on John*, 2 vols. (Darlington, UK: Evangelical Press, 2001), 1:453.

of every Christian. "If we were dead in our sins, and if over us a voice has cried, 'Come forth,' and if we have risen to newness of life and the Master has said, 'Unbind him, and let him go,' so that now we are free, then we have become unanswerable arguments for Jesus Christ."[7]

Lazarus was a threat to the rule of the leaders who hated Jesus, as well as to the fragile peace they sought with the Romans. For this reason, the fact that he had so publicly died and been raised by Jesus was a serious problem for them. J. C. Ryle writes: "They could not deny the fact of his having been raised again. Living, and moving, and eating, and drinking within two miles of Jerusalem, after lying four days in the grave, Lazarus was a witness to the truth of Christ's Messiahship, whom they could not possibly answer or put to silence."[8] For this reason, "the chief priests made plans to put Lazarus to death as well" (John 12:10). Matthew Henry observed, "God will have Lazarus to live by a miracle, and they will have him to die by malice."[9] Caiaphas had begun by declaring that it would be better for one man to die for the nation (11:50), but already there would be two. Before the Caiaphases of history are finished, millions of Christ's followers will die for their witness to Jesus, yet not one Christian death will effectively stop the spread of the gospel.

Christians should not be surprised to be similarly threatened for their Christian witness. Burying the evidence is a tactic as ancient as Caiaphas and as modern as the daily newspaper. But realize that it is only the guilty who take such a course of action. And since Satan wants above all to bury or at least obscure the evidence of God's saving power at work in the world, Christians not only should be zealous to give their witness but should feed their own faith on the proofs for the claims of Christ, both those in the Bible and those living among us in the church today.

So does your faith in Christ challenge others to consider the gospel? Is your godly life threatening to unbelief? Are you able to tell people why they should believe on Jesus, and are they able to find convincing proofs of salvation in your conduct? If we continue in the noble line of Mary and Lazarus, we can be certain that others will see the truth of Jesus in our lives,

7. R. Kent Hughes, *John: That You May Believe* (Wheaton, IL: Crossway, 1999), 295.

8. J. C. Ryle, *Expository Thoughts on the Gospels: John*, 3 vols. (Edinburgh: Banner of Truth, 1999), 2:350.

9. Matthew Henry, *Commentary on the Whole Bible*, 6 vols. (Peabody, MA: Hendrickson, 2009), 5:864.

and what was said of Lazarus will be said of us, too: "On account of him many . . . were . . . believing in Jesus" (John 12:11).

DEVOTION REWARDED

The devotion for Jesus that was modeled by Mary, challenged by Judas, and threatened by the corrupt leaders was richly rewarded by the Lord. One reward of devotion to Christ is seen in Mary's apparent understanding of his saving mission. In Mark's Gospel, Jesus defends Mary's lavish outpouring of expensive oil by stating, "She has done what she could; she has anointed my body beforehand for burial" (Mark 14:8). This indicates that Mary, perhaps alone among the disciples, understood Jesus' approaching cross and shared its anticipation with him. Another reward is seen in the experience of Lazarus. Having already experienced a literal resurrection, Lazarus would have been emboldened to a life of strong faith and would have been greatly comforted by his personal experience of resurrection when it came time for him to enter into death a second time. Surely Lazarus would have lain down in death, eagerly expecting the call of Christ that would raise him up to everlasting glory.

Yet I think the chief reward of devotion to Christ is seen in one last detail that John provides from this lovely episode. He writes that after Mary anointed Jesus' feet and washed them with her hair, as she moved about, "the house was filled with the fragrance of the perfume" (John 12:5). Her devotion to Jesus was *fragrant*, and wherever she went the aroma of her gift to Jesus was spread. What greater reward could we have than this! And what greater blessing could we give to others! If we will see Jesus in his divine glory and grace, and if we will break the bottle of our hearts to pour out in devotion to him, then our lives will bear the fragrance of his salvation, spreading gospel mercy wherever we go. There can be no greater reward than to be used in this way to share the glory of Christ in the world, knowing that as we pour out our devotion to him, he will pour out through us the grace of his gospel for the salvation of those we know and love.

79

BEHOLD, YOUR KING IS COMING!

John 12:12—19

*Jesus found a young donkey and sat on it, just as it is written,
"Fear not, daughter of Zion; behold, your king is coming, sitting
on a donkey's colt!" (John 12:14–15)*

ext year in Jerusalem!" These words from the traditional
Jewish Passover express the fervor with which Jews long
for their ancestral home. Jerusalem was where the true
Passover was celebrated, at the holy temple on Mount Zion, with the holy
Levitical priesthood. There were three festivals at which ancient Jews were
expected to be present in Jerusalem: Passover, Pentecost, and Tabernacles.
Tabernacles might have been the most festive occasion, being the feast for
the completion of the annual harvest. But Passover was the most solemn,
remembering the exodus deliverance when the blood of the lamb had protected God's people from the angel of wrath.

Jesus' entry into Jerusalem for the Passover in his third year of ministry
is one of the great, dramatic events of his earthly life. The triumphal entry
is one of the few events recorded in all four Gospels. Yet it is probably the
most poorly understood. It is marked by a strange departure from Jesus'
usual behavior. Elsewhere Jesus withdraws from public confrontation, as he

did immediately after raising Lazarus, since the authorities had published what amounted to an arrest warrant for him. Many think that Jesus now entered with such fanfare as a final appeal for the people to accept him as King. But Jesus entered Jerusalem so publicly not to garner public approval for a secular throne. Instead, because the time had finally come, he was goading the leaders of the Jewish Sanhedrin into acting on their wicked plans. J. C. Ryle explains Jesus' intent:

> The time had come at last when Christ was to die for the sins of the world. The time had come when the true Passover Lamb was to be slain, when the true blood of atonement was to be shed, when Messiah was to be "cut off" according to prophecy (Dan. 9:26), when the way into the holiest was to be opened by the true High Priest to all mankind. Knowing this, He placed Himself prominently under the notice of the whole Jewish nation. . . . He died in a week when by His remarkable public entry into Jerusalem He had caused the eyes of all Israel to be specially fixed upon Himself.[1]

THE GRAND ENTRY

History has known many grand entries: conquerors returning home from war, kings and queens arriving for coronation, and sports and media stars celebrating their triumphs. But none is as remarkable as the triumphal entry of Jesus into Jerusalem.

For one thing, it is likely that the assembled crowd was truly vast. The first-century Jewish historian Josephus recorded that one census taken at Passover counted 2,700,000 people in the small city. A count of the lambs brought for slaughter numbered 256,500, with one lamb slain for at least ten people present. If those numbers seem hard to believe—and many scholars doubt them, since Josephus does seem to inflate his numbers—few deny that there would have been at least half a million people thronging the streets of Jerusalem.

The name of Jesus would have been on practically everyone's tongue. One reason was the public notice made by the rulers calling for his arrest (John 11:57). Another reason was the spread of the news from Bethany. Jesus' friend

---

1. J. C. Ryle, *Expository Thoughts on the Gospels: John*, 3 vols. (Edinburgh: Banner of Truth, 1999), 2:365.

Lazarus had died. Four days after Lazarus was laid in the tomb, Jesus called him forth from the grave. Numerous witnesses attested to the fact, and an even greater number of people had seen Jesus and Lazarus together just the day before Jesus' entry, at the dinner given in his honor (12:9).

Therefore, as Jesus approached Jerusalem on what we remember as Palm Sunday, the effect was explosive: "The next day the large crowd that had come to the feast heard that Jesus was coming to Jerusalem. So they took branches of palm trees and went out to meet him, crying out, 'Hosanna! Blessed is he who comes in the name of the Lord, even the King of Israel!'" (John 12:12–13).

John's Gospel is the only record to note the palm branches, so it seems that he wanted to emphasize this feature. As Jesus approached, the people draped the road with their cloaks (see Matt. 21:8) and with palm branches. This is a curious detail, since palms played no role in the Passover Feast but rather in the Feast of Tabernacles. Why, then, did the people wave and place palm branches before Jesus?

The answer is that the palm branch had been for the previous two hundred years a general symbol for Jewish nationalism. When Simon Maccabaeus drove the Syrians out of Jerusalem and restored the temple a hundred and fifty years earlier, he was heralded with waving palms. During the wars of Jewish rebellion a generation after Jesus, coins were struck by the insurgents with an image of palm branches. The palm was the Jews' emblem for a conqueror, an association that they also made with the promised Messiah. William Barclay writes that the Jews who waved these palms

> were looking on Jesus as God's Anointed One, the Messiah, the Deliverer, the One who was to come. And there is no doubt that they were looking on Him as the Conqueror. To them it must have been only a matter of time until the trumpets rang out and the call to arms sounded and the Jewish nation swept to its long delayed victory over Rome and over the world.[2]

This idea is reinforced by the cries lifted up at Jesus' approach: "Hosanna! Blessed is he who comes in the name of the Lord, even the King of Israel!" (John 12:13). "Hosanna!" means "Save us now!" Most significantly, it comes from Psalm 118, a messianic psalm sung during the Passover Feast: "Save

2. William Barclay, *The Gospel of John*, 2 vols. (Philadelphia: Westminster, 1975), 2:136.

us, we pray, O LORD! O LORD, we pray, give us success! Blessed is he who comes in the name of the LORD! We bless you from the house of the LORD" (Ps. 118:25–26). So frequently were these words sung and repeated during the various feasts of Israel that they had become practically the fight song for the Jewish independence party. That this was the spirit of those welcoming Jesus is evident from the fact that they added the words "even the King of Israel!" As Britons hail their monarch with "God Save the King!" and Americans greet their President with "Hail to the Chief," the Jews welcomed Jesus with the "Hosanna" from Psalm 118.

THE KING OF PEACE

People have different mental images of how Jesus responded to this welcome. Those who envision him as exulting in the attention, like a modern hero riding through a ticker-tape parade, are clearly wrong. But those who envision a stoic Jesus, passively going his way as if he barely noticed, are also wrong. A key to understanding this event is that Jesus did not begin his entry mounted on a donkey. The other Gospels make it clear that Jesus anticipated what would happen, and had made miraculous provision for an unridden donkey to await him on the Mount of Olives (see Matt. 21:2). But as Jesus arrived in full view of the crowd, he was walking. It was only atop the last ridge that he mounted the donkey in a clear symbolic statement. Moving forward, he observed the city itself soon coming into his view. Jesus stopped and, Luke tells us, wept over it, saying, "Would that you, even you, had known on this day the things that make for peace! But now they are hidden from your eyes" (Luke 19:42), and then Jesus prophesied Jerusalem's coming destruction (19:43–44). This proves that Jesus lamented the palm branches, or at least the kind of salvation they proclaimed.

Jesus did present himself as Israel's true King, but not as the king whom the people were seeking. This was the provocative point made by the donkey on which he rode. The horse-mounted king came bent on war; the donkey was ridden by a king who came with peace. Therefore, the point Jesus made was clear to all. His manner of entry could not have more strongly renounced the Zealots' militant idea of what the Messiah should be. Jerusalem was offering Jesus the kingship, only a kind of kingship that Jesus pointedly rejected in the manner of his coming. This explains how this crowd that so excitedly welcomed Jesus could call for his crucifixion just days later. Jesus had rejected their offer of a warbound kingship on Palm Sunday; they rejected his kingdom of peace on Good Friday.

John reminds us that Jesus' entry on a donkey perfectly fulfilled an important Old Testament prophecy. This alone provided a good reason for Jesus to act as he did: the minute fulfillment of so many ancient prophecies is a strong proof of Jesus' claims. The prophecies foretold the character that the Messiah would exhibit in his coming. One of the most important was given by the prophet Zechariah about five hundred years before Jesus. John writes that Jesus sat on the donkey "just as it is written, 'Fear not, daughter of Zion; behold, your king is coming, sitting on a donkey's colt!'" (John 12:14–15).

John is referring us to the prophecy of Zechariah 9:9: "Rejoice greatly, O daughter of Zion! Shout aloud, O daughter of Jerusalem! Behold, your king is coming to you; righteous and having salvation is he, humble and mounted on a donkey, on a colt, the foal of a donkey." When New Testament writers quote an Old Testament verse, they are normally referring us to the entire passage in which the verse is found, wanting us to read the verse in its full original context.

Zechariah's prophecy provides a rich understanding of the coming Messiah. It describes the coming King as righteous and having salvation, humble and bringing peace. The next verse continues by foretelling the end of warfare and the bringing of peace to all the nations of the earth: "I will cut off the chariot from Ephraim and the war horse from Jerusalem; and the battle bow shall be cut off, and he shall speak peace to the nations; his rule shall be from sea to sea, and from the River to the ends of the earth" (Zech. 9:10). Against the backdrop of this well-known prophecy, we see how strongly Jesus' manner of entry served as a rebuke to Jerusalem's mood. Little did the Jews appreciate that the kind of Messiah they sought was directly contrary to the Savior whom God had promised to send. What a warning this is to us, as Christians and churches, that our spiritual agenda be the one that God has actually mandated in his Word!

The Jews in Zechariah's time did not have a king, their last monarch having perished in the Babylonian captivity. So in that kingless era, God's people were told to look for the coming of the Ruler whom God would send, One who fits and fulfills the messianic expectation of the Old Testament.

Here is a King who is just and having salvation, and who comes in meekness and affliction. David Baron writes:

> This prophecy was intended to introduce, in contrast to earthly warfare and kingly triumph, another Kingdom, of which the just King would be the Prince of Peace, who was meek and lowly in His Advent, who would speak peace to the heathen, and whose sway would yet extend to earth's utmost bounds. . . . If [there] ever was a true picture of the Messiah-King and His Kingdom, it is this: and if ever Israel was to have a Messiah, or the world a Saviour, He must be such as is described in this prophecy—not merely in the letter, but in the spirit of it.[3]

The only person in all of history who fits this description is the Lord Jesus Christ. Here is a wonderful portrayal of his person, the Messiah who comes as King. First, Jesus is righteous. Many commentators think this simply states that his reign will be just, but it must also touch upon him as a person, that he is himself righteous. Isaiah 42:1 said of him: "Behold my servant, whom I uphold, my chosen, in whom my soul delights; I have put my Spirit upon him; he will bring forth justice to the nations." The One who establishes righteousness is the One who is pleasing in God's sight, who is himself righteous in all his ways. Jesus accomplished perfect righteousness as the personal qualification for serving as God's righteous King.

Second, God's coming King is "humble and mounted on a donkey, on a colt, the foal of a donkey." The donkey was a royal mount in Israel's earlier days. The judges, as well as David, rode a donkey, and Solomon, the king of peace, rode one in his coronation ceremony. This, therefore, is associated with royalty, characterized by humility and gentleness of spirit. Comparing this to the war horses ridden by worldly kings, Thomas McComiskey writes:

> The donkey stands out . . . as a deliberate rejection of this symbol of arrogant trust in human might, expressing subservience to the sovereignty of God. Jerusalem's king is of humble mien, yet victorious, and so it has always been that the church does not effectively spread the gospel by sword or by arrogance, but by mirroring the humble spirit of its king and savior.[4]

---

3. David Baron, *The Visions and Prophecies of Zechariah* (Grand Rapids: Kregel, 1918), 303–4.
4. Thomas E. McComiskey, *The Minor Prophets: An Exegetical and Expository Commentary*, 3 vols. (Grand Rapids: Baker, 1998), 3:1166.

Such is the entrance of this messianic King, One who is righteous, with salvation, but who comes not in worldly might but in the weakness of the cross. One of our Palm Sunday hymns expresses it well:

Ride on, ride on in majesty!
In lowly pomp ride on to die:
O Christ, your triumphs now begin
O'er captive death and conquered sin. . . .

Ride on, ride on in majesty!
In lowly pomp ride on to die;
Bow your meek head to mortal pain,
Then take, O God, your pow'r and reign.[5]

Just as these words rebuke the ancient Jews who rejected Jesus for refusing their worldly agenda, they also rebuke us today if we are seeking a militant savior in Christ. How easy it is for Christians to get so caught up in the so-called culture war—the contest today between policies promoting Christian values and those of pagan unbelief—that we mount a war horse to ride against our sinful neighbors. But the Jesus who rode into Jerusalem on a humble donkey would have his followers likewise minister his truth in loving humility. As Christians face an increasingly hostile secular society, we must resist the temptation to wage war, but instead we must represent the Prince of Peace in his truth and love. As we interact with unbelieving neighbors—including even such flagrant culture-war enemies as abortionists, homosexuals, and evolution proponents—we must reach out to them with the same loving desire for their salvation that drove Jesus into Jerusalem to take up the cross.

We should meditate on the contrast between the person of Christ and that of every earthly king. Whereas earthly kings rule for their own riches and glory, Christ rules for our salvation. Earthly kings reign from above the people, in haughty power, but this King condescends to dwell among us. Jonathan Edwards writes, "His condescension is great enough to become their friend, to become their companion, to unite their souls to Him in spiritual marriage. . . . Yea, it is great enough to abase Himself yet lower for

5. Henry H. Milman, "Ride On, Ride On in Majesty!" (1827).

them, even to expose Himself to shame and spitting; yea, to yield up Himself to an ignominious death for them."[6]

In Jesus' life and ministry we find one example of humble meekness after another. A. W. Pink remarks, "Notice it in the men selected by Him to be His ambassadors: He chose not the wise, the learned, the great, the noble, but poor fishermen for the most part. Witness it in the company He kept: He sought not the rich and renowned, but was 'the Friend of publicans and sinners.' See it in the miracles He performed: again and again He enjoined the healed to go and tell no man what had been done for them. Behold it in the unobtrusiveness of His service: unlike the hypocrites who sounded a trumpet before them, He sought not the limelight, shunned advertising, and disdained popularity. . . . When He, in fulfillment of prophecy, presented Himself to Israel as their King, He entered Jerusalem 'lowly, and riding upon an ass.'"[7]

Such a King is worth shouting over, which is why the prophet enjoins the people: "Rejoice greatly, O daughter of Zion! Shout aloud, O daughter of Jerusalem! Behold, your king is coming to you." On the day her King did come, when Jesus rode in on the back of a donkey, this prophecy was fulfilled. Luke tells us, "The whole multitude of his disciples began to rejoice and praise God with a loud voice . . . . 'Blessed is the King who comes in the name of the Lord! Peace in heaven and glory in the highest!' And some of the Pharisees in the crowd said to him, 'Teacher, rebuke your disciples.' He answered, 'I tell you, if these were silent, the very stones would cry out'" (Luke 19:37–40).

PERSPECTIVES ON THE COMING KING

John concludes his account of Jesus' triumphal entry by showing the different perspectives held by the different participants. This is something that John likes to do, knowing how helpful it is for placing ourselves inside the story.

First, John tells us of Jesus' closest disciples, those who had long followed him and had close access to him: "His disciples did not understand these

6. Jonathan Edwards, *Altogether Lovely: Jonathan Edwards on the Glory and Excellency of Christ* (Morgan, PA: Soli Deo Gloria, 1997), 18–19.

7. Arthur W. Pink, *Comfort for Christians* (Grand Rapids: Baker, 1993), 75.

things at first, but when Jesus was glorified, then they remembered that these things had been written about him and had been done to him" (John 12:16). The ignorance of the disciples is remarkable, since Jesus had so clearly told them what was about to happen. Matthew tells us that on the brink of Jesus' entry, he said to his disciples: "See, we are going up to Jerusalem. And the Son of Man will be delivered over to the chief priests and scribes, and they will condemn him to death and deliver him over to the Gentiles to be mocked and flogged and crucified, and he will be raised on the third day" (Matt. 20:18–19).

This shows that Jesus was far from a passive victim of the events about to unfold. He was the Lord of them, and everything that happened was by God's sovereign intention. But despite Jesus' clear statements, the disciples were puzzled by the triumphal entry, just as they were by the cross. Only later, when they had been enlightened by the Holy Spirit, did they understand the meaning of Jesus' ministry.

Christians today are not much different from the disciples. Most of us have little idea how God's saving kingdom is being extended and served through the affairs of our lives. Indeed, one of the joys of heaven will be learning how God used something we said or some encouragement we gave to a struggling sinner that made all the difference in the person's life. J. C. Ryle observes, "We shall then discern with wonder and amazement the full meaning of many a thing in which we were unconscious agents during our lives."[8] Indeed, much of the excitement that gains the attention of the world will be shown to be of little significance, while much unnoticed but faithful Christian worship and service will be seen in its glorious importance. Realizing this, we should make it our business simply to serve the Lord in keeping with his Word and in reliance on his sovereign grace. Whether we are employed in the workplace, raising children in the home, mingling with neighbors in society, or joining together in the church, Jesus calls us to a purposeful life of humble obedience, sacrificial love, and gospel witness.

Second, there were many who hailed Jesus because they had either witnessed or heard of his great miracle in raising Lazarus from the grave. The relationship between Lazarus's resurrection and the triumphal entry is seldom appreciated. Yet it is obvious that many, if not most, of the crowd

---

8. Ryle, *John*, 2:372.

drew the wrong conclusion. They saw in Jesus a power that they hoped to harness to their own purposes. Instead, they should have recognized his deity and simply come to worship and serve him. This is a perennial problem in the world: a desire to receive the blessings that Christ might offer, without first embracing the true purpose of his saving grace. This prompts me to ask what you see in Jesus. Do you see only a power to help in your worldly pursuit of security and success? Or do you hear his call to humbly come, confessing your sins, finding forgiveness through his blood, and serving him in humble, holy faith?

The crown that Jesus came to wear was not a crown of gold but of thorns. The throne that he came to ascend was a cross. Jesus says to all who would seek his blessings: "If anyone would come after me, let him deny himself and take up his cross daily and follow me. For whoever would save his life will lose it, but whoever loses his life for my sake will save it" (Luke 9:23–24). Unless we are willing to meet Jesus at the cross, finding our life not only in his death, but in our own death to sin and self, then we are rejecting Jesus as he has really come.

Finally, John presents the perspective of the Pharisees. They said to one another: "You see that you are gaining nothing. Look, the world has gone after him" (John 12:19). As always, Jesus has mastered the situation. One of his main purposes in the triumphal entry was to force the hand of those who sought to kill him. Unnerved by Jesus' apparent popularity, the religious leaders were primed to accept Judas's offer of betrayal. But they were playing Jesus' game all along.

Even their concluding remark, the final word on Jesus' dramatic entry into Jerusalem, is made to serve the glory of Christ. They complained, "The world has gone after him." How profoundly have these words come true. Jesus had not come to rescue a puny nation tucked in a corner of the world. Rather, he had come to rescue his people from their sins in every tribe and nation throughout the globe. That his people still gather together today in his name is proof of his success. For as Zechariah prophesied, "Behold, your king is coming to you; . . . and he shall speak peace to the nations; his rule shall be from sea to sea, and from the River to the ends of the earth" (Zech. 9:9–10).

Jesus is not finished. When he returns in the glory of his kingdom, when all who reject him are judged and all sin is put away in hell, then

Jesus will look upon a whole world that he has saved. For the King is coming again, and the book of Revelation depicts him then as riding not a donkey but a horse for war. And when he has conquered and judged all that stands against him, then there will be peace forevermore. "Behold, I am coming soon," Jesus declares in the last chapter of the Bible. "Blessed is the one who keeps the words of the prophecy of this book" (Rev. 22:7).

80

THE HOUR OF GLORY

John 12:20–26

Jesus answered them, "The hour has come for the Son of Man to be glorified." (John 12:23)

In his sermon on this passage, James Montgomery Boice reflected on the various pulpits in which he preached in his many travels. He pointed out that while from the front pulpits are often quite beautiful and ornate, on the preacher's side they are often less glamorous. There are wires to trip on, buttons to push, books stacked up, and even fans or heaters. Sometimes there are signs that say, "When the light comes on you have two minutes!" But there was one pulpit that he particularly enjoyed preaching from because of a sign pasted inside. It read, "Sir, we would see Jesus." Boice commented, "That is a good word for any preacher. I could wish that every preacher and teacher of the Word of God might have those words before him constantly as he prepares his messages and as he speaks them."[1]

THE GRAND ENTRY

The saying "Sir, we wish to see Jesus" comes from the passage that we are now studying in John's Gospel. It was spoken by a group of unnamed

1. James Montgomery Boice, *The Gospel of John*, 5 vols. (Grand Rapids: Baker, 1999), 3:934.

Greeks who wished to meet the Lord. John tells us: "Now among those who went up to worship at the feast were some Greeks. So these came to Philip, who was from Bethsaida in Galilee, and asked him, 'Sir, we wish to see Jesus.' Philip went and told Andrew; Andrew and Philip went and told Jesus" (John 12:20–22).

Living in Palestine at this time were many Greeks, some of whom were proselytes to Judaism who came to Jerusalem for Passover. The region where Philip and Andrew grew up, Bethsaida in Galilee, was close to a large Greek population. So these Greeks could have been acquaintances. Still, it seems that Philip did not know how to respond to their request, so he consulted with Andrew. This is the third time we find Andrew bringing someone to Jesus. The first was his brother Simon Peter, to whom he said, "We have found the Messiah" (John 1:41). The second was the boy whose few fish and loaves Jesus used to feed the hungry crowd (6:8–9). Andrew's exemplary reputation for bringing others to Jesus is confirmed here, for he took Philip to Jesus with news of the Greeks.

Jesus' reply to this news was as remarkable as it was unexpected. "Jesus answered them, "The hour has come for the Son of Man to be glorified" (John 12:23). He looked upon the arrival of these Greeks as "a sign that the climax of his mission had at last arrived."[2]

First, Jesus declared, "The hour has come." This is remarkable, given earlier statements in John's Gospel. During a wedding feast at the beginning of his ministry, his mother, Mary, wanted Jesus to reveal himself in glory. He replied, "My hour has not yet come" (John 2:4). Later, at the Feast of Tabernacles, his brothers urged him to glorify himself by performing miracles. Jesus answered, "My time has not yet come" (7:5). Later, the authorities failed to arrest him "because his hour had not yet come" (8:20).

So why has the arrival of these Greeks caused Jesus to say, "The hour has come"? The answer recalls us to the building conflict between Jesus and the Jewish authorities. The crisis is coming quickly, orchestrated by Jesus himself. Now these representatives of the Gentile world appear, asking for him, and Jesus sees that the decisive turning point of his mission in the world is at hand. For, as Peter would later preach, God intended for the gospel to go to "the Gentiles, to take from them a people for his name" (Acts 15:14).

2. Ibid., 3:935.

In the previous passage, the Pharisees lamented, "Look, the world has gone after him" (John 12:19). With typical irony, John reports the arrival of these Greeks to show that this was Jesus' very intention: to gain his converts from the whole world. The coming of the Greeks signified that Jesus' victory was at hand. "This was the point," says Boice, "at which literally the entire world, represented by these Greeks, was beginning to go after him."[3]

Jesus adds to this a most striking description of what this hour entails: "The hour has come for the Son of Man to be glorified" (John 12:23). The title "Son of Man" comes from the vision of Daniel 7, which showed that "there came one like a son of man, and he came to the Ancient of Days and was presented before him. And to him was given dominion and glory and a kingdom, that all peoples, nations, and languages should serve him" (Dan. 7:13–14). This was a popular image among the Jews; their literature in the preceding centuries includes numerous references to the "Son of Man." Jesus took this name for himself, especially when speaking about his second coming in glory (cf. Matt. 13:41; 16:27–28; 19:28; 24:27; 26:64; John 5:27). But he also pointed out what the Jews had forgotten: that for the Son of Man to ascend, he first must descend (see John 3:13). This is why Jesus so often used this name in association with his predictions about the cross (see Matt. 12:40; 17:12; 20:28; 26:2, 45; John 3:14; 6:53).

So there is both drama and irony in Jesus' exclamation: "The hour has come for the Son of Man to be glorified." His Jewish hearers would imagine trumpets blowing and the marching of God's people in world conquest. This was the glory they sought. But Jesus was referring to his coming cross. D. A. Carson comments, "Jesus' death was itself the supreme manifestation of Jesus' glory."[4]

"Glorifying" always involves "revealing" or "displaying." We glorify someone's artwork by displaying it prominently. So what displays the true glory of the Son of Man? Jesus' answer is his crucifixion: his self-sacrifice in making atonement for sin. All questions about the purpose, character, and glory of God were about to receive their answer. Not only was Daniel's vision to receive its clearest explanation, but the whole Old Testament would be explained and fulfilled when Jesus took up the cross. What the world sees as the deepest humiliation, Jesus understood as his highest glory. As

---

3. Ibid., 3:936.
4. D. A. Carson, *The Gospel of John* (Grand Rapids: Eerdmans, 1991), 437.

he put it on the night of his arrest, "Now is the Son of Man glorified, and God is glorified in him" (John 13:31).

This is why there is no clearer distinction between the Christian and the unbeliever than their respective views of the cross. Paul wrote that to the Jews the cross was a "stumbling block," and to the Gentiles "folly" (1 Cor. 1:23). But, the apostle continued, "to those who are called, both Jews and Greeks," the cross is "the power of God and the wisdom of God" (1:24). Charles Spurgeon writes:

> Christ's death is *his* glory and it ought also to be *ours*. . . . To spiritual eyes, the Christ of God was never more glorious than when he was nailed to the cross of Calvary . . . . A glory, never equaled, shone around the Conqueror of death and hell when he bowed his head, and said, "It is finished."[5]

The Principle of Glory

John does not tell us whether the Greeks ever met with Jesus. But whether Jesus' response was made to them, to the disciples, or before the crowds, he clearly wanted his hearers to understand what it means to come to him. Therefore, he amplified his meaning about his hour of glory with an example from nature: "Truly, truly, I say to you, unless a grain of wheat falls into the earth and dies, it remains alone; but if it dies, it bears much fruit" (John 12:24). Just as a seed must be buried in the ground and decay to give birth to a plant, the Son of Man is glorified and bears his fruit through his suffering in death.

Just taking this saying as a general principle, it makes an important point about life. John L. Girardeau identifies this as "a great and universal law in this world of sin—the law that sorrow is in order to joy, and death in order to life."[6] The way to really live is not to indulge yourself but to discipline yourself. The way to achieve things of value is to engage in self-denial. And unless there are things you will die for, then your life is really not worth living.

During his last visit to northern Virginia, the great Christian general Robert E. Lee was approached by a young mother who asked him to bless

5. Charles H. Spurgeon, *Metropolitan Tabernacle Pulpit*, 63 vols. (Pasadena, TX: Pilgrim, 1978), 53:50.
6. George A. Blackburn, ed., *The Life & Work of John L. Girardeau* (Columbia, SC: The State Company, 1916), 172.

her baby son. Lee held the baby and gave this blessing: "Teach him he must deny himself."[7] It was by applying that same principle to himself in Christian faith that Lee's life made such a difference.

Of course, the greatest example and fulfillment of this principle was the death that Jesus was about to suffer. J. C. Ryle writes:

> This sentence was primarily meant to teach the wondering Greeks the true nature of Messiah's kingdom. . . . Our Lord would have them know that He came to carry a cross, and not to wear a crown. He came not to live a life of honour, ease, and magnificence, but to die a shameful and dishonoured death. The kingdom He came to set up was to begin with a crucifixion, and not with a coronation. Its glory was to take its rise not from victories won by the sword, and from accumulated treasures of gold and silver, but from the death of its King.[8]

It was only by dying that Jesus became our Savior. Unless Jesus had borne our sins on the cross, there would be no Christianity and no church. There is no Christianity if the cross is absent from our message and faith, regardless of what symbols we wear or hang on the wall. We are not saved by following Jesus' example. Some people will say, "My Christianity is the imitation of Christ." Certainly, Christians are to follow Jesus' example, but one cannot become a Christian this way. Those who wish to be saved by imitating Jesus must present themselves as perfectly righteous in God's presence, as Jesus did (Heb. 1:8–9). Can you hope to do this? The same is true of Jesus as an ethical teacher. But Jesus' ethic was explained in the Sermon on the Mount: "You therefore must be perfect, as your heavenly Father is perfect" (Matt. 5:48). This standard of ethics for salvation is simply higher than we can hope to achieve.

Moreover, Jesus taught that salvation depends on what only he could accomplish, namely, his atoning death for our sin. Our true and greatest problem is not poor information or bad examples, but God's righteous condemnation of our sin. The issue is not how we can find God, but how the God we find can accept guilty sinners like us. For this reason, Jesus is glorified as our Savior when we confess our great need for his cross. Therefore,

7. Douglas Southall Freeman, *Lee* (1934; repr., New York: Simon & Schuster, 1991), 588.
8. J. C. Ryle, *Expository Thoughts on the Gospels: John*, 3 vols. (Edinburgh: Banner of Truth, 1999), 2:376.

to deny or reject the cross is to deny Christ. To refuse to confess your sin and your need for Jesus' atoning blood is to refuse the only way of salvation that he came to offer.

This is what Jesus wanted these Greeks to know. They were right to come to Jesus. But they must know that it is from his atoning death that eternal life comes to men and women. Like the seed that first is buried and dies, Jesus bears the fruit of his kingdom through the cross and the tomb in which his body was laid. Having died for us, Jesus has gained and is still gaining his fruit—a great harvest—to the praise of his grace. Donald Grey Barnhouse writes: "Because of His death, multitudes of every tongue and nation would come forth to eternal life in Him, as fruit. How true this has been as we survey the pages of church history. Wherever the message of Christ's atoning death has gone, it has borne fruit in abundance. This is the very heart of the Christian gospel."[9]

THE PRINCIPLE APPLIED TO US

It is true, however, that those who are saved by faith in the cross must take up the cross for themselves. The principle of Jesus as Savior is also the principle for the salvation he gives. To make this point, Jesus continued: "Whoever loves his life loses it, and whoever hates his life in this world will keep it for eternal life" (John 12:25).

What was true for Jesus is true for his followers. Jesus says that we are not to love our lives, but to hate our life in this world. We need to understand this rightly. Jesus is not saying that we should hate life itself, nor that we should not love the good things that God has placed in this world. Jesus' meaning is made clear when we note the two different Greek words he uses for *life*. In the first clause, when Jesus tells us not to love our "life," he uses the word *psyche*. This gives us our word *psychology*. Jesus means that we are to reject the worldly way of thinking and feeling. We are to reject the life of ego. But then when Jesus speaks of gaining "eternal life," he uses the word *zoe*. When joined to the word *eternal*, this refers to the divine life in us. So we are to turn from the former—worldly ego—to the latter, the divine life that enters us through the Holy Spirit whom Jesus sends.

9. Donald Grey Barnhouse, *Illustrating the Gospel of John* (Grand Rapids: Revell, 1973), 155.

A recent controversy over *lordship salvation* has made clear the importance of Jesus' teaching. The question is whether a Christian can have Jesus as Savior without receiving him as Lord. Sadly, many theologians and church leaders have answered in the affirmative. Some actually wrote that so long as one has believed in Jesus, even if he never shows any change in his life and never turns away from sin in the least, he can still be assured of heaven. To teach otherwise, they claim, is legalistic. But those who emphasize lordship salvation are not teaching salvation *by* works. Rather, they are rightly teaching salvation *to* works. That is, they insist on Jesus' own teaching that to be a Christian requires that we turn from sin and the world to possess eternal life. This is the very point on which Jesus laid such stress in John 12:25.

How, then, should we understand what it means to turn from a worldly life and seek a heavenly one? Jesus' point about the grain of wheat dying makes it clear that we are saved by trusting in Christ's death for us. This leads to a death that we also experience, which we should understand in at least two ways.

First, Christians must *die to self.* We experience a death to our own will as we surrender our lives to Jesus. We all have our ideas and desires for life. But Christians are called to surrender our plans to Jesus. Where Jesus would have us go, we go. What Jesus would have us do, we do. Especially, being a Christian means relinquishing worldly values and goals, most of which center on money, success, fame, and pleasure. Are you willing to do this? If you are a Christian and are still living for the things of the world, you will never prosper spiritually or be truly useful for Christ until you let them go.

One man who learned this lesson was George Mueller, who became famous in nineteenth-century England for the great number of orphanages he built and maintained, all through the power of prayer. Mueller was once asked his secret. He replied: "There was a day when I died. Died to George Mueller, his opinions, preferences, tastes, and will; died to the world, its approval or censure; died to the approval or blame even of my brethren or friends; and since then I have studied only to show myself approved unto God."[10] George Mueller showed us that to die to self is to lead a life of service to both God and man.

Second, the follower of Christ must *die to sin.* Paul explained: "So you also must consider yourselves dead to sin and alive to God in Christ Jesus. Let not sin therefore reign in your mortal body, to make you obey its passions.

10. Ibid., 156.

Do not present your members to sin as instruments for unrighteousness, but present yourselves to God as those who have been brought from death to life, and your members to God as instruments for righteousness" (Rom. 6:11–13). We die to sin by starving it and by presenting our lives to God. We offer our feet to take us into wholesome and holy places, not places of sin. We offer our hands not to iniquity but to good works. We offer our lips no longer to gossip, slander, and coarse speech but to praising God, uplifting others, and spreading the gospel. We offer our eyes not to gaze in lust or envy but to glorify God. We offer our minds no longer to the ways of the world, but to being filled with the light of God's Word.

This presents a great challenge. Joel Nederhood rightly assessed: "We are deeply in love with the world. We play the game of life according to the rules the world lays down. Sometimes we drink of the trough with which it satisfies its ordinary swine. We relish certain things that heaven despises."[11] Since this accurately describes many Christians today, we ought to make it a matter of fervent prayer and serious application. Perhaps above all, we need to devote ourselves to a life of regular communion with God through the study of his Word, which alone can make us "wise for salvation" (2 Tim. 3:15) and transform us through the renewing of our minds (Rom. 12:2).

On the day that she was put to death for her faith in Christ, the teenage princess Lady Jane Grey sent her personal Bible to her sister Katherine, along with a note that included these words:

> If you with good mind read it, and with an earnest desire follow it, no doubt [it] shall bring you to an immortal and everlasting life; it will teach you to live and learn you to die[,] . . . my good sister, and more again let me entreat thee to learn to die; deny the world, defy the devil, and despise the flesh, and delight yourself only in the Lord . . . with whom even in death there is life.[12]

THE PATH OF GLORY

Jesus has presented us with the principle of his glory, namely, that of his cross. He said that the hour of his glory came as his cross approached.

11. Joel Nederhood, *The Forever People: Living Today in the Light of Eternity* (Phillipsburg, NJ: P&R Publishing, 2000), 113.

12. Quoted in John E. Marshall, *Life and Writings* (Edinburgh: Banner of Truth, 2005), 108–9.

We might echo his words, since for us the time has now come for the Son of Man to be glorified in our lives, that we might participate in that glory. With this in mind, Jesus concluded by laying out the path of glory for those who come to him in faith: "If anyone serves me, he must follow me; and where I am, there will my servant be also. If anyone serves me, the Father will honor him" (John 12:26).

First, Jesus said, "If anyone serves me, he must follow me." This was his message for the Greeks who sought him. J. C. Ryle comments: "As the soldier follows his general, as the servant follows his master, as the scholar follows his teacher, as the sheep follows its shepherd, just so ought the professing Christian to follow Christ. Faith and obedience are the leading marks of real followers, and will always be seen in true believing Christians."[13] We follow Jesus in a life of cross-bearing self-denial. We follow him in a life of service to God and man. We follow Jesus by holding fast the doctrines of his Word and pursuing a holy life through the power of his Holy Spirit.

Second, Jesus stated: "And where I am, there will my servant be also." This is not a command but a promise. This is our great reward and our pleasure in this life: to have Christ's encouragement, to know Christ's approval, and to live by Christ's power. Christ is with every Christian; even when we stray, the Good Shepherd watches over us. But only those who are following Jesus are able to experience his presence. So we must ask ourselves, "Would I rather have pleasant circumstances without the presence of Christ? Or do I realize that the worst this world can give me is nothing compared with the surpassing greatness of living with Christ?" A. M. Hunter wrote, "It has been said that *follow me* is the whole of a Christian's duty, as to *be* where Christ is is the whole of his reward."[14]

Last, and greatest, Jesus promises, "If anyone serves me, the Father will honor him." Much of our problem is that we do not aim high enough in life. We settle for earthly happiness, when Christ calls us to holiness. We settle for earthly success when we were made and redeemed for heavenly glory. Boice writes, "Jesus tells us that God will honor those who follow him in this life. In this life his way often involves suffering. Sometimes it involves death for his sake. It always involves self-denial. But, says Christ,

---

13. Ryle, *John*, 2:378.
14. Quoted in Leon Morris, *Reflections on the Gospel of John* (Peabody, MA: Hendrickson, 1986), 447.

the suffering will be followed by honor and the self-denial by praise."[15] Following Jesus, our praise will come from God; why, then, would we need the applause of the world?

The Greeks said, "Sir, we wish to see Jesus." Do you wish to see Jesus? If you do, realize that Jesus answers by showing you his cross, as he did the visiting Greeks. He tells you to confess your guilt before God and embrace his atoning death as your own way of salvation. Is this the Jesus you expected? Do you still wish to see him, when he calls you to find glory in his death for your sins? Are you still willing to come, when Jesus calls you to deny yourself and follow him? You should be, because to turn from the cross is to forfeit the only true Savior and thus to lose your soul. If you come to Jesus, it will lead to your own death, but that death leads to everlasting and glorious life. And if we wish to show Jesus to others—if we want to make real to them the glory of his cross—the best way is for us to carry it, living out a life of death to self and sin, and of resurrection life to the glory of our Lord.

15. Boice, *John*, 3:944.

81

LIFTED UP

John 12:27–34

*"And I, when I am lifted up from the earth,
will draw all people to myself."* (John 12:32)

The Christian faith involves a number of high mysteries. We think of the doctrine of the Trinity, which teaches that God exists in one being and in three persons, and we realize that this is beyond our comprehension. The same might be said about the incarnation of Christ and the inspiration of Holy Scripture. Both Jesus and the Bible are fully human: Jesus possessed a truly human nature, and the Bible contains truly human documents. But they are also fully divine: Jesus possessed a truly divine nature, and the Bible is the very Word of God. How one can be both fully human and fully divine is a high mystery that we cannot understand.

These are all mysteries for the mind, but there are also mysteries for the heart. One is the question of Jesus' suffering on the cross. There, Jesus suffered not only at the hands of men but also at the hands of God. Can we ever appreciate the price Jesus paid to redeem us from our sins? Surely we cannot. Yet in the Gospels we can gaze in wonder and adoration at Jesus' own trepidation as he prepared to suffer and die for our sins. The Synoptic Gospels present Jesus' anguished prayer in the garden of Gethsemane:

"Father, if you are willing, remove this cup from me" (Luke 22:42). John shows us Jesus' anxiety earlier, after Jesus had seen the hour of his cross in the arrival of some Greeks to see him. He exclaimed, "Now is my soul troubled" (John 12:27).

JESUS' SOUL TROUBLED

It might seem surprising at first that such a man as Jesus would approach his death with such trembling of soul. After all, other men have approached their death tranquilly. Socrates was stoic as he drank his hemlock. History records many Christians as facing even a torturous death with calm repose. So why is Jesus' soul so greatly troubled about the coming cross? Especially when we remember how much greater Jesus is than any other man, being God the Son in his divine nature, and when we remember his miraculous powers, we wonder why Jesus should say, "Now is my soul troubled."

The answer is that terrible though his physical sufferings were, by far the greatest part of Jesus' suffering on the cross was spiritual, entailing his receipt of God's full wrath for our sins. A. W. Pink comments on Jesus' anguish: "And what occasioned this? The insults and sufferings which He was to receive at the hands of men? The wounding of His heel by the Serpent? No, indeed. It was the prospect of being 'made a curse for us,' of suffering the righteous wrath of a sin-hating God."[1] At the thought of this, as all the Gospels tell us, Jesus began to tremble and have trouble in his soul. As other men feel their stomachs turning and their palms sweating before some dreadful ordeal, so also our Lord trembled as he contemplated the judgment of God that he would bear. William Hendriksen writes, "The realization of the inexpressibly dreadful character of his impending descent into hell shook the human soul of Jesus to its very depths."[2]

If Jesus' troubled spirit shows his solidarity with human suffering, the spirit of his faithful resolve sets an example for us. "Now is my soul troubled," he prayed. "And what shall I say? 'Father, save me from this hour'? But for this purpose I have come to this hour. Father, glorify your name" (John 12:27–28).

1. Arthur W. Pink, *Exposition of the Gospel of John* (Grand Rapids: Zondervan, 1975), 679.
2. William Hendriksen, *Exposition of the Gospel according to John*, 2 vols., New Testament Commentary (Grand Rapids: Baker, 1953), 2:200.

Where did Jesus gain the resolve needed not to shrink away from his ordeal? His answer shows that he found strength in his knowledge of God the Father's will for him. It was the very purpose of his life to come to the hour of his cross. Jesus had been born to die, as signified by his given name: the angel told Joseph, "You shall call his name Jesus, for he will save his people from their sins" (Matt. 1:21). Moreover, Jesus' submission to the Father's will was not recently attained, for this had been the guiding principle of Jesus' entire life. All along he had been committed to the will of God, so now in the hour of his trial he was fortified in his resolve by this same commitment. We, too, will have strength under trials if we have long practiced submission to God's will.

We might think that Jesus found the strength to face the cross in his knowledge of God's will to redeem us from our sins. That is doubtless true (cf. Heb. 12:2). But Jesus points to an even higher motive: "Father, glorify your name." James Montgomery Boice comments: "To glorify God is his chief end. . . . He will not shrink from following whatever way the Father chooses to have the Son glorify him."[3] The highest motive in our salvation is always that God should be glorified in his power and grace, and it was this desire that primarily strengthened Jesus' trembling soul before the cross. He literally loved God's glory more than his own soul, and thus he found strength to overcome the infinite suffering of the cross. Thus, he prays, "Father, glorify your name."

The response to Jesus' prayer was jarring to his listeners: "Then a voice came from heaven: 'I have glorified it, and I will glorify it again'" (John 12:28). On previous occasions, God spoke from heaven in order to express his approval of Jesus. At Jesus' baptism, God's voice was heard saying, "This is my beloved Son, with whom I am well pleased" (Matt. 3:17). God spoke similar words from heaven during Jesus' transfiguration on the mount (Matt. 17:5). In this case, God is also expressing his approval of Jesus, only now he says, "I have glorified [my name], and I will glorify it" (John 12:28). Jesus' desire for God's name to be glorified in his life has already been gratified, and it will be again in his cross.

God was glorified in Jesus' birth, which is why the angels sang, "Glory to God in the highest" (Luke 2:14). God was glorified in Jesus' perfect life;

---

3. James Montgomery Boice, *The Gospel of John*, 5 vols. (Grand Rapids: Baker, 1999), 3:947.

from earliest childhood he had perfectly kept God's law. God was glorified in Jesus' ministry. Jesus displayed the kingdom of God in his miracles, his teaching, and his life. But it would be especially at the cross that Jesus would glorify God, displaying the perfections of attributes such as his justice, mercy, wisdom, and love.

JESUS LIFTED UP

When we think of works of glory, we tend to think of mankind's great achievements. The ancient world would probably have said that the most glorious achievement in construction was the Hanging Gardens of Babylon. But those great gardens no longer exist, and their glory has long since faded. Or we might think of military glory. Alexander the Great achieved colossal glory, yet for him it ended with his youthful death, after which his empire fragmented. A similar story might be related about the great Roman conquerors. In more recent times, we remember the glory of the war rallies staged by Adolf Hitler, which ended in the destruction of the German nation. Today, we attach glory to the exploits of sports stars, movie stars, or corporate giants. The tabloids sell their millions on the endless stream of the fallen lives of those they had only recently glorified. Yet when Jesus Christ sought to glorify his heavenly Father by his death on the cross, he attained a glory that will never end. Indeed, it is a glory that is shared and celebrated by more and more people each year, just as Jesus said, "And I, when I am lifted up from the earth, will draw all people to myself" (John 12:32).

In noting this, we cannot help but observe a significant difference between the way in which Jesus attained eternal glory for God and the way in which men and women gain fleeting glory for themselves. Worldly glory is attained by ascending some kind of throne. But Christ achieved his glory by ascending the cross.

When the voice from heaven spoke to Jesus, what the crowd heard was something like thunder. John says that some of them concluded that "an angel has spoken to him" (John 12:29). But Jesus informed them that the voice was intended as a communication not to him but to them. He explained, "Now is the judgment of this world; now will the ruler of this world be cast out" (12:31). This is one important way in which Jesus' death would bring glory to God—by the judgment of this world and the casting out of Satan.

How does the cross of Christ judge the world? First, by showing the sinfulness of sin. Why, after all, did God's perfect Son die in such cruel humiliation and, beyond that, suffer such terrible wrath from God? The answer is "sin." J. C. Ryle writes:

> Terribly black must that guilt be for which nothing but the blood of the Son of God could make satisfaction. Heavy must that weight of human sin be which made Jesus groan and sweat drops of blood in agony at Gethsemane and cry at Golgotha, "My God, My God, why hast Thou forsaken Me?" (Matt. 27:46).[4]

The world writes off sin as only a small thing. Today, sin is excused as dysfunction; no longer viewed as evil, sin is written off as the inevitable result of poor environments. But the cross of Jesus exposes the evil of the world's sin and in that way judges the world.

Second, the world's attitude toward Jesus is judged at the cross. Why, after all, was Jesus crucified? On the Godward side, he was crucified as a Sacrifice for our sin. But on the manward side, Jesus was being removed by a world that hated him. If you want to understand the world, consider what it did to Jesus Christ. He lived a perfect life of truth and love, healing and teaching the people. So the world killed him. Therefore, Jesus anticipated the cross by saying, "Now is the judgment of this world."

But not only did the cross judge the world, it also overthrew "the ruler of this world." This refers to the devil. The irony is that the cross was Satan's greatest triumph. The Messiah had been put to death by the will of his own people. But in the greatest reversal ever, Jesus instead overthrew Satan's reign. Satan reigns through sin, and he holds sway over men and women through the power of their guilt before God and by lying to us about God's goodness (cf. Gen. 3:4–5). But Jesus' death removes our sin by paying the debt of our guilt. Moreover, when believers come to Christ for their forgiveness, Christ also sends his Holy Spirit to deliver them from Satan's power. Donald Grey Barnhouse notes: "When a person becomes a Christian, he is delivered from Satan's grasp, and the chains of sin which had shackled him are instantly broken."[5] The cross secured not only the judgment of the world that rejected Jesus, but also the overthrow of his enemy, the devil.

4. J. C. Ryle, *Holiness* (Durham, UK: Evangelical Press, 1979), 6.
5. Donald Grey Barnhouse, *Illustrating the Gospel of John* (Grand Rapids: Revell, 1973), 160.

But there is a more positive way in which the cross glorified God the Father: its power to draw sinners and restore them to God. Jesus continued: "And I, when I am lifted up from the earth, will draw all people to myself" (John 12:32).

This is one of the great verses on the power of the cross for the salvation of sinners. By saying "when I am lifted up from the earth," Jesus is clearly referring to the dreadful events of the cross that would take place in a few short days. That cross would glorify not only God's righteous judgment, but also his gracious power to draw men and women into fellowship with himself.

In this respect, the cross is the greatest display of God's love to the world. The Puritan Jeremiah Burroughs writes: "Behold the infinite love of God to mankind and the love of Jesus Christ that, rather than God see the children of men to perish eternally, would send His Son to take our nature upon Him and thus suffer such dreadful things. Herein God shows His love. . . . Oh, what a powerful, mighty, drawing, efficacious meditation this should be to us!"[6]

And yet the cross's power does not consist in the sentiments it inspires in men's and women's hearts. It should inspire our love to God, but because of our sin it does not. Instead, it is by the ministry of the Holy Spirit, which Christ secured by his obedience on the cross, that sinners are drawn to God. William Hendriksen comments: "By means of his crucifixion, resurrection, ascension, and coronation Jesus attracts to himself all of God's elect, from every age, clime, and nation. He draws them by means of his Word and Spirit. This activity of the Spirit is the reward for the Son's being lifted up."[7] As the Holy Spirit presses the cross of Christ upon our hearts, the prophecy of old is fulfilled: "I will pour out on the house of David and the inhabitants of Jerusalem a spirit of grace and pleas for mercy, so that, when they look on me, on him whom they have pierced, they shall mourn for him" (Zech. 12:10).

It is those who are born again by the Spirit's ministry of God's Word who are drawn to God by the cross. The lesson we learn of God's love is seen in a story about a boy and his model sailboat. Longing for such a toy, the boy got a kit and spent weeks laboring to build it. When it was finally complete, he took it down to the lake. It sailed so beautifully that it kept going, right

6. Jeremiah Burroughs, *Gospel Worship* (1648; repr., Morgan, PA: Soli Deo Gloria, 1990), 353.
7. Hendriksen, *John*, 203.

out of sight. Despite all his efforts, the boy could not find the boat. Several weeks later he was walking past a store window when to his amazement he saw that boat. Only it had an expensive price tag on it. He went into the store and explained to the shopkeeper, but the owner said, "I'm sorry, but I paid a great deal of money for this toy boat and I cannot give it to you for free." So the boy took up jobs and worked and worked until he finally had enough money to buy back his boat. At last, he walked out of the store with his precious boat in his hand. And he said, "Now you are twice mine—once because I made you and once because I bought you." So it is with God. He created us, and then when we were lost in sin he purchased us with the precious blood of Jesus on the cross. How wonderful is the love of God revealed in the cross of Christ![8]

Lifting Up the Cross

Jesus' statement that "I, when I am lifted up from the earth, will draw all people to myself," contains a wealth of truth concerning the gospel. First, it declares the necessity of faith in his atoning death for sin. This comes through in his reference to "all people." When Jesus says that he will draw all people through his cross, he does not mean that he died for everyone's forgiveness. We know this because of the Bible's frequent insistence that not all will be forgiven and saved. John's Gospel is clear that "whoever does not believe is condemned" (John 3:18). When John's Gospel refers to "all people," it means all kinds of people, from all nations, races, and tongues. But note that Jesus says that their salvation will occur "when I am lifted up from the earth." Kent Hughes writes: "Christ was not saying that the whole world would be saved, but that all who will be saved will be saved by looking to and relying upon him. If you are not yet a believer, see his troubled soul as he became a curse for you, as he suffered separation from the Father, as he lovingly bore the penalty of your sins."[9]

Moreover, salvation happens as we are "drawn" to Jesus. The Greek word *elko* is used for the dragging of a heavy object. Jesus taught this truth in negative form earlier in John's Gospel: "No one can come to me unless the Father who sent me draws him. And I will raise him up on the last day"

8. Illustration from R. Kent Hughes, *John: That You May Believe* (Wheaton, IL: Crossway, 1999), 308.
9. Ibid.

107

(John 6:44). So great is sin's power over us that only if God extends his own power to draw us to himself can we be saved.

This should have a profound effect on our approach to evangelism. Jesus says that he will draw people to himself, not drive them. The preaching of God's wrath and his law plays an important role in evangelism, since it is through the law that we learn of our sin. Yet we should not seek to terrify people into conversions. This is especially true of those who are burdened with the misery of a life in sin. We remember Jesus' treatment of the woman by the Samaritan well in John 4. His evangelism began with a human connection. He told her, "If you knew the gift of God, and who it is that is saying to you, 'Give me a drink,' you would have asked him, and he would have given you living water" (John 4:10). Jesus did not skirt the subject of sin, but still he boldly offered the woman God's gift of eternal life. It is especially the sweetness of Christ and the grace of his gospel that God uses to draw sinners to himself. James Montgomery Boice writes, "The uplifted Christ draws sinful, ignorant, and rebellious men and women to him, conquering them by the unimaginable, unfathomable love that is so clearly displayed there."[10]

Finally, if Jesus will draw all people to himself through his cross, then let us preach his cross. It is true that many are offended by the cross's message of judgment on sin. But from that cross, as we proclaim it, Christ will draw many. This was the apostolic example of witnessing the gospel. Paul explained, "Jews demand signs and Greeks seek wisdom, but we preach Christ crucified, a stumbling block to Jews and folly to Gentiles, but to those who are called, both Jews and Greeks, Christ the power of God and the wisdom of God" (1 Cor. 1:22–24).

When Our Souls Are Troubled

In the coming of the Greeks to see him, Jesus had seen the hour of his cross. His soul was deeply troubled, but as he found his resolve in his submission to God's will, we have seen how God's glory shines through the cross. We have a similar calling when we face the kinds of trials that trouble our souls. What do we do when circumstances seem to have turned against us? When a job is lost, or sickness has come, or a loved one is lost? The example of Jesus tells us what we should do as well.

---

10. James Montgomery Boice, *The Gospel of John*, 5 vols. (Grand Rapids: Baker, 1999), 2:636.

First, we should remind ourselves of the anguish that Jesus willingly endured for us. Ours is a Savior who willingly suffered unimaginable violence so that we might be saved. This was something that the Jews of his day could not comprehend. Their idea of a Savior was only of one who conquers and reigns forever. But Jesus instead suffered for us. Remembering this makes us peaceable under trials.

Not understanding the cross, the Jews asked, "We have heard from the Law that the Christ remains forever. How can you say that the Son of Man must be lifted up? Who is this Son of Man?" (John 12:34). The Old Testament did indeed make great promises of the eternal reign of God's Messiah (see 2 Sam. 7:12–13; Isa. 9:7; Ezek. 37:25). But the Jews forgot the many other passages that showed that he must first suffer for his people. For instance, Daniel 9:26 spoke of a Messiah who "shall be cut off and shall have nothing." Isaiah prophesied about the cross, saying that the Messiah "shall be high and lifted up, and shall be exalted." The prophet elaborated, "His appearance was so marred, beyond human semblance, and his form beyond that of the children of mankind . . . . It was the will of the LORD to crush him; he has put him to grief; . . . his soul makes an offering for guilt" (Isa. 52:13–14; 53:10). Jesus was probably referring to this passage when he spoke of himself as being "lifted up." The listening Jews hoped for a different Messiah and a different salvation. "Who is this Son of Man?" they asked.

Christians should know better than to think we can be saved without our sins' first being forgiven, and we should know better than to think our salvation will keep us from carrying our own crosses. But we can look to Jesus lifted up for us, think of the suffering he endured for our salvation, and remember that in this way he secured an eternal salvation that will never fail us.

Second, when trouble assails us we should follow Jesus' example in looking to the Father in prayer. Paul wrote, "My God will supply every need of yours according to his riches in glory in Christ Jesus" (Phil. 4:19). Too often, we respond to distress with frantic and fearful action, when Jesus would have us turn trustingly to the Father in prayer.

Third, we should resolve, as Jesus did, for God's name to be glorified through our affliction. "What shall I say?" he asked. " 'Father, save me from this hour'? But for this purpose I have come to this hour" (John 12:27). The Christian, thankfully, will never bear Christ's cross, for he has put away

God's wrath from our sin. But we will have our own crosses to bear, and our primary concern should be to bring glory to God by the faith we display in times of trouble.

The Bible teacher Ralph Keiper struggled all his life with extremely poor eyesight. It handicapped his studies when he was entering the ministry, and he frequently complained about it to God. But one day, as he was dwelling on this, he felt that the Holy Spirit was saying to him, "Keiper, what is the chief end of man?" He knew the answer from his study of the catechism: "The chief end of man is to glorify God and enjoy him forever." "And is that your chief end?" the Holy Spirit prodded. "Of course," he replied. "At this point, the Spirit drove home his point to Keiper's conscience: "Which would you rather have, perfect eyesight or the privilege of glorifying me?" Keiper realized that his ailment provided him with an opportunity to glorify God by showing a joyful attitude in affliction, and this realization radically transformed his response to his trial.[11]

That is a question that could be suitably asked of each of us in our discouragement and affliction. And when we resolve, as Jesus did before us, to endure the struggle in faith, we may look forward to the same response that God pronounced to our Lord: "I have glorified [my name in you], and I will glorify it again" (John 12:28).

---

11. Ibid., 3:949.

82

DARKNESS AND LIGHT

John 12:35—43

Jesus said to them, "The light is among you for a little while longer. Walk while you have the light, lest darkness overtake you. The one who walks in the darkness does not know where he is going. While you have the light, believe in the light, that you may become sons of light." (John 12:35–36)

t was a dark, dark night in Jerusalem. At least it was dark in the prophet Isaiah's heart, for the king had died. King Uzziah had ruled Judah for fifty-two years, a time characterized mostly by godliness and divine blessing. But now Uzziah was dead, and Isaiah entered the temple seeking light for the darkness of his grief and dismay. What happened that dark night would determine the course of Isaiah's life. He later recalled, "In the year that King Uzziah died I saw the Lord sitting upon a throne, high and lifted up" (Isa. 6:1).

As John the apostle draws down the curtain on the ministry of Jesus before the cross, he thinks of Isaiah. For through the mystery of the inspiration of Scripture, John had come to realize that in Isaiah's vision of the Lord, the eighth-century B.C. prophet had seen the Lord Jesus Christ. Quoting him, John observes, "Isaiah said these things because he saw his glory"—that

111

is, Jesus' glory—"and spoke of him" (John 12:41). The long-ago experience of Isaiah—a pivotal moment in the Old Testament—was focused on what would later happen to the Messiah. For like Isaiah, Jesus spoke of light to a world in darkness, and of a darkness that would seek to put out that light.

THE OFFER OF LIGHT

John 12:35–36 records the final public appeal of Jesus to God's ancient people Israel. After Jesus spoke, "he departed and hid himself from them" (12:36), and he would not be seen publicly until his trial and crucifixion. The final words of any great man are important, but the final public teaching of Jesus is especially significant. It forms a summary of his entire message as presented by John. Jesus began: "The light is among you for a little while longer. Walk while you have the light, lest darkness overtake you" (12:35).

From the beginning of his Gospel, John has used light to describe Jesus. Light is an ancient symbol for God, and by applying it to himself, Jesus declared his deity. "The LORD is my light and my salvation," David sang (Ps. 27:1). Moreover, Jesus' claim to be a light shining in the world teaches that he is the One who makes God known. It is in this way that Jesus meets the need of this world. James Montgomery Boice writes, "[Men] do not know God. Jesus comes; his light shines upon men. Now those who were in darkness have the light of the knowledge of the glory of God in the face of Jesus Christ."[1] Therefore, it is by following Christ's light that those in darkness are led to God.

But now Jesus warns that his light will soon be taken away: "The light is among you for a little while longer." This made it urgent for anyone who would be saved to believe on him. "Walk while you have the light," he exhorted, "lest darkness overtake you. The one who walks in the darkness does not know where he is going" (John 12:35). This is Jesus' warning: the Pharisees and other Jews who were opposing him did not realize what they were bringing onto themselves. To reject the light is to be plunged into a greater darkness. Alexander Maclaren writes: "Rejected light is the parent of the densest darkness, and the man who, having the light, does not trust it, piles around himself thick clouds of obscurity and gloom, far more doleful

1. James Montgomery Boice, *The Gospel of John*, 5 vols. (Grand Rapids: Baker, 1999), 3:965.

and impenetrable than the twilight that glimmers round the men who have never known the daylight of revelation."[2]

The Pharisees were themselves the greatest example of this principle. It is clear that in the last phase of Jesus' ministry, the Pharisees no longer seriously doubted the truth of his claims. They knew that he really had given sight to the man born blind and raised dead Lazarus from the grave. But still they rejected the light of Christ, preferring the petty darkness in which they exalted themselves. The result was that darkness overtook them, and they became far more hardened to God in the end than we could have imagined at the beginning.

This presents a challenge to those today who have heard and understood the gospel, but who have not yet committed themselves to Jesus in saving faith. Their encounter with the rejected Jesus will not leave them with a little light but rather with a much deeper darkness. If you have not yet turned to Christ in faith, you must realize that you will regress from darkness to greater darkness unless you believe on him—the One who is the Light of the World.

John 12:36, which records Jesus' final public statement, is both wonderful and dreadful at the same time. It is wonderful because Jesus' final words consist of an invitation to his light: "While you have the light, believe in the light, that you may become sons of light." It says much about Jesus' heart that he wanted his final words not to drip with the acid of condemnation, but to flow with the sweet offer of God's grace. His departure would take the light from the world, so he leaves behind the gospel offer to become children of God by believing in his light.

But even so, the aftermath of Jesus' gospel offer is dreadful. John says, "When Jesus had said these things, he departed and hid himself from them" (John 12:36). The time comes for unbelievers when the gospel is no longer available to believe. This time might come with death, but it could also come when their hearts have become so hardened through practiced unbelief that they are no longer able to believe. Jesus "hid himself from them." When we realize that Jesus is the one true light, the only Savior for a world lost in sin, his withdrawal from those who will not believe portends their final condemnation in eternal darkness.

2. Alexander Maclaren, *Expositions of Holy Scripture*, 17 vols. (Grand Rapids: Baker, 1982), 7:162.

THE TRAGEDY OF DARKNESS

Jesus' final plea to the Jews was straightforward. But their refusal to believe raises some questions. First, if these Jews, who alone in their world knew the Holy Scriptures and lived in God's holy city, would not believe in Jesus, then what hope is there for anyone else? Another question deals with God. If God has gone to such pains to send his only Son to offer salvation to the world, only to be so broadly rejected, does this not suggest that God has somehow failed?

Such questions are obviously on John's mind, so he adds a postscript to Jesus' final sermon. First, he states the problem: "Though he had done so many signs before them, they still did not believe in him" (John 12:37). This refers to Jesus' miracles, especially the great miracles of healing the man born blind and raising Lazarus. Even after this, the bottom line was the unbelief of the Jews. What does it take to win people's belief, if even this didn't work among the Jews?

To answer these questions, John turns back to the prophet Isaiah. Jesus' earlier remarks in chapter 12 referred to Isaiah's prophecy of the Suffering Servant, in Isaiah 53, and John returns to that passage. The Jews did not believe, he explains, "so that the word spoken by the prophet Isaiah might be fulfilled: 'Lord, who has believed what he heard from us, and to whom has the arm of the Lord been revealed?'" (John 12:38). Jesus had referred to this quotation from Isaiah 53 in explaining that he would be "lifted up" and "exalted" (Isa. 52:13). John points out that the same passage included Isaiah's lament that this message would be rejected. The prophet complained: "Who has believed what he has heard from us? And to whom has the arm of the LORD been revealed?" (53:1). This is the very travesty that Jesus experienced, with both his message and his miracles rejected by almost everyone. John's point is that the same Old Testament prophecy that foretells the cross also foretells the rejection of Jesus' message. The Jews of Jesus' day did not believe in him "so that the word spoken by the prophet Isaiah might be fulfilled."

This raises some questions, because it seems to say that the reason the Pharisees and other Jews rejected Jesus was that an earlier prophecy had foreordained it. This suggests that God had predestined the Jews' unbelief. Many writers recoil against such a suggestion, lest God be thought to compel people to sin. William Barclay objects: "It seems to say that God has ordained that certain people must not and will not believe. Now in whatever way we are going to explain this passage, we cannot believe that. We cannot believe that the God whom Jesus told us about would make it impossible for His children to believe."[3] Barclay suggests that we read John not to say that the Jews did not believe "so that" Isaiah's prophecy would be fulfilled, but rather "with the result that" the prophecy was fulfilled. The unbelief of the Jews was the kind of thing that Isaiah was complaining about, rather than something that Isaiah was specifically prophesying. Some stalwart Reformed commentators take the same view, including F. F. Bruce, J. C. Ryle, James Montgomery Boice, and A. W. Pink.

The problem with this view, however, is what John actually says. He concludes his reference to Isaiah's complaint by saying, "Therefore they could not believe" (John 12:39). In some meaningful sense, then, it must be that in light of Isaiah's seven-hundred-year-old prophecy, the Pharisees were not able to believe in Jesus. Their unbelief did not defeat God's purpose; rather, it achieved God's purpose.

Perhaps John anticipates questions about this, because he elaborates by quoting another passage from Isaiah, this time in Isaiah 6: "For again Isaiah said, 'He has blinded their eyes and hardened their heart, lest they see with their eyes, and understand with their heart, and turn, and I would heal them'" (John 12:39–40). There is no way to avoid the fact that here it is God who is acting to blind and harden the people and that he does so for a reason: lest they should see, understand, and turn, "and I would heal them."

John paraphrases the original language, which records God's commission to Isaiah: "Go, and say to this people: 'Keep on hearing, but do not understand; keep on seeing, but do not perceive.' Make the heart of this people dull, and their ears heavy, and blind their eyes; lest they see with their eyes, and hear with their ears, and understand with their hearts, and turn and be healed" (Isa. 6:9–10). Isaiah had seen the vision of the Lord's glory and offered his services to God. God responded by commissioning him to a preaching ministry that was designed to harden the hearts, close the ears, and blind the eyes of Israel. By explaining the unbelief of the Jews toward Jesus with this passage, John is relating Jesus' unbelieving generation to the earlier generation of idolatry and unbelief to which God sent

3. William Barclay, *The Gospel of John*, 2 vols. (Philadelphia: Westminster, 1975), 2:153.

Isaiah to preach judgment. Now, as before, it was God's sovereign purpose that his judgment would consist in the hardening of the people against the gospel offer of peace.

There are three ways in which we should understand God's hardening of the Jews. First, we should realize that the Jews' rejection of Jesus was part of God's sovereign plan for our salvation. God purposed for the Jews to reject Jesus so that he might be crucified for our sins. This rejection involved both the will of the unbelieving Jews and the will of God. As Peter later preached, Jesus was "delivered up according to the definite plan and foreknowledge of God," yet he said to his Jewish hearers, "you crucified and killed [him] by the hands of lawless men" (Acts 2:23). Peter accuses his hearers of their culpable guilt and also ascribes what happened to God's sovereign plan.

Do we object to this? If we do, we are objecting to the very plan of God that achieved redemption through the crucifixion of Jesus. Moreover, the Jews' rejection of the gospel brought salvation to the Gentiles, which includes most Christians today. So if we object to God's will in hardening Jesus' Jewish hearers, we object to God's plan for our salvation. We would do better to follow Isaiah's example when he accepted God's commission for his own ministry of hardening: Isaiah had seen the Lord's sovereign majesty and knew better than to pit his puny wisdom against the Lord's holy will.

Second, John's teaching reminds us that the gospel is a "two-edged sword" (Heb. 4:12; Rev. 1:16), giving eternal life to those who believe but conveying judgment to those who are hardened in unbelief. This is why Jesus warned, "Walk while you have the light, lest darkness overtake you" (John 12:35). Gordon Keddie explains: "Those unwilling to believe become progressively unable to believe."[4] Leon Morris writes, "They have rejected the gracious invitation of God, and it is God, none less, who has decreed that those who act in this way have their eyes blinded and their hearts hardened."[5]

Third, it is clear in this passage that the hardening effect of unbelief is not merely a natural cause and effect but God's judicial response. J. C. Ryle comments, "God had given over the Jews to judicial blindness, as a punishment for their long continued and obstinate rejection of His warnings."[6]

---

4. Gordon J. Keddie, *A Study Commentary on John*, 2 vols. (Darlington, UK: Evangelical Press, 2001), 1:485.

5. Leon Morris, *Reflections on the Gospel of John* (Peabody, MA: Hendrickson, 1986), 460.

6. J. C. Ryle, *Expository Thoughts on the Gospels: John*, 3 vols. (Edinburgh: Banner of Truth, 1999), 2:416.

This presents us with a sober reality, since God has not changed over the years. People think they can wait to commit themselves to Jesus. They want a few more years to enjoy their sin, and they think that at the time of their own choosing they can become Christians and start living as they know they should. But they do not realize the hardening effect of unbelief on their hearts, so that it will be increasingly difficult for them to believe. They might come to a time when it is impossible for them to believe. Moreover, since God is offended by their disdain for his Son, it is quite possible for God to give such people over to ultimate reprobation. The time came when God gave over the Jews to a judicial hardening, so that, John says, "therefore they could not believe" (John 12:39). This argues that when God presents you with the invitation of his gospel—the gracious offer to forgive your sins and grant you eternal life through faith in Jesus Christ—that is the time when you should believe, accepting the gospel in trusting faith. The same is true for professing believers who gain some benefit from Christianity but have never truly reckoned with God and surrendered their lives to him. The longer you wait, the greater risk you take.

While unbelief has the effect of hardening our hearts to the gospel, faith works in the opposite way. When our eyes accept the truth revealed in Scripture, our spiritual perceptiveness increases. When we sorrow over our sin and seek grace to repent, our hearts are made more tender and pure. When our ears are frequently attuned to the Word of God, they become sharper in hearing his voice. Through such saving faith, we turn to God and are healed. Our sins are washed away by the cleansing blood of Christ. Just as the blind man of John 9 received his sight and Lazarus was brought from death to life, our souls are restored by God's grace until in the end we will be fully healed of every vestige of sin and corruption.

All of this shows the eternal significance of how we respond to the gospel whenever it is proclaimed and offered. This is why Paul exhorted, "Behold, now is the favorable time; behold, now is the day of salvation" (2 Cor. 6:2). To put off belief in Christ is to reject him. Jesus calls you to walk in his light and offers that in this way you will receive eternal life as a child of God. But, writes William Hendriksen, "when people, of their own accord and after repeated threats and promises, reject him and spurn his messages, then—and not until then—he hardens them, *in order that* those who were *not willing* to repent may *not be able* to repent."[7]

THE CHALLENGE OF FAITH

Part of the good news of the gospel is that God is always at work in surprising ways to bring salvation to those in darkness. This was true even in the gloomy setting that John has described. He concludes the passage by telling us that "many even of the authorities believed in [Jesus]" (John 12:42). It is hard to imagine a more difficult ministry setting than that of the Pharisees and Sadducees who were seeking to put Jesus to death. Yet when Jesus offered them salvation one last time, even among this hostile group there were some who began to see his light.

But there was a problem with these budding converts. John says that while they had believed in Jesus, "for fear of the Pharisees they did not confess it, so that they would not be put out of the synagogue" (John 12:42). This reminds us that there is a price to following Jesus. Jesus offers a free salvation, but it comes with the possibility of the world's rejection. These budding believers were reluctant to be cast out of Jewish society, which was what expulsion from the synagogue entailed. But Christ demands that his followers not be secret disciples; sooner rather than later, a true believer must go public with his faith in Jesus, regardless of the cost. Jesus had said, "Whoever is ashamed of me and of my words in this adulterous and sinful generation, of him will the Son of Man also be ashamed when he comes in the glory of his Father with the holy angels" (Mark 8:38).

Moreover, John tells us that these men remained silent because "they loved the glory that comes from man more than the glory that comes from God" (John 12:43). This is a particular temptation to those who are high in the eyes of the world; John Calvin writes that "earthly honours may be called golden shackles binding a man."[8] A. W. Pink comments of these compromised believers:

They preferred the good will of other sinners above the approval of God. O the shortsighted folly of these wretched men! O the madness of their

---

7. William Hendriksen, *Exposition of the Gospel according to John*, 2 vols., New Testament Commentary (Grand Rapids: Baker, 1953), 2:212.

8. John Calvin, *New Testament Commentaries*, trans. T. H. L. Parker, 12 vols. (Grand Rapids: Eerdmans, 1959), 4:49.

miserable choice! Of what avail would the good opinion of the Pharisees be when the hour of death overtook them? In what stead will it stand them when they appear before the judgment-throne of God? "What shall it profit a man if he gain the whole world, and lose his own soul?"[9]

Many, if not most, Christians struggle with these same temptations. This is one of the reasons why we are tempted to blend in with the world in our manner of living. We fear to be ostracized if we live openly and boldly as followers of Christ. We are reluctant to speak to people about the only Savior who can redeem their souls. What will break this spell of our fear of man and love of the world?

The answer is found in the word that appears in both verses 41 and 43. The word is *glory*. These cowardly Pharisees were afraid to admit their belief in Jesus because they were enthralled by the glory of this world. But in contrast, Isaiah committed himself to the Lord "because he saw [Jesus'] glory" (John 12:41). If we go back to Isaiah 6, we read that he "saw the Lord sitting upon a throne, high and lifted up; and the train of his robe filled the temple" (Isa. 6:1). It was Jesus that he saw in a seat of ultimate sovereignty, high and majestic over every power and authority. He saw that Jesus' robe filled the temple, so that there was no room for any other sovereign in his kingdom. Isaiah also saw holy angels, the seraphim, and they were singing in rapturous praise: "Holy, holy, holy is the LORD of hosts; the whole earth is full of his glory!" (6:3). He says, "The foundations of the thresholds shook at the voice of him who called, and the house was filled with smoke" (6:4). Isaiah saw the weightiness of Christ, the awesomeness of Christ, the holiness of Christ, and the consuming fire that burns in the heart of our Lord.

As a result, Isaiah no longer feared the world or stood in thrall to its tarnished glory. He would stand against the world with Jesus and speak to the world for Jesus. If the same is not true of us, then the logical explanation is that we have not seen what Isaiah saw. We are more concerned with our lifestyle, our comfort, with getting by in the unholy world. This is why we are more interested in "practical matters" and consider theology boring and irrelevant. This is why we fear the world and love its glory.

This shows that our greatest need is to see the glory of Christ, as Isaiah did. J. C. Ryle comments: "The expulsive power of a new principle, making

9. Arthur W. Pink, *Exposition of the Gospel of John* (Grand Rapids: Zondervan, 1975), 692.

us see God, Christ, heaven, hell, judgment, eternity, as realities, is the grand secret of getting the victory over the fear of man."[10]

Isaiah received his vision of Christ by direct revelation, as the Lord revealed his glory to the grieving prophet in the temple. How, then, are we to see the glory of Christ? The answer is that for believers today, the glory of Christ is found shining through the Word of God. This is what Peter emphasized in his second letter. He admitted that he had the privilege of witnessing miracles and seeing visible displays of Christ's glory. But, he insists, "we have something more sure, the prophetic word, to which you will do well to pay attention as to a lamp shining in a dark place, until the day dawns and the morning star rises in your hearts" (2 Peter 1:19). This is what the two disciples discovered on the Emmaus road. Jesus appeared to them on the day of his resurrection, yet his chief display of glory was in explaining the Bible. The disciples exclaimed: "Did not our hearts burn within us while he talked to us on the road, while he opened to us the Scriptures?" (Luke 24:32). The Lord has given to his Word the power to convey the glory of Christ to our souls. When the Bible becomes that for us—the revelation of divine glory to our faith—then we will no longer have to worry about the danger of our hearts' becoming hardened, we will no longer fear what man might do, and the spell of worldly glory will be broken. For Christ will be high and exalted on the throne of our hearts, and the train of his robe will fill the temple of our souls.

10. Ryle, *John*, 2:420.

83

CHRIST VINDICATED

John 12:44–50

*"For I have not spoken on my own authority, but the Father
who sent me has himself given me a commandment—what to
say and what to speak. And I know that his commandment is
eternal life. What I say, therefore, I say as the Father has told me."*
(John 12:49–50)

The expression "the passion of Christ" is usually reserved to describe Jesus' ordeal in suffering on the cross. Yet all through this Gospel, John has frequently presented Jesus' passion, in the sense of his emotional response to people and events. It certainly was a passionate Jesus who took a whip and drove the money-changers out of the temple (John 2:13–16). And it was a passionate Jesus who stood amid the festival attendees and cried out, "If anyone thirsts, let him come to me and drink" (7:37). Because of his zeal for the Father's glory and his love for sinners, Jesus was anything but dispassionate in his earthly ministry.

As we conclude John 12, we arrive at the main transition in John's Gospel. We recall that the first twelve chapters are referred to as *The Book of Signs*, since they present Jesus' ministry in terms of seven great miracles. Chapter 13 begins *The Book of the Passion*, detailing the events of the cross and resurrection. As we now consider the final words recorded by John before his account of the events of the cross, we are not surprised to find great passion in them.

Jesus' public teaching was now over. John says that after his last appeal to the Jews, "he departed and hid himself from them" (John 12:36). Presumably, Jesus withdrew to the company of his closest disciples, perhaps back with his friends at Bethany. But Jesus was anything but withdrawn from the drama of the occasion. Indeed, it must have been a heartbreaking time, for the words that John wrote in his prologue had proved true: "He came to his own, and his own people did not receive him" (1:11). On the brink of the great storm into which he was about to walk, Jesus vindicates himself against those who will soon condemn him and gives encouragement to those who will remember his words after the cross.

WHY JESUS SHOULD HAVE BEEN RECEIVED

In only five places in the Gospels is it recorded that Jesus "cried out." Two of them arise from his sufferings on the cross (Matt. 27:46, 50; Mark 15:34). Another was when Jesus appealed to the crowd at the Feast of Tabernacles, calling for them to come to him as the giver of living water (John 7:37). A fourth occasion was when Jesus "cried out" to Lazarus in the tomb, calling him back to life (11:43). The fifth occasion is here at the very end of his public ministry, when Jesus responds to the Jews' final rejection of their Messiah.

Here, Jesus' passionate concern is not just with the people's failure to believe, but also with the overwhelming reasons why they should have believed. In John 12:44–46, he gives three reasons, starting with the fact that he had come as God's messenger: "Whoever believes in me," Jesus cried, "believes not in me but in him who sent me" (12:44).

Three times in these final verses of chapter 12, Jesus refers to God as the One who sent him. This truth bears both on Jesus' credentials and on the honor of God that is offended by unbelief. People complain that God does not seem to do anything about the great problems of our world. But in fact, he has sent his Son as the giver of grace, with good news of salvation. Yet the world rejected him!

It is true that Jesus' message was surprising and even confrontational. He challenged men such as the Pharisees, who were relying on their supposed goodness to win their way to heaven. Jesus' coming exposed their sin and confronted their false teaching. None of us enjoy having our beliefs corrected and our sins exposed. But the true question is whether Jesus really spoke for God. The answer is that he did, the proof of which was his miracles. By giving sight to the man born blind and then raising Lazarus from the grave, Jesus sufficiently proved that he had come from God, as it seems clear the Pharisees realized. Their rejection of Christ was thus a rejection of God.

Jesus not only spoke for God but also revealed God to us. For this reason also, he deserves to be believed. He said, "And whoever sees me sees him who sent me" (John 12:45).

This is the Bible's answer to the greatest of all questions: "What is God like?" Inevitably, we all ask whether God is concerned about us. We wonder what God demands and what he offers. The answers are found in the coming of his Son. Jesus is, Paul wrote, "the image of the invisible God" (Col. 1:15), so that by a sincere study of Jesus, we learn the great truths about God himself.

Jesus said, "Whoever *sees* me *sees* him who sent me," using the Greek verb *theoreo*. From this, we get our words *theory* and *theorize*. Jesus did not mean that merely by laying eyes on him we see God, true though that is. Rather, he means that those who studiously reflect on his person and work will come to know God. We learn that God is love by seeing the love of Jesus, especially as he offers himself on the cross. We see what it means that God is holy when we observe Jesus' actions. Jesus lives out God's wisdom and displays God's saving power. John Owen wrote, "In Christ we behold the wisdom, goodness, love, grace, mercy and power of God all working together for the great work of our redemption and salvation."[1]

Man was made by God in his own image. This means that "humanity was designed to be the perfect vehicle for God's self-expression within this world."[2] It was because sin ruined man for this God-imaging role that God sent his Son into the world as a man. In this respect, Jesus not only reveals God to us but also reveals true humanity. When we see Jesus in the Scriptures, not only should we say, "This is what God is like!" but we should also conclude, "This is what I was meant to be like!" Jesus reveals God by speaking and acting in perfect conformity with the character of God. The

1. John Owen, *The Glory of Christ* (1684; repr., Edinburgh: Banner of Truth, 2000), 25.
2. N. T. Wright, *Colossians and Philemon* (Grand Rapids: Eerdmans, 1986), 70.

reason Jesus can do this is that he is himself God, fully partaking of the divine nature.

The true disgrace of sin is that we who were made to reveal God need to have God revealed to us. We have lost contact with our Maker. So Jesus came to restore to us the knowledge of God and reconcile us to God through the forgiveness of our sins. How great, then, is the tragedy of unbelief! All that is left to those who reject Jesus is a godless life of increasing darkness. But the opposite is true of faith in Christ. William Hendriksen summarizes: "Knowing Christ means knowing the Father. Loving Christ means loving the Father. Receiving Christ means receiving the Father. Christ and the Father are one."[3]

Jesus gave a third reason why he should be believed, dealing with his mission in the world: "I have come into the world as light, so that whoever believes in me may not remain in darkness" (John 12:46). He came to lift us out of darkness and bring us into his marvelous light. J. C. Ryle summarizes his meaning: "I have come into a world full of darkness and sin, to be the source and centre of life, peace, holiness, happiness to mankind; so that everyone who receives and believes in Me, may be delivered from darkness and walk in full light."[4]

When we consider these three reasons, we see why Jesus was so grieved that his own people did not receive him. He was sent by God, he revealed God, and he brought light to the world. If you have not believed, will you not face the reality of who and what Jesus is? If you have believed, then these are reasons why you must press on in faith, despite whatever difficulties you experience in this world.

UNBELIEF JUSTLY CONDEMNED

Jesus' tone is not one of vindictive anger but of frustrated good will. He knows, however, that the result of unbelief is condemnation. To believe in him is to believe the Father who sent him, to see and understand God, and to be lifted out of darkness. But Jesus continued, "The one who rejects me

3. William Hendriksen, *Exposition of the Gospel according to John*, 2 vols., New Testament Commentary (Grand Rapids: Baker, 1953), 2:214.

4. J. C. Ryle, *Expository Thoughts on the Gospels: John*, 3 vols. (Edinburgh: Banner of Truth, 1999), 2:427.

and does not receive my words has a judge; the word that I have spoken will judge him on the last day" (John 12:48).

The purpose of Jesus' coming was not condemnation. He explains, "If anyone hears my words and does not keep them, I do not judge him; for I did not come to judge the world but to save the world" (John 12:47). This statement has confused some people because there are other passages making it clear that Jesus will judge the world on the last day. Paul says that Jesus will "judge the living and the dead" (2 Tim. 4:1). Jesus himself taught, "When the Son of Man comes in his glory, and all the angels with him, then he will sit on his glorious throne. Before him will be gathered all the nations, and he will separate people one from another as a shepherd separates the sheep from the goats" (Matt. 25:31–32). Jesus is not now denying his role in the future judgment. His point is that while rejecting him leads to condemnation, it was not for condemnation that he came: "I did not come to judge the world but to save the world," he asserts (John 12:47).

Jesus likely has the Pharisees specifically in mind, along with other Jews who had heard and understood his message, yet denied him. Therefore, he says that the message they rejected will judge them: "The word that I have spoken will judge him on the last day" (John 12:48). Jesus uses the word *rhema*, which indicates his actual words, rather than merely the substance of his meaning. Jesus' words will be used in the final judgment of those who have refused him. People who have never heard the gospel will be judged for all their sins (see Rev. 20:12). But those who rejected the gospel will especially be judged for the words of grace that they spurned. They will be made to remember that Jesus declared himself to be "the light of the world" as they enter the absolute and eternal darkness earned by their unbelief.

From this we may draw some important applications. The first is that we should realize that there will be a "last day" (John 12:48). Martyn Lloyd-Jones comments:

> From beginning to end the message of the Bible . . . is that there is to be an end to the world, and that the end is judgment. The Christ of God will come back into this world and he will return to judge it. . . . The world is under judgment. And it is going to perish. All that is opposed to God is going to be judged and it is going to be destroyed. . . . There is a day

coming when astonished humanity is going to hear this cry: 'Babylon is fallen, is fallen" (Rev. 14:8).[5]

If this is true, then we should live with the judgment day in mind. Those who are not able to face that day should search for a Savior, in which case Jesus Christ alone can speak good news. He alone died for the forgiveness of our sins. But even we who have found salvation should live in light of the great coming day. If the unbelieving world seems so happy and well off, we should not envy but remember that the end of it all is near. We should live for the things of heaven, "for the present form of this world is passing away" (1 Cor. 7:31).

Second, Jesus makes it plain that unbelievers are responsible for their rejection of his gospel. Earlier, he taught, "This is the judgment: the light has come into the world, and people loved the darkness rather than the light because their works were evil" (John 3:19). This means that at the back of unbelief is a moral cause. People want to be their own master, so they reject the lordship of Christ. Why else would they have crucified a man who went about healing and teaching light? Why else would people not want the holy life to which Christians are called? Unbelievers are too staunchly committed to self and sin. So even while Jesus can prove to have come from God, while Jesus meets our greatest need by showing us God, and while Jesus shines light to lift us out of darkness, people still will not bend the knee to him. For this they are responsible. As A. W. Pink wrote, "Every man who hears the Gospel *ought* to believe in Christ, and those who do not will yet be punished for this unbelief."[6]

To hear the gospel is to be responsible to God for your response; on the last day, God will vindicate Christ's gospel and hold to account those who held it in contempt. Jesus once said that the judgment would be more bearable for pagan cities like Tyre and Sidon, which never heard the gospel, than for the Jews who rejected him (Matt. 11:21–22). The same point was made by an old minister who wrote a book of instruction in Christian truth. At the end he asked what would happen to one who disregarded the gospel contained in his book. He answered that condemnation would surely result to those who would not believe, and then he concluded, "And so much the

5. D. Martyn Lloyd-Jones, *The Cross* (Westchester, IL: Crossway, 1986), 102.
6. Arthur W. Pink, *Exposition of the Gospel of John* (Grand Rapids: Zondervan, 1975), 695.

more because thou hast read this book."[7] So it is for everyone who hears the teaching of Jesus' salvation: you are responsible for all your sins, but especially for rejecting the gospel that you have heard.

JESUS' ULTIMATE VINDICATION

It was the eve of Jesus' arrest and crucifixion, and his last words are meant to prove his ultimate vindication: "For I have not spoken on my own authority, but the Father who sent me has himself given me a commandment—what to say and what to speak. And I know that his commandment is eternal life. What I say, therefore, I say as the Father has told me" (John 12:49–50). With these words, John draws the curtain on the first half of his Gospel, *The Book of Signs*.

People have different opinions of Jesus and the New Testament. But Jesus has asked and demanded nothing more than what God the Father has authorized him to ask and demand. Does it seem extreme for Jesus to call for faith in him as Son of God and Savior? Then realize that God has authorized him to call for such faith. Does it bother you that Christianity insists that salvation comes only through Jesus (Acts 4:12)? But this claim is made by the authority of God himself, who has provided no other Savior.

Christians need to claim this same authority when speaking to the world. Too often we debate matters of truth and morality in accordance with the world's standards. In arguing against abortion, some Christians will try to show the economic value of an increased birthrate. When arguing against homosexuality, they will present a sociological or psychological argument. But these arguments, even when true, lack authority. Christians should instead speak forth the Word of God, unashamedly pointing out the teaching of Holy Scripture, which comes with the authority of God himself. Especially when presenting the gospel of salvation, we should avoid arguing on the basis of worldly benefits, but should speak in such a way as to be able to say with Jesus: "I have not spoken on my own authority," but on the authority of God. Then, even if the world rejects us, God will vindicate all we have said on his behalf.

Second, Jesus vindicated himself by the character of his message: "And I know that his commandment is eternal life" (John 12:50). We might say this

---

7. William Barclay, *The Gospel of John*, 2 vols. (Philadelphia: Westminster, 1975), 2:158.

broadly about the whole teaching of God's Word. God's Word is life and it is light. To turn from our sins and seek the way of God is to set ourselves on the path of blessing that leads to everlasting life. Whether we are speaking about moral standards in general, our conduct in marriage and the family, our performance of duties as citizens, or our interactions with other people, God's Word vindicates itself by the fruit it bears. Therefore, Psalm 1 says of the man or woman who delights in the law of the Lord: "He is like a tree planted by streams of water that yields its fruit in its season, and its leaf does not wither. In all that he does, he prospers" (Ps. 1:3).

But Jesus probably has the gospel specifically in mind. After all, what commandment especially determines eternal life? It is the command to believe on Jesus. "Believe in the Lord Jesus, and you will be saved" (Acts 16:31). Earlier, Jesus was asked, "What must we do, to be doing the works of God?" He replied, "This is the work of God, that you believe in him whom he has sent" (John 6:28–29).

We customarily express the gospel as an invitation from God, and rightly so. But it is also true that God demands that men and women receive his Son. When preaching to the Athenians, Paul noted God's patience over the ages with rebel mankind. But with the coming of his own Son, Paul said, "now he commands all people everywhere to repent" (Acts 17:30). James Montgomery Boice comments: "This is not something to be toyed with; this is not something to be delayed. God is our master, and he orders us to turn from sin and to respond to him."[8]

Our postmodern world likes to make sport of nearly every failing of the church and of Christians over the years. Yet the record still stands that the spread of Christianity has literally brought life, light, and freedom throughout the world. Even today, it is Christian faith that prompts the greatest amount of charitable giving and doing of works of mercy throughout the world. Each of us should commit to being lifesavers, peacemakers, and help-givers, to show that God's commands bring life. And especially we should spread the gospel of Jesus Christ, God's commandment that brings eternal life.

Finally, Jesus vindicated himself by his obedience to the Father's will: "What I say, therefore, I say as the Father has told me" (John 12:50). Jesus

---

8. James Montgomery Boice, *The Gospel of John*, 5 vols. (Grand Rapids: Baker, 1999), 3:992.

might have said this about every aspect of his life. What he said, what he did, where he went, and how he lived was always "as the Father has told me." Obedience to the Father was Jesus' ultimate vindication.

The story is told of a virtuoso pianist who performed his first concert at Carnegie Hall. The crowd was awed by his playing and demanded an encore. Afterward, nearly the entire audience rose to their feet, cheering. But when asked to go out and take a final bow, the pianist refused. When challenged about this, he peered between the curtains and pointed to a small man in the balcony who remained seated. He said, "Do you see that one man up there? When he stands up and applauds, then I will take my bow." "But it is only one man!" they replied. "Why will you not take your bow until that one man applauds?" "Because that man is my teacher," the pianist replied.

So it was with Jesus, who ultimately vindicated himself by his obedience to the will of God the Father. The world might hate him (and it did) and might scoff at his teaching (and it still does), but he would content himself with the applause of one person only: his heavenly Father. And throughout his ministry, the Father gave his applause to Jesus over and over. In fact, earlier that very day, God had audibly expressed his approval from heaven. Jesus, feeling great anxiety over the cross, prayed, "Father, glorify your name." And the Father spoke from above: "I have glorified it, and I will glorify it again" (John 12:28). That was all the vindication that Jesus ever needed.

The same should be true for us. "If God is for us, who can be against us?" (Rom. 8:31). So let us resolve to speak and live so as to be able to say, "What I have done, I have done as God has taught me in his Word." If we can say that, we will not need the applause of the world and we will not fear its scorn. For in the end it will be revealed that only one opinion really matters: that of the God who holds eternity in his hand and gives eternal life to all who receive his beloved Son.

PART 5

Jesus' Parting Ministry to the Disciples

84

LOVE TO THE END

John 13:1

*Now before the Feast of the Passover, when Jesus knew that his
hour had come to depart out of this world to the Father, having
loved his own who were in the world, he loved them to the end.*
(John 13:1)

ohn 13:1 stands at the very center of the teaching of John's Gospel. Not only does it begin the second half of the Gospel, but it looks both backward to what John has written and forward to what is yet to come. John's key statement is that "having loved his own who were in the world, [Jesus] loved them to the end."

For many Christians, the Gospel of John is the spiritual high point of the entire Bible, which is why John is often recommended as a first book to read for those new to Scripture. Within John, the chapters that present Jesus' final teaching to his disciples, his arrest, and his crucifixion are especially precious to believers' hearts. F. W. Krummacher describes the events of the second half of John in terms of the Israelites' entry into the temple sanctuary. First, there is the outer court, which describes Jesus' Last Supper teaching to the disciples; then comes the Holy Place, the outer room with its sacred objects, which Krummacher compares to the account of Jesus' arrest and trial; and finally we enter the Most Holy Place, the inner sanctum where God's glory dwelt, which he compares to John's account of the crucifixion of Jesus.[1]

The first section of John's *Book of the Passion* presents material found nowhere else in the New Testament. It is now the night of the Passover Feast, at which Jesus would celebrate his Last Supper with the disciples. This momentous evening, the eve of the cross, is unfolded in John chapters 13–17. Chapter 13 relates Jesus' symbolic act of washing the disciples' feet. It is followed by a lengthy instruction dealing with Jesus' coming departure and God's provision in his absence, from the end of chapter 13 through chapter 16. Chapter 17 concludes the section with Jesus' High Priestly Prayer, in which he commits his disciples into the care of the heavenly Father. In all these events, Jesus was motivated by the knowledge "that his hour had come to depart out of this world to the Father" (John 13:1). Of this matchless material, James Montgomery Boice writes:

> Nowhere in the entire Bible does the child of God feel that he is walking on more holy ground. For here, more than in many other portions of Scripture, he hears the voice of Jesus leading him into a greater understanding of his new place before the Father and consequently also of his new position in the world. These chapters contain teaching about heaven, the new commandment, the person and work of the Holy Spirit, the mutual union of Christ with the disciples and the disciples with Christ, and prayer.[2]

CHRIST'S PARTICULAR LOVE FOR HIS OWN

One reason that these chapters are precious to believers is that they highlight Jesus' particular love for "his own." This touches on a truth emphasized throughout John's Gospel, that there is a people set apart by God the Father for his Son and that these elect people are the objects of a special and saving love. Not that Christ loved only his own. Christ's love for the whole world is strikingly revealed in John. But there is a difference between Christ's love for the world and his love for his own, just as there is a difference in a man's love for his bride compared to his love for others. Boice explains this difference: "God has done *some things for all men* . . . [but] on the other hand,

1. F. W. Krummacher, *The Suffering Saviour* (1856; repr., Edinburgh: Banner of Truth, 2004).
2. James Montgomery Boice, *The Gospel of John*, 5 vols. (Grand Rapids: Baker, 1999), 4:995–96.

God has done *all things for some men.*"[3] It is Christ's all-saving love for those who are "his own" that is the concern of these chapters.

How did believers come to be Christ's own? The first answer is that Christ chose them. Jesus says in John 15:16, "You did not choose me, but I chose you." Charles Spurgeon comments: "A man may surely choose his own wife, and Christ chose his own spouse, he chose his own church; and while the Scripture stands, that doctrine can never be eradicated from it."[4] Having chosen us in his gracious love, Jesus made us his own by purchase, redeeming us from our sins through the blood of his cross. Therefore, Paul writes to believers: "You are not your own, for you were bought with a price" (1 Cor. 6:19–20).

A second answer is that believers are Christ's own because we were given to him by the heavenly Father. Jesus said: "All that the Father gives me will come to me . . . . And this is the will of him who sent me, that I should lose nothing of all that he has given me, but raise it up on the last day" (John 6:37, 39). This presents the biblical doctrine of election, which states that in eternity past God predestined particular people to be joined to his Son for their salvation and his glory. Paul writes that God "chose us in [Christ] before the foundation of the world, that we should be holy and blameless before him" (Eph. 1:4). Therefore, Jesus prays in his High Priestly Prayer: "Yours they were, and you gave them to me" (John 17:6).

The first and second reasons why Christians are "Christ's own" center on God the Son and God the Father. It makes sense that the third reason focuses on God the Spirit. We are Christ's own because we were born again as children of God through the Holy Spirit. The effect of this is that we have taken Christ for our own and given ourselves to him, so that for us life holds no more glittering crown than to be called "Christ's own." Spurgeon exults:

> The fact that you are truly Christ's is the fountain of innumerable plea-
> sures and blessings to your heart. Jesus calls us "his own"—his own sheep,
> his own disciples, his own friends, his own brethren, the members of his
> body. What a title for us to wear, "His own"! . . . Thus he distinguishes
> us from the rest of mankind, and sets us apart unto himself. "My name

3. Ibid., 998.
4. Charles H. Spurgeon, *Majesty in Misery*, 3 vols. (Edinburgh: Banner of Truth, 2005), 1:16.

shall be named on them," says he[;] . . . surely, this is the highest honour that can be put upon us even in the last great day.[5]

Knowing that we are Christ's own is even more glorious when we realize how great is the love of Christ for his own. This is the theme of these chapters: "having loved his own who were in the world, he loved them to the end."

The love of Christ for us is mirrored in the love he showed to his first disciples, despite their great unworthiness. Consider these men whom Christ loved! How often they had been foolish, wayward, and unbelieving! All this would be especially revealed in the hour of the cross. Yet, observes J. C. Ryle, "knowing perfectly well that they were about to forsake Him shamefully in a very few hours, in full view of their approaching display of weakness and infirmity, our blessed Master did not cease to have loving thoughts of His disciples." This tells us that we can look to the love of Christ despite our failures and sins. However we might fall short of our calling, believers are still Christ's own and enjoy his unfailing love. How this ought to motivate us to please him in the manner of our lives.

Moreover, if there were ever a time when we might excuse Jesus for turning his thoughts away from his disciples and turning inward to his own problems, this would be such a time. Spurgeon writes: "If you and I had to bear all that Christ had to suffer, it would engross our thoughts, we should not be able to think of anything else but that; but it did not engross our Lord's thoughts. He still thought of 'his own.' "[6]

What is closest to one's heart is usually made apparent in the hour of his death. Some are preoccupied with their business affairs, so there is a rush to get affairs settled before dying. Some reveal their love for family, and others for the fleeting pleasures of life. Likewise, Jesus revealed what is closest to his heart as his cross came near. It was his love for his own that dominated his thoughts and feelings, and "having loved his own who were in the world, he loved them to the end." Does this not prove that there is no greater blessing than to be called one of Christ's own? While Christ has chosen his own, it is equally true that anyone who takes him for Lord and Savior is one of those chosen. If you will yield your faith to Jesus, then you may know the incomparable blessing of being loved as one of his own.

5. Ibid., 1:18.
6. Ibid., 1:21.

HAVING LOVED THEM

I said that John 13:1 stands at the very center of John's Gospel. His key phrase, "having loved his own who were in the world, he loved them to the end," looks both backward and forward on Jesus' love. What, then, do we see if we look backward from the cross on the love of Christ? How has he "loved his own"?

This quest will take us all the way back to the creation of the world. John's Gospel began with a statement of Christ's deity that deliberately reflected the creation account in Genesis 1. John wrote: "In the beginning was the Word, and the Word was with God, and the Word was God. He was in the beginning with God. All things were made through him, and without him was not any thing made that was made" (John 1:1–3). Therefore, when Genesis 1 recounts that "God said, 'Let us make man in our image'" (Gen. 1:26), Christ was that Word by which man came into being. We were made as spiritual beings capable of fellowship with our Creator and called to reflect his glory in the world. Boice writes: "He created us, not to a meaningless existence but to an existence that is the highest existence possible for any created object, namely, communion with the One who created it."[7] This is the fundamental dignity stamped onto every human soul, the result of Christ's love for us in creation.

Following with John's prologue, we see that Christ loved us in his incarnation. John writes, "The Word became flesh and dwelt among us, and we have seen his glory, glory as of the only Son from the Father, full of grace and truth" (John 1:14). It was for love that Christ left the glories of heaven for the miseries of earth. And it was a mark of his love that he was born not in a palace amid jewels and gold, but in the poverty of a stable in the midst of the world in need. Krummacher writes: "He associated with sinners, that He might bear them eternally on His heart."[8]

The particular love of Christ for his own was seen in the calling of his disciples. They came at his invitation: "Come and you will see" (John 1:39). Matthew, the tax collector, was sitting in his sin when Jesus approached and called, "Follow me" (Matt. 9:9). Peter, James, and John were tending their nets when Jesus promised them: "From now on you will be catching men"

7. Boice, *John*, 4:1003.
8. Krummacher, *The Suffering Saviour*, 29–30.

(Luke 5:10). Every Christian can look to the same love that called him or her to faith with effectual grace. Jesus called us not because of what we can give to him but because of what he can do for us and what he can make of us. "You were called to freedom, brothers," wrote Paul (Gal. 5:13): freedom from worldliness, misery, bondage, and sin. We were called to "the riches of his glorious inheritance in the saints" (Eph. 1:18), all by the love of Christ for his own.

Furthermore, Jesus loved his own by teaching and leading them during the three years of their discipleship. The Twelve could never have imagined the things they would hear from the loving lips of Jesus. How often had he called them aside for a special word of truth, or patiently borne with their questions and objections. "If you abide in my word, you are truly my disciples," Jesus told them, "and you will know the truth, and the truth will set you free" (John 8:31–32). Likewise, Christians are taught the Word of truth in the Scriptures by the ministry of Christ through his Spirit.

Had the disciples been told at the start the dangers and threats they would face in Jesus' company, they would have probably fled in terror. But Jesus guided them through all these trials. Ever the Good Shepherd, he constantly brought them beside still waters, restored their burdened souls, and led them in paths of righteousness (Ps. 23:2–3). All for love! Every Christian can look back on the life of faith, with many joys and trials, and say of that same love: "The LORD is my shepherd; I shall not want" (23:1).

How Jesus Loved to the End

But now John turns to the future, and the immediate future facing Jesus and his disciples was as dark as could be. What would become of Christ's own in this dreadful hour? What provision would there be for them in light of the cross? John answers, "Having loved his own who were in the world, he loved them to the end."

The expression "to the end" (Greek *eis telos*) can be taken in a number of ways. It can mean that Jesus loved them perfectly or thoroughly, and that is certainly true, for Jesus was about to show the disciples the full extent of his love. But probably the best way to take this is by its temporal meaning. Jesus did not just love them up to this point, but kept on loving them to the end.

First, Jesus loved his own to the end of his own life. Undoubtedly, this was John's major point of view, since this passage takes place in the shadow of the cross. If love for his own required Jesus to die for their sins, then he loved them to that end; the cross was indeed the fullest extent of his love. "Greater love has no one than this," Jesus explained, "that someone lay down his life for his friends" (John 15:13). Krummacher comments:

> O how He loved them, when He took their sins with Him into judgment, and cast Himself into the fire which their transgressions had kindled! How He loved them, when His own blood did not seem to Him too dear a price to be paid for them, although it was they who were the transgressors; He loved them to the end; and to this day He loves them that are His in a similar manner![9]

What should the love of Christ on the cross mean to us? An analogy is presented in the movie *Saving Private Ryan*. It tells of a rescue operation after the Allied invasion of Normandy in June 1944. The War Department has learned that three out of four boys in a family named Ryan died in battle on the same day. So the Army's top general orders that the fourth son be rescued from behind German lines, where he parachuted. An elite squad of Army Rangers is assigned to find Private James Ryan. Their search leads to a bridge where German tanks are attacking, and the squad is destroyed as their quest finally succeeds. As the captain who saved him lies dying on the bridge, surrounded by the bodies of the men from his squad, he draws Ryan close and gasps, "Earn this. Earn it." The movie concludes with Ryan, as an old man, walking across a field of crosses, marking the graves of men who died for him. Falling to his knees at Captain Miller's grave, he says to the white plaster cross, "Every day I think about what you said to me that day on the bridge. I've tried to live my life the best I could. I hope that was enough. I hope that at least in your eyes, I earned what all of you have done for me."

Of course, none of us could ever earn the death of God's own Son for our sins. Our forgiveness in Christ's blood is a free gift, received not by works but by simple faith alone. Yet it ought to open up a fountain of gratitude and love in our hearts. Every believer should turn to Christ's wooden cross and

9. Ibid., 30.

pray, "If you, with all your glory, died for me, I can live for you today." We are called to live for him because he loved us to the end that was his cross, because he died for us.

But this expression "he loved them to the end" can be taken a second way. Jesus loved his disciples not only to the end of his life but also to the end of their lives. The striking of the Shepherd on the cross would scatter the sheep; the disciples would cower in fear, Peter even denying Christ three times on the night of his arrest. Yet far more would be demanded of them in years to come. They would be persecuted, afflicted, tempted, and tried as they served their Master in the world. How could they even hope to endure, much less to conquer in faith? The answer is that the risen and ascended Christ would continue in his love to the end of their lives.

This is why the chapters to come focus heavily on the ministry of the Holy Spirit, whom Christ would send to his own from heaven after his own departure. Indeed, Jesus himself would continue to disciple them—teaching, guiding, disciplining, and strengthening his own—through the ministry of the Spirit. And from his throne of authority and power in heaven, Jesus would intercede for his own with the Father. In John 17, Jesus prayed:

> I am no longer in the world, but they are in the world, and I am coming to you. Holy Father, keep them in your name, which you have given me . . . . While I was with them, I kept them in your name, which you have given me. I have guarded them, and not one of them has been lost . . . . But now I am coming to you, and these things I speak in the world, that they may have my joy fulfilled in themselves. . . . I do not ask that you take them out of the world, but that you keep them from the evil one. . . . Sanctify them in the truth; your word is truth. (John 17:11–17)

Note the key expression "in the world." "The world" is mentioned eighteen times in Jesus' prayer. The same expression, "in the world," occurs in John 13:1: "having loved his own who were in the world, he loved them to the end." Jesus knows that he has left us "in the world," that is, in the midst of sin, darkness, misery, temptation, and affliction. Spurgeon writes: "The church of God . . . is nothing but a camp in the midst of heathendom."[10] In

---

10. Spurgeon, *Majesty in Misery*, 1:22.

this world we will suffer losses and bear crosses. Like Lot living in Sodom and the Israelites journeying through the barren desert, without the love of our Lord we would never make it through. But Jesus knows where we are—he knows what temptations bring us down, what doubts beset us, what furnaces try our faith—and he loves us to the very end of our lives, providing all that we need to continue unto salvation. He not only grants us the great privilege of prayer, but prays with and for us, sending the Spirit to help us in our weakness.

That leads us to a third and final way to understand Jesus' love "to the end." He loves us to the very end of history, all the way to our eternity in glory. In Hebrew, the expression "to the end" means "forever." And Jesus' love for us abides forever. When this world has passed away, when God's enemies have been judged, and when the cosmos is renewed in the glory of the final reign of Christ, his love for his own will not have changed. Therefore, Paul could extol:

> Who shall separate us from the love of Christ? Shall tribulation, or distress, or persecution, or famine, or nakedness, or danger, or sword? . . . I am sure that neither death nor life, nor angels nor rulers, nor things present nor things to come, nor powers, nor height nor depth, nor anything else in all creation, will be able to separate us from the love of God in Christ Jesus our Lord. (Rom. 8:35–39)

What an encouragement this is for us to rely on Jesus' love now. Do you turn to Jesus' love with your joys and sorrows, with your wants and your needs? He who loved you to his own end on the cross has promised to love you to the very end. Do you realize that being saved by Christ means far more than going to heaven in the end—all-important though that is—that it also means that his love is resting on you all through this present life? If you do not realize this, then it is no wonder that you struggle with spiritual weakness, that you feel dry and distant from the Lord, or that you fear to return to Christ when you falter or fall into sin. Yet his nail-scarred hands are held out to you even now, marked with eternal emblems of a sin-conquering love. More fundamental than our faith in Jesus and our will to live in obedience to him is the unchanging, unending, unfailing love of Christ for his own. No one is more devoted to your good, more sympathetic to your plight, or more interested in your heart than Jesus Christ, who loves his own to the end. Every one of his own should therefore daily sing:

> Jesus, lover of my soul,
> Let me to thy bosom fly.[11]

LOVE WORTH HAVING

The final words in our reflection on this glorious verse should therefore be directed to those who have not yet known the love of Jesus for his own. If Jesus loves like this, and if in his divine power and unending life he will always love his own to the very end, how can you afford not to receive this great and saving love? Can even parents or spouses, can children or friends, offer you a love that will save your soul and endure forever, to the very end of all things? Do you know a love that gladly accepts death in your place? Do you have a love that will even bear your sins before God, so that you may stand spotless in his holy presence, a love that will win you through to an eternity in heaven? In the end, without the love of Christ, you will be lost. But the day of God's grace is still present, and today should be the day of your salvation through faith in the love of Jesus Christ. Then you will discover how much he has loved you, and how faithfully he will love you as one of his very own, to the very end.

11. Charles Wesley, "Jesus, Lover of My Soul" (1740).

85

WASHING THE DISCIPLES' FEET

John 13:2–11

He laid aside his outer garments, and taking a towel, tied it
around his waist. Then he poured water into a basin and began
to wash the disciples' feet and to wipe them with the towel that
was wrapped around him. (John 13:4–5)

I have learned a great many things in ministry. Among them is the value of letting people know that you care. Preachers would like to believe that people in church will receive our teaching based on the authority of God's Word, and to a certain extent they do. But many people are not willing to receive God's Word until they learn from experience that the minister loves them. Once they realize how much their pastor cares for them, they are often willing to receive even the most difficult Bible teaching from his lips.

This is something that Jesus understood very well. Having arrived at his pivotal last night with the disciples, as John relates, Jesus knew "that the Father had given all things into his hands, and that he had come from God and was going back to God" (John 13:3). So the teaching that Jesus was going to give at this Last Supper was of great importance, which is why it occupies four chapters in John's Gospel. Some of what Jesus would say would be hard for them to receive. So on this last opportunity to teach the disciples about God's saving love, Jesus began not with words but with action. Before speaking about God's love, he showed it to them. Jesus did this with the most remarkable behavior, taking up the place of a servant and washing the disciples' feet. D. A. Carson comments that by this stunning act of humility, our Lord offered "a display of love (v. 1), a symbol of saving cleansing (vv. 6–9), and a model of Christian conduct (vv. 12–17)."[1]

THE TOWEL-BEARING SAVIOR

The foot-washing took place according to established cultural practices. It was considered the duty of a host to provide a servant who would greet guests with a basin and wash towel. The roads were not paved, and since almost everyone wore sandals, the guests' feet would often be quite dirty and unpleasant. Moreover, since dinner was eaten at a low table, with the guests reclining on pillows with their feet extended outward, it was understandably important that feet be washed. Just as we give our dinner guests an opportunity to "freshen up" before a meal, it was the custom for a servant to be provided to wash people's feet.

On this occasion, Jesus had borrowed a room to celebrate the Passover dinner with his disciples, so there was no servant to greet them. There would likely have been a basin and a towel by the door, and we can imagine the twelve disciples each maneuvering away, none volunteering to perform the odious task. This being the case, John writes that after they were seated, Jesus "rose from supper. He laid aside his outer garments, and taking a towel, tied it around his waist. Then he poured water into a basin and began to wash the disciples' feet and to wipe them with the towel that was wrapped around him" (John 13:4–5). Jesus was placing himself in the position considered too menial for even a Jewish slave, stripping down to his loincloth and wrapping a towel around his waist, making himself the most humble servant of those he loved. Approaching his disciples one by one, he poured the water and wiped the dirt from their feet. Ever since, Jesus' washing of the disciples' feet has been an enduring symbol of humble, sacrificial servanthood.

1. D. A. Carson, *The Gospel of John* (Grand Rapids: Eerdmans, 1991), 462–63.

John makes a couple of significant comments that provide context for what Jesus did. First, he notes that "the devil had already put it into the heart of Judas Iscariot, Simon's son, to betray him" (John 13:2). This shows the satanic inspiration for Judas's betrayal. It is curious that John points this out here; he seems to be contrasting the spirit within Judas with the spirit displayed by our Lord. Judas was moved by Satan, whereas Jesus was moved by the loving will of God. What a contrast they present! The pride of Judas is contrasted with the humility of Jesus. We remember how Judas complained when Mary used expensive perfume to wipe Jesus' feet; what must he have thought of their Master's bowing in the place of a servant! Furthermore, before coming to the meal, Judas had transacted to betray Jesus for thirty pieces of silver (Matt. 26:15). But Jesus' treasure is the hearts of his people. Judas thought only of his own self-interest, whereas Jesus was expending himself in service to others.

The contrast between the way of Satan and the way of Christ endures to this day. It does not require a government study to show that it is largely the values of Satan, revealed in Judas, that motivate worldly society. This is why Paul refers to Satan as "the god of this world" (2 Cor. 4:4). Jesus offers the only true alternative, a life of loving servanthood that follows Jesus' example. Paul exhorts us: "Do nothing from rivalry or conceit, but in humility count others more significant than yourselves. Let each of you look not only to his own interests, but also to the interests of others" (Phil. 2:3–4).

The other significant statement is found in John 13:3: "Jesus [knew] that the Father had given all things into his hands, and that he had come from God and was going back to God." John says that Jesus was intensely conscious of the authority that God had given him, as well as his imminent return to his divine glory. With this awareness in his mind, we would expect Jesus to rise up from the supper and stake his claim to supremacy and homage. According to our way of thinking, he would insist, "Now you wash my feet!" But how different is the reality. F. W. Krummacher writes, "Think of the Holy One, who came down from heaven, thus engaged with sinners; the majestic Being, whom angels adore, abasing Himself to the occupation of a menial servant!"[2] The truth is that we would never have imagined this

2. F. W. Krummacher, *The Suffering Saviour* (1856; repr., Edinburgh: Banner of Truth, 2004), 31.

scenario on our own, and Jesus' display of divine servanthood constrains us to humble adoration, renewed faith, and heartfelt repentance.

By this one act, Jesus challenges our understanding of the glory of God. Later that very evening, he would tell the disciples, "Whoever has seen me has seen the Father" (John 14:9). The God that Jesus reveals is tender, compassionate, and servant-hearted toward the needs of his people.

This being the case, how are Christians to display God to the world? Is it by denouncing the wicked ways of the world? We do need to speak truth to the lies of our culture, just as Jesus often confronted falsehood and evil. Do we display God by winning arguments with unbelievers? Jesus debated with false religious teachers, although we seldom see him arguing with common people. But what about this? If Jesus, with his soul filled with the consciousness of deity, took up the place of the most menial servanthood to wash his disciples' feet, then any authentic display of God must be characterized by humility, tenderness, and sacrificial love. And if this is the truth about the God that we are called to glorify in the world, how we ought especially to take up the towel of Jesus in our marriages, in our home life, and in our fellowship in the church! It will be when the world sees us ministering with humble, tender love to the stinky feet of each other's lives—the places where there is pain, ugliness, failure, and need—that it will realize that the Spirit of God is in our midst. To do this, just as Jesus took off his garments, we must take off all our pride, all our envy, and everything else that hinders us from taking up the basin to wash the feet of others.

THE NECESSITY OF CLEANSING

We can only imagine what was going through the various disciples' minds as Jesus washed their feet, one by one. But we do not have to wonder what was in Peter's mind, because as usual his thoughts came immediately out of his mouth. Peter was confused and astonished: "He came to Simon Peter, who said to him, 'Lord, do you wash my feet?'" (John 13:6). His meaning is more emphatic in the Greek text, where "you" and "my" are placed together. Literally it reads: "You, my feet to wash?" The idea of the Lord of glory washing his dirty feet simply did not fit with Peter's way of thinking.

Jesus patiently responded: "What I am doing you do not understand now, but afterward you will understand" (John 13:7). Jesus was referring to after his death and resurrection, which fulfilled all that the foot-washing symbolized. This reminds us that we Christians will often find it hard to understand what the Lord is doing in our lives. He might lay a calling on us that we would never have chosen, or he might answer our prayers in ways that are perplexing to us. Jesus' response to Peter forms a good rule for us all: "It's true that you don't understand now. But trust in me, believe my Word, accept my providence, and in the end you will understand."

Peter was not yet ready to patiently await the unfolding of Christ's purpose. With his characteristic inconsistency, Peter was too humble to allow Jesus to wash his feet, but proud-hearted enough to rebuke his Master's actions: "Peter said to him, 'You shall never wash my feet'" (John 13:8).

It is a good rule in general that when we find ourselves arguing with or rebuking the Word of the Lord, we are getting ourselves into trouble. Peter was shocked when Jesus showed just how wrong was his attitude: "Jesus answered him, 'If I do not wash you, you have no share with me'" (John 13:8).

This was a most serious response from the Lord. The Greek word for *share* (*meros*) generally indicates an inheritance. So Jesus was telling Peter that unless he washed him, Peter could not enter into Jesus' inheritance—that is, he could not enter into heaven.

With these words, Jesus advances from the symbol of the foot-washing to the reality symbolized by it. For Jesus' act of servanthood was more than a mere demonstration of humility; it was a prelude to the greater humiliation of the cross. Jesus "was giving a dramatic illustration of his entire ministry,"[3] in keeping with the great summary that he had given earlier: "The Son of Man came not to be served but to serve, and to give his life as a ransom for many" (Matt. 20:28).

If we follow the sequence of events that John recalls in Jesus' foot-washing, we can see how closely they correspond to Jesus' ministry in the world. First, Jesus rose from his seat, just as he rose from his heavenly throne in order to come into our world. Second, he "laid aside his outer garments." This closely echoes Paul's words in describing how Christ set aside his glory: "though he was in the form of God, [he] did not count equality with God a thing to be grasped" (Phil. 2:6). Next, Jesus took a towel and tied it around his waist. Likewise, Paul states that Jesus "made himself nothing, taking the form of

---

3. James Montgomery Boice, *The Gospel of John*, 5 vols. (Grand Rapids: Baker, 1999), 4:1010.

a servant, being born in the likeness of men" (2:7). Fourth, Jesus "poured water into a basin and began to wash the disciples' feet, just as in a few short hours he was to pour out his blood for the washing away of human sin by the atonement."[4] Fifth, Jesus completed his enacted parable by rising again and taking his seat back at the table, which corresponds with Jesus' resurrection and ascension into glory after the finished work of his cross. Hebrews 1:3 states, "After making purification for sins, he sat down at the right hand of the Majesty on high."

This is why Jesus responded the way he did to Peter. If Peter was not willing to allow Jesus the partial humiliation of washing his feet, how was he to embrace the full and complete humiliation that would be Jesus' agonizing death on the cross the very next day? And unless Jesus cleanses us with the true washing of his shed blood for our sins, we cannot have any part of the salvation that he offers.

This is the most grave and significant matter that any of us can ever face. Despite his infant faith, Peter did not fully understand the one way to be restored to God. How else might we partake of the salvation that God offers? Can it be through good works? Religious exercises? Service in Christ's name? Notice that Jesus insists that even Simon Peter, the chief of his apostles, cannot partake of his salvation unless he is cleansed by the blood that Jesus would shed on the cross.

People often tell jokes about what will happen when they try to get into heaven. Usually, those jokes involve meeting St. Peter at the pearly gates, based on the false teaching of the Roman Catholic Church that Peter decides who gains entry into heaven. But if you were to meet Peter at the pearly gates, what right would you claim to be received into the inheritance of Christ? Most people answer that they have been basically good people. But Peter, now perfected in glory, and unquestionably remembering what Christ taught him with the basin in his hands, would surely reply: "Unless you have been washed by Christ, you have no part in him!"

Christ, having now died on the cross, comes to each of us, no longer with symbolic water but with the shed blood of his cross. He comes to cleanse you. What will you say? Will you turn away, unwilling to admit your need of cleansing for your sins? Will you echo Peter: "You, my sins to cleanse?"

4. Ibid.

Will you proudly insist that you will decide your own way into eternal life? If you respond in any of those ways, Christ, having now fully taken up his power and authority as Lord of heaven and earth, the divine Son enthroned in glory, will say to you: "If I do not wash you, you have no share with me" (John 13:8). Leon Morris writes:

> Jesus was about to die, to die the atoning death that meant cleansing for his people. There is no other way of being Christ's than in receiving the cleansing he died to bring. If he does not wash us in this way, we have no part with him. . . . It is only in accepting the truth that we cannot secure our salvation by our own effort, but that Christ can cleanse all who trust him, that we are freed from our sin and brought into Christ's salvation.[5]

CLEAN SOULS, DIRTY FEET

Peter loved Jesus and trusted him enough to realize that his Lord was speaking in deadly earnest. Immediately, his opposition to the foot-washing fell away. Instead, he blurted out his new idea about what Jesus should do: "Lord, not my feet only but also my hands and my head!" (John 13:9).

Once again, Peter would have done better simply to allow Jesus to minister to him in grace and tell Peter what needed to be done. But it was still a good response; realizing his need to be cleansed, Peter wanted to be cleansed all over. Yet Jesus answered: "The one who has bathed does not need to wash, except for his feet, but is completely clean. And you are clean" (John 13:10).

This is an important statement that tells us much about the daily walk of followers of Christ. First, Jesus insists that those who come to him in faith receive a once-for-all cleansing that need never be repeated. Jewish dinner guests would bathe at home, and it was only because they walked through dirty streets that their feet needed to be washed. Likewise, whoever receives the cleansing ministry of Christ's atoning blood is clean once for all.

Jesus is referring to our standing before the presence of God's holiness. He declares to all who belong to him through saving faith: "You are clean." This means that with his shed blood Jesus paid the debt of all the sins of those who trust in him. This means that as God sees you in Christ, you are completely clean forever. If you have confessed your need of the cleansing

---

5. Leon Morris, *Reflections on the Gospel of John* (Peabody, MA: Hendrickson, 1986), 469.

that Jesus offers and believed on him for the forgiveness of your sins, you will never be more clean in the sight of God than you were at that moment and than you are right now. Moreover, the Bible teaches that Christ's own perfect righteousness is imputed, or reckoned, to us, so that believers in Christ stand before God dressed in the perfect righteousness of Jesus himself. Paul explains the great transaction by which Christ took our sins to the cross and placed his own cleanliness upon us: "[God] made him to be sin who knew no sin, so that in him we might become the righteousness of God" (2 Cor. 5:21). A. W. Pink comments:

> The moment a sinner, drawn by the Holy Spirit, comes to Christ, he is completely and finally cleansed. It is the apprehension of this which gives a firm rock for my feet to rest upon. It assures me that my hope is a stable one; that my standing before God is immutable. It banishes doubt and uncertainty. It gives the heart and mind abiding peace to know that the benefits I have found in Christ are never to be recalled. I am brought out from under condemnation and placed in a state of everlasting acceptance. . . . I stand resplendent in the sight of God in all the Saviour's beauty and perfections. God looks upon believers not merely as forgiven, but as *righteous*: as truly as Christ was "made sin" for us, so we have been "made the righteousness of God in him."[6]

Second, just as dinner guests got their feet dirty on the way to the meal, Jesus says that only our feet need to be cleansed as we walk through this world: "The one who has bathed does not need to wash, except for his feet" (John 13:10).

Jesus was pointing out that believers still live in a dirty world. We are touched by it, are impacted by it, and continue to be infected by its sins. We are clean in the sight of God, but our feet are soiled as we walk through this world. Therefore, it is not our standing before God that needs ongoing cleansing, but our walk as Jesus' disciples that compels us to bring our feet to the towel-wearing Savior. This is why Jesus taught believers to pray regularly, "Forgive us our debts . . . . Lead us not into temptation, but deliver us from evil" (Matt. 6:12–13).

There is not a single Christian whose walk in this world is not polluted by sin. Jesus knows this. He knows that we fall into sin. He knows that our

---

6. Arthur W. Pink, *Exposition of the Gospel of John* (Grand Rapids: Zondervan, 1975), 712–13.

minds are polluted with the evil of the world. He knows that our hearts are poisoned by foul streams, so that we are brought into confusion, grief, and sometimes even despair. John Calvin observes that the term *dirty feet* is metaphorically applied to "all the passions and cares by which we are brought into contact with the world. . . . Thus Christ always finds in us something to cleanse."[7]

These two principles, taken together, are keys to the spiritual life of Christians. First, we must know that our standing with God is never in jeopardy once we have been cleansed by the ministry of Christ's atoning blood. As water cleanses the body, Jesus cleanses us with his blood from the stain and the guilt of our sins. We are not accepted by God on Monday because we think we performed at an acceptable level, but cast out on Tuesday because we were swept up by the world. In Christ, through sincere and saving faith in Christ's blood, we are fully and finally accepted every day and forever, not because of the sufficiency of our performance but because of the perfect sufficiency of Jesus' performance for us on the cross. The second principle is that we must return to Christ again and again, daily bringing the dirty feet of our hearts to the basin in his loving hands. John writes in his first epistle: "The blood of Jesus [God's] Son cleanses us from all sin. If we say we have no sin, we deceive ourselves, and the truth is not in us. If we confess our sins, he is faithful and just to forgive us our sins and to cleanse us from all unrighteousness" (1 John 1:7–9).

Not Every One

A postscript to the foot-washing impresses upon us the defining seriousness of the cleansing ministry of Christ. Jesus said, "You are clean, but not every one of you" (John 13:10). John explains, "For he knew who was to betray him; that was why he said, 'Not all of you are clean'" (13:11).

Judas had received many benefits as Jesus' disciple. He was there for many of the miracles and the teaching of God's holy Son. But in the pride of his heart, he never opened his heart for cleansing. In his love for money and worldly position, he never sought a place in the family of God. Therefore, though Jesus washed his feet, the blood of the cross was never applied to the

7. John Calvin, *Calvin's Commentaries*, trans. William Pringle, 22 vols. (Grand Rapids: Baker, 2009), 18:59.

record of his sins, and because of the privilege of his discipleship he was all the more condemned before the holy justice of God.

It is remarkable that Jesus washed Judas's feet along with the others'. He thus exemplified his command to love our enemies. This also means that when Judas departed to meet with the chief priests and Pharisees who plotted Jesus' death, hatching his plan to betray Jesus with a kiss, he went with feet that had been washed by Jesus' hands. How many people are like that today! They enjoy the benefit of participation in the church or of fellowship with God's people. Their hearts are temporarily lightened by singing songs of praise or by listening to prayers. But their guilt is never washed away and their souls are never renewed, for the simple reason that they refuse to humble themselves before the cross of Christ. How dirty was Judas's guilty soul. How black was his record before God as he passed into condemnation. How quickly his feet became dirty again as he walked through the garden of Gethsemane to betray the Savior.

If Judas were among us today, he would be baptized, a member of the church, and chairman of the deacons. After all, here is a man who preached the kingdom and even performed miracles (see Luke 10:1–19)! Yet with his soul uncleansed by the blood of Christ, he would still be lost. Let us learn the lesson of the washing of the disciples' feet. Jesus is a humble, servant Savior. He came into the world not to be served, but to serve, and to give his life as a ransom for our sins (Matt. 20:28). Let us therefore, with all of Peter's impetuous faith, though without his impetuous folly, submit ourselves to Jesus with joy. "Cleanse me, Lord," let us cry. "Wash me whiter than snow with the blood of your cross, and cleanse me daily from my sins."

86

BLESSED SERVANTHOOD

John 13:12—17

*"You call me Teacher and Lord, and you are right, for so I am.
If I then, your Lord and Teacher, have washed your feet,
you also ought to wash one another's feet."* (John 13:13–14)

while back, I received an e-mail that recounted the life philosophy of Charles Schulz, famous for his *Peanuts* cartoon. Schulz's philosophy was communicated in two sets of questions. First, the reader is asked to name the following: the five wealthiest people in the world, the last five winners of the Heisman Trophy, the last five Miss Americas, ten people who have won the Nobel or Pulitzer Prize, the last half-dozen Academy Award winners for best actor and actress, and the teams who won baseball's World Series over the last ten years. The point of these questions was to show that we remember few of these famous achievers because they are not important to our lives.

The second series of questions asked the reader to name a different class of people: a few teachers who aided your journey through school, three friends who helped you through a difficult time, five people who have taught you something worthwhile, a few people who have made you feel appreciated and special, and five people you enjoy spending time with. These are questions for which we have answers! Why? The e-mail concluded: "The people who make a difference in your life are not the ones with the most credentials, the most money, or the most awards. They are the ones that care."

I do not know whether Charles Schulz really was the source of that philosophy, but since Schulz was known as a believer in Jesus Christ, I would not be surprised if he was. After all, it was this very philosophy that Jesus set forth when he donned a servant's towel and washed the dirty feet of his disciples. Jesus made the point that what really matters is the kind of humble, sacrificial, and personal ministry he had provided. John recounts: "When he had washed their feet and put on his outer garments and resumed his place, he said to them, 'Do you understand what I have done to you? You call me Teacher and Lord, and you are right, for so I am. If I then, your Lord and Teacher, have washed your feet, you also ought to wash one another's feet'" (John 13:12–14).

THE TOWEL-BEARING SAVIOR

Having washed his disciples' feet, Jesus asked the Twelve: "Do you understand what I have done to you?" (John 13:12). One might give a good theological answer: "Jesus, you have shown that salvation requires us to be cleansed by your atoning blood, just as you have cleansed our dirty feet with water." That answer would be correct. Jesus made that point when he told Peter, "If I do not wash you, you have no share with me" (13:8). But if we stop with the theological lesson, we miss the full meaning of Jesus' foot-washing. Therefore, he added: "For I have given you an example, that you also should do just as I have done to you" (13:15).

The washing of his disciples' feet, then, was intended by Jesus as an example for his apostles and for all Christians. Having used the foot-washing as a paradigm for his own atoning death, Jesus also employs it as a model for our sacrificial service in his name. He was not establishing a ritual whereby lofty church officials would playact at foot-washing during Holy Week, as their annual gesture of humility. Rather, Jesus' intent was to set forth a lifestyle that emulates the example he set by this humble act of service.

There are two ways in which we should think of this example that we are to follow. First, Jesus provided his followers with an example in *attitude*. "You call me Teacher," Jesus asserted, and his instruction includes an attitude by which Christians are to live.

If we go back to the beginning of this chapter, we can appreciate the attitude of ministry that Jesus assumed in the foot-washing. First, a Christlike attitude will be aware of the hour in which we live. John 13:1 says, "Jesus knew that his hour had come to depart out of this world to the Father." This suggests that Christians should be attuned to the spiritual needs of whatever situation they are in. In times of doubt, they should minister faith. In times of division, they should pursue peace and unity. When there is distress, the Christ-minded will minister comfort. Like Jesus, we should minister with a sense of our setting and the needs of the people in it.

In this case, Jesus was specifically aware that during the next twenty-four hours he would be seized, tried, and put to death on the cross. Therefore, he centered his efforts on gospel priorities. Christians should likewise look on the times of their lives as days of gospel urgency. We know neither the time of Christ's return to judge the earth nor the time of our deaths. But we do know that we are living in the time when eternal destinies are decided. Should we, then, live for the things of the world? Should we devote ourselves to building worldly empires, reputations, or riches, all of which are destined to pass away? Jesus knew "that he had come from God and was going back to God" (John 13:3), and his followers should likewise know that this life is a brief pilgrimage on our way to heaven. Our attitude to life in this world should reflect the gospel urgency of Christ.

John 13:1 also states that Jesus, "having loved his own who were in the world, . . . loved them to the end." Jesus did not love the disciples based on their worthiness, for they were unworthy of his love. Likewise, Christ-minded disciples will have an attitude of love even for the unworthy and the unlovely. We will not pick and choose our friends based on what they can do for us, but we will befriend and minister to difficult, unpleasant people as well. Jesus was criticized by the Pharisees for supping with tax collectors and prostitutes—the greatest undesirables of his time. He answered, "Those who are well have no need of a physician, but those who are sick" (Matt. 9:12).

This marks the difference between a community and a club. In a club, you choose the people with whom you will associate, whereas a community is a place where the person that you least want to associate with also lives. The church is a community, not a club. A true church will exhibit an attitude of love that is based on Christ's sacrificial love for us, not on the attractiveness of others.

This is the problem with the "homogeneous unit principle" that is practiced by so many churches today in a quest for rapid numerical growth. The idea is to target a certain demographic group—usually a group such as upwardly mobile suburban whites or hip, progressive young adults—and design everything according to their tastes: the building, the worship style, and even the minister. Churches that follow this approach can quickly grow to an enormous size, although others that follow this approach would prefer to remain very small. The problem is what such churches are designed to be: self-serving spiritual clubs, instead of the communities of grace that Jesus desires. Philip Yancey asserts, "Anyone can form a club; it takes grace, shared vision, and hard work to form a community."[1]

A third feature of Jesus' attitude was that he was not absorbed with his own profound concerns, but that even in the shadow of his cross, his heart was fixed on the needs of others. Jesus could do this because he had committed his concerns into the hands of his sovereign, almighty Father. The same is true of Christians: we have the sovereign Lord of heaven to look after our own affairs. He calls us, therefore, "in humility [to] count others more significant than yourselves. Let each of you look not only to his own interests, but also to the interests of others" (Phil. 2:3–4). According to Paul, this is what it means to have the mind of Christ (2:5).

Jesus showed a fourth attitude that believers should emulate, namely, his special love for his own. He "loved his own who were in the world" (John 13:1). Realizing this, believers should make Christ's own our own. While we are called to love the whole world in Jesus' name, we have a special calling to one another in the family of God. Paul therefore wrote: "As we have opportunity, let us do good to everyone, and especially to those who are of the household of faith" (Gal. 6:10).

This ought to have a profound influence on our attitude toward the church. As Christians, we are called to love the church of Jesus Christ and the people in it. If we love the Shepherd, we are bound to love his flock. Remembering that the church is Christ's own body and bride, we should be, "with all humility and gentleness, with patience, bearing with one another in love, eager

1. Philip Yancey, "Why I Don't Go to a Megachurch," *Christianity Today*, May 20, 1996, 80.

to maintain the unity of the Spirit in the bond of peace" (Eph. 4:2–3). This means that out of love for Christ, we will gladly suffer irritation and disappointment rather than do anything that would harm the body of believers. Douglas Jones points out that many Christians today "think it acceptable to skip around churches as if they were fast food stands."[2] But if we remember Christ's love for our fellow Christians, we will think less of our own preferences and more of the purity and peace of the church. Moreover, we will serve in the church as Christ has served us.

"Just as I have done to you" (John 13:14), Jesus said. This is the rule of Christ that should shape the attitude of his followers. Therefore, in our attitude toward our times, toward the needs of people, and especially toward other Christians and the church, Christians are directed "to Jesus' self-sacrificial love for them as the source and driving force for their love for each other."[3]

AN EXAMPLE IN ACTION

"You call me Teacher and Lord," Jesus observed (John 13:13). Bruce Milne writes, "One of the primary expressions of our submission to Jesus as our 'Lord' is our willingness to allow him to be our 'Teacher.'"[4] Here, Jesus teaches his own example as the guide not only for our attitude but also for our *action*: "If I then, your Lord and Teacher, have washed your feet, you also ought to wash one another's feet" (13:14).

It is important to note that Jesus is calling his disciples not to do "what" he has done, that is, simply to wash each other's feet, as if that exhausted his example. Rather, we are to do "as" he has done (John 13:15), that is, to embrace a lifestyle of humble, sacrificial, and personal ministry. Christians are to live in a way that gladly stoops to perform even menial tasks that will convey the love of Jesus to the world.

Jesus directs us here to "one-anothering" in the church. He said, "If I then, your Lord and Teacher, have washed your feet, you also ought to wash one another's feet" (John 13:14). This should be the pattern of our interactions

2. Douglas Jones, *Angels in the Architecture* (Moscow, ID: Canon Press, 1999), 93.
3. Herman Ridderbos, *John: A Theological Commentary* (Grand Rapids: Zondervan, 1997), 463.
4. Bruce Milne, *The Message of John: Here Is Your King!* (Downers Grove, IL: InterVarsity Press, 1993), 199.

as fellow Christians. Instead of a proud, critical spirit, always eager to point out failings or weaknesses in one another, we are to act to bless one another especially as we are difficult, unworthy, or soiled. Christians should act to cover up one another's faults, strengthen one another's weaknesses, comfort one another's sufferings, and provide for one another's needs. Meanwhile, we are called to encourage one another in faith in Christ, provoking one another to good works and growth in grace. And if any one of us falls into sin, Paul exhorts us: "You who are spiritual should restore him in a spirit of gentleness" (Gal. 6:1).

It will be impossible for us to follow Christ's example unless we are watching for one another's needs. How often have we learned that a family left the church because of lack of friendship, or a young person dropped out of school because he or she didn't fit in, or a neighbor struggled with problems that could have been helped, but we learned only after it was too late? These kinds of things usually happen because we are so self-occupied that we are not thinking about the needs of others.

The needs within any church are far greater than the ministry staff, elders, and deacons can possibly meet. It takes a community committed to the love of Christ, serving together in humility and compassion. Milne comments wisely: "In a world desperately searching for the secret of community this passage speaks most powerfully. . . . It is those who have been humbled at the cross, and come to Christ as helpless sinners seeking his cleansing, who are the raw material of the community of humble servants. The cross is both the way of salvation and the key to community."[5]

Spiritual needs ought to be our special priority. Jesus' cleansing of dirty feet was related to his atoning death on the cross; it was with the shedding of his own precious blood that Jesus could say to the disciples: "You are clean" (John 13:10). He was referring not just to their feet but to their souls. And the cleansing of souls remains the greatest need of people today. This is why it is a mistake for a church to respond to Jesus' foot-washing by neglecting its gospel mission in order to respond to social and material needs. Certainly, the church must not be unmoved by poverty, suffering, or injustice. But ministries to these needs must flow out from rather than replace the ministry of the gospel for the salvation of souls.

5. Ibid., 199.

Whether we are meeting spiritual or material needs, let our ministry be characterized by humble servanthood. This is especially important for those called to positions of leadership in the church. Too often, church leaders are mainly focused on church management and institutional decision-making. These are necessary, but they are not what makes a church strong. It is spiritual ministry that is humbly and personally directed to souls that most pleases Christ and builds his church. Church members should personally feel the hearts of those called to shepherd them. Just as David prayed, "The LORD is *my* shepherd," church members should be able to say, "That is *my* pastor," and "That is *my* elder," because they have personally benefited from their spiritual encouragement and prayers.

We may wonder how well the disciples learned the lesson of Jesus' example. The answer is found in the book of Acts. There we read that under their leadership, the early Christians

> devoted themselves to the apostles' teaching and fellowship, to the breaking of bread and the prayers. . . . And all who believed were together and had all things in common. And they were selling their possessions and belongings and distributing the proceeds to all, as any had need. And day by day, attending the temple together and breaking bread in their homes, they received their food with glad and generous hearts, praising God and having favor with all the people. (Acts 2:42–47)

Given that kind of humble one-anothering, centered on the apostles' teaching of Jesus' Word, focused through worship and prayer, and expressed in mutual ministry among believers, there is little reason to wonder why the passage concludes: "And the Lord added to their number day by day those who were being saved" (Acts 2:47). The biblical model for true church growth is not a spiritual club but a gospel-centered community that is inspired in attitude and actions by the self-sacrificing grace of Jesus.

THE KEY TO HAPPINESS

In giving his example as the rule for our attitude and actions, Jesus was not imposing a lifestyle of drudgery, but instead he was offering a life of blessing. He thus concluded, "If you know these things, blessed are you if you do them" (John 13:17). According to our Lord, knowing and doing the way of Jesus is the key to happiness.

We can briefly note five things that Jesus wants us to know in order to lead a blessed life. First, we must know that *Jesus is our Lord.* This is most important, because the whole premise of Jesus' teaching is that his position as Teacher and Lord mandates that we follow his example. This is the greatest problem for many Christians: while they call Jesus "Lord," they do not follow his example or obey his commands. The result is that their lives are in chaos and they do not receive the blessing that ought to be theirs.

James Montgomery Boice compares this problem to the ancient Ptolemaic system of astronomy, which dominated until the time of Copernicus. This system assumed that the earth was the center of the universe, with the stars and planets revolving around it. This is exactly how most people, and many Christians, live their lives: they act as though they were the center of the universe. The Ptolemaic system was able to accomplish certain things. It could predict sunrise and sunset, as well as new moons. It had some success at charting the planets. But it was not always accurate and did not permit progress, since new discoveries always went against it. Ptolemaic astronomers devoted themselves to calculations, but the problem was at the very heart of the system.

We experience the same thing when we place ourselves at the center of our spiritual universe. Through selfishness, we can gain many things we desire. But the system is fatally flawed and permits no growth or progress. The longer we live this way, the worse things get until our lives break down. The only way to straighten out our lives is to remove ourselves from the center and place the Lord Jesus Christ there, not only calling him Lord but obeying him as our Teacher and Master.[6] Jesus says that only in this way can we really be blessed.

The second thing we must know is that *Jesus made himself a servant.* Though himself the Lord of glory, he humbled himself to die for us on the cross. This was the lesson of the foot-washing, and our ascended Lord in heaven continues in servant ministry to us even now.

Third, we must realize that *Christians are not greater than Christ.* Jesus said, "Truly, truly, I say to you, a servant is not greater than his master"

6. James Montgomery Boice, *The Gospel of John*, 5 vols. (Grand Rapids: Baker, 1999), 4:1015.

(John 13:16). We therefore should not consider ourselves above servant roles that were not beneath Jesus. Whenever we place our own desires first, we are acting as if we were above the Lord Jesus Christ, who "came not to be served but to serve" (Matt. 20:28).

Fourth, *what was proper for Jesus to do is proper for us to do.* Princes and princesses might consider servanthood improper for their station. But "if the king has stooped to serve, then it is not unreasonable for his subjects to do so also."[7] Whenever we think our station in life makes it improper for us to humble ourselves in menial service, we should remember the example of King Jesus. A pastor is not too reverend to change a diaper. A father is not too exalted to empty the dishwasher. A professionally accomplished Christian woman is not too highly qualified to teach children's Sunday school.

Fifth, we must realize that having been saved and served by Jesus, now *we are sent by him to serve in humility and love* (John 13:16). Skip Ryan writes: "There will be a quality of 'sentness' about our lives. Being a missionary doesn't always mean that we go on mission trips . . . . It may mean we are sent to the hospital to care for a friend who is lonely. We are sent next door with a pot of soup when someone is sick. We are sent to care for one another as the Lord has cared for us, as the Lord gave up His rights. . . . We have been commissioned, initiated into the fraternity of the water basin, the order of the towel."[8]

BLESSED IF WE DO

Jesus said that knowing these things is the key to happiness. Yet there is still one more thing to be said: Jesus concluded, "If you know these things, blessed are you if you do them" (John 13:17). Not only must we *know*; we must also *do.* In our academic age, there is always a tendency to be satisfied merely with knowing. But that is not enough. We must act on what we know. And if we do, Jesus assures us that we will have seized not only the key to usefulness but also the key to happiness.

Remember the philosophy of Charles Schulz? He showed that the key to happiness is not in worldly achievements, all of which are quickly forgotten. The key to being a person whose life has meaning is to be a person who

7. Mark G. Johnston, *Let's Study John* (Edinburgh: Banner of Truth, 2003), 178.
8. Joseph "Skip" Ryan, *That You May Believe* (Wheaton, IL: Crossway, 2003), 298.

161

cares. Isn't this why we love Jesus so much? We hold him in awe because of his divine glory. But we trust him as our Savior and Lord because he cared so much for us. Jesus gained our love by giving us his love. The same will be true for us: love is the one thing you can gain only by giving it away.

There is a second reason why humble service in Christ's name leads to happiness. This is because this lifestyle develops the character that God desires to bless. Jesus taught this principle in his Sermon on the Mount: "Blessed are the poor in spirit . . . . Blessed are those who mourn . . . . Blessed are the meek . . . . Blessed are those who hunger and thirst for righteousness . . . . Blessed are the merciful . . . . Blessed are the pure in heart . . . . Blessed are the peacemakers . . . . Blessed are those who are persecuted for righteousness' sake" (Matt. 5:3–10).

You might say that this makes no sense. Everyone knows that exactly the opposite is true: it is the boastful who win, not the poor in spirit. Happy are those who dominate. Blessed are the movers and shakers who place themselves before others. Like the Ptolemaic system of astronomy, that approach works in some ways at least for a while. But notice what Jesus says at the beginning of John 13:16: "Truly, truly, I say to you." Jesus came to teach us the truth. He showed his disciples the truth when he wrapped the servant's towel around his waist, and especially when he extended his hands and feet to be nailed to the cross. What is the truth? The truth is that the only way truly to be blessed and achieve real happiness is to be served by the Lord Jesus Christ in his death for our sins, and then to make his example of humble servanthood the model for our own lives.

87

ONE TO BETRAY

John 13:18—30

"The Scripture will be fulfilled, 'He who ate my bread has lifted
his heel against me.' I am telling you this now, before it takes
place, that when it does take place you may believe that I am he."
(John 13:18–19)

When the Samaritan woman spoke of her faith in Jesus as the Savior, she based her claim on his legitimacy as a prophet: "Come, see a man who told me all that I ever did. Can this be the Christ?" (John 4:29). She probably had in mind God's promise to Moses to send a prophet like him in the future (Deut. 18:18). In this she was right, and she reminds us that Jesus as Messiah not only offers the perfect priestly sacrifice for sin and perfectly fulfills the kingship of the Davidic throne, but also comes as the true and final Prophet who declares God to the world. This is a strong theme in John's Gospel, right from the opening words that said of Jesus, "In the beginning was the Word" (John 1:1).

Fulfilled prophecy plays an important part in validating the God of the Bible. This is what the Lord declares in Isaiah: "Who is like me? Let him proclaim it. Let him declare and set it before me, since I appointed an ancient people. . . . Have I not told you from of old and declared it? And you are my witnesses! Is there a God besides me?" (Isa. 44:7–8). This is a serious claim, in which the Bible presents evidence offered by no other religion. All through the Bible we see specific prophecies that have come true—prophecies about God's people Israel, about pagan empires, about major historical events, and especially about the promised Savior, Jesus Christ—and our ability to validate the fulfillment of what Scripture foretold demonstrates that the God of the Bible is the true and sovereign God.

JESUS' PROPHETIC LAMENT

John 13:18–19 presents Jesus both as a Prophet who foretells and as the One whose life is foretold in the Bible's prophecies. In the preceding passage, when Jesus washed the disciples' feet, he told them, "You are clean." He then added: "but not every one of you" (13:10). The verses that continue deal with the one who was not one of the true disciples and thus was not clean: Judas Iscariot. Jesus continues: "I am not speaking of all of you; I know whom I have chosen. But the Scripture will be fulfilled, 'He who ate my bread has lifted his heel against me.' I am telling you this now, before it takes place, that when it does take place you may believe that I am he" (13:18–19). The point of Jesus' prophecy was to prove himself to his true disciples by specifically foretelling what was about to take place. Gordon Keddie explains:

> Jesus knew how much Judas' duplicity would shake the faith of the other eleven disciples. Perhaps they might think that Judas had outwitted Jesus. They needed to be assured that this was the outworking of God's plan and that Jesus was fully aware of what was about to transpire. That is why he tells them "before it comes".[1]

Jesus not only stakes his reputation on his own prophecy, but he also points out that these events were already predicted in the Scriptures. Specifically, he quotes Psalm 41:9, which states, "Even my close friend in whom I trusted, who ate my bread, has lifted his heel against me."

This was a psalm attributed to King David, in which David calls upon God for deliverance from a great personal betrayal. The most likely setting is

---

1. Gordon J. Keddie, *A Study Commentary on John*, 2 vols. (Darlington, UK: Evangelical Press, 2001), 2:24–25.

the revolt of his son Absalom, which so surprised David that he was driven out of Jerusalem in the most desperate circumstances. But what David finds most painful is the betrayal of close and trusted friends who shared his very table. Most prominent among these was his counselor Ahithophel, who advised Absalom in his war against David. When David learned of this, he feared greatly because of the wisdom of Ahithophel's schemes, and he prayed, "O LORD, please turn the counsel of Ahithophel into foolishness" (2 Sam. 15:31). God answered David's prayer, for even though Ahithophel counseled Absalom wisely, the rebel prince disregarded his advice. The parallel between Ahithophel and Judas is made particularly strong in that when Ahithophel realized what Absalom was doing, he went home, put his affairs in order, and hanged himself (17:23), just as Judas hanged himself after betraying Jesus.

What is particularly noteworthy in Jesus' quotation of David's psalm is the anguish that he experienced over so personal a betrayal as that of Judas. I have found that there are few bitter pills to rival that of a close friend or loved one who uses that position to betray. I am not talking about someone who merely does not do what we wish or who disappoints us in some way or another. Rather, I am referring to one who intentionally uses a relationship of trust and intimacy to act falsely and maliciously. It can be a spouse who cheats or otherwise betrays. It can be a trusted business associate who embezzles. It can be a child who mocks parental love or a parent who abuses it. These are among life's most bitter blows, precisely because of the relationship and trust that are violated.

The danger on such occasions is that we might turn to bitterness and malice, but Jesus did not do that with Judas. Yet it is clear that our Lord suffered emotionally at the betrayal. Jesus prophetically lamented, "He who ate my bread has lifted his heel against me" (John 13:18). And John reports, "Jesus was troubled in his spirit" (13:21). Therefore, when we are abandoned by loved ones or betrayed because of our Christian convictions, we may take solace in the fellowship we have with our Lord, who was even more wickedly betrayed. The same disciple who had expressed alarm that a jar of alabaster worth three hundred denarii was being wasted now sold his Master, the Lord of glory, for the slave price of thirty silver pieces! George Herbert attempted to capture Jesus' feelings in a poem:

Mine own Apostle, who the bag did beare,
Though he had all I had did not forbeare
To sell me also, and to put me there:
Was ever grief like mine?[2]

JESUS AND THE DISCIPLES

It was with this troubled spirit that Jesus announced the betrayal to the disciples: "Truly, truly, I say to you, one of you will betray me" (John 13:21). The effect of this announcement places three relationships in bold relief. The first of them is the relationship of Jesus and his disciples. John recounts: "The disciples looked at one another, uncertain of whom he spoke. One of his disciples, whom Jesus loved, was reclining at table close to Jesus, so Simon Peter motioned to him to ask Jesus of whom he was speaking. So that disciple, leaning back against Jesus, said to him, 'Lord, who is it?'" (13:22–25).

Notice, first, that the fellowship of the disciples centered on their mutual relationship with Jesus. This is why they responded with such immediate alarm at the idea that one of them should betray Jesus. The same is true today, that the linchpin of any Christian fellowship is the relationship of the individuals to Jesus. This is what makes a church—not the quality of the preaching, not the music ministry, not the value of its programs, but the relationship of the body to its Head, Jesus Christ. What binds any Christian fellowship is a shared commitment to Jesus, to the teachings of his Word, and to his mission in the world. It is when other agendas intrude that fellowship and unity are broken. Thus, the thought of one of them betraying Jesus caused the disciples to look at one another with uncertainty.

This account also gives us insight into the dynamics of the original band of twelve disciples. One of them was personally close to Jesus, and he "was reclining at table close to Jesus" (John 13:23). The others do not seem to resent Jesus' strong emotional connection with this disciple "whom Jesus loved"; Peter, at least, seems to accept it without concern. They were all loved by Jesus in their own way, and all had a place in his fellowship.

The question naturally arises as to the identity of this Beloved Disciple. The overwhelming consensus is that it is none other than the apostle John himself. It had to be one of the Twelve, since only they were present, and it

---

2. Quoted in D. A. Carson, *The Gospel of John* (Grand Rapids: Eerdmans, 1991), 476.

makes sense that John would avoid naming himself in his own Gospel as one especially loved by Jesus. John was unquestionably the youngest of the disciples, perhaps only a teenager at the time, and the relationship of John and Peter to Jesus is highlighted again later in this Gospel. Finally, at the end of the Gospel, John says of the disciple loved by Jesus: "This is the disciple who is bearing witness about these things, and who has written these things" (John 21:24). So we may confidently regard the Beloved Disciple as the author of the Gospel, John the apostle.

Peter's relationship with Jesus appears somewhat differently. He often emerges as the acting leader of the group, the first among a band of equals. Peter is bold and full of action, sometimes in faith and sometimes in folly, and Jesus devotes a great deal of attention to shaping his faith and character. Here, Peter breaks the ice by asking the Beloved Disciple to make use of his closeness to Jesus to gain some clarification: "Simon Peter motioned to him to ask Jesus of whom he was speaking" (John 13:24). This does not mean that Peter had a formal supremacy, as is claimed by the Roman Catholic Church. This passage is cited as proving Peter's supremacy, but in reality it shows the opposite: Peter is seen relying on John's intercession with the Lord to gain information unavailable to himself.

John sets a good example, showing that those who draw near to the Lord's heart are best able to gain his truth. Therefore, it is John who speaks for the others, and from his place next to Jesus he asks, "Lord, who is it?" (John 13:25). This might be taken in a number of ways, but Matthew's Gospel gives us the true sense: "They were very sorrowful and began to say to him one after another, 'Is it I, Lord?'" (Matt. 26:22).

This is the proper attitude that every Christian should take whenever turmoil or trials arise in the church. By our worldly nature, we are prone to focus our attention on what others will do. "How will the others handle themselves, Lord?" we ask. "Who is going to be the troublemaker who spoils it for everyone?" Instead, our focus should be on ourselves and our own spiritual attitude. "Lord, might I be one who will hinder your work? Is my attitude improper, my devotion to you compromised, or my focus on the wrong things?" It is virtually certain that those who inquire of the Lord about their own hearts will not be the ones to bring trouble.

Luke tells us that Jesus spoke of the betrayal again. But this time "they began to question one another, which of them it could be who was going to do this" (Luke 22:23). Now, the disciples returned to their sinful ways, looking for others to blame and accuse. What was the inevitable result? "A dispute also arose among them, as to which of them was to be regarded as the greatest" (22:24). Whenever this happens it is disastrous to a church, and on this occasion it was the prelude to the scattering of the disciples after Jesus' arrest.

JESUS, SATAN, AND JUDAS

The worst response came from Judas himself. Matthew 26:25 records that he said, "Is it I, Rabbi?" Judas knew very well that he was the one, and it was his hypocritical deceit that was destined to break the fellowship of the disciples, however temporarily. In John's Gospel, Jesus unmasked Judas in answer to John's question. "Jesus answered, 'It is he to whom I will give this morsel of bread when I have dipped it.' So when he had dipped the morsel, he gave it to Judas, the son of Simon Iscariot" (John 13:26).

A couple of things stand out in this second relationship, between Jesus and Judas. First, it is clear that Judas was seated close to Jesus. At an Oriental banquet of this kind, the table was likely set up in the form of a U, with the host at the head of the central table and those in positions of honor at his side. John was clearly at Jesus' right hand, since the literal reading of verse 23 states that he was leaning on Jesus' breast. We should understand that, quite in contrast to Leonardo da Vinci's famous portrait of *The Last Supper*, the disciples were not seated on chairs but were reclining on mats around a low table. Everyone's head was leaning into the chest of the neighbor on his left. This means that John was on Jesus' right and suggests that Judas was seated at or near Jesus' left, which was the place of honor. So, knowing full well that Judas had already plotted to betray him, Jesus seated him in a place of prominence and favor.

Second, in that culture, for the host to take food off his own plate and offer it to a guest with his own hands was an expression of high favor. Jesus was thus offering his personal blessing to Judas. A similar example is found in Ruth 2:14, where Boaz says to Ruth: "Come here and eat some bread and dip your morsel in the wine."

These two features tell us that even at this late hour, knowing exactly what was in Judas's heart, Jesus was still exercising every opportunity for the redemption of his betrayer. Painful as it was for Jesus to be betrayed by one who ate from his own table, he did not give himself over to bitterness but continually sought the spiritual blessing of the one who abused his trust. This provides a model for how we should respond in Christian grace to those who betray us.

The great tragedy is that while Judas took the morsel from Jesus, he continued to close his heart even to this last offer of mercy and grace. John writes: "After he had taken the morsel, Satan entered into him. Jesus said to him, 'What you are going to do, do quickly'" (John 13:27).

This is the third relationship revealed: between Satan and Judas. John is not saying that Satan came to Judas only now, for earlier in the chapter John stated that "the devil had already put it into the heart of Judas Iscariot, Simon's son, to betray him" (John 13:2). Long beforehand, Judas had revealed Satan's influence on his life, for instance, by using his position in charge of the disciples' money to steal from Jesus (12:6). James Montgomery Boice writes: "Judas, I am convinced, was not just a mistaken individual. He was a deceiver, a devil, a hypocrite *par excellence*. Judas lived with the others and pretended that he was one with them, while deep in his heart he was rebelling against everything that Jesus Christ had taught."[3]

Judas shows us much about how the devil works in anyone's life. J. C. Ryle comments: "First he suggests: then he commands. First he knocks at the door and asks permission to come in: then, once admitted, he takes complete possession, and rules the whole inward man like a tyrant."[4] James 4:7 provides us with the remedy: "Submit yourselves therefore to God. Resist the devil, and he will flee from you." These two go together: we must submit ourselves to God's authority and grace. Then, as we resist the impulses of sin and unbelief, Satan will flee in search of more convenient targets.

This shows us that even while in thrall to the devil, Judas was responsible for his actions. Matthew 26:24 records Jesus as saying, "Woe to that man by whom the Son of Man is betrayed! It would have been better for that man if he had not been born." Even those who may point to Satan's power over their lives are responsible for their sins and will be judged if they do

---

3. James Montgomery Boice, *The Gospel of John*, 5 vols. (Grand Rapids: Baker, 1999), 4:1028.

4. J. C. Ryle, *Expository Thoughts on the Gospels: John*, 3 vols. (Edinburgh: Banner of Truth, 1999), 3:34.

not turn to Christ, for Satan has gained power over them as a result of their openness to his influence.

As we consider the interplay between Jesus, Satan, and Judas, we must not fail to notice the sovereignty that Jesus exercises throughout. We see this in verse 27, where, realizing that Judas's last chance had passed, Jesus said to him, "What you are going to do, do quickly." So Judas even departed to betray Jesus at Jesus' command. Our Lord was not caught unawares by Judas's betrayal. Jesus did not fall into Judas's or Satan's trap. Instead, Jesus was obeying and even orchestrating events according to the foreordained will of God the Father. This reminds us that when we see Satan triumphing in the world today, and sometimes even in the church, we should not be shaken from our reliance on the Lord. When our own lives begin to resemble that of Job, that man most tormented by the devil, it is not because God's sovereign grace has been overturned. Rather, the cross of Jesus shows that even in apparent foolishness, God is wiser than the devil and men, and in apparent weakness, Paul writes, "the weakness of God is stronger than men" (1 Cor. 1:24–25).

Satan's greatest triumph ended in his ultimate defeat. God, in his infinite wisdom, made the worst thing that ever happened on earth the best thing that ever happened for sinful men. This is the right way to understand Jesus' statement in John 13:20: "Truly, truly, I say to you, whoever receives the one I send receives me, and whoever receives me receives the one who sent me." If we stand for Christ, we stand with Christ, and with Christ stands God the almighty heavenly Father. The Savior who triumphed through his own cross will lead us to salvation through whatever crosses he calls or permits us to bear.

LESSONS TAUGHT BY JUDAS

This last encounter between Jesus and Judas before the actual betrayal teaches us a number of important lessons. The first is the absolute necessity of the new birth as the sovereign act of God's grace. Judas shows that even the best Christian example simply cannot save. He had the example of Jesus close at hand for three years, yet his heart remained cold. Even the most powerful teaching of the gospel, such as Judas often heard from the very lips of Jesus, cannot result in faith unless God himself first opens the heart. "No one can come to me unless the Father who sent me draws him," Jesus had said (John 6:44). Therefore, we must never try to manipulate or manufacture conversions by worldly means. And even our witness of God's Word, which God has commanded us to give, must be accompanied by prayers for God's sovereign grace, apart from which even one who spent three years with Jesus could not be saved.

Second, we note how difficult it is to accurately assess the state of anyone else's soul. Even when Jesus sent Judas out, the other disciples remained confused: "Some thought that, because Judas had the moneybag, Jesus was telling him, 'Buy what we need for the feast,' or that he should give something to the poor" (John 13:29). Until Judas actually betrayed Jesus, the other disciples do not seem to have suspected him. This shows the problem of those who seek to ensure a wholly regenerate church: it is so difficult to know who really is born again. Therefore, we accept others as Christians based on a credible profession of faith in Christ. If some depart from us or turn to the way of the devil, we should not be dismayed, even though it grieves us greatly, since we can expect some false professors like Judas. Ultimately, the only proof of the new birth is continuance in the faith until the end.

Third, Judas proves the danger of toying with sin. The betrayal was not the start but the result of his dabbling with the devil. We do not know where it began, but we can easily imagine how. Ryle explains:

> Trifling with the first thoughts of sin—making light of evil ideas when first offered to our hearts—allowing Satan to talk to us, and flatter us, and put bad notions into our hearts and minds—all this may seem a small matter to many. It is precisely at this point that the road to ruin often begins. He that allows Satan to sow wicked thoughts will soon find within his heart a crop of wicked habits. Happy is he who really believes that there is a devil, and, believing, watches and prays daily that he may be kept from his temptations.[5]

INTO THE NIGHT

Finally, Jesus' handling of his own betrayer shows his great patience and mercy as the Savior of sinners. Look at how Jesus bore with Judas even to the dreadful end of the hardened unbelief that claimed Judas's soul. Jesus

5. Ibid., 3:35.

still patiently continues to reach out to sinners. Seeing this in Judas's case urges us to respond to Jesus while his offer of grace remains for us. Judas little realized that he was orchestrating not merely Jesus' death but also his own. Likewise, all who reject the grace offered in Christ's gospel—the gospel that extends forgiveness and saving power received through faith alone—are consigning themselves to condemnation. If they persist in unbelief, the last opportunity for salvation will come and be gone, as it was for Judas, that most woeful of all who were ever born.

Surely this is the implication of John's final statement in this passage. He tells us that "after receiving the morsel of bread, [Judas] immediately went out." John then concludes, "And it was night" (John 13:30). So it is for all who turn away from Jesus, rejecting his offer of grace from God through his own blood, shed in payment for our sins. In his first chapter, John said, "In him was life, and the life was the light of men" (1:4). It is because Jesus is the true light that anyone who turns from him enters into eternal night. "To refuse the light means to choose the darkness where no light will ever shine again."[6]

The good news is that for all who still hear the gospel of Jesus, the night has not yet come eternally. Jesus still extends the bread of life from his own table to the most unworthy sinners. He calls to everyone: "I am the light of the world. Whoever follows me will not walk in darkness, but will have the light of life" (John 8:12).

6. Bruce Milne, *The Message of John: Here Is Your King!* (Downers Grove, IL: InterVarsity Press, 1993), 204.

88

A New Commandment

John 13:31–35

"A new commandment I give to you, that you love one another:
just as I have loved you, you also are to love one another."
(John 13:34)

One of the things I most enjoyed when I lived in Florida was the beauty of its skies. I would often stop and look upward, entranced by the deep-blue canopy and the luminous sunshine. But the best moments were when the clouds that had burdened the sky all parted. Especially in the first moments when the sky was clear, the beauty of its color and the radiance of light refreshed the heart and lifted it with joy.

Something similar takes place in a gathering of friends that has been burdened by the presence of one with a contrary spirit. While he is present, the fellowship is tense and strained. But immediately upon his leaving, there is a lightening of spirits and an elevation of the conversation, like a symphony that has changed to a higher key. This evidently was the effect of the departure of Judas Iscariot from the gathering of Jesus and his disciples in the upper room. Immediately after the exit of Judas, Jesus turned to the highest of all themes. John recounts: "When he had gone out, Jesus said, 'Now is the Son of Man glorified, and God is glorified in him'" (John 13:31).

GOD'S LOVE GLORIFIED

The departure of Judas not only unburdened the fellowship of Jesus and his disciples, but also set in motion a train of events that would lead directly to the cross. Jesus foresaw his betrayal and told Judas to do his deed quickly (John 13:27). But Jesus saw beyond his ordeal to the ultimate result: "Jesus said, 'Now is the Son of Man glorified, and God is glorified in him'" (13:31).

This plainly states that Jesus saw his coming cross as his glorification. What irony this involves! In the eyes of men, Jesus' crucifixion was his lowest humiliation. The soldiers mocked him with the crown of thorns and scarlet robe. Matthew records how they reviled him: "'Hail, King of the Jews!' And they spit on him and took the reed and struck him on the head" (Matt. 27:29–30). Many today still think Jesus a weak and pathetic figure as he meekly embraced his torment and murder. But the reality is that the cross of Christ is mankind's deepest humiliation, not Christ's. God sent his beloved Son, full of life and light, and sinful man abused him with all his deadly scorn. Here, the judgment is proved: "The light has come into the world, and people loved the darkness rather than the light because their works were evil" (John 3:19). Yet in the midst of that dreadful scene, Jesus found his highest glorification. "Now is the Son of Man glorified," he exulted (13:31).

How is Christ glorified in the cross? First, Jesus is glorified because his atoning death is the central moment of all history. James Montgomery Boice writes: "Nothing that has happened in the world's history from the beginning of creation until now, or will ever happen before that day when all things will be wrapped up in Christ, is as significant as the crucifixion."[1] In his cross, Jesus fulfilled the only hope of man's salvation. And from his cross flow all the spiritual blessings for which man was originally created and that Christ's own will enjoy forever.

Second, Christ is glorified in his cross by reversing the great calamity that befell mankind when Adam, our first father, sinned. Paul states: "As one trespass led to condemnation for all men, so one act of righteousness leads to justification and life for all men" (Rom. 5:18).

Third, at the cross, Jesus overthrew man's greatest enemy: the devil. He also conquered death and condemnation for all who believe in him. This

---

1. James Montgomery Boice, *The Gospel of John*, 5 vols. (Grand Rapids: Baker, 1999), 4:1033.

is why the symbol of the cross has been most precious to all Christians throughout the long centuries of our religion. What is it that most glorifies Christ in the eyes of his people? The answer was foretold by Isaiah: "He was wounded for our transgressions; he was crushed for our iniquities; upon him was the chastisement that brought us peace, and with his stripes we are healed" (Isa. 53:5).

Not only is Jesus glorified in his cross, but the glory of God the Father is also revealed. "Now is the Son of Man glorified, and God is glorified in him" (John 13:31). *Glorifying* means "revealing" or "displaying," and the cross displays the glory of the Father to the world. John Calvin comments: "In the cross of Christ, as in a splendid theatre, the incomparable goodness of God is set before the whole world."[2]

What does the cross tell us about God? First, it reveals God's perfect justice, for even when it was his own Son who bore the guilt of our sins, God did not withhold the righteous sentence of death. Men might well have questioned God's justice, for during all the long ages it seemed that people had sinned and gotten away with it. Paul admits that "in his divine forbearance [God] had passed over former sins" (Rom. 3:25). Why wasn't David punished for his adultery with Bathsheba? Why wasn't Moses condemned for his many sins? These biblical figures did suffer temporal punishments, such as the death of David's child and Moses' bar from entering the Promised Land. But they did not suffer the eternal consequences of their sins, just as we have not suffered the hell that our sins deserve. Is this because God is not just to uphold his law? The cross of Christ displays that God is perfectly just, for he has passed judgment on his Son, dying in our place.

But God is also glorified at the cross in his perfect faithfulness. All through the Old Testament, God promised a solution to the problem of sin. Adam gave his wife the name *Eve* because he believed God's promise to send a Deliverer through her womb (Gen. 3:15). Abraham received God's covenant because God promised him a multitude of spiritual offspring as numerous as the stars in the sky. Year after year, the Israelites celebrated the Passover, celebrating the blood of the lamb that promised provision for the guilt of their sin. The priests daily sacrificed sheep and goats, knowing that mere animal blood could never suffice for their sins but believing in God's promise

2. John Calvin, *New Testament Commentaries*, trans. T. H. L. Parker, 12 vols. (Grand Rapids: Eerdmans, 1959), 5:68.

of a better Savior. There at the cross, God made good on all his promises of salvation, so many of which seemed hard to believe and for which God's people had so long labored in belief. Had God forgotten his promises? Would God be faithful to the only hope of salvation? At the cross, God is shown to be faithful to every last promise of his Word. As Paul declares, "All the promises of God find their Yes in [Christ]. That is why it is through him that we utter our Amen to God for his glory" (2 Cor. 1:20).

We might go on to touch upon every single attribute of God to see how they are all glorified in the cross of Jesus: God's power, God's holiness, God's wisdom, God's sovereignty. But in Jesus' teaching here, we can see that one attribute of God is glorified above all the rest in the cross: the love of God. The reason for this is that God's love answers the question "Why?" Other attributes tell us how it is that God could offer his own Son to die for our sins. But only God's love explains why he would do it. God so loved the world that if the only way for sinners to be redeemed from the penalty of sin was for his Son to suffer divine wrath in their place, God was willing to do it. Indeed, so brightly is the love of God glorified in the cross that it is practically never mentioned in the New Testament apart from a reference to Christ's death for us. John writes in his first epistle: "In this is love, not that we have loved God but that he loved us and sent his Son to be the propitiation for our sins" (1 John 4:10). Nothing in all of time or eternity reveals the love of God so clearly as the cross of Calvary. Therefore, Jesus exulted in his coming torment and death: "Now is the Son of Man glorified, and God is glorified in him" (John 13:31).

Despite the great blessings we accrue through the cross, its greatest significance is the glory it brings to God the Father and God the Son. J. C. Ryle comments: "The Son shows the world, by His death, how holy and just is the Father, and how He hates sin. The Father shows the world, by raising and exalting the Son to glory, how He delights in the redemption for sinners which the Son has accomplished."[3] This mutual glorification is essential to the inner relations of the divine Trinity. Thus Jesus continues: "If God is glorified in him, God will also glorify him in himself, and glorify him at once" (John 13:32). God the Father is glorified in God the Son, and God the Son is glorified in God the Father, a glory that shines at the cross and then in the resurrection

---

3. J. C. Ryle, *Expository Thoughts on the Gospels: John*, 3 vols. (Edinburgh: Banner of Truth, 1999), 3:50.

of Jesus. Surely this makes us realize that as we are brought into fellowship with this same triune God, the grand purpose of our redemption is that we should glorify Father and Son together. And as we become children of God, God will glorify us as he is glorified in us. As the early Reformer Wolfgang Musculus noted, "Those who glorify God shall be glorified by God."[4]

A NEW SITUATION

As marvelous as it is to think about these things, the best way for us to glorify God's love is not merely by contemplating it. As Jesus continues, he insists that the new situation occasioned by his departure demands the new commandment of love among his followers, according to the new priority that the world should know that they are his disciples.

This teaching marks the formal start of Jesus' Farewell Discourse. The background for all the teaching in chapters 14–16 is the reality that Jesus is about to be separated from these men who had followed him for three years. It occasions a word of tender care, as Jesus begins by addressing them as "little children." He then informs them that "yet a little while I am with you. You will seek me, and just as I said to the Jews, so now I also say to you, 'Where I am going you cannot come'" (John 13:33).

All during the time of their discipleship, these men had relied on Jesus' loving ministry for them. But now that love would be taken away by the cross. Not only was Jesus' love departing from the disciples, but his love was also leaving the world. His was the only example of true love that the world had ever seen. So how were men and women to know the great love of God without the example provided by Jesus? Up to this point, the disciples themselves had hardly shown anything like Jesus' love. One of the reasons that Jesus had washed their feet was that each of them had bypassed the water basin, refusing to minister to one another. So a new situation would be brought about by Jesus' death on the cross, and the solution would be that the disciples must direct the love that they had for Jesus to one another. William Barclay summarizes: "He was taking a road that He had to walk alone; and before He went, He gave them the commandment that they must love one another as He had loved them."[5]

---

4. Quoted in ibid.

5. William Barclay, *The Gospel of John*, 2 vols. (Philadelphia: Westminster, 1975), 2:173.

A New Love

It was because of this new situation that Jesus gave his disciples what he called "a new commandment": "A new commandment I give to you, that you love one another: just as I have loved you, you also are to love one another" (John 13:34).

The first question is in what sense this commandment is "new." This is hardly the first time that the Bible commands God's people to love. After all, it was through Moses that God said, "You shall love your neighbor as yourself" (Lev. 19:18). Some people think love is only a New Testament virtue, but they are wrong. The God of the Old Testament is a God of everlasting love, and the people of God have always been commanded to love God and their neighbors. Jesus himself gave this two-sided obligation to love as the summation of the whole Old Testament law (Matt. 22:37–40). But just as the "new" covenant Christ brings does not replace but rather perfects the old covenant that preceded it, the new commandment to love brings to true fulfillment the obligation that believers always have to be a people of love. J. C. Ryle points out, "It is called a 'new' commandment, not because it had never been given before, but because it was to be more honoured, to occupy a higher position, to be backed up by a higher example than it ever had been before."[6]

We can make three observations about the newness of this command to love, starting with the *new object* to which Christian love is directed. The command from Leviticus directed one's love to a fellow Jewish neighbor. The whole context of Leviticus is that of the covenant community of Israel. But the death of Christ opens salvation for all the world, and the ancient commandment to love now includes any believer in Jesus of any class, race, or nationality. Christian love is not exclusive love, just as the Christian church is not an exclusive organization. Christians have not joined a club in which they are expected to love people that they have chosen to associate with. Instead, we are a community of believers of all kinds, some of whom we find more difficult to love than others. But the new commandment in Christ has a new object that is as broad as the offer of salvation that Jesus sends out into all the world. Alexander Maclaren comments insightfully as to what a difference this has made in history:

6. Ryle, *John*, 3:46.

178

When the words were spoken, the then-known civilized Western world was cleft by great, deep gulfs of separation, like the crevasses in a glacier.... Language, religion, national animosities, differences of conditions, and saddest of all, differences of sex, split the world up into alien fragments.... The learned and the unlearned, the slave and his master, the barbarian and the Greek, the man and the woman, stood on opposite sides of the gulfs, flinging hostility across. A Jewish peasant wandered up and down for three years in His own little country, which was the very focus of narrowness and separation and hostility, as the Roman historian felt when he called the Jews the "haters of the human race"; He gathered a few disciples, and He was crucified by a contemptuous Roman governor, who thought that the life of one fanatical Jew was a small price to pay for popularity with his troublesome subjects, and in a generation after, the clefts were being bridged and all over the Empire a strange new sense of unity was being breathed, and "Barbarian, Scythian, bond and free," male and female, Jew and Greek, learned and ignorant, clasped hands and sat down at one table, and felt themselves "all one in Christ Jesus."[7]

In our world today, which is as segregated as it has ever been, the fellowship of Christians is to display a love that transcends every earthly difference. Christians of every kind are bound together in love, since, as the apostle Paul explained: "Now in Christ Jesus you who once were far off have been brought near by the blood of Christ. For he himself is our peace, who has made us both one and has broken down in his flesh the dividing wall of hostility" (Eph. 2:13–14).

Second, the old commandment to love has received a *new measure* in the atoning death of Jesus. F. F. Bruce explains: "The standard of the love which the disciples are to have one for another is the love which their Lord has lavished on them."[8] "Greater love has no one than this," Jesus taught, "that someone lay down his life for his friends" (John 15:13). In other words, our love for one another is to be marked by the same sacrificial love that Jesus has shown for us. Seldom will it be the case that any of us are literally called to die in the place of a fellow Christian. But true Christian love involves a long sequence of little deaths as we set aside our own pride, our own preferences, our own sense of privilege. Jesus laid down his rights for

---

7. Alexander Maclaren, *Expositions of Holy Scripture*, 17 vols. (Grand Rapids: Baker, 1982), 10:227–28.
8. F. F. Bruce, *The Gospel of John* (Grand Rapids: Eerdmans, 1983), 294.

our salvation, and we are to lay down whatever we think we are entitled to for the sake of our fellow Christians and the church.

Paul described this new love that Christ has brought into the world in the famous words of 1 Corinthians 13: "Love is patient and kind; love does not envy or boast; it is not arrogant or rude. It does not insist on its own way; it is not irritable or resentful; it does not rejoice at wrongdoing, but rejoices with the truth. Love bears all things, believes all things, hopes all things, endures all things" (1 Cor. 13:4–7). Those words are usually read at weddings and applied in a romantic setting, but Paul's primary reference was the love of Christ among fellow Christians in the church.

Third, the old commandment to love has been infused with a *new power* through Christ's death and subsequent resurrection. The source of this power will occupy much of Jesus' teaching in this Farewell Discourse, namely, the coming of the Holy Spirit. When a sinner is born again and believes in Jesus, the Holy Spirit gives birth to the life of Jesus and also to the love of Jesus in his or her heart. This is what makes possible the new kind of love that Christians are to display: the power of the God of love in our newly born hearts.

Moreover, as Christians grow, this will be seen in an increased capacity to love. Increased knowledge of the Bible is not the primary mark of a growing Christian. Rather, increased knowledge of God's Word is tested by whether or not our love is growing. Paul went so far as to say that the thing that matters above all is "faith working through love" (Gal. 5:6). This does not mean that doctrine doesn't matter, for Jesus and the New Testament place a very high priority on truth. But true doctrine—true faith—breeds love. If you cannot love, then you are believing lies. If you are reacting to a situation in hatred rather than in love, then you are not trusting Christ. Indeed, the two great issues of our lives are to learn more and more to know and trust the Lord and to love one another.

The key words in this command are "just as I have loved you" (John 13:34). How humbling this is, because the truth is that none of us loves as Christ has loved us. This is our recurring problem in the home, the church, and the world: how little we know about Christlike love! But if we seek to grow in love through God's Word and if we pray for God to give us the love of Christ, then our capacity to love will grow as we become more and more like Jesus.

A NEW PRIORITY

Jesus would soon depart from his beloved disciples. His teaching was therefore given an added force as he gathered with them one last time before the cross. It would be a new situation for them, no longer walking through this world in company with their Master. The new situation required that the old commandment to love be given new urgency and power. And it set before them a new priority as the church graduated from its infancy in the days of Christ's earthly ministry. Jesus therefore concluded: "By this all people will know that you are my disciples, if you have love for one another" (John 13:35).

What is the priority for a Christian? Is it that he or she rise in affluence and worldly power? Is good health the priority, or increased knowledge? The same might be asked of a church. What is the top priority: the size of the attendance, the extent of the budget, or the excitement of the worship service? According to Jesus, addressing his own on the night of his arrest, the priority for his followers is that the world should know that we are his disciples.

So the question arises: "How is the world to know that we are followers of Jesus Christ?" A number of answers could be given. We might say, "Because we preach and believe the New Testament teachings." That certainly is important—so important that we are not even Christians unless we believe the apostolic witness of the New Testament. But that is not how the world knows that we are Christians. Or we might say, "Because we are engaged in good works to help the poor and needy." That, too, is important, and we are failing in our Christian duty if we are not doing it. But even good works are not the distinctive mark of the disciples of Christ.

Francis Schaeffer considered this question in a famous essay entitled "The Mark of the Christian":

> Through the centuries men have displayed many different symbols to show that they are Christians. They have worn marks in the lapels of their coats, hung chains about their necks, even had special haircuts.
>
> . . . But there is a much better sign—a mark that has not been thought up just as a matter of expediency for use on some special occasion or in some specific era. It is a universal mark that is to last through all the ages of the church until Jesus comes back. . . .

Love—and the unity it attests to—is the mark Christ gave Christians to *wear* before the world. Only with this mark may the world know that Christians are indeed Christians and that Jesus was sent by the Father.[9]

This says that we can be Christians without showing that we are. But if we want the world to know that we belong to Jesus, and if we want the reality of Jesus to appeal to the broken and the lost in a cruel and loveless world, then we have to love one another. As the early-church leader Tertullian commented, it was this that impressed the pagan world of his day: "'See,' they say, 'how they love one another,' for they themselves are animated by mutual hatred; 'see how they are ready even to die for one another.'"[10]

Perhaps most importantly, when we remember that this was the commandment to which Jesus gave priority in his last meeting with the disciples, we will realize that when we love one another, we please our Lord. How will we love our Lord Jesus, who is not physically present? By giving to one another the sacrificial love that Jesus has given to us.

Jesus said of his cross, "Now is the Son of Man glorified, and God is glorified in him" (John 13:31). This prompts us to ask: "How may God the Father and God the Son be glorified in us?" The answer is that when we die to sin and to self, taking up our own cross to follow after Jesus, and love one another, God is glorified by his people. And this—the glory of God—is our highest calling as followers of Christ.

9. Francis A. Schaeffer, *The Complete Works of Francis A. Schaeffer*, 5 vols. (Westchester, IL: Crossway, 1982), 4:183, 204.
10. Tertullian, *Apology*, 39.

89

Before the Rooster Crows

John 13:36—38

*Jesus answered, "Will you lay down your life for me? Truly,
truly, I say to you, the rooster will not crow till you have denied
me three times." (John 13:38)*

Those who teach the Bible find that many people are more interested in matters of curiosity or controversy than in the straightforward message of God's Word. An example is provided by Simon Peter during Jesus' Farewell Discourse. Jesus had told the disciples that he would soon leave them. Because of this, he urged, "A new commandment I give to you, that you love one another" (John 13:34). That is the kind of biblical teaching that is not hard to understand, but is seldom valued. Thus Peter distracted Jesus and returned to the mysterious issue of his departure: "Lord, where are you going?" (13:36). Gordon Keddie points out how Peter is like so many of us: "Speculation about prophetic predictions seems much more exciting than just living a quiet upright life, ordinary day after ordinary day."[1]

1. Gordon J. Keddie, *A Study Commentary on John*, 2 vols. (Darlington, UK: Evangelical Press, 2001), 2:53.

Peter's interruption occurred at the moment when Jesus was seeking to inform the disciples about what he would provide for them after his departure into glory. But Peter was not ready to accept these words. "Lord, why can I not follow you now? I will lay down my life for you" (John 13:37), he blurted out. Yet Peter needed to understand where Jesus was going and what Jesus was doing for him—far more important things than what Peter would do for Jesus.

Christians are indeed to follow Christ, yet there are things that only Jesus can do, such as dying on the cross for our sins. Moreover, Jesus is able to do his works without needing our help. In contrast, the demands placed on any of us simply in following Christ are more than we can achieve in our own strength. To make this point clear to Peter, Jesus replied with a statement that was simultaneously a prophecy, a rebuke, and a ministry. "Jesus answered, 'Will you lay down your life for me? Truly, truly, I say to you, the rooster will not crow till you have denied me three times'" (John 13:38).

JUDAS AND PETER

The apostle John undoubtedly intended for us to reflect on Judas and Peter together as he reported the events of Jesus' last night with his disciples. In doing this, we might be surprised to realize how much the two men had in common. Judas and Peter had both spent three years in Jesus' company, seeing his miracles and receiving privileged instruction. They had both received Christ's love and had both served him in return. Both men would fail Jesus in appalling ways in the hour of his greatest trial. We are told that Jesus "was troubled in his spirit" (John 13:21) over Judas's betrayal; Peter's denials must surely have pained him even more.

The similar behavior of Judas and Peter shows us that anyone can fall to temptation, even when it comes to denying Christ. If Peter, who heads the list of Christ's disciples, could fall and deny Jesus, then any of us can. The lesson of Peter's failure was thus intended not merely for him but for all of Christ's disciples.

If Peter had much in common with Judas, the differences between the two men are even more important. Most significantly, one of them was saved and the other was not. Even though both of these men betrayed Jesus on the night of his arrest, Peter was ultimately restored by Jesus, whereas Judas received nothing but the Lord's prophetic woe (Luke 22:22). When Judas faced the enormity of his heinous sin, he responded not with repentance but with suicide; Peter, instead, mourned, repented, and was restored.

The difference between Judas and Peter is best seen in the motives behind their actions. Judas sinned with a treacherous heart, using piety as a cloak for his intended evil. Peter sinned with a boastful heart that was led into folly by his real love for the Lord. What a difference there is between a true disciple who lacks the strength to live up to his or her faith, and a false disciple who has no faith. Ultimately, the faithless betrayer, having no saving relationship with Jesus, must face the bitter consequences of sin by himself, as Judas did in taking his own life and then entering unforgiven into hell. In contrast, Peter, who belonged to the Lord Jesus, had a Savior to uphold him even in his sin and then to rescue him when he had fallen. So just as Peter shows that any of us can fall, he also appeals to each of us as to the necessity of our having Jesus as our Savior.

PETER'S "SUDDEN" FALL

Having learned from Peter that any of us can fall, we should next consider the steps that led to his fall. As often happens, his betrayal of Jesus happened suddenly. Yet as is usually the case, his "sudden" fall was the result of what had long been brewing in his heart.

This scenario is what we frequently find when believers fall into gross sin. For instance, King David looked out his palace window and gazed on the beautiful figure of lovely Bathsheba. The latter half of David's reign was greatly marred by the sin that followed, yet it happened so quickly. In three terse verses we simply read that "he saw . . . [he] sent . . . and [he] took" (2 Sam. 11:2–4). How sudden a fall! Yet in reality, the corruptions of pride and lust had crept unchallenged into David's heart long beforehand, awaiting the opportunity to strike. Peter's denial of Jesus warns us of the same. No wonder the wise man of Proverbs exhorts us: "Keep your heart with all vigilance, for from it flow the springs of life" (Prov. 4:23).

In studying John's Gospel, we have come to expect some folly and sin from Peter, the lovable fisherman. But one sin we might not have expected was that of denying his Lord. What could have caused this true-hearted man to fail Jesus so badly? The first answer was Peter's *ignorance*, which resulted in part from his tendency to speak when he should have been listening to Jesus.

Consider what Peter said to Jesus, here in the very shadow of the cross: "Lord, why can I not follow you now? I will lay down my life for you" (John 13:37). This statement reveals an astonishing ignorance of what lay before our Lord, despite repeated explanations. How often Jesus had spoken of the necessity of his death! Earlier that very week, Jesus had spoken of being "lifted up from the earth" (12:32), thus telling the disciples "by what kind of death he was going to die" (12:33). This was added to numerous occasions when Jesus had plainly informed them of what must soon happen: "The Son of Man . . . will be delivered over to the Gentiles and will be mocked and shamefully treated and spit upon. And after flogging him, they will kill him, and on the third day he will rise" (Luke 18:31–33). That very evening, Jesus had instituted the sacrament of the Lord's Supper, during which he passed them the cup and said, "This cup . . . is the new covenant in my blood" (22:20). If it discourages us to see how little of Jesus' teaching his disciples were able to understand and absorb, then we should realize how difficult it is for men and women to believe truths that contradict their preconceived notions. Seeing Jesus' frustration with his students should drive every preacher and Bible teacher to his knees for prayer!

Given all that he had taught about his coming death, we can imagine some irony in Jesus' voice when he replied to Peter, "Will you lay down your life for me?" (John 13:38). It was not Peter who would lay down his life for Jesus, but Jesus who would lay down his life for Peter. Even when it came to the obligation of all disciples to follow Jesus and carry their cross, Peter betrayed a cavalier ignorance of the true cost of being a Christian. Therefore, writes Leon Morris, "when the crunch came he was not ready to die; he ran away with the others and went further by denying his Lord."[2]

Peter not only was ignorant of what Jesus was about to do, but also revealed an astonishing ignorance of himself. How little he calculated the truth of his weakness when faced with a real challenge! How little he recognized the infirmity of his corrupted nature! A. W. Pink comments, "Peter knew and really loved the Lord, but how little he as yet knew himself!"[3] When Jesus told him, "Where I am going you cannot follow me now" (John 13:36),

---

2. Leon Morris, *Reflections on the Gospel of John* (Peabody, MA: Hendrickson, 1986), 487.
3. Arthur W. Pink, *Exposition of the Gospel of John* (Grand Rapids: Zondervan, 1975), 749.

Peter should have recognized how ill equipped he was not merely for what Jesus was called to do but also for the far lesser deeds that Peter himself was called to do.

This ignorance of our spiritual weakness is not restricted to Peter. Christians think they can toy and dabble with forbidden pleasures, and then are dismayed when they become overwhelmed in moral catastrophe. Peter's duty that evening was simply to admit before the world that he was a follower of Christ: how far beyond our cowardly flesh even that is for the best of us! J. C. Ryle thus writes:

> We never know how far we might fall if we were tempted. We fancy sometimes, like Peter, that there are some things we could not possibly do. We look pitifully upon others who fall into certain sins, and please ourselves in the thought that at any rate *we* should not have done so! We know nothing at all. The seeds of every sin are latent in our hearts, even when renewed, and they only need occasion, or carelessness, or the withdrawal of God's grace for a season, to put forth an abundant crop.[4]

The way for biblically informed Christians to avoid falling into devastating sins is to realize how able we are to do such things. Being properly informed about ourselves, we will then shun temptation, starve our sinful desires, and daily pray as Jesus taught us, "Lead us not into temptation, but deliver us from evil" (Matt. 6:13).

A second contributor to Peter's "sudden" fall was his *overconfidence*. This was, in part, a result of his ignorance, but it was also simply an aspect of his own sin and folly. Luke's Gospel tells us that this episode took place right after the disciples had been disputing over which of them was the greatest (Luke 22:24). Mark tells us that Peter not only claimed that he would die for Jesus, but also emphasized how much more faithful he would be than the others: "Even though they all fall away, I will not," he boasted (Mark 14:29). Peter thus set himself up as an example of the famous proverb: "Pride goes before destruction, and a haughty spirit before a fall" (Prov. 16:18).

Jesus' rebuke thus had the intention of humbling Peter. His pride was a threat not only for the dark night to come, but even more importantly for

---

4. J. C. Ryle, *Expository Thoughts on the Gospels: John*, 3 vols. (Edinburgh: Banner of Truth, 1999), 3:47–48.

his future ministry as an apostle. Peter thought the Lord needed him. What he had yet really to learn was how much he needed the Lord. A humbling failure would best teach this vital lesson. Therefore, Jesus told him, "Truly, truly, I say to you, the rooster will not crow till you have denied me three times" (John 13:38).

In saying this, Jesus displayed his sovereign foreknowledge of detailed events, including the number of Peter's denials and the immediate crowing of the rooster, so that this accurate prophecy is yet another proof of his deity. But Jesus also showed his wise handling of his servants. Jesus knew what Satan would think of Peter's pompous self-confidence. Luke tells us that he said, "Simon, Simon, behold, Satan demanded to have you, that he might sift you like wheat" (Luke 22:31). Peter's abject weakness would be displayed in that Satan would overcome the fisherman not at his weakest point but at his strongest: the matter of Peter's courage. It was imperative, then, for Peter to learn, as it is for us, that we are far too weak to withstand the sifting of Satan even in our greatest strength. The sooner we know this, the sooner we will become strong in the Lord, so that he will uphold us even at the points of our greatest weakness. This is what Paul meant when he said, "Therefore I will boast all the more gladly of my weaknesses, so that the power of Christ may rest upon me" (2 Cor. 12:9).

Peter's "sudden" fall into sin had a third component that builds on the previous two. Peter was ignorant of the Lord's saving work and of his own weakness. He was thus overconfident in relying on his own strength. The third cause of his fall was his *neglect of spiritual resources*. This mistake occurred later on this same evening, when Jesus took Peter and the others to the garden of Gethsemane for prayer. Before drawing away for his own period of the most intense pleading with the Father, Jesus advised the disciples three times: "Pray that you may not enter into temptation" (Luke 22:40). Yet when the Lord returned from his own prayers, he found Peter and the others not praying but sleeping.

Peter's was the sleep of a falsely confident man, who little considers his need of God's help. How true this is today of parents who pray little for the Lord's help with their children, of pastors who pray little for God's power to build and protect their congregations, and indeed of all Christians who pray little, spend little time in God's Word, and fail to be consistent in attending the worship of the church. Such a neglect of spiritual resources reveals an ignorance and overconfidence when it comes to the grave matter of temptation to sin. John Calvin exhorts us from Peter's example: "Let us learn to distrust our own strength and betake ourselves early to the Lord, that He may support us by His power."[5]

Fallen but Not Forsaken

Just as we need to be warned by the fall of Peter, we should also be heartened by the fact that while Peter would fall, he would not be forsaken. Peter shows us that anyone can fall into temptation and even deny the Lord. But Peter also proves that when a true believer falters, Jesus will nonetheless save him or her in the end.

We can know that Peter was not forsaken by reading ahead in the story to when Jesus, after his resurrection, restores Peter to faith and apostleship (John 21:15–19). But we need not even look ahead, for it was clear even here, as Jesus predicted Peter's denials, that the fisherman would not finally be lost. The reasons that Peter was not lost pertain to every believer in Christ, so that while we must be vigilant lest we fall, we can yet have the peace of knowing that we will never be forsaken in Christ.

We know that Peter will not ultimately be lost, first, because of the *declaration* that Jesus made concerning his salvation. Jesus said, "Where I am going you cannot follow me now, but you will follow afterward" (John 13:36). At the time, Peter might have heard only the first half of that statement— "You cannot follow me now"—but it is the second half that contained his salvation: "you will follow afterward."

We can read this declaration in two ways, both of which are probably intended. First, since Jesus was going ahead of his disciples into glory, he declared that Peter would follow there himself. This is the theme that Jesus goes on to in the next verses, seeking to give assurance to all the disciples: "Let not your hearts be troubled. . . . In my Father's house are many rooms. . . . And if I go and prepare a place for you, I will come again and will take you to myself, that where I am you may be also" (John 14:1–3). In answer to Peter's question, Jesus flatly declared this of him personally: Peter would follow Jesus into heaven.

5. John Calvin, *New Testament Commentaries*, trans. T. H. L. Parker, 12 vols. (Grand Rapids: Eerdmans, 1959), 4:72.

Not only was Jesus headed to heaven, but he would first pass through his death on the cross. This is why Peter was being so presumptuous when he asked to follow the Lord and then glibly offered to die for him. Yet the time would come for Peter to follow his Master to the cross in order to die. After Christ's resurrection and his restoration to service, Peter would follow Jesus in so many ways. Peter would declare Jesus' gospel to Jerusalem and perform miracles in Jesus' name. Peter would go on to share in the fellowship of the sufferings of the Lord and, according to the witness of church tradition, to die on a cross during Nero's persecution in Rome. At the end of John's Gospel are words from Jesus that allude to Peter's future crucifixion (John 21:18–19). But "now" was not the time for Peter to face that test. Indeed, an important step in Peter's apostolic preparation was his failure on this night, which would teach him so many things about himself and the grace of the Lord.

Just as Jesus made a declaration concerning Peter's salvation, he has done the same for everyone who believes in him. Many of these statements are found in the Gospel of John. Jesus said: "This is the will of him who sent me, that I should lose nothing of all that he has given me, but raise it up on the last day. For this is the will of my Father, that everyone who looks on the Son and believes in him should have eternal life" (John 6:39–40). Similarly, after declaring himself the Good Shepherd, Jesus stated that his sheep will know him and follow his voice. He added, "I give them eternal life, and they will never perish, and no one will snatch them out of my hand" (10:28).

Whenever the fall of Judas and Peter is preached, many Christians will worry over their souls. Just as the disciples worried when Jesus said that one would betray him, each of them asking, "Is it I?" (Mark 14:19), Christians today worry, "Will I betray Jesus and be lost?" The way to answer the question is to determine whether you are a Judas or a Peter now. The key difference is that Judas never believed in Jesus—whether he outwardly professed faith or not—whereas Peter was a genuine believer in Christ, for all his failings. Despite all your own failings, if you are a believer in Christ, he has declared your salvation just as he declared that Peter would follow him into heaven.

Second, Luke's Gospel adds an important detail that will be helpful to include here: Jesus' *prayer* for Peter's repentance and restoration. "Simon, Simon, behold," he said, "Satan demanded to have you, that he might sift you like wheat, but I have prayed for you that your faith may not fail" (Luke

22:31–32). Satan might be able to overcome Peter's courage, but he could not defeat Jesus' prayer.

We, too, as believers in Christ, are shielded by his priestly intercession, as Jesus prays for us in heaven from his throne at the right hand of God. While Peter, in his foolish self-confidence, would fail to pray on this dreadful night, Jesus would remember to pray not only for himself but also for his sifted disciple. Paul applies this to us: "Who is to condemn? Christ Jesus is the one who died—more than that, who was raised—who is at the right hand of God, who indeed is interceding for us" (Rom. 8:34). Jesus' ministry for every believer continues even now, safeguarding in heavenly prayer those whom he purchased on earth with his own blood.

Third, Jesus' warning to Peter included a *provision* that was intended to provoke his repentance: "Truly, truly, I say to you, the rooster will not crow till you have denied me three times" (John 13:38). Later that night, when Peter had denied Jesus for the third time, "immediately, while he was still speaking, the rooster crowed" (Luke 22:60). At that moment, Jesus turned and looked at his disciple. "And Peter remembered the saying of the Lord, how he had said to him, 'Before the rooster crows today, you will deny me three times.' And he went out and wept bitterly" (22:61–62).

I do not know how you or I or any other Christian might fail our Lord, even doing something so dreadful as to deny him before the world. But I know that if we do, and if we have sincerely believed in Jesus despite our failure, Jesus has already made provision for our repentance and restoration, just as he did for Simon Peter.

What a hope this gives to parents, spouses, and friends of those who once sincerely professed faith in Jesus and gave credible evidence of that faith, but since have fallen away. None of us is able to read anyone's heart but our own, and just as the disciples were fooled by Judas, we could easily have been fooled by others' false profession of faith. But we know that those who truly belong to Christ will never be lost and that he has made provision for the repentance of his most wayward sheep.

WITNESSES OF THE SAVIOR

Remember that Peter fell in part because he confused roles with Jesus: Peter was never meant to be a savior but only a witness to the Savior, Jesus

Christ. Overconfident in himself, Peter then did not rely on the Lord, nor did he avail himself of the privilege of prayer. His experience proves to us that we are never the savior but always those who are saved. Knowing that Jesus will be faithful to us no matter how waywardly we might stray or how grievously we might fall, we have the privilege of doing the very thing that Peter failed to do. We are to be witnesses for Jesus in the world. It is our privilege to be asked what Peter was asked: "You are one of his disciples, are you not?" and to answer, "Yes, I am," and then to tell all who will hear about the grace and glory of Jesus Christ.

If we overcome our ignorance with the teaching of God's Word, if we humble ourselves in constant reliance on the Lord's grace, and if we make diligent use of prayer and other spiritual resources, we can be confident even in our weakness that we will not deny our Lord. In this way, not merely before the rooster crows but before the trumpet sounds to summon all mankind to appear at the return of Christ in his glory, we may be used to tell many of Jesus and his salvation.

90

IN MY FATHER'S HOUSE

John 14:1–3

"In my Father's house are many rooms. If it were not so, would I have told you that I go to prepare a place for you?" (John 14:2)

Christians are, or at least should be, the world's great realists. Consider, in contrast, the attitude of today's secularism, as expressed by the lyrics of a once-popular song, "Don't worry, be happy." Since this life is all that there is, we should just *keep* trying to have a good time. Or consider stoic philosophy. Stoics seek to remain calm during trials because they despair of the future. Life has no meaning, and therefore problems are not faced but ignored. Christians, however, face their troubles, finding a great hope in our confidence for the future. Christians are the world's great realists, but also the world's great optimists: trusting God to uphold us, we can be honest about the world and life, since we look ahead to heaven where our hopes are held fast and secure.

Consider the matter of death. Christians are not reduced merely to saying that someone has "passed away," but we face the truth that he or she has died. To die is to suffer death, and we know that death is real. The same is true of life's other woes: sickness, poverty, injustice, loneliness, and fear. Christians can be realists about all these ills because of the great hope that we have with the Lord.

Do Not Be Troubled

It was from this perspective that Jesus sought to comfort his disciples after the Last Supper, saying, "Let not your hearts be troubled" (John 14:1). Jesus said this because it was obvious that the disciples' hearts *were* troubled. In fact, Jesus' own heart had been troubled. In chapter 12, in light of his approaching cross, Jesus had declared, "Now is my soul troubled" (12:27). Earlier during this last meal, Jesus had foretold his betrayal and was "troubled in his spirit" (13:21). After Judas departed, Jesus foretold Peter's three denials, and we can only imagine how troubling this was to the Lord. Jesus was contemplating the atoning death by which he would suffer the full wrath of God for his people's sin. He faced a bitter betrayal from one who shared his table, and one of his closest followers would deny him. Of course this troubled Jesus! Just as our hearts are troubled by fearful prospects, personal betrayals, and painful disappointments, Jesus in his true humanity was troubled in heart.

The disciples, too, were troubled, which is why Jesus spoke this way. They were still trying to grasp the prediction of Judas's betrayal and Peter's denials. Moreover, in the midst of the dangerous and fearful situation in Jerusalem, Jesus now told them that he was departing and that they could not follow. Their lives had been so wholly focused on Jesus for three years that the sudden prospect of his leaving must have been devastating.

Troubled hearts are so common today as to be nearly epidemic. Even in a society where food, shelter, and medical care are almost universally available, many people are yet deeply troubled in spirit. All around us, men and women are plagued by distress, loneliness, and fear, with no peace of mind and no comfort for their souls.

Like Jesus, we need to face the truth about our troubled hearts. If we find ourselves counseling a Christian friend, we should avoid the mistake of wrongfully minimizing that person's problems. Instead, we should listen and face the reality of his or her troubles, and when appropriate we should acknowledge our friend's distress as understandable.

This does not mean, however, that all we can do is to face the reality of troubles. Jesus' point was that there are nonetheless overwhelming reasons not to remain troubled by them. "Let not your hearts be troubled," he said, and then gave the reason: "Believe in God; believe also in me" (John 14:1).

According to Jesus, Christians are to be realists not only about our troubles but also about the power and goodness of God and his Son, Jesus Christ. Being realistic about our God and our Savior is the antidote to the troubles that we honestly face.

According to Jesus, the cure for a troubled heart is belief. He refers not merely to belief itself: Christianity does not teach the mere "power of positive thinking."[1] Rather, Jesus reminded his disciples that they have God to believe in. A. W. Pink elaborates that God "is possessed of infinite power, wisdom, and goodness. He knows what is best for [you], and He makes all things work together for [your] good. He is on the Throne, ruling amid the army of heaven and among the inhabitants of the earth, so that none can stay His hand."[2] It was with such thoughts that David wrestled with his troubles: "Why are you cast down, O my soul, and why are you in turmoil within me?" he asked. In answer to his troubled soul, David argued: "Hope in God, for I shall again praise him, my salvation and my God" (Ps. 42:11).

There is a question as to how we should translate verse 1, since the verb *believe* can be read in either the indicative or the imperative mood (the Greek for both is the same). Did Jesus command the disciples, "Believe in God and believe in me?" Or did Jesus simply point out their faith: "You do believe in God and in me." Or is Jesus combining an indicative statement with an imperative command, "Since you believe in God, believe also in me"? Most commentators believe that at least the call to trust Jesus is an imperative, since Jesus' point is that the disciples should trust him just as they trust God.

This statement provides a clear affirmation of Jesus' deity, since he identifies God and himself equally as objects of the disciples' faith. Jesus' point is not merely that through faith we are saved, true though that is, but that by exercising our trust in God and his Son, believers gain comfort for their troubled hearts.

What is it about trusting Jesus that gives peace to troubled hearts? The answer is taught to children by means of a necklace with colored beads, each of which corresponds to a Scripture verse and its teaching. The first bead is colored black, representing the guilt of our sin (Rom. 3:23). The second bead is red, for the blood of Christ that was shed for our forgiveness (John 3:16).

---

1. Norman Vincent Peale, *The Power of Positive Thinking* (New York: Ballantine, 1996).
2. Arthur W. Pink, *Exposition of the Gospel of John* (Grand Rapids: Zondervan, 1975), 755.

The third bead is white, since Isaiah 1:18 tells us that our sins are washed and made "as white as snow." Fourth is a gold bead (John 14:2–3), which corresponds to the glory that awaits all whose sins are forgiven by Jesus. Along with the necklace goes a song with these comforting words:

> Once my heart was black as sin, until the Savior came in.
> His precious blood I know has washed it whiter than snow;
> And in this world I'm told I'll walk the streets of gold.
> Oh, wonderful, wonderful day; He washed my sins away.[3]

THE FATHER'S HOUSE PREPARED

That children's song, with its final golden bead, leads to the second source of comfort that Jesus brought before his troubled disciples. The first was their ability to trust in God and in himself. The second was the belief that a place has been prepared for them in heaven. Jesus added, "In my Father's house are many rooms. If it were not so, would I have told you that I go to prepare a place for you?" (John 14:2).

If we know what he has taught about our future in heaven, Jesus states, this belief will overcome other troubles that beset us in life. This highlights a great problem today, that Christians think so seldom about heaven and in many cases do not understand the Bible's teaching about it. When we are moving to a new city or even vacationing somewhere new, most of us will do extensive research. We will pore over maps and books, studying the geography, history, and culture. If this is how we respond to places on earth where we will briefly live or visit, how much more interested should Christians be about heaven! How strange it is that so few believers seem to have interest in the place where they hope to live forever with Christ.

Some years ago, I knew a woman named Helen who had spent many decades as an overseas missionary. Now elderly, she worked as missions secretary in our church. Helen became ill with cancer, and one day when I was praying with her, she told me that the doctors had not given her long to live. I asked, "How are you feeling about this?" Helen beamed and answered, "Well, I am just getting so excited!" She had long been thinking about heaven

3. Quoted in R. Kent Hughes, *John: That You May Believe* (Wheaton, IL: Crossway, 1999), 336–37.

and now was comforted in anticipation. This is the attitude that we will have if we know the Bible's teaching on our hope in heaven.

We can glean four truths about heaven from Jesus' teaching in this passage, truths that will replace the anxiety in our hearts with great joy. The first teaching is that heaven is *the beloved home for the family of God*. This is why Jesus refers to heaven as "my Father's house" (John 14:2). Home is a place, writes J. C. Ryle, "where we are generally loved for our own sakes, and not for our gifts or possessions; the place where we are loved to the end, never forgotten, and always welcome. . . . Believers are in a strange land and at school in this life. In the life to come they will be at home."[4]

Most of us will admit that our hearts greatly long for home. We deeply desire a place where we fully belong, where we are safe and secure, where we are loved, and that we love in return. In the hypermobility of our society today, how many people are troubled by the absence of anywhere that is truly home. Christian psychologist Paul Tournier spoke of this in his book *A Place for You*. He wrote of a young man he was counseling who came from an unhappy home, developed a sense of failure in relationships, and could never really settle down. At one point, the man expressed his inner longing: "Basically, I'm always looking for a place— for somewhere to be."[5]

This young man is not alone in that troubled feeling, for ours is an exiled race. The Bible's story begins with our first parents, Adam and Eve, falling into sin against God the Creator. The result was that they were expelled from their home in the garden of Eden, where they had formerly enjoyed the blessing of God's presence (Gen. 3). When their son Cain fell further into sin by murdering his brother, God cursed him by making him "a fugitive and a wanderer on the earth" (Gen. 4:12). Later, his descendants sought to make a home and a name for themselves in rebellion against God. But God cast down the Tower of Babel and scattered rebellious mankind across the face of the earth (11:1–9). So it has been throughout human history that men and women feel a longing to be home. Augustine thus prayed that "thou hast created us for thyself and our heart cannot be quieted till it may find

---

4. J. C. Ryle, *Expository Thoughts on the Gospels: John*, 3 vols. (Edinburgh: Banner of Truth, 1999), 3:57.

5. Quoted in James Montgomery Boice, *The Gospel of John*, 5 vols. (Grand Rapids: Baker, 1999), 4:1066.

repose in thee."[6] Jesus tells us that this longing for home will be met in his Father's house in heaven.

Second, we should know that heaven is *our permanent and eternal dwelling*. This means that heaven is a real place. Too many Christians think of heaven as a wispy, ethereal state of being. But since Jesus ascended into heaven in his human body, heaven must be a material location. Jesus did not describe heaven's physical details, but he said that "in my Father's house are many rooms" (John 14:2). Older versions render this as saying that heaven includes many "mansions." This translation arises from the fact that Jerome used the Latin word *mansiones* in the Vulgate version, so that the King James translators used the closest English word: *mansions*. But both the Latin word and the Greek in John's text simply mean "lodging places." Heaven is the place where our eternal lodging will be.

C. S. Lewis wrote a book, *The Great Divorce*, about our wrong ideas of heaven. A group of English tourists are taken on an imaginary bus trip to heaven. Once there, the tourists get off the bus, only to realize that they appear as ghosts. They are stunned at how solid and real everything in heaven is compared to earth. The grass is so real that it hurts their feet to walk on it, and they learn that while people in heaven are "solid people," it is those on earth who are ethereal.[7]

Heaven is filled with dwelling places that will endure for all eternity. This is what Abraham was looking forward to. As a sojourner in Canaan, Abraham longed for a real home. By faith, we are told that he was looking forward to heaven, described as "the city that has foundations, whose designer and builder is God" (Heb. 11:10).

Third, and Jesus' main point here about heaven, is *the spacious provision made there for Christ's people*. The Father's house, Jesus said, has "many rooms." In ancient Palestine, a patriarch would often live in a large villa, with wings and rooms constantly being added on for children, grandchildren, and their families. The image is that of "a large compound centered around a communal courtyard."[8] Likewise, there is plenty of room in heaven for all of God's family. Ryle comments that "there will be room for all believers

---

6. Augustine, *The Confessions*, trans. William Watts (Cambridge: Harvard University Press, 1999), 1.1.

7. C. S. Lewis, *The Great Divorce* (New York: Macmillan, 1946).

8. Andreas J. Kostenberger, *John* (Grand Rapids: Baker, 2004), 426.

and room for all sorts, for little saints as well as great ones, for the weakest believer as well as for the strongest. The feeblest child of God need not fear there will be no place for him. None will be shut out but impenitent sinners and obstinate unbelievers."[9]

Fourth, heaven is *where Jesus went to prepare a place for us.* He told the disciples that he would depart for his Father's house "to prepare a place for you" (John 14:2). Chiefly, Jesus prepared a place for us in heaven by removing the obstacle of our sin. Jesus entered into heaven after shedding his blood on the cross for our purification. The Old Testament priests would sprinkle the altar in the temple with the sacrificial blood, and the book of Hebrews tells us that Jesus likewise "entered once for all into the holy places [that is, heaven], . . . by means of his own blood, thus securing an eternal redemption" (Heb. 9:12). The point is, as Charles Simeon said, "heaven would have been defiled . . . by the admission of sinners into it; he therefore entered into heaven to sanctify it by his blood."[10] Do you hope to enter into heaven? Then realize that only those for whom Christ has made this preparation may dwell in those holy halls, that is, those who have trusted in the blood he shed for the forgiveness of our sins.

How wonderful it is to find a room prepared after a long journey. All who believe and trust in Christ can know that heaven has been prepared for their arrival. Our Mediator and Savior has carried our names into heaven and made a reservation there for us. No Christian will ever appear in heaven either unknown or unexpected, for Jesus has prepared a place there for each and every one of his own. Knowing and trusting in our prepared home in the Father's house is Jesus' antidote to the troubles and anxieties of life.

CHRIST'S RETURN PROMISED

There is yet another reason why Jesus' disciples should not be troubled by fear and distress. Our third comfort is knowing that not only has Jesus gone ahead of us to prepare heaven, but he will return to receive us to himself. "If I go and prepare a place for you," he promised, "I will come again and will take you to myself, that where I am you may be also" (John 14:3).

9. Ryle, *John*, 3:57.
10. Quoted in Gordon J. Keddie, *A Study Commentary on John*, 2 vols. (Darlington, UK: Evangelical Press, 2001), 2:79.

The book of Hebrews says that "Jesus has gone as a forerunner on our behalf" into heaven (Heb. 6:20), appearing before God the Father as "the founder and perfecter of our faith" (12:2). Right now, Jesus is preparing heaven for us and preparing us for heaven. But in a day to come, Jesus will return to this world. The Bible calls this day "our blessed hope, the appearing of the glory of our great God and Savior Jesus Christ" (Titus 2:13). This is our comfort amid so many troubling threats in this present evil age. Bruce Milne comments: "History is not at the mercy of the whims or passions of politicians or tyrants. The reins are firmly in the hands of the Lord of history, and 'he has set a day when he will judge the world with justice'" (Acts 17:31).[11]

It is particularly wonderful that Jesus says, "I will come again and will take you to myself" (John 14:3). Jesus is returning to take us with him into heaven, but that is not how he phrases it. As Jesus sees our great future, he is coming to take us "to himself." William Hendriksen writes: "So wonderful is Christ's love for his own that he is not satisfied with the idea of merely bringing them to *heaven*. He must needs take them into his own embrace."[12] Hearing these words, we look forward to heaven not merely to escape our trials today, but to be with the Lord. We will be forever with Jesus. After Jesus returns, our salvation will come into its crowning glory, and those crowns will be given to us by his nail-scarred hands, and we will place them at his nail-scarred feet with praise and glory. John writes in his first epistle: "Beloved, . . . what we will be has not yet appeared; but we know that when he appears we shall be like him, because we shall see him as he is" (1 John 3:2). It is in anticipation of our great future with him that Jesus says to us now: "Let not your hearts be troubled. Believe in God; believe also in me" (John 14:1).

LIVING IN LIGHT OF ETERNITY

To be a Christian is to be a realist about our present lives, but also to be realists about the promised future that we have in Christ. It is in the light

---

11. Bruce Milne, *The Message of John: Here Is Your King!* (Downers Grove, IL: InterVarsity Press, 1993), 211.

12. William Hendriksen, *Exposition of the Gospel according to John*, 2 vols., New Testament Commentary (Grand Rapids: Baker, 1953), 2:266.

of eternity that we gain our perspective on today, a perspective that should transform our lives. Let me conclude by noting some of the effects in our lives that should result from Christ's promise about heaven and his soon return.

First, we have a strong incentive to *behave as followers of Christ*, obeying his teachings and living in love. Paul declared, "The hour has come for you to wake from sleep. For salvation is nearer to us now than when we first believed. The night is far gone; the day is at hand. So then let us cast off the works of darkness and put on the armor of light" (Rom. 13:11–12).

Second, we are greatly encouraged to *witness boldly to the gospel of Christ*. Jesus proclaimed, "All authority in heaven and on earth has been given to me. Go therefore and make disciples of all nations, baptizing them in the name of the Father and of the Son and of the Holy Spirit" (Matt. 28:18–19). Jesus soon returns to judge the living and the dead, so just as now is the only time of salvation, now is also the time of urgent need for the spreading of the gospel.

Third, our hope of heaven encourages us to *labor for the building up of the church and the advancement of the kingdom of Christ*. Jesus urges us to "seek first the kingdom of God" (Matt. 6:33). Speaking of his return, Jesus said, "Blessed is that servant whom his master will find [serving] when he comes" (Luke 12:43).

Fourth, we are called by Christ to *love one another as he has loved us*. Our fellow believers are our brothers and sisters with whom we will live in the Father's house forever. The relationships we forge now in Christian worship, fellowship, and service will literally last forever. And the most valuable thing that you and I will ever behold before seeing Jesus in glory is one another: precious saints purchased with the blood of Christ.

Finally, Jesus' teaching provides an imperative to *come to Christ in saving faith*. The comfort of which Jesus spoke is only for those who have believed in him. Entry into the Father's house is only for those for whom Jesus has been preparing rooms. Being a realist means admitting that just as Jesus said he must depart, every one of us must also depart this life and this world. Do you have a loving home where you are going? Receive the Lord Jesus Christ as your Savior now, and he will prepare a place for you in the Father's house, and when he returns in his glory, he will receive you, together with all the saints, into his never-ending fellowship of love.[13]

---

13. These concluding points are paraphrased from Keddie, *John*, 2:90–91.

91

I Am the Way, the Truth, and the Life

John 14:4—6

Jesus said to him, "I am the way, and the truth, and the life. No one comes to the Father except through me." (John 14:6)

Christians are sometimes dismayed by the world's opposition to our gospel. For this reason, many Christians emphasize having a nonoffensive attitude toward unbelievers and seek to use expressions that avoid giving offense. So long as we do not compromise our message or biblical standards of behavior, it is proper for believers to show such care in their dealings with non-Christians. Yet as we do this, we will soon find that the gospel's real offense is one that we cannot easily avoid. Christianity's true offense is none other than Christ himself. This is especially true when we consider Jesus' exclusive claims as the one Lord and only Savior of mankind.

One modern critic has spouted contempt for Christianity's exclusivity in these words: "Christianity is a contentious faith which requires an all-or-nothing commitment to Jesus as the one and only incarnation of the Son of God." We can endorse this author's assessment, though not perhaps all that he goes on to say: "[Christians are] uncompromising, ornery, militant, rigorous, imperious and invincibly self-righteous."[1] This is not a recent opinion of our faith: Philip Ryken asserts that "for the past 2,000 years, Christianity's claims about the unique truth of Jesus Christ have aroused no end of opposition from Jews, pagans, Muslims, Communists, humanists, and atheists."[2]

We might think this opposition to have lessened with the advent of postmodernity, given its emphasis on tolerance. Instead, the opposite has happened. Postmodern unbelievers grant tolerance to every religion *except* Christianity, precisely because the gospel is seen as the ultimate intolerant creed. The gospel's message that only Jesus can save offends postmodernity's relativist mantra, since Christians insist that all other religions are false and any other route to God is a dead end. Objections to these doctrines have marked the world's hatred for Jesus ever since he spoke the words that John's Gospel continues to proclaim today: "I am the way, and the truth, and the life" (John 14:6).

Uncompromising Exclusivity

This is the sixth of Jesus' seven famous "I am" sayings, each of which is radically exclusive in setting Jesus apart as the one and only Savior. In each of these statements, Jesus uses the word *the* rather than *a*. He is *"the* bread of life" (John 6:35), not *a* bread of life: that is, Jesus is the one and only source of satisfaction for the hunger of our souls. Likewise, Jesus is *"the* light of the world" (8:12), the only guide who can lead mankind out of darkness into the light of God. Jesus said, "I am the door" (10:7), since through him alone we can enter the fold of God, and "I am the good shepherd" (10:11), who alone lays down his life for the sheep. To these, Jesus added the remarkable statement, "I am the resurrection and the life" (11:25), claiming to be the Conqueror even of death—a claim that he backed up by raising Lazarus from the grave (11:43–44). Each of these statements is radically exclusive, asserting that none but Jesus can save us from sin, bring us to God, and grant us eternal life.

This same focus on the person of Jesus is seen all through this portion of John's Gospel, which centers on four questions asked by the disciples, each

1. Alan Watts, *Beyond Theology* (New York: World Publishing, 1967), xii.
2. Philip Graham Ryken, *Is Jesus the Only Way?* (Wheaton, IL: Crossway, 1999), 11.

of which Jesus answered by directing them to himself. Peter asked, "Lord, where are you going?" (John 13:36). Thomas continued, "How can we know the way?" (14:5). Philip added, "Lord, show us the Father" (14:8), and Judas (not the betrayer) asked, "Lord, how is it that you will manifest yourself to us, and not to the world?" (14:22). These are slightly different questions, and each receives a slightly different answer. But each of the answers is a variant on John 14:6: "I am the way, and the truth, and the life."

Despite the world's disdain for John 14:6, the content of this saying tells us why we must not surrender Christ's exclusive claims, however offensive they may be. For not only is John 14:6 true, but it offers the only real answer to the great needs of the world. Man's tragic plight is that we are alienated from God, ignorant of truth, and condemned to both physical and spiritual death. Jesus has come as the answer to sin's dreadful predicament. He is the way for sinners to be reconciled to God, the truth that God has revealed to correct our ignorance, and the life that we need to regenerate us from the power of death.

THE WAY: RECONCILIATION

There is an obvious priority to the first of Jesus' descriptions. While Jesus is the way, the truth, and the life, the context focuses on Jesus as the way. We can see this in the dialogue, going back to John 13:33. Jesus informed the disciples that he would soon depart, adding, "Where I am going you cannot come." This was disturbing to the disciples, so Peter demanded, "Lord, where are you going?" Jesus answered, "Where I am going you cannot follow me now, but you will follow afterward" (13:36). Jesus was referring to his return to the glory of heaven, and perhaps also to the cross that he would bear on the way. But Peter was not settled, insisting that he would follow Jesus even to death (13:37). This statement prompted Jesus' prophecy of Peter's three denials that very evening. Then, to comfort the disciples, Jesus told them that he was going to his "Father's house" to prepare a place for them and that he would return to get them (14:1–3). He concluded in verse 4, "And you know the way to where I am going." This time it was Thomas who answered: "Lord, we do not know where you are going. How can we know the way?" (14:5). He meant that if one does not know the destination, he cannot know the way there. To clarify his meaning that the disciples' relationship to himself was the way of which he spoke, Jesus said, "I am the way, and the truth, and the life. No one comes to the Father except through me" (14:6).

Like Thomas, if we are to understand what Jesus means, we have to know the destination to which he was referring. Verse 6 makes it clear that Jesus is speaking of God the Father and his glorious presence in heaven. That is where Jesus was going, and that is where we are to follow him. But we need also to know where we are. A *way* is the path between a starting point and an ending point. So, spiritually speaking, where does man start? In what condition does man find himself in his search for God? According to the Bible, mankind is utterly ruined. We are condemned before God for the guilt of our sin. Paul writes, "All have sinned and fall short of the glory of God" (Rom. 3:23), and are thus barred from God's holy presence and his blessing. Our need is to be reconciled to him.

So bad is our condition that there is nothing we can do to reconcile ourselves to God. Even if we should turn a new leaf and begin leading a morally upright life, we still have the guilt of our previous sins to pay for. Moreover, we are not only condemned in sin, but utterly corrupted by sin. Therefore, we are not able to perform an adequate moral reformation. In the light of the Bible's teaching of God's unrelenting justice, our past haunts us, our present confounds us, and our future dismays us. For this reason, not only is it true that sinful mankind cannot come to God, but sinful mankind does not even want to come to God. Just as Adam and Eve clothed their shame with fig leaves and fled from God in the garden, we are alienated not only by God's justice but by our own God-loathing consciences.

We see now where the true offense of Jesus' gospel lies. Christianity scandalizes because the gospel declares that man's alienation from God is humanly hopeless because of sin. The gospel says that we could be reconciled only if God sent a Savior to die for our sin. Only Jesus, as God's sinless Son, could atone for sin through his death. His way of salvation requires us to confess our sin, humble ourselves seeking pardon, and surrender our claims to self-rule: the very acts that sinful mankind refuses to do. Man hates the message that he cannot save himself! Man would come to God, but not by this way! Jesus offers only a salvation from sin, and a world that will not confess its sin takes offense in him and refuses reconciliation with the God who sent him.

Yet it remains good news that Jesus came from heaven to earth in order to reconcile sinners to God. Jesus said that he was returning to his Father's house, and this makes us wonder why God's Son departed the glory of heaven to live in our world. The answer is given in all the Gospels, which record Jesus' explanation for why he came. Luke records: "The Son of Man came to seek and to save the lost" (Luke 19:10). In Matthew, Jesus explained: "The Son of Man came not to be served but to serve, and to give his life as a ransom for many" (Matt. 20:28). John's Gospel records another of Jesus' explanations: "I came that they may have life and have it abundantly" (John 10:10).

Thus, when Jesus said that he is "the way," he meant that sinners may come to God only through the ministry of reconciliation for which he came. Jesus is the way because God in his grace has provided for sinners to be justified in his sight through faith in his Son. "All have sinned and fall short of the glory of God," Paul laments. But the good news is that we may be "justified by [God's] grace as a gift, through the redemption that is in Christ Jesus" (Rom. 3:23–24).

Skip Ryan tells of having served on a special project for the United States Department of State. The working group to which he was assigned once held a briefing at the White House. The meeting took place in the Roosevelt Room, a conference room across the hall from the Oval Office. After the meeting, the State Department official in charge asked whether Ryan would like to see the Oval Office, the official working place of the President of the United States, since the President was out of town. Ryan recalls two things about that visit. The first was the awe he felt at being in such a place. The second was that he could not possibly have entered the Oval Office unless he was taken there by someone authorized to bring him.[3]

If that is true of the office of the President of the United States, how much more true is it of the glorious presence of almighty God in heaven? People who would never think to enter the White House simply assume that they will go to heaven after they die. But heaven is far more restricted than any high-security location here on earth. Heaven is guarded by mighty angels armed with swords of divine power (Gen. 3:24). Entry into heaven is governed by the perfect and unyielding justice of God's holy law. How much more true of heaven are the words that Psalm 24 spoke about God's temple in Jerusalem:

3. Joseph "Skip" Ryan, *That You May Believe* (Wheaton, IL: Crossway, 2003), 301–2.

Who shall ascend the hill of the LORD?
    And who shall stand in his holy place?
He who has clean hands and a pure heart,
    who does not lift up his soul to what is false
    and does not swear deceitfully.
He will receive blessing from the LORD
    and righteousness from the God of his salvation. (Ps. 24:3–5)

To enter heaven and approach God on your own rights requires you to present hands that have never sinned, a heart that has never known impure thoughts, and lips that have never spoken falsely. None, of course, can meet this holy standard. For us, therefore, there must be someone authorized to bring us into heaven, and it was for this that Jesus came: he said, "I am the way" (John 14:6). It is through his perfect life and atoning death that we may "receive blessing from the LORD and righteousness from the God of his salvation" (Ps. 24:5).

THE TRUTH: REVELATION

The second and third statements that Jesus made about himself in John 14:6 are rightly seen as subordinate to the first. Jesus is first the way, and coordinated with this is his claim to be the truth and the life. Some scholars have therefore wanted to translate the verse to read, "I am the true and living way." But that is not what Jesus said. He said that he is the way, and that he is the truth and the life.

Man needs the revelation of truth because it was through ignorance and lies that we first fell into sin. Our first parents did not merely happen to sin, but they were led into sin by Satan. The Serpent of the garden beguiled Eve by asking, "Did God actually say, 'You shall not eat of any tree in the garden'?" (Gen. 3:1). God had *not* said that: they could eat of every tree in the garden except one, the Tree of the Knowledge of Good and Evil (2:16–17). Satan's lie suggested that God's commands are not for our good and that the way for mankind to experience freedom and blessing is by breaking God's commands. This lie has marked the way of sin ever since.

A great part of mankind's plight in sin is ignorance of God and blindness to God's truth. Paul explained, "They are darkened in their understanding,

207

alienated from the life of God because of the ignorance that is in them, due to their hardness of heart" (Eph. 4:18). In order for us to be saved, we must therefore be enlightened by the revelation of God's truth, the fullest expression of which comes through Jesus Christ.

Most specifically, Jesus is the truth "because he embodies the supreme revelation of God—he himself 'narrates' God (1:18), says and does exclusively what the Father gives him to say and do,"[4] and is himself one with God the Father as his only begotten Son. Jesus is the way to God not only by what he did for lost mankind, dying on the cross for our sins, but also in revealing the truth of God so that we might believe and come to God through faith in him.

God had been revealing the truth about himself and his salvation before the coming of Christ. But Jesus is *the* truth in that all that God ever revealed points to Jesus and comes into focus in him. D. A. Carson writes, "The test of whether or not Jews in Jesus' day, and in John's day, *really* knew God through the revelation that had already been disclosed, lay in their response to the supreme revelation from the Father, Jesus Christ himself."[5] This is why the writer of Hebrews said that God had previously spoken in many ways through the prophets, "but in these last days he has spoken to us by his Son" (Heb. 1:1–2). All that God ever revealed comes into clarity, focus, and ultimate truth in the coming of his Son, Jesus Christ.

We must expand this principle beyond the realm of mere religious knowledge, for when Jesus said that he is "the truth," he spoke of all truth. Even when men and women know things and those things are true, unless this knowledge is held through faith in Christ, it is not known truly. Truth itself is known falsely if opposed to Jesus. It is out of accord with its true purpose and meaning. The great model of this falseness is Satan, who knows many truths but knows none of them truly. "There is no truth in him" (John 8:44), Jesus said about Satan, for despite his great genius and vast knowledge, in his rebellion to God and his Son there is no truth.

This reality explains so much of the darkness and ignorance of our well-educated times. For all of mankind's increasing knowledge, unless it is held in obedience to him who is the truth, there can be only ignorance, folly, and darkness. Ultimately, as A. W. Pink wrote, "Truth is not found in a system

---

4. D. A. Carson, *The Gospel of John* (Grand Rapids: Eerdmans, 1991), 491.
5. Ibid.

of philosophy, but in a Person—Christ is 'the truth': He reveals God and exposes man. In Him are hid 'all the treasures of wisdom and knowledge' (Col. 2:3)."[6]

The obvious application of this teaching is that Christians must therefore be students of Jesus, which means that we must be devoted in study of his Word in the Bible. "Heaven and earth will pass away," Jesus said, "but my words will not pass away" (Matt. 24:35). "If you abide in my word, you are truly my disciples," he taught, "and you will know the truth, and the truth will set you free" (John 8:31–32). In the light of heaven, Christians will wish they had read their Bibles more frequently and looked at newspapers or the Internet less often. How much more true will this be of unbelieving men and women who neglected him who is the truth and thus entered into eternity unsaved and unforgiven by God.

THE LIFE: REGENERATION

Jesus' third claim is that he is "the life" (John 14:6). "The wages of sin is death" (Rom. 6:23), and man in sin has fallen under death's power and curse. Apart from Christ we are spiritually dead (Eph. 2:1–3), unable to do anything spiritually for our salvation, so that life increasingly becomes a living death, without satisfaction or hope. But Jesus came "that they may have life and have it abundantly" (John 10:10). John said of him at the beginning of his Gospel: "In him was life, and the life was the light of men" (1:4).

Jesus is the source of eternal life for those who believe and follow him. It would not have been enough for Jesus as the way to gain our reconciliation with God, tearing down the veil by his death on the cross for our sins. It likewise would not be enough for Christ the truth to grant us a revelation of God. We would yet remain dead, morally corrupt, and spiritually disabled, so that we would never be able to follow in the way that he has made or believe the truth that he has revealed. Jesus made this known to the Pharisee Nicodemus, saying, "Unless one is born again . . . , he cannot enter the kingdom of God" (John 3:3, 5). In order to be saved, we must be not only forgiven but also regenerated. We must be made alive spiritually, so that we believe and are made willing and able to follow after Jesus.

6. Arthur W. Pink, *Exposition of the Gospel of John* (Grand Rapids: Zondervan, 1975), 763.

Jesus is the source of the life that we need, and he conveys his power of life through his Word. Thus he called to dead Lazarus, who had been four days in the grave, "Lazarus, come out," and "the man who had died came out" (John 11:43–44). All who are saved come to Jesus by the power of life in his call through the gospel. And those who come to Jesus as the way of salvation and believe him as the Revealer of God's truth receive life in him. His is the way of truth that brings life. Jesus said, "Whoever hears my word and believes him who sent me has eternal life" (5:24). For "whoever believes in the Son has eternal life; whoever does not obey the Son shall not see life, but the wrath of God remains on him" (3:36).

ONLY JESUS

Jesus' answer to Thomas's question was, according to James Montgomery Boice, "probably the most exclusive statement ever made by anyone."[7] Jesus' claims so assume deity that we must either reject Jesus or worship him as Savior and Lord. Just in case we missed his radical claim to be the exclusive and only Savior, Jesus added, "No one comes to the Father except through me."

Little wonder that this Jesus has aroused such opposition and hatred from the world. How bold were these words on the eve of the cross! Leon Morris comments: "'I am the Way,' said one who would shortly hang impotent on a cross. 'I am the Truth,' when the lies of evil people were about to enjoy a spectacular triumph. 'I am the Life,' when within a matter of hours his corpse would be placed in a tomb."[8] How could Jesus speak so boldly when he knew what was about to happen? The answer is that Jesus also knew that he would rise from the grave, that his truth would be proclaimed with power across the world, so that multitudes who believed and followed—in the earliest times they were called followers of "the Way" (Acts 19:9, 23)— would be reconciled to God and enter into glory with him. As the bearer of resurrection life, Jesus can give eternal life to those under death's power. As the incarnate truth, Jesus can reveal the truth amid the errors and lies of the world. And as the only way to the Father, Jesus has the right to demand our

7. James Montgomery Boice, *The Gospel of John*, 5 vols. (Grand Rapids: Baker, 1999), 4:1076.
8. Leon Morris, *The Gospel according to John*, rev. ed., New International Commentary on the New Testament (Grand Rapids: Eerdmans, 1995), 570.

faith and exclusive devotion, as our only Savior and Lord. No wonder the apostle Paul stated of salvation that "no one can lay a foundation other than that which is laid, which is Jesus Christ" (1 Cor. 3:11). For as Peter declared, "there is salvation in no one else, for there is no other name under heaven given among men by which we must be saved" (Acts 4:12).

Since only Jesus is the way, the truth, and the life, he calls us to faith in himself. Notice that when Thomas asked the way to the Father, Jesus did not hand him directions, or point out a path of good works or spiritual achievements that must be followed. He directed Thomas, and us, to himself. "I am," he declared, and we are not saved by following a way, believing a truth, or seeking after life. We are saved by Jesus, and he is the way, the truth, and the life. We therefore do not need to discover or make a way for ourselves, but we need to trust in Jesus and follow him. We do not need to master all truth, but we need to know Jesus and then grow in his truth. We do not need to achieve the life that we desire, but we need to receive Jesus and the life that he gives.

The question may be asked what kind of life we will have if we simply trust in Jesus. The answer is that as he is the way, he will lead us to the Father and we will gain a life of love as dear children. As Jesus is the truth, he will teach us the wisdom of salvation so that our lives are freed from the darkness of ignorance and folly. As he is the life, he will grant us entry into the courts of heaven and we will know an increasing measure of life as we draw nearer to him. Apart from Jesus, the world offers many things, but they are all godless, darkened, and deadly. "I am the way, and the truth, and the life," Jesus said (John 14:6). He presents himself to us, demanding no achievements, not waiting for our improvement, but calling us simply to receive him in trusting faith, and ready to give to us by grace all that he has and all that he is. We will never receive a better offer, and we will never have a better time to receive Jesus than now.

92

WHOEVER HAS SEEN ME

John 14:7–11

"Whoever has seen me has seen the Father. How can you say,
'Show us the Father'?" (John 14:9)

ost Christians have known the feeling expressed by Philip's plea, "Lord, show us the Father" (John 14:8). For there are times when God seems distant from us, and our hearts desire a tangible sign of God's presence and reality. Jesus' disciples were confused and distressed about Jesus' impending departure, so Philip asked Jesus for an experience that would make their belief in God real. Bruce Milne writes, "His plea articulates the longing of the heart of humanity across all the ages to see and to know the living God."[1]

Not only does this scene connect with experiences that many of us have had, it more generally addresses the situation of all Christians in this current age. Jesus was preparing his disciples for that time when he would no longer be physically with them, after his death, resurrection, and ascension into heaven. This is the very time in which we experience our entire Christian lives. We have come to faith in Christ through God's Word, so we love and

---

1. Bruce Milne, *The Message of John: Here Is Your King!* (Downers Grove, IL: InterVarsity Press, 1993), 213.

follow him. Yet not only have we never seen God, but we have never seen Jesus or heard his human voice in our ears. God the Father and Jesus in heaven *are* distant from us, so we need a way to experience their presence. This is the great subject of John chapters 14–16, in which Jesus tells of his provision precisely for our situation today.

SHOW US THE FATHER!

Philip's question not only was prompted by the occasion, but also was provoked by Jesus. Having told the disciples that he was going to the Father's house to prepare a place for them, Jesus wanted to further awaken their knowledge of the Father. He told them, therefore, "If you had known me, you would have known my Father also" (John 14:7). The disciples did know Jesus, of course, having spent three years in his company. Yet their poor understanding of the Father showed their inadequate grasp of Jesus himself. Leon Morris explains: "They had known him well enough to leave their homes and friends and livelihood to follow him wherever he went. But they did not know him in his full significance."[2]

The events that were about to transpire would change this situation. Jesus thus added, "From now on you do know him and have seen him" (John 14:7). His expression "from now on" indicates that the events that were about to take place would change the situation. Through Jesus' death, resurrection, ascension into heaven, and outpouring of the Holy Spirit at Pentecost, the disciples would gain a deep and profound knowledge of God. In anticipation of these certain events, Jesus said, "You . . . have seen [the Father]" (14:7).

However certain this future knowledge was, Philip showed that it had not yet happened, pleading, "Lord, show us the Father, and it is enough for us" (John 14:8). Philip was evidently thinking about Old Testament saints who had been granted an immediate revelation of God's being. Moses had asked God, "Please show me your glory" (Ex. 33:18). God replied, "I will make all my goodness pass before you and will proclaim before you my name 'The LORD'" (33:19). Elijah was also granted divine theophanies. Exhausted from his confrontation with the false prophets and wicked Ahab and Jezebel, Elijah had fled to Mount Sinai, probably seeking the experience of God's

---

2. Leon Morris, *The Gospel according to John*, rev. ed., New International Commentary on the New Testament (Grand Rapids: Eerdmans, 1995), 570.

nearness. God then shook the mountain with a great wind, an earthquake, and a raging fire (1 Kings 19:11).

Probably with events such as these in mind, Philip expressed his belief that if the disciples could only experience an audiovisual divine display, it would be "enough for us" (John 14:8). Such a confirming experience would pull the disciples through whatever ordeal lay ahead of them, Philip reasoned, just as so many Christians today seek spiritual experiences to propel them through the travails of faith and life.

"Seeing" Jesus

Another way to understand Philip is to realize the connection he was making between *seeing* and *believing*. His whole point was that if the disciples could see the Father, then they would be able to believe in him. Jesus challenged this assertion by asking, "Have I been with you so long, and you still do not know me, Philip?" (John 14:9). There was probably a bit of exasperation in Jesus' statement, marveling, "Can you really not understand these things, having known me for so long?" But Jesus was also making an important point. Philip said that he could believe if only his eyes could take in a visual display of the Father. But Philip had seen Jesus in this way for roughly three years, yet he had not thereby come to understand him and fully believe. Jesus thus refutes the idea that seeing is believing, at least when it comes to the kind of seeing that Philip had in mind.

It is helpful, in this respect, to realize that the Greek language of the New Testament employs a number of different words for *seeing*. We can compare these words by observing how they are all used in a later account in John's Gospel, the story of Peter and John's inspection of the empty tomb after Jesus' resurrection.

The most basic word for *seeing* is *blepo*, meaning "a visual apprehension of physical objects." This word is used when we are told that John "saw the linen cloths" (John 20:5) in the empty tomb. Then a second word for *seeing* is used when Peter arrives at the tomb. Pushing in after John, Peter "saw the linen cloths lying there" (20:6). Here the Greek word is *theoreo*, from which we derive our word *theory* or *theorize*. Peter not only saw the cloths, but marveled over them and wondered what they meant. How could Jesus' body be gone, and why were the graveclothes still in the tomb? Later that evening, Jesus appeared in the room where the disciples were staying, showing them his hands and side. We read that "the disciples were glad when they saw the Lord" (20:20). Here, the Greek word is a form of *horao*, which means "to see with comprehension." The disciples used this word in speaking to Thomas when he later arrived, telling of their faith in Jesus: "We have seen the Lord" (20:25).

The distinction between these words for *seeing* becomes important for understanding Jesus' answer to Philip's request to see the Father: Jesus replied, "Whoever has seen me has seen the Father" (John 14:9). The word for *seen* here is a form of *horao*: Jesus means that anyone who has *comprehended* or *understood* him has also *understood* the Father. Philip asked for a vision, using the verb *deiknumi*, signifying a demonstration of God. All this time, Jesus had been providing the demonstration that Philip sought! If Philip had understood Jesus, he would have comprehended the Father in Christ.[3]

Jesus' answer to Philip is a most significant statement concerning the Christian faith: "Whoever has seen me has seen the Father" (John 14:9). This is the very heart of our belief, that Jesus Christ came to this world to reveal God to mankind: to show us in his life and ministry what God is like and to reveal to us by his Gospel what God intends for our salvation. This teaching is so important that John cited it in the prologue to his Gospel: "No one has ever seen God; the only God, who is at the Father's side, he has made him known" (1:18). This truth is one of the most important elements of our witness to others about Christ: in proclaiming Jesus, we must explain that he is the One who came from heaven to show us God.

Jesus might have shown us God in a number of ways, two of which are particularly noteworthy. One is by demonstration. If you know someone personally and have spent time with that person, then you are able to depict him or her to others. I had an experience of this a few years after my father died. My uncle, his only brother, was visiting my mother on an occasion when I was with her. As the conversation progressed, I found that I could not pull myself from his presence. Why? Because, as my father's brother, he looked like my dad and his voice sounded like the voice I had not heard since my father's death. The way he stood and his mannerisms were precisely

---

3. These paragraphs are drawn from James Montgomery Boice, *The Gospel of John*, 5 vols. (Grand Rapids: Baker, 1999), 1:1089–90.

those of my father. Seeing him, it was as though I were looking at my dearly missed dad, and the experience was overwhelming.

In a similar way, Jesus represented God the Father to mankind. Because of our alienation from God in sin and because of our own idolatrous tendency to erect false images of God, our race had lost contact with our Maker. But Jesus came into the world, and his posture, his tone of voice, his attitude, and his reaction to events were those of God. Jesus was familiar with God the Father, having come from the presence of God's glory in heaven. Indeed, Jesus is God's own Son, so he possesses all the family traits and mannerisms. Each of us has a desperate need to know God, and John 14:9 makes the vitally important statement that Jesus reveals God the Father.

To see Jesus and comprehend his mind and heart, his character and his habits, is to comprehend God. God is always and only Christlike, so that the more we know of Christ, the more we know of God. This revelation of God is the impetus to our faith, for to comprehend God in Christ is to trust and adore him. "Whoever has seen me," Jesus declares, "has seen the Father." William Barclay exclaims, "Jesus is the revelation of God, and that revelation leaves the mind of man staggered and amazed into wonder, love, and praise."[4]

It is not enough, however, to state that Jesus represents God because of his intimate familiarity with the Father. Jesus grounds his revelation of the Father more deeply, speaking of the mutual indwelling of the Father's being with his own being. Jesus said, "How can you say, 'Show us the Father'? Do you not believe that I am in the Father and the Father is in me?" (John 14:9–10). Not only does Jesus show us what the Father is *like*, but Jesus shows us the Father, since the Father is *in him*. While Father and Son are distinct persons, they possess a unity of being so that Jesus *reveals* God because he *is* God. Jesus reveals the Father because the Father is in him, as they not only collaborate in their works but also share the interpenetration of their being. George Hutcheson writes, "The true ground of our knowing the Father in the Son is his unity in essence with the Father."[5] Jesus has come to earth as more than a divine envoy, a servant who brings a message from God. Were he only a messenger, Jesus would never say that by seeing him we see the Father. Instead, the Father has come to us in his Son, that

---

4. William Barclay, *The Gospel of John*, 2 vols. (Philadelphia: Westminster, 1975), 2:187.

5. George Hutcheson, *Exposition of the Gospel of John* (Lafayette, IN: Sovereign Grace Publishers, 2001), 299.

we might know him who cannot be seen and be reconciled to him through faith in Jesus Christ.

When it comes to knowing God, Jesus is like the Rosetta Stone. This was part of a second-century B.C. Egyptian monument discovered during Napoleon's Nile campaign in 1799. Its value comes from being inscribed with a text in three languages, including hieroglyphic and Greek. Given the Greek translation of the ancient hieroglyphic, scholars were able to greatly advance their understanding of the ancient Egyptian language, which would otherwise have remained a mystery to them.

Likewise, God the Father would remain a mystery to us unless Jesus had come. We had learned God's basic character and requirements in the Old Testament. But we could not see God and have a personal knowledge of him until Jesus came. Just as linguists looked at the Greek on the Rosetta Stone and were able to read the hieroglyphic, so also we see Jesus and are able to interpret God the Father.

Therefore, any idea of God that does not square with the Bible's portrait of Jesus is false. Likewise, any questions you have of God are answered by seeing Jesus. You may wonder whether God is compassionate. Look at Jesus touching the mottled arm of a leper who had called to him for mercy, healing him with tenderness and love (Luke 5:13). You may wonder whether God is able to handle your problems. Look then at Jesus standing amid the storm, calming the winds and the waves with his mere voice (Matt. 8:26). You may doubt that God could ever forgive you and receive you back when you repent. Then listen as Jesus cries out from the cross, seeking mercy for the very men who had crucified him, "Father, forgive them, for they know not what they do" (Luke 23:34). God's attitude to children is seen when Jesus receives them for blessing (Matt. 19:14). God's grief over death is revealed in Jesus' weeping at the tomb of his friend Lazarus (John 11:35). God's desire for our salvation is displayed in Jesus' gospel call: "Come to me, all who labor and are heavy laden, and I will give you rest" (Matt. 11:28). "Whoever has seen me," Jesus declares, "has seen the Father" (John 14:9).

WHAT IS ENOUGH?

We hear Jesus' claim and we return to Philip's question: "Lord, show us the Father, and it is enough for us" (John 14:8). Philip wanted a display of divine power. Jesus' answer confronts this thinking: a sensory experience of the divine presence is not what we need. It is not in such demonstrations that we perceive God and are thus enabled to face our challenges. This was God's message to Elijah, when that great prophet came speeding to Mount Sinai, wearied and frightened from his battles with wicked Ahab and Jezebel, and needing reassurance of God's presence. God put Elijah on the mountain and gave him what he wanted: demonstrations of power. But the prophet learned that the Lord was not in them:

> The LORD passed by, and a great and strong wind tore the mountains and broke in pieces the rocks before the LORD, but the LORD was not in the wind. And after the wind an earthquake, but the LORD was not in the earthquake. And after the earthquake a fire, but the LORD was not in the fire. And after the fire the sound of a low whisper. (1 Kings 19:11–12)

Where did Elijah "see" God? The Lord was in the "low whisper": the quiet revelation of his Word. How, then, do we overcome our sense of God's distance? Where do we turn to see God and gain strength and hope? The answer is in God's Word, by understanding Jesus Christ. We will see God in the Bible, open on our laps, often in a quiet place, as we study his Son Jesus Christ. If we want to experience power to tear down strongholds, Paul says that it comes from God's Word, which will "destroy arguments and every lofty opinion raised against the knowledge of God" (2 Cor. 10:5). If we want the fire of God to burn in us, let us remember the words of the downcast disciples whom Jesus had taught on the road to Emmaus: afterward they said, "Did not our hearts burn within us . . . while he opened to us the Scriptures?" (Luke 24:32). While spectacular displays and spiritual highs are not enough to carry us through our trials, the knowledge of God through Jesus Christ as he is comprehended in the Scriptures is more than enough for us.

Does this suggest a rationalistic spirituality? The answer is no, for the reason that Jesus went on to give later in this chapter. "The Helper, the Holy Spirit, whom the Father will send in my name," Jesus said, "he will teach you all things" (John 14:26). It is the third member of the Trinity, whom the Father and Son send, who gives the Word of God power in our lives: by his presence, the Father and Son live in us as well. True spirituality, then, is biblical faith, seeking diligently to know and understand Jesus, in this way seeing God, and receiving the Spirit's power to live in accordance with the teaching of God's Word.

In his second epistle, the apostle Peter reminded us of the divine displays that he had received. Peter refers to being present at the Mount of Transfiguration, where "the voice was borne to him by the Majestic Glory," and "we ourselves heard this very voice borne from heaven, for we were with him on the holy mountain" (2 Peter 1:17–18). Did Peter then say that we need the same: an audiovisual display of divine glory, and that will be enough for us? To the contrary; he continues: "We have something more sure, the prophetic word, to which you will do well to pay attention as to a lamp shining in a dark place, until the day dawns and the morning star rises in your hearts" (1:19). God's Word is enough for us, Peter says, and it will make God present and real to us, if we will see and understand Jesus in the Bible. For, Jesus declared, "whoever has seen me has seen the Father" (John 14:9).

REASONS TO BELIEVE

Jesus concludes his thought with two reasons to believe, which together supply our calling as his witnesses in the world. The first is the compelling authority of his Word: "The words that I say to you I do not speak on my own authority, but the Father who dwells in me does his works" (John 14:10). Jesus does not mean that he is like a ventriloquist's dummy, with strings attached to his mouth. Rather, because of his obedience to the Father and the unity of being in the Godhead, when Jesus speaks it is God who is acting in and through his Son. Those who have believed on Jesus know this, since it was by God's power in Christ's Word that we came to new life and saving faith. The way that we press on in faith, knowing that God is near to us, is to hear Christ's voice and to know it as the truth of God.

Christ's Word is and should be enough for our faith, Jesus says. But if we think we need more, he points us to his works: "Believe me that I am in the Father and the Father is in me, or else believe on account of the works themselves" (John 14:11). We think immediately of Jesus' miracles, which he often pointed to as proof of his identity (cf. 5:36). But we can more fully grasp Jesus' meaning here by remembering his answer to John the Baptist, when the great forerunner was tempted to doubt during his dark days in prison. Messengers came from John, inquiring: "Are you the one who is to come, or shall we look for another?" (Matt. 11:3). Jesus answered, "Go and tell John what you hear and see: the blind receive their sight and the lame walk, lepers are cleansed and the deaf hear, and the dead are raised up, and the poor have good news preached to them. And blessed is the one who is not offended by me" (11:4–6).

If Jesus of Nazareth was not the Savior sent from God, then there will never be any Savior. But Jesus is the Savior. He validated his coming by fulfilling all that was foretold of him in the prophecies, and he displayed in his words and deeds the work of God for the salvation of men. His dual testimony—his words and his works—leaves us without excuse if we remain in unbelief: there is literally nothing that God can do for our salvation if we will not believe in his Son through his teaching and his saving deeds.

These reasons to believe reveal to us how we are to serve as Christ's witnesses today. Jesus said that those who see him see God. So what do we need to show the world today, but Jesus as he is revealed in the Scriptures? What good do we do the world if we give money, help, and encouragement but do not show them Jesus? The world today is asking, "Where is God?" By proclaiming Christ's Word and doing his work— both of them together as one witness—we provide not only what the world really needs but what will truly be enough for all who believe. Our calling is to show them Jesus and through Jesus to bring them to a knowledge of God in saving faith.

ENOUGH FOR US

It was enough for Elijah to hear God's Word in the quiet voice on the mountain, and the prophet went down from the mountain back into the world to do God's work. It will also be enough for us to see and comprehend Christ through faith in his Word: to feed on his promises, bow our heads before his commands, and receive his saving benediction on our hearts. Yet how easy it is to live without comprehension of Jesus, just as the earlier disciples did: "Have I been with you so long, and you still do not know me?" Jesus might lament of us (John 14:9). Let us ensure that we do know him, that we hear his call, that we comprehend what he has revealed to us about the Father, most especially his grace for our salvation through so costly a gift as his own Son.

"Show us the Father," our hearts cry with Philip. In answering, Jesus says, "Whoever has seen me has seen the Father" (John 14:9). This means that the key to the Christian life—to endurance in faith and growth in grace—is looking always to Jesus and in him to see God displayed. We will never advance from needing to be with Jesus, and we will never graduate from looking at him for the answer. We will never grow out of needing the life and power that only he can give. Jesus is himself God's provision for us, through the Holy Scriptures, that we might feel the presence and know the reality of God in our lives. In this way, Jesus really is enough for us.

93

GREATER WORKS THAN THESE

John 14:12

*"Truly, truly, I say to you, whoever believes in me will also do
the works that I do; and greater works than these will he do,
because I am going to the Father." (John 14:12)*

Usually, if something seems too good to be true, it is. The surefire real estate deal that will net large profits without risk usually isn't. The weight-loss pill that promises lost pounds without effort usually doesn't deliver, despite the persuasive before-and-after testimonies. But there are too-good-to-be-true promises in the Bible that really are true, for their testimonial comes from Jesus Christ. Indeed, when it comes to the Christian faith, the problem is that we often find it too hard to believe the promises that are indeed true because they are given by the Son of God.

In his last meeting with the disciples before his arrest and crucifixion, Jesus gave them one of his most remarkable promises. "Truly, truly, I say to you," he declared, "whoever believes in me will also do the works that I do; and greater works than these will he do" (John 14:12). This would rightly seem too good to be true, were it not for the explanation that Jesus gave, an explanation that changes everything in the Christian life: "because I am going to the Father" (14:12).

What Kind of Work Will We Do?

Jesus' promise concerning the "greater works" that we will do raises immediate questions. The most significant question concerns the nature of these works.

First, we must ask whether Jesus was specifically referring to his miracles. Jesus sometimes spoke of his "works" in a way that pointed to the miracles (see John 5:36). For this reason, some scholars believe that the works that Jesus said the disciples would do after his resurrection are miracles. A. W. Pink takes this view: "The 'works' of which Christ here spake were His *miraculous* works . . . , works to which He appealed as proofs of His Divine person and mission."[1]

There are some problems with this view, however. The main problem is that if Jesus was referring to his miracles, then this promise did not come true. It is true that the disciples, as Jesus' apostles, performed many great miracles. So it might be said that they did the miracles that Jesus did. But it is not possible to say that their miracles were greater than Jesus' miracles. "Greater works than these will he do," Jesus said of the one who believes in him. But the book of Acts records no miracles performed by the apostles that were greater than Jesus' greatest miracles, including his feeding of the five thousand and the raising of Lazarus from the grave.

More significant is the problem that believers in Christ do not perform miracles today. We believe that God may answer our prayers with miracle-working power, but none today has power personally to perform supernatural acts of divine power. Pink responds to this concern by asserting that Jesus' promise was given exclusively to the original disciples for their apostolic ministry. This fits the statement of Hebrews 2:4 that the apostles' preaching was attested to "by signs and wonders and various miracles." But this answer does not take seriously what Jesus actually promised. He said, "Whoever believes in me" will do his works and even greater works (John 14:12). Some interpreters would argue that this promise is true, provided that we believe fervently enough to perform miracles. Under this view, the reason that you and I do not raise the dead and calm the winds is that our faith simply is not strong enough. But if this were Jesus' meaning, the only way that we could do greater miracles than he did would be by believing more than Jesus

1. Arthur W. Pink, *Exposition of the Gospel of John* (Grand Rapids: Zondervan, 1975), 770.

did, which is a preposterous suggestion. Jesus did not say, "Whoever has a sufficient degree of faith or a faith intense enough to perform miracles will do my works." Rather, he said, "Whoever believes," that is, all Christians, will do his works and more because he has gone to the Father.

If Jesus was not referring to his miracles, then what are the works that believers will do in his name? To answer this, we need to consider how God measures greatness. We think a work is greater if it is visually more spectacular, but is this how God reasons? One place we can find the answer to this question is Luke chapter 10, where Jesus responds to the return of the seventy-two disciples from their first preaching mission. The disciples rejoiced that they had power to cast out demons, which replicated one of Jesus' most common miracles. Jesus replied that he had given them "authority to tread on serpents and scorpions, and over all the power of the enemy," just as he later gave the apostles a unique power to perform miracles. But Jesus added, "Nevertheless, do not rejoice in this, that the spirits are subject to you, but rejoice that your names are written in heaven" (Luke 10:19–20). This shows that the works of Christ that are greater than the miracles are the works that lead to the salvation of souls. When we turn to the book of Acts, which records the disciples' ministry as apostles, we see this same priority. While Acts records numerous apostolic miracles, the emphasis is placed on the preaching of the gospel and the conversion of multitudes to faith in Christ.

The work of the gospel, then, is the work of Jesus that we who believe will do. This is a work that has indeed been achieved in greater measure since Jesus departed for heaven. During his three years of ministry, Jesus gathered a relatively small group of believers. Before ascending into heaven, Jesus said farewell to a gathering of about five hundred believers (1 Cor. 15:6). Afterward, a group of one hundred twenty disciples obeyed Jesus' command to gather for prayer in Jerusalem (Acts 1:15). These were relatively small numbers. But what happened after Jesus poured out God's Spirit at Pentecost? That very day, Peter's preaching of the first Christian sermon resulted in the conversion of over three thousand people (2:41). Moreover, while Jesus' ministry was confined to a relatively small portion of Palestine, the gospel spread across the ancient world through the apostles, with communities of believers established as far as the empire's capital in Rome. Believing in Christ, Peter and the others were empowered to do the works of Christ in greater measure and with greater spiritual results to the glory of God.

By properly identifying the works of which Jesus spoke, we may summarize his great promise. First, "the works Christ refers to are spiritual works, primarily the work of regeneration that takes place when the gospel is proclaimed through the power of God's Holy Spirit."[2] Second, Jesus says that these works will be achieved by every Christian. It will be true, he said, for "whoever believes in me" (John 14:12). This does not mean that every believer is equipped or called to be a great evangelist. But it does mean that we are all sent to be witnesses and that we are in a position now to do more for salvation than Jesus did before his death, resurrection, and ascension.

The third thing for us to understand is that we can accomplish only so much, Jesus said, "because I am going to the Father" (John 14:12). It is because of Jesus' mediation for us with God the Father in heaven, because of Christ's intercessory prayers, because, as he said in the Great Commission, "all authority in heaven and on earth has been given to me" (Matt. 28:18), and because of the power of the Holy Spirit that Jesus would send that we will enter into his works and achieve so great a spiritual harvest in the saving of souls. John Calvin explains: "The reason why the disciples will do greater things than Christ is that when He has entered into possession of His kingdom, He will demonstrate His power more fully from heaven."[3]

The New Testament book that records the disciples' later ministry appears in our Bibles under the name *The Acts of the Apostles*. But Luke wrote in the opening verse that he had recorded in his Gospel "all that Jesus began to do and teach, until the day when he was taken up" (Acts 1:1–2). The clear implication is that while the Gospel of Luke recorded what Jesus "began to do and teach," the book of Acts recorded what Jesus "continued" to do and teach through the ministry of his apostles. The book really records the acts of the ascended Jesus Christ through his apostles. So it is with us: believers will do what Jesus did and more because the exalted Christ continues his work in and through us by the Spirit he has sent.

2. James Montgomery Boice, *The Gospel of John*, 5 vols. (Grand Rapids: Baker, 1999), 4:1095.
3. John Calvin, *New Testament Commentaries*, trans. T. H. L. Parker, 12 vols. (Grand Rapids: Eerdmans, 1959), 5:80.

GREATER WORKS THROUGH FAITH AND PRAYER

The obvious application of this promise is that Christians should take up the work of Christ's gospel with great confidence and high expectations. Yet how could any of us, or all of us together, believe that we can accomplish things of value for God and even be used for the saving of many souls? The answer is that Christ promised that we would do his works, and with greater impact than he did while on earth. But the works that we will do are *his* works. Jesus did not promise that we would be able to raise great volumes of money, build magnificent cathedrals, seize political power in the nation, and overthrow all resistance to the Christian faith. He promised that we would do his work of salvation with great success. Sometimes this will involve raising money, erecting buildings, and working in society for Christian principles. But the work that Jesus promised to empower is especially the sending forth of the gospel for the saving of souls. Likewise, on an individual basis, Jesus did not promise financial security, personal success, good health, or comfortable circumstances. But he did promise that "whoever believes in me will also do the works that I do; and greater works than these will he do, because I am going to the Father" (John 14:12). So while we do not know whether the Lord wills for us to be rich or poor, healthy or afflicted, successful or downtrodden, we do know that the Lord intends for us to be effective in leading others to faith in him through the gospel.

The question is rightly asked, "How are we to do these great works for Christ?" The answer can be seen in the broader context of Jesus' teaching in this chapter, which presents four steps for doing great things for Christ. The first step is that we must *have faith* in him: "Whoever believes in me," Jesus said (John 14:12). This tells us that the promise is irrelevant until we have believed on Jesus and trusted him as our Lord and Savior. Until we have come to Christ in faith for our own salvation, we can be of little use in the salvation of others. Moreover, while Jesus did not distinguish here between strong and weak faith, it is nonetheless true that we will be useful to the Lord's work as and to the extent that we believe his Word and trust in him. The writer of Hebrews thus wrote: "Without faith it is impossible to please him, for whoever would draw near to God must believe that he exists and that he rewards those who seek him" (Heb. 11:6).

Second, we will do Christ's work greatly as we *pray*. We see the importance of prayer as Jesus adds a second promise about prayer: "Whatever you ask in my name, this I will do" (John 14:13). Therefore, it is through Christ's answers to our prayers that we will do his work and achieve great results.

The importance of prayer to evangelism is seen all through the New Testament. Jesus often withdrew for intimate communion with the Father in prayer, especially at crucial times of ministry. Before Jesus walked on water, he was up on the mountaintop praying (Matt. 14:23). More notably, before submitting to the cross, Jesus went to the garden of Gethsemane to pray with the Father (26:39). Indeed, Jesus specifically identified prayer as one of the important works that are necessary for the spread of the gospel: "The harvest is plentiful, but the laborers are few; therefore pray earnestly to the Lord of the harvest to send out laborers into his harvest" (9:37–38).

One of the greatest examples of the primacy of prayer in the work of Christ is the life of the apostle Paul. The first thing said of Paul after his conversion was this report: "Behold, he is praying" (Acts 9:11). Paul's letters are filled with accounts of his prayers for the churches, for people, and for gospel success. Paul shows the direct link between gospel teaching and prayer in Ephesians chapter 1. The first half of the chapter contains some of the most elevated and intense gospel teaching in all the New Testament, and the second half of the chapter contains Paul's prayer for God's blessing on the teaching of the first half. The Puritan Jeremiah Burroughs saw in Paul's example a fixed principle for every servant of the Lord. He commented, "We read that Moses was upon the mountain forty days with God, and when he came down his face so shone that the people were not able to bear it. . . . Converse much with God, be often with God, bear near to Him and that will make you shine as lights in the midst of a crooked and perverse generation."[4]

Prayer is important not only for great and public works of gospel ministry, but also for the individual work that God has given each of us to do. We are to pray for the opportunity to witness to specific people and for our gospel witness's success in leading them to faith. We are to pray for the work of Christ in our families and homes. R. A. Torrey tells of a case in which a mother approached him about her son, who was the most difficult boy

4. Jeremiah Burroughs, *Gospel Worship* (1648; repr., Morgan, PA: Soli Deo Gloria, 1990), 55–56.

that Torrey had ever known. The woman asked whether Torrey knew the boy, and when he said that he did, she added, "You know he is not a very good boy." "Yes," Torrey answered, "I know he is not a very good boy." The heavy-hearted mother continued, asking, "What shall I do?" "Have you ever tried prayer?" he asked. "Why, of course I pray," she replied. Torrey went on by asking whether she had made specific prayer requests, including a prayer for God definitely to regenerate her son, and whether she had then trusted that God would do it. "I do not think I have ever been as definite as that," she answered. "Well," Torrey told her, "you go right home and be just as definite as that," and the mother later reported that as she began praying not just generally for her child but definitely naming specific requests, especially the boy's conversion, things began to change in his life, including his regeneration to faith in Christ.[5]

This is not to say that our prayers will automatically achieve all that we desire. Yet it does say that we are to make specific requests of Christ, and that through such prayers we will accomplish his work in great power and abundance.

Keep My Commandments

Third, we will accomplish great works in Christ through *loving obedience* to his commands. This is the next step in the progression of Christ's teaching in this chapter. Having told us that he will grant things that we pray for in his name, he continued, "If you love me, you will keep my commandments" (John 14:15). It is as we obey Christ out of love for him that he will accomplish great works for the salvation of many through us.

Let me give some examples of how our obedience to Christ is essential to our works in his name. First, it is by our refusal to assimilate into the sinful culture and adopt its values that we are able to represent Christ in the world. Jesus compared our moral purity to salt and its preserving influence on meat. "You are the salt of the earth," he told the disciples, "but if salt has lost its taste, how shall its saltiness be restored?" (Matt. 5:13). Likewise, if Christians compromise our obedience to Christ by engaging in sin, then we lose our influence for others' salvation.

5. Illustration from Boice, *John*, 5:1096–97.

On the other hand, our refusal to join with sin leaves a salty taste in people's mouths that will cause some to drink from the gospel fountain. I experienced this not long before my conversion as a young adult. I had met a couple who were engaged to be married, but the young woman had recently converted to faith in Christ. Some months later, as she deepened her relationship with Jesus and her fiancé continued in unbelief, she broke off the engagement despite her strong affection for the man. She explained that her discipleship to Christ was the most important relationship in her life and that, despite the heartbreak involved, she had to obey his command to marry only another believer (see 1 Cor. 7:39). As an acquaintance of the unbelieving man, I was amazed at the young woman's choice of obedience to Christ over romantic love. And that was one small factor in my openness to the gospel when I was converted later that same year.

A second way that our obedience relates to accomplishing Christ's work has to do with our fidelity to the Bible's doctrine. We realize that the world is hostile to certain biblical teachings, so that many harden their hearts to the Lord. In response, many well-meaning Christians have sought to tone down doctrines such as man's total depravity in sin, God's wrath in judgment of sinners, and the Bible's depiction of the torments in hell. Others have sought to emphasize worldly benefits from believing in Jesus, while downplaying the cost of discipleship and the cross that every follower of Jesus must bear. But we can do Christ's gospel work only by proclaiming Christ's actual gospel. We therefore must follow the example of Paul, who wrote that he was "not ashamed of the gospel" because it alone "is the power of God for salvation to everyone who believes" (Rom. 1:16). If we want God to use us in the salvation of souls, we must not trim the biblical message but obey the Bible's doctrine in our evangelism.

Finally, loving obedience to Christ will often mean persevering wherever he has placed us. As products of a quick-fix culture, we might find this to be the most difficult thing to do. But if we want to accomplish great things for the Lord, not only must we trust him, pray, and obey the teaching of the Bible, but we must persist in doing so. Some Christians will be in a troubled marriage, perhaps with an unbelieving spouse or a believing spouse who is difficult. They will often want to flee, but obedience to Christ requires them to stay, continue to pray, and lovingly minister as Christ has called his people to do. We might have children who have turned from the faith, and we are to continue to love them, pray for them, and speak to them about the good news of Christ. Our hearts' desire in such cases will sometimes be achieved only when bathed with many tears and many prayers and through long-term obedience to Christ. We will often be like Paul in Corinth, where he was wearied of failure in ministry and repulsed by deeply entrenched sin. But Christ appeared to Paul and said, "Do not be afraid, but go on speaking and do not be silent, for I am with you, and . . . I have many in this city who are my people" (Acts 18:9–10). Gospel success in a certain place will sometimes require the intimate acquaintance and fellow-feeling that can be gained only after a lifetime's commitment and built-up trust.

Because I Am Going to the Father

Christ has promised that we will do even greater works for salvation than he did before taking up the cross. He calls us to trust in him and in his Word, to pray with bold requests, and to show our love by obeying his commands. This raises a question: are these really enough? Following this plan, can we, in our own strength, do what Jesus did and more? The obvious answer is No. This is why Jesus points to a fourth item in his program for our carrying on his works. Indeed, what Jesus promises to do is not only something that is too good to be true but something that no one ever imagined possible. He promises to *send the Holy Spirit* to us from heaven. "I will ask the Father," Jesus said, "and he will give you another Helper, to be with you forever, even the Spirit of truth" (John 14:16–17).

This simple fact changes everything for us. Can any of us believe that our preaching of the gospel will succeed in gaining someone a new nature, so that he or she is born again to faith and eternal life? Certainly not. But if Christ will send the Holy Spirit to exert his power from heaven, we can offer our feeble witness to save the lost. In a difficult marriage, can we persevere in faithful love, believing that it will change the attitude of our spouse? The answer is No, since people never really change. But what if Christ will send the Holy Spirit, who can change the heart? Do we have enough love for Jesus to say No to long-cherished sins, so that through our obedience others will be inspired to trust in Christ? No, none of us really possesses sufficient love for that or enough power to overcome our temptations. But what if Jesus has promised to send the Spirit? What if our departed Lord has commissioned a Helper to give divine aid to our feeble faith? That changes everything, so that Christ's promise will be found true in us: "Whoever believes in me will also do the works that I do; and greater works than these will he do" (John 14:12).

Jesus directs these words individually to us. He tells us that while he was on earth he did many things in weakness: healing the sick, feeding the hungry, preaching good news to the poor. After three years, he permitted the people to put him to death on a cross. Now he is the risen Lord, in full possession of his divine and royal authority. He now desires to continue those works, especially the spread of the gospel, through us. Will you trust his promise? Will you pray? Will you show your love by obeying his commands? If you do, it is not true that these will achieve great things for the Lord. What is true is that Jesus will send the Holy Spirit and that in his power, Christ will do great things through you. Not great things that the world will notice, perhaps. But whenever a sinner comes to faith in Jesus and is saved, in part through our witness, we will rejoice, knowing that eternal life is not only good but forever true.

94

ASK IN MY NAME

John 14:13—14

"Whatever you ask in my name, this I will do, that the Father
may be glorified in the Son. If you ask me anything in my name,
I will do it." (John 14:13–14)

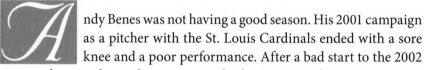ndy Benes was not having a good season. His 2001 campaign as a pitcher with the St. Louis Cardinals ended with a sore knee and a poor performance. After a bad start to the 2002 season, the team began hinting to Andy that it was perhaps time to start thinking of retirement. Instead, Benes accepted a demotion to the minor leagues, where he could seek to regain his form. A Christian, Andy and his wife began praying that the Lord would enable him to pitch well enough to remain in St. Louis and retire with his reputation intact.

One day in the minor leagues, Benes began toying with throwing a split-fingered fastball. This is an effective but difficult pitch that few can master, yet Andy seemed to pick it up immediately. Instead of spending the months and even years normally required to master a new pitch, Benes threw the split-fingered fastball that night and began retiring batters. Within a few weeks, he was back up in the major leagues, and with his new pitch he contributed to a division championship and then retired at the top of his game. Believing that God had answered his and his wife's prayer, Benes commented just six months later: "That pitch was like a gift God dropped from heaven. If I had to throw a split-fingered fastball today, I'm not sure I would know how to do it."[1]

Hearing this story, Christians might wonder, "Is this the kind of request that we are to make of the Lord?" Are such prayers what Jesus had in mind when he promised, "Whatever you ask in my name, this I will do" (John 14:13)?

Ongoing Communion with Christ

In his last meeting with the disciples, Jesus made a number of revolutionary promises designed to uphold the disciples' faith, revealing his plans to provide for their needs after his departure. First, Jesus promised to prepare a place for us in heaven and return to take us there with him (John 14:3). The second promise assured believers that they would carry on Christ's work, saying that even "greater works than these will [they] do, because I am going to the Father" (14:12). Immediately following was a third great promise: "Whatever you ask in my name, this I will do" (14:13). Here, our Lord assured the disciples of ongoing communion with him after his death, resurrection, and ascension into heaven.

The importance of Christ's promise can be understood by asking what it means to be a Christian. What is a Christian? One answer is that a Christian is someone who believes the Bible's teaching about Jesus Christ. This definition was emphasized in Peter's Great Confession, declaring his belief in Jesus: "You are the Christ, the Son of the living God" (Matt. 16:16). Another definition of a Christian is one who has become, through faith in Jesus, a forgiven and beloved child of God. John emphasized this definition, writing that "to all who did receive him, who believed in his name, he gave the right to become children of God" (John 1:12).

Another essential definition is that a Christian is a man or woman in a personal relationship with Jesus Christ. The "I am" statements of Jesus in John's Gospel make this point: "I am the light of the world. Whoever follows me will not walk in darkness, but will have the light of life" (John 8:12);

---

1. Quoted in Daniel M. Doriani, *Matthew*, 2 vols., Reformed Expository Commentary (Phillipsburg, NJ: P&R Publishing, 2008), 1:218–19.

"I am the good shepherd. I know my own and my own know me" (10:14); and "I am the true vine . . . . Abide in me, and I in you" (15:1, 4). These and many other statements in John's Gospel define the Christian life as a personal and saving relationship with Jesus Christ.

Yet the question is raised as to how we have a personal relationship with someone who is not physically present. This was the question gnawing at the disciples. Jesus was departing and they could not follow: how could they remain in communion with him? Jesus' answer was that he was entering into heaven to take up his kingdom and power. This being the case, just as believers are able to speak to the Father through prayer, so may we also commune with Christ his Son in prayer. Prayer is talking to God, and we may through faith talk with Jesus just as the disciples spoke with him during his days on earth. A. W. Pink writes, "True, He would be in Heaven, and they on earth, but *prayer* could remove all sense of distance, prayer could bring them into His very presence at any time," and prayer was thus essential to the "greater works" of which Jesus spoke in John 14:12.[2]

For this reason, just as a personal relationship with Jesus is essential to Christian salvation, prayer is essential to our discipleship and life of faith. Martin Luther thus insisted, "A Christian without prayer is just as impossible as a living person without a pulse."[3] Without prayer, there is no communion with Christ; without a personal relationship with Christ, there is no Christianity.

Present, personal, ongoing discipleship with the risen Lord Jesus is not only the believer's obligation but his or her great privilege as well. Peter Lewis tells of a Chinese pastor who was placed in a labor camp for his faith. His captors denied him a Bible and punished him when he prayed or sang. Out of malice they made him clean the camp latrine. Every day the pastor would take the excrement out and scatter it as fertilizer over the fields. The smell was so foul that the guards would withdraw and give him plenty of space, enabling him to sing and pray to the Lord. For this reason, he came to love his malodorous occupation because of the communion that he could openly enjoy with the Lord Jesus. The dunghill became his "garden," and he sang:

2. Arthur W. Pink, *Exposition of the Gospel of John* (Grand Rapids: Zondervan, 1975), 773.

3. Martin Luther, *Luther's Works*, vol. 24, *Sermons on the Gospel of St. John, Chapters 14–16* (St. Louis: Concordia, 1957), 89.

I come to the garden alone, while the dew is still on the roses . . . .
For he walks with me and he talks with me, and he tells me I am his own;
And the joy we share as we tarry there, none other has ever known.[4]

Many Christians today are just as tyrannized by our schedules and life-styles, and would do well to spend our own time in the "garden" with the Lord. Moreover, each of us can and should live in constant communion with our Lord, as Paul instructed us: "whatever you do, in word or deed, do everything in the name of the Lord Jesus, giving thanks to God the Father through him" (Col. 3:17).

THE SCOPE OF OUR PRAYERS

The promise of John 14:13 goes further, however, than merely assuring us of ongoing communion with Christ in prayer. Jesus states not only that we may pray to him, but that "whatever you ask in my name, this I will do." It is the scope of this promise that takes our breath away: "whatever you ask," Jesus says, "this I will do."

It is commonly and correctly stated that prayer does not mean that we get everything that we asked for exactly as we asked for it. Sometimes we pray foolishly, and we can be grateful that God's wisdom is not overruled by our folly. Furthermore, since the Lord's priorities are spiritual, he usually places our spiritual well-being ahead of our material well-being. The apostle Paul, for instance, prayed three times for God to remove a thorn from his flesh—whatever that was—and three times the Lord answered not by removing the thorn but by giving Paul grace to bear the affliction. God was teaching him a vital lesson: "My grace is sufficient for you, for my power is made perfect in weakness" (2 Cor. 12:9). Unanswered prayers might also be a matter of timing, as for various reasons the Lord desires that we wait for what we have requested.

Having understood these standard explanations for why our prayers do not always seem to be answered, we need to realize that this is not the emphasis given by Jesus in this promise. Jesus emphasized that he *will* give *whatever* we ask of him in prayer.

4. Peter Lewis, *God's Hall of Fame* (Fearn, Ross-shire, UK: Christian Focus, 1999), 32.

An illustration from the reign of Alexander the Great might help to show Jesus' emphasis. The Macedonian conqueror was once approached by a man who pleaded his need of a large sum of money. Alexander immediately sent the man to his treasury, telling him to request whatever he needed. Some time afterward, the treasurer appeared with the horrified report that the man had taken a vast sum from the royal hoard. Alexander confirmed that he had authorized this, explaining, "He has asked me as a king, and I have given to him as a king." How much more is this true of our Lord Jesus, who "is able to do far more abundantly than all that we ask or think, according to the power at work within us" (Eph. 3:20). There is literally no limit placed on the scope of our requests to Christ in prayer: "Whatever you ask," he says, "this I will do" (John 14:13). John Newton thus urges us:

> Thou art coming to a King, large petitions with thee bring;
> For his grace and pow'r are such, none can ever ask too much.[5]

THE CONDITION FOR OUR PRAYERS

But a condition is placed on our prayers. Jesus says that he will do whatever we ask "in my name" (John 14:13). "If you ask me anything in my name, I will do it" (14:14).

For some believers, praying "in Jesus' name" means nothing more than appending the words "in Jesus' name" to the end of their prayers. This is a good practice, so long as we are serious about what it means. When we pray "in Christ's name," we are coming to God the Father through the mediation of his Son, relying on his shed blood for our acceptance and his intercession for our admittance to God's throne. To pray in any other name, or simply to pray in no name at all, is to have no legitimate reason to expect God to answer your prayers.

R. A. Torrey tells of receiving a note at a conference from a man who was embittered by God's failure to answer his prayers. The note read: "I have been a member of the Presbyterian Church for thirty years, and have tried to be a consistent one all the time. I have been superintendent of the Sunday school for twenty-five years, and an elder in the church for twenty years; and yet God does not answer my prayer and I cannot

---

5. John Newton, "Come, My Soul, Thy Suit Prepare" (1779).

understand it." Torrey read the note from the pulpit and stated that an explanation was simple:

> This man thinks that because he has been a consistent church member for thirty years, a faithful Sunday school superintendent for twenty-five years, and an elder in the church for twenty years, that God is under obligation to answer his prayer. He is really praying in his own name, and God will not hear our prayers when we approach Him in that way. We must, if we would have God answer our prayers, give up any thought that we have claims upon God. There is not one of us who deserves anything from God. If we got what we deserved, every one of us would spend eternity in hell. But Jesus Christ has great claims on God, and we should go to God in our prayers not on the ground of any goodness in ourselves, but on the ground of Jesus Christ's claims.[6]

Praying in Christ's name therefore means praying on the basis of his claims with God. The name of Christ, however, also refers to the whole of his self-revelation, including his character and known will. Leon Morris points out that this "means that prayer is to be in accordance with all that that name stands for. It is prayer proceeding from faith in Christ, prayer that gives expression to oneness with Christ, prayer that seeks to glorify Christ."[7] Donald Grey Barnhouse adds, "To pray in the name of the Lord Jesus Christ is to seek an endorsement of our request, and to bring into consideration that what we ask is consistent with the nature and purposes of our Saviour."[8]

This means that we should never expect selfish, petty, worldly, foolish, self-glorifying, self-pitying, or, especially, sinful prayers to be fulfilled by our Lord. But on the other hand, when our prayer coincides with the known will of Christ, with his character, purposes, and attitude—that is, when we are praying in a way that Jesus would pray for us—then we should be confident to offer all kinds of prayers to our risen Lord. Such prayers would include Christ's blessing on his Word as it is preached and witnessed. Christ's will also extends to prayers such as that of Andy Benes, who desired to finish his

6. Quoted in James Montgomery Boice, *The Gospel of John*, 5 vols. (Grand Rapids: Baker, 1999), 4:1101.

7. Leon Morris, *The Gospel according to John*, rev. ed., New International Commentary on the New Testament (Grand Rapids: Eerdmans, 1995), 574.

8. Donald Grey Barnhouse, *Exposition of Bible Doctrines, Taking the Epistle to the Romans as a Point of Departure*, 10 vols. (Grand Rapids: Eerdmans, 1952), 1:96.

career with a positive reputation so as to foster his long-term witness to his city. Praying in Christ's will extends to our seeking good health to continue serving the Lord and financial provision to take care of our families and support our church. Christ's will does not, however, endorse prayers for self-glorifying success, for the kind of self-serving riches that the Bible tells us not to seek (1 Tim. 6:17), or for committing or covering up sin.

Ralph Keiper gives an illustration about praying in Christ's name, based on the work of the Colony of Mercy, a Christian rehabilitation center for alcoholics. The founder of this colony was William Raws, and it was directed by successive generations of Raws' sons. Suppose, Keiper suggests, that one of the men in the colony departs from the grounds and enters a bar at the nearby town. He steps up to the bar and calls out, "Give me a shot of whiskey in Raws' name." At this, the bartender turns around and asks, "Do you mean William Raws, founder of the Colony of Mercy, or his sons who have continued the work of freeing men from bondage to alcohol?" "That's right," the drunk demands; "give me a shot of whiskey in Raws' name!" Such a bartender would refuse, saying, "How dare you charge this drink to Raws? If you were really acting in Raws' name, you would have passed by this tavern or come in only to lead someone else back with you to the Colony of Mercy to learn about Jesus Christ. Dr. Raws is not a drinking man, and those who name his name are not customers of ours."[9]

Keiper commented: "To pray in the name of Christ is a serious matter, not to be taken lightly. We ask for many things without regard for our Lord, because we would please ourselves instead of Him." When we do, we find our prayers unanswered, because they were not truly "in Christ's name."[10]

The best way that we can be confident of praying in Christ's name is to pray for the things that the Bible tells us to seek. We should pray for love, joy, peace, patience, and other fruits of the Holy Spirit (Gal. 5:22–23). We should pray for power to withstand temptation, since God has promised to respond with the help that we need (1 Cor. 10:13). Parents should pray for their children to come to faith. All Christians should pray for opportunities to witness the gospel, and many more Christ-honoring matters. When we pray for things such as these—matters that we know are "in Christ's name" because they are taught in Scripture—we should

---

9. Quoted in Boice, *John*, 5:1102.
10. Quoted in ibid.

pray with expectations of our Lord's mighty answer, in his wise manner and timing, since he has promised, "If you ask me anything in my name, I will do it" (John 14:14).

Moreover, we will find, as we consider Christ's name in our prayers, that the subject matter of our prayers begins to change from a worldly to a godly and Christ-centered perspective. Newton models a Christ-centered prayer:

With my burden I begin: "Lord, remove this load of sin;
Let thy blood, for sinners spilt, set my conscience free from guilt.

"Lord, I come to thee for rest, take possession of my breast;
There thy blood-bought right maintain, and without a rival reign."[11]

As we pray with an increasing focus on the gospel and its work in our lives, we will know in increasing measure the power of Christ in answering our prayers.

THE GOAL OF OUR PRAYERS

There is one more matter to be considered in Christ's promise, however. Whatever we pray in Christ's name, we must seek above all else to bring glory to God the Father through his Son. Jesus said, "Whatever you ask in my name, this I will do, that the Father may be glorified in the Son" (John 14:13).

This is exactly what we should expect if we are to pray in accord with Christ's will. For what is the great desire of God the Son but the glory of God the Father? For this reason Jesus viewed the cross not as a horror to be avoided but a sacrifice to be embraced. Thus, when Jesus prayed on the night of his arrest, the glory of God was his chief preoccupation. "Father," Jesus began, "the hour has come; glorify your Son that the Son may glorify you" (John 17:1). James Montgomery Boice comments: "This is a new thought for many people, for we are so filled with the idea that prayer is getting something from God, that we rarely consider that prayer is actually a means by which God gets something from us. What he wants from us is glory, a glory that will lead others to trust him."[12]

11. Newton, "Come, My Soul, Thy Suit Prepare."
12. Boice, *John*, 4:1103.

We see Christ's commitment to the glory of God in its most holy intensity when he prayed in the garden of Gethsemane about the torments that he would endure to atone for our sins. His example shows that when we are afraid, anticipate suffering, or are sifted by trials, we may pray for God to take them away, since Jesus did the very same thing in anticipation of the cross. "Father, if you are willing," Jesus pleaded, "remove this cup from me." But Jesus did not stop there, for his prayer was guided by faith in the Father's will and zeal for the Father's glory. He therefore concluded, "Nevertheless, not my will, but yours, be done" (Luke 22:42). Therefore, writes A. W. Pink, "To ask in the name of Christ is, therefore, to set aside our own will, and bow to the perfect will of God."[13]

To believe in Christ's name, and to pray in Christ's name, is to walk in Christ's way. His is a path that leads to glory and to unending pleasures at God's right hand. But his also is a path that enters into glory by way of the cross. Jesus taught, "If anyone would come after me, let him deny himself and take up his cross daily and follow me" (Luke 9:23). We therefore cannot pray in Christ's name and seek an exemption from the cross, but instead are called to "share in suffering for the gospel by the power of God" (2 Tim. 1:8).

We will therefore suffer many things that are common to life in this world, as well as some trials that result directly from our faith in Christ. We and others close to us will suffer and sometimes die. Our lives will include many disappointments, some of which will produce keen sorrow. Before much time has passed, we ourselves will die. How will we respond to these circumstances? Will we complain to God and blame him for the reality of life in a world that he made good but that mankind ruined by sin? Or will we receive the circumstances that God decrees as his good and gracious will for our lives, through which our souls are saved through faith in Christ? Boice writes: "If we choose the latter, we will be able to demonstrate the reality of God's great grace and peace, produced by God's sovereign choice in suffering Christians."[14]

Understanding our calling as believers in Christ, therefore, not only should we conclude our prayers with "in Christ's name," but we should append to all our requests, "Father, not my will, but yours be done." Then, if we pray in Christ's name, for God's glory above all else, we may confidently know the reality of Jesus' promise: "Whatever you ask . . . , this I will do" (John 14:13).

13. Pink, *John*, 775.
14. Boice, *John*, 4:1104.

95

IF YOU LOVE ME

John 14:15

"If you love me, you will keep my commandments." (John 14:15)

t might seem surprising that in a chapter filled with promises intended by Jesus to comfort his disciples, we also encounter so many uses of the word *if*. All through John 14, Jesus not only tells us of his provision for the disciples during his absence from earth, but also tells us the conditions by which we may be certain of these promises. In verse 3, Jesus said, "If I go and prepare a place for you, I will come again and will take you to myself." Here, Christ's return to gather us into glory is conditioned on his first departing from earth in his ascension. In verse 7, Jesus answered Thomas, "If you had known me, you would have known my Father also." Knowing Jesus is the required condition for knowledge of God the Father: we can experience the latter only if we possess the former. Likewise, in verse 14, Jesus conditions his actions on our behalf with the *if* of prayer: "If you ask me anything in my name, I will do it."

The *ifs* of John 14 do not make our salvation less certain but more certain, as long as the conditions are met. Christians must comprehend Christ, and then we will understand God. Christians must pray, and then Christ will answer. These are cause-and-effect relationships in God's economy of which we may be absolutely certain and from which we may derive great comfort. Particularly important among this list of *if*-conditions is one that pertains to our love for Christ. In this case, the result of our love for Jesus is as certain as it is important: "If you love me, you will keep my commandments" (John 14:15).

LOVE AND THE LAW

Many people, including some Christians, have difficulty thinking of love and obedience together: we may act either in love or according to law, but not both. Among liberals, who are willing to dismiss the Bible's teaching, it is often said that what matters is not law but only love. On this basis, recent generations have been taught a "new morality" in which the only guideline is love. Anything is permissible so long as it does not seem to hurt anyone. This has been the driving idea behind the "situational ethics" approach that now dominates contemporary society. Its originator, Joseph Fletcher, said, "Only love is a constant; everything else is a variable."[1] As a result of this thinking, marriages may be casually dissolved, adultery may be celebrated, contracts may be broken, parents may be disregarded, and worldly things may be coveted—and all may be justified on the grounds that no one is being hurt and that love is the motive.

There are two major problems with this view, however. The first is that we must ask how to define love. In the new morality, love is generally defined according to the 1960s philosophy of Jerry Rubin: "If it feels good, do it." But as the drug culture of the '60s proved, there are things that feel good that are not loving, but that destroy the person who does them and others. The Bible says that the heart is "deceitful above all things" (Jer. 17:9), so in reality we cannot trust our own feelings as a guide to love. Thus, a young man who seduces a woman into sexual sin is not loving her, however good it may feel at the time. Likewise, a young woman who tempts men into lust by her immodest way of dressing is not loving her neighbor, however good the attention might feel to her at the time.

---

1. Quoted in Peter Barnes, "Do We Need the Ten Commandments in the 21st Century Church and World?" in *Love Rules: The Ten Commandments for the 21st Century*, ed. Stuart M. Bonnington and Joan Milne (Edinburgh: Banner of Truth, 2007), 9.

This raises a question: has God provided us with an objective guide to love? The answer is Yes, God has done this very thing in his law. Jesus summarized God's law in terms of love. The first great commandment, he said, is to "love the Lord your God with all your heart and with all your soul and with all your mind." The second great commandment is to "love your neighbor as yourself" (Matt. 22:37–39). This division corresponds to the two halves of the Ten Commandments, the first half of which pertains to love for God and the second half to love for our neighbor. The way to love one another, then, is to observe the commandments, not only in their prohibitions but also in terms of their positive agenda. Not only do we not murder, but we protect; not only do we not steal, but we provide. Compared to God's law of love, the "new morality" is revealed as justifying a self-love that does indeed hurt other people.

This leads to a second problem with the "new morality" of love, namely, that it utterly excludes the value of love for God. According to Jesus, this is the very first priority, so we must not have a view of love that conflicts with God's definition and standards of love. Our society asks, for instance, what is wrong with telling a few harmless lies. The first answer is that the practice shows no love for God, who is a God of truth and hates lying lips (Prov. 6:16–17). The second answer is that we are not loving our neighbor when we speak falsely and deceive. For these reasons, the antinomianism of liberal theology (*antinomianism* combines the words *against* and *law*—"against law") is not in fact an ethics of love, and its prevalence in our society in recent decades has brought misery and ruin to millions of people.

There is, however, an antinomianism of another kind among Bible-believing Christians, namely, those who conceive a radical contrast between law and grace in such a way that Christians are no longer to obey God's law. This can be seen among some dispensationalists, who tend to see the Old and New Testaments as teaching different approaches to God and salvation, and by Lutherans, who tend to react against law-keeping out of concern for legalism. Noting that the Ten Commandments are part of the Old Testament, and also noting that we are justified through faith alone in Christ, who kept the law for us, these Christians will assert that we are therefore saved in such a way as to be free from obedience to God's law. All we need for salvation is to trust and love the Lord Jesus Christ.

The first problem with this Christian antinomianism is that the New Testament strongly emphasizes the Christian's duty to obey God's law. Paul writes that while we are saved from our failure to keep God's law, we are justified through faith in Christ "in order that the righteous requirement of the law might be fulfilled in us," as we walk in the power of God's Holy Spirit (Rom. 8:4).

The second problem with the view that we need only love, but not obey, is Jesus' own teaching on love for him: "If you love me, you will keep my commandments" (John 14:15). According to Jesus, the Christian's bond of love with Jesus does not free us *from* keeping God's law, but frees us *to* keeping his commandments. If we love Jesus, that love will draw us to thoughts and actions that conform with Jesus' thoughts and actions, and please him. William Barclay comments, "It was by His obedience that Jesus showed His love to God; and it is by our obedience that we must show our love to Jesus."[2]

LOVING AND OBEYING JESUS

John 14:15 makes a number of important points about Christian obedience. The first is that our obedience to Christ's commands is *personal* obedience. That is, we do not obey a cold legal code, but we offer obedience to Jesus himself. He calls us to obey "my commandments." This shows the divine lordship of Jesus Christ. Moses never called Israel to obey "my commandments," but Jesus unreservedly calls us to personal obedience out of love for him. Charles Spurgeon wrote: "There are some men for whom you would do anything: you will to yield to their will. If such a person were to say to you, 'Do this,' you would do it without question. Perhaps he stands to you in the relation of a master, and you are his willing servant. Perhaps he is a venerated friend, and because you esteem and love him, his word is law to you. The Saviour may much more safely than any other be installed in such a position."[3] Both in his person as the perfect Son of God and in his work, having shown us the highest love by dying for our sins, Jesus has earned the right to call us to personal obedience: "If you love me, you will keep my commandments."

2. William Barclay, *The Gospel of John*, 2 vols. (Philadelphia: Westminster, 1975), 2:193.

3. Charles H. Spurgeon, *The Metropolitan Tabernacle Pulpit*, 63 vols. (Pasadena, TX: Pilgrim, 1974), 32:653.

Second, we note in Jesus' words the intimate connection between love for and obedience to him. The only kind of true obedience to the Lord is *loving* obedience. That is, we must obey Christ's commands willingly, gladly, and freely, as an intentional expression of our thanks and love to him. Spurgeon comments, "The essence of obedience lies in the hearty love which prompts the deed rather than in the deed itself. . . . Love is the chief jewel in the bracelet of obedience."[4] How dead and useless is obedience to the letter of God's law without love to Christ! As Paul said, "If I give away all I have, and if I deliver up my body to be burned, but have not love, I gain nothing" (1 Cor. 13:3). We see this in those who obey the letter of Sabbath observance but never rest their hearts in Jesus on the Lord's Day. We see it again in those who are careful to tithe but take no delight in giving to the gospel work of Christ's church. We could say the same about sexual purity, obedience to marital duties and church-membership vows, and many other matters. Obedience to the Bible is obedience to Christ only when given out of love for him.

Third, Jesus teaches the *certainty* of obedience when there is love for him. It is important to note that John 14:15 does not express a command, as rendered by the King James Version: "If ye love me, keep my commandments." Jesus uses the future tense, rather than the imperative, pointing out that "if you love me, you *will* keep my commandments." A desire to walk in his way and embrace his teaching is the inevitable result of loving Christ. Indeed, it is *only* love that will motivate us to keep Christ's commands, since to do so we must, like him, take up the cross, crucifying our love of self so as to love the Lord and love one another as he has loved us. This means that the key to obeying Christ is to cultivate a love for him, which comes from reflecting on his love for us. John wrote in his first epistle: "We love because he first loved us" (1 John 4:19). This love for Christ will necessarily and inevitably result in a desire to obey his commands.

How We Know That We Love Jesus

Jesus' teaching plainly shows how essential it is that believers love him. Spurgeon writes, "He that believes in the Lord Jesus Christ for his salva-

4. Ibid., 32:652–53.

245

tion produces as the first fruit of his faith love to Christ; this must be in us and abound, or nothing is right."[5] This priority is confirmed in the New Testament. What was it that Jesus asked Peter when he restored him to discipleship? Since Peter fell away before the cross, did Jesus ask, "Peter, do you now understand the doctrine of the atonement?" Understanding doctrine is essential, especially when it comes to the meaning of Christ's death, but that is not what Jesus asked Peter. Nor did Jesus ask about his plans for spiritual improvement: "Peter, have you taken steps to make sure that this problem doesn't arise again?" What did Jesus ask Peter? He asked, "Simon, son of John, do you love me?" (John 21:16).

This raises the important question: "How do we know that we love Jesus?" The answer is found in our verse, which we may reverse to say, "We know that we love Jesus if we keep his commandments." This is how Jesus puts it in John 14:21: "Whoever has my commandments and keeps them, he it is who loves me."

To what, then, is Jesus specifically referring when he speaks of his commandments? To answer, we should note how Jesus touches on this same matter throughout this chapter. In verse 21, Jesus speaks again of his "commandments," but in verses 23 and 24 he expands his meaning to include his whole teaching: "If anyone loves me, he will keep my word . . . . Whoever does not love me does not keep my words." Thus, we must understand Jesus' commands to embrace all his teaching, whether it is doctrinal or ethical. Indeed, when we realize that the New Testament apostles spoke for Jesus and that the Old Testaments prophets were servants of Christ's covenant, we rightly expand Jesus' commands to embrace the whole of the Bible. A. W. Pink explains: "The whole revelation of the Divine will, respecting what I am to believe and feel and do and suffer, contained in the Holy Scriptures is the law of Christ. . . . The commandments of Christ include whatever is good and whatever God hath required of us."[6] There is no division between the will of Christ and the will of God, so the Word of God is the Word of Christ. This does not mean that we do not love Jesus unless we are perfectly obeying every line in the Bible. Rather, a love for Christ will instill in us a loving, obedient, and willing attitude toward all that is taught in God's Word. The Bible will become God's Word for us, and we will love it as that

---

5. Ibid., 32:653.

6. Arthur W. Pink, *Exposition of the Gospel of John* (Grand Rapids: Zondervan, 1975), 776.

which both leads us to Christ and teaches us how to obey the commands of our dearly beloved Lord.

Does this mean, therefore, that if we find ourselves struggling with sin, or if we find it difficult to obey God's Word, we therefore must have no love for Jesus? The answer is No: a struggle to obey does not rule out love for Christ. We all struggle with sin, as John emphasized in his first epistle (1 John 1:8), because we all are still sinners and must contend with our sinful nature. But if we love Jesus, we *will* struggle and not give ourselves over to sin. This means that if you are a teenager, you might sometimes think your parents hopelessly ignorant, but because you love Jesus you will nonetheless seek to obey and respect your father and mother. If you are a husband, your sinful flesh might desire to neglect your wife in favor of your hobbies or career ambitions. But in loving Jesus, you will turn your heart to your wife and children so as to be a faithful servant of the Lord. Similarly, Christian wives might sometimes resent the Bible's teaching to submit to their husbands and will grow weary of expending themselves in ceaseless service to their families. They might look out the window at other women who are living for themselves, to the detriment of their husbands and children, and feel a twinge of envy. But because they love Jesus, Christian women will turn back to their husbands with respect and to their families with devotion, doing it all "as to the Lord" (Eph. 5:22).

Struggling with sin does not mean that we do not love Jesus; if we love Jesus, we will struggle and we will seek Christ's power in prayer that we might obey his commands. The good news is that those who love Jesus will be helped by the mighty Holy Spirit whom Jesus sends. As Jesus continues in John 14:16: "I will ask the Father, and he will give you another Helper, to be with you forever." Loving Jesus, we are not left to obey him in our own small strength, but he gives us his strength from heaven through the ministry of the Spirit, so that our love for him is enabled to express itself in obedience to his commands.

Having noted that Jesus' commands must be seen as encompassing the whole Bible, we should still note his special emphasis on our love for one another. Jesus earlier taught, "A new commandment I give to you, that you love one another: just as I have loved you, you also are to love one another" (John 13:34). Later, Jesus repeats this special command: "This is my commandment, that you love one another as I have loved you. Greater love has no one than this, that someone lay down his life for his friends" (15:12–13).

With this in mind, we realize that love for Jesus is certain to yield obedience to him in the form of *service to others*. We remember how Jesus began his teaching at this last gathering of his disciples before the cross by taking up the servant's towel and washing the disciples' feet. Jesus said, "You call me Teacher and Lord, and you are right, for so I am. If I then, your Lord and Teacher, have washed your feet, you also ought to wash one another's feet" (John 13:13–14). James Montgomery Boice comments: "This is the picture Jesus gave of true Christianity. It is the attitude that divests itself of its own prerogatives in order to serve others."[7]

Moreover, our love for Jesus will produce an obedience that involves *sacrifice*. "This means that we are not called to serve only when we can do so conveniently and at no cost to ourselves. It means that we are called to serve at our cost when we would much rather do something else."[8] In other words, our love for one another in Christ's name is modeled on his sacrificial love for us. "Love one another as I have loved you," Jesus said (John 15:12), and he loved us by offering his life for our sake on the cross.

Finally, the love for others that reflects Christ's love will involve *sharing*. We are to share ourselves with others, freely giving of our time, talents, and spiritual gifts. We are to share the provision that God has given to us, so that others might have their needs provided for. Most importantly, the love of Jesus calls us to share the good news of salvation through faith in him, so that others may know and love Jesus Christ and find eternal life in him. Here, the command to love merges with the last of Jesus' commandments, given just before he ascended into heaven: "Go into all the world and proclaim the gospel to the whole creation" (Mark 16:15). How can we claim to love Christ if we neglect this great command to share his love with others?

Love, Obedience, and Assurance

We should conclude our study of this important verse by considering the relationship between love, obedience, and our assurance of salvation. This is important because love for Christ is integral to our faith in Christ, and it is

7. James Montgomery Boice, *The Gospel of John*, 5 vols. (Grand Rapids: Baker, 1999), 4:1109.
8. Ibid.

only through faith in Christ that we are saved. Because this is so important, in his first epistle John made explicit the link between our love for Jesus, our obedience to Jesus' commands, and our assurance of salvation: "By this we know that we have come to know him, if we keep his commandments. . . . Whoever keeps his word, in him truly the love of God is perfected. By this we may know that we are in him" (1 John 2:3, 5). John does not say that we are saved by obeying Christ's commands, since salvation is by faith alone, but rather that we *know we are saved* only through a love for Christ that obeys his Word.

This teaching makes two vital statements concerning our assurance of salvation. First, if we have no motivation to obey Jesus Christ and thus are not living a life of increasing obedience to his Word, we should have serious concerns about our salvation. To trust Christ is always to love Christ, and he adds, "If you love me, you will obey my commandments" (John 14:15).

Merely professing faith in Jesus, without bearing the fruit of that faith in obedience, provides no grounds for the assurance of salvation. In the Sermon on the Mount, Jesus spoke to those who practiced religion but did not obey him in love: "I never knew you; depart from me, you workers of lawlessness" (Matt. 7:23). He explained, "Not everyone who says to me, 'Lord, Lord,' will enter the kingdom of heaven, but the one who does the will of my Father who is in heaven" (7:21). This was not to establish a works basis for salvation, but rather to point out that a saving love for Jesus will always yield the fruit of a life of obedience to his commands. Therefore, if you have professed faith in Christ, but have neither made progress in biblical obedience nor gained a desire to do so, you should reconsider what you mean by faith in Christ. Biblical faith is never a bare assent to beliefs, but always includes a trust in Christ that yields a personal commitment and surrender to his holy will. If you have not offered yourself wholeheartedly to Christ, then you are not saved, and he calls you to a true faith, trusting in his love, that will yield salvation.

Second, if you love Christ and sincerely desire to honor him through obedience to his Word, this can only be because you are born again to a new and eternal life in Jesus. This is the point of John's teaching in his first epistle: not to cause true believers to doubt their salvation but to encourage weak and faltering believers to have assurance through the evidence of their faith. Even if your obedience is flawed and incomplete, do you find yourself desiring to change in a Christlike direction? How can this be if you are not a true believer? Do you not realize that it is mankind's nature, apart from Christ, to rebel against God and resent his commands? Paul writes, "The mind that is set on the flesh is hostile to God, for it does not submit to God's law; indeed, it cannot" (Rom. 8:7). How is it, then, that you are not hostile to God's law, but that you desire to show your love to Christ by obeying him, that you are frustrated by your failure to obey God's law, and that you are in fact increasingly finding that you do keep God's law and find great joy in doing so? The only reasonable answer is that you must be a Christian. James Montgomery Boice explains, "When a man or woman begins to obey God, first in responding to his offer of salvation in the Lord Jesus Christ and then in a growing desire to live a Christlike life, this is evidence of a divine and supernatural working in his or her life. It is proof that God is present and that he has already begun a regenerative work within the individual."[9]

Be greatly encouraged, then, if you desire to show your love to Jesus by obeying his commands. Take heart, and be assured of God's saving work in your life. Now press on in new obedience, and enter into the joy of yielding yourself more and more fully in loving embrace of Christ's commands, knowing that in this way you not only prove your love of Christ to yourself but show your love to him who has loved you and laid down his life for your sins.

9. Ibid., 4:1108.

96

THE OTHER HELPER

John 14:16—17

"I will ask the Father, and he will give you another Helper, to be
with you forever, even the Spirit of truth." (John 14:16–17)

*I*t is not hard to see how the disciples became so devoted to Jesus
and dependent on his personal presence. During the three or
so years of his ministry on earth, he had guided them, taught
them, rescued them, and revealed God's power to them. According to Jesus,
however, one of the most important things that he would ever do for his
disciples was to leave them. Jesus explained why his departure to heaven
was for the benefit of his followers: "I will ask the Father, and he will give
you another Helper, to be with you forever, even the Spirit of truth" (John
14:16–17). In heaven, Jesus would be seated in power at the right hand of the
Father for their sakes, and in his place on earth he would send the Holy Spirit,
who not only would "dwell with you," but would even "be in you" (14:17).

MEET THE HOLY SPIRIT

Most Christians today are well informed about the person and work of
Jesus Christ, at least knowing that he is the Son of God who died on the cross

for our sins. But, writes J. I. Packer, "the average Christian is in a complete fog as to what work the Holy Spirit does."[1] Errors abound among Christians when it comes to the Spirit, and, perhaps just as concerning, many are like the impoverished believers whom Paul met when he first arrived in Ephesus. These Ephesians stated, "We have not even heard that there is a Holy Spirit" (Acts 19:2).

The first thing for us to know about the Holy Spirit is that he is a divine person. His personhood can be seen throughout the New Testament, in which the Spirit is said to decide (1 Cor. 12:11), act (Rom. 8:26), speak (1 Tim. 4:1), and feel (Eph. 4:30), just as any other person does. When Jesus says that he will send "another Helper," he means not a different kind of Helper but the same kind of Helper as himself. The Holy Spirit is thus a divine person who takes the place of the divine person who leaves.

The importance of the Spirit's personhood cannot be overstated, since the alternative is to think of the Spirit as an impersonal force. Thinking this way, many Christians desire to get more of the Spirit in the same way that one gets power from an electrical outlet. They speak of "plugging into" the Spirit and emphasize spiritual techniques or experiences that will "tap into" the Spirit's power. The Holy Spirit is not a mere power, however, but the third person of the divine Godhead, coequal with God the Father and God the Son. James Montgomery Boice comments: "If we think of the Holy Spirit as a mysterious power, our thought will continually be, 'How can I get more of the Holy Spirit?' If we think of the Holy Spirit as a person, our thought will be, 'How can the Holy Spirit have more of me?' The first thought is entirely pagan. The second is New Testament Christianity."[2]

In Acts 8:9–24, we read of Simon the Magus, a spiritual figure who professed faith in Christ and then sought to purchase the Holy Spirit. Peter rebuked Simon, saying, "May your silver perish with you, because you thought you could obtain the gift of God with money!" (8:20). Acts later tells of the calling of Paul and Barnabas to be the first missionaries. While the believers in Antioch were worshiping, "the Holy Spirit said, 'Set apart for me Barnabas and Saul for the work to which I have called them'" (13:2). Simon was one who wanted to gain and use God's Spirit as a magical force, but instead it is the Spirit who gains us and uses us for Christ's work.

1. J. I. Packer, *Knowing God* (Downers Grove, IL: InterVarsity Press, 1973), 60.
2. James Montgomery Boice, *The Gospel of John*, 5 vols. (Grand Rapids: Baker, 1999), 4:1112.

The Spirit as *Paraklete*

In addressing his forlorn disciples, Jesus made a second statement about the Holy Spirit. He said that the Holy Spirit is sent by the Father and the Son together as a result of Jesus' finished work on earth. "I will ask the Father," Jesus said, "and he will give you another Helper, to be with you forever" (John 14:16). Jesus had just told the disciples that they would do "greater works" than he had done (referring to the spread of the gospel), that they would pray effectual prayers, and that out of love for him they would obey his commands (14:12–15). The promise of the Holy Spirit continues that teaching. The sending of the Holy Spirit is not a reward for good behavior, but rather is Jesus' part of this relationship of mutual devotion. He would send the Holy Spirit to empower the disciples' life of gospel witness, prayer, and good works. Together in a joint council of grace for our salvation, the Father would give the Spirit and the Son would send the Spirit, to carry forward Christ's saving work in the gospel after his resurrection and ascension into heaven.

This teaching highlights the importance of the word *another*. Herman Ridderbos states, "This [Helper] will take Jesus' place after Jesus' departure and in his activity as [Helper] will do nothing other than what Jesus has been doing, except that in doing it he will continue and advance Jesus' work."[3] The Holy Spirit thus comes as another Jesus, not in his person but in his work. It is because of the Spirit's ongoing ministry on Christ's behalf that Christians are not impoverished by Jesus' departure but in fact are greatly helped.

What exactly, then, does the Spirit do to provide for Christ's disciples and their work for Jesus? The answer is found in a word that Jesus will mention four times in his Farewell Discourse, but that is not easily translated from the original Greek into English. The King James Version describes the Spirit as "another Comforter." The New International Version calls him "another Counselor." The English Standard Version renders this description as "another Helper." All of these offer a valid perspective, so long as they are rightly understood. In the Elizabethan English of the King James Version, a *comforter* was not a sympathetic listener but a legal advocate who supported a person in his affairs at court. To call the Spirit a *Counselor* is in

3. Herman Ridderbos, *John: A Theological Commentary* (Grand Rapids: Zondervan, 1997), 500.

accord with his mission of conveying Christ's truth, and the word *Helper* perhaps best conveys the meaning by being most general, speaking of the whole help that the Spirit provides.

In order to understand Jesus' meaning, we must consider the Greek word itself. Jesus describes the Holy Spirit as a *paraklete* (Greek *parakleton*), a word that combines the prefix *para* (meaning "alongside of") with the verb *kaleo* (meaning to "call out"). The form of the word is a passive participle, so we might literally describe the Holy Spirit as the One "who is called alongside." It is also valid to translate *paraklete* in terms of the Spirit's action, in which case he would be One "who calls from alongside." If we take these two ideas and combine them, we have the basic meaning of Jesus' designation of the Spirit as a *paraklete*. The Spirit is the divine person who is called to our side to continue the ministry that Jesus began. There at our side, the Spirit calls out to us, in the words of the Puritan John Owen, "to support, cherish, relieve, and comfort the church."[4]

I thought of the idea of a *paraklete* recently as one of our younger daughters began to ride her bicycle without the training wheels. She was able to take this important step in life only with a good deal of help. The "helper" was her mother, who acted out both senses of the word *paraklete*. First, she raced to our daughter's side as one called to answer the need. Once there, she guided the handlebars, balanced the bike as it got going, and called out the encouragement that our daughter needed to ride on her own without the training wheels. With the help of her mother as a *paraklete*, our daughter was able to accomplish what she otherwise lacked the ability to do on her own. In a like manner, the Holy Spirit provides the enabling help for Christians to achieve their potential as born-again followers of Jesus.

The Spirit's Inward Ministry

The primary difference in the manner of Christ's ministry and the Spirit's ministry as our Helper is seen in John 14:17. "You know him," Jesus said of the Spirit, and he "dwells with you," referring to the Spirit's presence in Christ himself. Jesus was born by the miraculous conception of the Holy Spirit (Matt. 1:20), and though he was himself fully divine, Jesus received

4. John Owen, *The Spirit and the Church*, abr. R. J. K. Law (Edinburgh: Banner of Truth, 2002), 147.

the equipping of the Holy Spirit at his baptism (Matt. 3:16). Jesus was the beginning of a new humanity in the Holy Spirit, which is why Paul refers to him as "the last Adam" who "became a life-giving spirit" (1 Cor. 15:45). In the person of Christ, the Spirit had been present all along, so by knowing Jesus, the disciples knew the Spirit. Now, after Jesus departed, his continued ministry of grace would be by means of the *indwelling* Spirit. Jesus here refers to the future when the Holy Spirit would come upon the church at Pentecost, saying that the Spirit then "will be in you" (John 14:17). This is why Jesus said that it was better for his disciples that he depart, for then the other Helper whom he would send would indwell believers with saving power.

The Spirit carries on Jesus' work as the *Christ*, meaning "Messiah" or "Anointed One," a title that gathers together the three anointed offices of the Old Testament. It is in terms of these offices that the Spirit carries on *within us* the work that Jesus accomplished *for us*.

First, the Spirit takes up Christ's office as the great and true Prophet of God's people. John began his Gospel by designating Jesus as "the Word" (John 1:1), and Jesus told his disciples that "whoever has seen me has seen the Father" (14:9). His revealing work carries on in the church by means of the Holy Scriptures, which Jesus appointed his apostles to write. It was the role of the Spirit to come alongside the apostles in this calling, divinely inspiring them so that their words would be the very words of God. Benjamin Morgan Palmer commented that Christ carried on his work of revelation as the Spirit's "mysterious power [was] exerted upon the minds of prophets and apostles, in order that they may safely conceive in thought and accurately represent in language all that the Revealer [made] known."[5] Peter likewise stated that in writing the Scriptures, "men spoke from God as they were carried along by the Holy Spirit" (2 Peter 1:21).

Christ's work of revelation did not conclude with the Spirit's inspiration of the Bible, but he continues to reveal God and his salvation today through the Spirit's illuminating work. It is only as the Spirit shines on the heart that anyone comprehends and believes God's Word today and is saved. Palmer explained that the Spirit "does this by lighting up the Scriptures to us with the glory which beams from the Savior's person and throne above."[6] As the *paraklete* that we need, the Holy Spirit comes alongside and works on

5. B. M. Palmer, *Sermons*, 2 vols. (1875; repr., Harrisonburg, VA: Sprinkle, 2002), 1:208.
6. Ibid., 1:209.

Christ's behalf within us so that, as Paul put it, the Word shines "in our hearts to give the light of the knowledge of the glory of God in the face of Jesus Christ" (2 Cor. 4:6).

Second, Christ is the Great High Priest who brings his cleansed people before God's holy throne. The New Testament teaches that it was "through the eternal Spirit" that Jesus gave himself as a spiritual Sacrifice for our sins (Heb. 9:14), offering his own blood to pay our debt to God's justice and secure our forgiveness. This great and pivotal work was about to take place, since Jesus' arrest lay mere hours beyond this last teaching to his disciples. For us as the true High Priest, Jesus made the sacrifice for our sin, and after his ascension he offered that sacrifice once for all in heaven. It is in this context that the New Testament uses the term *paraklete* to describe Jesus himself: "if anyone does sin, we have an advocate [Greek *parakleton*] with the Father, Jesus Christ the righteous" (1 John 2:1).

Since Jesus' sacrifice was offered once for all, what is the further priestly role of the Spirit? The answer is seen in the inward application of Christ's priestly blessings to the individual believer's spirit. Palmer explains:

> Christ procures for His people all spiritual blessings by His death. He then, by His intercession, sues them out before the throne of the Father. The decree is granted in their favor under this pleading; and then it is handed over to the eternal Spirit, whose function it is to work it into the actual experience of the believer.[7]

Jesus ministers as our High Priest today by his effectual intercession at the right hand of the Father. Paul asks, "Who is to condemn? Christ Jesus is the one who died—more than that, who was raised—who is at the right hand of God, who indeed is interceding for us" (Rom. 8:34). While Jesus, now in heaven, intercedes for us at the throne of grace, reaching out to the Father with the hands that were pierced for us, the other Helper, the Holy Spirit, performs this same work within us, bringing peace to our consciences as he presents the wounds of Christ to our minds. The pardon of sins was achieved for us by Christ our *paraklete*, and the application of this pardon within our hearts is carried out by the other *paraklete*, the Spirit whom Christ has sent from the Father.

7. Ibid., 1:210.

Christ's third office is that of the great King over all God's people. According to answer 26 of the Westminster Shorter Catechism, Christ executes his kingly office "in subduing us to himself, in ruling and defending us, and in restraining and conquering all his and our enemies." Jesus reigns in us today by means of the Holy Spirit within us. Jesus said, "Unless one is born again, he cannot see the kingdom of God" (John 3:3). Thus, he subdues the elect from their unbelief by sending the Holy Spirit to regenerate their souls. "Being born of the Spirit, we become the living subjects of Jesus the King,"[8] who rejoices along with the host of heaven as his sheep are called into the fold of salvation.

This kingly ministry is necessary for our strength under trials and temptations. Palmer comments, "The strength by which we are sustained, and through which we conquer at the last, is purchased for us by Christ our Lord, and is communicated through the agency of the Holy Spirit."[9] This principle pertains to the whole of our sanctification. Jesus said that the Holy Spirit whom he sends will be "with you forever" (John 14:16), because he is able to preserve us in faith by working into us all the graces of Christian character that we need for our pilgrimage to heaven. It is by the Spirit that believers are set free from their bondage to sin. It is by the Spirit that we receive assurance of our sonship to the Father and our inheritance with Christ in glory. Paul thus calls him the "Spirit of adoption," by whom we cry out, "Abba! Father!" (Rom. 8:15). And it is by the Spirit within us that Christ conveys his peace to our hearts, calling, "Come to me, all who labor and are heavy laden, and I will give you rest" (Matt. 11:28).

THE SPIRIT OF TRUTH

One thing that all these ministries have in common is that they are revealed to us by Christ through his Spirit by means of the Word. This reality explains the emphasis that Jesus gives in describing the *paraklete* as "the Spirit of truth" (John 14:17). As we continue in Jesus' Farewell Discourse, the role of the Spirit in revealing Christ's truth will be explained in detail. It was by the Spirit that these disciples were able to write the New Testament: "The Helper, the Holy Spirit . . . , will teach you all things and bring to your remembrance all that I have said to you" (14:26). It is by the same Spirit that

8. Ibid., 1:213.
9. Ibid., 1:212.

the glory of Christ is revealed to believers in the Word: "He will glorify me, for he will take what is mine and declare it to you" (16:14).

Without delving into Jesus' later teaching, for now we should observe the close connection between the Spirit of God and the Word of God. Christianity is not a religion of mystical insight, intuition, or ritual technique, but of revealed truth through the Word of God. It is largely because of erroneous views regarding the Holy Spirit that so many Christians today are suspicious of believers who are devoted to knowing Christ's truth and who revere the Bible as the very Word of God, given by the Spirit to lead us into a true knowledge of divine revelation. For many, being spiritual means being nondogmatic and imprecise. But according to Jesus, to be spiritual is to be biblical, for the Spirit is the "Spirit of truth" who through the Scriptures "will guide you into all the truth" (John 16:13). To be sure, this revelation will give us more than head knowledge! But it will not give us less. Thus, Paul says that the way for us to progress spiritually is to "be transformed by the renewal of your mind," so that we may "discern what is the will of God" through the truth of God's Word (Rom. 12:2).

Indeed, according to Jesus, it is by means of the truth that the great division within mankind is revealed. He says of the Spirit that "the world cannot receive [him], because it neither sees him nor knows him" (John 14:17). John Calvin commented: "The Holy Spirit is only a dream to earthly men, because they rely on their own reason and despise heavenly illumination."[10] Without the regenerating work of the Holy Spirit, man in sin is spiritually dead, so that he not only *will not* but *cannot* accept the things of God's Spirit. Paul elaborates: "The natural person does not accept the things of the Spirit of God, for they are folly to him, and he is not able to understand them because they are spiritually discerned" (1 Cor. 2:14). This gives believers all the more reason to prize the truth given us by Christ through the Spirit, relying not on worldly wisdom but on God's revealed Word.

EMPOWERED TO SERVE

Given Jesus' statement about the Spirit and the world, the first application of this passage should be made to unbelievers. Why is it that you, if

10. John Calvin, *New Testament Commentaries*, trans. T. H. L. Parker, 12 vols. (Grand Rapids: Eerdmans, 1959), 5:83.

you do not believe on Jesus Christ, know nothing of the reality and power of God's Holy Spirit? The answer, according to the Bible, is that through sin you are alienated from God. This alienation is within you, so that your heart is hostile to God, in the way that a reckless driver resents a trailing police car. According to the Bible, this alienation is even more severe on God's part, for our sins have offended him personally and transgressed his holy law, and as sinners we now lie under the awful wrath of the holy God who warns, "The wages of sin is death" (Rom. 6:23).

What hope is there for you if you cannot know the Holy Spirit or even understand God's Word? The answer is the very work of Christ that we have considered in this study. Christ is the Prophet, and he sets himself before you as the perfect revelation of the glory and grace of God. Moreover, through the Spirit-inspired Scriptures he declares to you his priestly work to gain the pardon of sins through his own blood. As King of heaven, he calls you to salvation through simple faith in his Word. As Prophet, Priest, and King today, Jesus invites you to receive all his work for you, which he will then continue in you by his Spirit, if you will receive him in humble, repentant faith. "Behold, now is the favorable time," he says; "behold, now is the day of salvation" (2 Cor. 6:2).

What is the application for believers? Jesus' teaching was designed to comfort his disciples with the knowledge of his continuing work in them by the Holy Spirit. We should thus be greatly encouraged by the power of Christ available to us through the Spirit, who comes alongside us and calls within us so that we can achieve our potential as born-again citizens of the kingdom of Christ.

So far in this chapter, Christ has told his disciples of three things they will do after he departs, and it turns out that these correspond to his own threefold office. Jesus said that whoever believes "will also do the works that I do," even "greater works than these" (John 14:12), referring mainly to the spread of the gospel through the world. But how are we to take up Christ's prophetic office, telling people today about his gospel of salvation? The answer: by the mighty help of the Holy Spirit, who gives us words to say (Matt. 10:19–20). Jesus added that we would pray in his name and receive what we ask. But can we really be mighty in the priestly ministry of prayer? The answer is found in the indwelling help of the Holy Spirit. Not that we always know what we should pray, but, Paul writes, "the Spirit helps us in our weakness" and intercedes for us even in our own prayers (Rom. 8:26–27). Finally, Jesus said, "If you love me, you will keep my commandments" (John 14:15). Can we reign with Christ, obeying the commands of God's Word, especially Christ's new commandment that we should love one another? The answer must surely be No if we were left to our own strength. But Jesus said, "I will ask the Father, and he will give you another Helper, to be with you forever, even the Spirit of truth" (14:16–17). With the Spirit of our King subduing our sin and granting us power from the armories of heaven, we have what we need through faith to do his royal will on earth as it is in heaven.

So how do we receive the Spirit? Remember that he is a person, not an impersonal force that we tap. According to the Bible, we receive the Spirit by trusting in Jesus Christ. Paul asked the Galatians, "Did you receive the Spirit by works of the law or by hearing with faith?" (Gal. 3:2). The answer was by faith alone. We then experience the Spirit's power through the Word that he inspired, which "is breathed out by God and profitable for teaching, for reproof, for correction, and for training in righteousness, that the man of God may be competent, equipped for every good work" (2 Tim. 3:16–17). Finally, we receive the Spirit's work in our lives by asking. In his great parable on prayer, Jesus commented that even earthly fathers give good gifts to their children. "How much more," he concluded, "will the heavenly Father give the Holy Spirit to those who ask him!" (Luke 11:13).

97

Because I Live

John 14:18–24

"I will ask the Father, and he will give you another Helper, to be with you forever, even the Spirit of truth." (John 14:16–17)

f all the promises of Jesus Christ, one that is most precious to me is not even recorded in any of the Gospels. Instead, it comes from the Old Testament, although Hebrews 13:5 attributes it to Christ, who promises: "I will never leave you nor forsake you" (see Deut. 31:6; Josh. 1:5). On many occasions when I have felt alone, unworthy, or defeated, I have retreated into this promise for shelter and strength: Jesus will never leave or forsake me!

The Puritan Thomas Watson described all of Christ's promises as "the water of life to renew fainting spirits." He said that "as in the ark manna was laid up, so promises are laid up in the ark of Scripture."[1] Thus, as we study and come to know Christ's promises, and then as our hearts feed on this manna for faith, we are sustained, renewed, strengthened, and comforted from fear.

Given their power, it is not surprising that Jesus' Farewell Discourse was filled with promises. Jesus promised to make a home for his followers

1. Thomas Watson, *A Body of Divinity* (Edinburgh: Banner of Truth, 1958), 36.

in heaven, to return for them in due time, to answer their prayers, and to strengthen them by sending the Holy Spirit. In John 14:18–24, Jesus heaps on four more precious promises. Together they address the problem of his soon departure, with promises regarding *what* Christ will do, *when* he will do it, *how* it will happen, and *why* it is given to believers. At the heart of these promises is one that seals Christ's ability to fulfill them all: "Because I live," Jesus assured his disciples, "you also will live" (14:19).

A SOLUTION PROMISED

As Jesus prepared to depart from his disciples, he summoned one of the most heart-wrenching images to capture their fears: "I will not leave you as orphans," he said (John 14:18). Orphans are perhaps the world's most destitute class of people, lacking even the love and care of family. This is why images of orphaned children pull at the heart and gain sympathy from virtually everyone.

Jesus stood on the very brink of the cross, when he would hang alone in contempt and agony before the hatred of the world. He was about to be forsaken, yet his concern focused on the disciples and how they would feel abandoned when their Master was cruelly slain. Their disappointment would be summed up by the words of the downcast disciples whom Jesus would later meet on the road out of town: "we had hoped that he was the one to redeem Israel" (Luke 24:20–21). Jesus knew that his closest disciples would especially feel abandoned and lost after he died, as alone in the world as helpless orphans.

This forlornness is often felt by followers when their leader dies or departs. Plato said, for instance, that when the great philosopher Socrates died, his disciples "thought that they would have to spend the rest of their lives forlorn, as children bereft of a father, and they did not know what to do about it."[2] Therefore, seeking to strengthen them for the coming dark hours, Jesus had a promise: "I will not leave you as orphans; I will come to you" (John 14:18). He promised to come to his disciples in their need, taking them swiftly back under the wings of his care so that they would not wander as lost orphans in the world. Earlier, Jesus had promised great things to his

---

2. William Barclay, *The Gospel of John*, 2 vols. (Philadelphia: Westminster, 1975), 2:196.

disciples: after going to heaven he would return for them, and while he was gone he would answer their prayers and send the Holy Spirit. But here was a promise more tangible and direct, certain to address the immediate need of those who relied on him: "I will come to you" (14:18).

THE RESURRECTION APPEARANCES PROMISED

In a passage of great promises, the first promise is foundational, stating clearly the *what* of Jesus' provision for his disciples. But this leads to some vital questions, the first of which is *when?* Jesus said that he would come, so when would that take place?

Scholars have disputed the answer to this *when*-question. Some argue that Jesus referred to his second coming, noting that this section began with a promise of his return at the end of the age (see John 14:3). Another view sees this promise as signaling the coming of the Holy Spirit at Pentecost, since the surrounding verses speak very definitely about the coming Holy Spirit. The previous verses state, "I will ask the Father, and he will give you another Helper, to be with you forever, even the Spirit of truth" (14:16–17). Both of these blessed events are occasions when Jesus promised to come to his disciples in need.

Nonetheless, the best understanding of Jesus' *when*-promise is that he refers to his appearances to the disciples after his resurrection from the grave, an event that would happen in a few days. Jesus says that his coming will be in "a little while" and that it will follow his removal from the world's sight: "Yet a little while and the world will see me no more, but you will see me" (John 14:19). That statement was fulfilled in the death and burial of Jesus, followed by his resurrection and appearances to the disciples, producing the very result that Jesus cites here: that the disciples would finally comprehend who he was in relation to the Father. Speaking to the disciples on Thursday night, knowing that he would be taken from them and crucified on Friday, Jesus looked ahead to the first Easter Sunday and said, "You will see me." The Greek word here for *see* is *theoreo*, which means a seeing of perception: "You will perceive me," Jesus meant.

What a difference it made to the disciples when Jesus appeared among them in his resurrected body, displaying his wounds, inviting them to touch him, and even eating a fish to prove that he was really alive (Luke 24:39–43).

Jesus invited Thomas to place his fingers in Jesus' side and hands to enable him to believe (John 20:27), prompting the model profession of faith: "My Lord and my God!" (John 20:28). Having seen Jesus in the flesh, the same Peter who had denied him before his trial was emboldened to proclaim his resurrection in the first Christian sermon at Pentecost (Acts 2:23–24). What a difference Christ's postresurrection appearances made in the lives of the disciples: this was when he came to them so that they would know themselves not forsaken.

But there is more to Jesus' coming than his resurrection, for another result was the disciples' own spiritual resurrection. This interpretation is demanded by Jesus' statement that "because I live, you also will live" (John 14:19). Having risen from the grave in the power of the Holy Spirit, Jesus gave spiritual life that enabled the disciples to see him with eyes of faith. The principle in this promise may be applied to the whole range of our salvation. Because Jesus rose in resurrection life, he will raise our bodies into resurrection glory, and he now grants spiritual life to those who belong to him. "Because I live," he assures us, "you also will live" (14:19). "His resurrection is the guarantee that they will not be overcome by death. His life means life for them (cf. 6:57)."[3]

The immediate result of Jesus' resurrection was that the disciples would perceive, as Jesus put it, "that I am in my Father" (John 14:20). This shows that Christ's resurrection life imparts faith in him. The disciples' failure to understand the meaning of the cross highlighted their need for a spiritual resurrection of their own. The same is true for each of us. It is only when Christ grants us his resurrection life that we understand the truth about him and respond in faith, joyfully trusting him for our salvation. This granting of spiritual life from God is called our new birth, which precedes and causes faith (3:3).

The result of our new life is our initial, saving knowledge of Jesus. Here, Jesus says that the disciples will know that he is in the Father. Later, Jesus says that we will grow in our personal knowledge of him as he manifests himself, but at first we gain the perception that he is who he said he is. It was because of Christ's unbreakable unity with the Father as the divine Son that death could not conquer him. For while he died in his human nature,

---

3. Leon Morris, *The Gospel according to John*, rev. ed., New International Commentary on the New Testament (Grand Rapids: Eerdmans, 1995), 579.

his divine nature—eternally joined in being with God the Father—was incapable of dying. This saving deity is what we know when we first believe: "that I am in my Father."

Jesus comes to us today in the gospel message and in the ministry of the Holy Spirit. When he calls us to new life and faith, we, too, are brought into saving union with God's eternal life. Thus, when we come to know that Christ is one with the Father, we also realize that "this union is in turn the pattern for the relationship between Christ and his followers."[4] Jesus says in full, "In that day you will know that I am in my Father, and you in me, and I in you" (John 14:20). This is why Christians will live forever: not because we have become intrinsically immortal ourselves, independent of Christ, and certainly not because we have ourselves become divine, but because we are joined to the eternal life of the incarnate Son of God—as Paul put it, God "made us alive together with Christ" (Eph. 2:5)—and because he will live forever. The writer of Hebrews celebrates his reign, saying, "You, Lord, laid the foundation of the earth in the beginning, and the heavens are the work of your hands; they will perish, but you remain; . . . you are the same, and your years will have no end" (Heb. 1:10–12). Through our bond of faith with him, Christ has granted us resurrection life so that we will live and reign with him forever, beginning at the moment of our new birth into saving faith.

INCREASED KNOWLEDGE OF CHRIST PROMISED

Jesus has promised the disciples that they will not be left as orphans, and that his renewed fellowship with them will begin after his resurrection. These were his promises in answer to the questions of *what* and *when*. This raises another question: *how* will the disciples, after the resurrection, grow in their knowledge of Jesus? His answer is that, having begun our new life by knowing that Jesus is who he said he is, we grow in our knowledge of him personally through a life of love for him that obeys his commands. "Whoever has my commandments and keeps them, he it is who loves me," Jesus said (John 14:21).

This is the second time in this Farewell Discourse that Jesus has emphasized obedience to his commands. The first was in verse 15: "If you love

4. William Hendriksen, *Exposition of the Gospel according to John*, 2 vols., New Testament Commentary (Grand Rapids: Baker, 1953), 2:280.

me, you will keep my commandments." Here is sufficient proof to refute the idea that Christians, having been saved by faith alone, need not obey. To be sure, a cold, outward, or proud adherence to the Bible is not true obedience, since only love is able to keep Christ's commands. Yet Jesus maintains that one who truly loves him will obey his Word. Alexander Maclaren wrote: "There are two motives for keeping commandments—one because they are commanded, and one because we love Him that commands. The one is slavery and the other is liberty. The one is like the Arctic regions, cold and barren, the other is like tropical lands, full of warmth and sunshine, glorious and glad fertility."[5] Real and living Christianity always involves a free and happy obedience out of love for Jesus.

Jesus' point was not merely to repeat his teaching on obedience, however, but rather to show that by this loving obedience, believers come to know him better. The first reason for this is that an obedient life pleases our heavenly Father: Jesus said, "He who loves me will be loved by my Father" (John 14:21). This does not mean that we earn God's love by loving Jesus. The whole New Testament emphasizes that we are saved because "God so loved the world" (3:16). In his first epistle, John reminds us that "we love because he first loved us" (1 John 4:19). It is helpful to consider an older distinction: between God's love of *compassion*, whereby he sent his Son to die for our sins, and God's love of *complacency*, an old term that means his pleasure and delight in the love and obedience of his people. This is why obedience to God's Word always results in spiritual blessing, not merely because God's Word is right and good but also because God sovereignly blesses obedience. Just as the Father was well pleased with the obedience of his Son, so he is also pleased when we glorify his Son through loving obedience.

The second reason that obedience yields increased knowledge of Christ is explained in yet another promise: "He who loves me will be loved by my Father, and I will love him and manifest myself to him" (John 14:21). The word for *manifest* occurs seldom in the Bible, normally referring to a vivid display of divine glory. It was the word used by Moses in the Greek translation of the Old Testament (known as the *Septuagint* or *LXX*) when he pleaded with God for a visible display of his deity (Ex. 33:13). In the years that

5. Alexander Maclaren, *Expositions of Holy Scripture*, 17 vols. (Grand Rapids: Baker, 1982), 11:347.

followed his resurrection, as the disciples poured out their lives in faithful service as apostles, Jesus appeared to them many times in visions, giving them encouragement, further revelation, and strength to endure. He did not leave them as orphans, and not only appeared to them after his resurrection, but manifested himself to them for increasing knowledge in years to come.

How does this promise apply to us today? Jesus is saying that he will respond to our obedience by making himself increasingly real to us. He does not manifest himself bodily, having ascended into heaven, and nothing in the Bible encourages us to expect visions. Instead, Christ will make himself real to us and manifest his glory in the Bible and through the Holy Spirit's witness to Scripture in the hearts of those who love and obey Jesus. Jesus mentions his Word four times in John 14:21–24, making it clear that those who seek him out in Scripture will be given an increased knowledge of Jesus through his Word.

This teaching is vitally important for Christians. Notice that Jesus does not prescribe a life of monastic seclusion that will enable us to know him better. Jesus does not send us to some mountaintop away from life that we might see his glory. Instead, he calls us to a lifestyle of loving obedience in which we will increasingly know him as the Father responds in pleasure and as Christ reveals his glory in the Word. Paul expressed our duty in these classic terms: "I have been crucified with Christ. It is no longer I who live, but Christ who lives in me. And the life I now live in the flesh I live by faith in the Son of God, who loved me and gave himself for me" (Gal. 2:20). Notice that we walk with Christ and grow in knowledge while living "in the flesh"—that is, in our normal earthly life—as we lovingly obey him in our jobs, homes, families, marriages, and communities.

If you are a new or young believer, this highlights the importance that you start following Christ sincerely, applying his teaching in the Bible to your daily life. We are not merely to learn his teaching but also to put it into practice. We are to pray and take an interest in the salvation of others; we are to love others and pursue personal holiness. In this way, obeying Jesus out of love for him, he promises to disclose his glory increasingly as we walk with him in faith.

This teaching is equally important for many who have long called themselves Christians. James Montgomery Boice comments:

Many Christians would be willing to do spectacular things if by that means they could come to know Christ better. But they are unwilling to do the commonplace things that are involved in simple obedience. Will you do them? If you will, you will most certainly grow in God's grace. If you obey, Christ will increasingly unveil his heart to you.[6]

If we find that our relationship with Christ has dulled, it is probably because we have turned our passions back to the world, ceased our hunger for biblical truth, and settled for the initial spiritual gains of our first days as a Christian. Dry-souled and barren-hearted Christians should be motivated to renew their passion for Christ by his promise to respond with a greater knowledge of him and display of his glory.

COMMUNION WITH GOD PROMISED

We remember that this chain of promises began with Jesus' teaching of *what* he will do (not leave us as orphans), then *when* he will come (to the disciples after the resurrection and to us in our new birth), and then *how* we will enjoy this fellowship with him (through his increased disclosure as we love him and obey his commands). The passage concludes with Jesus' answer to a question that came from Judas—not Judas Iscariot but Judas the son of James (Luke 6:16), also known as Thaddeus (Mark 3:18)—regarding *why*: "Lord, how is it that you will manifest yourself to us, and not to the world?" (John 14:22). This question revealed Judas's confusion regarding Christ's saving work, thinking that it would be better for Jesus to display his glory before the world, perhaps recalling the ways in which God had awed both pharaoh and Israelite with visual displays during the exodus.

Jesus answered with a promise that clarifies God's intentions in saving his people. He said, "If anyone loves me, he will keep my word, and my Father will love him, and we will come to him and make our home with him" (John 14:23). Here we find that Jesus' plan to be with us involves the fulfillment of God's ancient purpose: to make his home in the hearts of those who love him and keep his Word. God's plan never envisioned winning over a hard-hearted, unbelieving world with overwhelming audiovisual displays. Rather, he planned to redeem a people for himself,

6. James Montgomery Boice, *The Gospel of John*, 5 vols. (Grand Rapids: Baker, 1999), 4:1145.

a people who, by his grace and by the power that he would work in them, would love him in holiness so that he might dwell in them in love. Paul stated this, saying that Christ "gave himself for us to redeem us from all lawlessness and to purify for himself a people for his own possession who are zealous for good works" (Titus 2:14).

Within such a people, chosen by God's sovereign election, bought by Christ's atoning blood, and sanctified by the Holy Spirit, both Father and Son design to come and "make our home with him." So far from being forsaken or orphaned, those who receive the gospel in faith, loving Jesus and obeying God's commands, will become, individually and together with the church, a holy temple in which God will dwell (cf. 1 Cor. 6:19; Eph. 2:21–22). In this way, both God and his people begin now a communion of love that anticipates the glorious communion that he has prepared for eternity: "Behold, the dwelling place of God is with man. He will dwell with them, and they will be his people, and God himself will be with them as their God" (Rev. 21:3). The chief blessing that God can give is himself, and the purpose of our redemption is that he might be glorified in us as we enjoy communion with him by the Spirit and through the Word as God dwells in our hearts.

BECAUSE HE LIVES

At the heart of this great series of promises is Jesus' claim and pledge, "Because I live, you also will live" (John 14:19). This suggests that there are two kinds of Christians. There are those who live as if Christ is alive and those for whom Jesus is little more than a figurehead for their religion. Which one are you? Christians who realize that Jesus is now living at the right hand of God and that we can know him better will make this privilege the overriding passion of their lives. We still have to do our jobs, raise our children, and engage in all manner of worldly activities. But all will be done unto our living and present Lord, who loved us and calls us into love for him. Such Christians will seek to please Jesus rather than the world; they will want to be close to Jesus rather than sinful pleasures. They will live by his strength and not by their own resources or by the power of the world. The Bible will be for them a living book of communion, in which they hear the voice of Christ, on the pages of which his glory and grace are manifested to our souls.

Other Christians—nominal Christians, even if their profession of faith is biblical—will live as if Jesus were not alive or present. Their concern is what they can get from their faith rather than the giving of themselves through it. Their delight is found in the things of this world, the will of which they find it hard to refuse. If they read the Bible, they do so out of cold duty, learning facts but not hearing the voice of Christ. So on it goes, with prayer, worship, and other Christian duties: all is Arctic frost or at least a Midwestern chill.

If any of this describes you, then listen to Jesus: he says, "Because I live, you also will live" (John 14:19). Not only will you live after you die, but through communion with the living Christ you will experience the life he gives now. Come to him, seek him, ask him to make himself real to your faith. Seek him in his Word, love him by obeying his commands, and remember that those who are faithful in little things are always entrusted with more (Matt. 25:21).

Finally, if you are not a believer in Christ, then the last verse was written for you. Jesus said, "Whoever does not love me does not keep my words" (John 14:24). Your indifference to Christ's gospel and your neglect of his commands reveal a cold heart toward the Son of God and Savior. He adds, "And the word that you hear is not mine but the Father's who sent me." Will you not seek the life that Jesus gives, and will you not accept the message that he brings from God the Father? The danger is that once you have turned away, you, like the men who crucified him, may see Jesus no more (14:19). Yet he offers you salvation now, offering to be with you always, conquering sin and death by his atoning blood, and living in you by the Holy Spirit he sends. Isn't this more than the world can offer you? Jesus lives forever, whether you believe or not. But if you believe, giving your love to Jesus Christ, by his life you will have life forever. He promises, "Because I live, you also will live," starting right now.

98

MY PEACE I GIVE

John 14:25—31

"Peace I leave with you; my peace I give to you. Not as the world
gives do I give to you." (John 14:27)

Edward Hicks was a nineteenth-century American folk painter, and a minister in the Society of Friends, also known as the Quakers. Nearly all his many paintings were devoted to the same subject: the "Peaceable Kingdom" of Isaiah 11:6 wherein "the wolf shall dwell with the lamb . . . , and the calf and the lion and the fattened calf together; and a little child shall lead them." Hicks's paintings had two goals: to show that Christians could be practicing artists and to express his hope for peace on earth.

Art historians group Hicks's paintings into four periods. The first period, known as the "Border Peaceable Kingdoms," for their surrounding borders with the text of Isaiah 11:6, depicted the lions and lambs mingling sweetly, with Quakers enjoying peaceful pursuits in the background. The second phase, the "Banner Peaceable Kingdoms," features banners of Isaiah 11:6 wrapped around the human figures. Now, however, there is disquiet and anxiety, with the people not gathering but dispersing. These paintings reflected a division within the Society of Friends between those who sought a rural lifestyle and those Quakers who lived prosperous city lives. The last two phases, the "Middle" and "Late Peaceable Kingdoms," reflect Hicks's abandonment of any hope for peace on earth because of increased division among the Quakers, with the animals fighting and humanity divided. In Hicks's very last painting, his own depression is depicted by a lion hunched over in sheer exhaustion.

What do these works of art tell us about Edward Hicks? Seeking peace on earth through the labors of men, he discovered nothing but division and strife, even in a society of religious friends.[1] His quest for peace failed because he looked to men and not to Jesus Christ. What Hicks longed for, Jesus promised to give: "Peace I leave with you," he said; "my peace I give to you" (John 14:27).

PEACE IN THE STORM

When Jesus told the disciples, "Let not your hearts be troubled, neither let them be afraid" (John 14:27), they were on the brink of a great storm, with much to fear. Jesus was about to lead them out toward the garden of Gethsemane, where Judas and the temple guards would find them. They therefore needed to be reassured with reasons not to be afraid.

Being a Christian does not preserve us from the storms and trials of this world. Instead, Christ will himself often send us into storms, just as he was now leading the disciples to the place of his arrest. Perhaps the most vivid illustration of this principle was when Jesus sent the disciples onto the wind-swept Sea of Galilee. Mark records that as the storm was about to capsize their little boat, Jesus stepped forward and "rebuked the wind and said to the sea, 'Peace! Be still!'" (Mark 4:39), and the winds and waves obeyed his sovereign voice. This was the same Jesus who now prepared his disciples for the great storm surrounding his arrest and crucifixion. He said to them again, "Let not your hearts be troubled, neither let them be afraid" (John 14:27).

Jesus followed with the reason they should not fear: "Peace I leave with you; my peace I give to you" (John 14:27). A peaceful state of mind is not something that the disciples were to achieve by their own will or devices, but rather, Jesus would grant peace as his parting gift. Jesus did not promise

1. Philip Graham Ryken, *My Father's World* (Phillipsburg, NJ: P&R Publishing, 2002), 117–20.

to leave his disciples an inheritance of money, worldly influence, or safety. Instead, he gives "inward peace of conscience, arising from a sense of pardoned sin and reconciliation with God."[2] Matthew Henry remarks:

> When Christ was about to leave the world He made His will. His soul He bequeathed to His Father; His body He bequeathed to Joseph, to be decently interred; His clothes fell to the soldiers; His mother He left to the care of John; but what should He leave to His poor disciples, that had left all for Him? Silver and gold He had none; but He left them what was infinitely better, His peace.[3]

The peace that Jesus gives may be considered in two ways, in keeping with the biblical language. First, Jesus gives *peace with God*. This is what Paul referred to as the result of our justification through faith: "Therefore, since we have been justified by faith, we have peace with God through our Lord Jesus Christ" (Rom. 5:1). Jesus ended the war between the believer and God, paying in his blood the price of peace in the courts of divine justice. Yet Christ's peace is not merely the absence of our former conflict with God. It also entails the positive experience of the *peace of God*, which results from the ministry of the Holy Spirit whom Jesus sends. Paul wrote that we receive this peace when we pray, for then "the peace of God, which surpasses all understanding, will guard your hearts and your minds in Christ Jesus" (Phil. 4:7). This peace of blessing comes from a right relationship with God, the awareness of his loving presence in our lives, and the receiving of his grace through faith. It was in the *peace of God*, Christ's having made *peace with God* on the cross, that the disciples were to be untroubled in the storm.

PEACE DESPITE AN UNLOVING WORLD

When Christians begin speaking of the blessings of spiritual peace, we are sometimes accused of pie-in-the-sky escapism. But as Jesus promised peace, he did anything but avoid the real threats to the disciples. He dealt with three threats to our peace, including one that would become obvious in the coming hours: the hostility and violence of an unloving world.

2. J. C. Ryle, *Expository Thoughts on the Gospels: John*, 3 vols. (Edinburgh: Banner of Truth, 1999), 3:98.

3. Matthew Henry, *Commentary on the Whole Bible*, 6 vols. (Peabody, MA: Hendrickson, 2009), 5:903.

Jesus said, "My peace I give to you. Not as the world gives do I give to you" (John 14:27).

James Montgomery Boice characterized the giving of the world as *insincere*, since the motives seldom match the words; *impotent*, since our peacemaking seldom achieves more than a hostile truce; *scanty*, always giving less than was possible; and *selfish*, often giving with a true desire of receiving in return.[4] It is in large part because of the world's manner of giving that there is no peace. Discovering this reality caused Edward Hicks increasingly to depict strife in his "Peaceable Kingdom" paintings. As the prophet Jeremiah complained about Jerusalem's worldly leaders, "Peace, peace," they say, "when there is no peace" (Jer. 6:14).

One of the great eras of worldly peace was the Pax Romana of Augustus Caesar. After his conquests in western Europe, Augustus returned to Rome and built an altar to peace, the Ara Pacis, which remains today. Fittingly, he placed his peace monument on the field of Mars, the Roman god of war. The Roman historian Tacitus gave the most fitting commentary, quoting the words of a Scottish chieftain who had warred against the Roman legions: "They make a desolation, and call it peace."[5] George Beasley-Murray described Augustus' peace altar as "a monument to the skill of its sculptors and to the empty messianic pretensions of its emperors."[6]

How different is the peace that Christ gives. Jesus did not make peace for himself at the expense of others, but he gives peace to his people at his own expense. His peace altar was not built of marble on the field of war but consisted of two wooden beams in the shape of a cross on Calvary's hill. Whereas the peace of the world is *insincere*, Christ gives peace with the coin of his heart's blood; the world's peace is *impotent*, but Jesus' death for sin achieved true reconciliation with God; the world gives *scantily*, but Jesus gave his very life and body for us; the world gives *selfishly*, but Jesus' peace is one of self-sacrifice and self-giving. "Greater love has no one than this," he explained, "that someone lay down his life for his friends" (John 15:13).

Christ's peace differs from that of the world in terms of its *certainty*. Unlike man, who gives but takes back, Paul writes that "the gifts and the calling of God are irrevocable" (Rom. 11:29). The peace that Jesus gives is

4. James Montgomery Boice, *The Gospel of John*, 5 vols. (Grand Rapids: Baker, 1999), 4:1154.
5. Tacitus, *Agricola*, 30.
6. George R. Beasley-Murray, *John*, Word Biblical Commentary 36 (Waco, TX: Word, 1987), 262.

thus an eternal peace. The peace of Christ contrasts with worldly peace in its *character*: "his peace is not the absence of conditions that intimidate but rather is the composure to be faithful in the face of adversity."[7] Finally, the peace of Christ is unique in its *conclusion*. Beasley-Murray writes, "'My peace' is Jesus' bequest of the peace which is no less than the salvation of the kingdom of God."[8]

PEACE DESPITE CHRIST'S ABSENCE

A second threat to our peace is the problem of Jesus' departure. Would Christ's absence remove the disciples' peace, and does Jesus' physical absence nullify his peace for us today?

Jesus addressed this problem in a way that might be surprising to us. He said: "You heard me say to you, 'I am going away, and I will come to you.' If you loved me, you would have rejoiced, because I am going to the Father" (John 14:28). Knowing the agony that lay ahead of Jesus, we might forget his crowning joy that was just beyond, as the faithful Son of God returned to the heavenly Father in glory! If dying Christians are often excited about seeing God face-to-face for the first time, Christ would have been no less thrilled about, as D. A. Carson put it, "returning to the sphere where he belongs, to the glory he had with the Father before the world began (17:5), and to the place where the Father is undiminished in glory."[9]

John 14:28 is a favorite verse of Unitarians, Jehovah's Witnesses, and others who seek to deny Jesus' true deity, since he states that "the Father is greater than I." This statement, they assert, specifies that Jesus is something less than fully God. The main problem with this view is that the Gospel of John is filled with direct assertions to Jesus' full deity, as is the entire New Testament. In John 10:30, for instance, Jesus stated, "I and the Father are one," claiming deity so clearly that the Jews sought to stone him for blasphemy. John Calvin explains that when Jesus says that the Father is greater, he "does not here make a comparison between the Divinity of the Father and of his own, nor between his own human

---

7. Andreas J. Kostenberger, *John* (Grand Rapids: Baker, 2004), 444.
8. Beasley-Murray, *John*, 262.
9. D. A. Carson, *The Gospel of John* (Grand Rapids: Eerdmans, 1991), 508.

nature and the Divine essence of the Father, but rather between his present state and the heavenly glory, to which he would soon afterwards be received."[10]

An implication of Christ's return to heaven is a second reason why Jesus' absence would be no barrier to his gift of peace. As he insisted throughout this farewell teaching, Jesus' return to the Father would benefit the disciples in every way. Christ's return to the Father, who is "greater," can only mean the beginning of a new era of grace that would exceed all that had previously been known. Christ's return in glory is good news for his followers, since "it will mark the Father's approval and acceptance of all that he has achieved on earth."[11]

The final reason that Christ's absence will not mar the disciples' peace is "the Helper, the Holy Spirit, whom the Father will send in my name" (John 14:26). This is the second of four passages in this Farewell Discourse regarding the person and work of the Holy Spirit, each naming him the *paraklete*, or "Helper." We are reminded here of what we observed in our study of John 14:16–17, that the Holy Spirit is a divine person who is sent, not an impersonal power that is seized or manipulated. It is by means of the Spirit's ministry on his behalf that Jesus bequeaths peace to his followers, even in his absence.

In particular, the Holy Spirit will minister peace by means of Christ's revealed Word. Jesus said, "He will teach you all things and bring to your remembrance all that I have said to you" (John 14:26). This statement has particular reference to the original disciples, who as Christ's apostles would later write the New Testament under the inspiration of the Holy Spirit. Verse 26 explains much regarding this inspiration: the Spirit would teach the apostles the doctrine that they would pass on in Scripture and cause them to remember the things that Jesus had taught them during his earthly ministry. John is, of course, letting us in on his own experience in writing this Gospel. He has occasionally noted that the disciples did not understand an event or saying of Jesus until after his resurrection (cf. 2:22; 12:16; 14:26; 15:20). But the Spirit will come and help them, bringing to their minds the whole saving revelation of Jesus for his church.

---

10. John Calvin, *Calvin's Commentaries*, trans. William Pringle, 22 vols. (Grand Rapids: Baker, 2009), 18:103.
11. Mark G. Johnston, *Let's Study John* (Edinburgh: Banner of Truth, 2003), 196.

We should make a number of important observations from these verses. First, the Holy Spirit teaches us today nothing but the same message that Jesus gave his disciples. John Calvin emphasized this principle because of his battles with the Roman Catholic Church, which then (as now) claimed special revelation from the Holy Spirit that enabled it to contradict the Bible. Jesus insisted, instead, that the Holy Spirit would convey "all that I have said to you" (John 14:26). Calvin comments, "By this single word we may refute all the inventions which Satan has brought into the Church from the beginning, under the pretence of the Spirit. . . . But the spirit that introduces any doctrine or invention apart from the Gospel is a deceiving spirit, and not the Spirit of Christ."[12] Today, Christians face claims by liberal scholars that the New Testament cannot convey the actual message of Jesus because he did not himself write it. Our answer is the Holy Spirit, who taught the apostles and brought to their remembrance all that Jesus had done and said. We also face extremists within the church who claim special revelation from the Spirit contrary to the Bible. The Spirit, however, teaches nothing but what Christ taught and had recorded in the Scriptures.

Second, we are reminded that our apprehension of God's Word is a spiritual matter and not a merely intellectual pursuit. We therefore must pray for an understanding of Scripture, and we will sometimes wait for the Spirit's illumination. Likewise, the bare preaching of the gospel accomplishes nothing unless the Spirit brings the Word of salvation to bear upon the heart, so that we must not only preach and witness God's Word but also bathe our ministry in prayer.

Third, Jesus' emphasis on the teaching ministry of the Holy Spirit indicates that we receive his peace today in large part through the ministry of the Word of God. Just as the Israelites of old ate the entire Passover lamb, Jesus said that we gain peace from "all that I have said to you" (John 14:26). Jesus' teaching on sin and forgiveness, on justification, sanctification, and glorification, on life and death, and on the church and the world is all necessary for our peace. If we are not experiencing the peace that this gives, we should seek his peace in prayer (Phil. 4:7) and drink from the fountain of peace that flows through the whole of his Word.

12. Calvin, *Calvin's Commentaries*, 18:101.

PEACE DESPITE SATAN'S ATTACKS

As Jesus prepared to depart from the upper room, not only was his mind focused on the unloving world that would soon crucify him and on the disciples whom he loved so well, but he also heard the coming footsteps of his greater adversary, Satan. Indeed, while Jesus was delivering this very teaching, the devil was busily working through Judas the betrayer, the scheming Jewish leaders, and the temple soldiers who were then arming for their appointment with Jesus on the Mount of Olives. Thus Jesus mentioned one last threat to the disciples' peace: "I will no longer talk much with you," he said, "for the ruler of this world is coming" (John 14:30).

Satan is called the "ruler of this world" not because he wrested actual dominion from the hands of God, but because "by God's permission, he exercises his tyranny over the world."[13] This is the same devil who asked to "sift" Peter that very evening, resulting in his three denials (Luke 22:31), and whom Peter would later describe as "a roaring lion, seeking someone to devour" (1 Peter 5:8). So why would Satan's attacks not threaten the peace of Christ's people? Jesus answered, "He has no claim on me" (John 14:30).

Long beforehand, Satan had come in serpent form to tempt our first parents into sin and ruin. In the first garden, the devil had found Adam and Eve apt to his influence. But how different it would be when Satan came to the garden in which Jesus presented himself to be arrested and put to death. With Jesus, the new Adam and the fountain of a new, Spirit-empowered humanity, Satan could gain no handhold. Satan could find no chink in the armor of the Son of God, no flaw to exploit, no weakness to tempt, and especially no sin to condemn. This can be said only about Jesus Christ, which is why he alone could offer himself for the sin of others and why we need him to redeem us from the power of sin and of Satan.

C. S. Lewis captured Satan's inability to master Jesus in his famous novel *The Lion, the Witch, and the Wardrobe*. In that tale, the evil White Witch knows the way in which she can gain the right to slay the Lion King, Aslan. With what lurid evil she delights in every moment of his agony and disgrace. His death is the great triumph for which her heart has long lusted. But the deeper mystery that she has never fathomed is that he would by his death

13. Ibid., 18:104.

overthrow her kingdom utterly.[14] So it was with the true subject of Lewis's allegory, the Lord Jesus Christ in his atoning death, by which he conquered sin, overthrew the power of death, and laid Satan's kingdom in ruins. The writer of Hebrews explains: "Since therefore the children share in flesh and blood, he himself likewise partook of the same things, that through death he might destroy the one who has the power of death, that is, the devil, and deliver all those who through fear of death were subject to lifelong slavery" (Heb. 2:14–15).

Instead of being conquered by the devil, Jesus went to the cross of his own choosing, in obedience to the Father's will for our salvation. He said, "I do as the Father has commanded me, so that the world may know that I love the Father" (John 14:31). As Jesus now prepared to depart the upper room and head to that garden confrontation, he wanted people to know not merely how much he loved them but, even more importantly, how much he loved the Father. Jesus was not tricked or overpowered in his murder but sovereign in his obedience to the will of God for our salvation. Already hearing the footsteps of Satan, Jesus lifted up his head, rejoicing to obey his Father and knowing that Satan's attacks could not thwart the peace that he gives, and declared, "He has no claim on me" (14:30).

PEACE THROUGH FAITH IN CHRIST

With this teaching, Jesus concluded his discourse to the disciples in the upper room, urging them, "Rise, let us go from here" (John 14:31). On the way to the Mount of Olives, Jesus would teach them more things, yet this promise of peace was central to his overall message. Jesus stated the reason: "Now I have told you before it takes place, so that when it does take place you may believe" (14:29). What ultimately matters is that his followers believe, since the peace that Christ gives can be received only through saving faith.

Jesus, with the whole New Testament, was clear in stating that his shed blood would savingly benefit only those who believe on him, not the entire world. Indeed, the Gospel of John has throughout emphasized the necessity of faith in Christ for salvation (cf. John 20:31). John summarized Jesus' gospel offer: "Whoever believes in the Son has eternal life; whoever does not obey

14. C. S. Lewis, *The Lion, the Witch, and the Wardrobe* (New York: Collins, 2000).

the Son shall not see life, but the wrath of God remains on him" (3:36). This means that we gain peace with God only by confessing our need for Christ to pay the penalty of our sin, finding our forgiveness in his shed blood.

The progressive despair of Edward Hicks's "Peaceable Kingdom" paintings seems to indicate that he never turned to Jesus and thus never found the peace that he desired. But he must at some time have been told about Christ and his peace. I say this because in one early painting, Hicks depicts a child holding a branch with a cluster of grapes. That is a reference to Christ, the grapes pointing to the blood that he would shed on the cross. In this painting alone, among all of Hicks's artwork, the banner of peace flows from Christ, whom Hicks depicts on high before all the world.[15] That painting is true, since the banner of peace comes only from the cross of Christ, who says now, "Peace I leave with you; my peace I give to you" (John 14:27). If you confess your need of his atonement for your sins and trust him for forgiveness and salvation, he will grant you peace with God. Then, as you live by faith through prayer and God's Word, "the peace of God, which surpasses all understanding, will guard your hearts and your minds in Christ Jesus" (Phil. 4:7).

Finally, we should notice that because of the peace that he gives, not only was Jesus able to face the hatred of an unloving world and the assaults of the devil, but he also called his disciples to join him. "Rise, let us go from here," he called, summoning them to go with him on his way to the cross. Likewise today, Christ gives us peace so that we may rise and go to the world, unfazed by its scorn and undaunted by Satan's opposition, so that others might know the glory of God, who is great above all, believe in the gospel of Christ, and receive through faith his matchless gift of peace.

15. Ryken, *My Father's World*, 120.

99

I Am the True Vine

John 15:1—5

"I am the true vine, and my Father is the vinedresser.
Every branch in me that does not bear fruit he takes away,
and every branch that does bear fruit he prunes, that it
may bear more fruit." (John 15:1–2)

*J*ohn 15 begins a new phase of Jesus' farewell teaching, signaled by Jesus' departure from the upper room with the disciples. In John 14, Jesus sought to comfort the disciples' fears in light of his imminent departure. Now Jesus gives the corresponding teaching regarding the disciples' duty and obligation during his absence. Jesus did this by means of the seventh and last "I am" statement in the Gospel of John: "I am the true vine" (John 15:1).

The True Vine

The route from Jerusalem to the Mount of Olives, east of the city, would have afforded Jesus and the disciples the sight of the great temple atop Mount Zion. One of the temple's notable features was the large decorative vine affixed above the entryway into the Holy Place. Over the years, wealthy Jews had brought gifts of gold and jewels to add tendrils, grapes, and leaves to this gigantic piece of art. According to Josephus, some of the grape clusters were the height of a man.[1] We do not know for certain, but it is possible that this sight prompted Jesus' use of the vine to make his last "I am" statement. Having led his disciples out toward the Mount of Olives, Jesus began teaching them again, saying, "I am the true vine" (John 15:1).

The vine was the symbol of Israel, which is why the temple was adorned with this image. Psalm 80 is one of many Old Testament passages employing this symbol: "You brought a vine out of Egypt; you drove out the nations and planted it. You cleared the ground for it; it took deep root and filled the land" (Ps. 80:8–9). The idea of the vineyard expresses God's labor and care in planting his people in the Promised Land. The vine was the Lord's people, from which he desired a rich harvest of fruit.

The problem was that Israel never produced the fruit that the Lord had desired. This is the point of most of the biblical references to Israel as a vine. Isaiah's famous Song of the Vineyard makes this point: "For the vineyard of the LORD of hosts is the house of Israel, and the men of Judah are his pleasant planting; and he looked for justice, but behold, bloodshed; for righteousness, but behold, an outcry!" (Isa. 5:7). In Jeremiah 2:21, God complained, "I planted you a choice vine, wholly of pure seed. How then have you turned degenerate and become a wild vine?"

It was in comparison to Israel's failure that Jesus declared himself the "true vine." Israel became a false and wild vine through idolatry and wickedness. In contrast, how pleasing was the life of Jesus to God the Father! As Isaiah foretold, Jesus "grew up before him like a young plant" (Isa. 53:2), and out of his humble circumstances he brought delight to the Father through perfect obedience. Thus God praised Jesus at his baptism: "a voice from heaven said, 'This is my beloved Son, with whom I am well pleased'" (Matt. 3:17). The fruit that God desired from Israel but did not find, he gained for himself by sending his own Son to be the true vine, from which his new and righteous people would live and bear good fruit.

When we consider the life of Jesus, we can see in how many ways "the true vine" is an apt emblem for our Lord. The vine grows from a modest beginning to display great beauty with its leaves and grapes. So also does Jesus

1. Gary M. Burge, *John*, NIV Application Commentary (Grand Rapids: Zondervan, 2000), 416.

overflow with a beautiful character and love. Just as the vine is the source of life for its branches, Jesus is the true vine, the source of true and everlasting life for those who believe. Jesus taught, "I came that they may have life and have it abundantly" (John 10:10). Just as the fruit of the vine brings joy and refreshment to the hearts of men (Ps. 104:15), Jesus came to give true joy and spiritual rest to heavy-laden hearts (Matt. 11:28). Moreover, the wine that comes from the vine was the emblem that Jesus used that evening for the blood he would shed to cleanse us from our sins. As the true vine, he provides his blood as the source of the new life for believers.

This passage is unique among the "I am" sayings of Jesus in that it forms the basis for an extended metaphor or parable. Jesus said that he is the true vine, the Father is the vinedresser, and the disciples are the branches. Believers are the tendrils or branches that are to bear good fruit from Jesus the true vine. Paul thus writes that Christians were saved "in order that [we] may bear fruit for God" (Rom. 7:4). Jesus here emphasized the good fruit that believers are to bear for the Lord, along with the Father's loving activity in pruning the branches, and his own life as the source of believers' fruitfulness.

The contrast with idolatrous Israel and the context of Jesus' teaching in chapters 14–16 show that our fruit is to consist mainly in devotion to God and obedience to his commands. It was because of idolatry and injustice that God promised to remove Israel's hedge, break down its wall, trample down the vineyard, and make it a waste (Isa. 5:5–6). In addition to praise (Heb. 13:15) and righteousness (Phil. 1:11; Heb. 12:11), the New Testament adds the fruit of good works (Col. 1:10) and the fruit of the Spirit in our inward character (Gal. 5:22–23). Not only does the Lord desire such fruit from us, but Jesus depicts how determined God is to gain it from our lives.

FRUITLESS BRANCHES TAKEN AWAY

Anyone who knows about vineyards can tell you that they require a great deal of tending, lest they grow wild and become fruitless. Here, Jesus depicts the Father's personal activity in tending his cherished vine. This description emphasizes the Father's protective care, watchfulness over the daily condition of each branch, and faithfulness in not permitting any true branch to go to ruin. A. W. Pink comments, "He does not allot to others the task of caring for the vine and its branches, and this assures us of the widest, most tender and most faithful care of it."[2]

Jesus description requires us to distinguish between two kinds of branches: "Every branch in me that does not bear fruit he takes away, and every branch that does bear fruit he prunes, that it may bear more fruit" (John 15:2). There are branches in Christ, the true vine, that flow with life and bear fruit. But there are other branches connected to Jesus that do not bear fruit. What are these other branches "in me" that do not bear fruit?

John 15:2, which depicts the removal of fruitless branches from the vine, is a favorite verse of Arminians, who cite this verse as proof that true believers who are savingly joined to Christ may yet fall away and be lost. It must be agreed that these fruitless branches are lost: verse 6 says that they "are gathered, thrown into the fire, and burned." Arminians teach that this verse describes true believers who lose their salvation by ceasing to bear fruit.

The first problem with this interpretation is the Bible's clear teaching of the eternal security of genuine believers in Christ. For instance, in Jesus' teaching on himself as the Good Shepherd, he said of his true sheep: "I give them eternal life, and they will never perish, and no one will snatch them out of my hand" (John 10:28). This is in keeping with Jesus' teaching in John 6:39 that "this is the will of him who sent me, that I should lose nothing of all that he has given me, but raise it up on the last day." These, and many other clear Bible passages, directly refute the Arminian doctrine.

The second problem with the Arminian view is seen in the functioning of this very parable, which presumes that branches containing the life of the vine will certainly go on to bear good fruit: "Whoever abides in me and I in him, he it is that bears much fruit" (John 15:5). The problem with dead branches is that they do not possess the sap of the vine. Vinedressers remove these dead branches to preserve the vine's strength for the fruitful branches. Thus, Jesus said, "Every branch in me that does not bear fruit he takes away" (15:2).

So what kind of branches are connected to Christ without possessing his saving life? The answer is nominal Christians: that is, those who call themselves Christians, attend church with Christians, and engage in many

---

2. Arthur W. Pink, *Exposition of the Gospel of John* (Grand Rapids: Zondervan, 1975), 805.

actions that Christians do, but who nonetheless do not possess the life of Christ through true and saving faith.

This teaching makes a vitally important point for us. According to Jesus here, and throughout the Gospels, the true mark of those who belong to him and are saved is the bearing of good fruit. We are saved not by good fruit or any other work of our own, but by faith in Christ alone. The good fruit, however, is the only proof that our profession of faith is true and saving. Being present in the church, receiving the rite of baptism, having membership on the church rolls, and being part of a godly family are not proofs of salvation and new life. Moreover, it is possible for a person to affirm the basic truths of Christian belief, yet to possess none of Christ's life. The true and only proof of salvation is fruit. This is the sole distinction between the two kinds of branches that Jesus mentions. Both are connected to him in some sense. But one does not bear fruit, and it is taken away while the fruitful branch is tended. "You will recognize them by their fruits," Jesus taught elsewhere (Matt. 7:20), and so will God.

It follows that we should never encourage a person to have assurance of salvation through a bare profession of faith, until that faith has proved itself by bearing fruit. The best Christians are imperfect and flawed in many ways, but all true Christians bear some true fruit in the form of obedience to God's commands, faithfulness to Christ before the world, and the cultivating of inward spiritual grace.

I once met with a woman, a longtime church member and the wife of an elder, who was nonetheless worldly in her speech and conduct. I asked her how she was doing and she answered, as was her custom, "I am ornery." I pointed out that orneriness is not among the fruit of the Spirit listed by Paul in Galatians 5:22–23. "Read me the list," she asked, "and see if I possess any of those qualities." I therefore read, "The fruit of the Spirit is love, joy, peace, patience, kindness, goodness, faithfulness, gentleness, self-control" (Gal. 5:22–23). "Which of these do you see in yourself?" I asked. She had to reply, "I see none of them in myself." I pointed out that this indicated the possibility that she was not truly joined to Jesus Christ and began discussing her need to trust in Christ's blood for forgiveness and new life. Taking offense at my reply, the woman demanded that we change the subject.

Do you see any of the fruit of the Spirit in your life? If you are a Christian, the honest answer should be Yes. You should be able to identify an increasing righteousness, peace, and joy (Rom. 14:17), with a growing love for God and his people. No doubt there is a mixed report in these areas, but a true Christian will be able to see some fruit of inward change, to go along with obedience to God's Word, fidelity to Christ before the world, and good works. Christians who know the fruit of Christ in their lives should thus be assured that their profession of faith is real, since the life of the vine is bearing fruit in the branch.

The question may be raised as to how God "takes away" the fruitless branches. Charles Spurgeon suggests that in some cases the Lord might allow a false professor to become rich so as to no longer feel his need for religion. In other cases, a dead branch might fall into open sin that leads to pride and rejection of Christ. Others will be drawn by the world into unbelief and will "discover" that Christianity is not true after all, particularly after such activities as golfing on Sundays and travel have slowly turned their heart to the world. Though Christians may plead with God over such persons, Spurgeon delivers the Father's answer: "Take them away . . . : if they had through saving faith been made to bear the fruit of the Spirit, they should have been saved; but as there was not fruit, take them away."[3] God does this for the good of the vine and for the life of the true branches, so that each will bear more and better fruit.

FRUITFUL BRANCHES PRUNED

While Jesus mentions the fruitless branches that are removed, he emphasizes God's pruning activity on the fruitful branches. Jesus said, "Every branch that does bear fruit he prunes, that it may bear more fruit" (John 15:2). It might seem surprising that God prunes the fruitful branches, since pruning sounds painful, until we realize that the purpose of pruning is to gain the maximum amount of fruit from the vine.

Grapevines require aggressive pruning. After each year's harvest, the fruitful branches are cut back significantly. The idea in pruning is to remove whatever inhibits growth, and Jesus applies this principle to the Father's pruning of our spiritual lives. He strips away things that are spiritually detrimental, even if they are otherwise good things. He takes the knife to our

3. Charles H. Spurgeon, *The Metropolitan Tabernacle Pulpit*, 63 vols. (Pasadena, TX: Pilgrim, 1969), 13:560.

bad habits and assails our prayerlessness by giving us things to pray about. The Father applies the pruning knife to our priorities and values, and strips away relationships that would hinder our faith. It is important to note that this is not punishment, but vinedressing. The writer of Hebrews said: "He disciplines us for our good, that we may share his holiness" (Heb. 12:10).

This pruning might take place by means of God's providential arrangement of our circumstances: we might suffer loss, face a temptation, or experience a reproof. The purpose of all these is to make us fruitful through an increased faith. Peter wrote that his readers had "been grieved by various trials," the purpose of which was "that the tested genuineness of your faith . . . may be found to result in praise and glory and honor at the revelation of Jesus Christ" (1 Peter 1:6–7). James reminds us how much better off Christians are because of the trials we have endured: "Count it all joy, my brothers, when you meet trials of various kinds, for you know that the testing of your faith produces steadfastness" (James 1:2–3). In his years of dark suffering in Pharaoh's prison, Joseph was having his character prepared for his reign over Egypt. More recently, the severe afflictions suffered by Christians in China under the Communists have borne fruit in a remarkable explosion of spiritual power and gospel success. It is true that the Father's pruning involves afflictions known only to Christians, the like of which the world knows nothing. But neither does the world know the joy of the harvest in the fruit of eternal life.

This tells us that when we endure trials in life—when we find biblical parenting to be overwhelming, when loving our spouse is difficult, when integrity in the workplace is hard, and when we experience the more severe trials involved with sickness, grief, joblessness, or persecution—we should lift our faces to the Lord and ask him to do his work in our life, that we might bear the fruit that he desires. Mark Johnston comments that while "the process may be painful . . . , it will always be worthwhile as it leads to a better and more profitable life in Christ."[4] Thus, the saintly and much-afflicted Elizabeth Prentiss wrote to a friend who was suffering under grief: "My dear friend, don't let this tragedy of sorrow fail to do everything for you."[5] David similarly sang, "Before I was afflicted I went astray, but now I keep your word" (Ps. 119:67).

---

4. Mark G. Johnston, *Let's Study John* (Edinburgh: Banner of Truth, 2003), 202.
5. Quoted in Susan Hunt, *The True Woman* (Wheaton, IL: Crossway, 1997), 93.

Cleansed by the Word

We rightly think of God's pruning in terms of outward trials, but it seems that Jesus refers also to the ministry of God's Word. He continued, "Already you are clean because of the word that I have spoken to you" (John 15:3). The word for *clean* is the noun form of the same word he used in verse 2 for *prunes*. The basic idea of the word (verb, *kathairo*; noun, *katharos*) is "cleansing," but with the idea of pruning, it means the removal of unwanted materials. It is primarily the Word of God, Jesus said, that produces this cleansing. Therefore, when he speaks of the Father's pruning, he refers to the Scriptures as the agent of our spiritual change and growth. His meaning is similar to that of Hebrews 4:12: "For the word of God is living and active, sharper than any two-edged sword, piercing to the division of soul and of spirit, of joints and of marrow, and discerning the thoughts and intentions of the heart." God intends for his Word to penetrate our hearts, unmask our true thoughts and desires, and cut away all that hinders our growth. It was with this in mind that Paul said that the Bible is not only "breathed out by God" but also "profitable for teaching, for reproof, for correction, and for training in righteousness" (2 Tim. 3:16).

This means that we must come to God's Word not merely to learn spiritual facts but to bring our hearts under the pruning knife of our loving Father, the vinedresser. The saying is true that "soft preaching creates hard hearts, but hard preaching creates soft hearts." Therefore, we should not seek only comforting and uplifting messages when we attend to preaching in the church or when we read our Bibles. Rather, we should seek the truth that will cut away our sin and the challenging teaching on holiness that will stimulate spiritual growth. Most significantly, we should seek in God's Word to see the glory of the Lord in the face of his Son, Jesus, so that God's grace would teach us "to renounce ungodliness and worldly passions, and to live self-controlled, upright, and godly lives in the present age, waiting for our blessed hope, the appearing of the glory of our great God and Savior Jesus Christ" (Titus 2:12–13).

The One Principle of Fruitfulness

So far, Jesus has used the symbolism of the vine to describe himself and the vinedresser to depict God's pruning activity for our growth in holiness. He concludes the metaphor by referring to his disciples as the branches, and he provides a single key principle for our fruitfulness: "Abide in me, and I in you" (John 15:4). This saying was likely meant as a command: believers are commanded to abide in Christ in order to bear our fruit.

What does it mean, then, to abide in Christ? To *abide* is to dwell in, with close communion and fellowship. The basic idea, Gordon Keddie writes, is "the active cultivation by every professing Christian of a living spiritual relationship to Christ."[6] As Paul put it, "For to me to live is Christ" (Phil. 1:21). He explained, "I live by faith in the Son of God, who loved me and gave himself for me" (Gal. 2:20).

Abiding in Christ means that we draw near to Christ spiritually and hold fast to his teaching. Jesus earlier taught, "If you abide in my word, you are truly my disciples, and you will know the truth, and the truth will set you free" (John 8:31–32). Abiding in Christ's Word involves more than a bare adherence to Christian doctrine and the discipline of Bible reading; it also involves a yearning trust in its promises and a serious application of its lessons to our lives. Abiding in Christ likewise involves a fervent communion with the Lord in prayer. It includes a devoted participation in the worship and work of Christ's church, joining together with other members of the body of Christ for communion with and service to the Lord.

Jesus makes two vital statements connecting our fruitfulness to our abiding in Christ. The first is that by abiding in him we will bear fruit, for the same reason that a living branch bears the fruit of the vine. When we abide in Christ, he abides in us and his Spirit works in us with power. This means that the Christian life is not a calling to self-improvement. Our calling is to abide in Christ, following him through his Word, prayer, worship, and service, and he will bear his fruit in us. The solution to many of our problems is thus simply to walk with Christ over many years. He will lead us, change us, and transform us by the power of his Spirit. This does not mean that Christians are not to strive against sin and labor for holiness. What it means is that the way that we seek our own holiness and fight sin is by trusting Christ, drawing from his strength, and living in loving, personal obedience to him. "Whoever abides in me and I in him," Jesus said, "he it is that bears much fruit" (John 15:5).

A vital corollary to this principle is that apart from abiding in Christ, we can bear no fruit: "As the branch cannot bear fruit by itself, unless it abides

6. Gordon J. Keddie, *A Study Commentary on John*, 2 vols. (Darlington, UK: Evangelical Press, 2001), 2:156.

in the vine, neither can you, unless you abide in me. . . . Apart from me you can do nothing" (John 15:4–5). By this Jesus did not mean that we literally do nothing: apart from Christ, we can do many things! We can recruit large numbers, raise huge sums of money, erect glorious buildings, and secure worldly power. On a personal level, we can accomplish many things for ourselves and for others apart from Christ. The problem is that apart from Jesus, all that we accomplish is nothing. Only by the means that God has ordained—chief among them God's Word and prayer—and through a conscious dependence on Christ do we accomplish anything of real spiritual value. However glorious it might be to our own eyes and to the world, all that we do apart from Christ, and all that the church accomplishes by worldly means, is really chaff and dead branches, fit only in the end to be gathered up and burned (cf. 1 Cor. 3:13–15).

Much Fruit

In the upper room, Jesus told the disciples of all that he would do to provide for them in his absence. Now, as they walked to the Mount of Olives, Jesus stressed the disciples' duty. As Jesus is the true vine, God seeks and demands true spiritual fruit from his disciples. If we will abide in Christ, his life will accomplish wonders of spiritual power in and through us, and the Father will tend us with his pruning knife to bring forth our fruit.

Does this sound intimidating? Do you doubt that someone like you, with all your weakness and sin, could really bear fruit for the Lord? The good news is the promise essential to this teaching. If you will but abide in Jesus, he will bear great fruit through you. If you doubt yourself, do not doubt our Savior and Lord. In one of his earlier parables, Jesus spoke of those to whom his Word came so that they believed and were saved. Jesus admitted that some of these bore more fruit than others, saying of the believer, "He indeed bears fruit and yields, in one case a hundredfold, in another sixty, and in another thirty" (Matt. 13:23). There is a difference between a very fruitful Christian and a less fruitful Christian, but both have this in common: they bear much fruit, some a hundredfold and some thirtyfold. If you will abide in Christ and live with him and for him, out of your life, your witness, and your prayers you will make a godly difference in a great many lives and in you God will grow much spiritual fruit, to his own glory. Jesus said as a simple statement of fact: "I am the vine; you are the branches. Whoever abides in me and I in him, he it is that bears much fruit" (John 15:5).

100

ABIDING IN CHRIST

John 15:6—11

*"If you abide in me, and my words abide in you, ask whatever
you wish, and it will be done for you. By this my Father is
glorified, that you bear much fruit and so prove to be my
disciples." (John 15:7–8)*

As Jesus prepared to depart from his disciples, he taught them
a parable consisting of three parts, spelling out the conditions
of their spiritual fruitfulness in his absence. The first two
parts depicted God's provision on our behalf. First, Jesus would himself be
"the true vine," securing by his obedience eternal life to give to those who
come to him in faith. Second, the Father would be the vinedresser, tending
to our spiritual growth primarily by pruning the fruitful branches. Both
of these are divine actions, accomplished for our benefit by God's grace.

The third element of the parable presents believers' responsibility. In
order to bear fruit as living branches, Christians are commanded to abide
in Christ. "Abide in me, and I in you," Jesus said. "As the branch cannot
bear fruit by itself, unless it abides in the vine, neither can you, unless you
abide in me" (John 15:4).

THE MEANING OF *ABIDE*

Jesus' teaching on abiding in him is evidently of great importance, as seen not only by the fact that Jesus taught this parable on so pivotal an occasion as the night of his departure but also in the extended treatment he gave to the subject. It is clearly important for Christians to understand what it means to abide in Christ. The Greek verb *meno* means "to dwell or remain." J. C. Ryle explains how it speaks of our relationship with Christ:

> To abide in Christ means to keep up a habit of constant close communion with Him, to be always leaning on Him, resting on Him, pouring out our hearts to Him, and using Him as our Fountain of life and strength, as our chief Companion and best Friend. To have His words abiding in us, is to keep His sayings and precepts continually before our memories and minds, and to make them the guide of our actions, and the rule of our daily conduct and behavior.[1]

Jesus amplifies his own teaching by relating our abiding in him, first, to our resting in his love: "As the Father has loved me, so have I loved you. Abide in my love" (John 15:9). This informs us that the Christian who abides in Christ is one who believes, trusts, relies on, and rests within Christ's love for his own. Even while Christ's love for his disciples is unbroken, it is still possible for Christians to "live without being mindful of Christ's love for them and so break the closeness of their fellowship."[2] This is why Jesus urges us to remain in his love. John wrote of this in his first epistle, emphasizing that "we know and rely on the love God has for us" (1 John 4:16 NIV). To be a Christian is to know the love of God in Christ, who died on the cross for our sins. To abide in Christ is then to rely on that love, so that in all things we draw near to him, look to him in faith, and confidently expect his saving grace to be at work in our lives. Jesus has proved his love for us forever on the cross; now we are to abide in his love.

Jesus points out to us an analogy between his relationship of love with the Father and our relationship of love with him: "As the Father has loved

---

1. J. C. Ryle, *Expository Thoughts on the Gospels: John*, 3 vols. (Edinburgh: Banner of Truth, 1999), 3:116–17.

2. Leon Morris, *The Gospel according to John*, rev. ed., New International Commentary on the New Testament (Grand Rapids: Eerdmans, 1995), 597.

me, so have I loved you" (John 15:9). This reminds us that Jesus' love for us consists of more than mercy and compassion, since the Father does not pity the Son but rather delights in the Son, approves of his Son, and desires the fellowship of his Son. Likewise, then, Jesus delights in his people, approves of those who are cleansed by his blood (1 John 1:7), and delights in those whom he takes as his disciples.

How many Christians are paralyzed in their spiritual lives by a dread of Christ's disfavor and disapproval. They see a constantly frowning face in heaven. But Jesus says that his love for us is like the Father's love for him. We might say that Jesus not only loves us but likes us. Indeed, the primary biblical metaphor for Christ's love for the church is that of a groom for his bride. A groom longs for his bride with great delight and piercing joy. The Bible tells us that since believers are robed in the perfect imputed righteousness of Christ (Gen. 3:21; 2 Cor. 5:21), then "as the bridegroom rejoices over the bride, so shall your God rejoice over you" (Isa. 62:5). No man marries a woman simply because he feels sorry for her, and Jesus' love for us is one of joy in fellowship, delighting in our redeemed persons for his own sake.

Christians who know and rely on Christ's love will respond by obeying his commands. This is the second relationship that Jesus identifies with abiding in him: "If you keep my commandments, you will abide in my love, just as I have kept my Father's commandments and abide in his love" (John 15:10).

Jesus is not saying that we are saved by obedience, since we are saved by faith alone in his perfect saving work for us. What he is saying is that as we rely on his love for us and respond with loving obedience to his commandments, the result is that we are drawn near to abide in his love. Ours should be the grateful, devoted attitude of David in Psalm 40:8: "I desire to do your will, O my God; your law is within my heart." The source of this submitted will is our knowledge of God's love for us, and its effect is our abiding in Christ.

These very words were ascribed to Jesus in the New Testament (Heb. 10:7), so that his obedient love to the Father sets the pattern for our obedient love to him: "just as I have kept my Father's commandments and abide in his love" (John 15:10). Jesus took great pleasure on earth in showing his love to the Father by obeying his commands. Likewise, our love for Christ and our abiding in him involves the submission of our will to his will, so that on the path of obedience that Jesus himself walked we have close fellowship with him. Realizing this, we are warned against thinking that abiding in Christ manifests itself in mystical experiences. Instead, abiding in Christ manifests itself in devoted obedience to his Word.

Jesus is describing a lifestyle of abiding in him that moves from love to love. In the fourth chapter of his first epistle, John enlarges on this theme, stating that "in this the love of God was made manifest among us, that God sent his only Son into the world, so that we might live through him" (1 John 4:9). Our defining reality as Christians, he says, is God's love for us in Christ and Christ's love for us on the cross. Both the Father and the Son continue to love us so that believers live through Christ, abiding in his love, living for his pleasure, and accepting his will as our own. John sums up the Christian life, saying, "We love because he first loved us" (4:19), and the way that we show our love is through joyful obedience to Jesus' commands.

This mentality was displayed by the aged bishop Polycarp, when the Roman proconsul urged him to renounce Jesus in order to escape being thrown to the beasts in the arena. Polycarp answered, "Eighty and six years have I served him, and he never did me any injury: how then can I blaspheme my King and my Savior?"[3] Every Christian should reason likewise: what wrong has Jesus ever done so that I might disobey the commands of him who loved me so?

ABIDING IN CHRIST DELIVERS US FROM JUDGMENT

Having defined *abiding in him* in terms of his love and our obedience, Jesus also sets before the disciples four great results that ensue from our abiding in him. The first is that abiding in Christ *delivers us from the judgment of God*. Jesus expressed this truth in negative terms, speaking of false professors who do not abide in him: "If anyone does not abide in me he is thrown away like a branch and withers; and the branches are gathered, thrown into the fire, and burned" (John 15:6).

Throughout the New Testament, fire is used to depict the torments awaiting those who stand under God's judgment for sin. An important example is Jesus' parable of the weeds in Matthew's Gospel. Jesus said that he has planted his good seed in his field, but the evil one has come and planted

---

3. *Martyrdom of Polycarp*, in *Ante-Nicene Fathers*, ed. Alexander Roberts and James Donaldson, 10 vols. (Peabody, MA: Hendrickson, 1994), 10:41.

weeds there also. The weeds in that parable represent false professors and correspond to the fruitless branches in John 15. Jesus said that we should not concern ourselves with trying to sort the wheat from the weeds, but that we should leave the task for when the harvester comes. He explained, "The harvest is the close of the age, and the reapers are angels. Just as the weeds are gathered and burned with fire, so will it be at the close of the age. The Son of Man will send his angels, and they will gather out of his kingdom all causes of sin and all law-breakers, and throw them into the fiery furnace. In that place there will be weeping and gnashing of teeth" (Matt. 13:39–42). This is one of many places where hell is described as a place of personal, physical, and perpetual torment as God's just penalty for sins (see Matt. 3:12; 5:22; 7:19; Mark 9:47; etc.).

Jesus speaks here of God's judgment not on sinners generally but on professing believers who did not possess his saving life and bear good fruit. In the context of the Farewell Discourse, we think of Judas Iscariot as the classic example of a false professor who was first removed and then condemned by God. Jesus referred to him as the "son of destruction" (John 17:12), that is, one doomed to eternal judgment for his betrayal of Christ.

The Old Testament background for Jesus' teaching on the burning of the fruitless branches is Ezekiel 15:1–6. The prophet pointed out that the wood of the vine is good for nothing unless it bears fruit. "Is wood taken from it to make anything? Do people take a peg from it to hang any vessel on it?" he asked (15:3). The wood of the vine is so useless that it will not even serve as a peg. Therefore, if it will not bear fruit, it can be used only for fire, and even then it burns too quickly. Since the vine was a symbol of Israel, this was a warning of God's judgment, which soon fell on fruitless Jerusalem through the siege of Nebuchadnezzar and the city's destruction. God warned, "Like the wood of the vine among the trees of the forest, which I have given to the fire for fuel, so have I given up the inhabitants of Jerusalem" (15:6).

Christians should look on the fall of Jerusalem and realize how useless to God is fruitless religion. A profession of faith in Christ is of no interest to God unless it goes on to bear the fruit of a godly life, and such an empty profession of faith renders us fit only for the fires of God's judgment. It was with this in mind that James wrote that "faith by itself, if it does not have works, is dead" (James 2:17). He did not mean that we are saved by a combination of faith and works, but rather that saving faith is always a faith that goes on to bear the fruit of good works, along with a changed life. According to Jesus, then, false professors of faith will sooner or later be taken away by God (John 15:2), and they will ultimately be subjected to God's fire, all because they never truly embraced Jesus as Savior and therefore died without their sins' being forgiven.

In contrast, to abide in Christ is to be delivered from God's judgment, since the branches that abide in him bear fruit through their possession of saving life. How urgent it is that every professing believer actually abide in Christ—relying on his love, living in close fellowship with Jesus, and bearing the good fruit of obedience to the commands of the Bible—which is the only kind of faith that actually saves us from the just wrath of God on our sins.

Abiding in Christ Leads to Power in Prayer

A second result is that abiding in Christ *leads to power in prayer*. "If you abide in me, and my words abide in you," Jesus taught, "ask whatever you wish, and it will be done for you" (John 15:7).

This promise is essentially the same as the one made in John 14:13–14: "Whatever you ask in my name, this I will do, that the Father may be glorified in the Son. If you ask me anything in my name, I will do it." The difference here is the nuance of Christ's words abiding in us. Jesus earlier said that if we ask in his name, he will answer our prayers; now he insists that we must pray with his Word abiding in us.

A. W. Pink explains that Jesus refers here to a life that is "regulated by the Scriptures." Jesus speaks of his "words," which refers to "the precepts and promises of Scripture personally appropriated, fed upon by faith, hidden in the heart. . . . It is . . . constant and habitual communion with God through the Word, until its contents become the substance of our innermost beings."[4]

In God's Word we find that Jesus tells us not to expect comfortable circumstances or the absence of trials and temptations. What we should seek is faith to trust Christ, strength to obey God's will, grace to transform our lives, and compassion to care for a lost world. In John 15, Jesus has stressed the vital importance that we abide in him, relying on his love and obeying his commands. Surely abiding in him, then, is something for which we

---

4. Arthur W. Pink, *Exposition of the Gospel of John* (Grand Rapids: Zondervan, 1975), 825.

should pray, with confidence that Jesus has promised to bless prayers that are offered according to his Word. According to Jesus' promise, whenever we pray for the priorities he has taught in Scripture, we should pray with an absolute certainty of divine answers. Do we pray for grace to believe, for compassion on the lost world so that we will witness the gospel, or for courage to stand against the pressures of the world and of sin? We must pray for these things, and when we pray Jesus' own words back to our Lord, when his teaching forms the substance of our pleas, we can be assured that they will be heard with favor in heaven.

If we wonder why we do not seem to enjoy greater power in prayer, we are given a vital clue in this passage. Perhaps our lack of power in prayer stems from a lack of abiding in Christ and in his Word. F. B. Meyer writes: "If you abide in Christ in daily fellowship, it will not be difficult to pray aright, for He has promised to abide in those who abide in Him; and the sap of the Holy Ghost securing for you fellowship with your unseen Lord, will produce in you, as fruit, desires and petitions similar to those which He unceasingly presents to His Father."[5] The "secret" to power in prayer, then, is to live closely enough to Christ that our own desires, expressed in prayer, have been molded by his Word.

An example of how abiding in Christ works with prayer was given by Corrie ten Boom in one story of her poor but godly father, Casper. Living under Nazi occupation in Holland, their family faced many difficulties and great poverty. On one occasion, they had prayed for God to send a customer to buy a watch so that they could pay their overdue bills. A customer did come, picking out a quite expensive watch, and casually remarked as he paid that another merchant had sold him a defective watch. Corrie's father asked the man whether he could examine that watch, and pointed out that only a minor repair was needed. He assured the man that he had been sold a fine-quality watch by the other merchant and gave his money back as the man returned the watch that he had been going to buy.

Little Corrie asked, "Papa, why did you do that? Aren't you worried about the bills you have due?" Her father replied that it would not honor the Lord to allow another man's reputation to be wrongly harmed, especially since the other merchant was a believer. He assured the little girl that God would

5. F. B. Meyer, *The Life of Love* (Old Tappan, NJ: Revell, 1987), 296.

provide, and just a few days later a man came and bought the most expensive watch they had, the sale of which not only paid their bills but also paid for two years of Corrie's education.[6] How simple it would have been for Casper to take the man's money and claim God's answer to prayer! But he put obedience to Christ first, and then did not lack for anything, since abiding in Christ produced not only obedience but also great power in prayer.

ABIDING IN CHRIST GLORIFIES THE FATHER

The Westminster Shorter Catechism begins by telling us that man's chief end is "to glorify God." This highlights the importance of the third result of abiding in Christ, that in this way we *glorify the Father*. Jesus added, "By this my Father is glorified, that you bear much fruit and so prove to be my disciples" (John 15:8).

This is an important statement, first, because it reminds us that we "prove" our discipleship by bearing fruit to the Lord. Jesus adds that the same fruit that grants us assurance of salvation also brings glory to the Father. This indicates that if we are not abiding in Christ and bearing the fruit of changed lives, then we are denying God glory that ought to be his. It is easy for us to speak of praising God and to sing hallelujahs, but the way that God especially desires to be glorified in us is by our transformed lives. That our lives might contribute to the glory of the one, true, and eternal God ought to fill our hearts with wonder and amazement. Moreover, that we might give something back to the God who has given his own Son for our salvation ought to spur us with great zeal for the glory of the Father.

Christ's fruit in our life glorifies the Father before the holy angels, who Peter says long to look into the things of the gospel (1 Peter 1:12). Our changed lives vindicate God's saving purpose before the accusations of the devil. Back in the garden, God cursed Satan, declaring that he would be made to eat dust (Gen. 3:14). One of the chief ways in which God feeds the Serpent dust is by first forgiving our sin through Christ's blood and then actually making us holy, so that even Satan must glorify God in our salvation. The fruit of our lives further glorifies God before the watching world. Gordon Keddie writes that even the hard-hearted world "cannot but see the hand of

---

6. George Guthrie, *Hebrews* (Grand Rapids: Zondervan, 1998), 449.

God in the saving change of an otherwise corrupt and condemned sinner." The unbeliever "may pour contempt on his friend who is converted and gives up his former wicked ways, but he knows somehow that he protests too much and is really covering a deeper amazement at a change that he cannot explain."[7]

When Jesus says that our fruit proves our discipleship, a corollary principle is that many professing Christians lack assurance and peace in their salvation, some living with great doubt and fear, because they are careless about abiding in Christ. Ryle observes, "Men are content with a *little* Christianity, and a *little* fruit of the Spirit, and do not labour to be 'holy in all manner of conversation' (1 Peter 1:15). They must not wonder if they enjoy little peace, feel little hope, and leave behind them little evidence."[8] The way for us to receive the most benefit from our faith is the same way that we are of maximum usefulness to the Lord: if we will abide in Christ, we will bear much fruit so as both to glorify the Father and to prove our discipleship.

ABIDING IN CHRIST FILLS US WITH JOY

Fourth, Jesus states that *abiding in Christ fills us with joy*: "These things I have spoken to you, that my joy may be in you, and that your joy may be full" (John 15:11). The world insists that turning from sin to follow Christ is bound to take all the pleasure out of life. Jesus insists that exactly the opposite is in fact true. The way to possess true and abiding joy—not the joy of the world, but what Jesus calls "my joy"—is to abide in him.

It is obvious from this that we may fail to know the joy that ought to be ours. We lose our joy when our fellowship with Christ is broken through worldly distractions. Disobedience and unbelief steal our joy. This is why David pleaded in his great prayer of repentance, "Cast me not away from your presence, and take not your Holy Spirit from me. Restore to me the joy of your salvation" (Ps. 51:11–12). David missed the spiritual joy that he had previously known, and he pleaded with God not only to forgive him but also to restore his presence and therefore his joy. Jesus found his joy in pleasing the Father through obedience. Leon Morris comments: "It is not

7. Gordon J. Keddie, *A Study Commentary on John*, 2 vols. (Darlington, UK: Evangelical Press, 2001), 2:161.

8. Ryle, *John*, 3:118.

cheerless, barren existence that Jesus plans for his people. But the joy of which he speaks comes only as they are wholehearted in their obedience to his commands."[9]

Jesus stated his desire that by abiding in him, "your joy may be full" (John 15:11). Jesus was not speaking here of a fairy-tale happiness in which all our worldly dreams come true. Jesus never promised a carefree life to his followers, but he did offer us fullness of joy as his life grows in us. Hebrews 12:2 says that "for the joy that was set before him" Jesus endured the cross, so that even that great baptism of suffering could not snuff out the eternal flame of his joy. Abiding in him, as a living branch in the true vine, we experience his life flowing into us through the ministry of the Holy Spirit, so that our deep experience of blessing matures into the rich wine of spiritual joy as we abide in him.

Do you find that you long for the fullness of Christ's joy in your life? It is evident that Jesus longs for this, too. Indeed, there can be no greater object in love than for the One we adore to have joy in our fellowship. We do not need to live joyless lives, but we do need to abide in Christ, relishing his love, offering our obedience in return, and then abounding in the perfect divine joy that he has eternally possessed and that he delights to give to those who abide in him.

9. Morris, *The Gospel according to John*, 598.

101

NO GREATER LOVE

John 15:12—17

"Greater love has no one than this, that someone lay down his life for his friends. You are my friends if you do what I command you." (John 15:13–14)

here are people who speak very casually about "the imitation of Christ," some foolishly attempting to gain their way to heaven by being like Jesus. An example of this emphasis is the once-popular WWJD jewelry and paraphernalia that boiled down the Christian faith to this question: "What Would Jesus Do?" The idea is that all we have to do in any situation is to know what Jesus would do and then do it ourselves. The problem with this approach is that it fails to realize that Jesus is unique in both his person and his saving mission. In most situations, Jesus would do what we cannot do and, in some cases, should not do. The most important example is how Jesus responds to the sins of his people, laying down his uniquely perfect life as the once-for-all Sacrifice to atone for sin. For this reason, the very heart of the Christian faith is what Jesus did for us, precisely because we could never do it for ourselves. We are saved not by doing what Jesus did but by trusting what Jesus did for our salvation.

Certainly, Christians are commanded to follow and imitate Christ (Luke 9:23; Eph. 5:1). Yet the Bible does not tell us to do *what* Jesus did; he commanded his disciples to do *as* he did. This is above all true when it comes to Jesus' love. Having been loved by him with so great a redeeming love, we are to love others in a way that reflects his matchless grace. Jesus emphasized this truth to the disciples, saying, "This is my commandment, that you love one another as I have loved you" (John 15:12).

CHRIST'S FRIENDSHIP FOR US

When we think about the greatness of Christ's love for us, which Paul said "surpasses knowledge" (Eph. 3:19), we find that one of its more amazing features is that Jesus loves his people so as to take us as his friends. This is amazing because it is the Son of God who speaks this way. In human society, it is not common or easy for men and women of different stations to enjoy friendship. Learned men are seldom close companions with the unlearned. People in high positions are isolated from others and isolate themselves, often being more admired than known and loved. But no person is higher above others to the extent that Christ, God's holy Son, is high above us all. He spoke the simple truth in Isaiah 55:9: "For as the heavens are higher than the earth, so are my ways higher than your ways and my thoughts than your thoughts." Yet for all his infinite superiority in terms of his being, station, majesty, authority, knowledge, holiness, and power, Jesus says to us, "You are my friends" (John 15:14). J. C. Ryle marvels, "For sinful men and women like ourselves to be called 'friends of Christ,' is something that our weak minds can hardly grasp and take in. The King of kings and Lord of lords not only pities and saves all them that believe in Him, but actually calls them His 'friends.'"[1]

We became Jesus' friends not because we had some affinity for him but because of what he did for us. We are brought near to his heart, he says, by the greatest love imaginable: "Greater love has no one than this, that someone lay down his life for his friends" (John 15:13).

This verse adorns countless war memorials, honoring soldiers who made the supreme sacrifice for their nation. We will likewise occasionally hear

---

1. J. C. Ryle, *Expository Thoughts on the Gospels: John*, 3 vols. (Edinburgh: Banner of Truth, 1999), 3:125.

of a father who runs back into a burning building, perishing in search of a trapped child, or a grandparent who jumps into a lake to save a fallen boy and ends up drowning. These sacrifices are justly celebrated, but there are differences when it comes to Christ that makes his death the greatest expression of love ever.

First, we should realize that Jesus did not have to die, since his life alone was not intrinsically destined for the grave. Every heroic sacrifice of life that any other person makes is the gift of a life that was going to die sooner or later anyway. This by no means diminishes the sacrifice of those who die for others. But Jesus' death was in a higher category. He alone possessed a life over which death had no power: he suffered death when the grave was perfectly avoidable if he had so willed.

Moreover, Jesus' sacrifice differs from others in that he intentionally gave his life. When a person gives his life to save another, he normally does not know that he is going to die, and usually hopes to escape death. But Jesus' death was especially priceless because he knew and intended that he would die to save us from our sins.

Furthermore, Jesus died for us when we were not really his friends. He was our friend, but he died to save men and women who had done nothing but wrong to him and would in fact hate him until he saved us. Paul said, "God shows his love for us in that while we were still sinners, Christ died for us" (Rom. 5:8).

A clear implication of Jesus' statement is that he did not die in order to save all persons, but died to save only those who, though his enemies at the time, had been chosen by God to be Jesus' companions through his redeeming work. This doctrine is called *limited atonement*, which limits Christ's saving death only in terms of the scope of persons for whom it was intended: Jesus spoke of his coming death in this way, saying that he laid down his life not for everyone but "for his friends" (John 15:13). Limited atonement does not denigrate but rather exalts Christ's death: while the atonement was limited in terms of the persons for whom he died, it was unlimited in terms of its power to save those who believe. Christ really and fully saved his people when he died on the cross, but it was only for them that he made atonement for sin.

When other men or women sacrifice their lives for another, that person is almost always someone particularly beloved. But Jesus died for us, knowing all the details of our wickedness, knowing all our sins and every corrupt twist in our hearts, but loving us nonetheless and giving his life for our salvation. There are no dirty secrets for Jesus to learn about us later that will cause him to turn his love from us. Christ's friendship "is unchangeable, resting upon His knowledge of what we are by nature, and of what He means His grace shall make us to be."[2] We may therefore rest on Christ's friendship, knowing that it originates in his sovereign, unchanging grace and not in ourselves.

The greatness of Jesus' sacrifice is understood when we remember the nature of what he suffered. Jesus suffered intense physical anguish on the cross. But so infinitely intense were his spiritual sufferings that his physical pains must have been relatively insignificant. Popular accounts sometimes emphasize Jesus' physical suffering, often going far beyond the Scriptures in their graphic details. But primarily, Jesus suffered the infinite wrath of God on our sins that he bore. Not only was Jesus' death physically degrading, but it included what was for him the horrifying separation from the Father as he bore our curse and suffered divine wrath. Recognizing the uniquely anguishing experience that Jesus underwent for us in death, we can then appreciate the truth of his claim, "Greater love has no one than this" (John 15:13). This is the love that God's Son has for us even now, having proved his unparalleled love on the cross.

Our Friendship with Christ

Recognizing Christ's love for us, we receive his friendship as the single greatest possession of our lives, and also as the great calling on our lives. Jesus spoke of our friendship with him, saying, "You are my friends if you do what I command you. No longer do I call you servants, for the servant does not know what his master is doing; but I have called you friends, for all that I have heard from my Father I have made known to you" (John 15:14–15).

The New Testament shows that the disciples as apostles continued to know themselves as Christ's servants. Peter identified himself as "a servant and apostle of Jesus Christ" (2 Peter 1:1), and Paul delighted to refer to himself as the bondservant of Jesus (Rom. 1:1; Titus 1:1). One of our chief privileges

2. B. M. Palmer, *Sermons*, 2 vols. (1875; repr., Harrisonburg, VA: Sprinkle, 2002), 2:272.

as Christians is to be personal servants of so great a Lord as God's Son, Jesus. Among our fellow servants are not only the apostles but Moses, who at his death was described simply as a "servant of the LORD" (Deut. 34:5); Joshua, who declared, "As for me and my house, we will serve the LORD" (Josh. 24:15); and David, whom God identified as "my servant" (Ps. 89:20).

Clearly, then, Jesus did not intend to convey that Christians are no longer his servants, for in this very passage he speaks of the necessity of our obeying his commands. What he does mean is that our relationship with him is not merely one of hierarchical submission. Even when a friend is in a subordinate position, he is a confidant and companion. Jesus emphasizes the idea of our entering into his confidence and his full disclosure of his plans and practices. Jesus opens up his heart to his friends, telling us through the Scriptures what he earlier confided personally to the original disciples. Jesus thus contrasts his disciples with *mere* servants: "the servant does not know what his master is doing; but I have called you friends, for all that I have heard from my Father I have made known to you" (John 15:15),

It is probably noteworthy that only Abraham is described in the Bible as God's "friend." God spoke to Abraham so that he understood God's purpose; this is what especially marked him as a "friend of God" (James 2:23; see Isa. 41:8). God said, "Shall I hide from Abraham what I am about to do, seeing that Abraham shall surely become a great and mighty nation, and all the nations of the earth shall be blessed in him?" (Gen. 18:17–18).

We have likewise been entrusted with the revelation of Christ. He said, "All that I have heard from my Father I have made known to you" (John 15:15). Friends bare their souls, and Jesus has opened his mind to us in the Scriptures. Through God's Word, Paul said, "we have the mind of Christ" (1 Cor. 2:16). Friends will often spend long hours sharing ideas and talking about their plans for the future, and Jesus wants to do this with us. Some of us have diaries in which our most cherished thoughts are kept secure. This is what Jesus has given to us in the Bible, with faith as the key to open it. The Bible is not only the holy book for us to revere, but also Jesus' disclosure of his own heart for us to treasure as his friends.

In the Bible, Jesus has clearly told us the purpose of history and of his kingdom, informing us of his plans, explaining his works, and entrusting to us his promises. Paul notes that this is important, for instance, so that we are "not . . . outwitted by Satan," for by Christ's revelation "we are not ignorant of his designs" (2 Cor. 2:11). Neither are we ignorant of Jesus' designs. We hear today from advocates of innovative worldly strategies for the church that the Bible gives only vague principles for Christian ministry. But a serious study of Scripture will reveal clear instructions for doing Christ's work in his way and with his power. We are to receive his teaching not as reluctant servants but as eager friends and partners in Christ's kingdom, knowing that his commands are good and filled with blessing for us and for others. We should never listen to those who tell us that we must compromise the Bible in order to be relevant or that careful obedience to the Bible will stifle our ministry.

Our requirement for ongoing obedience to Jesus is confirmed by his repetition of this obligation: "You are my friends if you do what I command you" (John 15:14). Jesus has repeatedly stressed our obedience to him in this Farewell Discourse, and the relationship between our obedience to and our love for him. He is obviously determined for us to realize that obedience is the true test of Christian faith and the path on which we abide with him. For us to speak about being Christ's people, while we are obeying the commands of our sinful world instead of those of Christ, does us little good. Jesus said, "Not everyone who says to me, 'Lord, Lord,' will enter the kingdom of heaven, but the one who does the will of my Father who is in heaven" (Matt. 7:21). This is not teaching salvation by works, but rather a salvation that necessarily involves obedience to our Savior and Lord, since, as branches in the vine, we have his Spirit working in us.

Having reiterated this principle, we should also note here that Jesus' emphasis seems to be on his special command that we are to love one another. "This is my commandment," he stressed, "that you love one another as I have loved you" (John 15:12). He concludes this section on the same note: "These things I command you, so that you will love one another" (15:17).

There is an oft-abused dictum of Augustine: "Love God and do what you like." Sadly, this statement has been made to say that so long as we love God, we are then free to do whatever pleases us, whether it is sinful or not. Augustine in fact was stressing the opposite. He was saying that if we really love the Lord, then we will hardly need any other guide to Christian living, since genuine love will lead us rightly, and guided by love we will not sin.[3]

---

3. Leon Morris, *Reflections on the Gospel of John* (Peabody, MA: Hendrickson, 1986), 523.

Yet we do have a clear guide for love: the Ten Commandments are God's mandate for love, and they teach us how to love one another in tangible and specific ways. The sixth commandment not only says that we are not to murder, but necessarily implies that we are to preserve one another's well-being. The seventh commandment tells us not to sin sexually and also to purify our minds. The eighth commandment tells us not to steal but also to provide; the ninth commandment requires us not only not to lie but also to preserve all truth and uphold our neighbor's good name; and the tenth commandment teaches us contentment so that we will not hate our neighbor in covetous envy.

At the heart of our obedience to Christ, then, is our treatment of other people, especially our fellow believers. How far it is from Jesus' brand of obedience for us to attain some man-made code of conduct while scorning or neglecting other Christians. Loving one another requires us to bind our temper, to speak in ways that build others up, to turn from envy and contempt to respect and goodwill, and to sacrifice readily for the well-being of others. Ryle states: "The weakest, the lowest, the most ignorant, the most defective disciples, are not to be despised. All are to be loved with an active, self-denying, self-sacrificing love. He that cannot do this, or will not try to do it, is disobeying the command of his Master."[4] Indeed, a chronic failure to obey Jesus' command to love presents troubling evidence about our salvation. John thus wrote in his first epistle: "Anyone who does not love does not know God, because God is love" (1 John 4:8).

Appointed for a Purpose

Jesus follows up his command to obey through love with another statement that is well known to many Christians: "You did not choose me, but I chose you" (John 15:16). This is, on the one hand, a simple statement of fact, as the record of the disciples' calling in John chapter 1 reveals. Jesus called them to follow him; they did not apply to him for the position of disciples. On the other hand, this statement joins up with many other similar statements to teach clearly that all who are saved have benefited from God's sovereign grace in salvation.

4. Ryle, *John*, 3:124.

Some commentators take these words as referring to the disciples' appointment as apostles instead of as referring to their receipt of salvation and eternal life. Yet the privileges spoken of by Jesus here are not those distinct to apostleship, but rather those held in common by all believers. It is certainly true that Jesus sovereignly chose and appointed these disciples, but it is equally true that Christ sovereignly chose all believers before their conversion and that he appointed them all to "go and bear fruit" (John 15:16). Paul clearly taught this sovereign choosing, writing to the Ephesians that God "chose us in [Christ] before the foundation of the world" (Eph. 1:4). The Greek word for *chose* is *eklego*, from which we derive our word *election*.

While it is true that to believe in Christ is to choose him, the greater reality is that he first elected or chose us, and we decided for him only as a response to his choosing of us and as the result of his own grace first working in our lives. Paul explains, "For by grace you have been saved through faith. And this is not your own doing; it is the gift of God, not a result of works, so that no one may boast" (Eph. 2:8–9). If we think that we first chose Christ, then we display great ignorance of the true depravity of our sinful nature. We were not Christ's friends but his enemies, having rebelled against his sovereign rule and rejected his love. It was God's sheer prior grace—a free gift based only on his own sovereign love—that called us to Christ, and therefore the whole glory for our salvation belongs to him.

Jesus added that he not only chose the disciples but "appointed you that you should go and bear fruit and that your fruit should abide" (John 15:16). This is consistent with the Bible's constant teaching on election, that believers have been chosen, Paul said, "that we should be holy and blameless before him" (Eph. 1:4). Christians often wonder what is God's will for them, even though the Bible states clearly, "This is the will of God, your sanctification" (1 Thess. 4:3). Since God has chosen believers for holiness, then those who are chosen *will* advance in holiness. Moreover, Jesus said, he appointed the disciples to bear good fruit. This is in keeping with Paul's teaching that "we are [God's] workmanship, created in Christ Jesus for good works, which God prepared beforehand, that we should walk in them" (Eph. 2:10).

Three things should be noted here. The first is that Jesus is probably emphasizing the gospel mission of his disciples as apostles. We have often described the fruit of a Christian in terms of a transformed, Christlike character, as well as general obedience. But here the expression "go and bear fruit" reminds us of the Great Commission, in which Jesus commanded us: "Go therefore and make disciples of all nations" (Matt. 28:19). We remember as well that when Jesus called these first disciples, many of whom were fishermen, he said, "From now on you will be catching men" (Luke 5:10). This gospel mission is our calling as well, and Jesus has appointed all Christians to bear the fruit of salvation through our witness of the gospel and service to the church.

Second, we might wonder about Jesus' purpose in reminding us about sovereign election. Evidently, he intended to remind us of the grace he has had for us so that we will share it with others. The doctrine of election reminds our tender consciences that we are not saved by our works but by God's sovereign grace. This then becomes the greatest message that we can share with non-Christians. We can tell what Jesus did for us and how we, though sinners, are saved by the grace of God in Christ. Correspondingly, being aware of God's sovereign mercy, you can best show your gratitude by sharing that same mercy by bringing the gospel to the lost around you. The word for *appointed* means "set apart," and everyone who was chosen by God from eternity past and called by Christ through the gospel to salvation is also set apart for the gospel. Through our witness we bear fruit that will truly abide, enduring forever through eternal life for all who believe.

Third, Jesus links our abiding in him and our bearing fruit to his promise to answer our prayers: "so that whatever you ask the Father in my name, he may give it to you" (John 15:16). This is the third time in this Farewell Discourse that Jesus has made essentially the identical promise about prayer (cf. 14:13–14; 15:7). This repetition indicates the emphasis that Jesus places on our prayer. We tend to think of prayer as a privilege, but here we find that it is a duty. We are not to be prayerless! In the context of Jesus' reminder of his matchless love for us and his calling us to be his friends, we are no doubt to remember that his friends are our friends and that we must pray as an essential ministry of our love for others. More than this, we find in Jesus' emphasis that prayer is not merely a means to an end. Note that Jesus does not say that we are to pray in order to bear good fruit—true though that is—but that we are to bear fruit so as to pray. Leon Morris comments: "We ought not to think of prayer as something in the nature of a tool that enables us to do better service. Rather, we do better service in order that we may pray more effectively. . . . Jesus is here telling his followers that it is important that we should all have set before us the goal of being more effective in our praying."[5]

LOVE AS THE SUM

If we notice Jesus' repeated summons to prayer, we must certainly notice his ceaseless emphasis on love: "These things I command you, so that you will love one another" (John 15:17). Why the repetition? One reason is that our unwilling hearts obviously need the repeated emphasis. Moreover, it is evident that everything to which Jesus calls his disciples is summed up in love. Our salvation originates in the love of God and manifests itself in love for God and others. This means that we may gauge the quality of our Christianity by our loving treatment of others, our loving concern for the needs around us, and our loving prayers for God to help one another. It suggests that the measure of a church is not merely the faithfulness of its doctrine but also the fervency of its love; indeed, Jesus indicates that the efficacy of the doctrine is measured in the love of the believers. "The aim of our charge," Paul wrote, "is love that issues from a pure heart and a good conscience and a sincere faith" (1 Tim. 1:5).

Consider, for instance, each of the mandates in this passage without love. What is service to Christ without love, but tyranny and self-righteousness? What is evangelism without love, but winning arguments and defeating enemies? How little prayer there will be without love! It is surely in part our lack of love that accounts for our lack of prayer. Prayer stirs up our love for one another, and especially our love for God, with whom we speak in prayer. To realize that while we are yet sinners, God receives us with love at his throne of grace, and that he cares for and meets the needs we express in prayer, is to grow in our love for both the Father to whom we pray and Jesus in whose name we ask. Jesus commands us to obey his commandment to love, to bear good fruit in the gospel, and to pray "so that you will love one another," knowing that in this same way we express and grow in our love for him as well.

---

5. Morris, *Reflections on the Gospel of John*, 527.

102

Hated without a Cause

John 15:18–25

*"If the world hates you, know that it has hated me before
it hated you."* (John 15:18)

esus' Farewell Discourse contains some of the most encouraging
material in the New Testament. In John 14, Jesus told how he
would provide for the disciples during his absence from earth,
primarily by sending the Holy Spirit to guide and empower them. John 15
transitions to the disciples' responsibility, but that, too, involves the great
encouragement of knowing that if we abide in Christ, as a branch in the
vine, then we are sure to bear fruit that glorifies God and blesses others.

Jesus' final topic was less encouraging, though equally important. According to Jesus, there is a cost to following him that must be faced: his followers
will be hated by the world. Just as Jesus was savagely opposed by the people
of his time, despite his loving ministry and godly life, so also must those
who follow him expect hostility and persecution from the world.

This cost of discipleship is a subject that is often left out of evangelistic
appeals today, and even from instruction on Christian discipleship. This
is true at least in the Western nations, where persecution has been mostly
mild. Western Christians are often concerned for fellow believers who are

persecuted in other lands. But they, in turn, express concern for us, that our easier setting has fostered a shallow spirituality. Consider the words of Peter Kusmic, a Yugoslavian Christian who suffered under Communist persecution:

> So much popular Western evangelical religiosity is so shallow and selfish. It promises so much and demands so little. It offers success, personal happiness, peace of mind, material prosperity; but it hardly speaks of repentance, sacrifice, self-denial, holy lifestyle and willingness to die for Christ.[1]

According to Jesus, such an easy, persecution-free Christianity is far from normal. Indeed, a kind of Christian faith that involves no sacrifice and produces no opposition from the world is, according to the New Testament, not true Christianity at all. Paul stated plainly: "All who desire to lead a godly life in Christ Jesus will be persecuted" (2 Tim. 3:12).

HATED BY THE WORLD

Jesus taught the inevitability of the world's hostility in a comparison from the greater to the lesser: "If the world hates you, know that it has hated me before it hated you" (John 15:18). He was not suggesting that the world might not hate Christians, but rather assuming with certainty that as the world hated him, it would also hate his followers.

In speaking of "the world," Jesus referred to the world system that is opposed to God. "The world" is not the physical earth but the controlling mentality of unbelieving mankind, with its rewards and sanctions, its expectations, ideologies, and practices, all of which are in rebellion to God and his rule. In the context of Jesus' meeting with the disciples, "the world" was present in the form of the Jewish leaders who opposed his teaching of grace. In later years, when John wrote this Gospel, "the world" was operating in the form of the hedonistic Roman Empire. There were many differences between the Jews and the Romans, one being moral and the other immoral, but they were united in their opposition to God and his gospel.

---

1. Quoted in Bruce Milne, *The Message of John: Here Is Your King!* (Downers Grove, IL: InterVarsity Press, 1993), 226.

According to Jesus, a defining characteristic of "the world" is its hatred for him. "It has hated me," he said (John 15:18). How vital it is for Christians to realize the world's hostility to Christ. What danger we court when we think that the world is safe and that its attitudes and ways are compatible with faith in Christ. Martyn Lloyd-Jones commented: "If you want to know what this world is like, look what it did to him. . . . He gave himself to healing people and to instructing them. . . . He went about doing good. What was the response of the world? It hated him, it persecuted him, it rejected him. It chose a murderer before him. It crucified him, it killed him. And there on the cross he exposed the world for what it is."[2]

This being the case, Christians who think they can live openly, faithfully, and fruitfully for Jesus and yet enjoy the favor of the world are deceiving themselves. "If the world hates you," Jesus said, "know that it has hated me before it hated you" (John 15:18). The word *hate* is a strong one, and Jesus chose it to convey the true feeling of the world for those who authentically follow him. He uses the word eight times in this passage (seven in the original Greek), so that hatred is the dominant response of the world to Jesus and his people.

This hatred for Christ is expressed in a myriad of ways. On a personal level, worldly people casually blaspheme the name of God's Son with such contempt that for them *Jesus Christ* is primarily a curse. Less dramatically, people shun any exposure to the Bible's teaching and react with outrage to the doctrines that Jesus taught. An example was shown in John 6, when Jesus fed the hungry crowd and then taught them about his atoning death for sin. At this teaching, the people grumbled and turned away (John 6:61, 66). This hatred for Jesus' teaching would ripen until the crowd in Jerusalem shouted for Pontius Pilate to crucify him (Luke 23:18–23), an event that would take place the next day after Jesus' teaching in John 15.

And this hatred for Christ is being seen in a case brought before the United States Supreme Court, concerning a cross that was erected in the Mojave Desert. In 1934, the Veterans of Foreign Wars (VFW) erected the cross as a monument to fallen soldiers in World War I, and that cross has been standing for over seventy years. In 2001, the American Civil Liberties Union (ACLU) filed a suit on behalf of a man named Frank Buono, who

---

2. D. Martyn Lloyd-Jones, *The Cross* (Westchester, IL: Crossway, 1986), 99–100.

was offended by the emblem of Christ's atoning death. Since the VFW had donated its monument to the U.S. Parks Service, the suit claimed that the cross violated the separation of church and state. In response, the Department of the Interior transferred the ownership of the monument back to the VFW. Far from being satisfied, the ACLU filed a new suit, opposing the transfer of the land and demanding that the cross be taken down. At the time of this writing, the cross is covered by a plywood box, and the matter awaits the Supreme Court. It is implausible to imagine any other religious figure than Jesus Christ receiving such hatred that he inspires a well-financed legal assault demanding the removal of his symbol from a war monument on a hill in the middle of a desert.[3]

The world does not stop at hatred, however, Jesus insisted. "Remember the word that I said to you: 'A servant is not greater than his master.' If they persecuted me, they will also persecute you. If they kept my word, they will also keep yours" (John 15:20). Earlier that evening, Jesus had pointed out that servants are not greater than their master, on that occasion reminding the disciples to serve one another as Jesus had served them by washing their feet. This principle holds true for the world's hatred as well. The world that crucified Jesus will not leave his followers and heralds unscathed. The world that responded to Jesus' teaching with anger will respond likewise to our preaching of his gospel.

An immediate application of this teaching is that we should not make a pretense of following Jesus unless we are prepared for the world's scorn and persecution. For many of us, this persecution will involve little more than social ostracizing and unfair harassment. These things can hurt very deeply, as anyone who has been slandered and mocked can attest. For Jesus' disciples in Jerusalem, this persecution quickly developed into official demands for silence, which we might also receive. The apostles and their followers at first enjoyed "favor with all the people" (Acts 2:47), just as Christian love will win us many friends. But as soon as the gospel was publicly preached, the world struck back. Acts 4:18 records the Jewish Sanhedrin as ordering Peter and John "not to speak or teach at all in the name of Jesus." When the apostles refused to comply, they were publicly beaten (5:40). Before long, the Jews stoned to death Stephen the deacon for his preaching (7:58) and then

---

3. After this chapter was written, the case was ultimately decided in favor of allowing the cross to stand.

launched a full-scale assault of intimidation, arrest, and violence against Christ's followers. By the time that John wrote this Gospel, Christians faced death all over the Roman Empire for their profession of faith. Virtually all the apostles died from acts of violence and official persecution.

This raises two questions for us. The first is whether or not we are willing to be hated and persecuted for Jesus. Many believers wonder, "Would I remain faithful to Jesus if threatened with death?" The way to answer is your response to whatever persecution you face right now. If you hide your confession in the face of social shunning or unfair harassment, then it is not likely that you would hold fast to Jesus in the face of death. It is of the greatest importance that we not shrink from persecution, for Jesus said, "Everyone who acknowledges me before men, I also will acknowledge before my Father who is in heaven, but whoever denies me before men, I also will deny before my Father who is in heaven" (Matt. 10:32–33).

A second question is whether there is any reason for the world to notice and persecute us. The world does not hate a false Christianity that differs little from itself. The world will tolerate a Christian who remains silent and fits in, but it hates a living testimony to saving grace and a truly holy life. If you were arrested today on a charge of discipleship to Jesus, would there be enough evidence to sustain the charge against you?

REASONS FOR THE WORLD'S HATRED

At the end of this passage, Jesus says that the world "hated me without a cause" (John 15:25), but this does not mean that there were no reasons for the world's hatred. Jesus provides three reasons for the world's opposition, beginning with the fact that Christians no longer belong to the world: "If you were of the world, the world would love you as its own; but because you are not of the world, but I chose you out of the world, therefore the world hates you" (15:19).

According to Jesus, the world loves its own, that is, those who share its self-centered, man-exalting, sin-permissive values. It is not the weakness and failures of Christians that the world hates: the world actually loves these. This is not to say that Christians who are being obnoxious should blame others for the opposition they experience. The point is that Christians must realize that their allegiance to heaven through biblical thinking and living will generally infuriate a world in rebellion to God. The Puritan Jeremiah Burroughs commented:

> The world would have all to be like themselves and, for any kind of people to make a profession as if they were called out of the world, and live after another kind and fashion, and have other sorts of hopes, comforts, ends, and rules by which they live, oh, this the world cannot endure! . . . There is nothing more provoking to the world than separation from the world, and, therefore, it is no marvel that the people of God are hated in the world and looked upon as the ringleaders of sedition.[4]

After the 2004 U.S. presidential elections, humorist Garrison Keillor spoke on government- financed National Public Radio in favor of a "constitutional amendment to deny voting rights to born-again Christians." This shows the particular hatred of the world for Jesus; it is impossible to imagine that such a statement would avoid outrage if Keillor had stated that Jews, Muslims, or homosexuals should not be permitted to vote. Keillor was not punished, of course, because he was speaking against the rights of Christians. But notice his reasoning, which conforms exactly to Jesus' explanation: "I feel if your citizenship is in heaven—like a born-again Christian's is—you should give up your citizenship."[5] They do not belong to us, they do not think and vote like us, he was saying, so we should exclude and persecute them. This is characteristic of how the world is always infuriated by even the influence of those who serve God.

Not only are Christians hated because they are not of the world, but second, Jesus said, because "I chose you out of the world, therefore the world hates you" (John 15:19). If there is one biblical doctrine that is loathed by the world above all others, that is the doctrine of predestination, or election. The idea that God, by his own good pleasure and sovereign choice, selected some to be saved and permitted others to perish is maddening to a worldly mind. So offensive is this teaching to the natural man that even many Christians object on humanistic grounds to the Bible's clear teaching of election. Jesus taught, "You did not choose me, but I chose you" (15:16), and this above all the world hates.

---

4. Jeremiah Burroughs, *Gospel Conversation* (1648; repr., Morgan, PA: Soli Deo Gloria, 1995), 249–50.

5. Quoted in Michele Malkin, *Unhinged* (Washington, DC: Regnery, 2005), 130.

Not only is the doctrine of election a source of worldly hatred, but so are the effects of God's sovereign grace in the lives of his people. Christians possess a new and heavenly nature by the new birth, they enjoy peace with God through his forgiveness in Christ's blood, and they possess a sure hope of an eternity in glory. These privileges of our election receive a great hostility from the world, which thereby acknowledges their existence. As long as our election out of the world and into Christ's kingdom remains an in-house doctrine bearing little evidence in our lifestyles, the world can ignore and therefore tolerate our doctrine. But, writes A. W. Pink, "when the 'I have chosen you out of the world' becomes a *practical* reality, then the world's rage and ban will be displayed."[6]

The third reason for the world's hatred of Christians sums up the whole: Jesus said, "All these things they will do to you on account of my name" (John 15:21). This is the great point that Jesus wants us to know: the world hates his disciples because of *him* and therefore only because we bear *his* name. This is our single greatest privilege, and it ought to be our greatest joy: to bear Christ's name amid the world's hatred and persecution. When we are persecuted simply because of our faith in Jesus, our love for him, and the power of his kingdom at work in us, this blesses us richly. It proves as little else can do that we must be children of God and citizens of the heavenly kingdom. J. C. Ryle comments, "Persecution, in short, is like the Goldsmith's hallmark on real silver and gold: it is one of the marks of a converted man."[7]

There are several reasons why we must not betray our allegiance to Jesus under persecution, including fear for our own souls and simple loyalty to the cause of our Lord. But the blessing of suffering not only *for* but *with* Jesus is one for which we may be truly thankful. Notice how Paul expressed this idea to the Philippians: "For it has been granted to you that for the sake of Christ you should not only believe in him but also suffer for his sake" (Phil. 1:29). Likewise, when Peter and John were publicly beaten for their refusal to cease preaching Christ's gospel, they departed, "rejoicing that they were counted worthy to suffer dishonor for the name" (Acts 5:41). Therefore, in the face of persecution for our faith, we ought to pray like the early believers.

6. Arthur W. Pink, *Exposition of the Gospel of John* (Grand Rapids: Zondervan, 1975), 843.
7. J. C. Ryle, *Expository Thoughts on the Gospels: John*, 3 vols. (Edinburgh: Banner of Truth, 1999), 3:132.

Not only did they not decide to scale back their public witness of the gospel, as some Christians advocate for us to do today, but they did not even ask the Lord to remove the persecution. Instead, they prayed only, "Lord, look upon their threats and grant to your servants to continue to speak your word with all boldness" (4:29).

THE WORLD CONDEMNED FOR HATING JESUS

For believers, the world's persecution of Christians works for blessing through sanctification, but for the unbelieving world it leads to a great condemnation. Jesus earlier told the disciples that he came as the true revelation of God the Father: "Whoever has seen me has seen the Father," he asserted (John 14:9). The world's hatred of him therefore exposes its ignorance of God. Jesus said, "All these things they will do to you on account of my name, because they do not know him who sent me" (15:21).

This explains why it was the religious leaders who most opposed Jesus, since their religion had long since lost touch with God and served only their own purposes. This ignorance is a defining characteristic of this age of the world, seen both in those who crucified Jesus then and in those who deny him now. Paul said, "None of the rulers of this age understood this, for if they had, they would not have crucified the Lord of glory" (1 Cor. 2:8).

Not only does the world's hatred for Jesus prove that it does not know God, but its response to his teaching reveals that the world hates God. Jesus said, "If I had not come and spoken to them, they would not have been guilty of sin, but now they have no excuse for their sin. Whoever hates me hates my Father also" (John 15:22–23). Jesus does not mean that apart from his teaching the world would not have sinned, but simply states that the world's guilt is compounded by its hateful reaction to his teaching.

Consider how remarkable it is that Jesus' teaching is rejected by the world. We could understand if Jesus had been arrogant in tone, since people rightly object to such an attitude. But Jesus was instead humble and gentle in his teaching, especially when dealing with brokenhearted sinners. We might likewise understand if Jesus' words were selfish, revolving completely around his own interests. But Jesus taught that he came "not to be served but to serve, and to give his life as a ransom for many" (Matt. 20:28). Some people's words are harsh and others hypocritical. The world would be justified in rejecting either. But Jesus' ministry was one of love for the weak and rejected, offering grace to sinners. "Come to me, all who labor and are heavy laden," he called, "and I will give you rest" (Matt. 11:28). "If anyone thirsts, let him come to me and drink," he cried. "Whoever believes in me, as the Scripture has said, 'Out of his heart will flow rivers of living water'" (John 7:37–38). For men and women to resent the teaching of Jesus, especially as he presents God's saving grace through the shedding of his own blood, reveals a perverse hatred that must incur a just and awful debt to the wrath of God.[8]

Third, Jesus adds his works to his words: "If I had not done among them the works that no one else did, they would not be guilty of sin, but now they have seen and hated both me and my Father" (John 15:24). The religious leaders who crucified Jesus had seen his great miracles: John's Gospel highlights Jesus' giving of sight to the man born blind (9:24–25) and his resurrection of dead Lazarus (11:44–46), both of which were miracles that the Pharisees knew to be true. Years earlier, at the beginning of his ministry, the Pharisee Nicodemus had admitted what was obvious about Jesus' mighty works: "Rabbi, we know that you are a teacher come from God, for no one can do these signs that you do unless God is with him" (3:2). This awareness, which ultimately drove Nicodemus to saving faith, condemned those who recognized the divine origin of Jesus' miracles and yet opposed, hated, and persecuted him. It is similarly true today for those who cannot deny the power of God at work in the lives of Christians, yet because of their love of sin and hatred for Christ go on to hate and persecute Christ's disciples all the more.

If you are not a Christian, then you should reckon with these condemnations. Jesus reveals your unbelief as willful, culpable ignorance. The good news for you, however, is Christ's merciful grace for those who denied him. On the cross, Jesus prayed to the Father, "Father, forgive them, for they know not what they do" (Luke 23:34). Moreover, your hatred of Christ's teaching—especially his gospel message of forgiveness for sins through faith alone, apart from any works or merit of your own—can be remedied by believing the gospel as it continues to be proclaimed. At Jesus' command, Peter first preached to the very religious leaders who had crucified

---

8. This paragraph is adapted from James Montgomery Boice, *The Gospel of John*, 5 vols. (Grand Rapids: Baker, 1999), 4:1192.

Jesus, and "a great many of the priests became obedient to the faith" (Acts 6:7). You, too, may believe the gospel that you previously rejected, and by this means alone receive salvation through faith in Christ. Finally, there is hope for you in that Jesus is continuing to perform his mighty, saving works. Just as he gave sight to the man born blind, you may ask him to enable you to see. And just as Jesus raised Lazarus from the dead, he can give you new life through the power of his Word (1 Peter 1:23). Christ has power to change your heart, so you should pray to him for the free gift of forgiveness and eternal life.

WITHOUT A CAUSE

There are professing Christians who fall away under the threat of the world's hatred and persecution, reasoning that the cost is too high. Such people fail to reckon on the value of their immortal souls. Others continue to believe in Christ but live close to the world and fear to challenge its judgment. But Jesus concludes his teaching with a reminder that the true judgment belongs not to the world but to God. We see this in his statement that by the world's persecution, "the word that is written in their Law must be fulfilled: 'They hated me without a cause'" (John 15:25).

Jesus is referring here to the Pharisees who would crucify him, speaking of the Old Testament as "their Law." The important point is to realize that, so far from the world's being in control in its hatred and persecution of Christ and his people, the world is instead merely fulfilling what was foreordained and prerecorded by God in the Bible. This quotation is from either Psalm 35:19 or Psalm 69:4, but the chief point is that it came from God, just as the world's persecution of Jesus was ordained by God. It was their malice that would nail Jesus to the cross, but it was God's grace at work that through his death believers would be forgiven of our sins (cf. Acts 2:23). We should not, therefore, fear the judgment of a world that even in its wrath can work only for the praise and glory of God and the salvation of his people (see Ps. 76:10). Instead, we should fear God, that is, we should concern ourselves with his judgment and seek his salvation through a costly faith in Jesus Christ.

Finally, this is not a warrant for Christians to hate the world. God loved the world and sent his Son to be our Savior when we were worldly sinners

(John 3:16). Let us love the world enough to be bold and gracious witnesses of his salvation. Moreover, Jesus' statement that he was "hated . . . without a cause" reminds us that if the world is to hate us, it should not be because of any arrogance or sin on our part. Let our discipleship to Jesus, the evidence of his grace in our lives, and our witness to his gospel of salvation be the only cause the world has to hate and persecute us, so that Christ may receive glory through our sufferings and that we might have the joy of suffering truly for and with him.

103

WITNESS TO THE WORLD

John 15:26—16:4

*"But when the Helper comes, whom I will send to you from
the Father, the Spirit of truth, who proceeds from the Father,
he will bear witness about me. And you also will bear
witness, because you have been with me from the beginning."*
(John 15:26–27)

t is not mere coincidence that the Greek word for *witness* is
martyr, the word in our language that identifies one who loses
his life for his religious testimony. To be a witness for Christ
in our world is to suffer hatred and sometimes violence. But *witness* and
martyr also go together because it is largely through our willingness to
suffer for Christ that the Christian witness advances. As the early-church
leader Tertullian stated frankly to the persecuting powers, "The blood of
the martyrs is the seed of the church."[1]

In the final chapter of his Farewell Discourse, Jesus prepared his disciples
for martyrdom. He began his farewell teaching in chapter 14 by comforting
the disciples regarding his ministry to them after departing for heaven. In

1. Tertullian, *Apology*, 50.

chapter 15, Jesus exhorted them to abide in him so as to bear fruit. Now in the final section of the Farewell Discourse, beginning roughly with chapter 16, Jesus turns to prediction of the Spirit's effective witness of the gospel through the disciples.

The fact that Jesus told the disciples that his forewarnings were given "to keep you from falling away" (John 16:1) tells us that their sufferings would be great indeed. The record of history confirms this, but also shows that what Christ promised to provide was more than enough to sustain his tiny flock. Looking back over the spread of the gospel in its first two centuries, despite the most bloody persecutions, Tertullian wrote to his Roman opponents: "We are but of yesterday, and we have filled every place among you—cities, islands, fortresses, towns, market-places, the very camp, tribes, companies, palace, senate, forum—we have left nothing to you but the temples of your gods."[2]

The great work of gospel witness that would change the world would begin with Christ's band of weak and unimpressive disciples. It would be in his strength that his church would advance, and his followers' witness would be empowered by the Spirit of truth whom he would send.

THE SPIRIT'S WITNESS

The later victories of the gospel were yet in the future when Jesus spoke with his disciples one last time before facing the cross. The disciples had been troubled to learn that Jesus was departing from them. Now came the additional shock that they were going to be hated and persecuted for his sake. This reminds us of Jesus' and the Bible's honesty about the cost of following Christ in this present world. This honesty contrasts with false religions, which usually promise present advantage and ease; Jesus spoke frankly about not only spiritual blessings but also worldly troubles. For this reason the disciples needed encouragement in their appointed roles as ambassadors for Christ. Matthew Henry observes:

Christ having spoken of the great opposition which his gospel was likely to meet with in the world, and the hardships that would be put upon the preachers of it, . . . he here intimates . . . what effectual provision was made for

2. Ibid., 37.

supporting it, both by the testimony of the Spirit (v. 26), and the subordinate testimony of the apostles (v. 27).[3]

To equip the disciples for their witness, Jesus said that he and the Father would send the Holy Spirit: "When the Helper comes, whom I will send to you from the Father, the Spirit of truth, who proceeds from the Father, he will bear witness about me" (John 15:26). Before considering the ministry of the Spirit, we should note three things that Jesus says here about the third person of the Trinity.

First, Jesus names the Spirit "the Helper," which in Greek is the *paraklete*. We saw in our study of John 14:16 that *parakletos* speaks of One who is called to our side with empowering help and who calls out to us on Christ's behalf. One nuance of this word is that of a legal advocate, and here Jesus employs the term with respect to the Spirit's declarative and testifying mission. The world convicts and condemns Christ's followers, but the Spirit comes to bear divine testimony to the gospel in and through the human testimony of Christ's disciples, validating their witness.

Second, along this same line, Jesus refers to the Spirit as "the Spirit of truth." The Spirit came into the world not only that the truth might be revealed and known but that it might conquer by the inward persuasion that he alone can impart.

Third, Jesus spoke of the relationship between the Spirit's mission and the mission of Christ and his Father: "I will send to you from the Father, the Spirit of truth, who proceeds from the Father" (John 15:26). This statement has placed this verse at the center of one of the great controversies in church history, regarding the "procession" of the Holy Spirit, resulting in the long division of the Eastern and Western churches. The issue concerns "the essential inner relationships of the persons in the Godhead."[4] The original version of the fourth-century Nicene Creed declared that the Spirit "proceeds from the Father," mirroring Jesus' language in verse 26. Later, however, and heavily influenced by Augustine, the Latin churches began inserting an additional phrase, known as the *filioque clause*, stating that

3. Matthew Henry, *Commentary on the Whole Bible*, 6 vols. (Peabody, MA: Hendrickson, 2009), 5:914.
4. Sinclair B. Ferguson, *The Holy Spirit*, Contours of Christian Theology (Downers Grove, IL: InterVarsity Press, 1996), 73.

the Spirit proceeds from the Father "and the Son." Unable to resolve their differences over this rather obscure doctrinal debate, among other causes, in 1054 the Eastern and Western churches formally separated, a split that has continued for what now approaches a thousand years.

One of the ironies of this controversy is that the key Bible verse, John 15:26, does not speak directly to the subject. The *filioque* debate pertains to the eternal personal relationships of the members of the Trinity. Jesus' statement, however, pertains not to eternal relationships within the Trinity but rather to the Spirit's mission in history. Western Christians have argued, however, that we must account for Jesus' additional teaching that the Son sends the Spirit. Moreover, the *filioque* argument makes an important point about the relationship between who God is eternally (called the *ontological* Trinity) and what God does in time (called the *economic* Trinity). The principle for relating the two is that "the economic Trinity is a true, however accommodated, reflection of the ontological Trinity."[5] The way that the triune God reveals himself in his works reveals truth regarding who God is in himself.

While noting these implications of John 15:26, we must focus on Jesus' actual emphasis, which is the Holy Spirit's mission as his witness: "he will bear witness about me." In the face of worldly hatred and persecution, the disciples would rest on the truth of Christ as established in and through them by God's Spirit. John Calvin wrote: "Christ now, in opposition to the wicked fury of those men, produces the testimony of the Spirit, and if their consciences rest on this testimony, they will never be shaken."[6]

Much could be said about the Spirit's witness in and to the world, but we should mainly understand it as an *objective* and a *subjective* witness. The Spirit would present an objective witness to Christ through the inspired writings of the apostles in the New Testament. Peter later stated that the Scriptures came into being as "men spoke from God as they were carried along by the Holy Spirit" (2 Peter 1:21). The Spirit would also provide a subjective witness to the souls of men and women. The Spirit's witness would be not only *to man* but also *in man*. This is what Paul meant when he said that he did not rely on "lofty speech or wisdom" in his preaching, but

5. Ibid., 75.
6. John Calvin, *New Testament Commentaries*, trans. T. H. L. Parker, 12 vols. (Grand Rapids: Eerdmans, 1959), 5:130.

rather "in demonstration of the Spirit and of power" (1 Cor. 2:1, 4). By the witness of the Spirit of truth, not only do believers possess external proofs of God's Word but, as Westminster Confession of Faith 1.5 puts it, "our full persuasion and assurance of the infallible truth and divine authority [of Scripture], is from the inward work of the Holy Spirit bearing witness by and with the Word in our hearts." Thus, when Jesus said that "the Spirit of truth . . . will bear witness about me," this was a mighty provision for the success of the gospel in the world.

THE APOSTLES' WITNESS

Jesus immediately linked the witness of the Holy Spirit to the witness that the disciples would themselves bear to the world: "And you also will bear witness, because you have been with me from the beginning" (John 15:27). The apostles' witness was not superseded by the Spirit's witness, but rather it was only through their witness that the Spirit would give his witness to Christ.

Jesus makes the comment that the disciples would witness "because you have been with me from the beginning." Christ has provided for himself the potent testimony of eyewitnesses who lived closely with him for three years. The things written in the New Testament are not attested by hearsay, but as the true record of men who were present and had every reason to be truthful. The apostles died for their witness, and men do not die for a testimony that they know to be untrue. Along these lines, John began his first epistle by pointing out that he had been present with Jesus "from the beginning, which we have heard, which we have seen with our eyes, which we looked upon and have touched with our hands" (1 John 1:1). He adds, "That which we have seen and heard we proclaim also to you" (1:3). It is impossible to imagine the Christian message as possessing its same power were it not attested by such eyewitnesses. Peter said: "We did not follow cleverly devised myths when we made known to you the power and coming of our Lord Jesus Christ, but we were eyewitnesses of his majesty" (2 Peter 1:16).

The disciples and the Holy Spirit share this status as eyewitnesses who were present with Jesus from the beginning of his ministry. The Holy Spirit was with Jesus from the moment of his conception in the virgin womb of Mary: "The Holy Spirit will come upon you, and the power of the Most

High will overshadow you," the angel informed her (Luke 1:35). When Jesus started his ministry by being baptized, the Holy Spirit came to equip him especially for his ministry (3:22). Jesus preached his first sermon on this theme, beginning with the words: "The Spirit of the Lord is upon me" (4:18). Sinclair Ferguson thus comments: "The Spirit is ideally suited to be the chief witness for Christ because he was the intimate companion of Jesus throughout his ministry."[7]

Jesus' teaching on the witness of the Spirit and the apostles provides us with at least four applications. The first is that a true Christian witness is always a witness to Jesus Christ. The Holy Spirit "will bear witness about me," Jesus said (John 15:26). The disciples were qualified as witnesses because of what they had seen and heard about Jesus. A Christian witness today must likewise be a testimony to the person of Christ in his glory as the divine Son and the work of Christ centered on his humble sacrifice to atone for our sins. John stated of his Gospel: "These are written so that you may believe that Jesus is the Christ, the Son of God, and that by believing you may have life in his name" (20:31). Jesus as the Christ speaks to his saving work, and Jesus as the Son of God refers to his person: we receive eternal life through him as God's Son and as our sin-bearing Savior. Our witness must therefore not be to a Christian lifestyle, to our own experiences, or to our opinion of current affairs, but must center on the biblical testimony to the person and work of Jesus Christ.

Second, consider the great mercy of Christ in providing this witness to a world that had rejected and hated him, and was about to put him to death in a torturous and shameful fashion. A. W. Pink writes: "Marvelous grace was this. Neither hostility nor hatred had quenched the compassion of Christ. The world might cast Him out, yet still would His mercy linger over it."[8] Our witness must therefore flow from and bear the marks of Christ's mercy for lost sinners.

Third, we see here the foundational importance of the apostolic ministry. These disciples, who would shortly take up the office of Christ's apostles, performed an essential and unrepeatable role on which all Christians rely today. Empowered by the Holy Spirit for preaching the gospel and the divinely inspired writing of the New Testament, the apostles gave the once-for-all

7. Ferguson, *The Holy Spirit*, 37.
8. Arthur W. Pink, *Exposition of the Gospel of John* (Grand Rapids: Zondervan, 1975), 852.

testimony to the life and work of Jesus. Just before ascending into heaven, Jesus told them, "You will receive power when the Holy Spirit has come upon you, and you will be my witnesses" (Acts 1:8). It is true that all believers receive the Holy Spirit when we come to faith in Christ (2:38), but the apostles were uniquely equipped by the Spirit to give the foundational testimony and to corroborate it with mighty miracles. The writer of Hebrews explains that the gospel "was declared at first by the Lord, and it was attested to us by those who heard, while God also bore witness by signs and wonders and various miracles and by gifts of the Holy Spirit" (Heb. 2:3–4).

Jesus' promise to the disciples was fulfilled on the day of Pentecost, when they not only received the Holy Spirit but began their public witness to Christ. Acts 4:33 tells us that "with great power the apostles were giving their testimony to the resurrection of the Lord Jesus." This tells us that there are no apostles today, since this foundational work of the resurrection-witness could be done only by eyewitnesses and their circle, and that to be a Christian is to accept the apostolic testimony concerning Jesus Christ. Christianity is the faith witnessed to us through the apostles in the New Testament, both in the events of history and in their saving significance. Ours is an apostolic faith: Christian truth comes from the Bible, since that is where the apostles recorded their witness.

Fourth, while there was a uniqueness to the testimony of the original disciples as Jesus' apostles, the Holy Spirit continues to witness through our testimony today. William Hendriksen writes: "Whenever a true servant of God bears witness against the world, this witness is the work of the Spirit. Whenever a simple believer, by word and example, draws others to Christ, this too is the work of the Spirit."[9] We, like the apostles, may fully rely on the power of the Holy Spirit in our preaching, teaching, and evangelism, and we may share their glory as colaborers with God in the ongoing witness to Jesus Christ.

THE APOSTLES' SUFFERING WITNESS

Anticipating the witness of his disciples and those who would come after them, Jesus foretold how the Christ-hating world would persecute them.

---

9. William Hendriksen, *Exposition of the Gospel according to John*, 2 vols., New Testament Commentary (Grand Rapids: Baker, 1953), 2:314–15.

Jesus went so far as to indicate that the assault would deliver blows of such pain and doubt that apart from his advance warning the disciples would be in danger of abandoning the faith. He therefore told "all these things to you to keep you from falling away" (John 16:1). The word for "falling away" is *skandalizo*, which carries the idea of being offended in such a way as to apostasize and abandon the faith. In John's Gospel, Jesus has emphasized his and the Father's sovereign care of the disciples. He promised, "They will never perish, and no one will snatch them out of my hand" (10:28). Here, however, we are reminded that God exercises his sovereignty through means, among which was this warning so that the disciples would not be caught unawares. The only true threat to the disciples was that they might fall away under trial, for, like us, they would soon triumph if only they would persevere in faith.

We may take the two persecutions that Jesus mentions here as representatives of the whole range of afflictions that the first Christians would experience, representing both those that cause doubt and those that instill fear. Jesus foretold: "They will put you out of the synagogues. Indeed, the hour is coming when whoever kills you will think he is offering service to God" (John 16:2).

First, Jesus refers to the threat of excommunication because of their faith in him. Excommunication, properly administered, declares the fearful state of alienation from God and his people. But in the Judaism of Jesus' time, it meant not only separation from the spiritual life of Israel—including the sacrifices, prayers, and Scripture reading—but also separation from the social and even economic life of the nation. A man who was cast out of the synagogue could not get a job and, if he owned a business, would lose all his customers. Excommunication meant being cut off from family, church, and nation, a dreadful punishment.

We have already seen the abusive manner of the Pharisees in wielding this terror. In chapter 9, the man whose eyes Jesus restored was cast out of the synagogue simply for praising his healer. Jesus came to the man afterward and asked him the more essential question: "Do you believe in the Son of Man?" (John 9:35). This was the answer to wrongful excommunication: refuge in the saving work of Jesus Christ.

Condemnation from the church is a fearful thing, and sensitive Christians must necessarily question themselves if the church should cast them out. But many who stood for Christ have been excommunicated from churches that had lost their testimony to Jesus and his gospel. Martin Luther and many other Protestant Reformers were excommunicated, and it burdened their conscience until they realized that the papacy had fallen from Christ and could no longer be considered a true church. I have a friend who was deposed as a minister in a conservative Reformed church because he taught the free offer of Christ's gospel. At his trial he was accused, "You speak too much about Christ." That was the moment that relieved his soul, for he realized then the cause of his rejection. The Jews ultimately excommunicated all the Christians, and by the time that John wrote this Gospel they had inserted a curse on the Nazarenes, by which Christians were kept from attending their synagogue prayers. The intent was not only to condemn the teaching, but also to cause Jewish Christians to doubt the apostles' teaching.

Second, Jesus said that "the hour is coming when whoever kills you will think he is offering service to God" (John 16:2). The book of Acts records the fulfillment of this promise, as pious Jews stoned Stephen to death and then sought the apostles' lives. Paul later stated that this attitude of religious hatred had governed him in his persecuting: "I myself was convinced that I ought to do many things in opposing the name of Jesus of Nazareth" (Acts 26:9). Paul was a living testimony to Jesus' explanation, that they will do these things "because they have not known the Father, nor me" (John 16:3). Only when Jesus displayed his glory to Paul on the Damascus road did the Pharisee gain the blinding insight that he had not been serving but rather persecuting the Lord (Acts 9:4). The disciples were to face a legion of men like Paul had been, not only facing death but, like Jesus, having to die as those considered accursed by God before all the people.

So it has been all through church history, including our present time, which is numerically the greatest era of Christian martyrdom. A typical example is that of the English Reformer Thomas Cranmer, who showed his faith in Christ by submitting to death by burning rather than forsake the gospel, and whose papal persecutors showed their ignorance of Christ by preaching a sermon gloating over the martyrdom of Christ's witness.

Jesus foretold these things to his disciples so that they would be forewarned: "I have said these things to you, that when their hour comes you may remember that I told them to you" (John 16:4). By referring to their persecution as an "hour" that would come, Jesus invested the future sufferings of his apostles with prophetic significance. The book of Acts records that when these things came to pass, the disciples were in fact prepared to face them. When the Sanhedrin ordered Peter and John to cease preaching about Jesus, these Spirit-filled witnesses refused to relent. When they were beaten for their testimony, they left "rejoicing that they were counted worthy to suffer dishonor for the name" (Acts 5:41). Moreover, when they prayed, they asked only for the courage to keep up their witness (4:29). Not only did they remember what Christ had said, but they remembered Christ, and desired only to bear witness to him.

OUR APOSTOLIC WITNESS

One of the famous lines in the Nicene Creed proclaims that we believe in "one holy catholic and apostolic Church." This means that the church is unified in Christ, holy to God, and universal in all places (*catholic* means "universal"). But the fourth statement declares that we are part of a church that is apostolic. *Apostolic* means that as Christians, we uphold the apostles' teaching in the New Testament. To be apostolic is to be biblical, and an apostolic church today will be like the first church in Jerusalem, which we are told was "devoted . . . to the apostles' teaching" (Acts 2:42).

But there is more to being apostolic than merely upholding biblical truth. We must also be willing to embrace apostolic suffering for the spread of the apostolic witness to Jesus.

Five men who learned this truth were young seminary graduates from Switzerland, returning home to France after spending time in Geneva with John Calvin. Upon entering France they were arrested, and in the months that followed they corresponded often with Calvin. One letter, in March 1553, spoke of their blessing in suffering for Christ:

> We want you to know that although our body is confined here between four walls, yet our spirit has never been so free and so comforted, and has never previously contemplated so fully and so vividly as now the great heavenly riches and treasures, and the truth of the promises which God has made to his children; so much so that we seem not only to believe and hope in them but even to see them with our eyes and touch them with our hands, so great and remarkable is the assistance of our God in our bonds and imprisonment. So far, indeed, are we from wishing to regard our affliction as a curse of

331

God, as the world and the flesh wish to regard it, that we regard it rather as the greatest blessing that has ever come upon us, for in it we are made true children of God, brothers and companions of Jesus Christ, the Son of God, and are conformed to his image.[10]

By simply standing for Jesus they had suffered persecution, but through that persecution they had learned to be witnesses for Christ. Their letter continues with these words:

By bringing us out before men to be His witnesses and giving us constancy to confess His name and maintain the truth of His holy Word before those who are unwilling to hear it, indeed, who persecute it with all their force—to us, we say, who previously were afraid to confess it even to a poor ignorant labourer who would have heard it eagerly.[11]

On May 16, 1553, these five Christian martyrs, through whom the Holy Spirit bore testimony to Christ in power, were taken out and burned at the stake. Theirs was a boldness for Christ that shook the world. This is the apostolic witness that stands boldly before the world, proclaiming the death and resurrection of Jesus for forgiveness and new life, fearlessly answering hatred and death with grace and truth. Where can we gain such boldness? Jesus said to remember his words so that we will be ready when persecution comes. The apostles responded by praying for boldness to bear witness to Christ in the power of the Holy Spirit: "Now, Lord, look upon their threats and grant to your servants to continue to speak your word with all boldness" (Acts 4:29). What would happen in and through our lives if we remembered Jesus' words and prayed as the apostles did?

---

10. Ronald S. Wallace, *Calvin, Geneva and the Reformation* (Eugene, OR: Wipf & Stock Publishers, 1998), 217.

11. Ibid.

104

THE SPIRIT'S MINISTRY
TO THE WORLD

John 16:4–11

*"If I go, I will send him to you. And when he comes, he will
convict the world concerning sin and righteousness and
judgment." (John 16:7–8)*

One of the blessings of being a Christian is knowing that God is
at work in our lives in such a way that even our losses end up as
gains. This is true of earthly calamities such as the loss of a job, a
serious illness, or a severed relationship. Time and again, serious Christians
who turn to the Lord in times of loss come through praising God, saying
with David, "It is good for me that I was afflicted" (Ps. 119:71). They find
that God often takes material goods from us in order to give spiritual riches
to us. Christians can know that this principle is true in our lives because we
see its truth in the great affairs of redemptive history. There is no greater
example than the disciples' great loss in the departure of Jesus to take up
the cross and then return into heaven.

Christ's departure is the main theme of his Farewell Discourse. Jesus had
previously told the disciples about his need to die for sin, but he withheld

many details of the doctrine of his departure until it drew near. "I did not say these things to you from the beginning," he explained, "because I was with you" (John 16:4). Now, on the brink of his arrest, Jesus fully explained his departure, and as he noted, "sorrow has filled your heart" (16:6). Their three years with Jesus had been the high point of the disciples' lives. Jesus had meant everything to them, and they had left all to be with him. If we do not appreciate their dismay over his leaving, we little consider the glory of Jesus even before his exaltation. Jesus insisted, however, that they would be compensated for losing his bodily presence. "I tell you the truth," he said: "it is to your advantage that I go away, for if I do not go away, the Helper will not come to you. But if I go, I will send him to you" (16:7).

The apostle John's love of irony is richly present in this statement, for Jesus echoes the high priest Caiaphas's argument when the decision was made to have Jesus killed: "It is better for you that one man should die for the people" (John 11:50). Cynical Caiaphas meant that the nation could avoid trouble with the Romans if Jesus was killed. Now, using the identical words in the original Greek, translated "better for you" and "to your advantage," Jesus tells the disciples that this will really be true in their case. If they thought it was better for Jesus not to die, they completely misunderstood his entire mission, which centered on his atoning death for sin. This is why Jesus expressed surprise that, while they had asked about his leaving them, they had not inquired of his destination: "Now I am going to him who sent me, and none of you asks me, 'Where are you going?'" (16:3). If they had understood his mission, they would have been fascinated with the work he was going to do at God's right hand in heaven.

Likewise, if we think it would be better to have Jesus physically with us now, or that the disciples had an advantage over us today, we ignore the enormous blessing that has come through his exaltation in heaven. The choice is not between Christ present and Christ absent, but between Christ present in body and Christ present in the Holy Spirit. The latter is far better, Jesus said, explaining that when the Spirit came, he would "convict the world concerning sin and righteousness and judgment" (John 16:8).

THE SPIRIT'S CONVICTING

There is debate concerning how we should understand Jesus' use of the word *convict*, and thus concerning the Spirit's ministry to the world. This ministry is so important that it makes Jesus' physical departure worthwhile, so we need to understand what it is.

There are two main options for how the Spirit convicts the world: one negative and one positive. Negatively, it might be that the Spirit comes to condemn the world of its guilt, as a prosecuting attorney seeks to convict criminals today. The main problem with this view is that there is no judge in this teaching. Moreover, when Jesus says that the Spirit will convict the world "concerning . . . righteousness," that does not fit the idea of condemnation. An alternative negative view holds that the Spirit will convict the world in the sense of making it see that it is wrong about sin, righteousness, and judgment. There is no doubt that this sense captures at least part of Jesus' meaning. To make sense of the passage, however, it must be joined to a positive understanding of conviction. The Spirit convicts the world of its error concerning sin, righteousness, and judgment, so as to convince people of Christ's truth in such a way that many repent, believe, and are saved.

The best commentary on Jesus' teaching is the record of the apostles' work immediately upon the receipt of the Holy Spirit. The very day that Jesus sent God's Spirit upon the church, Pentecost, Peter preached the first sermon of the Christian church at the temple, emphasizing the guilt of his hearers: "You crucified and killed [Jesus] by the hands of lawless men" (Acts 2:23). Had Peter preached such a message even a day earlier, the only result would have been his abuse and arrest. No one would have tolerated what he said. But with the Spirit present to convict his hearers, the result was entirely different. Acts 2:37 might give us the best definition of the Holy Spirit's conviction: "they were cut to the heart." Convicted, they appealed to Peter, seeking a remedy: "Brothers, what shall we do?"

This is why it is better for us that Jesus has departed for heaven: he has sent the Holy Spirit, who performs the work of conviction that is essential to any sinner's salvation. While on earth, Jesus *accomplished* our salvation, chiefly by dying for our sins. But now he has gone to heaven to send the Spirit, who *applies* what Jesus achieved to the individual soul through the gift of faith. Such is the depravity of man in sin that unless the Spirit came to apply with divine power the saving benefits of what Jesus purchased on the cross, then no man or woman would ever believe and be saved. This passage, which is the greatest passage on the convicting ministry of the Spirit in all the Bible, is an enormous encouragement to both our ministry and our lives.

John Calvin remarked, "Far more advantageous and far more desirable is that presence of Christ, by which He communicates Himself to us through the grace and power of His Spirit, than if He were present before our eyes."[1]

CONVICTING THE WORLD OF SIN

Jesus not only encouraged the disciples with news of the Spirit's coming, but laid out the specifics of what and how the Spirit would convict the world. Jesus began, "When he comes, he will convict the world concerning sin and righteousness and judgment: concerning sin, because they do not believe in me" (John 16:8–9). This statement shows that the first work of the Spirit in any life is the work of conviction for sin. Robert Murray M'Cheyne described this conviction as follows: "to give him a sense of the dreadfulness of his sins, and to make him feel how surely he is a lost sinner."[2]

The great problem of mankind is sin. All other problems arise from sin, which has estranged our race from our Maker and brought the reign of death and evil into our midst. Jesus Christ was born and came into our world not to deal directly with problems of the economy, politics, education, psychology, or sociology, but to "save his people from their sins" (Matt. 1:21). Yet what man cares about are the very things that Jesus largely ignores: money, power, and societal problems, along with the lesser issues of sports and personal recreations. This is why so many people are indifferent to Christianity, since it concerns a matter about which they are not concerned. For our witness to bear fruit in their salvation, people must therefore be convicted concerning sin.

Both research and experience today show that the vast majority of people believe that they are basically good, that God is generally pleased with them, and that they can hope for some kind of heaven when they die. God's Word, however, reveals that exactly the opposite is reality. For this reason, the apostle Paul's long teaching on man's relationship with God in the book of Romans began by saying: "The wrath of God is revealed from heaven against all ungodliness and unrighteousness of men" (Rom. 1:18).

---

1. Quoted in J. C. Ryle, *Expository Thoughts on the Gospels: John*, 3 vols. (Edinburgh: Banner of Truth, 1999), 3:155.

2. Robert Murray M'Cheyne, *Sermons of Robert Murray M'Cheyne* (Edinburgh: Banner of Truth, 1961), 97–98.

People will agree in general that God ought to be upset about wickedness, but they believe that it is others who are wicked rather than themselves. So Paul went on to prove from Scripture that the standard of righteousness is God's holy law (2:12) and that by God's standard, "none is righteous, no, not one" (3:10). That's not so bad, people think, since God cannot be very much upset about our sins. But the Bible insists that he is. A sinner is "storing up wrath for yourself on the day of wrath when God's righteous judgment will be revealed" (2:5).

These are truths at the very heart of God's revelation in Scripture, but also truths that the world refuses to believe. This is why we rely on the supernatural convicting ministry of the Holy Spirit: it is by God's Spirit alone, through the Word of God alone, that men and women are convicted regarding sin. Conviction is not merely the admission that you have sinned, just like everyone else. Rather, it is the confession that you are a heinous breaker of God's righteous law and a rebel against God's holy rule, justly deserving eternal condemnation. Only the Spirit of God working on the soul can bring this conviction.

Sinners can be convicted in many ways, but Jesus says that the chief proof is "because they do not believe in me" (John 16:9). This is not to say that only unbelief in Jesus is sin, but rather that there is no better way to show man's sin than to reveal the wickedness of unbelief in God's Savior-Son. Jesus said, "This is the judgment: the light has come into the world, and people loved the darkness rather than the light because their works were evil" (3:19). How does unbelief convict of sin? F. B. Meyer writes:

> Here is the supreme manifestation of moral beauty, but man has not eyes for it. Here is the highest revelation of God's desire for man to be reconciled with Him, and be at one with Him, His happy child; but man either despises or spurns His overtures. Here is the offer of pardon for all the past, of heirship of all the promises, of blessedness in all the future, but man owns that he is indifferent to the existence and claims of God . . . . Here is God in Christ beseeching him to be reconciled, declaring how much the reconciliation has cost, but [unbelieving man] absolutely refuses to be at peace. No trace of tears in his voice, no shame on his face, no response to God's love in his heart.[3]

3. F. B. Meyer, *The Life of Love* (Old Tappan, NJ: Revell, 1987), 305.

Jesus' point is that there is no sin worse than this unbelief. To see Jesus, to hear his gospel offer, to learn of his wonderful life and works, and to remain coldly indifferent or hostile to God's Son is the quintessential act of depravity that must and will receive God's just retribution in the torments of hell. Rejecting Jesus involves choosing sin over salvation, the curse over the Christ, and is the stubborn denial of guilt over the humble reception of grace.

Since the Spirit's first work of conviction is to persuade the world of sin, this must also be our priority in gospel ministry. It is not an act of malice for preachers in their sermons and Christians in their witness to press home to sinners the heinous nature of their transgressions and their peril under divine wrath, but an act of mercy. If we neglect to seek conviction for sin, we can hardly expect the rest of the gospel to seem important or attractive, since it was for sinners that Jesus lived and died.

An example of this principle is seen in John Bunyan's classic book *The Pilgrim's Progress*, which begins on this very theme. Its first paragraph reveals a man with a Bible in his hand and a burden on his back—the burden of conviction for sin—reading, weeping, and trembling, asking pathetically, "What shall I do?" No Christian, not even the apostles, is able to bring a sinner to this conviction through our own eloquence or persuasion, but Jesus has sent the Spirit through our witness to "convict the world concerning sin" (John 16:8).

The answer to the question asked by Bunyan's pilgrim, "What shall I do?" is implied in Jesus' teaching. The Spirit convicts of sin because of unbelief; therefore, the intended remedy is faith in Christ's saving work. It is important for us to emphasize this remedy, because there are other ways for men and women to respond to conviction over sin. Bunyan provides one example in *The Pilgrim's Progress*. Convicted of sin and directed by the evangelist toward the cross, the pilgrim was nearly diverted along the way. Mr. Worldly Wiseman, from the town of Carnal Policy, asked him about the burden on his back. Learning about his conviction, Worldly urged him to visit the village of Morality, where a gentleman named Legality would help him feel better about himself through good works. Fortunately, the evangelist appeared and again directed the pilgrim to Jesus Christ, who would remove the burden of sin by the cross, paying in his blood the sin debt of those who trust in him.[4]

4. John Bunyan, *The Pilgrim's Progress* (Nashville: Thomas Nelson, 1999), 11–22.

Conviction of sin is necessary for salvation, but does not itself save. Meyer urges all who are convicted by the Holy Spirit: "Do not wait for more conviction, but come to Jesus as you are . . . . Do not stay away till you feel more deeply. Do not suppose that strongly roused emotions purchase His favor. His command is absolute—*Believe*."[5]

Convicting the World of Righteousness

The Spirit's second ministry to the world follows from the first: "he will convict the world . . . concerning righteousness" (John 16:8–10). This, like much else in this teaching, can be taken in at least two ways. First, Jesus could mean that the Spirit will convict the world regarding *its* righteousness. Jesus' earthly ministry condemned the petty righteousness of the Pharisees and other moralists by his perfect display of true righteousness, which is one of the reasons they hated and killed him, and the Spirit continues this work today.

James Montgomery Boice illustrates this idea of false righteousness by telling the story of a group of prisoners of war in World War II. They were permitted to receive care packages, and these included *Monopoly* games to help them pass the time. Soldiers being soldiers, they took the money to be used as their camp currency, which they primarily used for playing cards. As usually happens, one card player ended up getting almost all the money, amounting to thousands of dollars in *Monopoly* currency. When he returned home from the war, he brought this pile of paper, which he had long come to think of as real money, and tried to deposit it in a bank account. It was, of course, rejected as fraudulent. Likewise, mankind has developed a counterfeit system of righteousness that has no currency at all in the courts of heaven. Boice concludes: "Human righteousness is like Monopoly money. It has its uses in the game we call life. But it is not real currency, and it does not work in God's domain."[6] Jesus reveals true righteousness, and when the Holy Spirit convicts a sinner, his or her false righteousness is also revealed.

The Holy Spirit not only convicts the world regarding its counterfeit righteousness, but also, second, convinces the world of the true righteousness

5. Meyer, *The Life of Love*, 305.
6. James Montgomery Boice, *Romans*, 4 vols. (Grand Rapids: Baker, 1991), 1:292–93.

that is found in Christ. This is why Jesus spoke of conviction "concerning righteousness, because I go to the Father, and you will see me no longer" (John 16:10). Jesus' resurrection and ascension into heaven accomplished two great things regarding his righteousness. First, it reversed the verdict of the Jewish leaders who condemned Jesus (19:7), condemning them instead. Second, it proved that Christ's saving work for us was accepted by the Father. The resurrection set the Father's seal of approval on the life and death of his Son, and the sending of the Holy Spirit from the Father was the final proof that Jesus had succeeded in reconciling believers with God. Meyer comments: "The work of Jesus on man's behalf finished at the Cross, accepted by the Father—of which the resurrection is witness—presented by our Great High Priest within the veil, is the momentous truth which the Holy Spirit brings home to the convinced sinner."[7]

This is the gospel truth that those convicted of sin need and long to hear: there is forgiveness for sinners and righteousness in Jesus Christ. Jesus had taught this truth all through his ministry: "Whoever hears my word and believes him who sent me has eternal life. He does not come into judgment, but has passed from death to life" (John 5:24). Therefore, just as our Christian witness must begin with conviction for sin, it must always lead to righteousness by grace alone through faith alone in Christ. M'Cheyne preached:

> The second work of the faithful ministry is to do the very same [as the Spirit]—to lead weary souls to Christ—to stand pointing not only to the coming deluge, but to the freely offered ark—pointing not only to the threatening storm, but to the strong tower of safety—directing the sinner's eye not only inwards to his sin, and misery, but outwards also, to the bleeding, dying, rising, reigning Savior.[8]

Here again, the Spirit convicts so that sinners may believe. First, we must believe ourselves guilty under God's just condemnation; then we must believe that Jesus died for our sins and grants his righteousness through faith alone. Having departed to reign in heaven, Jesus has sent the Spirit to empower this conviction of righteousness in himself, a mighty provision for the gospel ministry of his disciples.

7. Meyer, *The Life of Love*, 306.
8. M'Cheyne, *Sermons*, 98.

Convicting the World of Judgment

The final convicting work of the Spirit pertains to judgment: "he will convict the world . . . concerning judgment, because the ruler of this world is judged" (John 16:8, 11). Typically for John, the meaning here may be rightly taken in a couple of ways. Jesus might be teaching that his overthrow of the devil, both by dying to destroy the power of sin and by rising from the dead to bring new and heavenly life into the world, has proved that there is a judgment on evil. Paul says that when Jesus nailed our sins to the cross, putting away our condemnation, "he disarmed the rulers and authorities and put them to open shame, by triumphing over them in him" (Col. 2:15). Christ saw his death and resurrection as the judgment of Satan, by which his falsehood is exposed and his demise achieved, and in the fall of Satan's reign we see that all the powers of sin and darkness must fall. Therefore, if you doubt that there is a judgment awaiting all evil in this world, excepting the sin that has already been judged on Christ's cross, then his defeat of Satan should prove your folly. It is the ministry of the Spirit to work this conviction concerning judgment.

Moreover, Jesus has judged all that is glorified in this Satan-ruled world: power, wealth, prestige, worldly glory, and carnal pleasure. Skip Ryan notes:

> In the triumph of Christ, the false one, the liar, the accuser who wants to hold up to us false standards of judgment has been defeated. Do you evaluate yourself by your appearance? Your wealth? Your standard of living? Your success? The opportunities that you have? The clubs to which you belong? The accuser lies and tells us to see ourselves in this way. Jesus comes to reveal him as the liar.[9]

The progression outlined for the Spirit's convicting ministry helps us to see the relevance of this final conviction for the lives of Christians. We are first convicted of our sin and guilt, and then of forgiveness and righteousness through Jesus Christ. What conviction do we then need as we live as Christ's people in the world? We need the Spirit's conviction that the reign of Satan really is over. Jesus had already told the disciples concerning his cross, "Now is the judgment of this world; now will the ruler of this world

9. Joseph "Skip" Ryan, *That You May Believe* (Wheaton, IL: Crossway, 2003), 320–21.

341

be cast out" (John 12:31). The cross to which we look for our salvation was also the judgment of the world we left behind to follow Jesus. Paul said that when we were dead in sin, we were under Satan's domination, living "in the passions of our flesh, carrying out the desires of the body and the mind" (Eph. 2:3). But Christ has judged and defeated Satan and his power, and we are now reborn in Christ "after the likeness of God in true righteousness and holiness" (4:24).

Do you believe that you are no longer under the dominion of Satan, no longer bound to sin, but now free in Christ to lead a new life of righteousness? It is the work of the Holy Spirit to convict believers that Satan and his reign are judged and cast down, so that our manner of acting and speaking, our treatment of one another, and our walk before Christ in the power of the Spirit will reflect the truth of his victory.

It is not possible even to be a Christian and to be saved from God's wrath without being convicted of sin and righteousness: we must confess our sins and seek refuge in Christ's blood. But if we want to be greatly used by the Spirit today—and his work of conviction always takes place through the witness of Christ's people—then we must also be convicted concerning the judgment of this world. Satan is defeated. The reign of sin is broken in Christ. The world's siren song of death need not be heeded. Do you believe that? Are you convicted of Christ's triumph and reign over all? Does your life show that you are? Let us pray for the Spirit's conviction of Christ's victory over Satan, sin, and the world, so that through the witness of our yielded lives the Holy Spirit might bring conviction and saving faith to many.

105

The Spirit's Ministry to the Church

John 16:12—15

"When the Spirit of truth comes, he will guide you into all the truth, for he will not speak on his own authority, but whatever he hears he will speak, and he will declare to you the things that are to come." (John 16:13)

J. I. Packer wrote in his valuable book *Keep in Step with the Spirit* that "the essence of the Holy Spirit's ministry, at this or any time in the Christian era, is to mediate the presence of our Lord Jesus Christ." Mediating Christ's presence, he explained, "is a matter of the Spirit doing whatever is necessary for the creation, sustaining, deepening, and expressing" of our relationship with Jesus.[1]

Since the Spirit mediates our relationship with Jesus, it is important that we understand his work in our lives. Errors about the Holy Spirit have led to any number of deviant approaches to the Christian life. Almost as harmful as the errors is the general ignorance of so many Christians about the

1. J. I. Packer, *Keep in Step with the Spirit* (Grand Rapids: Revell, 1984), 55.

Spirit, the result of which is a weakening of our confidence and experience as believers. Jesus' Farewell Discourse provides some of the Bible's most concentrated teaching on the Holy Spirit, and as we come to the final passage pertaining to the Spirit, it will be worthwhile to review our Lord's message.

Jesus refers to the Holy Spirit as "the Helper," which in the original Greek is *parakletos*. The *paraklete* is the third person of the Godhead, who is called to our side to minister on Christ's behalf. In the five passages of the Farewell Discourse dealing with the Spirit, Jesus taught that the Spirit: (1) is "another Helper" taking Christ's place in discipling his followers (John 14:16); (2) would enable the apostles to remember all that Jesus had taught them (14:26); (3) in the midst of persecution, would empower the believers' witness to Jesus (15:26); (4) would minister conviction of sin, righteousness, and judgment to the world (16:8–11); and (5) would guide the disciples into the whole of saving truth (16:12–13). This final point is the emphasis of our passage. Jesus, having spoken of the Spirit's convicting ministry to the world, adds the Spirit's revealing ministry to the church.

INTO ALL THE TRUTH

Jesus pointed out that there were truths that he had not taught the disciples because they were not yet ready or able to receive them: "I still have many things to say to you, but you cannot bear them now" (John 16:12). This inability reflects not merely the disciples' weakness, but also the reality that they were still living before the cross. The pattern of God's revelation is for his saving action first to happen, and then for the biblical teaching to record and explain it. In the forty days after the resurrection and before his ascension, Jesus would give an intensive course on biblical theology to the disciples. Still, he promised to send "the Spirit of truth" to complete their education after he had gone, guiding them "into all the truth" (16:13).

This statement indicates a progressive unfolding of God's revelation. We see this in the relationship of the Old Testament to the New. They present the same salvation, but there is growth in terms of clarity and maturity. In the Old Testament, Christ and his gospel are presented by symbols such as the temple, the feasts, and especially the animal sacrifices. At no time, however, did the Bible teach that sinners are forgiven because a lamb or goat died in their place. Rather, the sacrificial animals drew a picture of the true Savior and Lamb of God, Jesus, who would shed his blood for our sin. "Behold, the Lamb of God," cried John the Baptist, spying Jesus of Nazareth (John 1:29), and answering the great longing of the Old Testament. This shows the organic connection between the salvation doctrine of the Old Testament and that which has progressed in the New.

Seeing this progression within the Bible, some scholars erroneously conclude that this revelatory process continues beyond the Bible. This is the teaching of the Mormons, who hold that the nineteenth-century musings of Joseph Smith were the continued revelation of God to his church. The idea of new revelation from God is common to all the cults, including Mormonism and the Jehovah's Witnesses. A similar problem is seen in the Roman Catholic Church, with its emphasis on the extrabiblical and counterbiblical teaching passed down through the popes and councils. Another version of this problem is that which confuses the Holy Spirit's special inspiration of the apostles with the idea of human inspiration. William Barclay espouses this view, arguing that great poetry is inspired from God, as was George Frideric Handel in writing the "Hallelujah Chorus," and as is a scientist who makes a breakthrough in curing cancer. "There is no end to God's revelation," he writes. "God is *always* revealing Himself. . . . God is still leading us into a greater and greater realization of what Jesus means."[2]

A biblical understanding will agree that God still speaks to the world today, but will deny that God is still granting revelation. God speaks to us in the Scriptures, which are his final revelation to mankind before the return of Christ in glory. This realization is essential for the life and health of the church. Those who assert that God is continuing to give revelation consider the New Testament to be an incomplete and provisional revelation. Under this view, especially when linked to an evolutionary theory that grants those currently living a superior capacity for inspiration and understanding, the Bible's clear teaching on sexual morality, gender distinctions, and even the gospel of salvation are replaced with more current, worldly doctrines.

When Jesus spoke of a future revelation, he did not mean that there would be an endless progress in divine disclosure throughout history. James Montgomery Boice explains, "Jesus is teaching that the Holy Spirit would lead the disciples into a supplementary but definitive new revelation that thereafter

2. William Barclay, *The Gospel of John*, 2 vols. (Philadelphia: Westminster, 1975), 2:227–28.

would be the church's authoritative standard of doctrine."[3] The writer of Hebrews said that "in these last days [God] has spoken to us by his Son" (Heb. 1:2), indicating that the apostolic witness to Christ in the New Testament is the last revelation of God to mankind. Notice as well that Jesus tells the disciples that the Spirit will guide them into "all the truth" (John 16:13). Jesus was not promising to reveal "all truth" to them, as if they would know everything about everything. Nor was Jesus promising that the Spirit would teach them only some truths. Rather, it was "all the truth," that is, the whole of the fixed body of Christian doctrine that would be contained in the New Testament.

When the apostle Paul described Christ's gifts to the church, the first of these was the apostles (Eph. 4:7–11). Their work was primarily to provide the fixed revelation that would be the standard for the church in all subsequent ages, and for this work Jesus promised the teaching and guiding ministry of the Holy Spirit. As Paul tells it in Ephesians 2:20–22, this apostolic revelation laid the foundation for the church that would come afterward, with Christ as the chief cornerstone. Now that the New Testament has been revealed and laid down in writing as our foundation, we are not to lay new and different foundations but to build on the foundation that Christ has provided, by teaching and observing the commands of the Bible and by building churches based on the biblical message of the gospel.

THE CONTENT OF THE BIBLE

One of the reasons that the New Testament should be seen as God's final authoritative revelation is the nature of its content. When people describe modern poetry or science in terms that mirror the inspiration of God's Word, they fail to appreciate the distinctive content of Holy Scripture. The Bible does speak to a variety of matters, some of which touch on the sciences while others present details of secular history, always speaking truthfully in these cases. But these matters are incidental to the main message of the Bible, which focuses on God's redeeming work in history to save his people from the curse of sin. God's inspired revelation in Scripture pertains to the urgent matter of man's broken relationship with God because of sin and God's remedy in the sending of his Son, Jesus Christ.

3. James Montgomery Boice, *The Gospel of John*, 5 vols. (Grand Rapids: Baker, 1999), 4:1217.

In describing the Spirit's revealing ministry, Jesus also provided a summary of the kinds of materials found in the New Testament. The New Testament is not a handbook for worldly success and happiness, but God's final revelation concerning salvation through his Son. Jesus listed three categories of materials that make up this revelation.

First, the New Testament contains *recorded history* of the life and ministry of Jesus Christ, from his birth, through his public teaching and miracles, and culminating in his death, resurrection, and ascension into heaven. When Jesus said that the Spirit "will take what is mine and declare it to you" (John 16:14), he meant in part that the Spirit would tell who Jesus is and what Jesus has done. This reminds us that ours is a historical faith. We believe what we believe because of what has happened in history. Christian truth arises from Christ's actual life and ministry on earth. We do not believe the Bible because it is agreeable to our thinking or represents our particular myths, but because we believe the record of what has actually happened on this earth. Martyn Lloyd-Jones comments:

> The Bible . . . plainly shows that my comfort and consolation lie in facts—the fact that God has done certain things and that they have literally happened. The God in whom I believe is the God who could and *did* divide the Red Sea and the river Jordan. . . . If the facts recorded in the Bible are not true, then I have no hope and no comfort. For we are not saved by ideas; but by facts, by events. . . . Buddhism, Hinduism and other faiths rest upon theories and ideas. In the Christian faith alone we are dealing with facts.[4]

Any approach to Christianity, therefore, that is not grounded in the historical facts recorded in the Bible—especially Christ's saving work for us, centered on the cross—simply is not Christianity. We cannot have the message of Christianity without the life of Christ, beginning with his virgin birth and continuing to his sin-atoning death and bodily resurrection. To deny these facts is to cease to be Christian.

Second, the New Testament contains *doctrine*. This is what Jesus refers to when he says that the Spirit would lead the disciples into "all the truth" (John 16:13). Essential as the historical record of Jesus is, it would mean nothing without the doctrinal explanation. Why did Jesus offer himself to die? What

4. D. Martyn Lloyd-Jones, *Faith Tried & Triumphant* (Grand Rapids: Baker, 1953), 61.

347

did he accomplish on the cross? How do we benefit from what Jesus did? The apostles taught not only the historical record but also the authoritative meaning of Jesus' life, death, and resurrection. J. Gresham Machen writes: "'Christ died'—that is history; 'Christ died for our sins'—that is doctrine. Without these two elements, joined in an absolutely indissoluble union, there is no Christianity."[5]

Third, the New Testament provides *prophecy* of things yet to come. Jesus said that the Spirit "will declare to you the things that are to come" (John 16:13). An example is Jesus' clear warning about the destruction of Jerusalem, which happened in A.D. 70, and which the Christians escaped because of the Bible's prophetic teaching. The Spirit also revealed events future to us, recorded in the book of Revelation and elsewhere. What will happen when Christ returns? What will take place at the final judgment? Where will the church be living in the eternal glory yet to come? The prophecies of the New Testament remind us that God is still working in history, sovereignly guiding it to the glorious end of which we have been informed in his Word.

THE SPIRIT-REVEALER

Once we understand the New Testament as God's final revelation setting forth his salvation in Jesus Christ, we may then grasp the essential role played by the Holy Spirit. Jesus said, "When the Spirit of truth comes, he will guide you into all the truth" (John 16:13). This promise was given specifically to the eleven disciples, and provides the basis for their inspired writing of the New Testament. By describing the third person of the Trinity as "the Spirit of truth," Jesus was acknowledging his suitability for granting this God-breathed revelation. The Spirit's character is that of truth, the Spirit has an inherent love of truth, and the Spirit has perfect knowledge of the truth, which he would commit to the apostles for the church.

Jesus said that the Spirit would "guide" the apostles into the truth. Matthew Henry points out that a guide has two tasks. The first is to ensure that his charges do not wander or become lost. The Spirit thus ensured that the apostles taught and recorded the truth regarding Jesus, not any errors to which they might otherwise be prone. Second, a guide must ensure that his

---

5. J. Gresham Machen, *Christianity and Liberalism* (1923; repr., Grand Rapids: Eerdmans, 1996), 27.

charges arrive at their destination, and thus the Spirit caused the apostles to know and record "all the truth." When the pillar of fire guided Moses and Israel, God's people not only went where God desired but in due time arrived safely in the Promised Land. Henry comments, "The skilful pilot guides the ship into the port it is bound for."[6] The Spirit likewise guided the apostles into the whole counsel of God for our salvation, faith, and godliness (see Acts 20:27; 2 Peter 1:3).

While divine revelation was committed to the apostles, the Spirit who revealed God's Word to them continues to work today to enable us to believe, understand, and adore the apostolic doctrine. While none of us today is *inspired* by the Holy Spirit in the sense of revealing God's outbreathed Word, we still benefit from the Spirit's *illuminating* work. Just as the Spirit guided the apostles into the knowledge and teaching of the whole counsel of God— "all the truth"—the Spirit opens our eyes to the body of doctrine in the New Testament and enables us increasingly to embrace it and experience its power.

The Spirit is our guide today, which is why Paul urges us to "walk by the Spirit" (Gal. 5:16) and "keep in step with the Spirit" (5:25 NIV). We follow along with the Spirit's guidance as we study, believe, and obey his revealed Word in the Holy Scriptures. Just as the original disciples were not ready to receive Christ's full doctrine until they had received the Holy Spirit, men and women darkened through sin today need the light of the Holy Spirit to illumine the sacred page to our understanding. Gordon Keddie writes: "We need the Holy Spirit to teach us the Word and write it on our hearts,"[7] which reminds us that we should always study and teach God's Word with prayers for the Holy Spirit's aid and power.

This does not mean, however, that the Spirit gives us his own truth, distinct from the truth of God the Father. There have long been people who justify the most irreverent and God-dishonoring teachings and practices by appealing to the Holy Spirit. But Jesus says that the Spirit not only guides believers into all the truth, but faithfully declares what he has himself received from God the Father. Jesus said, "He will not speak on his own authority, but whatever he hears he will speak" (John 16:13). None of the Spirit's teaching originates

6. Matthew Henry, *Commentary on the Whole Bible*, 6 vols. (Peabody, MA: Hendrickson, 2009), 5:919.

7. Gordon J. Keddie, *A Study Commentary on John*, 2 vols. (Darlington, UK: Evangelical Press, 2001), 2:204.

with himself, nor does the Spirit teach anything novel or even original. Paul explained: "For the Spirit searches everything, even the depths of God. For who knows a person's thoughts except the spirit of that person, which is in him? So also no one comprehends the thoughts of God except the Spirit of God" (1 Cor. 2:10–11). Paul meant that, first, it is impossible to know what someone else is really thinking unless you have access to his or her inner spirit. Second, the Spirit provides us with just this insight with respect to God. The Spirit "searches" the truth of God, even to the depths, and he tells us the thoughts, actions, and will of God.

Jesus said, "Whatever he hears he will speak" (John 16:13). The Spirit is not a different God with a different agenda from that of the Father and the Son, but the Helper that they have sent to reveal their truth to their people. While the Spirit provided the final revelation through the apostles alone, his ministry is "poured out" on all believers so that he declares what is written in the Bible to our spirits in order to impart true and saving faith (see Joel 2:28).

THE SPIRIT OF CHRIST

The last thing Jesus tells us about the Holy Spirit might be the most important. The Spirit guides us into all the truth and declares God's truth to our spirits. His aim in doing so is to display the glory of Christ for our faith, adoration, and service. "He will glorify me," Jesus said, "for he will take what is mine and declare it to you" (John 16:14).

There are three important applications from this principle of the Spirit's Christ-centered witness. The first is that this rules out the Holy Spirit's being at work in any religion that denies Jesus Christ. We increasingly hear in our ecumenical world that Jesus must be at work in other faiths. We are told that to believe that the Spirit speaks only in Christianity is an intolerable arrogance. But Jesus states that the Spirit's ministry is directed toward the revelation of his glory, declaring only the things of Christ. Thus the Spirit is at work only where the biblical teaching of Jesus is believed and proclaimed.

What is true of false religions is also true of false professors of Christianity. Those who disobey the teaching of Scripture—for instance, by deserting a spouse, pursuing an agenda of greed or pride, teaching unbiblical doctrines, or worshiping according to worldly principles—only deceive themselves if they claim the leading of the Spirit, who serves and glorifies Jesus alone.

Second, this tells us that the hallmark of the Spirit's presence and activity is an intense focus and excitement about Jesus. When the focus is placed on the Spirit himself, rather than on the person and work of Christ—and especially his sin-atoning death on the cross—we can be sure that the Spirit is not in fact working. J. I. Packer illustrates this truth by telling of approaching a cathedral on which floodlights were illuminating a large stained-glass window. He realized that the Spirit is like the floodlights:

> When flood-lighting is well done, the floodlights are so placed that you do not see them; you are not in fact supposed to see where the light is coming from; what you are meant to see is just the building on which the floodlights are trained. The intended effect is to make it visible when otherwise it would not be seen for the darkness, and to maximize its dignity by throwing all its details into relief so that you see it properly.[8]

Floodlights work properly only when you are looking not into them but onto the object that they are bathing with light. To look into the floodlights is to be blinded; this happens spiritually for those who turn away from Christ to focus on the Holy Spirit. Packer concludes:

> It is as if the Spirit stands behind us, throwing light over our shoulder, on Jesus, who stands facing us. The Spirit's message to us is never, "Look at me; listen to me; come to me; get to know me," but always, "Look at *him*, and see his glory; listen to *him*, and hear his word; go to *him*, and have life; get to know *him*, and taste his gift of joy and peace."[9]

The third application is that the intent of the Spirit's work in our lives, and therefore the purpose of our study of the Bible and faith in its doctrines, is that we would be drawn closer to Jesus Christ. It is popular today to speak of spirituality and of being a spiritual person. But if we are speaking of the result of the Holy Spirit's work in our life, the result will and must always be a keener interest and delight in Jesus, a more fervent love and devotion for Jesus, a firmer trust and reliance on Jesus, and a life that is increasingly yielded in obedience and service to Jesus. John Calvin comments: "We receive the Spirit in order that we may enjoy Christ's blessings. For what does he

8. Packer, *Keep in Step with the Spirit*, 66.
9. Ibid.

351

bestow on us? That we may be washed by the blood of Christ, that sin may be blotted out in us by his death, that our old man may be crucified, that his resurrection may be efficacious in forming us again to newness of life, and, in short, that we may become partakers of his benefits."[10] This is why Jesus said, "It is to your advantage that I go away" (John 16:7), since once enthroned in heaven he would send the Spirit, and the Spirit working with power in our hearts will draw us to a closer discipleship to Jesus than was possible even for the original disciples. Thus, by the Spirit, we may possess a more blessed experience of the saving benefits that Jesus has provided for us.

TRUE RICHES IN CHRIST ALONE

Once we realize the purpose for which the Spirit was sent into the world, we will not only recognize that our calling is summed up in our relationship to Christ, but also realize that the treasures of God for us are all found in and summed up in Christ. Jesus concluded, "All that the Father has is mine; therefore I said that he will take what is mine and declare it to you" (John 16:15). Christian salvation is Trinitarian—it brings us the blessings of each of the persons of the glorious Godhead: God the Father to take us as his children, Christ the Savior-Shepherd to gain us salvation, and the Spirit-Helper to guide us into all the truth and unite us to Christ, in whom all divine blessings are found.

This raises the question: if we have Jesus through faith and in him we have the riches of God, what else do we need to lead lives of peace, joy, and spiritual power? Through the God-given means of his Word and of prayer, we receive the ministry of the Spirit. He has come not to deny us riches and pleasure that we could otherwise find in the world, but so that we might enjoy true riches and true life, by the Spirit and in Jesus Christ—the riches of eternal life and glory that God the Father has provided for us only in his Son.

10. John Calvin, *New Testament Commentaries*, trans. T. H. L. Parker, 12 vols. (Grand Rapids: Eerdmans, 1959), 4:146.

106

IN A LITTLE WHILE

John 16:16—22

"A little while, and you will see me no longer; and again a little while, and you will see me." (John 16:16)

O
ne of the most helpful things to know about biblical eschatology is that the Bible organizes history in two ages: "this present age" and "the age to come." The present age is one in which mankind lives in rebellion to God, God's Messiah is opposed, and God's people are frustrated by persecution, hardship, and disappointment. This is why the apostle Paul described it as "the present evil age" (Gal. 1:4), and why John said that this present world "lies in the power of the evil one" (1 John 5:19). The hope of God's people lies not in this world, or this age of the world, but in the age and world to come. Jesus taught that everyone who leaves family and comfort to follow him will receive "in the age to come eternal life" (Mark 10:30).

It is clear that Jesus' disciples believed that the age to come had arrived in his ministry. In important ways, their belief was correct. Jesus began his ministry, proclaiming, "The kingdom of God is at hand" (Mark 1:15), which is another way of speaking about "the age to come." His miracles involved an inbreaking of heaven's healing and liberating power. Through

353

his teaching, Jesus was able to say, "The kingdom of God is in the midst of you" (Luke 17:21).

We can see why the disciples, governed by this expectation, were so dismayed at Jesus' teaching in this Farewell Discourse about going away from them. Now he added, "You will weep and lament, but the world will rejoice" (John 16:20). It is no wonder that "some of his disciples said to one another, 'What is this that he says to us?'" (16:17). If the Messiah had come, why would there still be sorrow, if only for "a little while"?

Jesus answered the disciples' perplexity by explaining how the Bible's two-age eschatology would be mirrored in his own experience. "A little while, and you will see me no longer," he said, "and again a little while, and you will see me" (John 16:16). The disciples wondered what this meant: "they were saying, 'What does he mean by "a little while"? We do not know what he is talking about'" (16:18). Jesus' reply explained how he and they would first suffer through the cross, but how this sorrow would give way to salvation joy after a little while: "Is this what you are asking yourselves, what I meant by saying, 'A little while and you will not see me, and again a little while and you will see me'? Truly, truly, I say to you, you will weep and lament, but the world will rejoice. You will be sorrowful, but your sorrow will turn into joy" (16:19–20). This same pattern defines our situation as believers, for a little while longing for Jesus' coming and again in a little while rejoicing when he has returned to take us into heaven.

IN A LITTLE WHILE: SORROW AT THE CROSS

There is some debate among scholars as to Jesus' reference in this passage. Some, like John Calvin, think that Jesus refers to his bodily absence after ascending into heaven, followed by his coming at Pentecost, when he would dwell in the disciples by faith. This is possible, since so much of this Farewell Discourse deals with Christ's sending of the Holy Spirit. Others, such as Augustine, believe that Jesus speaks of the church age followed by Christ's second coming. It is most natural, however, to take Jesus' "in a little while" as referring to his crucifixion on the next day, since this dramatic event was immediately before them. Jesus was preparing the disciples for what they would experience literally within hours: "A little while, and you will see me no longer" (John 16:16).

Jesus said that his death would occasion weeping and lamenting. It is indeed not difficult to see why the disciples would be staggered by what was about to happen. First was the terrible injustice and horror of the crucifixion. For three years, the disciples had known Jesus to be the master of every circumstance, more than equal to the threats and plots of the religious leaders. But after his arrest later that evening, they would witness the shocking injustice of his mock trial, when Jesus stood mutely while falsely charged with blasphemy (Matt. 26:57–65). Jesus was handed over to Pilate, who had him scourged with whips, beaten by pitiless soldiers, and presented in mockery before the people (John 19:1–3). When Pilate then declared Jesus innocent, the Jews called out regarding the long-awaited Messiah, "Let him be crucified!" (Matt. 27:15–23). Charles Spurgeon writes: "Might not angels wish to weep in sympathy with him? Who can forebear to sorrow when Jesus stands insulted by menials, reviled by abjects, forsaken by his friends, blasphemed by his foes? It was enough to make a man's heart break to see the Lamb of God so roughly handled."[1]

Most shocking of all were the horrors of the crucifixion itself. Jesus' arms and legs were nailed in torment to the wooden beams, and then he was lifted up in shameful condemnation. The Gospel records do not dwell on the details of his physical agony, but simply state Jesus' awful torment. "My God, my God, why have you forsaken me?" he cried (Matt. 27:46). How much of this the disciples witnessed we are not told, but the very least of these scenes must have broken their hearts.

Looking back on Calvary today, we, too, can feel sorrow and lament for Jesus' arrest and crucifixion. Moreover, we can only continue to lament Jesus' treatment by this world. We hear his name spat out as a curse. We sorrow for the casual disregard of his claims on mankind, and we mourn for hard-hearted contempt of the truth and righteousness for which Jesus lived and died.

The fact of the cross was not the only reason for sorrow: second, the *cause* of Jesus' crucifixion should also break our hearts. Why should God's perfect Son suffer and die? The answer is that Jesus was crucified because of our sins. Spurgeon cries: "The sword which pierced his heart through and through was forged by our offences: the vengeance was due for sins

1. Charles H. Spurgeon, *The Metropolitan Tabernacle Pulpit*, 63 vols. (Pasadena, TX: Pilgrim, 1997), 24:617.

which we had committed, and justice exacted its rights at his hands."[2] The chief reason why Christians do not accuse the Jews or malign the Roman soldiers for their role in Jesus' death is that we are overcome with grief for our own primary role in the crucifixion of God's Son. What a horror it is to awaken to the reality that my sins caused Jesus Christ to suffer and die!

The disciples would also sorrow because of the loss that Jesus' removal would mean for them. All through the Farewell Discourse, they express alarm over this prospect. Peter earlier asked, "Lord, where are you going?" adding, "Lord, why can I not follow you now?" (John 13:36–37). This shows that for all their failings, the disciples loved Jesus, and the thought of being parted from him grieved them. They had left all to follow Jesus, and his absence would leave a void in their lives. Christians today feel some of this anguish. As we learn of Jesus in the Bible and as his grace grows in our lives, we love Jesus more and more. He is with us powerfully by the Holy Spirit, yet we long to see him face-to-face. Our hearts yearn for fuller communion with the Lord when we have passed through death to him or he has returned in glory to us. For all the joy we have as believers, for this "little while" our hearts are sorrowful over Jesus' bodily absence from earth.

A fourth reason for the disciples' sorrow was given by Jesus: "you will weep and lament, but the world will rejoice" (John 16:20). How galling it was for the Pharisees and scribes to stand gloating over Jesus' sufferings! Matthew recorded their mocking words: "If you are the Son of God, come down from the cross. . . . He saved others; he cannot save himself. He is the King of Israel; let him come down now from the cross" (Matt. 27:40–42). James Montgomery Boice observes, "The world, far from sorrowing at the loss of Jesus, actually rejoiced that he was now out of their way and would no longer be a bother to them."[3] So it remains today that people are glad for Jesus not to be in the world, preferring his crucifixion to his righteous reign.

Fifth, the disciples would sorrow because of their disappointment over Jesus' apparent failure in establishing God's reign and salvation. We gain insight into this disappointment through the words of the Emmaus road disciples: "we had hoped that he was the one to redeem Israel" (Luke 24:21). Many Christians today are likewise disappointed over the frustration often involved with serving Jesus in this world, and sometimes the apparent failure

2. Ibid., 24:618.
3. James Montgomery Boice, *The Gospel of John*, 5 vols. (Grand Rapids: Baker, 1999), 4:1223.

of gospel ministry. It seems that the more devoted we are to the cause of Christ and the spread of the gospel, the more difficult our lives are and the more disappointment we experience.

AGAIN IN A LITTLE WHILE: JOY IN THE MORNING

There are Christians who seem to think that the grief and apparent failure involved with the cross of Christ is a kind of scandal on Christianity. Such people struggle over the failure, frustration, and suffering that believers experience through following Christ in this present world. But Jesus did not look on the cross as his defeat—for all the sorrow and grief that it entailed first for him and then for us—but rather as the instrument of his victory. It was true that in "a little while" he would be taken from the disciples and they would weep and lament while the world rejoiced. But it would also be true that "again [in] a little while" they would see Jesus, and then, he said, "your sorrow will turn into joy" (John 16:19–20). Jesus refers to his triumphant resurrection from the grave. David sang, "Weeping may tarry for the night, but joy comes with the morning" (Ps. 30:5). So it would be for the disciples and then also for all who trust in Christ in this present world. "A little while, and you will see me no longer," Jesus said; "and again a little while, and you will see me" (John 16:16).

Notice that Jesus did not say that our sorrow would be compensated by a subsequent joy or even that our sorrow would be replaced by joy. Rather, he said, "You will be sorrowful, but your sorrow will turn into joy" (John 16:20). In this way, the resurrection does not do away with the crucifixion. Rather, it turns the sorrow of the cross into our joy and glory. This is why, when the apostles wrote in the Epistles regarding Christ's atoning death, they always expressed themselves with wonder, praise, and joy. It is not that they no longer felt the anguish of what Jesus suffered, but rather that the resurrection had transformed the very despair of the cross into delight.

This is why Christians today speak with unashamed happiness over the suffering death of Jesus and why true gospel churches rejoice in the cross, never ceasing to speak of Christ's death to redeem us from our sin and singing lusty songs of joy about the shedding of Christ's blood. This is why the apostle Paul resolved to preach nothing that was not centered on the cross (1 Cor. 2:2), and exclaimed, "Far be it from me to boast except in the cross of our Lord Jesus Christ" (Gal. 6:14). This is why Peter exulted in the "precious blood of Christ" (1 Peter 1:19). This is why the apostle John quoted the worship-song of heaven, with its joyful refrain to Jesus: "Worthy are you . . . , for you were slain" (Rev. 5:9). Far from undoing the cross, putting away the cross, or negating the cross, Jesus' resurrection has transformed the grief of Jesus' death into everlasting salvation joy.

Just as there were five causes for sorrow in Jesus' death, there are five reasons for great joy in his resurrection. First, by this means God the Father overturned the unjust verdict of mankind and publicly vindicated his Son before all history. After being indwelt by the Holy Spirit, Peter explained to the people of Jerusalem:

> The God of Abraham, the God of Isaac, and the God of Jacob, the God of our fathers, glorified his servant Jesus, whom you delivered over and denied in the presence of Pilate, when he had decided to release him. But you denied the Holy and Righteous One . . . , and you killed the Author of life, whom God raised from the dead. (Acts 3:13–15)

With what joy did the disciples greet the resurrection of Jesus, falling at his feet to worship him (Matt. 28:9)! Paul wrote that in the resurrection and ascension, "God has highly exalted him," and when Jesus returns in glory, how great will our joy be when "every tongue confess[es] that Jesus Christ is Lord" (Phil. 2:9, 11).

Second, we rejoice greatly in the resurrection because it proved God's acceptance of the redemption achieved by Christ's atoning death. Yes, it grieves us to realize that our sins nailed Jesus to the cross. But this very grief is transformed into joy when the resurrected Christ declares our guilt removed forever and God's justice satisfied once for all. Jesus did not regret dying for our sins. Hebrews 12:2 makes the remarkable statement that Jesus "for the joy that was set before him endured the cross, despising the shame." His joy was nothing less than knowing that his blood would redeem his people from the curse and power of death. Spurgeon writes: "Heartily do we lament our sin, but we do not lament that Christ has put it away nor lament the death by which he put it away; rather do our hearts rejoice in all his atoning agonies, and glory at every mention of that death by which he has reconciled us unto God. . . . It is a joy to think that he has taken on himself our personal sin and carried it right away."[4]

Third, after "a little while" the resurrection restored Christ's personal presence to the disciples. They grieved in his absence, but rejoiced in his restoration. Here is where Christians rejoice in the Spirit's coming at Pentecost, for while we do not have Jesus' bodily presence, we do have his Spirit dwelling within us. We therefore do not gaze on the Scriptures as a dead page, but with the Emmaus disciples after Jesus had taught them, we exclaim over the burning of our hearts through the Word of Christ (Luke 24:32). In yet a little while longer, our faith in Christ will give way to sight, transformed into so great a joy that we cannot begin to imagine it now. Job, who suffered so greatly in this present evil age, rejoiced at this mere thought:

> For I know that my Redeemer lives,
>   and at the last he will stand upon the earth.
> And after my skin has been thus destroyed,
>   yet in my flesh I shall see God,
> whom I shall see for myself,
>   and my eyes shall behold, and not another.
> My heart faints within me! (Job 19:25–27)

So great will be that transforming sight of Jesus in glory that, according to John, it will perfect our sanctification in glory: "we know that when he appears we shall be like him, because we shall see him as he is" (1 John 3:2).

Fourth, the disciples grieved for the world's rejoicing over Christ's death, but now in the light of his resurrection we rejoice in the conversion of many people from all over this same wicked world. The disciples would see many of the very men who conspired in Jesus' murder come to saving faith (see Acts 6:7), and even the chief of his persecutors would be won by the power of the risen Lord and, as Paul the apostle, would preach salvation grace to the very ends of the ancient world.

This is why the fifth cause of our grief in the cross has also been transformed into resurrection joy. Do we minister in weakness? Do we experience frustration and apparent failure? Do we ourselves fail to live up to our creed? The sad answer to all these is yes. The remedy for our disappointment as

4. Spurgeon, *Metropolitan Tabernacle Pulpit*, 24:619.

failed believers is the resurrection power of Christ, which transforms it all into joy. Paul thus writes that "we have this treasure in jars of clay, to show that the surpassing power belongs to God and not to us" (2 Cor. 4:7). Jesus showed the apostle that his resurrection power was great enough to overturn the greatest sorrow. When Paul prayed for his thorn to be removed, Jesus answered: "My grace is sufficient for you, for my power is made perfect in weakness." No longer sorrowful, Paul rejoiced: "Therefore I will boast all the more gladly of my weaknesses, so that the power of Christ may rest upon me" (12:9).

The Transforming Joy of New Life

To make his point clear to the disciples, Jesus concluded this promise of transforming joy with an illustration: "When a woman is giving birth, she has sorrow because her hour has come, but when she has delivered the baby, she no longer remembers the anguish, for joy that a human being has been born into the world. So also you have sorrow now, but I will see you again and your hearts will rejoice, and no one will take your joy from you" (John 16:21–22).

Jesus often referred to the coming cross as the arrival of his "hour" (John 2:4; 7:30; 8:20; 12:23; etc.). Here he compares his hour to the arrival of birth pains to a pregnant woman. Like an expectant mother, Jesus had been nurturing this defining act all through the years of his ministry, frequently speaking of it to the disciples. Long beforehand he had said, "The Son of Man came not to be served but to serve, and to give his life as a ransom for many" (Matt. 20:28). "The Son of Man must suffer many things and be rejected by the elders and chief priests and scribes, and be killed, and on the third day be raised," he had told the disciples (Luke 9:22). Now would come the crisis of suffering, not merely for him but for his disciples as well, and it would be dreadful beyond their fears. For "a little while," Christ and his people would suffer death and apparent defeat in the cross.

The resurrection changed this sorrow into great joy, just as the sound of a crying baby drives all thoughts of pain from its mother's heart. "When she has delivered the baby, she no longer remembers the anguish, for joy that a human being has been born into the world" (John 16:21). It was through struggle that the joy was born, even as the birth ends even an awareness of the labor. In like manner, Jesus said, "I will see you again, and your hearts will rejoice" (16:22).

This illustration supplies us with valuable applications from Jesus' teaching. What was Jesus' pastoral purpose in telling this to the disciples, and through John to us? First, Jesus reminds us not to be overthrown when our faith exacts a price in this present evil age. Just as Jesus foretold the necessity of his own death, he clearly told us about the cross that we must bear, not to atone for sin but to follow him in a world that hates his gospel. "If anyone would come after me," Jesus said, "let him deny himself and take up his cross daily and follow me" (Luke 9:23). Yet however greatly the cross might press down on our shoulder, we are strengthened to persevere by knowing that in "a little while" Christ will receive us into eternal glory. There, God "will wipe away every tear from their eyes, and death shall be no more, neither shall there be mourning, nor crying, nor pain anymore, for the former things have passed away" (Rev. 21:4). As the beloved hymn tells us, "The sands of time are sinking" and "the dawn of heaven breaks." Realizing this, we can sing:

> I have borne scorn and hatred, I have borne wrong and shame,
> Earth's proud ones have reproach'd me, for Christ's thrice-blessed name.
> Dark, dark hath been the midnight, but dayspring is at hand,
> And glory, glory dwelleth in Immanuel's land.[5]

Second, we should realize that it is by our experience of the cross and through it the resurrection power that Christians most closely fellowship with Jesus in this life. In his memorable passage of Philippians 3:8–11, Paul spoke of his reliance on Christ's righteousness for his justification, despising any merits or attainments of his own. He added that, having been justified through faith alone, he then desired to know greater fellowship with Christ by taking up his cross: "that I may know him and the power of his resurrection, and may share his sufferings, becoming like him in his death, that by any means possible I may attain the resurrection from the dead." Embracing the cross in our rejection of worldliness and sin, we know fellowship with Christ in this world through his resurrection life. In this way, though we are certainly too weak in ourselves, we receive Christ's resurrection power

---

5. Anne Ross Cousin, "The Sands of Time Are Sinking" (1857).

to lead godly lives that are useful to the gospel. Another hymn expresses our resolve:

> I take, O cross, thy shadow for my abiding place;
> I ask no other sunshine than the sunshine of his face;
> Content to let the world go by, to know no gain nor loss;
> My sinful self my only shame, my glory all the cross.[6]

Finally, Jesus wanted his disciples to know, on the eve of his crucifixion, that their sorrows in this present evil age, the grief of his cross, would last for only "a little while." Yet how different is the joy that comes through the cross by the resurrection. "You have sorrow now," Jesus said, "but I will see you again, and your hearts will rejoice, and no one will take your joy from you" (John 16:22). Knowing this, Jesus calls his followers to persevere by his power.

The joy we receive through the sin-atoning death of Jesus and his glorious resurrection power is a joy that will never end. The sorrow of the cross, so real and painful now, belongs only to this present evil age. But resurrection joy, which comes to us in the wonder of the new birth, will have no end. Which of the two, therefore, should have the greater power over our hearts: worldly sorrow or resurrection joy? Which should govern our daily thoughts and attitudes as we face the circumstances of this present evil age? Which should the world see reflected in our lives? Should we be overcome by the bitterness of this world, or overwhelmed by the joy of resurrection grace?

In this present age, for a little while, we have tears, sadness, disappointment, frustration, and even anguish. "In the world," Jesus will conclude, "you will have tribulation." But by his resurrection life, which shone through the empty tomb and reigns in the hearts of those who look to him in faith, Jesus says, "Take heart; I have overcome the world" (John 16:33). Is this not sufficient cause, is not the resurrection a sufficient power, for us to live now with joy, praise, and wonder with lives energized for the glory of Christ?

---

6. Elizabeth C. Clephane, "Beneath the Cross of Jesus" (1872).

107

Praying to the Father

John 16:23–27

"In that day you will ask nothing of me. Truly, truly, I say to you, whatever you ask of the Father in my name, he will give it to you."
(John 16:23)

O ne of the most demanding features of military life is the change of command. Every year or so, virtually every military unit receives a new commander. Commanding officers have an unusual amount of authority, so that their ability, personality, and training methods greatly shape the life of those under their orders. This is why the change of command is fraught with tension for the soldiers. Will everything change? Will they be punished in the future for actions that previously brought praise? Will the new regime be kind and humane or cruel and harsh?

As Jesus draws toward the end of his final teaching to the disciples, the atmosphere is comparable to that of a change of command. For three years, Jesus had been their Master and Teacher, and now he was speaking of his departure. He was going to the Father, and the care and oversight of his disciples would be in large part transferred. It was for this purpose that Jesus came into the world, that through his sacrifice for sin those who trust in him might be brought to the Father.

Unlike a military change of command, however, this transfer is not a cause for concern but for joy. Not only are Jesus and his heavenly Father perfectly united in character and purpose, sharing one divine and eternal nature, but the whole purpose of Jesus' ministry had been directed to our reunion with his Father. Jesus' departure would therefore not mean the end of one regime and the beginning of a strange and different one, but rather the fulfillment of his ministry in our restoration to the love and care of the Father.

A RELATIONSHIP OF PRAYER

The lens by which Jesus directs the disciples to the Father is that of prayer. This might be because the whole of the Christian faith can be understood through prayer. The relationship that we enter with God, the basis of our acceptance, the purposes of holiness, blessing, and glory, and the varied ministries of the three persons of the Trinity are all seen and experienced in prayer. Thus, as Jesus prepares for his great saving work on the cross to reconcile believers to his Father, he addresses their new relationship with God through the lens of prayer.

Jesus employed prayer with a similar didactic purpose at the beginning of his ministry, in the Sermon on the Mount. There, in what we have come to know as "the Lord's Prayer," the most radical and earthshaking statement Jesus made was the first. Jesus taught his followers to address the God of heaven as "our Father" (Matt. 6:9). So also now at the end of his ministry, Jesus directs the disciples to "ask of the Father in my name" (John 16:23).

The apostle Paul wrote of our salvation, "For through [the Son] we . . . have access in one Spirit to the Father" (Eph. 2:18). This pattern is experienced in prayer. Christian prayer is offered *to* the Father. We pray *through* the mediating ministry of Jesus, God's Son. Our prayer is spiritually empowered *by* the Holy Spirit. Paul explained: "The Spirit helps us in our weakness. For we do not know what to pray for as we ought, but the Spirit himself intercedes for us with groanings too deep for words" (Rom. 8:26). Prayer, like salvation, is *through* the Son, *by* the Spirit, and *to* the Father.

Jesus lived and died so that his people would be forgiven, justified, and restored to God the Father. This is why Jesus sees the fulfillment of his ministry and says, "I . . . will tell you plainly about the Father" (John 16:25). Jesus brings us into relationship with himself so that we can know and love the Father. He is our Mediator with the Father, the go-between who resolves all conflict, and his death and resurrection provide an open way for our restoration to God. Our relationship with the Father was severed by sin, so he sent Jesus, his Son, to "save his people from their sins" (Matt. 1:21).

It was with this in mind that after concluding this teaching, Jesus lifted his eyes to the Father. "I glorified you on earth," he prayed, "having accomplished the work that you gave me to do" (John 17:4). Jesus came to earth with a work to accomplish for the Father. This is why he says to the disciples, "I do not say to you that I will ask the Father on your behalf; for the Father himself loves you" (16:26). Jesus does not cause the Father to love his disciples, for it was God's love that sent Jesus to us. Christ does not cajole an otherwise unwilling deity, but rather achieves the great passion of God's own heart, that he might be restored as our Father and we as his beloved children.

During the three years of his ministry, Jesus had provided for the disciples. But once reconciled to the Father by his blood, they were restored to the Father's loving care. A father protects his children and provides for his family. All that a father possesses is granted to his children, and they receive a full inheritance from his riches. This is Jesus' message as he provides this last teaching on prayer. "The Father himself loves you," Jesus taught them, "because you have loved me and have believed that I came from God" (John 16:27). This does not mean that we earned God's love by loving Jesus, since the Bible repeatedly teaches the opposite. John wrote, "In this is love, not that we have loved God but that he loved us and sent his Son to be the propitiation for our sins. . . . We love because he first loved us" (1 John 4:10, 19). Jesus means that we can be assured of God's love for us through our love for and faith in him. Matthew Henry summarizes: "The disciples of Christ are the beloved of God himself. Christ not only turned away God's wrath from us, and brought us into a covenant of peace and reconciliation, but . . . brought us into a covenant of friendship" with the Father.[1]

---

1. Matthew Henry, *Commentary on the Whole Bible*, 6 vols. (Peabody, MA: Hendrickson, 2009), 5:925.

Asking in Prayer

If we wonder what it means to pray to the Father, Jesus answers by means of a single word, which he employs five times in these verses. Prayer is *asking* of God. Jesus said, "In that day you will ask in my name" (John 16:26).

Jesus emphasizes our direct access to the Father in prayer. He says, "In that day you will ask in my name, and I do not say to you that I will ask the Father on your behalf" (John 16:26). Jesus was not denying his priestly ministry of intercession for us from heaven (see Rom. 8:34), but simply means that after his death and resurrection—"in that day"— believers may pray directly to the Father, asking him as they once relied on Jesus to ask for them. Paul explains that the Holy Spirit implants an instinct of prayer to the Father, so that one of the distinguishing marks of being born again is a heart that prays to God: "you have received the Spirit of adoption as sons, by whom we cry, 'Abba! Father!' The Spirit himself bears witness with our spirit that we are children of God" (Rom. 8:15–16). Whereas spiritually dead people always ask others to pray for them (see Ex. 12:32; 1 Kings 13:6; Acts 8:24), believers in Jesus make their own requests directly to the Father in Christ's name. Christians follow the practice of the apostle Paul, who wrote, "I bow my knees before the Father" (Eph. 3:14).

Of course, prayer consists of more than a list of requests from God. A helpful approach to prayer is given in the acronym *ACTS*: adoration, confession, thanksgiving, and supplication. We should first praise God, confess our sins, and thank God for his many blessings. But then we should freely ask things of the Father. Jesus seems to be marking a parallel between how the disciples had been talking to him and how they would later talk to the Father. They had been asking Jesus all kinds of questions and making all kinds of requests: after Jesus' death and resurrection, they could speak directly to the Father in the same way. James Montgomery Boice rightly states: "Prayer must be lifted out of some mysterious realm of religious rites or practice, where only special people can go, and instead be brought down to the common experience of normal men and women. It means that prayer is essentially a conversation in which we talk to God."[2] It is good for pastors and elders to lead the congregation in prayer during gathered

---

2. James Montgomery Boice, *The Gospel of John*, 5 vols. (Grand Rapids: Baker, 1999), 4:1228.

worship, but every Christian must exercise the privilege of direct, personal prayer to the Father.

What kinds of things should we ask for in prayer? One good answer was given by Jesus in the Sermon on the Mount, in the Lord's Prayer. The first request that Jesus taught us pertains to the glorifying of God's name: "Our Father in heaven, hallowed be your name" (Matt. 6:9). This is asking for God's name to receive the glory it deserves. Next is a request for God's work in the world: "Your kingdom come, your will be done, on earth as it is in heaven" (6:10). After asking for God's glory and for the success of gospel ministry, Jesus urged us to pray for our daily needs: "Give us this day our daily bread" (6:11). This is not praying for our wants but for our needs! We should freely pray to the Father concerning our need of money for food, shelter, and clothing, of friendship, of work, and of the Spirit's help in understanding the Bible and leading a godly life. Our greatest need is to be forgiven of our sins, so Jesus tells us to ask God to "forgive us our debts, as we also have forgiven our debtors" (6:12). Finally, Jesus would have us pray for God's spiritual protection and help in resisting sin: "And lead us not into temptation, but deliver us from evil" (6:13).

While the Lord's Prayer is a very helpful guide, Jesus wants us to know that through his atoning death we have direct access to the Father for all matters of our needs. The story is told of a Union soldier with a great personal need who went to the White House to see the President during the Civil War. The secretaries refused to interrupt the nation's Chief Executive to deal with a personal problem, so the soldier sat in a hallway and began to weep. Soon a little boy came down the hall, and upon seeing the soldier, he asked what the problem was. "I need to see the President of the United States," the soldier explained, "but I cannot get in to him." At this explanation, the little boy took the soldier by the hand, walked him by the secretary's desk, past the armed guards, down another hallway, and into the oval-shaped office where Abraham Lincoln was working. Lifting up his head, the President said, "O my son, what can I do for you?" "This soldier needs to speak with you, Daddy," came the reply.[3]

We might often think ourselves to be like the soldier. For all our great needs, we are but one small person, and the great God is busy running the

3. Adapted from Michael Sigler, "Sunday School Lessons" (February 19, 2012), http://www .awfumc.org/console/files/oFiles_Library_XZXLCZ/SS_Lesson_February_19_R8XL5HKX.pdf.

universe. But Jesus tells us that through his ministry, and in his name, we have access to God the Father. Not only does God the Father say to Jesus, "My Son, what can I do for you?" so that Jesus tells our need to heaven's throne. More than that, God now says to the believer in Christ, "My son, my daughter, open your heart and ask me for what you need."

Two New Prayer Promises

In this concluding portion of his farewell address, Jesus was mainly summarizing teaching on prayer and salvation that he had already given. There are, however, two new promises here regarding prayer, or at least two new emphases on Jesus' promises of effectual prayer in his name. The first new promise addressed the disciples' lack of understanding. All through this last meeting, Jesus' followers revealed their inability to follow his meaning. He had not yet died on the cross, so it is natural that there should be confusion about this. Moreover, before the sending of the Holy Spirit at Pentecost, the disciples lacked the spiritual competence to understand Jesus' teaching. When the Spirit came, however, "in that day," Jesus said, "you will ask nothing of me" (John 16:23). Here, the Greek word for *ask* (*erotao*) is different than is used elsewhere in this passage, and has the connotation of asking a question for information rather than requesting a thing. Jesus means that after the Spirit has come in his revealing role, the disciples would no longer ask questions out of their ignorance because they would understand Christ's saving work.

This does not mean that neither the apostles nor we would have any further questions, but rather that the matters that Jesus had been teaching—his atoning death, resurrection, and ascension into heaven—would then be finally understood. "I have said these things to you in figures of speech," Jesus said. This has been true in this Farewell Discourse—consider Jesus' illustration of the woman bearing a child in the previous passage— Jesus' teaching all through the four Gospels was highly metaphorical and parabolic, often requiring a private explanation. But he continued, "The hour is coming when I will no longer speak to you in figures of speech but will tell you plainly about the Father" (John 16:25). Undoubtedly, Jesus was referring to the forty days after his resurrection and before his ascension. Luke tells us that after the resurrection, Jesus appeared to the disciples and "he opened their minds to understand the Scriptures" (Luke 24:45), focusing on the meaning of his death and resurrection and the preaching of the gospel to all nations. The result of this more direct teaching is seen in the clear doctrinal preaching of the book of Acts and the reasoned doctrinal explanations that fill the New Testament Epistles.

Since Jesus intends his disciples to understand the Bible clearly, we should pray for this understanding, always studying the Bible in an attitude of prayer. If we find the Bible sometimes hard to understand—or its clear teaching hard to accept—we should pray with confidence in Jesus' promise that if we ask, we will receive understanding and the ability to believe. He promised, "I . . . will tell you plainly about the Father" (John 16:25).

The second new promise concerns our experience of joy through a life of prayer: "Ask, and you will receive, that your joy may be full" (John 16:24). Jesus is not merely saying that when our prayers are answered we will have joy, but that through prayer itself we will receive joy. The reason is that in prayer God makes himself real to us and we experience communion with our Maker, receiving joy in our spirits. This is why so many Christians attest to an increase of joy in proportion to increased suffering: suffering prompts them to pray, and the leaning upon God in prayer brings great joy.

Consider the note that my wife received from a Christian friend who was struggling with cancer and had recently been near the point of death. Someone had asked her whether she was disappointed with God, since the Lord had permitted her to suffer and might soon allow her to die. "I realized that I could honestly say that I am in no way disappointed in or angry with God," she recounts. "The Lord has truly worked in my heart to reveal more of the deepness of his love and care for me. I have described to some that there is a sense of holy privilege in drawing near to God through suffering for which I can truly say I am grateful." What greater joy can there be than to be more deeply aware of God's love and care for our souls?

It is not necessary for us to suffer in order to experience the joy of the Lord in prayer. Paul wrote, "Rejoice always," and then immediately said, "Pray without ceasing" (1 Thess. 5:16–17). John Calvin commented that in saying that our joy will be filled through prayer, Jesus "means that nothing will be wanting which could contribute to a perfect abundance of all blessings, to the accomplishment of our desires, and to calm satisfaction, provided that we ask from God, in his name, whatever we need."[4] Sadly, however, the apostle James's lament is especially true when it comes to our experience of joy: "You do not have, because you do not ask" (James 4:2).

PRAYING IN JESUS' NAME

The goal of Jesus' teaching in these verses is that the disciples might realize the access to the Father that would soon be theirs. But just as important as this goal is the means by which Christians may ask of the Father. Jesus specifies the sole means by which we may come to the Father in verses 23, 24, and 27: "in my name." "Truly, truly, I say to you," Jesus said, giving his customary emphasis to what he considered an important matter, "whatever you ask of the Father in my name, he will give it to you" (John 16:23).

There are three important ways for us to understand prayer "in Christ's name." First, this means that we must pray to the Father as those who believe in the name of the Lord Jesus Christ. By believing on Jesus as Lord, we acclaim his deity as the covenant God of his people. *Lord* is the English equivalent of the Greek *kurios*, which translated the Hebrew name *Yahweh* or *Jehovah*. When the apostles referred to Jesus as "the Lord," they meant that he is the incarnate God and sovereign of his people. This is why the early Christians refused to praise the Roman emperors with the acclamation "Caesar is Lord" (*Kyrios Kaisar*), since to do so was to praise Caesar with the divine glory that belongs to Christ alone.

The personal name *Jesus* tells us something additional that we must believe. The name means "Yahweh saves" or "Yahweh is salvation." The angel therefore told Joseph that he was to call the child in Mary's virgin womb by the name *Jesus*, "for he will save his people from their sins" (Matt. 1:21). Finally, the name *Christ* is really a title or office, the Greek *Christos* translating the Hebrew *Meshiach*, which is *Messiah*. "The Messiah" was "the Anointed One," being a noun form of the verb *to anoint*, pointing to Jesus as the One who perfectly fulfills the three anointed offices of the Old Testament: prophet, priest, and king. To believe in Jesus, then, is to acclaim him as the incarnate God, the Savior, who reveals God to us (Prophet), cleanses us to bring us to God (Priest), and rules over us as sovereign (King).

4. John Calvin, *New Testament Commentaries*, trans. T. H. L. Parker, 12 vols. (Grand Rapids: Eerdmans, 1959), 4:155.

What we find in the name of the Lord Jesus Christ is the minimum truth that we must believe to be Christians. Therefore, to say that we must pray to the Father in his name is the same as to say that only true Christians have access to the Father in prayer. Boice writes: "It is a family privilege. God does not promise to hear the prayer of anyone who comes to him in any way but through faith in the person and work of his unique and beloved Son."[5]

Second, to pray in Christ's name is to approach God, relying on Christ's merit and atoning blood and not on any merit of our own. You and I have no right of our own to the favor and blessing of God, but we are invited to appeal to God in the name of his Son, who has every right to all the treasures of heaven. So when we pray "in the name of Jesus," the importance is not a phrase that we attach to our prayers but the reality that we are coming to God on the basis of Christ's saving work.

Reuben Torrey compares praying in our own name with presenting a check to a bank: it will not be cashed if we do not have sufficient funds to cover the amount. But if we go to the bank with a person's name signed to the check and that person has great resources in his account, then the check will be honored. Torrey concludes: "So it is . . . when I go to God in prayer. I have nothing deposited [in heaven], and if I go in my own name I will get absolutely nothing: but Jesus Christ has unlimited credit in heaven, and he has granted to me the privilege of going to the bank with his name on my checks, and when I thus go, my prayers will be honored to any extent."[6]

In recent years, some people have taken offense at the Christian insistence on praying in Jesus' name, demanding that in public settings we be willing to omit reference to Jesus. The idea is that we must acknowledge a multitude of perspectives on God and on prayer. But Christians cannot do this and remain faithful to our Lord. Gordon Keddie writes:

> Not to pray in Jesus' name—explicitly and unambiguously—is to conceal the necessity of his atoning death and faith in him as the sole ground of approach to God. It is to suggest by silence that there are other ways to God and that God will accept that prayer of those who do not know Christ as their Saviour.

5. Boice, *John*, 4:1230.
6. Reuben Torrey, quoted in Boice, *John*, 4:1230–31.

Christless prayer is godless prayer, however pious it may sound. No one can come to the Father except through the Son.[7]

Third, to pray in Christ's name is to pray in such a way that our requests are in line with his revealed will for us. Our prayers must reflect Jesus' character and objectives in order to be in his name. The best way for us to know how Jesus would have us pray is to carefully note the teaching of God's Word (see Rom. 12:2). This is why, as our hearts are increasingly shaped by God's Word, our prayers will grow in both fervor and effectiveness, being more and more in line with Christ's will.

THE FIRST AND GREATEST PRAYER REQUEST

If one thing is made clear by Jesus' teaching on the Christian's relationship to the Father and our privilege in prayer, this is the necessity that we believe on Jesus Christ and trust him for our salvation. For this reason, the first and greatest of all prayer requests, and one that we can know for certain will be answered by God, is the prayer for God to forgive us our sins and accept us as his children in the name of Jesus Christ. Jesus came to reconcile sinners through his atoning blood, granting us forgiveness, justification, and adoption into God's dearly beloved family. But only those who confess their sin and embrace Jesus in true faith receive these blessings. Have you asked God for salvation through faith in his Son? Jesus said, "The Father himself loves you, because you have loved me and have believed that I came from God" (John 16:27). This implies necessarily that if you refuse Jesus as your Lord and Savior, rejecting his claim to be God's unique Son, then you remain under God's wrath and condemnation. Why, then, would you refuse Jesus Christ, when in his name you may be cleansed, justified, and renewed with peace and joy, to stand in the glorious presence of God as his own beloved child, free to ask of the Father in Jesus' name?

7. Gordon J. Keddie, *A Study Commentary on John*, 2 vols. (Darlington, UK: Evangelical Press, 2001), 2:222.

108

CHRIST OVERCOMING
THE WORLD

John 16:28–33

*"I have said these things to you, that in me you may have peace.
In the world you will have tribulation. But take heart; I have
overcome the world." (John 16:33)*

s Jesus concluded the teaching of John 16, he was perhaps
drawing near to the garden of Gethsemane, where he would
offer up his High Priestly Prayer, awaiting his betrayal and
arrest. The time had therefore come for direct speaking. In the previous
passage, he had taught of an hour to come when he would speak "plainly
about the Father" (John 16:25). Now, poised at the brink of his own hour,
Jesus spoke plainly about himself: "I came from the Father and have come
into the world, and now I am leaving the world and going to the Father"
(16:28). Jesus pressed on the disciples the important realization that "in this
world you will have tribulation." His final words offered the antidote for
their troubles: "But take heart; I have overcome the world" (16:33).

EASY TO BELIEVE

Jesus began these final verses with a statement "concerning his true nature,
his heavenly origin, and his heavenly destiny, [that] is profound but, at the

same time, so simple that the disciples listening to him were led to exclaim, 'Now you are speaking clearly.' "[1] As Jesus recounts the basic facts of his life and ministry, we are struck that he spoke not as one acting under compulsion, but One who came and went by his free will and sovereign choice: "I came from the Father and have come into the world, and now I am leaving the world and going to the Father" (John 16:28). This statement sets forth Jesus' first coming in four great movements. He came from the Father, came into the world, is now leaving, and will return to the Father. These are vital facts that structure the truth of Jesus' person and redeeming work.

First, Jesus speaks of his eternal and divine origin, saying, "I came from the Father." This was a truth that the disciples clearly grasped, saying, "We believe that you came from God" (John 16:30). William Hendriksen explains: "This refers to Christ's perfect deity, his pre-existence, and his love-revealing departure from heaven in order to dwell on the sin-cursed earth."[2] Here is a direct claim to deity on the part of Jesus, presented as an essential element of saving faith.

Second, Jesus emphasizes his incarnation, the great miracle by which God the Son was born in the virgin womb and took up a human body and true human nature. It is noteworthy that Jesus spoke of his departure from heaven in the past tense, as a completed action. But he refers to his incarnation in the perfect tense, that is, as a past action with continued effects. "I . . . have come into the world," Jesus says (John 16:28). This includes his virgin birth, his sinless life, and his ministry with its miracles and teaching. Most importantly, Jesus came into the world to lay down his life as an atoning Sacrifice for sin. "The Son of Man came," Jesus stressed, "not to be served but to serve, and to give his life as a ransom for many" (Matt. 20:28). Donald Grey Barnhouse illustrates Christ's purpose in the incarnation with a judge who imposes strict justice on a convict, but then steps down from the bench to pay the fine himself. He does this because the guilty party is his own beloved child. Likewise, though very God, Jesus stepped down from heaven to pay in his blood the debt that his own divine justice demanded for our sins.[3]

1. James Montgomery Boice, *The Gospel of John*, 5 vols. (Grand Rapids: Baker, 1999), 4:1234.
2. William Hendriksen, *Exposition of the Gospel according to John*, 2 vols., New Testament Commentary (Grand Rapids: Baker, 1953), 2:339.
3. Donald Grey Barnhouse, *Let Me Illustrate* (Westwood, NJ: Revell, 1967), 170.

Moreover, Jesus came to reveal the glory and grace of the Father in his own person and work. We see why the perfect tense is rightly used for Jesus' incarnation: though he has departed from our world, his coming produced effects that not only continue today but will endure forever.

Third, Jesus moves to the present—the action that he was about to initiate—saying, "Now I am leaving the world," by way of the cross. Notice again that Jesus' death and departure was not thrust on him by some outward compulsion. Earlier, he had told the disciples, "I lay down my life that I may take it up again. No one takes it from me, but I lay it down of my own accord" (John 10:17–18). According to the New Testament, Jesus left the world via the cross in order to remove completely the guilt of his people's sins. Psalm 103:12 sings of him: "as far as the east is from the west, so far does he remove our transgressions from us."

Fourth, and last, Jesus declares that after departing the world, he is "going to the Father" (John 16:28). Jesus' resurrection from the grave reveals God's acceptance of his atoning death, so that we may be certain that satisfaction has been made for our sins. Moreover, in returning to the Father, Jesus assumed the place from which he can dispense spiritual gifts and blessings to his people. Most important of these gifts is our new birth into saving faith by means of God's Word (1 Peter 1:23). Finally, Jesus went to the Father that he might take up his ministry of intercessory prayer for all believers. Paul wrote that Christ "is at the right hand of God . . . interceding for us" (Rom. 8:34). There, Jesus displays in his body the marks of his atoning sacrifice, presenting our covenant claims through his blood. We sing:

Arise, my soul, arise, shake off thy guilty fears:
The bleeding Sacrifice in my behalf appears;
Before the Throne my Surety stands,
Before the Throne my Surety stands,
My name is written on his hands.[4]

These are the plain facts of the Christian faith, articulated by Jesus himself. We should notice that there is nothing difficult to grasp here; the gospel is easy to understand and believe. Jesus came from heaven, came to earth, departed the world, and returned to the Father. This shows that objections

4. Charles Wesley, "Arise, My Soul, Arise" (1742).

to the Christian gospel stem not from the obscurity of our teaching but rather from a moral objection to the claims made by Jesus. People reject the idea that God's Son came to this world from heaven because they refuse to surrender to him the reins of their lives. They object to Jesus' departure via the cross because they refuse to acknowledge the righteousness of divine condemnation and admit their need to be forgiven of their sins.

The disciples responded to Jesus with belief, stating that his words struck a chord in their hearts: "Ah, now you are speaking plainly and not using figurative speech! Now we know that you know all things and do not need anyone to question you; this is why we believe that you came from God" (John 16:29–30). It seems that Jesus had answered a question that was lurking in their minds. If we will open the Bible and read with an open mind, we will likewise find that the Scriptures lay bare the thoughts and motives of our heart (cf. Heb. 4:12). True faith in Jesus does not consist merely in intellectual understanding, but comes to life as the flint of Christ's words strikes the stone of our hearts and sets us inwardly ablaze.

THE HARD REALITY

It seems, however, that Jesus was not so impressed by their faith: "Jesus answered them, 'Do you now believe?'" (John 16:31). Some commentators see Jesus' reference to "now" as a complaint regarding their tardiness in believing, and others see a prediction that they would soon deny him. However Jesus meant "now," it is clear that he was challenging the disciples to realize that believing would not be as easy as it then seemed. Once God gives us eyes to see, the gospel is easy to believe. But there is a hard reality about following Jesus that every Christian must realize. Speaking of the trial facing the disciples—one in which their faith would waver—Jesus told them: "Behold, the hour is coming, indeed it has come, when you will be scattered, each to his own home, and will leave me alone" (16:32).

This reminds us that we should not take lightly the challenge of believing in Jesus in this world, nor should we indulge in self-confidence as Christians. The disciples failed to anticipate the weakness of the flesh, the power of Satan's afflictions, and their vulnerability in the hour of trial. J. C. Ryle comments: "Like young recruits, they had yet to learn that it is one thing to know the soldier's drill and wear the uniform, and quite another thing to be steadfast in the day of battle."[5] If we have felt the challenge of Jesus' words in our own lives—"Do you now believe?"—we will pray in earnest to be delivered from temptation, we will abide constantly in God's Word, we will regularly attend to the means of grace in the worship of Christ's church, and we will live in close communion with fellow believers who can encourage us to walk in the light through faith. Knowing that our faith will be tried by difficulties, the mature Christian is not one who has advanced beyond careful attention to God's Word, prayer, and regular worship in the church. Instead, mature believers have learned not to neglect the God-given means of grace that preserve our faith.

For the first disciples, these lessons would be learned in the events of that very night. Jesus foretold their scattering after his arrest, and the Gospels speak unanimously about the flight of the disciples. Matthew 26:56 reports, "Then all the disciples left him and fled" (cf. Mark 14:50). The only exceptions were Peter and John. Luke mentions that Peter followed Jesus at a distance (Luke 22:54), only to deny him three times outside the high priest's house. John, being acquainted with the ruling priests, entered into the courtyard to watch Jesus' mock trial (John 18:15) and later appeared with Jesus' mother at the cross. Still, Jesus' summary was borne out in general by the disciples: "you will be scattered, each to his own home, and will leave me alone" (16:32). This fulfilled the prophecy of Zechariah 13:7: "Strike the shepherd, and the sheep will be scattered."

Jesus mentions two dangers when Christians are troubled in the world: God's people, first, are scattered and, second, are tempted to renounce Jesus. Consider how Christians are scattered today, sometimes by persecution, sometimes by disagreements, and sometimes by false doctrines and practices. As the winds of heresy, worldliness, and fleshly pride blow across the church, we find ourselves scattered by argument, resentment, and suspicion. What is the way to reconciliation among scattered Christians? The answer is Jesus himself. To the extent that our doctrine and lives are centered on Jesus, we will avoid being scattered as believers, despite differing experiences and some differences in our teaching.

Second, since they would be scattered, Jesus said that the disciples would "leave me alone." This in part reflected the reality that, as Herman Ridderbos

---

5. J. C. Ryle, *Expository Thoughts on the Gospels: John*, 3 vols. (Edinburgh: Banner of Truth, 1999), 3:181.

explains, "Jesus must walk the road alone, and can do so as the good Shepherd who gives his life for his sheep so that not one of them is lost."[6] It remains true, however, that the disciples were torn away from Jesus by fear and self-concern, so that they abandoned him to face the cross alone.

How different was Jesus! Whereas the disciples were scattered, Jesus stood firm in his calling as our Savior. Whereas the disciples were confused, Jesus remained master of the situation. Whereas the Eleven departed, each to his own isolated refuge, Jesus said, "Yet I am not alone, for the Father is with me" (John 16:32). This is our hope: that Jesus persevered in his saving work in communion with the Father. Even when crying out on the cross, "My God, my God, why have you forsaken me?" (Matt. 27:46), Jesus was still one with the purpose and will of the Father in making the sacrifice for our sins. Bearing God's wrath by dying in his human nature, Jesus remained unified with the Father in his undying divine being.

Since Jesus died for sinners, there is hope for faltering but true disciples such as the original Eleven and us today. Thank God that we are not saved *by* our faith—as if our believing achieved our salvation—but we are saved by Christ *through* faith. Thus, a weak and failing faith is saved by a strong and faithful Savior. The disciples would fail Jesus and abandon their faith—how could they ever be restored? Paul answers: "If we are faithless, he remains faithful—for he cannot deny himself" (2 Tim. 2:13).

Meanwhile, whenever a Christian is scattered by persecution, failure, or even our own sin, we can know that we, too, are never truly alone. Whenever our faith turns to the Lord and our prayer reaches up for deliverance, God is near us to save. James wrote, "Draw near to God, and he will draw near to you" (James 4:8).

Christ's Promise of Peace

Because the Father would remain with him, and because he would be faithful in making his sacrifice for sins, Jesus followed his warning with words of comfort: "I have said these things to you, that in me you may have peace" (John 16:33). Though the disciples faced trouble, Jesus would leave them a legacy of his own peace. He had spoken of this same gift earlier,

---

6. Herman Ridderbos, *John: A Theological Commentary* (Grand Rapids: Zondervan, 1997), 545.

saying: "Peace I leave with you; my peace I give to you. Not as the world gives do I give to you. Let not your hearts be troubled, neither let them be afraid" (14:27).

Leon Morris describes a painting that matches Jesus' meaning. It depicts a storm beating against a rocky shoreline with waves crashing and foam flying high. A ship has been driven up against the rock and is falling apart, bodies falling into the deep. But in the foreground is seen a mighty rock with a crack. In the crack is a dove nesting securely, the storm unable to reach within. This expresses Jesus' gift of peace. Morris explains: "Believers are not immune to the storms of life. They must bear them . . . . But they are secure. The Rock of Ages is their sure refuge and there they have peace."[7]

Jesus qualifies his offer of peace in two ways. First, he says that we may have peace "in me." Believers have peace only in Christ; he is the Rock in the cleft of which we are secure. In Christ we enjoy peace *with* God, knowing that our sins are all forgiven. Believers also experience the peace *of* God, as the Holy Spirit works assurance and hope in our hearts. We gain this peace through prayer. Paul told us: "with thanksgiving let your requests be made known to God. And the peace of God, which surpasses all understanding, will guard your hearts and your minds in Christ Jesus" (Phil. 4:6–7). If you have not turned to Christ in saving faith, this might explain the restlessness of your heart. Our hearts were made to be given to him, and "he himself is our peace" (Eph. 2:14). James Montgomery Boice notes that not only do we gain peace by first coming to Christ in faith, but we must also realize that "a conscious dependence on him and staying close to him . . . is the prerequisite to joy and fruitfulness in the Christian life."[8]

Second, Jesus says that believers gain his peace through the teaching of his Word: "I have said these things to you," Jesus said, "that in me you may have peace" (John 16:33). "These things" that Christ has said refer to the whole of this Farewell Discourse, the purpose of which was to provide peace to the disciples in light of Jesus' coming death and departure. All through the Farewell Discourse, Jesus expresses his care and concern, which apply not only to the original disciples but also to us. Knowing Christ's loving care gives peace to our hearts. Jesus promised to secure a place for every believer in heaven: "In my Father's house are many rooms. . . . And if I go

---

7. Leon Morris, *Reflections on the Gospel of John* (Peabody, MA: Hendrickson, 1986), 563.
8. Boice, *John*, 4:1242.

and prepare a place for you, I will come again and will take you to myself, that where I am you may be also" (14:2–3). Believers know that whatever else happens to us as we follow Jesus in life, the destination will be our own prepared place in the glorious eternity of heaven. What a source of peace this should be to every Christian heart!

When it comes to following Christ in this world, Jesus also told about the provision of God's Holy Spirit to comfort, encourage, empower, and lead us. Not only will the Spirit "take what is mine and declare it to you" (John 16:14), but he will grant divine conviction to empower our ministry to the world: "he will convict the world concerning sin and righteousness and judgment" (16:8).

Finally, Jesus' teaching has repeatedly stressed our great privilege in prayer by appeal to his name. What a source of peace it is to know that God in heaven hears my cry and attends to my plea! Jesus taught, "Truly, truly, I say to you, whatever you ask of the Father in my name, he will give it to you" (John 16:23). This provides us with every incentive to try out our access to God in prayer, and to lay our anxieties into the Father's hands, requesting his gift of peace. Peter learned this in future years, urging us to cast "all your anxieties on him, because he cares for you" (1 Peter 5:7).

Are you living in the peace that Jesus has left to believers? If you are not a believer, you have every reason to turn to Jesus, seeking peace with the Father through the forgiveness of sin and the peace of the Father as he lives in you by his Spirit. If you are a believer living without peace, does this warn that you are not living in close communion with our Lord or that you are failing to derive the blessing of his teaching in God's Word? Many Christians struggle for peace in their hearts, some because of their sinfulness and others because of their weakness. All Christians should turn to Christ, turn from our sin, and seek his blessing. Jesus gives his people peace, and we should make sure that we receive this peace in him, through his Word, and in answer to our prayers.

Two Great Truths

John 16:33 concludes Jesus' farewell teaching with plain and direct words that emphasize two great truths that his disciples would need to know. Jesus began this final passage with plain teaching about his own mission, and he concludes with two direct statements that are to serve as watchwords for his church: "In the world you will have tribulation. But take heart; I have overcome the world" (16:33).

Are we surprised by the trials of this present life? We should not be, given Jesus' clear warning. Here is a promise that is certain to come true if only we live for a little while: "In the world you will have tribulation." The English word *tribulation* derives from a Latin word for the flail that was used to separate the wheat from the chaff. The world is the place of testing where our faith is revealed and made strong through trial. A. W. Pink writes: "While the Christian is left down here he suffers from the weakness and weariness of the body, from temporal losses and disappointments, from the severing of cherished ties, as well as from the sneers and taunts, the hatred and persecution of the world."[9] "Men design to cut [believers] off from the earth," notes Matthew Henry, "and God designs by affliction to make them [ready] for heaven; and so between both they shall have tribulation."[10] Though in Christ we have peace, in the world we have tribulation: we should therefore direct our hearts not to the things of the world but to the blessings of Christ, which alone convey peace.

The second great truth answers the need of the first. "Take heart," he says; "I have overcome the world." John's Gospel was written to display the whole range of Jesus' victory over sin, Satan, and death—all the powers of the world arrayed against Christians. It is probably best, however, to understand Jesus' victory in the terms that he gave the disciples in this final passage.

Jesus said, "I came from the Father and have come into the world" (John 16:28). Jesus overcame the world as the incarnate God-man by obeying the will of the Father in his perfect and sinless life, and by overthrowing the powers of Satan and sin. Jesus added, "Now I am leaving the world and going to the Father" (16:28). Jesus overcame the world in his death, because he offered his sinless life to pay the sin debt of all who trust in him, thus breaking the power of sin over us. Jesus then conquered death through his resurrection, and ascending to heaven he assumed "the throne of heaven from which he now rules the church and from which he will one day come again to put down all authority and power."[11] Because Christ has overcome

9. Arthur W. Pink, *Exposition of the Gospel of John* (Grand Rapids: Zondervan, 1975), 17.
10. Matthew Henry, *Commentary on the Whole Bible*, 6 vols. (Peabody, MA: Hendrickson, 2009), 5:927.
11. Boice, *John*, 4:1244.

the world, we now must only hold fast to him to gain our own victory, dividing his spoils by faith. John wrote in his first epistle, "Everyone who has been born of God overcomes the world. And this is the victory that has overcome the world—our faith" (1 John 5:4).

Notice two final points. Jesus said, "I have overcome the world" in the very shadow of Golgotha, where he would suffer God's wrath at the hands of evil men. Jesus spoke of victory as he stepped forward to embrace his apparent defeat, knowing that through his sacrifice God would grant salvation to his people. You may rely on his victory when you feel yourself at the end and on the brink of failure. Our victory is Christ crucified for our sins and Christ living with power at God's right hand. Take heart! Christ has overcome the world!

Finally, be encouraged that Jesus knew that his disciples would falter in their faith and foretold it in advance, yet did not forsake them. Jesus knows that you will have tribulations; your trials do not suggest that you have fallen outside of Christ's will or plan for your life. Jesus knows in detail every cross that you bear, especially when you bear it for him. The Eleven would return to faith because Jesus would return to them from the dead. You, too, through faith alone, are kept safe in his hand; even your faith is secured by Christ's unfailing grace (John 10:28). Take heart! Christ has overcome the world!

PART 6

Jesus' High Priestly Prayer

109

THE HOUR OF GLORY

John 17:1–2

When Jesus had spoken these words, he lifted up his eyes to heaven, and said, "Father, the hour has come; glorify your Son that the Son may glorify you, since you have given him authority over all flesh, to give eternal life to all whom you have given him." (John 17:1–2)

rises have a tendency to reveal what kind of person we really are. What do we do when trouble comes? How do we respond? Where do we turn? What concerns dominate our thoughts? This principle not only is true for us but was also true for Jesus Christ. John chapter 17 begins by declaring the arrival of the hour of crisis for Jesus. At numerous times in John's Gospel we read that Jesus' "hour had not yet come," so that his enemies were forbidden to lay hold of him. Now Jesus begins the great prayer of chapter 17 by declaring, "Father, the hour has come" (John 17:1).

We do not know exactly where Jesus was located during the prayer of John 17. Some commentators place Jesus and the disciples still in the upper room, where the Last Supper was held. But since John 14:31 records Jesus as calling the disciples to rise and depart, and since the parable of the vine in

John 15:1–11 suggests the background imagery of the temple with its decorative vine, it seems more likely that Jesus was now crossing the Kidron Valley and preparing to enter the garden of Gethsemane. There, he knew, Judas would come with soldiers to betray him. We can imagine Jesus as he stood on the very bank of the Kidron brook, about to take the fateful steps to the other side. He has concluded his vital instructions in his final sermon to the disciples, ending with a reminder that they would experience tribulation in the world (16:33). But now Jesus has his own tribulation to face: the hour of his cross. In this crisis, Jesus reveals the attitude of his heart by lifting "up his eyes to heaven" and praying to the Father (17:1).

Jesus' concerns in the prayer of John 17 show us the priorities of his heart. First, Jesus prays not that the world would acclaim him but that God would approve and glorify him. Second, Jesus prays that the events to come would glorify the Father. Third, Jesus devotes most of his prayer to petitions for the salvation and blessing of his people. The crisis of Jesus' cross reveals his dying passion for the Father's glory and for the salvation of the elect who belong to him.

THE TRUE LORD'S PRAYER

John 17 records what we might call the *true Lord's Prayer*. In the Sermon on the Mount, the disciples asked Jesus how to pray, and his answer is known as "the Lord's Prayer" (Matt. 6:9–13). That is really, however, a prayer for Jesus' disciples, while John 17 records the Lord's own prayer. Most Christians know this chapter as Jesus' *High Priestly Prayer*, a label dating back to Clement of Alexandria in the fifth century. More recently, scholars have pointed out that this prayer involves more than Jesus' priestly intercession for his people, that it also includes his own prayer of consecration before undertaking the cross. One useful suggestion labels this as Jesus' *Farewell Prayer*. This makes the point that as Mediator between God and man, Jesus first lays his hand on the people he would save and then lays his hand on God in praying on their behalf. Between the Farewell Discourse and the Farewell Prayer, Jesus performs his office as the Savior sent to reconcile his people to God.

Jesus' prayer may be divided into three sections. In John 17:1–5, Jesus prays for himself. In John 17:6–19, he prays for his disciples. In John 17:20–26, Jesus prays for all believers who would come to him in the centuries to come. The prayer contains five petitions: one for himself and four for his people. Moreover, James Montgomery Boice points out that the prayer sets forth "six distinctive marks of the church . . . : joy, holiness, truth, mission, unity, and love."[1] We will take special note of these in our study of his prayer.

Martin Luther commented, "This is truly, beyond measure, a warm and hearty prayer. He opens the depths of His heart, both in reference to us and to His Father, and He pours them all out. It is so deep, so rich, so wide, no one can fathom it."[2] Mark Johnston points out: "It was offered on the eve of the greatest event of history; it is found in conjunction with the greatest message ever heard in history; and its contents involve the greatest experience that history can ever provide. Furthermore, every sentence within the prayer is bound up with the honour and glory of God."[3]

Jesus' prayer is significant as a model and example of prayer for us. It is a *reverent* prayer, indicated by Jesus' lifting up his eyes to heaven and by his humble manner of address. It is a *reasoned* prayer, reflecting forethought and clear biblical thinking. It is a prayer that expresses Christ's *readiness* to do his Father's will, just as he would pray when he later arrived in the garden of Gethsemane. It is a *believing* prayer, asking God to perform the very things he has promised to do, a prayer that is centered on God's sovereign plan for salvation.

Finally, Jesus' priestly intercession is a prayer on which Christians may utterly *rely*. We may be sure that what Jesus asks in this prayer, he receives from his Father. His prayer was answered in the cross and resurrection, it is still being answered in the salvation of Christ's people today, and it will continue to be answered until God's mercy has brought in the last of those belonging to his Son. Here is a prayer that retains its potency through all the long centuries of the gospel age. Believers should therefore study Jesus' priestly prayer with the closest attention, since these are petitions that seal the certainty of our salvation through faith in Christ.

The Glory of Christ

Jesus' first petition, recorded in verses 1–5, asks the Father to glorify him so that he might glorify the Father in return: "Father, the hour has come;

1. James Montgomery Boice, *The Gospel of John*, 5 vols. (Grand Rapids: Baker, 1999), 4:1246.
2. Quoted in Arthur W. Pink, *Exposition of the Gospel of John* (Grand Rapids: Zondervan, 1975), 904.
3. Mark G. Johnston, *Let's Study John* (Edinburgh: Banner of Truth, 2003), 222–23.

glorify your Son that the Son may glorify you" (John 17:1). When Jesus asks to be glorified, it is possible that he was asking for his resurrection and ascension, which declared his divine sonship and royal authority after the humiliation of his cross. But it is more likely on this occasion that Jesus asks for the Father to glorify him in the events of the cross.

The glory of Christ is one of the main themes of John's Gospel, with John mentioning *glory* or *glorify* no fewer than forty-two times. John cited Christ's glory along with the other main themes in his prologue: "the Word became flesh and dwelt among us, and we have seen his glory, glory as of the only Son from the Father, full of grace and truth" (John 1:14). But John wishes to convey a specific idea of glory, namely, that divine glory that shines in humble, sacrificial service. Jesus' supreme act of humble service was performed in his atoning death on the cross, and that is where his glory is consummated in the hearts of his people. D. A. Carson writes, "The very event by which the Son was being 'lifted up' in horrible ignominy and shame was that for which he would be praised around the world by men and women whose sins he had borne."[4] Jesus spoke explicitly of his cross as the time of his being lifted up in glory: "The hour has come for the Son of Man to be glorified. . . . And I, when I am lifted up from the earth, will draw all people to myself" (John 12:23, 32).

Three Gifts for Christ's Glory

Since the glorification of Christ is the theme of the first five verses of John 17, we will explore it more fully in the coming studies. In these opening words of his prayer, however, Jesus emphasizes the resources that the Father has given to him in order that he might glorify the Father: "Father, the hour has come; glorify your Son that the Son may glorify you, since you have given him authority over all flesh, to give eternal life to all whom you have given him" (John 17:1–2). God's grace is biblically defined as a free gift, and here Jesus says that the Father has given him three gifts with which to glorify God's grace: authority over all flesh, a people to belong to Jesus, and eternal life for Jesus to give to his own.

4. D. A. Carson, *The Gospel of John* (Grand Rapids: Eerdmans, 1991), 554.

Probably the most difficult idea is the first: Jesus states that the Father has "given him authority over all flesh" (John 17:2). Here, the word *flesh* refers to all living creatures, most notably the entire human race. On the surface, this seems a remarkable claim, since Jesus was himself about to be given over into the authority of the Jewish priests and the Roman soldiers. Yet he prays to the Father regarding the "authority over all flesh" that has been given to him.

In understanding this, we should note that Jesus speaks of this gift in the past tense. He refers not to the authority that will be given to him in the resurrection or his ascension to the throne of heaven, but the authority that has already been given to him. What authority is this? It is the authority of the covenant Head of the human race in the place of fallen Adam. Frédéric Godet writes: "This gift consists in the decree by which God conferred the sovereignty over the whole human race upon the Son, when He sent Him to fulfill here on earth His mission of Saviour."[5] Jesus' appointment as King of kings and Head over all the earth was proclaimed at his birth, when the angels paid him homage. Isaac Watts's hymn adapts the angels' song:

Joy to the world! The Lord is come:
Let earth receive her King.[6]

The universal scope of Jesus' lordship was seen in the coming of magi from the east to worship the infant Messiah. The magi inquired, "We saw his star when it rose and have come to worship him" (Matt. 2:2). Jesus came as the Ruler of the destinies of all men and women. John Calvin writes, "Christ receives authority, not so much for himself as for the sake of salvation; and, therefore, we ought to submit to Christ."[7] J. C. Ryle summarizes: "The keys of heaven are in Christ's hands. The salvation of every soul of mankind is at his disposal."[8]

5. Frédéric Louis Godet, *Commentary on the Gospel of John*, 2 vols. (Grand Rapids: Zondervan, 1893), 2:325.

6. Isaac Watts, "Joy to the World!" (1719).

7. John Calvin, *New Testament Commentaries*, trans. T. H. L. Parker, 12 vols. (Grand Rapids: Eerdmans, 1959), 4:165.

8. J. C. Ryle, *Expository Thoughts on the Gospels: John*, 3 vols. (Edinburgh: Banner of Truth, 1999), 3:189.

If the Father's first gift to Christ is universal, the second gift is particular: "all whom you have given him" (John 17:2). This states that out of the great multitude of all humanity, there are particular persons who were specially given to Christ to receive salvation. This is one of many places in John's Gospel where Jesus refers directly to the doctrine of election, which teaches that God sovereignly chose certain people to belong to his Son and receive salvation. The elect are "given" by the Father to the Son (cf. 6:37–39).

If the question is asked when Christ's people were given to him, the answer is in eternity past. Theologians refer to the covenant of redemption, whereby the Father charged the Son to enter the human race and accomplish the work necessary for salvation, the reward of which was a particular people to belong to Christ and who would benefit from his saving work. This assumes that Christians were personally known to the Father and Son in eternity past, which was precisely Paul's teaching when he wrote that God "chose us in [Christ] before the foundation of the world . . . . In love he predestined us for adoption as sons through Jesus Christ" (Eph. 1:4–5). Christ's saving work encompasses all mankind, with all freely invited to receive salvation through faith in him, but is applied effectually to only the elect. These are all those, Jesus prays, "whom you have given" to him.

The Father's third gift to his Son was eternal life: "you have given him authority over all flesh, to give eternal life to all whom you have given him" (John 17:2). This states that the reason Jesus was appointed as sovereign over all mankind was so that he could give eternal life to those given to him by the Father.

Jesus has frequently mentioned eternal life in John's Gospel, and the next statement in his prayer will focus particularly on this greatest of God's gifts. If we peruse John's various references to eternal life, we find that to receive eternal life is *to prevail over death and live forever*. John 3:16 says, "For God so loved the world, that he gave his only Son, that whoever believes in him should not perish but have eternal life." The reason Christ's people live forever is that his saving gift *frees them from the deadly curse of God's judgment and wrath on their sins*. Thus John the Baptist preached that to lack eternal life from Christ is to perish in sin: "Whoever believes in the Son has eternal life; whoever does not obey the Son shall not see life, but the wrath of God remains on him" (3:36). Jesus said that the one who receives eternal life "does not come into judgment, but has passed from death to life" (5:24).

When Jesus was offering his gospel to the Samaritan woman, he emphasized eternal life as *a refreshing, life-giving power at work within us*. Contrasting eternal life with stagnant well water, Jesus told her that "whoever drinks of the water that I will give him will never be thirsty again. The water that I will give him will become in him a spring of water welling up to eternal life" (4:14). Finally, to receive eternal life is to participate in the great future resurrection at the end of days, then passing into the eternal glory. Jesus said, "For this is the will of my Father, that everyone who looks on the Son and believes in him should have eternal life, and I will raise him up on the last day" (6:40). The phrase *eternal life* appears seventeen times in John's Gospel, and a study of each of these verses will provide a well-rounded understanding of the salvation that Jesus came to give his people.

How do we receive eternal life? John's Gospel stresses two points. The first is that eternal life is received through faith in Christ alone. When Jesus was explaining the new birth to the Pharisee Nicodemus, he taught the necessity of his atoning death (John 3:14) and stated as its purpose that "whoever believes in him may have eternal life" (3:15). All through John's Gospel, eternal life is received only through faith in Jesus Christ, a point emphasized in each of the statements that I have referenced above.

How can we receive so priceless a gift merely by believing? The answer is that eternal life is Christ's free gift to those who belong to him and therefore respond to his gospel in saving faith. Jesus prays that the Father has given him "authority over all flesh, to give eternal life to all whom you have given him" (John 17:2). Leon Morris explains that eternal life "is not something that we achieve by our earnest endeavors, our good works, our devotional exercises, or the like. If we are to have eternal life, it will be because it has been given to us freely."[9]

We can understand this more clearly if we realize that the term *flesh* has a moral and spiritual nuance. God gave Jesus "authority over all flesh." In the New Testament, *flesh* sometimes refers simply to the human body. But it usually contrasts man's original spiritual calling with the fleshly life into which we have fallen by sin. In this sense, *flesh* means man in his sinful nature. Therefore, when God gave his Son authority over "all flesh," Jesus was assuming the lordship over a race that is unable to save itself because of

---

9. Leon Morris, *Reflections on the Gospel of John* (Peabody, MA: Hendrickson, 1986), 569.

the guilt and corrupting power of sin. The Bible does not teach that man in his sinful flesh is merely sick but rather that fleshly man is spiritually dead. Thus, fleshly man is unable to respond to God or accomplish anything for his own salvation. "You were dead in the trespasses and sins in which you once walked," Paul says, "following the course of this world, following the prince of the power of the air . . .—among whom we all once lived in the passions of our flesh" (Eph. 2:1–3). This being the case, the only way that the people given to Christ—people who are naturally wicked and opposed to God—can receive eternal life is as an unmerited gift, given to us freely by Jesus Christ and received simply in trusting faith. Eternal life—salvation—is, Paul writes, "by grace . . . through faith. And this is not your own doing; it is the gift of God, not a result of works, so that no one may boast" (2:8–9).

With so much at stake, how can we know that we have been given to Christ by the Father? The answer is found in realizing that the Bible promises eternal life to all those given to Christ and to all who receive the gospel in faith. These, therefore, are the same persons. Those who trust Christ and receive his gospel are none other than the elect people whom God has given to his Son. The doctrine of election is never taught in the Scriptures to prompt morbid speculation about our place in God's eternal decree. We are never told to wonder whether we are elect or not: we are instead told to believe in Christ to receive eternal life, and then we are told that believers are those chosen in eternity by God to be given to his Son. We know our election not by peering into God's inaccessible Book of Life but by believing in the Lord Jesus Christ.

GOD'S GLORY THE END OF SALVATION

If we learn nothing else from the opening words of Jesus' prayer, we should notice that in Jesus' mind, the chief end of his saving work—and therefore the primary goal of our salvation—is the glory of God the Father. Jesus refers to God's sovereign plan for our salvation, resulting in eternal life for those given to Christ, as the rationale for the glory that he will give to the Father: "Father, the hour has come; glorify your Son that the Son may glorify you, since you have given him authority over all flesh, to give eternal life to all whom you have given him" (John 17:1–2). This says that the grand purpose of God's eternal and sovereign plan of salvation, about to be accomplished by Christ on the cross, is the glory of the Father through the redeeming work of the Son.

This emphasis suggests that one of the reasons that Christians become overly concerned with ourselves is that we forget that the chief end of our salvation is God's glory. Forgetting this, we lose the greatness of the gospel by focusing on ourselves. When this happens, Christians are discontented when we suffer trials and setbacks, despite the infinitely valuable gift of eternal life given to us at such cost to God and his Son. Likewise, we sometimes present the gospel to others primarily in terms of the benefits it offers to the individual, producing believers who are interested only in something for themselves.

How different this idea of Christianity is from the heart and mind of Christ as he prepared to step across the Kidron brook and take up his cross. In Jesus' prayer, the great achievement, the chief end, and the primary benefit of the salvation he was about to accomplish was that through it God would be glorified. So it is with our own salvation! The chief and most exciting reality in being a Christian—in possessing eternal life—is that you and I might no longer be rebels who deny God's glory—which is the very essence of sin—and that we might no longer be blind to the awesome majesty of our Lord. Instead, we ourselves are made into those who display the perfections of God's attributes in the saving of our own souls. This was Paul's emphasis in Ephesians 1, writing that God "predestined us for adoption as sons through Jesus Christ, according to the purpose of his will, *to the praise of his glorious grace*" (Eph. 1:5–6).

When we take up Jesus' mind-set regarding salvation, our attitude toward everything changes. We no longer come to church primarily to get something for ourselves, insisting on our own preferences, but to render honor to God and grow in his grace. We no longer approach trials and tribulations as lamentable tragedies but as opportunities to show forth the glory of God's grace in our lives. James wrote: "Count it all joy, my brothers, when you meet trials of various kinds, for you know that the testing of your faith produces steadfastness" (James 1:2–3). As Jesus' hour of crisis approaches, he reveals the chief passion of his life. Martyn Lloyd-Jones writes: "Here he is, just before the cross, the crucial moment is at hand. He knows something about the agony and the sweat of Gethsemane, and his one desire is this: Father enable me to go on, give me strength to bear, give me all I need to do this, in order that your great glory in this matter of salvation can be revealed and made manifest. I have come to do that, enable me to do it that your name may be glorified."[10]

Here, then, is the astonishing thing about possessing eternal life. To receive eternal life is not only to be used by Jesus Christ in his great passion to bring glory to God the Father. It is marvelously true that Jesus' death achieved a display of God's eternal glory in the salvation of everyone who belongs to him. But there is more. To believe in Jesus Christ and receive eternal life means that we, too, can make the greatest of all ends—the glory of God— the chief aim of our lives. We can take up Christ's prayer, not in an atoning death, since Jesus died once for all for sins, but in a cross-bearing life as his disciples, offering ourselves up to God and his gospel. In this way, Jesus' prayer may be our own: "Father, glorify me, your son, so that I may glorify you." This request for glory, like Christ's, is a plea for grace to fulfill our calling in holy obedience to God's will, so that others may see God's glory in us and give praise to our Father in heaven. Our glory is a Christlike character and a cross-shaped, servant life of holy love, each of us carrying out the work that God has given us to do.

As we live in the crucified glory of Christ, we will gain no plaudits from the world: that is not the glory that Jesus had in mind. But we will gain something far greater: we will more and more be molded to behold and comprehend the glory of God. Moreover, the end for which we were made will be accomplished in our lives. God's glory will be magnified in us, and through our witness the good news of eternal life in Christ will be made known to all flesh.

10. D. Martyn Lloyd-Jones, *Saved in Eternity: The Assurance of Salvation* (Westchester, IL: Crossway, 1988), 47.

110

ETERNAL LIFE

John 17:3

"And this is eternal life, that they know you the only true God,
and Jesus Christ whom you have sent." (John 17:3)

O ne of the great benedictions in the New Testament concludes the apostle Paul's doctrinal teaching in the book of Romans. Paul exclaims with wonder for the mind of God: "Oh, the depth of the riches and wisdom and knowledge of God!" He concludes with one of the most God-centered statements in all the Bible: "For from him and through him and to him are all things. To him be glory forever. Amen" (Rom. 11:36).

That same God-filled attitude is seen in the prayer of Jesus Christ on the night of his arrest. Jesus began what is called his *High Priestly Prayer* by asking God to glorify him, so that he might glorify God in the gift of eternal life to those who belong to him. According to Jesus, his people were predestined by God, and eternal life was given by God for Jesus to grant to his people. In every sense, Jesus agrees with Paul that salvation is from God. He also affirms that salvation is through and to God. We see this conviction in the remarkable statement of John 17:3, in which Jesus declares that the eternal life that comes from God consists of nothing less than the knowledge of God.

This claim agrees with the whole message of the Bible. The prophet Jeremiah, for instance, urged: "Let not the wise man boast in his wisdom, let not the mighty man boast in his might, let not the rich man boast in his riches, but let him who boasts boast in this, that he understands and knows me, that I am the LORD who practices steadfast love, justice, and righteousness in the earth" (Jer. 9:23–24).

To experience the reality of Jesus' statement is therefore one of the most vital issues in life. J. I. Packer asks, "What were we made for?" He answers, "To know God." He continues: "What aim should we set ourselves in life? To know God. What is the 'eternal life' that Jesus gives? Knowledge of God. . . . What is the best thing in life, bringing more joy, delight, and contentment, than anything else? Knowledge of God."[1] We have this on the authority of Jesus, praying to the Father, "And this is eternal life, that they know you the only true God, and Jesus Christ whom you have sent" (John 17:3).

WHAT IS ETERNAL LIFE?

The term *eternal life* is one of the keys to John's Gospel, occurring seventeen times as a synonym for *salvation*. People tend to think of eternal life primarily in terms of its duration or *quantity*: it is life everlasting. The biblical idea, however, is focused more sharply on the *quality* of this life. There is a future in eternity for believers and unbelievers alike, although for the latter the Bible holds forth only eternal and everlasting death (Rev. 20:14; 21:8). Eternal life, therefore, is the life of heaven beginning in us now, granted by God at the moment of our coming to saving faith. William Barclay writes: "To possess eternal life, to enter into eternal life, is to experience here and now something of the splendour, and the majesty, and the joy, and the peace, and the holiness which are characteristic of the life of God."[2]

The prophet Ezekiel depicted eternal life as a river flowing out from the glorious presence of God, growing richer and deeper as we advance into it. At first, he said, the water was only "trickling out" (Ezek. 47:2), but as he went farther "it was ankle-deep" (47:3). A little farther and Ezekiel found that the water was "knee-deep," then "waist-deep" (47:4), and farther yet, it was "deep enough to swim in, a river that could not be passed through"

---

1. J. I. Packer, *Knowing God* (Downers Grove, IL: InterVarsity Press, 1973), 29.
2. William Barclay, *The Gospel of John*, 2 vols. (Philadelphia: Westminster, 1975), 2:243.

(47:5). Ezekiel's visionary river was a picture of the eternal life that God would grant through his Son, on the banks of which he saw "very many trees" that were green and growing (47:7). He said, "Their leaves will not wither, nor their fruit fail, but they will bear fresh fruit every month, because the water for them flows from the sanctuary" (47:12).

The apostle John would himself see the conclusion of this vision, recorded at the end of the book of Revelation: the blessed eternal Land of Promise, watered by "the river of the water of life, bright as crystal, flowing from the throne of God and of the Lamb" (Rev. 22:1), all bathed in the light of the knowledge of God: "They will need no light of lamp or sun, for the Lord God will be their light, and they will reign forever and ever" (22:5). This is the eternal life that begins in the heart of everyone who receives Jesus in faith. Jesus said that "whoever drinks of the water that I will give him will never be thirsty again. The water that I will give him will become in him a spring of water welling up to eternal life" (John 4:14).

This means that eternal life is not something that we merely add on to the person we were before. Eternal life is not a compartment that fits into a corner of our lives or a way that we live on Sunday but not on the other six days of the week. Rather, eternal life is an entirely new spiritual condition. It is "the life of God in the soul of man."[3] Faith in Christ creates an entirely new life, with a new power, new motives, and a new purpose. When someone becomes a Christian, that person does not receive new faculties—he or she remains a person with a mind, will, and affections—but the old faculties are governed by an entirely new spirit. Martyn Lloyd-Jones writes that "a new principle of life comes into us which produces in us a new nature, a new outlook, so much so that having received it, we are able to say with Paul . . . 'If any man be in Christ, he is a new creature' (2 Cor. 5:17)."[4]

ETERNAL LIFE AS KNOWING GOD

At the end of his first epistle, the apostle John makes the comment that God "is the true God and eternal life" (1 John 5:20). We may therefore say that eternal life consists of the knowledge of God. This is what the prophets foretold, that when God had brought his salvation, "the earth shall be full of

3. Henry Scougal, *The Life of God in the Soul of Man* (Harrisonburg, VA: Sprinkle, 1986).
4. Martyn Lloyd-Jones, *Saved in Eternity* (Westchester, IL: Crossway, 1988), 152.

the knowledge of the LORD as the waters cover the sea" (Isa. 11:9). Jeremiah foresaw the new covenant that would bring salvation, its ultimate blessing being the knowledge of God: "no longer shall each one teach his neighbor and each his brother, saying, 'Know the LORD,' for they shall all know me, from the least of them to the greatest, declares the LORD" (Jer. 31:34).

The question is therefore raised, "What does it mean to know God?" The first answer is that knowing God means being informed about the character and nature of the true God. What is God really like? Unless we know the truth about who God is, we can hardly be said to enjoy eternal life.

There are two ways in which we can know what God is like. The first is by means of the natural world around us, since God is the One who created everything. Paul says in Romans 1:20 that God's "invisible attributes, namely, his eternal power and divine nature, have been clearly perceived, ever since the creation of the world, in the things that have been made." The natural order, combined with God's rule working out in history, displays his goodness, power, and justice. Thus, no one is without excuse for withholding obedience to God, since God has designed the creation to be a theater for the display of his glory. Old Testament scholar E. J. Young put it this way:

> By regarding the universe which He has created we behold His glory, His perfection and His attributes . . . . The entirety of creation, visible and invisible, speaks with voices clear and positive of the glory of the Holy God. Wherever we turn our eyes, we see the marks of His majesty, and should lift our hearts in praise to Him who is holy. This is His world, the wide theater in which His perfect glory is displayed.[5]

It is the condemnation of the entire human race that we are so corrupted by sin that the display of God in creation brings eternal life to no one. Paul laments: "For although they knew God, they did not honor him as God or give thanks to him, but they became futile in their thinking, and their foolish hearts were darkened" (Rom. 1:21). Therefore, we require the saving revelation of God that he has graciously provided in the Holy Scriptures. The purpose of the Bible, then, is to reveal God so as to create faith. The Scriptures reveal God in his holiness, sovereignty, truth, power, justice, and mercy. Knowing about him is our urgent need: Hosea pointed out that

5. E. J. Young, *Isaiah*, 3 vols. (1965; repr., Grand Rapids: Eerdmans, 1992), 1:245–46.

the people of his day were "destroyed for lack of knowledge" (Hos. 4:6). The book of Judges tells of the calamities that resulted when a generation arose "who did not know the LORD or the work that he had done for Israel" (Judg. 2:10). Christians therefore have the urgent task of passing on to the next generation the Bible's revelation of God and his great works for our salvation. Likewise, every new believer needs to seek a thorough knowledge of the Bible, just as veteran Christians must continue their growth in the knowledge of God through his Word.

The importance of knowing the truth about God is underscored by Jesus' designation of him as "the only true God" (John 17:3). This reminds us that the opposite of knowing God is not knowledge of *no god*, but rather a belief in false gods. Thus, when John stated in his epistle that the Lord "is the true God and eternal life" (1 John 5:20), he concluded by writing: "Little children, keep yourselves from idols" (5:21).

This is what Paul was horrified to see when he arrived in the market of Athens. The city of the philosophers was literally "full of idols" (Acts 17:16). They had even erected an idol to "the unknown god" (17:23), thus admitting their ignorance. Today, few people worship idols of stone and wood, but they nonetheless worship vain philosophies such as evolution and secular human-ism. Carl Sagan, the famous physicist whose television show *Cosmos* declared the secular humanist mantra that "the cosmos is all there is, all there ever was, and all there ever will be," declared his belief that aliens populated the earth.[6] One of today's most prominent atheists, Richard Dawkins, admit-ted in an interview that he, too, replaces trust in God with belief in aliens.[7] Most people's idols are closer to earth: they worship money, pleasure, power, or love. If we say, "I could be happy and feel secure if I had _____," then whatever you put in that space is the god that you worship. How important it is that we learn that only the true and living God, the God and Father of Jesus Christ, is able to give eternal life, so that we may, as Paul put it, turn "from idols to serve the living and true God" (1 Thess. 1:9).

After we come to know *about* God, we must then *receive him* and render to him our worship and devotion. One example of this is the Gentile centurion Cornelius, to whom the apostle Peter was sent to preach. Cornelius was a

---

6. See Carl Sagan and Ann Druyan, *The Varieties of Scientific Experience: A Personal View of the Search for God* (New York: Penguin, 2007).

7. http://www.expelledthemovie.com/videos.php.

"God-fearer," that is, a Gentile who admired Judaism and its moral order and had thus expressed affinity for the Jewish religion and people. Cornelius had undoubtedly learned many Bible truths, yet he remained outside the covenant people of God and separate from the worship of the Lord. But when Peter preached the gospel of salvation in Christ, "the Holy Spirit fell on them" (Acts 11:15) and Cornelius received eternal life, accepting the Lord in personal faith and rendering worship to the true God. Have you done this? You might know many things about God and even believe that they are true. But you do not have eternal life unless you receive him as *your* God, offer him *your* personal faith, and worship him with *your* heart. Charles Spurgeon wrote that truly knowing God means "that we bow before him as worshippers, that we submit ourselves to his law, that we seek to do his pleasure. No man really knows God who does not know him as God, and does not accept him as his God; and to accept God as your God, is eternal life."[8]

Third, we should add that our knowledge of God leads to *a personal relationship* in which we walk with God as his people. As we live in fellowship with God, devoting ourselves to his Word, walking before him daily in faith, lifting our hearts to him in thankful prayer, and honoring him in practical obedience to his commands, we experience more and more deeply the knowledge of God and the power of his grace. Lloyd-Jones describes how such a personal relationship results in increased knowledge of God and the experience of eternal life:

> The Christian begins to realize that God is indeed his Father, that the hairs of his head are all numbered, and that his relationship to God is not something mechanical, it is experiential. That, of course, leads to a sense of dependence upon God, and the consciousness that, as time passes, we are in his hands. And that, further, means that we begin to look to him for strength, for power, and for everything.[9]

KNOWING GOD AS THE CAUSE OF ETERNAL LIFE

Just as we emphasize that eternal life *consists in* the knowledge of God, we can also declare that knowing God *causes* eternal life and advances its

8. Charles H. Spurgeon, *Metropolitan Tabernacle Pulpit*, 63 vols. (Pasadena, TX: Pilgrim, 1975), 41:28.

9. Lloyd-Jones, *Saved in Eternity*, 165–66.

power in our lives. As Paul said, "For from him and through him and to him are all things" (Rom. 11:36). Leon Morris thus comments that "to know God, really to know God, is to enter a transforming experience. If we come to know God, we can never be the same sinful people we were."[10] In this way, knowing God not only is the result of eternal life but also is its cause.

In his story "The Great Stone Face," Nathaniel Hawthorne tells of a boy living in a village beneath a mountain, on which was seen the stone image of a face. The village had a legend that someday someone who looked like the great stone face would come, bringing great blessing to the people. The story so fascinated the boy that he spent hours contemplating the stone face, wondering about the person who would come in that image. The years passed and the promise was not fulfilled, yet the boy, now a young man, continued looking at the stone face and thinking about the one who would come. So he continued through middle age, unable to get the legend and the beauty of the image out of his mind. Finally, one day he returned from gazing on the face on the mountain, now an old man, and as he walked through the village the people gasped and cried out, "He has come—the one who is like the great stone face!" The old man had become like the image he had contemplated.[11]

If we doubt the validity of that story in describing eternal life, then we should remember the case of Moses. When Moses spent time with God on the mountain, his face began to shine in glory, so that when he descended the people demanded that he veil the brightness of God's radiance shining from his face (Ex. 34:30). According to the New Testament, the same glorification results from our communion with Christ. Referring to Moses' reflected glory, Paul says of us: "We all, with unveiled face, beholding the glory of the Lord, are being transformed into the same image from one degree of glory to another" (2 Cor. 3:18).

Knowing God as we walk with him through this life, contemplating his glory in the Scriptures, we will find that like the man in Hawthorne's story, we increasingly bear the image of God in our spirits. This is, of course, what mankind was originally created to do and what we lost through our fall into sin: "God created man in his own image" (Gen. 1:27). The purpose of redemption is the restoration of this purpose, so that knowing God causes

10. Leon Morris, *Reflections on the Gospel of John* (Peabody, MA: Hendrickson, 1986), 571.
11. Cited in R. Kent Hughes, *John: That You May Believe* (Wheaton, IL: Crossway, 1999), 395–96.

God's life to shine in us. Charles Wesley celebrated the privilege of bearing God's glory, asking God to work in us more and more of this eternal life:

> Finish, then, thy new creation; pure and spotless let us be:
> Let us see thy great salvation perfectly restored in thee;
> Changed from glory into glory, till in heav'n we take our place,
> Till we cast our crowns before thee, lost in wonder, love, and praise.[12]

KNOWING GOD THROUGH JESUS CHRIST

I mentioned that in the last chapters of Revelation, the apostle John takes up and completes the prophet Ezekiel's vision of eternal life in its undying glory. There, God's people drink from the waters of the river of life and eat fruit from the tree of life. The description stirs the breast of all who are born again regarding the future that awaits us with God: "No longer will there be anything accursed, but the throne of God and of the Lamb will be in it, and his servants will worship him. They will see his face, and his name will be on their foreheads. . . . The Lord God will be their light, and they will reign forever and ever" (Rev. 22:3–5). Truly will it then be said that eternal life is knowing God.

All who come to enjoy that consummation of eternal life will be there for the same reason, that they came to know God here on earth: they learned the truth about God, they received and worshiped him as God, and they walked with God through life. Moreover, everyone who enters into that eternal bliss will have come to know God in the same way. Paul writes that "God, who said, 'Let light shine out of darkness,' has shone in our hearts to give the light of the knowledge of the glory of God in the face of Jesus Christ" (2 Cor. 4:6). It is only in and through Jesus Christ that any sinner comes to the knowledge of God. Indeed, it is only those who come to God through the saving work of his Son, especially his sin-atoning death on the cross, who receive eternal life. Jesus said, "I am the way, and the truth, and the life. No one comes to the Father except through me" (John 14:6). Thus, Jesus adds in his prayer his own saving mission: "And this is eternal life, that they know you the only true God, and Jesus Christ whom you have sent" (17:3).

12. Charles Wesley, "Love Divine, All Loves Excelling" (1747).

Jesus is himself the truest revelation of the Father, so that we come to know God most truly in the person of Christ. The writer of Hebrews began his book by pointing out that in former times God spoke in a variety of ways, "but in these last days he has spoken to us by his Son . . . . He is the radiance of the glory of God and the exact imprint of his nature" (Heb. 1:1–3). This means not only that Jesus is like the Father in every respect of his being, character, and will, but that the Father may equally be said to be like Jesus, his Son. "Whoever has seen me has seen the Father" (John 14:9), Jesus declared. Jesus therefore taught, "Truly, truly, I say to you, whoever hears my word and believes him who sent me has eternal life. He does not come into judgment, but has passed from death to life" (5:24). By sending his Son, God communicated the incarnate truth regarding himself. "The Word became flesh and dwelt among us, and we have seen his glory," John said, "glory as of the only Son from the Father, full of grace and truth" (1:14).

The knowledge of God comes not only through the person of his Son, however, but most especially through the saving work of Jesus Christ. In John 17:4, Jesus says to the Father, "I glorified you on earth, having accomplished the work that you gave me to do." That work was to grant eternal life through the knowledge of God to the people whom God had given to him.

It is not incidental, of course, that Jesus prays about granting eternal life through the knowledge of God as he prepares to undertake the great work of his cross. There, as never before, Jesus would reveal the glory of God so that we may know him for eternal life. On the cross, Jesus displayed the perfect holiness of God, pouring out the fullness of his wrath on our sins, even when they were borne by his perfect and well-beloved Son. What kind of God would pour out such wrath as Jesus suffered on the cross, such as to cause him to cry out, "My God, my God, why have you forsaken me?" (Matt. 27:46). On the cross, Jesus revealed a God of unyielding justice and holy wrath, before whom sinners must come with a fitting sacrifice or perish. But the cross reveals the mercy and love of this same holy God, in that he himself offered the sacrifice to free us from the penalty of our sin. Notice that Jesus says that eternal life is knowing God and Jesus Christ "whom you have sent" (John 17:3). God sent Jesus to lay down his life for the sake of his chosen people, bearing the curse and shame of our sin, revealing in this way the mercy and grace of an infinitely holy and loving God.

I mentioned earlier that Cornelius the centurion came to eternal life not merely when he learned about God but when he received God in personal faith. An even better example is that of the disciple Thomas, who doubted after Jesus was crucified. It was when Jesus appeared to him in his resurrection glory and displayed to Thomas the wounds of his cross, where Jesus had purchased forgiveness for our sins, that the doubting disciple believed and received eternal life. John writes that Thomas exclaimed to Jesus, "My Lord and my God!" (John 20:28). It is only when you look upon the atoning love of Jesus Christ, seeing by faith the marks of his death for your sins, that you truly know God in his glory and grace. In this way, if you will receive Jesus as Savior and Lord, worshiping him in his redeeming grace, you will know God and you will have eternal life.

111

MISSION ACCOMPLISHED

John 17:4–5

"I glorified you on earth, having accomplished the work that you gave me to do. And now, Father, glorify me in your own presence with the glory that I had with you before the world existed." (John 17:4–5)

ew satisfactions in life rival that of a job well done. Anyone who follows a task through to completion is rewarded with the approval of others and a personal sense of achievement. It is, of course, true that nothing we do in this life merits true and ultimate satisfaction, since none of our works is perfectly good. Moreover, our work is virtually never finished. An immaculately clean house soon gets dirty. Every workplace is constantly beset with new problems and challenges that must be met. For this reason, our job satisfaction is only partial and fleeting at best.

There is one person, however, who is completely and eternally satisfied with his work, having perfectly accomplished his mission in life. Jesus Christ prayed out of his own satisfaction and the Father's approval of the work that he achieved to perfection for our salvation: "I glorified you on earth," Jesus prayed to the Father, "having accomplished the work that you gave me to do" (John 17:4).

CHRIST RECEIVED A WORK

As Jesus faced his death on the night of his arrest, he looked upon his life with a perfectly clean conscience. Frédéric Godet comments: "He does not perceive in His life, at this supreme moment, either any evil committed, or even any good omitted. The duty of each hour has been perfectly fulfilled. There has been in this human life which He has now behind him, not only no spot, but no deficiency."[1] The words of Psalm 40:7–8 were the watchword of Jesus' life: "Behold, I have come; in the scroll of the book it is written of me: I delight to do your will, O my God; your law is within my heart.'"

Not only did Jesus perfectly obey the Father all his life, but he prays about a specific mission that he came into the world to fulfill. He prays to the Father, "I glorified you on earth, having accomplished the work that you gave me to do" (John 17:4).

When did Jesus receive this work from God the Father? There is ample evidence in the Bible that in eternity past the members of the Trinity entered into a pact for the redemption of the elect. This agreement is known by theologians as the *covenant of redemption*. We see evidence of this precreation covenant in John 17:4, where Jesus speaks of accomplishing a prearranged work, for which he receives a stipulated reward. He had previously told the disciples: "My food is to do the will of him who sent me and to accomplish his work" (4:34). The book of Hebrews concludes with a benediction appealing to "the God of peace who brought again from the dead our Lord Jesus, the great shepherd of the sheep, by the blood of *the eternal covenant*" (Heb. 13:20). This eternal covenant, fulfilled on the cross, is mentioned by Peter when he speaks of Jesus as the Lamb slain "before the foundation of the world" (1 Peter 1:20). Isaiah foretold Jesus' crucifixion in terms of this precreation pact, saying, "It was the will of the LORD to crush him; he has put him to grief; when his soul makes an offering for guilt, he shall see his offspring . . . . Out of the anguish of his soul he shall see and be satisfied; . . . he shall divide the spoil with the strong, because he poured out his soul to death and was numbered with the transgressors" (Isa.

---

1. Frédéric Louis Godet, *Commentary on the Gospel of John*, 2 vols. (Grand Rapids: Zondervan, 1893), 2:329.

53:10–12). These verses describe the cross in terms of Christ's reward for fulfilling his mission of salvation.

Louis Berkhof summarizes the biblical data concerning this precreation pact: "The Father required of the Son, who appeared in this covenant as the Surety and Head of His people, and as the Last Adam, that he should make amends for the sin of Adam and of those whom the Father had given him, and should do what Adam failed to do by keeping the law and thus securing eternal life for all His spiritual progeny." This mission involved the following particulars:

1. God the Son should take up a human nature by being born of a woman, thus experiencing all the weakness and infirmity of our nature, except for sin (Gal. 4:4–5; Heb. 2:10–15; 4:15);
2. he, the Son of God, would place himself under the law, making himself liable for his own obedience and for the penalty of his people's sins (Ps. 40:8; Matt. 5:17–18; John 8:28–29; Phil. 2:6–8); and
3. after securing forgiveness and eternal life for his people, he would send the Spirit to apply this salvation through the new birth into saving faith, through which his people would be saved by grace (John 10:16; 16:14–15; Heb. 2:10–13; 7:25).[2]

For his part, God the Father pledged a number of blessings to the Son:

1. the Father would give to the Son a people in reward for his accomplished work, "a seed so numerous that it would be a multitude which no man could number" (Pss. 22:27; 72:17);
2. the Father "would prepare the Son a body, which would be a fit tabernacle for him" (Luke 1:35; Heb. 10:5);
3. the Father would send the Holy Spirit to equip Jesus for his divine work in the flesh, and with the Son would send the Holy Spirit to regenerate and sanctify the people given to Christ;
4. the Father would, upon the Son's mission accomplishment, "commit to Him all power in heaven and on earth for the government of the world and of His Church (Matt. 28:18; Eph. 1:20–22; Phil. 2:9–11);

2. Louis Berkhof, *Systematic Theology* (Grand Rapids: Eerdmans, 1941), 269.

and would finally reward Him as Mediator with the glory which He as the Son of God had with the Father before the world was (John 17:5)."[3]

Understanding the covenant of redemption shows us how it is that Jesus secured our salvation: he fulfilled the eternal terms by which the Father has bound himself to grant Christ's people eternal life. Thus, our salvation does not rest on the brittle foundation of our personal faith. We receive salvation through faith alone, because Christ accomplished our salvation by his works, fulfilling a covenant with the Father that was sealed in eternity past.

Lest we think of the covenant of redemption as a matter of academic and abstract theology, the Puritan John Flavel reminds us of how personally this covenant involved each believer in Christ. He imagines a dialogue between the Father and the Son. The Father says, "My Son, here is a company of poor miserable souls, that have utterly undone themselves, and now lie open to my justice! Justice demands satisfaction for them, or will satisfy itself in the eternal ruin of them: What shall be done for these souls?" Christ replies, "O my Father, such is my love to, and pity for them, that rather than they shall perish eternally, I will be responsible for them as their Surety; bring in all thy bills, that I may see what they owe thee; Lord, bring them all in, that there may be no after-reckonings with them; at my hand shalt thou require it. I will rather choose to suffer thy wrath than that they should suffer it: upon me, my Father, upon me be all their debt." "But my Son," says God, "if thou undertake for them, thou must reckon to pay the last mite, expect no abatements; if I spare them, I will not spare thee." And Christ replied, "Content, Father, let it be so; charge it all upon me, I am able to discharge it: and though it prove a kind of undoing to me, though it impoverish all my riches, empty all my treasures . . . yet I am content to undertake it."[4]

Flavel concludes from that exchange, which resonates with the biblical record, that we cannot remain ungrateful to One so pure who bore our stain, One so rich who took our poverty, and One so innocent who paid the penalty for our guilt because of love. How can we, he asks, ignore so great a

3. Ibid., 270.

4. John Flavel, *The Works of John Flavel*, 6 vols. (1820; repr., Edinburgh: Banner of Truth, 1968), 1:61.

salvation or complain about the duty of obedience to Christ? Flavel writes, "O if you knew the grace of our Lord Jesus Christ in this his wonderful [compassion] for you, you could not do it."[5]

CHRIST COMPLETED HIS WORK

Throughout his life and ministry, Jesus referred constantly to being sent by the Father on a saving mission (John 3:16, etc.), saying that he "must work the works of him who sent me" (9:4). Now, praying on the brink of his arrest, Jesus sees the completion of the work given to him by God, speaking of having "accomplished the work that you gave me to do" (17:4). Jesus includes the cross among his finished works, since, as Augustine asserted, "Christ says He *has* finished that which He most surely knows He *will* finish."[6] Praying in the disciples' hearing, Jesus looked back on his taking up a human nature, his perfect, lifelong obedience to the letter and spirit of God's holy law, and his faithful rebuff of Satan's attempt to dissuade Jesus during his forty days in the wilderness. J. C. Ryle writes: "He did what the first Adam failed to do, and all the saints in every age fail to do: He kept the law perfectly, and by so keeping it brought in everlasting righteousness for all them that believe."[7] Paul explains Jesus' covenant perfection as the foreordained remedy for Adam's covenant failure and ours: "For as by the one man's disobedience the many were made sinners, so by the one man's obedience the many will be made righteous" (Rom. 5:19).

All that remained was for Jesus to bear the cross, as his sovereign will was committed to do. By his perfect life, lived on our behalf, Jesus provided the righteousness that his people lacked in themselves but need in order to stand in the holy presence of God. Now, Jesus would redeem us from the guilt of our sin. Isaiah foretold: "He was wounded for our transgressions; he was crushed for our iniquities; upon him was the chastisement that brought us peace, and with his stripes we are healed. . . . He poured out his soul to death and was numbered with the transgressors; yet he bore the sin of many, and makes intercession for the transgressors" (Isa. 53:5, 12).

5. Ibid.
6. Quoted in J. C. Ryle, *Expository Thoughts on the Gospels: John*, 3 vols. (Edinburgh: Banner of Truth, 1999), 3:199.
7. Ibid.

William Barclay, the often-helpful but sometimes quite liberal commentator on the Bible, compared Jesus' achievement to that of a courier boy who died delivering his message during the German bombing of Bristol. His dying words were: "I have delivered my message." Barclay mentions another example from the First World War, when a battlefield engineer was celebrated for sacrificing his life to connect the line that enabled the message to get through. Barclay compares this to what Jesus accomplished: "He had given his life that the message might get through. That is exactly what Jesus did. He had completed His task; He had brought God's love to men. For Him that meant the Cross."[8] It is true that Jesus delivered a message of God's love on the cross. But it is false that this was the sum of what Jesus achieved. Jesus did not die merely so that God's message of salvation would get through to us: God's Son died actually to achieve our salvation by laying down his life as an atoning Sacrifice for our sins. Therefore, while Jesus prays now of completing his work, he would not utter the decisive words, "It is finished" (John 19:30), until the moment came for him to die for our sins. Jesus died not merely to send a message but to complete a work, the result of which was salvation for those belonging to him.

We know that Jesus finished his work and accomplished his mission not only because he prayed in this way, but because the Father publicly declared his own satisfaction. I mentioned the satisfaction of a job well done: there has never been any satisfaction so infinitely great as the Father's satisfaction in the covenant-fulfilling work of his divine Son. The proof of God's satisfaction was Jesus' resurrection from the dead. Paul writes that Jesus was therefore "declared to be the Son of God in power according to the Spirit of holiness by his resurrection from the dead" (Rom. 1:4). The apostle adds that Jesus "was delivered up for our trespasses and raised for our justification" (4:25). This means that "by the resurrection God gave notice that Christ's death was that perfect substitution for sin he entered this world to make and that he, the Father, had accepted it in place of the condemnation of the sinner."[9] Since the Father has validated Jesus' mission accomplishment, we rejoice in Paul's declaration: "There is therefore now no condemnation for those who are in Christ Jesus" (8:1).

8. William Barclay, *The Gospel of John*, 2 vols. (Philadelphia: Westminster, 1975), 2:241.
9. James Montgomery Boice, *The Gospel of John*, 5 vols. (Grand Rapids: Baker, 1999), 5:1265.

CHRIST'S WORK GLORIFIED GOD

Not only was the Father satisfied by Jesus' job fulfillment, but Christ was himself satisfied by what he had done. This is why he prays, "I glorified you on earth, having accomplished the work that you gave me to do" (John 17:4). As Isaiah had foretold: "Out of the anguish of his soul he shall see and be satisfied" (Isa. 53:11). Jesus saw that his achievement would save his beloved people while bringing glory to the Father.

It is evident that Jesus has two different kinds of glory in mind in this prayer. In verse 5 he speaks of the divine glory he had before creation, and in verse 4 Jesus speaks of the glory he achieved on earth. The idea of glory in the latter sense is well expressed by the Greek word *doxa*, which stems from the verb *dokeo*, meaning "to seem." Paul uses this verb in Galatians 2:6 to speak of people who "seemed to be influential." The noun form was used for what one thinks. We have it in our word *orthodox*, which connotes thinking correctly, and *heterodox*, which connotes thinking differently. Over time, the word *doxa* stood for something that was of good repute so as to be especially praiseworthy. In this sense, *doxa* was used in the Greek translations to speak of God's glory. Psalm 24:10, for instance, states, "The LORD of hosts, he is the King of glory!" Today, we sing the *Doxology*, a hymn praising God's glory.

In this sense, to glorify God is to display his praiseworthy qualities or attributes. This is, of course, what Jesus did in the world, showing in himself the glory of what God is like. Jesus' life did not embrace worldly glory, but instead, through his life of humble obedience and ministry, Jesus displayed the infinitely praiseworthy character of God: his holiness, power, goodness, sovereignty, justice, truth, and mercy.

It would especially be in his self-sacrifice of the cross that Jesus would display the Father to the world. He began his prayer by asking the Father to enable him to do this: "Father, the hour has come; glorify your Son that the Son may glorify you" (John 17:1). On the cross, Jesus displayed the glory of God's love and grace for sinners. At the same time, Jesus displayed as never before the perfect justice of God as the Father poured out the whole of his wrath upon sin, even when borne by his beloved Son. The cross displays the sovereignty of God as reams of biblical prophecy are brought into focus and fulfillment. In like manner, Jesus displayed the perfections of the glory of all the attributes of God when he bore the cross to free us from our sins.

Just as Jesus glorified the Father on the earth by completing the work given him to do, we, too, will glorify God by doing the work that he has given us to do. We glorify the Father by believing the gospel of the Son whom he has sent. We glorify God by pursuing lives of holiness in obedience to his Word. We display God's glory by laboring together to build up the church and obey the Great Commission, making disciples of all kinds of people through our witness to the gospel. It is one thing to praise God with our lips, but quite another to praise God with our lives! J. C. Ryle comments: "To sing 'Glory, glory,' on a death-bed, after living an inconsistent life, is, to say the least, a proof that a man is a very ignorant Christian."[10]

CHRIST WAS GLORIFIED FOR HIS WORK

Christ received a work from the Father, he completed the work, and he brought glory to the Father by his work. Finally, Jesus prays to be glorified for his work with the glory he had with the Father in eternity past: "And now, Father, glorify me in your own presence with the glory that I had with you before the world existed" (John 17:5).

Matthew Henry points out four truths grounded in this request. First, Jesus asserts his full deity, coequal and coeternal with the Father. This is the truth expressed in the opening lines of John's Gospel: "In the beginning was the Word, and the Word was with God, and the Word was God. He was in the beginning with God" (John 1:1–2). Second, Christ was eternally full of glory, as was the Father. Henry writes: "He was from eternity the brightness of his Father's glory. . . . Christ undertook the work of redemption, not because he needed glory, for he had a glory with the Father before the world, but because we needed glory." Third, Jesus makes it clear that he divested himself of his outward glory in taking up a human nature. "He laid down this glory for a time, as a pledge that he would go through with this undertaking, according to the appointment of the Father." Fourth, having performed and fulfilled God's appointed

10. Ryle, *John*, 3:200.

work, Christ ascended into heaven and resumed his former outward glory, now glorified as both God and man. Henry urges us to seek after the glory of Christ rather than the tarnished glory of this world. "Let the same mind be in us," he writes; "Lord, give the glories of this world to whom thou wilt give them, but let me have my portion of glory in the world to come."[11]

Jesus' petition in verse 5 employs a second idea of glory. He speaks of a kind of glory that he temporarily laid down during his life on earth, even while he glorified the Father during his life and ministry. This second idea of glory is frequently seen in the Old Testament: glory as the radiance of the splendor of the light of God. Psalm 104:1–2 exclaims: "You are clothed with splendor and majesty, covering yourself with light as with a garment." When Moses descended from meeting with God on Mount Sinai, the people asked him to cover his face because of the brightness of the glory reflected on it. When Solomon dedicated the temple on Mount Zion, the glory cloud "filled the house of the LORD" (1 Kings 8:10). In many Jewish writings, this glory was called the *shekinah* glory, the outshining of the brilliance of the light of God. It is this visible glory, the splendor of divine radiance, that Jesus prays to resume as the reward for fulfilling God's work.

We know from the Bible that Jesus did take up this radiant glory upon his ascension into heaven. John himself would see it when Jesus appeared to him on the Isle of Patmos. In the book of Revelation, John tells us that he saw Jesus in glory,

> clothed with a long robe and with a golden sash around his chest. The hairs of his head were white, like white wool, as white as snow. His eyes were like a flame of fire, his feet were like burnished bronze, refined in a furnace, and his voice was like the roar of many waters. . . . His face was like the sun shining in full strength.
>
> When I saw him, I fell at his feet as though dead. But he laid his right hand on me, saying, "Fear not, I am the first and the last, and the living one. I died, and behold I am alive forevermore, and I have the keys of Death and Hades." (Rev. 1:13–18)

11. Matthew Henry, *Commentary on the Whole Bible*, 6 vols. (Peabody, MA: Hendrickson, 2009), 5:931.

This vision was given to encourage John and his friends in their great trials. It shows that Jesus has entered into the glory for which he prayed on the night of his arrest. He has ascended to the right hand of God, reigning with divine, sovereign power over heaven and earth (Matt. 28:18; Eph. 1:20–22). It is this glory of Christ that is heaven's great song and the joy of Christ's people forever: "Worthy are you . . . , for you were slain, and by your blood you ransomed people for God from every tribe and language and people and nation, and you have made them a kingdom and priests to our God, and they shall reign on the earth. . . . Worthy is the Lamb who was slain!" (Rev. 5:9–12).

Are We Satisfied?

In accomplishing the Father's mission, Jesus was satisfied, and he asked to receive the glory promised to him as the Son of Man. God the Father was satisfied, declaring in the resurrection his acceptance of Christ's saving work. The only remaining question is whether we are satisfied in the finished work of Jesus Christ. Are you looking for Jesus to do something more than living a perfect life on your behalf and shedding his life's blood for your sins? Do you desire the lesser, fleeting glory of the world, sin, and the flesh? If you realize your urgent need to be forgiven of your sins and for a righteousness to stand in the presence of God's glory, then you will be satisfied in the finished work of Christ. Realizing what Jesus has accomplished for us, we sing:

> Jesus paid it all,
> All to him I owe;
> Sin had left a crimson stain,
> He washed it white as snow.[12]

If we realize that Jesus finished his work, that his mission is accomplished, then we will cease trying to do something more for our salvation. Our great need now is not to add our works to Christ's finished work but for the glorious Christ to reign in us with his power. Seeing Jesus robed in the splendor of his heavenly glory becomes our hope and joy. We sing:

12. Elvina M. Hall, "Jesus Paid It All" (1865).

414

He ever lives above, for me to intercede,
His all-redeeming love, his precious blood to plead;
His blood atoned for ev'ry race, his blood atoned for ev'ry race,
And sprinkles now the throne of grace.[13]

God is satisfied in Jesus and has glorified his Son in heaven. The only thing that he desires even more is for Jesus to be glorified in our hearts. This is the goal of our salvation, which we receive by believing in him, so that God would shine in our hearts "to give the light of the knowledge of the glory of God in the face of Jesus Christ" (2 Cor. 4:6).

13. Charles Wesley, "Arise, My Soul, Arise" (1742).

112

THE PEOPLE OF CHRIST

John 17:6—8

"I have manifested your name to the people whom you gave me out of the world. Yours they were, and you gave them to me, and they have kept your word." (John 17:6)

he primary description that Jesus gives of his people in the prayer of John 17 is that they are those whom God the Father gave him in eternity past. He speaks of believers as the people "whom you gave me" no fewer than five times in this prayer.

This raises a vital question, namely, who are the elect, those who belong to Jesus by the sovereign, eternal choosing of God (cf. Rom. 8:30; Eph. 1:4)? In one sense, this is a question that we cannot answer and should not ask. We are not granted a peek at the Book of Life spoken of in Revelation (13:8; 20:15), the volume that records the identity of each of God's people. Likewise, the Bible never tells us to squander our anxious moments by wondering whether or not we are elect. The closest statement to this is 2 Peter 1:10, where the apostle urges believers to "be . . . diligent to make your calling and election sure." Yet Peter does not say to make ourselves elect but to give evidence of our election by a living faith. "Am I elect?" or "Is he or she elect?" is a question that the Bible never endorses.

Having made that qualification, Jesus' prayer does answer the question: "Who are the elect, those given to Christ?" He gives four marks of his people in John 17:6–8. The people of Christ are those to whom Jesus manifested the Father's name, whom Christ took out of the world, who have kept God's Word, and who received Jesus as the One sent from God.

Manifested God's Name

When God chose a people and gave them to Christ, those people were also brought into relationship with the Father and became important to God's saving mission in the world. "Yours they were, and you gave them to me," Jesus says. Therefore, he adds, "I have manifested your name" to them (John 17:6). This fulfilled Psalm 22:22, "I will tell of your name to my brothers; in the midst of the congregation I will praise you" (cf. Heb. 2:12).

In prior studies we have noted how Christ revealed the glory of God in terms of his perfect attributes: Jesus' life, and especially his atoning death, displayed God's power, holiness, truth, and love. But here we are reminded of the names by which God is revealed in the Old Testament. Leon Morris writes, "In biblical times it was widely held that 'the name' in some way sums up the whole person." To know the name of God is to possess a way of salvation; as Solomon wrote: "The name of the LORD is a strong tower; the righteous man runs into it and is safe" (Prov. 18:10). We know God because his name has been made manifest to us by Christ. Jesus revealed God's name "in a way that [the disciples have] never dreamed of before, and in doing this he has enlarged their understanding of the nature of God."[1]

We learn much about God by means of his scriptural names. The first is *Elohim*, which designates God as the Creator. It is used in the Bible's first verse: "In the beginning, God created the heavens and the earth" (Gen. 1:1). Later in the Bible, a derivative of this name is combined with other words to express more features of God's person and work. He is *El-Shaddai*, meaning "God Almighty" (17:1), and *El-Roi*, "the God who sees me" (16:13). Abraham named him *El-Elyon*, "God Most High" (14:22).

The other great name of God in the Old Testament is *Yahweh*, which is God's covenant name as Israel's Redeemer. Moses asked what name he

---

1. Leon Morris, *Reflections on the Gospel of John* (Peabody, MA: Hendrickson, 1986), 574, 576.

417

should give to the people for the God who was sending him to Egypt. "God said to Moses, 'I AM WHO I AM.' And he said, 'Say this to the people of Israel, "I AM has sent me to you"'" (Ex. 3:14).

In the Hebrew Old Testament, the name "I AM" is expressed through the four letters known as the *tetragrammaton*: YHWH. Jewish people came to speak of "the name of God" in reference to these letters, and in reverence to God they refused to utter the name aloud. In later years, when vowels were inserted into the Hebrew text, this name was given the vowel pointing for the word *adonai*, meaning "lord," in the place of the original vowels. The letters did not fit the consonants, which was the point, since it rendered the name unpronounceable. The best attempt rendered the name *Jehovah*. More recently, however, scholars are widely agreed that *Yahweh* is more likely the original name. Other versions of this name include *Yahweh-Yireh*, meaning "the LORD will provide" (Gen. 22:14), and *Yahweh Sabaoth*, meaning "LORD of hosts" (1 Sam. 1:3).

There can be no doubt that Jesus revealed the meaning of these names of God to the disciples. Some scholars argue that Jesus means here that he revealed a new name for God. If that is the case, then the name cannot be other than *Father*. It is true that Israel occasionally referred to God as "Father" (Isa. 64:8), but the idea that individual believers could call upon the Lord as Father was revealed only through Jesus Christ. Jesus himself constantly prayed to God as Father, and he urged the disciples to do likewise (Matt. 6:9). After the resurrection, Jesus says to Mary Magdalene, "I am ascending to my Father and your Father, to my God and your God" (John 20:17). As a result of his return to heaven, Jesus' disciples would enjoy the same relation to the Father that Jesus enjoyed.

Jesus' emphasis on manifesting God's name reminds us of the urgent importance of knowing God. Nothing is more important for us than to know God as he is revealed in the pages of Scripture and especially as he is manifested in Christ. The only way for Christians to live in faith, hope, and love is to know God as sovereign, loving, holy, powerful, just, and good. Knowing God's name is a priority that never takes a backseat: in this respect, our spiritual progress throughout life may be tracked by our growth in the knowledge of the name of the Lord.

The point in Jesus' prayer is that this knowledge of God's name is revealed only to his people, and this knowledge is a mark of the people of Christ.

Another way to say this is that Christians are not those who pray, "O high, exalted, and unknowable God, beyond our reach in majesty, aloof above the petty concerns of men," but we pray, "Our Father, the Almighty, most high, all-seeing God who is with us to save and to bless." Do you know God this way: as your Father? If you do not, then Jesus calls you to himself, for it is he who manifests the knowledge of God's name. As you come to know Jesus, receive him in true faith, and embrace the truth of his Word, Jesus will reveal to you the knowledge of the only true God, which brings eternal life.

TAKEN OUT OF THE WORLD

A second characteristic of the people of Christ is that they have been taken out of the world. Jesus prays, "I have manifested your name to the people whom you gave me out of the world" (John 17:6). Here we see that Christians have been separated out from the world and are called to live in a different way and by a new power. According to the Bible, there is a great division in mankind: there are some who belong to the world and others who have been separated by God out of the world. This relates to the doctrine of *sanctification*, from the Latin word *sanctus*, for *holy*. Christians are separated from the world and called to holiness.

We need to grasp three points to understand this teaching rightly. First, we tend to speak of sanctification (the process of becoming more holy) as something that follows justification (our acceptance with God through faith in Christ). This is true: those who believe in Jesus are forgiven of their sins, are justified before God, and then are called to holy living. Yet we must also realize that sanctification is not something that comes sometime later for believers, as an add-on to salvation. Rather, sanctification is a necessary component of salvation from its very beginning: Christians are those, Jesus says, "whom you gave me out of the world" (John 17:6). From the moment of our faith in Christ, we are set apart by God from the world; though still *in it*, we are no longer *of it*.

Second, sanctification means no longer living in a worldly manner. A worldly person is one whose mind is on the things of the world: money, prestige, pleasure, and fame. Christians no longer live for these things. Moreover, followers of Christ are no longer to live by the values of the world. John writes of these in his first epistle:

Do not love the world or the things in the world. If anyone loves the world, the love of the Father is not in him. For all that is in the world—the desires of the flesh and the desires of the eyes and pride in possessions—is not from the Father but is from the world. And the world is passing away along with its desires, but whoever does the will of God abides forever. (1 John 2:15–17)

Turning to Paul, we see sanctification addressed in a wide variety of ways. In Romans 6, Paul focuses on dying to sin so as to live to God. We are no longer to cultivate sinful practices and desires. He writes: "So you also must consider yourselves dead to sin and alive to God in Christ Jesus. Let not sin therefore reign in your mortal body, to make you obey its passions" (Rom. 6:11–12). In Philippians 3:20, Paul describes believers as being no longer citizens of this world but "citizens of heaven." Our allegiance is no longer to the world, for the world's authority over us has been supplanted by the authority of Christ. In Ephesians 4:22–24, Paul reminds us that we are taught "to put off your old self, which belongs to your former manner of life and is corrupt through deceitful desires, and to be renewed in the spirit of your minds, and to put on the new self, created after the likeness of God in true righteousness and holiness."

All these statements make it clear that one cannot be a Christian without being different from the world. We are given to Jesus "out of the world" (John 17:6) and are thus set apart from sin. To be sure, we continue to be plagued by sin throughout this life and we continue to be influenced by the world, but Christ's people no longer have the same relationship to sin and the world that they formerly did. Sinclair Ferguson writes: "They belong to a new family in which sin is not 'the order of the day.' Instead, righteousness, peace, and joy mark the family life of God's people (Rom. 14:17). We are 'the kind of people' who have begun to taste that deliverance from the reign of sin, which will be consummated at the regeneration of all things."[2]

Third, it is essential for us to realize that while we are separated out *from the world*, ultimately sanctification is separation *to God*. In the Bible, holy things were those that not only were taken away from worldly use but also were designated for God's possession and service. Mount Zion was holy because God's temple dwelt there. The temple vessels and utensils were holy because they were restricted for God's service, as were the holy men

2. Sinclair B. Ferguson, *Children of the Living God* (Edinburgh: Banner of Truth, 1989), 22.

who served as priests. To be holy is to be set apart and designated for God's possession, use, and pleasure. For us to be holy is to know the reality of Nehemiah's exclamation: "The joy of the LORD is your strength" (Neh. 8:10).

It is essential that we embrace this positive idea of sanctification, so that we do not ultimately define being holy as being different from the world but as offering ourselves to God. Paul writes that God "chose us in [Christ] before the foundation of the world, that we should be holy and blameless before him" (Eph. 1:4). The end of our election is our belonging to God for the sake of his glory. Realizing this distinction makes all the difference in our attitude to Christian living. We are not pursuing holiness merely by not attending movies or by avoiding certain worldly standards of dress. We are becoming holy as we increasingly desire to be near to God, living in such a way that is pleasing to God, more and more filling our hearts with the light of his truth and grace. The result of this positive holiness will most definitely include being different from the world, but in our consciousness we will be impressed not so much with how different or better we are than others, but with the thrill of knowing and serving God and growing in the wonder of his grace.

This, by the way, provides the key to Christian liberty. It is true that believers possess freedom when it comes to matters not forbidden in Scripture, including a proper use of alcohol, our manner of dress, and our enjoyment of the arts. But we must realize that the true freedom for which we were purchased by Christ is the liberty to draw near to God in holiness and love— as David sang, "to gaze upon the beauty of the LORD and to inquire in his temple" (Ps. 27:4). In all things, therefore, we should live in order to promote our nearness to God and to foster the spiritual blessing of others in Christ.

KEPT GOD'S WORD

The third characteristic of Christ's people is that they keep God's Word: "Yours they were, and you gave them to me, and they have kept your word" (John 17:6). The word *keep* means "to lay hold of and secure." Examples of its use in John will make Jesus' meaning clear. In John 12:47, Jesus warned of a person who "hears my words and does not keep them." Later, Jesus stated, "If you love me, you will keep my commandments" (14:15). He added, "Whoever does not love me does not keep my words" (14:24). It is clear

421

that Jesus means not merely assenting to his teaching, but embracing it in a lifestyle of obedience.

During Jesus' ministry there were multitudes who heard his teaching but did not keep his word. We think particularly of the great crowd that Jesus miraculously fed with a few fish and loaves, but that choked on his teaching. They complained, "This is a hard saying; who can listen to it?" (John 6:60). How different are the people of Christ! They keep God's Word! This does not merely mean that they do not walk away, that they do not offer objections, and that they nod their heads in agreement. Martyn Lloyd-Jones states: "You do not really keep the word of God unless you obey it. It is a word that cannot be kept only in your intellect; it has to be put in your heart and in your will also. The man who keeps the word of God is the man whose whole personality is keeping it, the man who is meditating and rejoicing in it, whose heart warms to it, and so obeys it."[3]

This reminds us that while we emphasize keeping as *obeying*, John's meaning includes *treasuring* God's Word. How will we be people of Christ, whose Word increasingly shapes our mind, will, and affections? The answer is by keeping the Scriptures as our prized resource. In Psalm 1, where the man of God is contrasted to the man who walks in the counsel of the world, we are told: "His delight is in the law of the LORD, and on his law he meditates day and night. He is like a tree planted by streams of water that yields its fruit in its season, and its leaf does not wither. In all that he does, he prospers" (Ps. 1:2–3).

RECEIVED CHRIST FROM GOD

The people of Christ are those to whom Jesus has manifested God's name, who are taken out of the world, and who keep God's Word. Finally, Christ's people are those who receive Jesus Christ as the Savior sent from God. Jesus says: "Now they know that everything that you have given me is from you. For I have given them the words that you gave me, and they have received them and have come to know in truth that I came from you; and they have believed that you sent me" (John 17:7–8). Jesus has described his people in their relationship to God, to the world, and to the Word of God. Finally, the

---

3. D. Martyn Lloyd-Jones, *Safe in the World* (Westchester, IL: Crossway, 1988), 78.

people of Christ are known by their receipt of Jesus himself as he has been given to us by the Father in heaven.

Many people in the world admire Jesus in some ways. But saving faith requires us to realize the relationship between Jesus and the heavenly Father. The disciples had noted all that was in Jesus: his grace, his power, his wisdom, his holiness, and his love. "Now," Jesus declares, "they know that everything that you have given me is from you" (John 17:7). The grace of Jesus is the grace of God, the power in Jesus is the power of God, the truth in Jesus is God's truth, and the blood of Jesus was offered by God for our cleansing and forgiveness.

Seeing that everything in Jesus is of God, his people receive Jesus as the sum and fulfillment of the Word of God. "For I have given them the words that you gave me, and they have received them" (John 17:8). It is an important truth that Christ's people keep God's Word, but Jesus here emphasizes that keeping God's Word directs us to Jesus himself. The Pharisees thought they were keeping God's Word, with their radical obedience not only to the law but to the layers of their own add-ons and traditions. Yet they rejected Jesus Christ! Christ said, "I am the good shepherd. I know my own and my own know me" (10:14); "he calls his own sheep by name and leads them out. . . . The sheep follow him, for they know his voice" (10:3–4). Because Christ's people hear the call of Jesus in God's Word, Jesus concludes, "they have believed that you sent me" (17:8).

Consider the response to the apostle Paul's teaching in the Greek city of Berea. The Jews there revered God's Word in the Old Testament. When Paul arrived, he as usual presented himself in the synagogue, showing the Jewish people how Jesus had fulfilled everything foretold in the Scriptures. Usually, Paul's teaching to Jews was returned with violent rejection; in fact, Paul had gone to Berea to escape violence from the Jews in Thessalonica. But his hearers in Berea were willing to pay attention and consider Jesus in light of the Scriptures. Luke writes: "Now these Jews were more noble than those in Thessalonica; they received the word with all eagerness, examining the Scriptures daily to see if these things were so. Many of them therefore believed, with not a few Greek women of high standing as well as men" (Acts 17:11–12).

This is the mark of Christ's people, that they have compared the claims of Jesus with the teaching of the whole Bible and have found that Jesus is in fact the One foretold by God. It might be that Christ's people sometimes do not understand everything in the Bible correctly, and they might have much yet to learn and much holiness still to attain. But they know that Jesus is the Savior promised by God in the Scriptures; Jesus prayed, "They have received them and have come to know in truth that I came from you; and they have believed that you sent me" (John 17:8).

This statement means that the way for you to join the people of Christ is by opening the Bible, reading its account of Jesus' life, ministry, and doctrine, and examining Jesus' claim to be the One who fulfills God's ancient prophecies and promises of salvation.

GIVEN BY GOD

According to Jesus, faith is not something attained by us but rather given to us by God. Notice the frequency with which Jesus uses the terms *gave* and *given* in this passage, occurring five times. This is why Paul says that salvation and faith are gifts of God: "For by grace you have been saved through faith. And this is not your own doing; it is the gift of God, not a result of works, so that no one may boast" (Eph. 2:8–9). This means that if you are struggling to receive Christ, or unsure that you are among the people of Christ, you should ask God to give faith and salvation to you.

The great Southern Presbyterian Benjamin Morgan Palmer tells of a meeting in his study with a man who had been attending church, without having yet believed on Christ. He entered and complained about Palmer's recent preaching that faith comes only as God's gift, yet that sinners must believe in order to avoid condemnation. Palmer, still looking down at the manuscript that he had been working on, answered, "Well, my dear [friend], there is no use in our quarreling over this matter; either you can [believe], or you can not; if you can, all I have to say is that I hope you will just go and do it." Still not looking at the man so as not to distract him, Palmer could hear the choke in his voice as he replied, "I have been trying my best for three whole days, and cannot." "Ah," said Palmer, now laying down his pen and facing the man, "that puts a different face upon it; we will go, then, and tell the difficulty straight to God." Here is how he reports it:

We knelt together, and I prayed in the most matter-of-fact style, as though this was the first time in human history this trouble had ever arisen; that here was a soul in the most desperate extremity, which must believe or perish, and hopelessly unable, of itself, to do it; that, consequently, it was just the case calling for Divine interposition; and pleading most earnestly for the fulfillment of the Divine promise. Upon rising I offered not a single word of comfort or advice . . . . So I left my friend, in his powerlessness, in the hands of God, as the only helper. In a short time he came through the struggle, rejoicing in the hope of eternal life.[4]

In the end, as in the beginning, faith in Jesus is the gift of God, just as the people of Christ are those whom the Father has given to his Son. Do you seek to be among them, receiving eternal life? Then ask of the Father, who gives grace in Jesus' name. For surely in this matter, above all others, Jesus' promise is true: "whatever you ask of the Father in my name, he will give it to you" (John 16:23).

---

4. Quoted in Iain Murray, *Revival and Revivalism* (Edinburgh: Banner of Truth, 1994), 373–74.

113

THE HIGH PRIESTLY PRAYER

John 17:9–13

*"I am no longer in the world, but they are in the world, and I
am coming to you. Holy Father, keep them in your name, which
you have given me, that they may be one, even as we are one."*
(John 17:11)

n his 1650 classic, *The Death of Death in the Death of Christ*,
the Puritan John Owen pointed out that the priestly ministry of
Israel required not one, but two essential tasks. First, an offering was made in blood to satisfy God's justice for sin. Second, intercession
was made to God on the basis of that sacrifice. Owen writes: "To offer and
to intercede, to sacrifice and to pray, are both acts of the same sacerdotal
office, and both required in him who is a priest." The Christian hope of
salvation therefore rests on both Christ's dying and Christ's praying. Owen
says, "By the one he hath procured all good things for us, and by the other
he will procure them to be actually bestowed, whereby he doth never leave
our sins, but follows them into every court, until they be fully pardoned
and clearly expiated."[1]

1. John Owen, *The Death of Death in the Death of Christ* (Edinburgh: Banner of Truth, 1967),
71, 74.

These words remind us not to discount Jesus' prayer on the night of his arrest. As God's Son came forth as the saving Priest for his people, he came both to die and to make intercession. This intercession would not end beside the Kidron brook, but would continue after Christ's resurrection into the eternal future. Paul therefore asks, "Who is to condemn? Christ Jesus is the one who died—more than that, who was raised—who is at the right hand of God, . . . interceding for us" (Rom. 8:34). Hebrews 7:25 exults, "He is able to save to the uttermost those who draw near to God through him, since he always lives to make intercession for them." Therefore, the High Priestly Prayer recorded in John 17, the heart of which is found in verses 9–13, was really the beginning of the eternal priestly intercession offered by Christ for us on the basis of his once-for-all atoning death. Another Puritan, John Flavel, writes, "In this prayer he gives them a specimen, or sample, of that his glorious intercession work, which he was just then going to perform in heaven for them."[2]

ONLY FOR HIS OWN

Having prayed for his own consecration in taking up the cross, Jesus now takes up his priestly intercession in prayer, and he begins by specifying precisely for whom he is praying: "I am praying for them. I am not praying for the world but for those whom you have given me" (John 17:9). This is the interceding prayer of the High Priest on behalf of the people whom he represents to God, namely, those whom God gave to him, who are the very people for whom Jesus was preparing to offer his own blood as an atoning Sacrifice.

Christ specifies that his priestly prayer is for particular persons, not for the world generally. Jesus *offers* salvation for the entire world, but he intercedes as Priest before God to *effect* salvation only for those who belong to him, dying to atone for *their* sins and then sending the Spirit to open *their* hearts to saving faith. Reformed theologians have emphasized that Jesus' entire priestly ministry, including the atoning Sacrifice of his blood, takes this *particular*, rather than *general*, shape. Since the priestly offering and the priestly intercession were always performed together, Jesus prays as High

---

2. John Flavel, *The Works of John Flavel*, 6 vols. (1820; repr., Edinburgh: Banner of Truth, 1968), 1:247.

427

Priest for the very people for whom he was about to die, namely, Jesus says, for the elect and not for the world in general. Charles Spurgeon comments: "Our Lord Jesus pleads for his own people. When he puts on his priestly breastplate, it is for the tribes whose names are there. When he presents the atoning sacrifice, it is for Israel whom God has chosen."[3]

The doctrine associated with Jesus' statement is *limited atonement* or, in its more positive label, *particular redemption*. The doctrine notes that while Jesus' death extends a gospel invitation to all the world, the actual atonement was offered only for his own people, whom the Father had given to him from all eternity. To teach otherwise is to assert that Jesus atoned for sins that are not actually forgiven. We see this *particular* focus throughout the Bible's teaching on his cross. The angel told Joseph to name Mary's Son *Jesus*, "for he will save *his people* from their sins" (Matt. 1:21). Jesus taught that he came "not to be served but to serve, and to give his life as a ransom for *many*" (20:28).

The pastoral value of particular redemption lies in realizing that Jesus did not make his atonement merely for the cause of salvation or only for the possibility of sinners' being forgiven. Instead, Jesus died to atone for the particular sins of his actual people. If you believe in Christ, you may say with perfect accuracy that "Jesus died for *me* and to pay the debt of *my* sins." Likewise, Jesus here specifies that his priestly intercession is not for the world in general but is offered for those elect people known personally to him in all eternity and given to him by the Father to be his precious own. To say, as many have done, that Jesus died generally for all, even though he prays here only for his own, is to disregard the unity of the Priest's sin-atoning work and to deny the clear implication of what Jesus here emphasizes.

Jesus not only states *that* he prays for his own, but also explains *why* he prays for his people. He gives two reasons, the first of which is that his people belong to the Father and were given to Jesus by the Father: "I am not praying for the world but for those whom you have given me, for they are yours. All mine are yours, and yours are mine" (John 17:9–10). Jesus realizes that he has been entrusted with the salvation of this people who belong to God and have been handed over to him on behalf of God's saving purpose for them.

3. Charles H. Spurgeon, *Majesty in Misery*, 3 vols. (Edinburgh: Banner of Truth, 2005), 1:89.

Since they belong to the Father and Jesus' role as their Savior comes from the Father, he is especially zealous to pray on their behalf.

Some of us have had the experience of staying in a house owned by a trusted and beloved friend or mentor. The fact that the property belongs to him makes us especially keen to take good care of it. While we might allow our own grass to grow a little long, we will be attentive to make sure that this grass is promptly cut. Any damage will be immediately repaired, and we will be glad to make any needed improvements. In this same way, Jesus is especially interested in us because we are chosen by the Father from all eternity (Eph. 1:4; Rom. 8:30), and he has been entrusted by the Father with our salvation. This, by the way, tells us how we should think of one another. Every fellow Christian is one who belongs to God, so that we should treat him with care and love, as God would have us to do.

The second reason Jesus prays for his own is that, as he prayed, "I am glorified in them" (John 17:10). Surely it should thrill believers to know that Jesus treasures us as belonging to the Father. But here he adds that he delights in us because his glory is invested in our salvation. How is Jesus glorified in his people? There are many answers, a few of which deserve to be emphasized.

First, Jesus is glorified *in his work of grace for our salvation.* Jesus offers himself for sinful, lost, blind, and unworthy sinners. He cleanses us from our sin by his blood and then renews our soul with his life-giving Spirit. The drunkard is made straight, the thief turns to hard work, the adulterer commits to chastity, and the blasphemer offers his tongue in praise to God. Surely, if the apostle Paul could refer to the church in Philippi as "my joy and crown" (Phil. 4:1), then Christ is glorified in every sinner cleansed and set free to live for God.

Second, Jesus is glorified in his people *to the degree that they lead holy lives and perform good works.* Jesus intercedes to "redeem us from all lawlessness and to purify for himself a people for his own possession who are zealous for good works" (Titus 2:14). This is our true incentive in turning from sin, cultivating holy graces, and pursuing good works in Christ's name: that Jesus might be glorified in our lives before the world.

Third, Jesus is glorified *by our bold confession of faith.* Are you living as a "secret Christian"? Are you frightened to let your coworkers and neighbors know that you trust and serve the Lord Jesus Christ? Ultimately, no true

Christian can remain "undercover," and desiring for Christ to be glorified, we should all live openly before the world in obedience to his Word.

Fourth, Jesus is glorified *by our work to extend his kingdom.* Spurgeon preached: "The tendency is, so often, to leave everything to be done by the minister, or else by one or two leading people; but I do pray you, beloved, if you be Christ's, and if you belong to the Father, if, unworthy though you be, you are claimed with a double ownership by the Father and the Son, do try to be of use to them. Let it be seen by your winning others to Christ that he is glorified in you."[4] Let Christ be glorified in your prayers for the church and for gospel success. Let Christ be glorified by your generous giving to support the gospel ministry. Let Christ be glorified by your sacrificial involvement in missions, or mercy, or hospitality, or spiritual encouragement. In whatever we do for the extension of Christ's kingdom, in the home or at work or in the world, Jesus is glorified in us.

With all these reasons ringing in our hearts, we should lift up our heads from Jesus' prayer, amazed at the honor that he has bestowed on us. As you depart from church and head back into the world, you should hear Jesus say to you, "You are the Father's and are given to me, and I am glorified in you." What greater incentive can there be for us to live for him than to know that he owns us and is glorified in us! Of what worth are the baubles and plaudits of the world to us, when God's Son speaks of his own glory in our lives?

THE SECOND PETITION

Jesus' having explained his particular focus in praying for his people and his reasons for doing so, verse 11 then contains his actual plea, the second petition of Christ's High Priestly Prayer: "And I am no longer in the world, but they are in the world, and I am coming to you. Holy Father, keep them in your name, which you have given me, that they may be one, even as we are one." This is a moving prayer. Jesus tells the Father that in coming to him, he is leaving his people behind in the world. So he appeals to the Father to watch over and protect them, placing their salvation into the care of the Father while he departs to take up the cross: "Holy Father, keep them," he pleads. We sense here the same quality of passion as when

4. Ibid., 1:100.

parents are separated from their children, entrusting them into the care of others. "Keep them safe," they plead. Or a newly married man must entrust the safekeeping of his bride to his parents when he goes off to war: "As you love me, show your love to her. Keep her until my return!"

Jesus' prayer proves that his people, as vulnerable sheep, require careful keeping. His prayer makes clear the dangers that he sees set against them. First is the danger of *the world*: "I am no longer in the world, but they are in the world" (John 17:11). Jesus is concerned about the corrupting influence of worldliness. The world is so barren a soil for the seedlings of grace, and its temptations so powerful to the flesh, that Christ prays for the Father to preserve them. He prays to the "Holy Father"[5] to preserve his people from the domination of sin. Marcus Rainsford notes: "The Lord does not ask riches for them, or honors, or worldly influence, or great preferments, but he does most earnestly pray that they may be kept from evil, separated from the world, qualified for duty, and brought home safely to heaven."[6]

Probably the best illustration of Jesus' praying for his church in the world is the story of his disciples' crossing the storm-swept Sea of Galilee. Jesus had sent them into the lake on a fishing boat, knowing that the sea would rage dangerously so as to threaten their lives. To the disciples in the boat, it seemed as though Jesus had abandoned them. But the Gospel writer reveals where Jesus was: he was above the storm high on the mountain, praying to the Father on their behalf. That is why the boat did not sink and why the disciples were not drowned (Mark 6:45–51). Likewise, though we struggle in the world, we know that Jesus is now in heaven, praying for his own in the world, so that their faith will hold firm. Peter therefore states that believers "by God's power are being guarded through faith for a salvation ready to be revealed in the last time" (1 Peter 1:5).

If the first danger that Jesus foresees is external, in the world, the second danger is internal, that Christians might suffer *division* and *disharmony* among themselves. Thus, he prays "that they may be one, even as we are one" (John 17:11). Jesus was not praying that Christians would form a single massive worldwide denomination; in fact, the darkest

5. This, by the way, is Jesus' only reference to the Father in these terms. With what blasphemy is the term *Holy Father*, which Jesus used to address God, applied today to a man who sits as the pontiff in Rome!

6. Quoted in James Montgomery Boice, *The Gospel of John*, 5 vols. (Grand Rapids: Baker, 1999), 4:1288.

times of the church have been when the church was outwardly most unified, as in the medieval era. Rather, Jesus prayed for a unity of spirit among his people, so that Christians would cooperate in their mutual edification and in their witness before the world. Isolated Christians are vulnerable to the world and to sin, so Jesus prays that his people would stay together in the world.

Christian unity may be compared to the tuning of violins in an orchestra. The violins are tuned to one another because they are each tuned to the same tuning fork. Believers likewise gain oneness not by striving for unity but by focusing on Christ. We are tuned to one another by each drawing near to the same Savior. A. W. Tozer notes, "So one hundred worshipers met together, each one looking away to Christ, are in heart nearer to each other than they could possibly be were they to become 'unity' conscious and turn their eyes away from God to strive for closer fellowship."[7]

Jesus' petition for God to keep his people upholds the doctrine of *the perseverance of the saints*. This doctrine states that Christ's true people *must* persevere in faith in order to be saved in the end, and that true believers *will* persevere because of God's faithfulness in keeping them.

How successful is Christ's prayer in securing the Father's care to keep his people? The answer is that Jesus' prayer is certain to be received in the heart of the Father, so that God will keep every one who belongs to his interceding Son. Flavel writes: "Can such a Father deny the importunity, and strong reasonings and pleadings of such a Son; O, it can never be! He cannot deny him: Christ hath the art and skill of prevailing with God."[8] Jesus' earlier words are made even more certain now, in light of his prayer: "I give them eternal life, and they will never perish, and no one will snatch them out of my hand. My Father, who has given them to me, is greater than all, and no one is able to snatch them out of the Father's hand" (John 10:28–29).

J. C. Ryle exclaims, "The special intercession of the Lord Jesus is one grand secret of the believer's safety. He is daily watched, and thought for, and provided for with unfailing care, by one whose eye never slumbers and never sleeps. . . . They never perish, because He never ceases to pray

---

7. Quoted in R. Kent Hughes, *John: That You May Believe* (Wheaton, IL: Crossway, 1999), 400.
8. Flavel, *Works*, 1:255.

for them, and His prayer must prevail. They stand and persevere to the end, not because of their own strength and goodness, but because Jesus intercedes for them."[9]

During his ministry, Jesus kept his disciples in the faith, with the sole exception of Judas: "While I was with them, I kept them in your name, which you have given me. I have guarded them, and not one of them has been lost except the son of destruction, that the Scripture might be fulfilled" (John 17:12). The point is not that Judas was Jesus' sole failure, but that he never was one who truly belonged to Christ, just as there are many false professors in churches today who neither obey nor belong to Jesus. As a "son of destruction," Judas was ordained for eternal condemnation, and his betrayal fulfilled God's Word. Just as the Scripture was kept in the loss of Judas, it will also be fulfilled in the final salvation of all who look to Jesus in true and saving faith. "He who began a good work in you," Paul writes, "will bring it to completion at the day of Jesus Christ" (Phil. 1:6).

Finally, we should note that Jesus asks the Father to "keep them in your name, which you have given me" (John 17:11). There are two ways of taking this statement. The first sees the name of God as his power for the salvation of his people. Proverbs 18:10 says, "The name of the LORD is a strong tower; the righteous man runs into it and is safe." True though this is, the second view seems to fit the context better, holding that Jesus prays that his people would be kept not *by* God's name but *in* God's name. Jesus prays that they would remain true to the revelation of God that he has given them, not falling away into unbelief or heresy. This is Jesus' ultimate concern: not that his people would be comfortable or at ease in the world, but that they would be true to God through faith in Christ's gospel. Matthew Henry paraphrases Jesus' meaning: "Keep them in the knowledge and fear of thy name; keep them in the profession and service of thy name, whatever it costs them. Keep them in the interest of thy name, and let them ever be faithful to this; keep them in thy truths, in thine ordinances, in the way of thy commandments."[10]

9. J. C. Ryle, *Expository Thoughts on the Gospels: John*, 3 vols. (Edinburgh: Banner of Truth, 1999), 3:205.

10. Matthew Henry, *Commentary on the Whole Bible*, 6 vols. (Peabody, MA: Hendrickson, 2009), 5:936.

THE FIRST MARK OF THE CHURCH: JOY

We have seen that Jesus' petition for the Father to keep his people is certain to be fulfilled. What, then, is the effect of Jesus' prayer in the hearts of those for whom he prays? Jesus continues, "But now I am coming to you, and these things I speak in the world, that they may have my joy fulfilled in themselves" (John 17:13). This prayer introduces the first of six marks of the church that we encounter in Jesus' Farewell Prayer: the mark of joy.

According to the Bible, it is essential that God's people live in this world with great joy. Paul issued it as a command: "Rejoice in the Lord always; again I will say, Rejoice" (Phil. 4:4). The prophets looked with wonder to the time of the coming of Christ, and they described it as a time of great joy: "The wilderness and the dry land shall be glad; the desert shall rejoice and blossom like the crocus; it shall blossom abundantly and rejoice with joy and singing" (Isa. 35:1–2). It is therefore not only our Christian privilege to live in joy, but also our duty to respond to the grace of Christ with hearts that rejoice in thanks to God. Jerry Bridges writes: "To be joyless is to dishonor God and to deny His love and His control over our lives. It is practical atheism. To be joyful is to experience the power of the Holy Spirit within us, and to say to a watching world, 'Our God reigns.'"[11]

Jesus prayed for believers to have joy because "now I am coming to you, and these things I speak in the world" (John 17:13). "These things" that Jesus speaks of and that give us joy can only be the matters about which he has been praying. Believers are not to find joy in the circumstances of the world, which often inflict pain and give joy with one hand while taking it away with the other. Instead, we gain joy in knowing that Christ our High Priest has died for our sins and is even now interceding for our salvation in heaven. We rejoice to know that we are kept by God for eternal glory, so that whatever else happens to us in life, we know that in Christ we are being ushered into everlasting delight in the presence of God. Do you struggle to rejoice as a Christian? Then perhaps you are focusing on the world and on your circumstances and trials rather than on Christ, who takes you as the gift of God, declares that his glory is found in you, and prays for God to keep you in the world so that you will be safe in eternity.

11. Jerry Bridges, *The Practice of Godliness* (Colorado Springs: NavPress, 1996), 119.

Second, Jesus emphasizes that the joy he desires for his people is his own joy: "These things I speak in the world, that they may have *my* joy fulfilled in themselves" (John 17:13). The way to rejoice is to live in close communion with Christ in God's Word and in prayer. Alexander Maclaren writes: "The only cheerful Christianity is a Christianity that draws its gladness from deep personal experience of communion with Jesus Christ. . . . If we abide in Christ, His joy will abide in us, and our joy will be full."[12] Jesus tells us that he rejoiced to do the will of the Father and bring glory to his name, and his rejoicing included his taking up the cross: Jesus "for the joy that was set before him endured the cross, despising the shame" (Heb. 12:2). We can experience Jesus' joy by committing ourselves to the will of the Father, anticipating with great excitement that eternal harvest that will soon be ours in Christ.

Finally, Christians can rejoice to know that we are now called and received into this same priestly ministry today, in the priesthood of all believers. Peter writes that believers are together "a chosen race, a royal priesthood, a holy nation" (1 Peter 2:9). What joy we have in praying for our fellow Christians, knowing as Jesus does that they belong to God and are beloved by him. What joy we have in knowing, as Jesus knew, that we are now brought into the great saving work of God's gospel, so that eternal destinies are gained through our witness and prayers. Finally, what joy there is in knowing, as Jesus states in this prayer, that our Lord is glorified through our own priestly ministry of prayer in his name. What a joy it is to pray, knowing that Jesus has promised, "Whatever you ask of the Father in my name, he will give it to you" (John 16:23). "Ask, and you will receive," Jesus had taught the disciples, "that your joy may be full" (16:24).

---

12. Alexander Maclaren, *Sermons for All Seasons* (Grand Rapids: World Publishing, 1995), 103.

114

SANCTIFIED IN THE TRUTH

John 17:14—17

"Sanctify them in the truth; your word is truth." (John 17:17)

rom time to time I hear a question that is frequently asked of pastors today: "What is your vision for your church?" I do not mean to denigrate this question, because it can be helpful for a congregation to think through its particular sense of identity and mission. Yet it must be emphasized that there is a far more important question than what is our vision: what vision Christ has for *his* church. However we may think of *our* church, we must acknowledge that the church belongs to Jesus, having been bought by his blood, and therefore his vision must be primary.

We may learn of Christ's vision for his church in a number of places. One is the seven letters to the churches in the book of Revelation, which emphasize moral purity, fidelity to truth, and zeal for gospel ministry. Perhaps the very best place, however, to see Christ's vision of the church, which should surely form the basis for any of our visions, is Jesus' prayer for the church in John 17.

THE THIRD PETITION

Jesus' Farewell Prayer is structured around a series of petitions to the Father, in which we learn what our Lord desires for his church. There are five requests, four of which pertain to the church, and in Jesus' prayer we can discern six marks of his church. These are joy, mission, unity, and love, along with the two marks emphasized in John 17:14–17: the marks of holiness and truth.

John 17:14–17 contains the third of Jesus' petitions. He has prayed to consecrate himself to the cross (17:1–5), and for the preservation of the church (17:11), with the result of joy, which is the first mark of Christ's people (17:13). Now, Jesus asks that his people be kept safe from the world, so that they might be sanctified in the truth. The third petition therefore asks for the holiness of his church.

The first threat that Jesus perceives to the church's holiness is the hatred of the world for his people: "I have given them your word, and the world has hated them because they are not of the world, just as I am not of the world" (John 17:14). This is a subject that Jesus went over with his disciples in his farewell sermon (16:18–25); now in their hearing, Jesus brings the matter to God. Jesus points out that his disciples are no longer like the world, since they have received God's Word in faith and been born again to new and eternal life. The holy values that they receive from God are a threat and a reproach to the world, which resents believers and wants to draw them back into sin. We are told that "Herod feared John [the Baptist], knowing that he was a righteous and holy man" (Mark 6:20). In a similar way, the world is bothered by Christ's people, and as they hated and killed Jesus, they hate Jesus' disciples, too. This is why believers require God's intervening protection. Hebrews 1:14 tells us that, among other things, God sends angels as "ministering spirits sent out to serve for the sake of those who are to inherit salvation." Therefore, just as the angel released Peter from Herod's prison (Acts 12:7f.), the world is not able to vent its hatred for Christ's people apart from God's permissive will.

A second threat from the world is moral and spiritual corruption. We see this concern in John 17:15, where Jesus asks the Father to "keep them from the evil one." Commentators debate whether Jesus refers to evil in general or to Satan as "the evil one." The latter is most likely, the point being that Satan corrupts the church by infusing it with worldly values. John elsewhere says that "the whole world lies in the power of the evil one" (1 John 5:19). Here is a threat to the church far greater than mere outward persecution: the spirit-destroying assimilation into the world's evil ways, as it is dominated by Satan.

Consider the way that churches and Christians are easily led into the *materialism* of our worldly culture. We see this tendency in the way that churches today typically measure success in materialistic ways: numbers of people, impressive buildings, and stockpiles of cash, often with little concern for faithfulness to the Bible, reverence to God, or holy living. The grossest example in the church today is probably the prosperity-gospel movement that makes material wealth practically the chief benefit of Christian salvation. More widespread is the situation forewarned some years ago by Francis Schaeffer, who worried that evangelical Christians primarily desire personal peace and enough money to enjoy it, not really caring about God or others. James Montgomery Boice cites a newspaper cartoon that was humorous in large part because it contained so much truth. The cartoon showed two pilgrims crossing to America on the *Mayflower*. One says to the other, "Religious freedom is my immediate goal, but my long-range plan is to go into real estate."[1] Today, America has large Christian denominations that are so materialistic that they literally care more for holding onto real estate than for holding onto God's saving truth.

We could multiply the *isms* that threaten to compromise Christ's church today. There is the *relativism* that has caused so many professing Christians to compromise on biblical doctrines. There is the *sensualism* of Hollywood-style entertainment in the place of biblical worship. There is the *humanism* of secular scholarship that denies the Bible's teaching on creation, gender, sexuality, and more, and the *consumerism* that some churches are importing from the advertising world of Madison Avenue. Jesus prays that his church would be kept by the Father from the ways of the world and of the evil one, so that his church may be holy.

THE CHURCH AND THE WORLD

Jesus' prayer is especially important in helping Christians understand our relationship to the world. We can deduce three statements about the church and the world from Jesus' prayer.

First, Jesus insists that Christians are *to live in the world*. This rules out reclusive monasteries, along with separationist communities such as the

---

1. James Montgomery Boice, *Whatever Happened to the Gospel of Grace?* (Wheaton, IL: Crossway, 2001), 23.

Amish. More subtly, evangelicals fall into the mistake of becoming what Rebecca Pippert calls "rabbit-hole" Christians. This is the kind of believer who "pops his head out of a hole, leaves his Christian roommate in the morning and scurries to class, only to frantically search for a Christian to sit by . . . . When dinner comes, he sits with the Christians in his dorm at one huge table and thinks, 'What a witness!' From there he goes to his all-Christian Bible study, and he might even catch a prayer meeting where the Christians pray for the non-believers on his floor."[2] The point is not that Christians should not seek fellowship with and support from one another. Rather, we should not escape from and avoid worldly contact altogether, madly dashing from one Christian context to another lest we somehow brush elbows with unbelievers.

It is noteworthy that three different Bible figures prayed to God to remove them from the world: Moses (Num. 11:15); Elijah (1 Kings 19:4); and Jonah (Jonah 4:3, 8). All three were illustrious servants of God, yet the Lord did not grant the request of any of them. Jesus told the Father regarding his church: "I am no longer in the world, but they are in the world" (John 17:11). He prayed, "I do not ask that you take them out of the world" (17:15), so Christians are to live in and interact with the world.

A second statement Jesus makes is that while the church is in the world, it is *not to be of the world*. As much as is prudently possible, we are to interact with the world and its people, but we are never to become like the world or unbelieving people.

James Montgomery Boice noted four ways in which the church and Christians tend to become secularized—that is, made like the world. The first is that churches begin to embrace the world's wisdom. When it comes to issues such as sexuality, marriage, parenting, financial management, leadership principles, personal counseling, and more, churches are tempted to incorporate the wisdom of the world with little or no consideration of God's Word. Embracing the world's wisdom is a sure way for Christians to be not only in but also of the world.

The second tendency is for the church to embrace the world's theology. Most of the theological challenges to sound biblical doctrine within evangelicalism today have their origin in secular and unbelieving academic

2. Rebecca Manley Pippert, *Out of the Salt Shaker* (Downers Grove, IL: InterVarsity Press, 1979), 113–14.

439

institutions. Evangelicals are influenced by worldly academia because they desire its approval and accreditation. The world believes that the Bible must have errors, that man is basically good and needs no redemption, that the celebration of Christ's cross promotes violence, that the Bible's creation story is a myth, and that the Bible's teaching on sexual purity and gender roles is out of date. These ideas show up within professedly believing churches and wreak a terrible havoc on Satan's behalf. Often, biblical terminology is retained but the meanings are twisted. Thus, *sin* no longer means rebellion against God but holding wrong political views. *Jesus* is no longer a sin-bearing Savior but a moral example. *Salvation* involves not getting right with God and receiving his blessing, but liberating society from oppressive social structures. With the world's theology, the church becomes not only in but also of the world.

Third, the church is secularized when it adopts the world's agenda. If the world is concerned with ending wars, then the church becomes a peace movement. A couple of years after the world begins stressing ecology, the church takes up this same cause. The energy crisis, homelessness, world hunger, tax relief, and Third World debt are worldly agendas that capture the focus of the church. Some of these causes may be noble and just. The point is, however, that when the church receives its agenda from the world, it becomes of the world. Instead, the church is called by Jesus to his agenda of the spiritual work of making disciples, baptizing them in the name of the Father, Son, and Holy Spirit, and teaching them the doctrines of Holy Scripture (Matt. 28:19–20).

Fourth, the church becomes of the world when it adopts the world's methods. Are we to seek political power to dictate laws? Are we to gain converts by employing emotional manipulation? Are we to grow our churches through man-centered entertainment or consumer-driven market campaigns? The answer is No, we are called to God's methods for bringing salvation through faith in Christ and for building up Christ's church.[3] These are, mainly, prayer and the Word of God. Paul wrote: "Though we walk in the flesh, we are not waging war according to the flesh. For the weapons of our warfare are not of the flesh but have divine power to destroy strongholds. We destroy arguments and every lofty opinion

---

3. This section was adapted from James Montgomery Boice, *The Gospel of John*, 5 vols. (Grand Rapids: Baker, 1999), 4:1301–3.

raised against the knowledge of God, and take every thought captive to obey Christ" (2 Cor. 10:3–5).

Christ's church is not to seek an escape from the world, and is to be in but not of the world. Third, Jesus' prayer makes it clear that the church *is to impact the world by being different from the world.* To be sure, Christians are not to ignore the culture as we pursue a kind of ghettoized faith. We must think of the world's culture, however, in biblical ways. Paul identified worldly culture as "the present evil age," from which Christ delivers us (Gal. 1:4). Many Christians today speak of "redeeming culture," but the Bible does not. At times of the church's greatest cultural influence, such as during America's Great Awakening in the eighteenth century, insightful Christians would assure you that the world remained under the evil one and the church under Christ. So it will always be until Christ returns. The world "lies in the power of the evil one" (1 John 5:19), and is consigned to judgment (1 Cor. 7:31; 2 Peter 3:10). Through the gospel we rescue sinners from the world so that they might enter into Christ's church culture. Therefore, we do not partner with the world or find salvation through collaboration with things of darkness (2 Cor. 6:14).

It is true that Christians have often influenced their society greatly. So how does this happen? Do we impact the culture by mirroring its expectations of dress, speech, conduct, gender roles, and doctrine so that the world will approve of and accept us? Jesus' answer is No. His people "are not of the world, just as I am not of the world" (John 17:16).

In reality, Christians most influence the culture when they are most different from the culture. Consider the example of Daniel and his three friends when they were exiled into the midst of the pagan culture of ancient Babylon. The book of Daniel reveals that these four young believers had a decided impact on Babylon, so that national expressions of praise and devotion were offered up to Israel's God. How did Daniel and his friends impact the culture? It was not by becoming like the world but *by remaining different from the world in obedience to God's Word.* This started with the Old Testament food regulations. Daniel and his friends asked permission to restrict their diet to conform to the law of Moses, and the result was that their health excelled that of all the other royal servants (Dan. 1:8–16). Later, when Nebuchadnezzar commanded everyone to bow before his golden statue, Daniel and his friends refused to worship the idol. When they were thrown into the furnace as punishment, God showed his power in saving them from the mighty flames, causing all of Babylon to take notice (3:1–30). (This prompts us to ask ourselves whether we really accommodate the world for cultural impact or to avoid the world's furnace.) Still later, when a royal decree forbade praying to the Lord, Daniel went on with his normal prayer life. When he was thrown into the lions' den for this "crime," God shut the lions' mouths and displayed his power to the Babylonians again (6:1–28). It might be objected that Daniel impacted the Babylonian culture because of God's mighty power at work through him. Exactly! God supernaturally blessed Daniel's obedience to Scripture, so that Daniel not only was rescued from the world's hatred but left a living testimony to the truth of his God.

We likewise will cause the world to notice our Lord as we live by biblical truth, and thus are different from the world. Martyn Lloyd-Jones wrote that "when the Church is absolutely different from the world, she invariably attracts it. It is then that the world is made to listen to her message, though it may hate it at first. . . . It should not be our ambition to be as much like everybody else as we can, though we happen to be Christian . . . . Our ambition should be to be like Christ, the more like Him the better, and the more like Him we become, the more we shall be unlike everybody who is not a Christian."[4] When Christians embrace not the world's but God's wisdom, theology, agenda, and methods, we gain the world's notice and God is glorified through his power at work in us.

The Marks of Holiness and Truth

Jesus' petition for the church is summed up in John 17:17, in which he presents the second and third marks of his church: "Sanctify them in the truth; your word is truth." First, Christ's church is to be holy: *sanctification* refers to the process by which God increasingly makes us holy, turning from sin and embracing practical godliness. And second, Christ's church is to be committed to the truth of God's Word.

Jesus began his petition by saying, "I have given them your word" (John 17:14). He concluded by declaring, "Your word is truth" (17:17). This means that the church has received God's Word of truth from Christ. The disciples

4. D. Martyn Lloyd-Jones, *Expositions on the Sermon on the Mount*, 2 vols. (Grand Rapids: Eerdmans, 1959), 1:37.

received the Word personally from Jesus; we receive it from the witness of Christ's servants the prophets and apostles in the Bible, which is our "only rule of faith and obedience."[5] Christians are not those who embrace every passing intellectual fad, therefore, but those who stand firm in the truth revealed to us by God through his written Word.

This means that the way for the church and for Christians to avoid being corrupted by the world and becoming secularized is to be people of God's Book, the Bible. We must submit to the authority of the Bible because it is God's holy, inspired, and inerrant Word. Whenever biblical authority is compromised, the dam is broken and the flood of secularism and worldliness breaks in. We must also embrace God's Word as wholesome and good, so that we desire to know it and eagerly put its teaching into practice. David wrote: "The law of the LORD is perfect, reviving the soul; the testimony of the LORD is sure, making wise the simple; the precepts of the LORD are right, rejoicing the heart; the commandment of the LORD is pure, enlightening the eyes" (Ps. 19:7–8). This should be our conviction as well. Therefore, whereas a worldly church derives its wisdom, theology, agenda, and methods from the world, Christ calls his church to derive its wisdom, theology, agenda, and methods from God's Word. The result of this commitment to Scripture will be a saving faith that is blessed with God's gift of eternal life, and a distinctively biblical lifestyle that identifies us as the people of Christ.

Not only does the Bible teach Christian holiness, but Jesus stresses that God's Word creates holiness within his people: "Sanctify them in the truth; your word is truth" (John 17:17). The way to be holy, then, is to study and apply the Bible.

All through Scripture, we find that life results from the going forth of God's Word. God said through Isaiah:

> For as the rain and the snow come down from heaven
> and do not return there but water the earth,
> making it bring forth and sprout,
> giving seed to the sower and bread to the eater,
> so shall my word be that goes out from my mouth;
> it shall not return to me empty,
> but it shall accomplish that which I purpose,
> and shall succeed in the thing for which I sent it. (Isa. 55:10–11)

5. Westminster Larger Catechism 3.

God's Word sanctifies because it conveys divine life from heaven, just as rain falls from the clouds and waters the soil so that life springs forth. This means that the way—the only way—for you to grow in holiness, becoming more like Jesus and gaining increased power to turn from sin to righteousness, is to commit yourself to the regular, serious, and believing study of God's Word. This means that the church must be fervently devoted to teaching and preaching God's Word, which is God's special means for our growth in grace and godliness. Donald Grey Barnhouse wrote: "It is the Word of God that can establish the Christian and give him strength to overcome the old forces and to live the new. It can never be done in any other way." Based on Jesus' teaching in John 17:17, Barnhouse went so far as to insist: "You cannot find even one Christian on this earth who has developed into strength of wisdom and witness in the Lord who has attained it by any other means than study and meditation in the Word of God."[6]

This was the experience of the prophet Ezekiel, who was called by the Lord to pastor the church of the "Valley of Dry Bones." He saw the valley scattered with the bleached bones of those who were dead. "Prophesy over these bones," God commanded, "and say to them, O dry bones, hear the word of the LORD" (Ezek. 37:4). So Ezekiel began to preach the Word, and as he did, the bones began to come together and the sinews were reformed. As he kept preaching, the bones, now alive again, took their feet, and they became "an exceedingly great army" (37:10).

Our generation needs legions of believers in Christ who are likewise enlivened by God's Word to holiness and spiritual might. We need a generation of Christians who are not captivated by the flesh and by sin but by the beauty of holiness, who are not daunted by the supposed sovereignty of the worldly culture but convinced of the power of God's Word. This was Paul's command to his young colleague Timothy, when Paul had warned him that times of unbelief, sin, and wickedness were coming. What should Timothy do when men would reject sound teaching and seek worldly voices to tickle their ears? Paul charged Timothy: "Preach the word . . . in season and out of season" (2 Tim. 4:2). No other power on earth compares with God's Word, for, as Paul writes, "All Scripture is breathed out by God and profitable for

---

6. Donald Grey Barnhouse, *Exposition of Bible Doctrines, Taking the Epistle to the Romans as a Point of Departure*, 10 vols. (Grand Rapids: Eerdmans, 1952), 1:137–38.

teaching, for reproof, for correction, and for training in righteousness, that the man of God may be competent, equipped for every good work" (3:16–17).

SANCTIFIED BY GOD THROUGH HIS WORD

If Christians impact our culture by being different from the world in a Christlike manner, then the need of our generation is churches and Christians who devote themselves to holy character and lifestyles. Furthermore, if holiness results from the truth of God's Word, the great need of our time is for churches and Christians to be devoted to the study, belief, and practice of Holy Scripture.

Do you desire to become more holy? Do you desire your life to make an eternal difference in our present world? Then, Paul says, "Do not be conformed to this world, but be transformed by the renewal of your mind" (Rom. 12:2). Devote yourself to the study of Scripture, not merely for a season but as a lifetime and lifestyle commitment. If you do, you will find that Jesus is right in saying that sanctification comes through the truth of God's Word. More than this, Jesus prays that God himself will sanctify his people through the truth of his Word. This means that as we humbly and expectantly place our hearts under the Scriptures, God's Holy Spirit will work in us with sanctifying power, just as rain falls to the earth and makes green things grow. Through his Word, God will himself work holiness into our lives so that we experience more and more of his life and shine more brightly the light of Jesus Christ into our dark world.

115

SENT INTO THE WORLD

John 17:18–19

"As you sent me into the world, so I have sent them into the world. And for their sake I consecrate myself, that they also may be sanctified in truth." (John 17:18–19)

*I*t is enlightening for pastors and churches to study Jesus' seven letters to the churches in the book of Revelation. These are real communications from the risen and exalted Christ to specific churches in Asia Minor. To read these letters is to be persuaded of Christ's overriding zeal for the holiness of his church, both in moral purity and in doctrine. To visit the ruins of these churches, which Christ seems to have given over to destruction, is to be brought to the fear of the Lord, who did not mince words when he threatened to remove their lampstands if they did not repent (Rev. 2:5).

Our study of Jesus' High Priestly Prayer in John 17 reveals an equally intense interest in the holiness of Christ's church. In the first lines of Jesus' prayer, he identifies the church as "the people whom you gave me out of the world" (John 17:6). A true disciple of Christ is "not of the world, just as I am not of the world" (17:16). Jesus petitions the Father to "sanctify them in the truth; your word is truth" (17:17). Now, in verse 19, Jesus identifies the holiness of his people as the intended result of his own mission and sacrifice: "for their sake I consecrate myself, that they also may be sanctified in truth."

In light of this strong emphasis, we must conclude that any churches or any Christians who take the matter of holiness lightly, casually adopting the stance of the world, are badly out of step with Jesus himself. At the worst, the present worldliness of evangelical churches suggests that many who consider themselves Christians are not actually saved. After all, Jesus warned that many will hear him say on the last day: "I never knew you; depart from me, you workers of lawlessness" (Matt. 7:23). For, he insists, "Not everyone who says to me, 'Lord, Lord,' will enter the kingdom of heaven, but the one who does the will of my Father who is in heaven" (7:21).

CHRIST SANCTIFIED FOR OUR SAKE

Jesus' emphasis on holiness warns us that we must take the matter of our sanctification seriously. His prayer in John 17:19 continues this emphasis. Jesus says, "For their sake I consecrate myself, that they also may be sanctified in truth." In the original Greek text, the word for *consecrate* and *sanctified* is the same. Jesus states, literally, that he sanctifies himself so that his people might be sanctified in him.

How can Jesus sanctify himself if he has never known sin? How can Jesus progress in holiness when he is and has always been the perfectly Holy One from on high? The answer is that while sanctification is generally understood as moral improvement, this being an essential component of holiness, its more basic meaning is being set apart for service to God. This is why the word for *sanctification* is often rendered as *consecrated*. This language was especially applied in the Old Testament to the priests, who were set apart for the ministry of offering atoning sacrifices to God. Thus, God told Moses to "put on Aaron the holy garments. And you shall anoint him and consecrate him, that he may serve me as priest" (Ex. 40:13).

Jesus did not need to put on outward holy garments, since he consecrated himself as our Priest through perfect obedience to the Father's will (see Heb. 10:7). This is why Jesus came before John the Baptist to receive the baptism of our repentance. John, his cousin, objected: "I need to be baptized by you, and do you come to me?" Jesus answered, "Let it be so now, for thus it is fitting for us to fulfill all righteousness" (Matt. 3:14–15).

447

Jesus was baptized to consecrate himself—set himself apart—for God's calling in Isaiah 53:12, to be "numbered with the transgressors." Now, on the brink of the garden of Gethsemane, Jesus sanctified himself to make the true atoning sacrifice. Israel's priests were sanctified with the sprinkling of the blood of lambs (Lev. 8:30), but when Jesus prays to sanctify himself as our Priest, he intends to do so in his own blood, shed for our forgiveness on the cross.

It is true that God calls Christians to a life of *progressive sanctification*, that is, a life of increasing godliness and turning from sin. Paul wrote that Christians are "to put off your old self," with all its sin and corrupt desires, "and to put on the new self, created after the likeness of God in true righteousness and holiness" (Eph. 4:22–24). In this important sense, sanctification results from our striving to put off sin and our putting on of holiness by the power that Christ gives. Jesus' prayer, however, reminds us that we must also think of our sanctification as the result of Christ's sanctification. "For their sake," he prays, "I [sanctify] myself, that they also may be sanctified in truth" (John 17:19).

As Jesus consecrated himself as our Mediator, he also consecrated us for holy service to his Father. In a vital sense, we may date our consecration even earlier, in the eternal predestination of God. God told Jeremiah, "Before I formed you in the womb I knew you, and before you were born I consecrated you" (Jer. 1:5). Equally vital is our consecration at the moment of our rebirth. When Christ sent the Holy Spirit to change our hearts so that we believed God's Word and were saved, he set us apart for himself and to the Father. Between God's ordination and the Spirit's application was Jesus' accomplishment of our sanctification through his priestly offering of his own blood for our sakes.

This setting of us apart, referred to by theologians as *definitive* sanctification, is in fact the New Testament basis for our *progressive* and ongoing sanctification. We are to pursue practical holiness not in order to be holy but because we have been made holy in Christ. Because we were set apart by Christ for God, we are therefore to pursue lives of corresponding holiness. Paul explained this in Romans, writing that our oneness with Christ is the basis and the motivation for our holiness: "For if we have been united with him in a death like his, we shall certainly be united with him in a resurrection like his" (Rom. 6:5). Therefore, he reasons: "So you also must consider yourselves dead to sin and alive to God in Christ Jesus. Let not sin therefore reign in your mortal body" (6:11–12).

One thing that this teaching means is that our sanctification corresponds to Jesus' sanctification. Christ consecrated himself to fulfilling God's calling on his life. We are likewise set apart for worship and service to God. Paul writes that we were saved "from idols to serve the living and true God" (1 Thess. 1:9). Perhaps with this in mind, Jesus says that he sanctified himself so that we might be "sanctified in truth" (John 17:19). This could mean simply that we are to be "truly" sanctified. But given the emphasis on "truth" in verse 17, it is more likely that, like Jesus, we are to be set apart for the truth of God. We are to believe God's truth, love God's truth, speak God's truth, and do God's truth in a world of ignorance, unbelief, and rebellion.

Our calling is not exactly the same as Jesus' calling. Our Lord was uniquely called to perform the work of salvation for God's people. But our consecration is like his in that we are to obey the Scriptures, to live a life of sacrificial, humble love, to witness and teach the truth of the gospel, and to offer our whole lives in worship to God. Within that general calling that all believers share, we are variously called to different kinds of work. Some are called to witness to Christ in the secular workplace. Some are called to minister to their families in the home. Our different spiritual gifts constitute various callings: some to service, some to administration, some to teaching, and some to encouragement. Some will be called into full-time gospel ministry or onto the mission field. What matters is that, like Jesus, we obediently embrace our own particular calling in service to God.

I was greatly challenged when a friend in ministry recently shared with me that when he wakes up each morning, he takes a moment to revel in his membership in Christ and to thank God for his saving mercy. He then prays that he will be enabled to live fully and unreservedly throughout the day for the sake of God's glory and in service to Christ's kingdom. This is not tyranny but true liberation! It is deliverance from a life not only of sin but also of trivia and vain pursuits. It is the whole consecration of self to which we were called when Jesus consecrated himself for us through the blood of his cross.

Moreover, our sanctification not only will be *like* Christ's but will be *in* Christ. The first words of John 17:19 are perhaps the most important: "for their sake." All that Jesus did and suffered was to sanctify his people to receive salvation and serve his Father. Having sanctified himself, Christ communicates his holiness to us through the Holy Spirit. John Calvin explains: "It is, because he consecrated himself to the Father, that his holiness might come to us; for as the blessing on the first-fruits is spread over the whole harvest, so the Spirit of God cleanses us by the holiness of Christ, and makes us partakers of it. . . . He has presented us to his Father in his own person, that we may be renewed to true holiness by his Spirit."[1]

Christ's blood was therefore shed not only for our justification but also for our sanctification: Paul says that he "became to us wisdom from God, righteousness and sanctification and redemption" (1 Cor. 1:30). Just as the high priest, having first sanctified himself, sprinkled blood to sanctify the objects in the temple, Christ offered his own blood and now consecrates us to draw near to God in the beauty of holiness (see Heb. 2:13; 9:11–14).

What this means to us is that for all our striving after holiness, this effort is never to be exerted in our own name but in Christ's, not in our own strength but in Christ's, nor even for our own sakes but for Christ's. The key to growing in godliness is to realize not only that in Christ we have a right to attain the holiness we seek, but that our striving rests on Christ's prior work of sanctification for us. Hebrews 10:14 explains, "By a single offering he has perfected for all time those who are being sanctified." We gain power for holiness as we rely on Jesus' prayer: "For their sake I [sanctify] myself, that they also may be sanctified in truth" (John 17:19).

The Fourth Mark of the Church: Mission

Jesus' prayer not only shows us his power for our sanctification, but also reveals his purpose in our sanctification. In other words, when Jesus says that he has sanctified his people, he has set us apart for a specific mission. We see this in John 17:18: "As you sent me into the world, so I have sent them into the world."

In our study of Jesus' prayer in John 17, we have been noting the marks of Christ's church that are seen in his requests to the Father. So far, we have noted the marks of joy, holiness, and truth. The prayer of verse 18 adds the fourth mark of Christ's church: mission. In our union with Christ, we take

1. John Calvin, *Calvin's Commentaries*, trans. William Pringle, 22 vols. (Grand Rapids: Baker, 2009), 18:181.

on his mission; as he was sent by the Father, now we are sent by Christ into the world. As Jesus has secured our place beside him in heaven, he calls us to take his place as witnesses on earth.

Verse 18 makes three essential points about the mission of Christ's people on earth. First, Christ has sent us. Therefore, we live in this world for Christ's work and kingdom. This calling applies most directly to the original disciples, whom Jesus sent as his apostles. The Greek verb for *to send* is *apostello*, the noun form of which gives us the word *apostle*, or "sent one." The apostles were uniquely sent as Christ's authoritative representatives. They continued Christ's work in the world, communicating Christ's gospel, healing in Christ's power, and recording Christ's message in the four Gospels and the Epistles of the New Testament. The apostles preached nothing but Jesus' own message of salvation by grace alone, and they confirmed his gospel with the same power from heaven that Jesus displayed in his own ministry.

While Christ's prayer in verse 18 is specifically directed to the original disciples, its general truth applies to all believers, who are sent by Christ on his mission in the world. Today's Christians carry on the apostolic ministry of the New Testament, teaching the same doctrine that the apostles taught and empowered by the same Holy Spirit sent from Christ. While we are not endued with the miraculous powers that the apostles wielded—casting out demons, healing the sick, and raising the dead—we carry on their work of mercy in Christ's name, and through the power of our prayers we receive help from the same Christ who gave his apostles the victory long ago.

Second, not only has Christ sent us, but we should be clear about where we are sent: into the world. This shows that while Jesus prays for the Father to protect his people in the world (John 17:11), and while John writes that we are not to love the things of the world or be like the world (1 John 2:15–17), yet the disciples' "mission to the world demonstrates that this Gospel is not introducing an absolute cleavage between Jesus' followers and the world."[2] If Jesus did not care for the world, he might have removed his disciples along with himself. But as the verses that follow show, the remainder of Christ's sheep must be called out from the world. For this reason, his holy people must yet remain in the world on his gospel mission of salvation.

2. D. A. Carson, *The Gospel of John* (Grand Rapids: Eerdmans, 1991), 567.

This calling into the world undoubtedly challenges many Christians. Because of the hostility of the world, along with the corrupting influences of worldliness on believers, we will be tempted to separate ourselves from the world almost completely. In the present moral collapse of the West, coupled with an aggressive, atheistic humanism, many Christians will decide to start their own schools or educate their children in their own homes. In time, an entire Christian subculture is created, with the effect that Christ's people are increasingly isolated from the world into which our Lord has sent us. James Montgomery Boice notes that it is possible today "to be born of Christian parents, grow up in that Christian family, have Christian friends, go to Christian schools and colleges, read Christian books, attend a Christian country club (known as a church), watch Christian movies, get Christian employment, be attended by a Christian doctor, and finally, one may suppose, die and be buried by a Christian undertaker on holy ground."[3] This might seem an entirely desirable approach were it not for Jesus' prayer: "As you sent me into the world, so I have sent them into the world" (John 17:18).

There is no standard corrective to this problem, except that our thinking about the world should be shaped by Jesus' missionary calling. At a minimum, there should be at least some meaningful ways in which we are living in the world and interacting with the world as Christ's witnesses—indeed, we should pursue this interaction in as many ways as is prudently possible. Boice advises: "We are to know non-Christians, befriend them, and enter into their lives in such a way that we begin to infect them with the gospel, rather than their infecting us with their worldliness."[4] Knowing the difference between the two will often be a matter of great discernment, and it will always need to be a matter of fervent prayer.

Jesus has sanctified us in order to send us, so that verses 18 and 19 go together in setting us apart for gospel mission in the world. It follows, then, that our sanctification is important to our witness. It is a holy witness that shines forth the light of Christ, and a holy ministry that shuts the mouths of demons and sends forth the gospel in power.

Not only must our mission be holy, but our holiness must also be missional. The best and truest kind of holiness is one that is intended to

3. James Montgomery Boice, *The Gospel of John*, 5 vols. (Grand Rapids: Baker, 1999), 4:1321.
4. Ibid.

452

communicate to the world the glory of Christ and the blessing of his salvation. What a difference there is for an unbeliever to live next door to a Christian whose holiness is intended as an affront versus a Christian whose holiness is intended as an invitation. Christ's holiness was always a breath of fresh air in the presence of sinners, intending offense only to the self-righteous and proud.

As Christ Was Sent

A third main point for us to take from Jesus' prayer in John 17:18 is that we are not only sent by Christ into the world, but, he says, sent into the world *as he was sent* by the Father. Therefore, if we consider what it meant to Jesus to be sent into the world, we can glean insight into what it means for us to be sent by him. In a sermon on this text, Charles Spurgeon highlighted four main examples.

First, Jesus came into the world *in subjection to the Father's will*. "I glorified you on earth," he said, "having accomplished the work that you gave me to do" (John 17:4). Though Jesus was coequal with the Father in deity and glory, he subordinated himself for our salvation. Spurgeon writes: "So long as he remained under his commission, he did not speak his own words, nor do his own deeds; but he listened to the Father's will, and what the Father said to him he both spoke and did. That is exactly where you and I have to place ourselves now, deliberately and unreservedly. Our Lord sends us, and we are to be, in very deed, subordinate to his command in all things. We are no longer masters; we have become servants. Our will is lost in the will of our glorious superior."[5]

Second, Christ's people in this world are *called to labor, not comfort*. In the days of his ministry, we constantly found Jesus wearied, burdened, thirsty, oppressed, and finally dying on the cross. Having been sent into the world, we are not to stake our claim for comfort and ease but for costly usefulness to Jesus and his gospel. We should embrace inconvenience for the sake of another's soul, and we are to undertake costly sacrifices for the work of Christ's church. As Jesus bore our burden, we are sent to take up the burden of others in his name.

5. Charles H. Spurgeon, *Metropolitan Tabernacle Pulpit*, 63 vols. (Pasadena, TX: Pilgrim, 1992), 36:267.

Third, Jesus' mission in the world *required him to defer the timing of his glory.* Jesus willingly laid down the glories of heaven in order to bring salvation to us. Many a Christian grows weary of this world and can scarcely wait to give it up, saying with Paul, "My desire is to depart and be with Christ, for that is far better" (Phil. 1:23). Yet we should remember what Christ gave up so that he could remain here to finish his work. Spurgeon exhorts us: "We must not sigh for heaven while so much is to be done on earth. The rest of glory will come soon; but just now we have to do with the work of grace."[6]

Fourth, just as Christ willingly accepted shame and disgrace, so we must also *accept humiliation* here while we advance toward glory there in heaven. Spurgeon says, "Expect to be misunderstood, misrepresented, belied, ridiculed, and so forth; for so was the Sent of the Father. . . . As the Father sent his Son into a world which was sure to treat him ill, so has he sent you into the same world, which will treat you in the same manner if you are like your Lord."[7]

Our Indispensable Mission

To Spurgeon's four applications, we should add two more in conclusion. The first is that we must always remember that, like Christ, we are *sent into the world with grace to reconcile sinners* with their holy God. A. W. Pink writes: "Christ was sent here on an errand of mercy, to seek and to save that which was lost; so we are here as His agents, His instruments, to preach His gospel, to tell a world dead in sin of One who is mighty to save. Christ was here 'full of grace and truth'; so we are to commend our Master by gracious and faithful lives."[8]

The last is perhaps most important. We must always remember that in God's saving plan—a plan that sent Christ for us and now sends us to the world—our mission in his name *is absolutely essential.* Your role is indispensable to Christ's saving mission in history: no one else can do the gospel work that Christ has set before your life. Never allow yourself to think that God's sovereignty makes your gospel witness optional or irrelevant. Far from it: Christ has sent you into your family, your workplace, your neighborhood,

6. Ibid., 36:268.
7. Ibid., 36:269.
8. Arthur W. Pink, *Exposition of the Gospel of John* (Grand Rapids: Zondervan, 1975), 950.

and the lives of those with whom you are in contact. Your prayers for their salvation, your life of holy joy and peace, and especially your testimony to the Bible's good news of grace in Christ for sinners are just as important in their own way as was Christ's death on the cross for our sins.

Of course, it is true that God is sovereign over our gospel failure as well as our gospel success, so that not one soul that he has predestined for glory will be lost and not one more soul gained (see Rom. 9:16). Yet God's sovereign plan of salvation requires both that Jesus should die and that we would witness in his name. "As you sent me into the world, so I have sent them into the world," Jesus prayed (John 17:18). Without the witness that he has sent you into the world to give, there cannot be salvation for those who thus would otherwise not hear the gospel. Paul asks, "How are they to believe in him of whom they have never heard? And how are they to hear without someone preaching?" (Rom. 10:14). In this light, we see the indispensable mission for which Christ sanctified each of us into the world. Romans 10:15 thus exclaims, "How beautiful are the feet of those who preach the good news!"

116

CHRISTIAN UNITY

John 17:20–23

*"I do not ask for these only, but also for those who will believe
in me through their word, that they may all be one, just as you,
Father, are in me, and I in you, that they also may be in us."*
(John 17:20–21)

tudents of the New Testament sometimes wonder where they fit
into what they are reading. It is a good question, and in our study
of the Bible we should always seek to apply the lessons directly
to ourselves. As we continue studying Jesus' Farewell Prayer in John 17, it
is not a great challenge to apply the message to ourselves, since Jesus prays
explicitly for today's believer in his Word. Having begun his prayer with a
request for his own consecration (John 17:1–5), and then continued with
his priestly prayer for the first believers (17:6–19), Jesus concludes with
petitions aimed specifically at the church that will follow in generations to
come (17:20–26). He prays: "I do not ask for these only, but also for those
who will believe in me through their word" (17:20). If you are a Christian,
you may be excited to realize that on the night of his arrest, Jesus prayed
specifically for your blessing as a member of his church.

Those Who Will Believe

Jesus' emphasis on the church that would span the generations after his coming was not a thought that he had only lately discovered. All through his ministry, Jesus had spoken in these terms. Consider his Good Shepherd Discourse in John 10. Jesus said, "I am the good shepherd. I know my own and my own know me . . . ; and I lay down my life for the sheep" (John 10:14–15). We can imagine Jesus standing with his hands outstretched toward the flock of Israel. But he immediately expanded his outreach: "And I have other sheep that are not of this fold. I must bring them also, and they will listen to my voice. So there will be one flock, one shepherd" (10:16).

This emphasis on a great worldwide church is seen from the beginning of Jesus' ministry. When he was rejected after preaching his inaugural sermon in his hometown of Nazareth, Jesus reminded his hearers that in the time of Elijah and Elisha, God had responded to hard hearts in Israel by sending his grace to the Gentiles. From the very beginning, Jesus knew that he was fulfilling God's original promise to Abraham in the covenant of grace: "in you all the families of the earth shall be blessed" (Gen. 12:3). This means that Jesus would not be astonished at the spread of the religion he had started so long ago in so humble a manner, as liberal scholars have often suggested. Instead, it was always the sovereign purpose of God the Son, in covenant with the Father and the Spirit, to erect a church through all ages for God's glory by redeeming a people with his atoning blood.

Earlier in his prayer, Jesus had asked the Father to make his church holy and protect it from corruption in the world (John 17:14–16). Christians are helped to resist being attracted to worldliness when we realize that we have been joined into a great, everlasting culture of Christian truth, worship, and life through faith in Christ. Jesus prayed that the Father would sanctify his church "in the truth" of his Word (17:17). Now, Jesus tells us that in praying for his future church, he is referring to "those who will believe in me through [the apostles'] word" (17:20). One may join an earthly church in a variety of ways, but there is only one way to join the great, redeemed, holy, and saved church for which Jesus prayed: by believing the Word of God as given through the apostles of Christ.

If Jesus looks forward in prayer to a great church that will consist of believers in his Word, then the way that we build and grow his church today is by the teaching and preaching of God's Word. Jesus originally founded the church by sending forth the apostles to preach and then to write down his gospel and its doctrines. People today are added to Christ's church in the same way: Peter said, "You have been born again, not of perishable seed but of imperishable, through the living and abiding word of God" (1 Peter 1:23).

In John 17:9, Jesus specified that he was not praying for the world but for those whom the Father had given to him. Now, in verse 20, we find that these elect people are those who will believe Christ's Word. This proves that the great issue in every life is belief or unbelief in the Word of God as it proclaims Jesus Christ. Jesus said, "Truly, truly, I say to you, whoever hears my word and believes him who sent me has eternal life. He does not come into judgment, but has passed from death to life" (5:24).

THE FIFTH MARK OF THE CHURCH: UNITY

In Jesus' prayer, our Lord sets forth his vision for the church. We see this in six marks of the church that are expressed in his petitions to the Father. So far, Jesus has prayed for the church to be marked by joy, holiness, truth, and mission. Now, he prays "that they may all be one, just as you, Father, are in me, and I in you" (John 17:21).

The topic of Christian unity has seen significant attention in recent decades. The words that Martyn Lloyd-Jones wrote a generation ago remain true today: "I suppose that if there is one thing that characterizes the life of the church and of Christian people more than anything else in this particular generation, it is the interest in what is called 'ecumenicity.' We are constantly reading about it and conferences and meetings are being held almost without intermission, with respect to it."[1] The word *ecumenism* comes from the Greek word *oikoumene*, which means "the inhabited world." Ecumenism, then, is the effort made for worldwide unity among professing Christians. Those involved in ecumenical action frequently cite Jesus' prayer in John 17:21, "that they may all be one." Christian unity is therefore an important item in Jesus' vision and must be important for Christians as well.

The first step in pursuing Christian unity, however, is defining it biblically. Here we immediately encounter the problem with ecumenism today, since

1. D. Martyn Lloyd-Jones, *Growing in the Spirit* (Westchester, IL: Crossway, 1989), 130.

it is usually assumed that Jesus was referring to an outward, physical, and organizational unity. This is the position of the Roman Catholic Church, which insists that Christian unity demands an institutional and bureaucratic oneness. Yet in looking at the early church in the book of Acts, we see the greatest spiritual vitality without a clear structural hierarchy. Rome insists that Peter was set above the other apostles by virtue of Jesus' description of his faith as the "rock" (Matt. 16:18). Yet Jesus granted his "binding" authority equally to all the apostles (18:18), and when Peter fell into error, Paul did not hesitate to rebuke him (Gal. 2:11f.). From the beginning, then, Jesus did not establish a formal hierarchy but founded his church through the conjoined action of all the apostles.

In fact, the worst periods of church history have been those with the strongest institutional unity. Consider the Middle Ages in Europe, for instance, when the church was united in a single ecclesiastical body under the papacy. James Montgomery Boice asks: "Was this a great age? Was there a deep unity of faith? Did men and women find themselves increasingly drawn to this faith and come to confess Jesus Christ to be their Savior and Lord?"[2] The answer is that under an institutional hierarchy, the gospel light was practically extinguished and the holiness, joy, truth, and mission of the church were grossly corrupted.

Reflecting on the New Testament generally, and on Jesus' prayer specifically, we may make three statements about the unity that Jesus had in mind. Christian unity is, first, *an organic, mystical unity*. The unity that Jesus defines in his prayer is patterned on the unity within the Godhead. Christians are to be one, Jesus said, "just as you, Father, are in me, and I in you, that they also may be in us" (John 17:21). I describe this as a mystical unity because we can already see that it transcends our understanding. How are three divine persons one single God, as the doctrine of the Trinity teaches? The answer is that we cannot know how this is, except to acknowledge a supernatural unity beyond our understanding.

What we can know is that this supernatural union is an organic one. We see this in the two main New Testament metaphors for the church: a body and a family. Paul wrote to the Corinthians, "For just as the body is one and has many members, and all the members of the body, though many, are

2. James Montgomery Boice, *The Gospel of John*, 5 vols. (Grand Rapids: Baker, 1999), 4:1328.

one body, so it is with Christ" (1 Cor. 12:12). Paul was stressing the mutual dependency of Christians within the church, just as a body relies on feet, hands, eyes, and ears. "The eye cannot say to the hand, 'I have no need of you,' nor again the head to the feet, 'I have no need of you'" (12:21). Moreover, like the human body, the whole church is affected by the experience of any part. "If one member suffers, all suffer together; if one member is honored, all rejoice together. Now you are the body of Christ and individually members of it" (12:26–27). Christian unity thus involves an organic oneness of service and sympathy.

The other main metaphor is that of the family, which is also an organic unity. One joins a family by being born into it: we likewise enter the true church of Christ through our new birth into saving faith. One can, however, join a family by adoption. We likewise join the family of the Trinity by being adopted into Christ (Eph. 1:5). Like any other family, the church expresses its unity by a bond of mutual commitment, affection, and common cause.

Second, we should observe that not only is church unity organic and mystical, but it is also a *spiritual union*. Jesus' prayer describes our unity by saying to the Father, "I in them and you in me, that they may become perfectly one" (John 17:23). If we ask how the Father is in the Son, the answer is complex. But if we ask how the Son is in the church, the answer is clear: through the indwelling presence of the Holy Spirit. This is exactly how Paul put it in Ephesians 4:3, saying that the church is joined by "the unity of the Spirit in the bond of peace." This is a unity that cannot be legislated or brought about by any human organization, but is rather a oneness created by the unifying presence of God's Holy Spirit.

Third, having unity in the Spirit, Christian unity is unity *in the truth*. We know that the Spirit indwells those who believe Christ's Word and, moreover, that the Word of Christ was inspired through the apostles by the Holy Spirit himself. This is what Jesus told the disciples to anticipate: "When the Spirit of truth comes, he will guide you into all the truth" (John 16:13). Jesus now prays "for those who will believe in me through their word" (17:20) that they may be one. This unity can only be, therefore, a unity in belief and in truth.

The mistake most commonly made in pursuing Christian unity today is to set aside matters of truth in order to gain unity. The reason that we cannot get along, it is argued, is an emphasis on doctrine. Since we are never going to agree on Christian truth, the only way to have unity is to dispense with doctrinal divisions.

This was the argument made by Anglican Archbishop George Carey, when he boasted of joining with Pope John Paul II and an Eastern Orthodox patriarch at a ceremony in Rome to celebrate the new millennium in the year 2000. Seeing this display of unity, we might rejoice if Carey had succeeded in winning doctrinal agreement with Rome, that the pope now embraced apostolic doctrines such as justification through faith alone and *sola Scriptura*, repudiating the unbiblical doctrines of Rome that had caused the original divide during the Protestant Reformation. But Carey did not announce accord in matters of truth; instead, he announced that for Christians to divide over doctrine is un-Christlike. "Polemics lead to hatred and division," he declared, so Christians must embrace unity without truth.[3]

This is, however, a denial of Jesus' teaching, as well as of Jesus' example throughout the Gospels. Jesus said that when the Spirit came, he would lead his church into truth (John 16:13). God's truth alone would sanctify the church, and Jesus prayed only for those who believe the truth. How can Christians, then, have unity without truth? The answer is that a unity without truth is something other than Christian unity. The unity that our Lord was concerned about is a spiritual unity in the truth of the gospel. Therefore, it is truth that determines the bounds of our unity, just as it is in the truth that the Spirit bonds us as one. Lloyd-Jones expressed the implications of truth for Christian unity:

> There are many people in this world who call themselves Christians, yet who, alas, regard the Lord Jesus Christ as nothing but a man. Well, all I can say to this is that I have no fellowship with such people. I have no unity with them for they take from the very foundation and basis of my faith, and my whole position and standing. What do these people believe about the work of the Lord Jesus Christ? What is their view of his death? . . . Is it a substitutionary death? Is it the Son of God dying because that is the only way whereby my sins may be forgiven, and therefore the essential preliminary to my becoming a child of God, and a partaker of the divine nature? If it is essential, and the other man says it is not, how can it be possible for there to be unity

3. Archbishop of Canterbury George Carey, *Sermon at Ecumenical Vespers, Anglican/Vatican Consultations,* May 17, 2000, http://www.archbishopofcanterbury.org.

between us? And the same is true with all these other cardinal doctrines of the Christian faith.[4]

Three observations will help us apply the principle of unity in the truth. First, Christian unity requires us to believe what the Bible says. To remove obedience to Scripture does not promote but rather destroys true spiritual unity. Second, Christian unity requires us not to add to the Bible. Sadly, man-made rules and extrabiblical doctrines have often divided Christians who should be one.

Third, unity in truth requires us to discern essential and nonnegotiable doctrines from those that are not essential to Christian oneness. This raises the question: does the Bible specify which teachings are essential? The answer is Yes. The New Testament explicitly identifies the following: the deity of Jesus (John 20:31), Jesus as the Christ, that is, the world's only Savior (1 John 2:22), Christ's death as a substitutionary atonement (1 Cor. 15:3), Christ's bodily resurrection (1 Cor. 15:4), and justification through faith alone (Gal. 1:8). Unity in truth also requires us to agree on the inspiration and inerrancy of God's Word, apart from which its authority is compromised. Doctrines other than these core teachings are not essential to Christian unity, however important and beloved they are. Among these is our view of baptism, eschatological positions, and precise details of church governance. Lloyd-Jones writes, "There are certain great doctrines about which there never has been unity in the Christian church and I take it there never will be, but I would not separate from any brother or sister on matters like that."[5] Francis Schaeffer agreed with this position, writing:

> The real chasm must be between true Bible-believing Christians and others, not at a lesser point. The chasm is not between Lutherans and everybody else, or Baptists and everybody else, or Presbyterians and everybody else.... The real chasm is between those who have bowed to the living God and His Son Jesus Christ—and thus also to the verbal, propositional communication of God's Word, the Scripture—and those who have not.[6]

4. Lloyd-Jones, *Growing in the Spirit*, 139.
5. Ibid.
6. Francis A. Schaeffer, *The Church at the End of the Twentieth Century*, in *The Complete Works of Francis A. Schaeffer*, 5 vols. (Westchester, IL: Crossway, 1982), 4:102.

We might observe that denominational distinctions are usually formed on a narrower basis than the bare essentials of Christian belief. For this very reason, denominations should encourage spiritual unity among all true Christians. As institutional unions, denominations not only foster unity within themselves, but permit a spirit of oneness that transcends detailed agreements on doctrine and practice. Consider the disagreement among Christians over the rite of baptism. Since Presbyterians and Baptists are not institutionally joined, they do not have to argue endlessly over this doctrine. Instead, despite our denominational boundaries, we can enjoy and cultivate a unity in spirit and mission with all others who believe God's Word and embrace the vital doctrines of the Christian gospel.

Once, when I was ministering in Philadelphia, I received a phone call from the new pastor of a notoriously liberal church. It turned out that the man was an evangelical, and he wanted fellowship and advice on introducing biblical faith to his congregation. Because we were not in the same denomination, we did not have to argue about the various lesser issues on which we differed, and it was my delight to meet often for prayer with this struggling brother, sharing a unity in gospel truth that transcended our denominational differences.

SO THAT THE WORLD MAY BELIEVE

Having defined Christian unity, we must now emphasize its importance in light of Jesus' prayer. Organic, spiritual unity in the truth is not an option for believers, especially within a local congregation. In working out the significance of Christian unity, Jesus highlights reasons why believers should prize and serve the cause of oneness in the church.

Jesus prays for the unity of his church, first, *for the sake of his people's blessing.* He asks "that they may all be one, just as you, Father, are in me, and I in you, that they also may be in us" (John 17:21). He adds, "The glory that you have given me I have given to them, that they may be one even as we are one" (17:22). This raises a question as to how we should understand the "glory" that Jesus has given to his church. The best answer is his manifestation of the character and blessing of God. Jesus has granted eternal life to his people, and this consists of the whole life of God within

463

their experience: a life of joy, peace, and love through faith in Christ. This experience of blessing in the church requires spiritual unity. Along these lines, Jesus concludes verse 23 by noting that the Father "loved them even as you loved me." D. A. Carson comments that "Christians themselves have been caught up into the love of the Father for the Son, secure and content and fulfilled because loved by the Almighty himself, with the very same love he reserves for his Son."[7]

The blessing of the Father's extravagant love forms a strong appeal for Christians to be one. We are loved by the Father in just the same way as and with just the same intensity and fervor with which the Father loves the Son. How greatly, then, we should dread that any grievance, preference, or agenda of our own should divide the family of God and diminish our experience of the divine love at work in us through our bond of faith in Christ.

There is, however, another great reason for Christians to prize and serve the cause of unity in the church. Jesus prays for unity, also, *for the sake of his people's witness.* He asks for our unity, "so that the world may believe that you have sent me" (John 17:21), and "so that the world may know that you sent me and loved them even as you loved me" (17:23). This prayer does not promise, as some ecumenists pedantically insist, that if we can achieve outward, institutional unity among Christian denominations, then the world will be converted to Christ. What it does say is that our gospel mission relies in large part on our unity in the faith.

It has always been those who are united in gospel truth who have turned the world upside-down for Christ. In Jesus' thinking, a church that adorns the gospel truth with a living testimony of God's supernatural love cannot fail to gain the world's attention. Such a world, even while persisting in unbelief, finds it difficult to argue against the reality that Christ was sent on God's mission of love to his people. Bruce Milne comments: "A group of Christians who are so knit together in the love of God that others can say of them, 'Look how they love each other,' is a church where the gospel will be 'the power of God for . . . salvation'" (Rom. 1:16).[8]

---

7. D. A. Carson, *The Gospel of John* (Grand Rapids: Eerdmans, 1991), 569.

8. Bruce Milne, *The Message of John: Here Is Your King!* (Downers Grove, IL: InterVarsity Press, 1993), 250.

A GOOD CHURCH

Even as we seek Christian oneness, we should remember that it is Christ's work, and Christ's prayer, that achieves our unity. Unity is a blessing that Christians have and are therefore to enjoy and protect. We *will* enjoy oneness as believers because Jesus prayed for this to happen and because the Father is sure to send the Holy Spirit to indwell all those who believe. It will therefore be our joy, and a cause of our praise to Christ, to experience a spiritual unity with all who love the truth of Christ through Spirit-wrought faith in God's Word.

Harry Ironside relates such an experience on a train ride he took in the early twentieth century. The first morning, he began his day as always by reading from his Bible. A German woman came by and asked him what he was doing. When he told her, she said, "Wait, I go get my Bible and we have it together." Sometime later, a Scandinavian man saw them. "Reading the Bible?" he asked. "Well, I think I'll get mine, too." Soon, a great number of people in their train car were taking part in the Bible study, which gathered every day during the long traverse of a continent. Before long, the conductor was advertising the Bible meeting to all the cars, hymns and prayers were added, and a service was started at which Ironside would preach. When they finally arrived at their destination and the passengers disembarked, the German woman who had started it all came to Ironside and asked, "What denomination are you?" He answered, "I belong to the same denomination that David did." "What was that?" she asked. "I didn't know that David belonged to any." Ironside replied, "I am a companion of all them that fear Thee and keep Thy precepts." The lady replied, "Yah, yah, that is a good church to belong to."[9]

---

9. Harry Ironside, *Ephesians* (1937; repr., Neptune, NJ: Loizeaux, 2000), 105–6.

117

To See My Glory

John 17:24

"Father, I desire that they also, whom you have given me, may be with me where I am, to see my glory that you have given me because you loved me before the foundation of the world."
(John 17:24)

I have been told that confession is good for the soul. I therefore want to confess that I am a glory-seeker. My flesh and heart cry out to see and enter glory. You might ascribe this longing to my upbringing, which did in part focus on achieving glory, or to quirks of my personality. However true these may be, there is a deeper and more fundamental explanation for my glory-seeking: God made me this way. Indeed, God made all mankind to be glory-seekers, for he said, "Let us make man in our image" (Gen. 1:26). God is himself a glory-seeker, and he made man to revel in and reflect his glory. What the Westminster Shorter Catechism says of man is equally true of God himself: God's chief end is to glorify God. Our own longing for glory explains mankind's otherwise mad obsession with sports championships, military triumph, Hollywood glitter, beauty-pageant splendor, and the shining radiance of new cars, houses, and other objects of glory. We crave glory!

The tragedy of mankind is not that we seek glory. Rather, the tragedy is that we swallow the false glory of sin, embrace the tainted glory of the flesh, and revel in the vainglory of the praise of men. The glory of the gospel is that Jesus came to redeem us to partake of his true glory that gives life. Jesus prayed to the Father for his people: "I desire that they also, whom you have given me, may be with me where I am, to see my glory that you have given me" (John 17:24).

THE ASSURANCE OF OUR SALVATION

As we eavesdrop on Jesus' prayer to the Father, we are first shown the source of our hope for glory, and the true source of our assurance in salvation. The question is rightly asked by many a troubled believer: on what ground may I be certain of arriving safe in the glories of heaven? The answer is never going to be found within ourselves. We know our weakness and our tendency to change. Our faith is strong today, but how will tomorrow's troubles shake it? Looking within ourselves for assurance of salvation can lead only to a fearful dread of what tomorrow may bring.

What if we listen to Christ's prayer on the night of his arrest? Here, we find the answer to our quest. Praying as High Priest for the people entrusted to his ministry, Jesus places the capstone in the bridge that will lead us into heaven. He prays, "Father, I desire that they also, whom you have given me, may be with me where I am" (John 17:24). The King James Version renders this idea more effectively, for Christ was not merely expressing a desire or wish in his prayer, but communicating his sovereign will for us to the Father. "Father," he prays, "I will that they . . . be with me where I am."

Our hope of salvation is held up by nothing less than the saving will of God the Son for the people given to him by the Father. Benjamin Morgan Palmer reflected:

When you see that High Priest coming up from the altar and standing before the throne, and in the very midst of that throne saying to His Father, "Father, I will," are we not safe? Let the devil howl; let him come with all his retinue from the depths of hell, and rage and raven all over this earth . . . , let the world enter into fatal conspiracy with the powers of darkness and rage around

us . . . , and in the midst of all this peril, in the power of intercession, in the
royalty and in the grace of our ascending Head, we are safe.[1]

When we realize our blessed reliance on the intercessory ministry of
Christ our High Priest, we perceive the vital significance of his resurrection.
Jesus prayed on the night of his arrest, expressing his will to the Father. We
may marvel: what an advocate his followers had! But what happened? Jesus
was arrested that evening, and on the next day he was cruelly put to death. If
he could not save himself, how then can his will succeed in saving us? Apart
from the resurrection, we must take up the lament uttered by the Emmaus
road disciples: "we had hoped that he was the one to redeem Israel" (Luke
24:21)—but those hopes were dashed in Jesus' death on the cross. In the
resurrection, however, we see a demonstration of Christ's power to achieve
the saving will he expresses in his prayer with the Father. This is what we
sing about on Easter morning:

> Hear the earth protest and tremble, see the stone removed with pow'r;
> All hell's minions may assemble, but cannot withstand his hour.
> He has conquered, he has conquered, Christ the Lord, the risen King![2]

Our assurance of salvation, then, is grounded in the will of Christ that
conquered sin and death in his resurrection.

The resurrection seems to provide the perspective for Jesus' prayer that
his people "may be with me where I am" (John 17:24). At that moment, the
disciples were with Jesus, probably in the Kidron Valley, just before their
entry into the garden of Gethsemane. It is evident, however, that Jesus was
looking forward to his victory, seeing already his triumphant return to the
glories of heaven. Jesus expresses his saving will in light of his foreordained
triumph in returning on high. He sees himself already resurrected and
ascended into heaven, and wills that believers in him will join him there
on high. Can a believer be sure of entering into heaven? The answer is Yes,
for Christ has set forth his will for us to be with him where he was going.

By what right, however, does Jesus express his will before the Father in
heaven? Is this prayer something more than a child's request, which a father

---

1. B. M. Palmer, *Sermons*, 2 vols. (1875; repr., Harrisonburg, VA: Sprinkle, 2002), 1:390.
2. Jack W. Hayford, "Worship Christ, the Risen King!" (1986).

may choose to answer or decline? What makes this petition a source of assurance for us? We can first answer by pointing out the heavenly Father's infinite delight in his holy Son. How often has the reader of the New Testament heard the Father say of him: "This is my beloved Son, with whom I am well pleased; listen to him" (Matt. 17:5). The Father who thus spoke to the disciples loves to hear the voice of his Son as well, and we can be sure that the holy Father will grant the petition of his beloved and holy Son.

But Jesus claims another right to exercise his will in the presence of the Father, namely, his redeeming work for our salvation. Jesus comes forth as High Priest for the people whose names he bears, offering his blood to fulfill his covenant with the Father. The writer of Hebrews grounds our blessing on "the blood of the eternal covenant" (Heb. 13:20), by virtue of which Christ speaks with the right of salvation on behalf of those for whom he came to die.

Seeing the believer's assurance in the priestly ministry of Christ, we see the necessity of belonging to Jesus if we desire to be saved. Who else but Jesus has the legal right to declare his saving will in the presence of God the Father? Who else has the standing that Jesus possesses as the wholly beloved, perfectly obedient and righteous Son, armed with the covenantal authority to save God's elect?

Many people reject turning to Christ as their Savior and imagine the conversation they will have as they stand before God. Each, in his own way, imagines expressing his will for his own salvation and his demands in vindicating his life. Some will claim their supposed merits, and others imagine that they will accuse God of his supposed faults or the supposed lack of evidence to compel them to believe. But none but Jesus can actually stand before God the Father and declare, "I will." All others will find themselves in Job's awestruck shoes when God finally revealed himself in his glorious majesty. Job foolishly imagined presenting his case before God until he finally saw him. Then he cried out, "I despise myself, and repent in dust and ashes" (Job 42:6). Those were the words of a foolish believer. What will be the case of those outside of Christ, those who spurned him as Savior and Lord? Will they stand before God to speak forth, "I will"? Instead they will cry out to the mountains and rocks: "Fall on us and hide us from the face of him who is seated on the throne, and from the wrath of the Lamb, for the great day of their wrath has come, and who can stand?" (Rev. 6:16–17). The reality is that only Jesus will stand to declare his sovereign will from the seat of heaven's throne. Only those who belong to him, who were given to him by the Father and who trust Jesus as Savior, will be saved by the will of Christ, who loves his own. We must, therefore, believe in Jesus Christ if we will be saved.

CHRIST'S HEART FOR HIS OWN

Christ's prayer in John 17:24 shows not only the assurance of salvation for all who believe in him, but also the love in Christ's heart for his people. Here is God the Son praying in the shadow of his deadly rendezvous with the cross, yet his heart is lifted up for his flock. Hebrews 12:2 declares that "for the joy that was set before him endured the cross, despising the shame," and that joy is expressed in his longing for his own to join him in glory: "Father, I desire that they also, whom you have given me, may be with me where I am."

We see here the remarkable reality of Christ's longing for the fellowship of his people. Jesus does not merely say that he wills for his people to enter into heaven but expresses his desire that they may be "with me." This plea should relieve us of the tendency to think of Jesus as something other than fully human, with all the right and God-given desires of the human heart, including the longing for loving companionship. Anyone with a shred of humanity knows the longing to be with one's own people, those whom we love and who love us. Who does not know what it is to grieve the parting of a dear one who has died? Whose face has not been streaked with tears at a cruel parting? Who has not known the joy of a long-awaited reunion with family and dearly beloved friends? Matthew Henry applies this principle to the heart of our Lord: "Christ speaks here as if he did not count his own happiness complete unless he had his elect to share with him in it."[3]

How many of us have found that unless we can share the great moments of our lives with others, then even our triumphs feel hollow? So it is for our greathearted Savior: "The triumph of the great day when he comes to judge the living and the dead will occasion a celebration like no other, and he wants his people to be there."[4] As much as we look forward to the fulfillment of

---

3. Matthew Henry, *Commentary on the Whole Bible*, 6 vols. (Peabody, MA: Hendrickson, 2009), 5:942.

4. Gordon J. Keddie, *A Study Commentary on John*, 2 vols. (Darlington, UK: Evangelical Press, 2001), 2:275.

God's promises for our salvation, so also does Jesus look forward to having us to "eat and drink at my table in my kingdom" (Luke 22:30) and, after conquering in his name, "to sit with me on my throne, as I also conquered and sat down with my Father on his throne" (Rev. 3:21).

Another way to understand Christ's desire for our presence in heaven is that the Redeemer longs to enjoy that love that he purchased at so great a cost. The book of Ruth tells of the love between the Moabitess Ruth and Boaz, a wealthy and godly Bethlehemite. Boaz sets his eye on Ruth, and she offers her love. But he must redeem her land in order to have the right of marriage. With what anxiety and energy Boaz set about his work! Naomi, Ruth's mother-in-law, observed, "The man will not rest but will settle the matter today" (Ruth 3:18). Boaz cheerfully made the necessary payment, just as Christ gladly freed us from our sin by his blood (1 John 1:7). As quickly as possible, Boaz then took Ruth as his wife, and they entered into God's blessing together. Christ likewise longs to enjoy that which he has redeemed, and he reveals the desire of his heart when he prays to the Father, "I desire that they also, whom you have given me, may be with me where I am" (John 17:24).

If Christ's *right* to win our salvation shows the *necessity* of belonging to him, his *desire* for us shows the *blessing* of belonging to Jesus. Christians, though often despised on earth, are desired by Christ in heaven. Believers, though often unlovely in appearance and even character on earth, will then be shining with the beauty of a perfected holiness. Anticipating the resurrection life that he has gained for us, Christ sees his bride even now dressed in all her glorious resurrection white. "With me" is Christ's language of love for his people, and his desire for our presence burned in his heart in the shadow of the cross.

In response, "with Christ" is the language of our longing for heaven. For to those who know Jesus and have drawn near to his love in faith, the joy of heaven is being there with Jesus in it. Indeed, to be "with Jesus" is the Christian's definition of heaven. We would agree with Samuel Rutherford, who declared, "O my Lord Jesus Christ, if I could be in heaven without thee, it would be a hell; and if I could be in hell, and have thee still, it would be a heaven to me, for thou art all the heaven I want."[5] George Hutcheson writes:

---

5. Quoted in Charles H. Spurgeon, *Morning and Evening: Daily Readings* (Grand Rapids: Zondervan, 1975), Devotional for January 17.

The glory and happiness of heaven to the elect will consist much in being in Christ's company, in whom they delight so much on earth, to follow the Lamb whithersoever he goeth, and to enjoy him fully, without separation any more; for so is heaven here described in Christ's prayer, "that they may be with me where I am."[6]

SEEING HIS GLORY

Finally, Jesus sets forth the crowning gift that he has prepared for his people. When we visit a friend's house, it is our custom to offer a small gift. But Christ has prepared a gift of infinite worth for his own when we enter into heaven: "to see my glory that you have given me" (John 17:24). This is what believers have to look forward to in the life to come: not streets paved with gold, but the utter and complete fulfillment of our very beings as creatures made in God's image; to see God the Son in his glory and to be elevated by him into a share of his inheritance in glory. Paul thus writes that as children of God, we are "heirs of God and fellow heirs with Christ, provided we suffer with him in order that we may also be glorified with him" (Rom. 8:17).

When Jesus says that we will see his glory, we may consider this in a number of ways. First, we will see true manhood glorified. When Jacob's sons went to Egypt seeking food, they trembled in awe before the majesty and power of the prince of Egypt. But the greater marvel was their realization that this prince was none other than their brother Joseph. We will likewise behold the glory of Christ in heaven and marvel with great joy that the Lord is our brother and fellow man. In the human form that he took up in the incarnation, humbling himself and setting aside his heavenly splendor while on earth, Jesus is now enabled to reveal his glory more perfectly to the objects of his love. Palmer writes, "When we are raised to sit with Him upon His throne, we shall behold His glorified humanity—behold Him, not as His disciples beheld Him, 'the man of sorrows and acquainted with grief,' but in that glorified human form in which He shall always be present to the sight and to the embrace of the saints above."[7]

6. George Hutcheson, *Exposition of the Gospel of John* (Lafayette, IN: Sovereign Grace Publishers, 2001), 370.

7. Palmer, *Sermons*, 2:399.

While we will see Jesus in human form in heaven, it will yet be the glory of his deity that shines on us. A vision of Christ's divine glory was granted to his disciples at certain key points in Jesus' earthly ministry. Most prominent was Christ's transfiguration upon the mount. Taking with him his three closest disciples, Peter, John, and James, Jesus went up to the mount. There, "he was transfigured before them, and his face shone like the sun, and his clothes became white as light" (Matt. 17:2). Interestingly, Jesus told them not to reveal what they saw until after his resurrection (17:9). It was in his postresurrection appearances that Jesus revealed his divine glory to all the disciples. Seeing him in splendor, "they came up and took hold of his feet and worshiped him" (28:9). We will do the same when Jesus brings us to himself and reveals his divine glory to our eyes. Not only will our worship of Jesus in the radiance of his personal glory be the consummation of our faith, but it will provide the ultimate satisfaction for our souls, of which our present worship on earth is the closest foretaste.

Jesus comments to the Father that the glory we will see in heaven is "my glory that you have given me because you loved me before the foundation of the world" (John 17:24). Therefore, it is not merely the glory of his incarnate manhood, which Jesus took to himself, nor merely the glory of his divine being, which Jesus possessed from all eternity. Ultimately, Jesus speaks of his mediatorial glory in the office that the Father has given him as Redeemer and Head over the church. Paul concludes his great chapter on the grace of God in Christ, Ephesians 1, with a crescendo of the glory that the Father has given to his Son in the resurrection and ascension: the Father

> raised him from the dead and seated him at his right hand in the heavenly places, far above all rule and authority and power and dominion, and above every name that is named, not only in this age but also in the one to come. And he put all things under his feet and gave him as head over all things to the church, which is his body, the fullness of him who fills all in all. (Eph. 1:20–23)

The glory given to Christ upon his return to heaven is that glory he earned by saving us from our sins and making himself our covenant Lord. Jesus adds the remarkable statement that the Father ordained this glory for his Son "because you loved me before the foundation of the world" (John 17:24). Here again, our salvation is grounded in God's love for his Son, by which the Father willed that Christ should be glorified as the Head of a redeemed people forever.

We see why the scenes of worship in the book of Revelation, which one day we will join above, show that it is the Lamb upon the throne who is worshiped with great awe and joy. John tells us that at the center of heaven's worship he saw "a Lamb standing, as though it had been slain" (Rev. 5:6). "Worthy is the Lamb who was slain," the heavenly chorus cried, "to receive power and wealth and wisdom and might and honor and glory and blessing!" (5:12).

It is therefore Christ as our Mediator, Christ the slain Lamb of God who purchased our redemption, who gains the worship of our hearts even now. It was the sight of Christ's pierced hands and feet that overcame Thomas's doubt, so that he worshiped Jesus, exclaiming, "My Lord and my God!" (John 20:28). Likewise, as Thomas Manton wrote, "We go to heaven to study divinity in the Lamb's face."[8]

With this glorious anticipation, we draw our final lesson from Jesus' great prayer in John 17:24. His petition to the Father reveals Christ's saving will as the ground of our assurance, so that we see the necessity of belonging to Jesus. His heart opens to show us his great longing for us, so that we perceive the remarkable blessing of belonging to Jesus. Finally, Christ has declared our inheritance with him, so that Christians may now see the destiny of all who belong to Jesus. Paul notes how this anticipation makes all the difference to us in a present world of woe: "this light momentary affliction is preparing for us an eternal weight of glory beyond all comparison" (2 Cor. 4:17).

HALLELUJAH!

A few days before his death, I had the privilege of meeting with a small group of friends in the home of the well-known Bible teacher James Montgomery Boice. We had come to see our pastor for one last time before he departed from us and entered into the glorious presence of Christ. It was because of our awareness of the occasion that we spent the majority of our time there singing. We sang a number of hymns that Dr. Boice had written,

8. Quoted in Keddie, *John*, 2:276.

a couple of which had only just been put to melody, so we wanted him to hear them sung before he died. Most moving was one of his hymns that had become a powerful testimony to us all during the brief period of his fatal illness. The hymn was titled "Hallelujah," and the lyrics were based on the great refrain at the end of Romans 8, where Paul reminds us that nothing can separate a believer from the love of God in Christ Jesus. One stanza of the hymn reads:

> Victors we're ordained to be
> By the God who set us free.
> What can therefore conquer me?
> Nothing. Hallelujah![9]

That hymn is not a testimony to self-confidence but rather to utter assurance of victory in Christ. Each verse of the hymn concludes with the words, "Nothing. Hallelujah!" and it was one of the great thrills of my life to see the eyes of the man who had led me to faith in Christ light up and his fist of victory held high when we came to the words: "Nothing. Hallelujah!" It was the dying testimony of a man who knew that he was only just beginning to live, since in Christ death for him would be merely a gateway into glory forever.

The burning question is how you can be sure of the same victory. How can you face death with the joy of certain glory? The answer is that you can know that you will be glorified with Jesus *then* if you glory in Jesus *now*. Do you believe that Jesus is the Son of God? Do you believe that God's Son came to earth in a human nature so that he could live a perfect life and then offer that perfect life as a Sacrifice to free you from your sins? Do you believe that, having died for sins, Jesus was raised from the grave and rose to the glory of his eternal kingdom on high, so that he reigns forever as Lord and King?

If you do not know the answer, then it is the urgent question of your life that you must seek. Ask Jesus to reveal his glory to you in the pages of Scripture, and to open your heart to believe the truth regarding God's Son and our Savior. If you will not seek the glory of Christ, should you

---

9. James Montgomery Boice, "Hallelujah!" in *Hymns for a Modern Reformation* (Philadelphia: Tenth Presbyterian Church, 2000), no. 5.

not marvel at the longing of your heart? Do you really think that the glory you desire is merely that of this world? If you do seek after Jesus, and if you believe on him for your own soul's salvation, you will learn that Christ has willed you to be with him in glory, so that you will spend eternity basking in the light of the glory of God—the glory for which we were made—in the face of a loving Christ forever. Living in the knowledge of that glory, you will be a victor now, with the privilege of offering your life as a hymn that says "Hallelujah" to the Lamb who was slain and rose from the dead.

118

GOD'S LOVE IN US

John 17:25–26

"O righteous Father, even though the world does not know you,
I know you, and these know that you have sent me. I made
known to them your name, and I will continue to make it
known, that the love with which you have loved me may be in
them, and I in them." (John 17:25–26)

T hroughout the centuries, men and women have employed different symbols to show that they are Christians. In the early days, believers used the fish symbol to identify themselves to one another, the Greek spelling of *fish* serving as an acronym for the words *Jesus Christ, Son of God, Savior*. In the medieval era, dedicated Christians received special haircuts. Today, some Christians wear a cross on their lapel or on a chain to identify themselves as followers of Christ. According to the New Testament, however, there is a better sign than any of these, given by Jesus to mark his people in all generations: the mark of love.

As we come to the end of Jesus' High Priestly Prayer, we are given the sixth mark of his church. Jesus asks the Father to fill his people with love: "that the love with which you have loved me may be in them" (John 17:26). Love is not only the last mark of the church, but also the greatest. This was, at least, the opinion of the apostle Paul. In his great "love" chapter, 1 Corinthians 13, he concludes: "So now faith, hope, and love abide, these three; but the greatest of these is love" (1 Cor. 13:13). If we desire a higher authority than Paul, we need only consult the Lord Jesus Christ. At the beginning of his farewell address, Jesus taught: "A new commandment I give to you, that you love one another: just as I have loved you, you also are to love one another. By this all people will know that you are my disciples, if you have love for one another" (John 13:34–35). Reflecting on the priority of love for a Christian, Francis Schaeffer commented: "Evangelism is a calling, but not the first calling. Building congregations is a calling, but not the first calling. A Christian's first call is to . . . return to the first commandment to love God, to love the brotherhood, and then to love one's neighbor as himself."[1]

THE SOURCE OF LOVE: KNOWING GOD

According to some people, the greatest threat to Christian love is Christian truth, especially distinctive doctrinal truths. There are two kinds of Christians, they argue: those who care about doctrine and those who show love. The problem with this viewpoint—this false dichotomy—is that Jesus indicates that the source of love among God's people is knowledge of the truth concerning the Father. Jesus says that in order for his people to have God's love, he has made the truth of the Father known to them: "O righteous Father," he prays, "I made known to them your name" (John 17:25–26).

Jesus' statement tells us three important things about truth as it relates to Christian love. The first is that *the knowledge of God is the source of Christian love*. In Jesus' understanding, knowing who God is, what God is like, and what God has done is an incalculable blessing. Jesus sums up his whole work in terms of revealing God and his name to his people: "even though the world does not know you, I know you . . . . I made known to them your name" (John 17:25–26). The "name" of God refers to his nature and character—who and what God is—and Jesus sees the revelation of God's name as the key achievement of his ministry before going to the cross.

Jesus highlights two features of God's character, both of which move us to love. The first is God's righteousness: "O righteous Father," Jesus begins.

1. Francis A. Schaeffer, *Genesis in Space & Time*, in *The Complete Works of Francis A. Schaeffer*, 5 vols. (Westchester, IL: Crossway, 1982), 1:85.

It is not obvious why Jesus notes God's righteousness here. He could be connecting with the prayer of the previous verse, in which Jesus claimed his right to bring his people into heaven with him. In that case, he is relying on God's righteousness to fulfill his covenant obligations. Jesus could also be noting God's distinction between the world and his church, since God separates the two groups based on righteousness. Whatever Jesus' precise intent, we realize that God's righteousness is essential to who God is—to his "name." One of the reasons the world does not know the Father is that it has no idea of his righteousness. The world never imagines that God will judge all sin in perfect justice. Even more tragically, the world does not realize that God offers righteousness as a gift to sinners who trust in the perfect life and sin-atoning death of Jesus. Believers, knowing God's righteous hatred of sin and delighting in the free gift of righteousness in Christ, respond with a great love for the God who loved us while we were yet sinners (Rom. 5:8). If you have realized God's mercy in extending righteousness to you at the cost of his own Son, then your heart has been moved by the marvel of God's grace and love.

When Jesus speaks of God's "name," he is appealing directly to God's love. We know this because of John's teaching in his first epistle, which serves as a commentary on the theology of his Gospel. There, John sums up the nature of God by writing, "God is love" (1 John 4:8). From this, John argues that we should "love one another, for love is from God, and whoever loves has been born of God and knows God . . . , because God is love" (4:7–8).

This leads to a vitally important point, namely, that an increased knowledge of God—that is, theology—must rightly result in a corresponding love for God and the love of God working in us. I noted that some Christians see an emphasis on truth as a barrier to Christian love. One reason for this opinion is personal experience with doctrinally motivated believers. People complain that our doctrine has impressed our minds but has not pierced our hearts. If that is so, then it can only be because we have not known the truth about God as well as we think we have. Paul warned Timothy about doctrinally argumentative people, insisting that "the aim of our charge is love that issues from a pure heart and a good conscience and a sincere faith" (1 Tim. 1:5). He warned the Corinthians that "knowledge puffs up, but love builds up" (1 Cor. 8:1). Paul was not saying that a loving Christian cares little for matters of truth: Paul himself was most fierce in defense of the great gospel truths, just as Jesus ferociously attacked the false teaching of the Pharisees. What Paul was warning against was an attitude toward truth that is clinical, cold, and proudly possessive.

Christian truth, in contrast, is never disconnected from the God who has revealed himself in Scripture: the God of mercy and love (see Ex. 33:19). Therefore, to grow in our knowledge of the character and being of God is to be changed with awe, humility, and joy in the Lord. To understand the doctrines of grace that Jesus has so strongly emphasized in this High Priestly Prayer—doctrines such as sovereign election, particular redemption, and the perseverance of the saints—is to be melted by the love of Christ so that our love for others grows. In this way, a true grasp of the knowledge of God can only instill in us a patient, merciful, Christ-honoring love for everyone that we know.

Jesus' second emphasis is that *knowing God accounts for the difference between Christ's people and the world*: "O righteous Father, even though the world does not know you, I know you, and these know that you have sent me" (John 17:25). The reason that Jesus was about to suffer the cross was the world's rejection of his revelation of God; the Jews charged him with blasphemy, since he claimed to speak and act for God. The religious leaders rejected the idea of God's righteousness for sinners, which is one reason why they had so little love in their proud, self-righteous hearts. The followers of Christ are those who know Jesus as the true revelation of God the Father, believing that the Father sent him to lead us into both truth and love.

This doctrinal difference accounts for the fundamental difference in the matter of love. Christians love one another the way they do—living in humble, servant fellowship as husbands and wives, parents and children, employers and employees, neighbors and church members—precisely because of what Jesus has taught them about God. Likewise, it is precisely because of its ignorance of God's character and of his saving work in Christ that the world lives in such perpetual selfishness, hostility, and mutual exploitation. Without a personal belief in the true and living God, there is no basis for a life of humble, servant, sacrificial love like that which was modeled and taught by Jesus. This means that if you desire to experience the love of which the Bible speaks, you must first come to know the God of the Bible through faith in the Son whom he sent, Jesus Christ.

Third, Jesus notes that *he will continue to lead his people into truth, that they may grow in God's love*. There was much for Jesus yet to reveal about

God, and in the cross, the resurrection, Christ's ascension, the sending of the Spirit at Pentecost, and the ministry of the apostles in founding the early church, Christ would "continue to make [God] known" (John 17:26). We should note that with the writing of the New Testament, the canon of God's revealed Word was brought to completion. Yet Christ continues today to lead his people into knowledge of the Father, through our study of the Word, our personal lives as disciples, and our service to God's kingdom.

This shows that every Christian is to be growing in the knowledge of God, especially through an openhearted study of Scripture, with the result that our love for God and others will expand and be enriched. How can you be a more loving husband or wife? How can you be a more devoted parent or a more obedient child? How can you have a better attitude at work and a more caring heart for people? The answer is through a growing knowledge of God's character and saving work as you study God's Word and devote yourself to prayer. Just as Jesus asked the Father to "sanctify them in the truth; your Word is truth" (John 17:17), he now promises the Father to "continue to make [him] known" (17:26).

THE SIXTH MARK OF THE CHURCH: LOVE

We have identified six marks of the church in Christ's prayer: joy, holiness, truth, mission, unity, and love. James Montgomery Boice points out the importance of love by imagining the other five marks of the church without love. He asks, "Suppose you take joy and subtract love from it? What do you have? You have hedonism. You have an exuberance in life and its pleasures, but without the sanctifying joy found in relationship to the Lord Jesus Christ."[2] We see something similar if we remove love from holiness. In this case, "You get self-righteousness, the kind of virtue that characterized the Pharisees of Christ's day. By the standards of the day the Pharisees lived very holy lives, but they did not love others and were ready to kill Christ when he challenged their standards, and actually did kill him. They were hypocrites."[3]

What happens when we take love out of truth? The result is the kind of bitter truth that I have already spoken against, the kind of truth that might

2. James Montgomery Boice, *The Gospel of John*, 5 vols. (Grand Rapids: Baker, 1999), 4:1348.
3. Ibid.

be accurate but repels people away from Christ rather than attracting them to him. What about mission without truth? Here we have imperialism, in which people are dominated in the name of Christ rather than set free and empowered to serve Christ to the utmost. Finally, what is unity without love? Here, the answer is tyranny. History notes many examples of church hierarchies that exhibit no compassion for people, no humility or accountability to others, and exploitation in the place of the ministry of God's grace in Christ.

On the other hand, we may see that the other marks of the church express the great principle of love in all our various relationships. What is the result of love for God as our Father? The answer is *joy*! What do love for and devotion to Jesus instill in our lives but a passion to please him in *holiness*? In his first epistle, John says that believers rejoice in the love of God that will someday make us like Jesus. He concludes, "Everyone who thus hopes in him purifies himself as he is pure" (1 John 3:3). What is the result of a love for the Word of God, but a commitment to *truth*? Love for the world breeds *mission*. And love for our fellow Christians expresses itself in true spiritual *unity*.[4]

It is no wonder, then, that Jesus concludes his great prayer for the church, in the hearing of his disciples, on the note of love. In this way, he fittingly wraps up the events of this most remarkable evening, before he goes forward to embrace the cross. John 13:1 began the account of Jesus' last meeting with his disciples by saying, "Having loved his own who were in the world, he loved them to the end." So it is not surprising that at the end of the prayer that accompanied Jesus' teaching, he concludes with an emphasis on love in his people.

LOVE AT WORK IN THE CHURCH

When we remember John's words about Jesus' love for the disciples at the beginning of the Last Supper, with Jesus stooping to wash the disciples' dirty feet, we are reminded that Christian love is always active and practical, never merely notional. So what does love consist of as it is actually lived out in the church? One apostolic leader who considered this matter was the writer of the book of Hebrews. He concluded his letter to persecuted Jewish believ-

4. Ibid.

ers with an exhortation to love: "Let brotherly love continue" (Heb. 13:1). The next verses work this principle out in two dimensions. Christians are to engage in loving fellowship and are lovingly to minister to the needs and burdens of others.

In terms of loving fellowship, the writer of Hebrews emphasized the essential Christian practice of hospitality: "Do not neglect to show hospitality to strangers, for thereby some have entertained angels unawares" (Heb. 13:2). The idea is that of bringing people into our homes for fellowship. In the ancient world, where traveling was dangerous and there were few inns, this was an important ministry. Today, with our compartmentalized lives, this is no less significant. Christians are to be actively reaching out to other Christians in pursuit of godly fellowship and encouragement. Earlier in Hebrews, the writer pointed out the spiritual significance of such fellowship, urging his readers to "exhort one another every day, as long as it is called 'today,' that none of you may be hardened by the deceitfulness of sin" (3:13). We are all vulnerable, if left alone with our sinful hearts, the temptations of the world, and the spiritual assaults of the devil, to the danger of hardening our hearts to God. The antidote is a close Christian fellowship that encourages, exhorts, and reproves in a loving way.

A loving church will therefore be a church whose members practice hospitality. This raises questions for us. How attentive are we to people who might need fellowship? How eager are we to set aside our own well-worn relationship paths to reach out to a new member in the church or someone who is struggling? How many people in your church (especially newcomers) could describe the inside of your home and the directions to your dinner table? At church gatherings, do you make room at your table or go out to sit with others who might feel left out, extending them fellowship because they are brothers and sisters in Christ who need encouragement and support? One of the best times for hospitality is Sunday afternoon, and a loving church will see its members often spending a portion of the Lord's Day by enjoying fellowship in their homes. While this exhortation applies mainly to other Christians, it includes all sorts of people whom, even if they are strangers, we must embrace with the love of God through Christian hospitality.

In addition to offering fellowship, Christian love is to minister to the burdens of others. Hebrews 13:3 gives the example of Christians imprisoned for their faith: "Remember those who are in prison, as though in prison with them, and those who are mistreated, since you also are in the body." Here we see the principle of sympathy for the trials experienced by others and a ministry that shares in suffering and relieves pains. In this ministry, Jesus is both our example and the ultimate recipient of our acts of love. "Truly, I say to you," he says, "as you did it to one of the least of these my brothers, you did it to me" (Matt. 25:40).

Notice the two key verbs in these exhortations. The writer says, "Do not neglect to show hospitality to strangers," and "Remember those who are in prison" (Heb. 13:2–3). "Do not neglect . . . remember." It seems that the problem is the way in which we view our lives and each other—the difficulty is that we forget to love other people, probably because we are too wrapped up in ourselves.

The writer includes an interesting statement about the spiritual value of these acts of love. "Thereby some have entertained angels unawares" (Heb. 13:2). The most prominent example is that of Abraham and Lot. Seeing strangers, Abraham rushed from his tent and slaughtered a calf for them, only later learning that they brought good news as messengers from the Lord. Lot defended two angels who visited him from the lustful mob of Sodom, and ended up being delivered from that city's destruction by those he had served.

The point is that there is more to the people we meet than meets the eye. I suppose it is possible that when you sit in church, the person next to you will really be an angel, but he or she is likely something even more wonderful. There beside you in the pew is probably a saint of God the Most High. Across the room are those destined to serve as priests and kings in the presence of the living God, who are now being prepared for their glorious raiment. To meet an angel might be wonderful, but in the church are those for whom angels are "ministering spirits sent out to serve for the sake of those who are to inherit salvation" (Heb. 1:14). A work is going on in their lives that angels wonder at and rejoice to see.

The most powerful force in the lives of such creatures, made in God's image, is love. Christopher Morley said (in the age before cellphones): "If we all discovered that we had only five minutes left to say all that we wanted to say, every telephone booth would be occupied by people calling other people to stammer that we love them."[5] Our job is to meet them outside the phone

5. Quoted in Ravi Zacharias, *Can Man Live without God?* (Dallas: Word, 1994), 105.

booth in the real world, there to contrast the self-gratifying exploitation of the world with the self-sacrificing love of Christ.

"AND I IN THEM"

The final thing that we need to know about both the knowledge of God and the love of God is that they come only through the saving ministry of the Son he has sent, Jesus Christ. Jesus said that while the world does not know God, his disciples know that the Father sent him. This reminds us that believers know God through Christ, since as Hebrews 1:2 states, God "has spoken to us by his Son." Likewise, the way that God's love animates Christians is through the personal presence of Jesus in our midst. It is on this theme that Jesus ends his great priestly prayer for his people, asking that "the love with which you have loved me may be in them, and I in them" (John 17:26). Matthew Henry comments: "There is no getting into the love of God but through Christ, nor can we keep ourselves in that love but by abiding in Christ . . . , nor can we have the sense and apprehension of that love but by our experience of the indwelling of Christ, that is, the Spirit of Christ in our hearts."[6]

We might understand Christ's petition to dwell in his disciples in two ways. The first notes that the word *in* may equally be taken to mean "among." In this case, Jesus is referring to his presence in the midst of his people as they gather for worship and live as a community. The dwelling of God in the midst of his people was the hope of Old Testament believers. This hope is fulfilled by the presence of Christ through his Word, in the shared faith of his people, and in the person of the Holy Spirit. This makes the point that a church that knows God and enjoys his love is a Christ-centered church in which the eyes of believers are fixed on Jesus for salvation, blessing, and service. We will know love and all the other marks of the church only as we obediently devote ourselves in discipleship to a living Christ.

Finally, when Jesus concludes by saying "and I in them," this corresponds to the indwelling presence of the Holy Spirit in our individual hearts as the result of our new birth into saving faith. Christians have been born again by Christ's power to the knowledge of God and his love. This means that

6. Matthew Henry, *Commentary on the Whole Bible*, 6 vols. (Peabody, MA: Hendrickson, 2009), 5:944.

if you wish to know God and be set free to love, you must first submit to Jesus as Lord and trust him as your Savior. It is our union with Christ that secures all the blessings about which Jesus prayed on this last night, so that we know God and enjoy his love at work in us.

This is where the hope resides for us: "and I in them." I say this because we tend to respond, "Can this really happen in my life? Can I be the kind of person who ministers Christ's love in the world—in my family, in my workplace, and in all my other relationships?" Jesus prays that he will live in us if we have embraced him in simple faith. Through his Word he intends to continue revealing the character of God to us and working the love of God in us. In this way, in loving fellowship, Christ's prayer will be fulfilled in our lives, so that we experience what Paul referred to as "the riches of the glory" of the mystery of salvation, "which is Christ in you, the hope of glory" (Col. 1:27).

PART 7

Crisis and Conquest through the Cross

119

THE ARREST OF JESUS

John 18:1—11

Then Jesus, knowing all that would happen to him,
came forward and said to them, "Whom do you seek?"
They answered him, "Jesus of Nazareth." Jesus said to them,
"I am he." (John 18:4–5)

C hapter 18 begins the final section of John's record of Jesus Christ. As we look back over this wonderful Gospel, we have seen John's prologue in 1:1–18, a period of witness and revelation in chapters 1–4, growing conflict with the religious leaders in chapters 5–8, Jesus' ministry among believers in chapters 9–12, and our Lord's parting ministry to the disciples in chapters 13–17. Now, as Jesus steps across the Kidron brook to enter the garden of Gethsemane, he not only embraces but orchestrates the crisis that will achieve his triumph through the cross.

If we are familiar with the other three Gospels, we will notice that John's record of Christ's passion offers different details from the other Gospels. Perhaps most noteworthy are his omissions. John omits Jesus' anguished prayer in Gethsemane, Judas's betrayal with a kiss, Simon of Cyrene's help in carrying the cross, and several of Jesus' cries during the crucifixion. John adds details previously unknown, however: Jesus' daunting of the soldiers in the garden, his conversation in the Jewish trial, Jesus' dialogue with Pontius Pilate, the inscription placed above the cross, the giving of Mary into John's care, the piercing of Jesus' side, and Nicodemus's apparent conversion at the cross.

What accounts for these differences? First, we should note that while John's account agrees in the main points, he notices different details, just as we would expect in a true eyewitness. Second, writing his Gospel later, John seems to assume our knowledge of the omitted material, writing his Gospel to provide items previously overlooked. More significantly, John has a message that he intends to convey through the details that he highlights. John wants us to realize that Jesus was not waylaid by evil people who were too strong for him. Instead, Jesus acted in obedience to the Father's will and sovereignly orchestrated the crucifixion and the events leading up to it. When John concludes the record of Jesus' death with the Savior crying, "It is finished" (John 19:30), he refers to the achievement of a carefully arranged plan, not to a tragedy that could not be averted.

To be sure, the passion of Christ is the greatest of all tragedies. For those involved, these were the most dismal of days. This young leader and teacher, more beautiful in character and more perfect in love than any other, a brilliant, compassionate, and mighty Savior, was unjustly arrested, cruelly betrayed, and savagely cut down in the prime of his manhood. Jesus' death represented the apparent victory of a corrupt establishment, behind which stood the specter of ultimate evil. Yet, John insists, its message is a gospel of hope for those who love him, good news of a triumph that breaks out of the tragedy. Not only is the tragic cross followed by triumph, but the cross *is* the triumph, and the apparent defeat emerges as Christ's great victory. As he unfolds these dramatic events, John highlights Jesus' sovereignty. Having concluded his great priestly prayer, the Messiah strides with a heavy heart across the Kidron brook not as a victim but as a determined Savior who has come to his most glorious hour.

BETRAYAL IN THE GARDEN

When John begins his account of the passion with Jesus' entering the garden, he likely intends for us to reflect on the significance. As the Savior enters the garden to redeem his people from sin, we remember that it was in the garden of Eden that mankind fell into sin. The contrast between the two—Christ and Adam in their gardens—is striking and instructive. Adam lived in a garden that was delightful, while Christ entered a garden that was fearful. Adam and Eve spoke to Satan, whereas Jesus devoted his time in the garden to prayer with the Father. One of the reasons Jesus came to this place was that he felt the need for prayer. In contrast, Adam and Eve committed the sin that condemned our race because they did not seek God in prayer, after which they fled from the presence of God. This leads to the most important contrast: in Eden, Adam fell in defeat, but in Gethsemane, Christ conquered. James Montgomery Boice explains: "Adam and Eve by their sin plunged the race into misery. They fell and carried their progeny over the cliff of sin into destruction. Christ, on the other hand, stood firm. He did not sin, nor did he shrink from his work. As a result, he saved all whom the Father had given him. In Adam all were lost. Christ could say, 'Those you gave me I have kept. None of them is lost.'"[1]

Jesus came to the garden not only to fulfill the covenant obligations that Adam had failed to keep, but also to be betrayed by his disciple Judas Iscariot. John tells us that when Jesus had finished praying, "he went out with his disciples across the Kidron Valley, where there was a garden, which he and his disciples entered" (John 18:1). The word for *valley* signifies an intermittent stream, so it seems that Jesus' work that evening called him to cross the brook, on the other side of which was the garden at the foot of the Mount of Olives.

It is noteworthy that this was a place where Judas might expect to find Jesus, since "Jesus often met there with his disciples" (John 18:2). Jesus had sent Judas out from the Last Supper, urging, "What you are going to do, do quickly" (13:27). Having then given Judas time to make his arrangements, Jesus went to a place where Judas would likely seek him. So Jesus was not avoiding arrest but went out of his way to make himself available. What a calloused heart Judas showed in betraying Jesus at a spot made precious by fellowship in prayer with Jesus himself.

Judas came to the garden supported by an impressive force of armed men: "So Judas, having procured a band of soldiers and some officers from the chief priests and the Pharisees, went there with lanterns and torches

---

1. James Montgomery Boice, *The Gospel of John*, 5 vols. (Grand Rapids: Baker, 1999), 5:1369–70.

and weapons" (John 18:3). The soldiers were Romans, since John uses the word for a Roman cohort, which was one-tenth of a legion. This force, commanded by a tribune, consisted of a thousand Roman soldiers, although it would often be smaller and this force might have been as small as a couple of hundred Roman troops. This was still an overwhelming show of force, probably assembled out of a concern for a disturbance among the people over Jesus' arrest. With the soldiers were "some officers from the chief priests and the Pharisees" (18:3). How fitting that a force of Jews and Gentiles together should come to apprehend the Savior of the world! John tells us that they carried "lanterns and torches and weapons" (18:3). Since the Passover always occurred at full moon, when there would be plenty of evening light, it is suggested that they expected to have to search out a hiding or fleeing Jesus. It would soon become obvious, however, that unless Jesus gave himself up, any human weapons would be useless against him.

The question is raised why it was necessary for Judas to betray Jesus. One answer is that Judas was needed to locate Jesus. Jesus, however, had placed himself in a likely location out of the way of public notice. The authorities could not possibly have desired a better scenario for arresting Jesus than he himself gave them. A better answer is that the religious leaders were afraid. They were afraid of an uprising among the people who had hailed Jesus so excitedly during his entrance to the city. More significantly, the leaders clearly feared Jesus himself. They were afraid that Jesus might make a bid for a messianic kingship during the feast (for which the people had begged Jesus in the triumphal entry; see John 12:13). Then there was the matter of Jesus' supernatural power. In earlier days, the religious establishment doubted the legitimacy of Jesus' miracles. By now, however, especially after Jesus had raised Lazarus from the grave in the nearby town of Bethany, the leaders acknowledged and feared Jesus' supernatural might (12:9–19). It is likely that the religious powers feared that Jesus might prove to be unarrestable. How could they oppose him if this were the case?

This concern probably explains the hurried series of events on the night of Jesus' arrest. It seems that when Judas approached the chief priests and informed them that he could lead them to a quiet place where Jesus could be arrested, they acted at once. This explains why the Jewish trial took place at night, despite the legal requirement that capital cases be tried only during the day. Moreover, it is possible that Judas conveyed the idea that Jesus was resigned to failure and death, since he had spoken of dying so often in the past few days (see John 12:27–33), and especially that very evening during the institution of the Lord's Supper (Matt. 26:26–29; Mark 14:22–25; Luke 22:14–23). Now was their opportunity, Judas reported, launching a flurry of ill-planned activity. The arrest would have to take place, the Sanhedrin had to be convened, and early in the morning Pontius Pilate would have to agree to meet with them to approve their death sentence, all so that Jesus could be put to death before the Passover and the Feast of Unleavened Bread. Yet all the while, as these hurried arrangements were made, Jesus was teaching his disciples one last time, committing them to the Father in prayer, and then waiting for Judas to arrive with the soldiers as he prayed to the Father in the garden.

JESUS' DIVINE MASTERY

Jesus proved himself to be not only the master of circumstances on that fateful evening, but also the master of souls. So large an armed force could not appear unseen at the foot of the Mount of Olives, so Jesus calmly awaited their arrival. As the other Gospels tell the story, Judas led the way, identifying Jesus with a kiss (Matt. 26:48). John tells us that Jesus, "knowing all that would happen to him, came forward and said to them, 'Whom do you seek?'" The soldiers answered, "Jesus of Nazareth." Jesus replied, "I am he" (John 18:4–5).

At these words, Jesus' mastery was revealed as the armed Roman legionnaires, most of them probably battle-scarred veterans, "drew back and fell to the ground" (John 18:6). Jesus' words here connect with some of the great moments in the Gospel of John, since he literally stated, "*Ego eimi*," the great "I am" declaration used to reveal his divine glory so many times before (the word *he* is not in the original Greek). "I am the bread of life," Jesus had earlier declared (6:35). "I am the light of the world" (8:12), "I am the way, and the truth, and the life" (14:6), and "I am the true vine" (15:1), Jesus had revealed. Now, standing in the light of the moon and the lanterns, Jesus answered the soldiers' query with divine authority: "I am" (18:6). Before the flame of arresting torches spoke the voice that Moses had heard from the burning bush: "I AM WHO I AM" (Ex. 3:14). Utterly daunted, the throng of armed veterans reeled back and fell to the ground, helpless even to stand before Jesus, much less to seize him. Alexander Maclaren comments: "I am inclined to think that here, . . . there was for a moment a little rending of the veil of his flesh, and an emission of some flash of the brightness that always tabernacled within him; and that . . . was enough to prostrate with a strange awe even those rude and insensitive men. When he said, 'I am He,' there was something that made them feel, 'This is One before whom violence cowers abashed, and in whose presence impurity has to hide its face.'"[2]

The majesty enfleshed by Christ's voice in the garden is just one instance of the glory revealed in his incarnation. At his birth, Jesus lay in the humility of a manger while angels lit the sky and sang the chords of heaven. Jesus was baptized, taking the posture of a sinner, while God's voice testified from heaven to his righteousness: "This is my beloved Son, with whom I am well pleased" (Matt. 3:17). Jesus slept with fatigue in the boat on the Sea of Galilee, and then rose to command the winds and the waves so that all was at peace. Now, in the garden, Jesus first prays in great anguish over the cup of death before him, and then rises to overwhelm his enemies with the sheer force of his divine presence.

John clearly intends for us to reflect on the implications of this situation. If Jesus could drive a cohort of Roman legionnaires to the ground by the mere projection of his deity, what could have hindered him from escaping the cross? Moreover, if this was the power of Jesus at the onset of his humiliation, how great will be his divine majesty when he returns in glory and power? What an appeal the awe of the soldiers is to us of the urgency of a trusting faith in Jesus Christ! F. W. Krummacher writes: "Their prostration in the dust before Him points out to unbelievers the situation in which they will one day be found. The homage which they refused to Jesus here below, He will in due time compel them to render Him. The knee that would not bow to Him in voluntary affection, will at length be constrained to do so by the horrors of despair."[3]

What a comfort this scene is to those who rely on Christ for salvation today. The same darkness lingers in this world. The same powers of corruption and evil seek to hinder and harm Christ and his people. The same conflict between light and darkness rages, with the people of God often cowering in weakness and fear. In his arrest, Jesus shows us his mastery over

2. Alexander Maclaren, *Expositions of Holy Scripture*, 17 vols. (Grand Rapids: Baker, 1982), 11:222.
3. F. W. Krummacher, *The Suffering Saviour* (1856; repr., Edinburgh: Banner of Truth, 2004), 124.

evil, unbelief, and idolatry. This example in the garden should encourage every believer, displaying that "at the will of your Defender, ev'ry foeman must surrender."[4] The spiritual war in which we are now enlisted was decided once for all in Jesus' coming, ultimately in his sovereign conquest in the garden and on the cross. "Be still, my soul," says another hymn to trembling believers today: "the waves and winds still know his voice who ruled them while he dwelt below."[5]

JESUS' PROTECTIVE CARE

With the Roman veterans fallen abashed on the ground, Jesus spoke again, recalling them to their mission. "Whom do you seek?" he asked. They answered, "Jesus of Nazareth" (John 18:7). Surrendering himself, Jesus replied, "I told you that I am he. So, if you seek me, let these men go" (18:8). This was a royal command, by which Jesus protected his disciples from arrest. John Calvin comments: "Here we see how the Son of God not only submits to death of his own accord, that by his obedience he may blot out our transgressions, but also how he discharges the office of a good Shepherd in protecting his flock."[6]

It seems likely that the soldiers intended to round up Jesus' followers along with him. This idea is supported by Mark's Gospel, which records the attempted arrest of a young man who was dressed in a linen cloth (Mark 14:51). This possibly explains Jesus' daunting of the soldiers with his deity, in order that they might be made pliable to his instructions to leave the disciples alone. John sees this protective action as a fulfillment of Jesus' statements in John 6:39 and 17:12 that "of those whom you gave me I have lost not one" (18:9). Some scholars balk at this claim, since these earlier references speak of the salvation of our souls and here Jesus only protects the disciples from bodily harassment. But John sees Jesus' action in the garden as a proof and example of his greater protection over our eternal destinies. Moreover, it likely was the disciples' eternal welfare that Jesus had in mind in the garden. Calvin explains: "The Evangelist does not speak merely of their bodily life,

---

4. Carolina Sandell Berg, "Children of the Heavenly Father" (1855).

5. Katharina von Schlegel, "Be Still, My Soul" (1752).

6. John Calvin, *Calvin's Commentaries*, trans. William Pringle, 22 vols. (Grand Rapids: Baker, 2009), 18:193.

but rather means that Christ, sparing them for a time, made provision for their eternal salvation. Let us consider how great their weakness was; what do we think they would have done, if they had been brought to the test? While, therefore, Christ did not choose that they should be tried beyond the strength which he had given to them, he rescued them from eternal destruction."[7] He knows which trials to permit us, too, so that we may be sure that every difficulty and challenge to our faith that we encounter is one that Jesus has sovereignly permitted for our eternal good.

The New Testament speaks clearly about Christ's promise to preserve the salvation of all who come to him in true faith. Hebrews 7:25 points out the significance of Jesus' unending intercession: "Consequently, he is able to save to the uttermost those who draw near to God through him, since he always lives to make intercession for them." Paul reminded Timothy that Christ "is able to guard until that Day what has been entrusted to me" (2 Tim. 1:12). Peter wrote that believers "by God's power are being guarded through faith for a salvation ready to be revealed in the last time" (1 Peter 1:5). Philippians 1:6 promises that "he who began a good work in you will bring it to completion at the day of Jesus Christ." Jude added a note of praise "to him who is able to keep you from stumbling and to present you blameless before the presence of his glory with great joy" (Jude 24).

What is the clear and encouraging message of these texts? The answer is that "Jesus shows his effective, persevering grace with us by lifting us from the darkness of this world into his own marvelous light, by interceding for us in heaven, by guarding our spiritual deposits, by seeing us through temptation, by saving even our bodies at the time of the last resurrection, and by bringing us at last and without blemish into the presence of his own and the Father's glory."[8] Just as Jesus interposed himself between the soldiers and his disciples in his arrest, he continues forever to place himself between us and our enemies.

SOVEREIGN SUBMISSION

One last episode in Jesus' arrest highlights his sovereign submission to the Father's will, while also showing Jesus' compassion and grace even for

7. Ibid., 18:194.
8. Boice, *John*, 5:1381–82.

496

his enemies. As the soldiers stepped forward to take Jesus into custody, "Simon Peter, having a sword, drew it and struck the high priest's servant and cut off his right ear. (The servant's name was Malchus.) So Jesus said to Peter, 'Put your sword into its sheath; shall I not drink the cup that the Father has given me?'" (John 18:10–11).

We can think of a few reasons why Jesus did not want Peter to strike his enemies with the sword. First, there was no benefit to this violence, since Jesus fully intended to be arrested, and thus there was no reason to harm this servant of the high priest. This is probably why Jesus healed the ear, as Luke 22:51 records. Second, Jesus continues to protect Peter, this time from his folly in raising his sword against so overwhelming a military force. Third, and the reason John highlights in verse 11, is that Jesus was determined to fulfill his Father's will: "shall I not drink the cup that the Father has given me?" (John 18:11).

The cup to which Jesus refers is the cup of God's judgment and wrath. This figure of speech is used several times in the Old Testament, contrasting the cup of judgment with the cup of blessing for obedience. Isaiah states to Jerusalem during the time of Israel's exile, "O Jerusalem, you who have drunk from the hand of the LORD the cup of his wrath, who have drunk to the dregs the bowl, the cup of staggering" (Isa. 51:17). Jeremiah and Zechariah also spoke of God's wrath in terms of a cup of judgment for his enemies to drink (Jer. 25:15–28; Zech. 12:2). This was the cup that Jesus was sovereignly determined to drink, taking into himself the last dregs of God's wrathful judgment for the sins of Christ's people.

Jesus' statement to Peter shows the beneficial result of Christ's earlier prayer in the garden, when he asked the Father if possible to remove his cup. Now, having submitted to the Father's will, Jesus is firm and fervent in embracing God's foreordained plan for his death. This reminds us that the way to be strong in faith when trials and crosses come our way is to be much in prayer with the Lord. Peter, on the other hand, depicts the vanity of human weapons in seeking to do the Lord's work. Jesus had commanded Peter to "watch and pray" (Matt. 26:41), and in prayer he would have wielded a sharper weapon than that which cut off Malchus's ear.

The great point, of course, is Christ's sovereignty in submitting to the Father's will for him to die on the cross. He would drink the cup of wrath so as to achieve our salvation. This is the true reason why Peter did not need his sword, since Jesus fully intended to be arrested. That he would give himself in this way for us encourages us to give ourselves to him in return. Seeing how he sought the glory of God's will through his own obedience reminds us of the significance of our obedience and witness, especially during trials.

Finally, when Jesus refers to the cup of wrath, he reminds us that every person who has ever lived will drink from one of the two cups that God has poured. If we look to Jesus for salvation, bringing our sins to his cross, we will enjoy the cup of blessing forever. In this way, believers will rejoice in the words of Psalm 23:5: "You prepare a table before me in the presence of my enemies; you anoint my head with oil; my cup overflows." But to spurn Jesus as Savior and Lord, to refuse his offer of salvation through a living faith, is to be left with no one else to drink the cup of God's judgment on your sins. Do you doubt God's wrathful judgment on your sins, if you refuse to trust in Christ? Why, then, would Jesus drink this wretched condemnation if there were any other way to save his people, who look to him in faith? Jesus prayed in the garden for some other way to save his people from their sins, but as the Bible insists, "without the shedding of blood there is no forgiveness of sins" (Heb. 9:22). How will you avoid the cup of God's just wrath on your sins if you reject Jesus as your Savior?

Psalm 75:8 tells us, "For in the hand of the LORD there is a cup with foaming wine, well mixed, and he pours out from it, and all the wicked of the earth shall drain it down to the dregs." To reject Jesus is to place our hands on this cup of wrath, with no choice but to drink its mixture of death and torment forever. Meanwhile, every believer who drinks from the cup of God's salvation receives it only because Jesus drank the cup of wrath in our place.

> In my place condemned he stood,
> Sealed my pardon with his blood:
> Hallelujah! what a Savior![9]

9. Philip P. Bliss, "Man of Sorrows! What a Name" (1875).

120

BEFORE THE ROOSTER CROWED

John 18:12–27

One of the servants of the high priest, a relative of the man
whose ear Peter had cut off, asked, "Did I not see you in the
garden with him?" Peter again denied it, and at once a rooster
crowed. (John 18:26–27)

t might be helpful in our study of John's account of Jesus' final hours before the cross to lay out the events recorded in the Bible. If Jesus was to be done away with, his execution must happen quickly, before the Passover and the weeklong Feast of Unleavened Bread, during which such proceedings were banned (see Lev. 23:5–8). To this end, Jesus was brought before Annas, head of the high priestly family, for a preliminary hearing. After this hearing proved inconclusive, Jesus was transferred to the acting high priest, Caiaphas, for a full trial by the Sanhedrin. Many false witnesses were brought forth, but a charge could not be established, so the high priest asked Jesus directly, "Tell us if you are the Christ, the Son of God" (Matt. 26:63). When Jesus confessed that he was, he was convicted of blasphemy and sent off to appear before the Roman governor, Pontius Pilate, whose endorsement was required to execute the sentence of death (see 26:57–66). By now it was early morning, and Pilate sought to relieve himself of the case, first by transferring Jesus to Herod, the ruler over Jesus' native Galilee, and then by offering the Jewish crowd that by now had assembled to have Jesus released in honor of the Passover. Finally, a frustrated Pilate agreed to the death sentence. By late morning Jesus was taken out by the Roman soldiers and crucified, dying in the midafternoon (see Luke 23:1–49).

John does not record all these events, perhaps assuming that we know them from the other Gospels. Instead, John focuses on details that will highlight his particular emphasis on Jesus' sovereign control and his voluntary self-offering as a Sacrifice for our sins. To this end, Jesus must be convicted and abandoned, cast out and isolated for his role as the atoning Lamb of God. To make his points, John draws together two simultaneous events, one inside the high priest's palace and one outside in the courtyard. In these intertwined scenes, the Jewish trial and the denials of Simon Peter, Jesus was abandoned to the cruelties of human injustice, as Isaiah foretold, "cut off out of the land of the living, stricken for the transgression of my people" (Isa. 53:8), all before the rooster crowed to end the dark night of Christ's arrest.

PETER'S FIRST DENIAL

The soldiers who arrested Jesus took him directly to the palace of Annas (John 18:12–14). Annas had been high priest from A.D. 6 to 15, when he was deposed by the Romans. In the following years, various members of his family held the office, including at present his son-in-law, Caiaphas. Most Jews considered Annas the legitimate high priest, although the acting office-bearer had to sit at formal tribunals.

Jesus was not alone at this hearing, since Peter and "another disciple" had followed him to the high priest's residence. This other disciple is traditionally considered to be the apostle John, who out of modesty declines to name himself. Critics of this view point out that a fisherman such as John would not likely be "known to the high priest" (John 18:15). The reply is that we know neither whether this was John nor how the high priest knew him. But since this manner of identification fits John's prior practice (see 13:23–25), since this account contains the kinds of details that an eyewitness might supply, and since we know from later in this Gospel that John did not abandon Jesus but was present at the cross (19:26–27), it seems best to consider this "other disciple" most likely to be John himself.

Being "known to the high priest," this disciple "entered with Jesus into the court of the high priest, but Peter stood outside at the door" (John 18:15–16). This situation was fraught with tension, with Jesus brought bound to the hostile court, John's having gone in with him, but Peter's being left outside the door. John, seeing this, "went out and spoke to the servant girl who kept watch at the door, and brought Peter in" (18:16).

As Peter entered the compound, the young woman at the door spoke to him, asking whether he like the other disciple was a follower of Jesus: "The servant girl at the door said to Peter, 'You also are not one of this man's disciples, are you?'" (John 18:17). This was only a casual remark; her acknowledgment that John was a disciple indicates her lack of violent hostility. Her question was, moreover, cast with the expectation of a negative answer: "You're not one of those disciples, are you?" Peter would have had to contradict the gatekeeper to state the truth, so the easiest answer for him, a stranger seeking permission to enter, was to agree. This he did, saying, "I am not" (18:17).

We remember Peter's earlier boasting: "Lord, . . . I will lay down my life for you" (John 13:37). John Calvin comments: "Now, at the voice of a single maid, and that voice unaccompanied by threatening, he is confounded and throws down his arms. Such is a demonstration of the power of man."[1] Calvin sees Peter's failure as an instance of the frailty that is common to us all. He continues: "Do we not continually tremble at the rustling of a falling leaf? A false appearance of danger, which was still distant, made Peter tremble: and are we not every day led away from Christ by childish absurdities?"[2] The servant woman did not ask Peter whether he was an insurrectionist, a heretic, a blasphemer, or an enemy of Judaism. She merely asked whether he was a disciple of Jesus. Peter, despite the humble station of the questioner and her unthreatening manner of speech, immediately abandoned his fidelity to Christ.

Peter might have looked upon his first denial as a necessary rite of admission to the courtyard. But once uttered, it was easy to repeat and hard to

1. John Calvin, *Calvin's Commentaries*, trans. William Pringle, 22 vols. (Grand Rapids: Baker, 2009), 18:199.
2. Ibid.

correct. This shows why it is always important for Christians to be up-front about our faith in Jesus, instead of giving an initial worldly impression that will be difficult to change later. Having identified himself as a stranger to Jesus, Peter had no reason to avoid keeping company with the others, so he joined a group of servants and officials of the high priest who were warming themselves at a charcoal fire (John 18:18). So it is with Christians today. In order to maintain a public denial of Christ, we will have to blend in with the unbelieving world. Seeing Peter sitting at the fire with the servants of those persecuting Christ, we remember the wisdom of Psalm 1, which warns that the blessed man neither "stands in the way of sinners, nor sits in the seat of scoffers" (Ps. 1:1). There was no doubt a great deal of mocking of Jesus at this fire, so Peter's denial had placed him in a situation in which it was all the more difficult to be faithful to his Lord.

How do we explain Peter's denial of Jesus? First, we note that Peter was there only because he had followed Jesus when all the others (except John) had scattered. The only reason that Peter was exposed to this trial was his love and devotion for Jesus and his courage in following the arresting soldiers. James Montgomery Boice reminds us: "This is no miserable specimen chosen from among the ranks of Christ's worst followers. This is the best. Yet it is precisely this one who falls, not only dreadfully but speedily and with slight provocation."[3]

What steps led to Peter's rapid downfall in denying his Master? First, we remember his overconfidence, which Jesus had checked back in the upper room (John 13:38). Mark's Gospel makes this problem even clearer, reporting that Peter boastfully compared himself with his fellow disciples: "Even though they all fall away, I will not. . . . If I must die with you, I will not deny you" (Mark 14:29, 31). This reminds us not to treat lightly those trials that we have not yet faced. Peter miscalculated his strength of will and courage, and therefore he trusted himself instead of reposing in God's strength and faithfulness. When Jesus told them earlier that evening that "apart from me you can do nothing" (John 15:5), he had meant what he said.

This leads to the second step in Peter's fall, namely, that he failed to pray when Jesus urged him to do so. An overconfident, self-reliant spirit will never be active in prayer. F. W. Krummacher writes: "Instead of [prayer] he

---

3. James Montgomery Boice, *The Gospel of John*, 5 vols. (Grand Rapids: Baker, 1999), 5:1414.

still depends upon himself, and upon the chance of accidents and circumstances. Satan and the world already stand armed against him on the field. He had no need to fear them, if he had only put on the breastplate of faith."[4] Boice points out the irony here that the person we think would least need to pray, namely, Jesus, was in fact the One most fervent in prayer. "If we were to pick someone who needed prayer, it would be Peter. Yet Peter is sleeping in the Garden while the Lord is pouring out his soul before his heavenly Father."[5] How like Peter we are, and how often we fail the Lord because of it. Paul urged believers to "pray without ceasing" (1 Thess. 5:17), yet we fail to arm and equip ourselves for spiritual warfare because, like Peter, we do not think we need God's help.

Third, we are told that when Peter came to the high priest's house, he followed Jesus "at a distance" (Luke 22:54). This can be understood in Peter's case, given the danger and Jesus' stated desire to protect his disciples. In our case, however, following Jesus at a distance is the cause of many spiritual failures. How many Christians are more determined not to be thought of as "fanatics" or "fundamentalists" than they are to live closely to Jesus? How many Christians are more interested in juicy tidbits on the Internet than regular study of their Bibles? Those who follow Jesus "at a distance" open themselves to worldly influences, deny themselves the grace they need, and expose themselves to the danger of falling into Peter's potentially damning sin of denying Jesus before the world.

The Jewish Trial

While Peter was warming himself at the fire outside the house, Jesus was being interrogated inside by Annas, the power-broking former high priest. This appears to have been an irregular hearing, since legal protocols were overlooked, probably intending to give Caiaphas time to assemble his false witnesses and gather the full Sanhedrin for a nighttime trial that would sentence Jesus to death.

John reports a twofold line of questioning: "The high priest then questioned Jesus about his disciples and his teaching" (John 18:19). Annas's evident purpose was to seek grounds to accuse Jesus of sedition by raising up a

---

4. F. W. Krummacher, *The Suffering Saviour* (1856; repr., Edinburgh: Banner of Truth, 2004), 160.
5. Boice, *John*, 5:1414.

rebel band against the Roman rule and of heresy by teaching doctrines that corrupted the Jewish faith. William Hendriksen notes that Annas's ordering of topics, citing Jesus' disciples over his doctrine, is typical of the world's way of thinking: "He was far more interested in the 'success' of Jesus—how large was his following?—than in the truthfulness or untruthfulness of that which he had been teaching."[6]

Jesus' response to Annas was both careful and pointed: "Jesus answered him, 'I have spoken openly to the world. I have always taught in synagogues and in the temple, where all Jews come together. I have said nothing in secret. Why do you ask me? Ask those who have heard me what I said to them; they know what I said'" (John 18:20–21). Notice that Jesus avoids the subject of his disciples, still protecting them from arrest. As for his teaching, Jesus pointed out that witnesses would be easy to find, since his doctrine had been heard in the open for three years, including synagogues and the temple. During all this time, his doctrine had never been refuted by the experts in the law.

Jesus' defense of his doctrine sets an example for all his servants, especially preachers of his gospel: "I have spoken openly to the world" (John 18:20). This is what Christians are to do. Paul expressed this principle as key to his ministry: "We have renounced disgraceful, underhanded ways. We refuse to practice cunning or to tamper with God's word, but by the open statement of the truth we would commend ourselves to everyone's conscience in the sight of God" (2 Cor. 4:2). There is no need for us to misrepresent or shade our doctrine in cunning or manipulative ways. Matthew Henry writes: "The doctrine of Christ, purely and plainly preached, needs not be ashamed to appear in the most numerous assembly, for it carries its own strength and beauty along with it. What Christ's faithful ministers say they would be willing all the world should hear."[7]

With his reply, Jesus demanded to be tried correctly under the law. Jewish law did not permit the direct questioning of the accused, but required a conviction to result from the testimony of eyewitnesses. Annas and his officials understood him, and one of the officers "struck Jesus with his

---

6. William Hendriksen, *Exposition of the Gospel according to John*, 2 vols., New Testament Commentary (Grand Rapids: Baker, 1953), 2:397.

7. Matthew Henry, *Commentary on the Whole Bible*, 6 vols. (Peabody, MA: Hendrickson, 2009), 5:953.

hand, saying, 'Is that how you answer the high priest?'" (John 18:22). Jesus, maintaining his sovereign composure, replied by simply reinforcing the illegality of this entire hearing: "If what I said is wrong, bear witness about the wrong; but if what I said is right, why do you strike me?" (18:23). Seeing that he was getting nowhere, "Annas then sent him bound to Caiaphas the high priest" (18:24).

This episode is all that John records of the Jewish trial, the most important parts of which took place later before Caiaphas and the full Sanhedrin, where Jesus was confronted with numerous false witnesses. Since Jewish law required witnesses to agree on even minute details, none of the trumped-up charges took hold. The best charge was that Jesus had promised to tear down the temple, raising it in three days, a reference to Jesus' teaching about his death and resurrection (Matt. 26:61), but this also could not meet the legal standards for a conviction. It was at this point that a desperate Caiaphas challenged Jesus directly to declare himself as the Messiah and Son of God. When Jesus confessed the truth of this claim, the Jewish court immediately convicted him on a capital charge of blasphemy.

John's brief treatment, however, is sufficient to make his points about the Jewish trial. Three things arise from even Jesus' brief hearing before Annas. The first is that these were *illegal* hearings. The breaches of Jewish legal proceedings are too numerous to be cited in detail.[8] Most prominent were these: Jesus was arrested without proper charges, based on the witness of an accomplice who had been bribed; Jesus was tried at night, whereas the law required daytime proceedings for capital cases, and contrary to the law the proceedings were held on the day before a feast; no testimony in favor of the accused was sought or permitted; Jesus was directly examined and called upon to testify against himself; and Jesus was convicted by a unanimous vote, which the Jewish legal rules considered evidence of a biased court. All of these were gross violations, but the last one is most pertinent. The Jewish system of law emphasized mercy and called on courts to do everything possible to exonerate the accused. The Jews' trial of Jesus was illegal precisely because it was conducted with no other aim than to unjustly convict Jesus and put him to death. William Hendriksen summarizes correctly: "This in reality is no *trial* at all. It *is murder!*"[9]

8. For a fuller discussion of the illegalities of the Jewish trial, see Boice, *John*, 5:1397–1402.
9. Hendriksen, *John*, 2:396.

Second, the Jewish trial was *cruel*. John notes the officer of Annas's court striking Jesus, probably with the flat of his hand. The Greek word, *rhaptisma*, originally denoted the use of a rod, so that John may see in this the fulfillment of prophecy: "with a rod they strike the judge of Israel on the cheek" (Mic. 5:1). Cruelty is usually performed by cowards, and so it was that Jesus was struck on the face while his hands were bound. This was just the beginning of his cruel abuse, yet Jesus meekly submitted to it all. How easily might Christ have consumed the insolent official with fire or withered his striking hand, yet this was the hour of his meek submission to injustice and cruelty. Though Jesus responded with words counseling justice and truth, he made no objection to his mistreatment. As Isaiah had foretold: "He was oppressed, and he was afflicted, yet he opened not his mouth; like a lamb that is led to the slaughter" (Isa. 53:7).

Above all, the Jewish trial was *unholy*. This appears not only in the ironic verdict of blasphemy upon the true Son of God, but also in the entire treatment of Jesus the Christ. Here, Annas represents the whole of apostate Judaism. Seated as the heir of all the old covenant leaders, the culmination of centuries of divine blessings, mighty deliverances, and covenant privileges, Israel's high priest now greets the long-awaited Messiah. In light of the Scripture's long anticipation of the coming Savior and King, we ache to see Israel's leader fall on his face in adoration and worship. Instead, Jesus is despised and beaten, and every trick in the book is employed to condemn him to death. Yet all of this was possible only by Jesus' self-effacing permission. J. C. Ryle notes: "He had only to command the confusion of His enemies, and they would at once have been confounded. Above all He was One who knew full well that Annas and Caiaphas, and all their companions, would one day stand before His judgment seat, and receive an eternal sentence. He knew all these things, and yet condescended to be treated as a malefactor without resisting!"[10]

JESUS ABANDONED

As John presents the dreadful events of that fateful night, the greater atrocity took place outside in the courtyard. There, Jesus' closest disciple,

10. J. C. Ryle, *Expository Thoughts on the Gospels: John*, 3 vols. (Edinburgh: Banner of Truth, 1999), 3:253.

Simon Peter, was awkwardly standing in the company of those who would persecute his Lord. John recounts: "They said to him, 'You also are not one of his disciples, are you?' He denied it and said, 'I am not.' One of the servants of the high priest, a relative of the man whose ear Peter had cut off, asked, 'Did I not see you in the garden with him?' Peter again denied it, and at once a rooster crowed" (John 18:25–27).

We observed Peter's weakness in his first denial to the humble servant girl, but how much clearer does his weakness appear at the fireside denials! To his previous self-confidence and self-reliant neglect of prayer, we now add the toxic ingredient of the fear of man.

Peter's second denial was given in answer to a direct question. Matthew's Gospel says that the servants recognized Peter's Galilean accent, so now they suspected him of being with Jesus (Matt. 26:73). What a blessing it is when our Christian "dialect"—that is, our whole manner of speaking and acting—gives us away as belonging to Jesus! How can believers, indwelt by the Holy Spirit, expect to fit in successfully with the world? Still, Peter denied Jesus again: "I am not," he insisted (John 18:25). One of the officials then looked into Peter's face in the poor light of the charcoal fire. This was one of those who had been present in the garden and who was a relative of Malchus, whom Peter had struck with a sword. Here is a truly menacing query, which Peter forcefully denied, saying, "I do not know this man of whom you speak" (Mark 14:71). Having yielded himself to the first, lesser temptation, how vulnerable Peter was in the second and third greater ones, especially having placed himself in such wicked company.

John's presentation of Peter's denials raises the question: why did the apostle arrange his material in the way that he did? Most sermons on this chapter treat the Jewish trial and Peter's denials separately, rearranging the text as needed. But why did John present these scenes intertwined together? The answer must surely be that for all our reflections on the corrupt unbelief of the Jewish leaders and the cowardly betrayal of his chief disciple, John seeks to direct our attention primarily to Jesus himself. A comparison is intended between Jesus and those both inside and outside the high priest's palace. The point of these comparisons is that Jesus alone is the One we can trust, the One who alone achieves God's will for justice, mercy, and salvation on the earth.

To put this more clearly, we should note that Jesus was not condemned by a corrupt system. He was "condemned to death by the most merciful and careful system of judicial processes known to our race."[11] How could this happen? The answer is the corrupt wickedness of the human race itself. Jesus' trial displays the dictum of Jeremiah 17:9, which is just as true of us today as it was of the Jewish rulers who condemned Jesus long ago: "The heart is deceitful above all things, and desperately sick; who can understand it?" Jesus did not submit himself to this unjust death because the Jewish priests and lawyers were corrupt but because the entire human race is corrupt. Jesus was not surprised by his treatment, because he came into the world to remedy the problem of our sin and to achieve the forgiveness of sinners whom he would call to himself in saving faith.

Prominent among these sinners was Simon Peter. Of all the blows struck against Jesus that night, Peter's denials must have wounded him most deeply, just as Jesus must watch in aggrieved sorrow when any of his people deny him today. But note how Jesus had made provision for the beginning of Peter's repentance and restoration. Earlier that evening, Jesus had told him, "Truly, truly, I say to you, the rooster will not crow till you have denied me three times" (John 13:38). What was the purpose of this foretelling, but to remind Peter of the truth! As Matthew tells us, when Peter heard the rooster crowing, he "remembered the saying of Jesus" and "went out and wept bitterly" (Matt. 26:75). John's Gospel ends with Jesus waiting for Peter by a fire, meeting Peter at the scene of his failure that he might restore him by his grace. It is no wonder that years later, when Peter told of the forgiveness of his sins and ours, he wrote of "the precious blood of Christ" (1 Peter 1:19), whereby his failure and betrayal was washed away in atoning love.

HOPE FOR SINNERS

Unless we can honestly show that we are different from the corrupt Jewish leaders and cowardly, unfaithful Peter, this passage not only seals our condemnation but also offers us hope. Perhaps the best way to view our situation is to compare Jesus' words to the soldiers in the garden and Peter's denials in the courtyard. Revealing himself to those who came to arrest him,

---

11. Boice, *John*, 5:1389–90.

Jesus declared his divine majesty, saying, "I am." Before the cock crowed, Peter denied Jesus three times, saying, "I am not." These words not only sealed the loneliness that was inevitable for the Savior who must embrace the cross alone in order to die for many. They also declare the failure of human self-reliance when put to the test by the power of evil.

Where, then, is the hope? The hope is found in realizing that Jesus walked his lonely road to the cross in order that he might be "wounded for our transgressions [and] . . . crushed for our iniquities," that upon him would be "the chastisement that brought us peace," and that "with his stripes" we would be healed (Isa. 53:5). This was Peter's own gospel hope, as expressed in his first epistle, a hope for all sinners who like the apostle so greatly need a Savior, and find that salvation only in Jesus himself. Peter exulted in the lonely achievement of the Savior whom he had failed, but who had never forsaken him, a victory that supplied gospel hope for himself and all who turn to Jesus in faith:

> He himself bore our sins in his body on the tree, that we might die to sin and live to righteousness. By his wounds you have been healed. For you were straying like sheep, but have now returned to the Shepherd and Overseer of your souls. (1 Peter 2:24–25)

121

KINGDOMS IN CONFLICT

John 18:28—38

*Jesus answered, "My kingdom is not of this world. If my
kingdom were of this world, my servants would have been
fighting, that I might not be delivered over to the Jews. But my
kingdom is not from the world." Then Pilate said to him, "So
you are a king?" (John 18:36–37)*

*J*n his monumental work *City of God*, the early-church theologian
Augustine of Hippo states that there are among men two cities,
the City of Man and the City of God. "Two societies," he writes,
"have issued from two kinds of love. Worldly society has flowered from a
selfish love which dared to despise even God, whereas the communion of
saints is rooted in a love of God . . . . The city of man seeks the praise of
men, whereas the height of glory for the other is to hear God in the witness
of conscience. The one lifts up its head in its own boasting; the other says
to God: 'Thou art my glory, thou liftest up my head' (Ps. 3:4)."[1]

Augustine's ideas are important for Christians today, because we still
live in these two cities. We are part of both the city of this world and the

---

1. Augustine, *The City of God*, trans. Gerald G. Walsh et al. (New York: Doubleday, 1950), xiv, 28.

city of God; we must render unto Caesar what belongs to him and to God what belongs to God.

In the Bible, these two cities are mainly described as two kingdoms, and there is no more telling interaction between these two kingdoms than in the Roman trial of Jesus Christ. Pontius Pilate, the Roman governor, sat in judgment, deciding the fate of this Jewish rabbi, Jesus of Nazareth, who had been arrested and convicted by the Jewish Sanhedrin on a capital charge of blasphemy. Little did Pilate appreciate that his meeting with Jesus involved a clash of two kingdoms, two value systems, and ultimately two judgments. While Pilate would decide Jesus' temporal fate, it was Pilate's eternal judgment that would be determined by his relationship to his prisoner, Jesus Christ.

Two Kingdoms

The passage begins as Jesus is led by the Jewish leaders to Pilate's residence in Jerusalem. Earlier in the morning the Jewish trial had taken place, in which Jesus was falsely accused of various crimes. When that attempt failed, the high priest asked whether he was the Christ and Son of God. Jesus admitted that he was, and on that basis he was convicted of blasphemy (Mark 14:61–63). On this charge, Jesus was brought to the Roman governor to be executed by him.

We know quite a lot about Pontius Pilate, both from the Bible and from other historical sources. All the evidence points to him as a man who was both morally weak and cruelly brutal. He was appointed governor of Judea by Tiberius Caesar in A.D. 26 and held that post until A.D. 37. His tactless policies often spurred public outrage and revolt, which he then savagely suppressed.

How fitting Pilate was, then, to represent the kingdom of this world as it encountered the kingdom of God in the person of Jesus Christ. Pilate shows us clearly what gives the worldly kingdom its power. Pilate held power by force of arms, by virtue of the legions of Rome. These soldiers required support, and so Pilate also relied on taxes. Worldly princes always rely on these things, along with pomp and ceremony, prestige, and alliances with other rulers. Modern governments have expanded this list to include manipulation of the press and propaganda, along with technological, scientific, and economic prowess. It is with such resources that the kingdom of the world exerts its rule, and we have to say that it is all quite impressive. Pilate's rule over the Jews was close to absolute; this was vividly portrayed as the religious leaders brought Jesus to him for disposition.

The Jews were hoping for a quick acceptance of their verdict, followed by Jesus' swift execution. Pilate, however, perhaps toying with them, did not go along so easily. He came out to them and asked, "What accusation do you bring against this man?" (John 18:29). This statement signaled that a real trial was going to take place, since the declaration of charges was the first step in the Roman legal procedure. "If this man were not doing evil," they replied, "we would not have delivered him over to you" (18:30). Pilate did not go along with this, but told the Jewish rulers to deal with the matter themselves. To this refusal, the Jews tellingly objected, "It is not lawful for us to put anyone to death" (18:31). The Old Testament law did, of course, give the Jews the right of capital punishment, but the Romans had taken this right away. John tells us that in this God was at work, ensuring that Jesus would die in the manner foretold, by the method of crucifixion, which only the Romans employed: "This was to fulfill the word that Jesus had spoken to show by what kind of death he was going to die" (18:32).

At this point Pilate returned to Jesus, who was inside, and asked him, "Are you the King of the Jews?" (John 18:33). The other Gospels tell us that the Jews specifically made this charge against Jesus, and now Pilate pursued the matter directly, having decided to investigate this charge. Jesus answered him, "Do you say this of your own accord, or did others say it to you about me?" (18:34).

This answer was not an evasion, as it may seem, but an important point that Jesus needed to make. The issue was the perspective from which Pilate was asking the question. Was he confronting Jesus on the charge of setting up a worldly kingdom opposed to that of Caesar? In that sense the answer would be No, for Jesus was not a rival to Pilate in Judea. But on the other hand, if the question was coming from the Jewish perspective, the answer must be Yes. Jesus was the Messiah, the long-awaited King from the line of David.

Pilate's answer revealed his disinterest: "Am I a Jew?" (John 18:35). He had no interest in purely religious matters, but only those that affected the sovereign rights of Caesar and his kingdom. It was in that sense that Pilate wanted to know, "What have you done?"

This exchange sets the stage for an important statement by Jesus regarding his kingdom. Jesus explained his position to Pilate: "My kingdom is not of this world. If my kingdom were of this world, my servants would have been fighting, that I might not be delivered over to the Jews. But my kingdom is not from the world" (John 18:36).

This statement tells us two vital things about Christ's kingdom, beginning with the words "my kingdom" (John 18:36). The point is that Jesus Christ is a King. This man, standing as a prisoner before the worldly governor, brought in as a criminal, bearing no emblems of worldly power, is a King. The audacity of this claim was not lost on Pilate. When the governor first questioned Jesus, he emphasized the contrast between the idea of Jesus' purported kingship and his lowly appearance. In the Greek text a very clear emphasis is placed on the pronoun *you*. "You," he says, "are *you* a king?" (18:33).

This is a way of thinking that is not restricted to Pontius Pilate. People today think the same way. Jesus might be a worthy fellow, a nice example in a spiritual sort of way, but he is not a power to be reckoned with. Jesus commands no armies, nor does he decide who gets promoted, who becomes rich, or who rises in rank in the world. He might be a nice religious model, but he is not really someone to take too seriously. So, at least, the thinking goes.

Yet Jesus insists that he is a King and that he has a kingdom. It is not, however, a kingdom like any other. "My kingdom," Jesus said, "is not of this world" (John 18:36). Jesus' kingdom is a spiritual one. It is not like the kingdom that Pilate represented. If Jesus' kingdom is not of this world, then it must be of some other origin, and that origin is heaven. Jesus reigns with spiritual and heavenly authority. That means that it is over the soul that Jesus reigns, through spiritual power and heavenly principles. As one hymn puts it:

For not with swords' loud clashing, nor roll of stirring drums—
With deeds of love and mercy the heav'nly kingdom comes.[2]

Let me ask a question: Does this mean that while you must respect earthly powers, you can afford to ignore Jesus' kingdom? If Jesus' rule is merely

2. Ernest W. Shurtleff, "Lead On, O King Eternal" (1888).

spiritual, does this mean that it has nothing to do with people who don't choose to be religious? James Montgomery Boice answers:

> Nothing is farther from the truth, for when we say that Christ's kingdom is not of this world, what we are really saying is that Christ's kingdom is of heaven and therefore has an even greater claim over us than do the earthly kingdoms we know so well. . . . Over these is Christ, and we flout His kingship not merely at the peril of our fortune and lives but at the peril of our eternal souls.[3]

As Jesus put it, "Do not fear those who kill the body but cannot kill the soul. Rather fear him who can destroy both soul and body in hell" (Matt. 10:28). Despite appearances, Jesus claims a kingship that is far more ominous and significant than any other power within this world.

THE VALUES OF THIS WORLD

This encounter between Jesus and Pilate was not only between two kingdoms and their respective powers, but also between two radically different value systems. In the actions of both Pilate and the Jewish leaders we clearly see the values of the kingdom of this world.

The first of these values is utilitarianism, or what we might call pragmatism. Our world believes in and practices whatever works. That is the religion of mankind, and especially of America. This value is clearly present in this encounter between Pilate and Jesus.

We see this value exemplified in the behavior of the Jews. Things were not going well for them this morning. First, Pilate demanded an actual charge rather than rubber-stamping their condemnation. John does not give the Jews' full reply, but we find it in the other Gospels: "We found this man misleading our nation and forbidding us to give tribute to Caesar, and saying that he himself is Christ, a king" (Luke 23:2). Two of those claims were outright lies. Jesus had done nothing to subvert the nation of Israel, and attempts to establish the claim with false witnesses during the Jewish trial broke down because of contradictions. With regard to paying taxes to Caesar, their earlier attempt to trap Jesus had failed miserably. When

---

3. James Montgomery Boice, *The Gospel of John*, 5 vols. (Grand Rapids: Baker, 1999), 5:1436.

asked whether it was lawful to pay taxes to Caesar, Jesus held up a coin with Caesar's inscription on it and gave the famous answer that says so much about church-state relations: "render to Caesar the things that are Caesar's, and to God the things that are God's" (20:25). Why did the Jews make these false charges? Because they thought it expedient to lie; they thought their scheme would work.

It did not work, however, for as John 18:38 tells us, Pilate acquitted Jesus of the charges against him. "I find no guilt in him." This was the formal ruling of this court of law. At this point, however, the Jews simply changed their complaint. In John 19:7 they gave their true charge: "We have a law, and according to that law he ought to die because he has made himself the Son of God." This accusation was no concern to Pilate, so the Jewish leaders changed their approach once again. We see this in John 19:12, when the Jews threatened, "If you release this man, you are not Caesar's friend. Everyone who makes himself a king opposes Caesar." This was a wholesale abandonment of any pretense to justice, in favor of direct intimidation. If Pilate did not go along with condemning Jesus, they would use it to discredit him with Caesar in Rome, something that had proved fatal in the case of other officials. In summary, the Jewish leaders threw justice aside, operating by pure expediency, which is the way of this world.

We find the same value governing Pilate's actions. He began his trial with care and propriety. He would not let Jesus be condemned without formal charges and a real trial. It is not completely clear why he acted so out of character in this manner, but the best suggestion seems to have to do with a message he received from his wife. Matthew 27:19 tells us, "While he was sitting on the judgment seat, his wife sent word to him, 'Have nothing to do with that righteous man, for I have suffered much because of him today in a dream.'"

In any case, Pilate began these procedures in keeping with the Roman tradition of law and justice. But when the pressure against him began to mount, he, too, responded with blatant expediency. Having declared Jesus innocent (John 18:38), Pilate did not release Jesus as he should, instead turning to a custom of granting free pardon to one prisoner in recognition of the Passover. Matthew's Gospel makes it especially clear that Pilate gave the people the choice between Jesus and a notorious insurrectionist named Barabbas. "Whom do you want me to release for you: Barabbas, or Jesus who is called Christ?" (Matt. 27:17). "Barabbas!" they cried, and Pilate therefore held onto Jesus. This injustice was compounded when Pilate then ordered the vicious scourging of Jesus with the bone-tipped Roman whip (John 19:1–5), followed by Pilate's assent to the crowd's demand that Jesus be crucified (19:14–16). Such is the way of this world in its self-serving pragmatism. St. Augustine was exactly right when he labeled love of self as the hallmark of the City of Man.

The second worldly value that this passage highlights is relativism, which is closely allied to utilitarianism. Jesus was explaining the nature of his kingdom: "For this purpose I was born and for this purpose I have come into the world—to bear witness to the truth. Everyone who is of the truth listens to my voice" (John 18:37). To this Pilate gave a reply that is both classic and revealing, admirably representing the values of this world. He replied, "What is truth?" (18:38).

"What is truth?" That might be the motto of our utilitarian, relativistic age. "It might be true for you," we hear, "but it isn't true for me." This assumes that there is more than one truth, or no real truth at all. Christians today are constantly told that it is okay to have our private beliefs as long as we don't insist that they are true for everyone. Indeed, the great offense of Christianity in our time is the claim that Christ is not merely *a* Savior, but the *only* Savior, the only way and truth and life.

Because relativism is the hallmark of our postmodern society, it is tempting to label Pontius Pilate as the first postmodern man. "What is truth?" he dared to say while staring into the face of truth itself! Yet what we call postmodernity is not really a new phenomenon, of which Pilate was a premature example. In reality, postmodern relativism is as old as unbelief, as Pilate shows so well.

Utilitarianism demands relativism: the two go together in the postmodern twenty-first century just as they did in the pagan first century. Self-serving pragmatists cannot afford the idea of absolute truth. Truth is an encumbrance if our highest aim is merely to serve our own apparent good. This is what lay behind the scorn of Pontius Pilate, a man whose power rested on the sword. To the kingdom of this world, truth is nothing; from the lips of those who serve nothing higher than self, we will ever hear the words of Pilate, "What is truth?"

Let me briefly observe what these two values produce, now as in the time of Jesus. They produce hypocrisy, injustice, and cruelty. Look at the Jewish leaders: could there be a more hypocritical sight? They are eager to hand over the sinless Son of God, coming to Pilate without a moment's hesitation with trumped-up charges and false testimony. Yet they are careful to stay outside the precincts of Pilate's house, lest they be defiled for the Passover (John 18:28). What could be more defiling than to betray the Messiah to a Gentile lord? What a picture they are of the hypocrisy of this world! The same may be said of Pilate's whole show of supposed justice. It was, at bottom, one great sham, just as hypocrisy is found in every corner of the kingdom of this world.

A second result of the world's value system is injustice. With everyone out for himself or at least his own interest group, with everyone treating truth as something to be manipulated, it is impossible that justice will ever prevail.

The injustices in this trial are rife. First there is the bringing of Jesus to Pilate in the first place: his treatment by the Jews was an enormity of false charges and lies. Pilate, for all his procedural correctness, was hardly any better. In John 19:4 he formally acquitted Jesus, but then had him savagely beaten, displaying the cruelty that goes along with hypocrisy and injustice. In the end, faced with the slightest threat to his personal well-being, the Roman trial ended with Pilate's words that condemn the justice of the kingdom he represents: "so he delivered him over to them to be crucified" (19:16).

THE REIGN OF TRUTH

The man whom Pilate examined was in fact a King, but a King as different from Pilate as the two men were in appearance. Christ's kingdom is everything that the kingdom of this world is not. This is why pragmatism and relativism in truth or morals are always the worst habits of mind for Christians to adopt. This is one reason why the New Testament consistently warns against the danger of Christians' falling prey to the kingdom of this world. "Do not love the world or the things in the world," John writes in his first epistle. "For all that is in the world . . . is not from the Father but is from the world. And the world is passing away along with its desires, but whoever does the will of God abides forever" (1 John 2:15–17).

Christ's reign is not of these values, but as Jesus said, it is a reign of truth. "For this purpose I was born," says our Lord, "and for this purpose I have come into the world—to bear witness to the truth. Everyone who is of the truth listens to my voice" (John 18:37).

For Jesus and his kingdom, truth is not something to be twisted or manipulated but revealed: "I have come . . . to bear witness to the truth." This explains why Jesus allowed himself to be falsely charged, brutally abused, and ultimately crucified. Why? To do the work of his kingdom, to reveal the truth.

Obviously, then, the truth that Christ's kingdom stands on is not like that of the world. His is not the truth of pragmatism, which is never willing to die; neither is it the truth of relativism, which has nothing to die for. Jesus has *the* truth because he *is* the truth. He is the great reality that shapes all things, the Word that became flesh and dwelt among us (John 1:14). His truth, therefore, is not constructed, and it is not discovered, partially and tentatively, like some new theory of men. It is the truth that always was and is and will be, the truth that Jesus brings into the world from God and reveals as light into darkness.

I am reminded of a story told by James Montgomery Boice. He was on a plane, and the woman seated next to him learned that he was a Christian minister. She began to bring out all her objections about Christianity. First she spoke of original sin, how it made no sense and how she would not accept it. Boice simply replied to her, "I see, but is it true?" Next, she went on to the idea of judgment and hell, how uncivilized and amoral all of it was. "I see how you feel, but is it true?" he replied. She went on to the next topic and then the next, each with the same response. Finally she erupted with her great distaste for everything taught in the Bible, how it wasn't modern or appealing to her way of thinking. As Boice began to open his mouth one last time, she exclaimed, "Oh, I know, I know, none of that matters. 'Is it true?' you are going to say!"

This is what we need to say. It is truth that Christians have to offer, and truth that we must be willing to stake our lives on. This is what our world needs and what a starving mankind is hungering for: truth we believe because it is true, because it is of God, and because it is revealed in Holy Scripture. This is also why Christians do not need to seek popularity in the world or measure success in worldly terms if we are to have a true relevancy in our age. As members of Christ's kingdom, we take our stand on the truth that is our greatest source of power in this world and measure our success in terms of fidelity to that truth. Paul thus writes: "For the weapons of our warfare are not of the flesh but have divine power to destroy strongholds. We destroy arguments and every lofty opinion raised against the knowledge of God, and take every thought captive to obey Christ" (2 Cor. 10:4–5).

Truth Revealed

Just as Pilate cynically answered Jesus, "What is truth?" (John 18:38), our postmodern world challenges if not the possibility of truth, then our ability to confidently know truth. We say, "What matters is knowing the truth," and the world challenges, "How can you claim to know the truth?" Jesus' words to Pilate offer a significant response to this challenge. According to Jesus, believers receive the truth not by their superior intelligence, investigative efforts, or experience, but by a divine act of revelation. His purpose for coming into the world was to give truth by means of revelation: "for this purpose I have come into the world—to bear witness to the truth" (18:37).

How are we to understand this statement? First, the subject matter of the Bible—the truth revealed in Scripture—is Jesus himself in his person and work. This is what Jesus emphasized to the Emmaus road disciples on the resurrection day: "beginning with Moses and all the Prophets, he interpreted to them in all the Scriptures the things concerning himself" (Luke 24:27). This is why Jesus says, "Everyone who is of the truth listens to my voice" (John 18:37), since to believe on Jesus is to belong to God's truth.

Second, Jesus commissioned his apostles to provide the truth to God's people in the form of a permanent written revelation. The New Testament does not contain merely the opinions and views of the apostles, with all their human limitations, but Christ's Word given by inspiration of the Holy Spirit. "The Helper, the Holy Spirit, whom the Father will send in my name," Jesus foretold, "he will teach you all things and bring to your remembrance all that I have said to you" (John 14:26). Jesus himself provided the written revelation of truth through the Holy Spirit's inspiration of the apostolic witness.

Finally, when you or I today pick up the Bible and read God's Word in faith, Jesus reveals the truth to our minds by the present ministry of the Holy Spirit. The same Holy Spirit who inspired the apostles' writing illuminates

Christ's Word to the believer's heart today. Why, then, do Christians disagree? The answer is that Christians do *not* disagree about Jesus and his saving work and other primary matters of faith and salvation. Where we differ in secondary matters, we trust Jesus to continue leading us into truth while he teaches us to bear with one another in love. For this reason, the Christian witness is one that sets forth the truth we have received by Christ's divine act of revelation. "If you abide in my word," Jesus promises, "you will know the truth, and the truth will set you free" (John 8:31–32).

I have a Bible given to me by a friend when I was preparing to enter seminary. In it he wrote these memorable words: "Know the truth. Live the truth. Tell the truth." That is the best advice that a Christian can receive, especially one entering the ministry. Atop all this, my friend wrote, "He is truth." This is what Jesus' reign and revelation are all about, Jesus himself as "the way, and the truth, and the life" (John 14:6). "Sanctify them in the truth," he prayed to the Father for his disciples; "your word is truth" (17:17).

"Everyone who is of the truth listens to my voice," Jesus told the Roman governor (John 18:37). Those who hold to his teaching, receiving the truth in faith, are saved by Jesus. All those who reject his truth in this life will be exposed by the truth in the judgment to come. On the last day, when every sin is exposed before the light of Christ, Pontius Pilate will face the truth in his own condemnation and judgment, while all those cleansed by the saving blood of Christ through faith in his revealed truth will enter into the glory of his kingdom forever.

122

BEHOLD THE MAN!

John 18:38—19:6

> *So Jesus came out, wearing the crown of thorns and the purple robe. Pilate said to them, "Behold the man!" When the chief priests and the officers saw him, they cried out, "Crucify him, crucify him!"* (John 19:5–6)

ccording to the New Testament, the crucifixion of Jesus Christ took place to fulfill the Passover Feast that was being celebrated in Jerusalem. Paul states this clearly: "Christ, our Passover lamb, has been sacrificed" (1 Cor. 5:7). This connection means not only that we may look at Jesus to understand the true meaning of the Old Testament Passover, but also that we may look at the Passover to gain a proper grasp of Christ's atoning work.

The Passover instructions specified that the sacrificial lamb "shall be without blemish" (Ex. 12:5), and this requirement is highlighted in the trial of Jesus. Just as the Passover lambs were kept in Israelite homes for a three-day examination, Jesus Christ was carefully observed during his three-year ministry. At his baptism, God the Father pronounced Jesus unblemished, speaking audibly from heaven, "This is my beloved Son, with whom I am well pleased" (Matt. 3:17). The disciples who lived closely with Jesus later described him as "holy" (Acts 2:27), "righteous" (1 John 2:1), and "without blemish or spot" (1 Peter 1:19). Judas Iscariot confessed, "I have sinned by betraying innocent blood" (Matt. 27:4). Last, the Roman procurator Pontius Pilate three times said of Jesus, "I find no guilt in him" (John 18:38; 19:4, 6). James Montgomery Boice observes: "It is as one uncondemned and, in fact, declared to be blameless that Christ goes to Calvary. It is as God's blameless Lamb that Jesus dies for the sin of this world."[1]

THE LAMB REJECTED

We might think that a spotless person like Jesus would be well received by those to whom he came. At the beginning of his Gospel, however, John warned us to expect the opposite, writing, "He came to his own, and his own people did not receive him" (John 1:11). Harry Ironside illustrates this truth with a story of two sermons preached at a church one Sunday. In the morning, a visiting preacher gave a marvelous oration on the beauty of virtue. He concluded, "Oh, my friends, if virtue incarnate could only appear on earth, men would be so ravished with her beauty that they would fall down and worship her." Many left impressed by the stirring oration and returned in the evening to hear a gospel minister preach about Christ crucified. He closed by saying, "My friends, Virtue Incarnate *has* appeared on earth, and men instead of being ravished . . . cried out, 'Away with him! Crucify him!'" As the preacher explained, man in his sin hates God's holiness and will do anything to rid himself of the light of Christ.[2] This is why Jesus the Lamb of God appeared before God's ancient covenant people only to be rejected and despised.

As John 18 comes to a close, Pilate has examined Jesus in light of the charges of the Jewish leaders and has acquitted him of all guilt. Instead of releasing him, however, Pilate turned to address the substantial crowd that had gathered outside the Praetorium, his official residence. "You have a custom that I should release one man for you at the Passover," he reminded them. It is clear that Pilate wanted to avoid making a decision over Jesus and yet was seeking some way to release his prisoner. Therefore, he put the matter in the people's hands: "So do you want me to release to you the King

---

1. James Montgomery Boice, *The Gospel of John*, 5 vols. (Grand Rapids: Baker, 1999), 5:1446.
2. Ibid., 5:1468.

of the Jews?" (John 18:39). According to Mark's Gospel, Pilate named Jesus "King of the Jews" to express his contempt for the priests' petty animosity toward Jesus (see Mark 15:10). Assuming that the crowd would call to have Jesus released, Pilate must have been surprised to hear instead their vehement answer: "They cried out again, 'Not this man, but Barabbas!'" (John 18:40).

John explains that Barabbas was, as most English translations render it, "a robber" (John 18:40). More accurately, John meant that he was an insurrectionist. Barabbas was most likely one of the Zealots who sought to oust the Roman power by means of guerrilla warfare; he would have been considered a terrorist by Pilate and his soldiers. Matthew tells us that Barabbas was "a notorious prisoner" (Matt. 27:16), and Luke added that he "had been thrown into prison for an insurrection started in the city and for murder" (Luke 23:19). Barabbas was therefore likely the last person Pilate desired to set free. Having been promised the release of a prisoner, however, the Jewish mob was intent, stirred up by the religious leaders who were present (Mark 15:11), so Barabbas would have to be released instead of Jesus.

Barabbas was the kind of savior that the Jews had wanted Jesus to be: a political and military deliverer from Roman rule. In riding into the city on a humble donkey, however, Jesus had declared not only his heirship to the Davidic throne (cf. 1 Kings 1:33–38) but also his rejection of a worldly, violent agenda. Jesus came not to overthrow Rome's legions but the guilt and power of sin. The people chose Barabbas over Jesus, salvation by the sword over salvation by the cross. In this way, J. C. Ryle observes, "They publicly declared that they liked a robber and a murderer better than Christ!"[3] The hypocrisy of the religious leaders was thus highlighted, as they incited the crowd to demand the release of a man who was guilty of the very crimes of sedition and rebellion that they had charged against Jesus. Peter would later lay this charge against Jerusalem: "you denied the Holy and Righteous One, and asked for a murderer to be granted to you" (Acts 3:14).

The crowd's rejection of Jesus involved not only the will of sinful men, but also the will of God for his sacrificial Lamb. On the Day of Atonement, Israel's high priest would lay his hands on the "scapegoat," transferring the guilt of the people's sins to it, and then rejecting it and removing it from the camp (Lev. 16:21–22). Thus Isaiah prophesied that Jesus would be "numbered

---

3. J. C. Ryle, *Expository Thoughts on the Gospels: John*, 3 vols. (Edinburgh: Banner of Truth, 1999), 3:295.

with the transgressors," bearing "the sin of many" (Isa. 53:12). Charles Spurgeon points out that in this capacity, the crowd's rejection of Jesus spoke forth the will of God, since "Christ, as he stood covered with his people's sins, had more sin laid upon him than that which rested upon Barabbas." It is true that in himself, Jesus was without guilt, as Pilate observed. Spurgeon notes: "holy, harmless, and undefiled is Christ Jesus, but he takes the whole load of his people's guilt upon himself by imputation, and as Jehovah looks upon him, he sees more guilt lying upon the Saviour than even upon this atrocious sinner, Barabbas."[4]

THE LAMB ABUSED

As procurator of Judea, Pontius Pilate had full authority to set Jesus free. That he did not do so, having declared Jesus' innocence, reveals Pilate's moral cowardice and corrupt misuse of power. But Pilate had another scheme for winning the crowd's agreement for releasing Jesus, the injustice of which is evident from the opening words of John 19: "Then Pilate took Jesus and flogged him" (John 19:1). Having been rejected by his people, the Lamb of God would now be abused by the worldly ruler, behind whom we may be sure was acting the malice of the prince of this world, Satan (Eph. 2:2).

The Roman practice of scourging was a horrific form of physical abuse, employing a whip with leather tails onto which bone fragments and pieces of metal were attached. There were three types of flogging practiced by the Romans. The lightest form was called the *fustigatio,* which was a milder beating intended as a severe warning to petty criminals. Next most severe was the *flagellatio,* a more brutal flogging for moderately serious criminals. Worst of all was the *verberatio,* a terrible and often fatal scourging that not only ripped the skin but dug into the tissue of the back, exposing arteries and bones. This savage scourging was employed as a preliminary to a crucifixion, intended both to inflict anguish and to hasten the execution.[5]

It seems likely that at this point Pilate inflicted Jesus with the lightest form of scourging. The other Gospels record that Jesus received the most severe form later, after Pilate had delivered him to be crucified, which explains why Jesus was physically too weak to carry his cross. But the flogging to

4. Charles H. Spurgeon, *Majesty in Misery,* 3 vols. (Edinburgh: Banner of Truth, 2005), 2:161.
5. D. A. Carson, *The Gospel of John* (Grand Rapids: Eerdmans, 1991), 597.

which John refers preceded Christ's condemnation. Pilate was still trying to save Jesus, administering a milder, though still terrible, beating that he hoped would slake the crowd's bloodthirst and teach the troublesome rabbi a lesson. The Gospels do not dwell on the details of Christ's physical agony, but we may be assured that the flogging displayed Jesus' bravery to go along with his innocence.

Added to this injury was the insult of the Roman soldiers assigned to flog Jesus. John briefly relates their mocking: "And the soldiers twisted together a crown of thorns and put it on his head and arrayed him in a purple robe. They came up to him, saying, 'Hail, King of the Jews!' and struck him with their hands" (John 19:2–3).

First, the soldiers pressed a "crown of thorns" on Jesus' holy brow. It is impossible for us to know which of the many kinds of thorns were used for this mock coronation. Many commentators suggest that it was made of branches from the date palm, since they contain sharp spikes as long as a foot. This crown not only would cause Jesus excruciating pain, but would also present an image of radiant beams extending outward, which was common for the crowns worn by rulers of that time.[6] To this royal mockery, the soldiers added a purple robe or cape to show contempt for the idea that Jesus might be a king. Finally, the soldiers came to Jesus one at a time in fake homage, rising from their mock bows to strike him in the head and face, no doubt aggravating the pain of the thorns and streaking Jesus' bruised face with lines of blood. According to Mark, the soldiers also spat on Jesus and used a reed that they had placed in his hands as a scepter to batter their prisoner.

How can we explain this savage treatment of one so holy and admirable as Jesus? One answer is that the Roman soldiers held the Jewish people in contempt, and since Jesus was called their king, they wanted to show their disdain for the Jewish messianic ideal.

This explanation alone, however, does not suffice. These soldiers were personally faced with the majesty of the Lord, a majesty that could only have continued to shine even in torment. On the head destined to wear heaven's crown of glory, mankind presses a torturous crown of unbelieving contempt. How great a condemnation the soldiers' mocking brings not only on them

6. Cf. Andreas J. Kostenberger, *John* (Grand Rapids: Baker, 2004), 530.

but on our entire cursed race! Mark Johnston reminds us of "that sobering theme that runs throughout this Gospel: 'People loved darkness rather than the light, because their deeds were evil' (3:19). This is the verdict of God. This is human nature as it really is."[7] Barbarous mankind ridicules divine humility; rebel mankind mocks Christ's reign as King of kings. Though Jesus is no longer physically present to abuse, the spirit of these Roman soldiers continues to raise its fist against him, and often raises its malice against his disciples still in the world.

We note here as well why the Apostles' Creed lists the abuse of Jesus among the great redemptive events of his atoning work: "he suffered under Pontius Pilate." This physical abuse and public ridicule was part of what Jesus suffered for us in bearing our sins. The thorns of his mock crown remind us of the curse on the creation for Adam's sin (Gen. 3:18). Not only was he "wounded for our transgressions" and "crushed for our iniquities" (Isa. 53:5), but he also bore the shame and reproach that our sins deserve. J. C. Ryle observes, "Our Lord was clothed with a robe of shame and contempt, that we might be clothed with a spotless garment of righteousness, and stand in white robes before the throne of God."[8]

The Lamb Condemned

When the soldiers' rough work with Jesus was completed, Pilate declared his purpose to the crowd: "See, I am bringing him out to you that you may know that I find no guilt in him" (John 19:4). We do not know what the people expected to see, nor how they initially reacted when "Jesus came out, wearing the crown of thorns and the purple robe" (19:5). His voice thundering through the corridors of history in ways that Pilate himself could hardly have known, the Roman judge presented Christ the King, battered, bloodied, and disgraced in mockery, crying out, "Behold the man!" (19:5). Rudolf Bultmann explains Pilate's action as an attempt

> to make the person of Jesus appear to the Jews as ridiculous and harmless, so that they should drop their accusation. Hence Jesus has to step forth as the caricature of a king, and Pilate presents him with the words, "This is the

7. Mark G. Johnston, *Let's Study John* (Edinburgh: Banner of Truth, 2003), 240.
8. Ryle, *John*, 3:305.

man! Look at the pitiful figure!" But to the mind of the Evangelist the entire paradox of the claim of Jesus is in this way fashioned into a tremendous picture. In very truth, it is just such a man who asserts that he is the king of truth! The declaration . . . "The Word became flesh" has become visible in its extremest consequence.[9]

Look, however, at how the Jewish crowd responded to its long-awaited Messiah. Pilate presented Jesus in the manner that Isaiah had foretold, "as one from whom men hide their faces" (Isa. 53:3). Seeing him, "they cried out, 'Crucify him, crucify him!' " (John 19:6). Not one of those speaking could point to any harm that Jesus had done; instead, he had often done them good, healing them, teaching them, freeing them from false doctrines and false shepherds. Why, then, did the Jews hate Jesus so much that they cried for him to be cruelly put to death on the cross? We have already noted their hatred for Jesus' holiness, which exposed their depravity. Paul adds that despite their privilege of possessing the Scriptures, they were blinded by sin, not recognizing Jesus as the Messiah that he was: "for if they had," Paul wrote, "they would not have crucified the Lord of glory" (1 Cor. 2:8).

The famous Latin words that translate Pilate's declaration, *Ecce homo* ("Behold the man!"), challenge us all to look upon Jesus, the sin-bearing Savior. We have noted that Pilate acknowledged him as sinless and without guilt. We have speculated about how the soldiers must have observed his sheer bravery. Would they also have seen his majesty shining through the misery? It is hard to imagine that they did not, yet still they crucified the Son of God.

Pilate's cry not only was heard by the Jewish crowd but resounds through the annals of Holy Scripture. In his words, "Behold the man!" we find the answer to the long-awaited expectation of God's people for the promised Savior who was to come. We remember the dreadful scene outside the garden of Eden, where Adam and Eve were expelled for committing the first sin, breaking God's covenant, and casting our race into the fall. But God in his grace had spoken of a Savior who would be the offspring of the woman. To Satan in the garden, God spoke of him: "he shall bruise your head, and you shall bruise his heel" (Gen. 3:15). "Here is the man," God declared, and the first thing we know is that he will be human, Son of a woman.

9. Quoted in George R. Beasley-Murray, *John*, Word Biblical Commentary 36 (Waco, TX: Word, 1987), 337.

The generations passed, and in the day of Moses God said once more, "Behold the man!" This time he is foretold as a prophet, one like Moses, who would speak from God to the people. God told Moses, "I will raise up for them a prophet like you from among their brothers. And I will put my words in his mouth, and he shall speak to them all that I command him" (Deut. 18:18). Later still, he is shown to David as a coming King, sitting on a throne wielding royal power. God told David, "He shall build a house for my name, and I will establish the throne of his kingdom forever" (2 Sam. 7:13). Behold the man: the Prophet and the King!

In the time of Zechariah, when the returning exiles were rebuilding the temple, the promised Savior was also revealed in his priestly office. Remarkably, Zechariah was told by God to make a crown woven with silver and gold, and to set it on the head of the high priest Joshua (the Hebrew name *Joshua* being rendered in Greek as *Jesus*). Once the crowned priest was seated on his throne, Zechariah was to point at him and cry out, "Behold, the man." God explained: "It is he who shall build the temple of the LORD and shall bear royal honor, and shall sit and rule on his throne" (Zech. 6:12–13).

Zechariah knew that his act was symbolic of another yet to come. Even as he cried out, "Behold, the man," he must have wondered when the Messiah would appear, his heart burning to see the day when the priestly King would be revealed before the watching eyes of God's people. With what horror, then, would Zechariah have stared as Pilate stood before Jesus where the prophet had stood before his earlier namesake. The purple robe was there and the crown, but it was all so horribly different. Yet the voice cried out, "Behold the man!" and the Messiah was presented to the people of God who, led by their chief priests and officials, answered, "Crucify him, crucify him!"

Would Zechariah have been mortified by his prophecy's fulfillment? Or would he have marveled to see in it the true message of the Bible? Would he have realized that God was building his true temple, where man may meet with God, in the person and work of his bloodied, sin-cursed Son? Why this? Because Jesus' suffering and death were suited to our need, that we as sinners might be forgiven and that we as rebels might be restored to God's love. Zechariah wove a crown of silver and gold for his priestly king, but how much more precious is the crown of thorns that Jesus wore for us! Behold the Lamb, our true Priest, who ministers peace between holy God and guilty man! Behold the thorn-crowned King, who out of love was willing to die! Behold the gospel of God's true Prophet, offering cleansing through faith in his own blood! Behold the man, Jesus Christ, God's Son, the true temple where God will meet with man, here and here alone, fulfilling his ancient plan to redeem a people from their sins.

IN MY PLACE

We should consult one last person. While Jesus stood before the crowd at the Praetorium, Barabbas sat imprisoned in the Tower of Antonia some fifteen hundred feet away. Barabbas would have been too distant to hear anything that Pilate said, but the loud answers of the crowd would have resounded in his cell. Pilate asked which prisoner the crowd desired to release, and Barabbas heard the loud cry of his name. Pilate responded, as Matthew records, "Then what shall I do with Jesus who is called Christ?" Barabbas heard nothing of that, but the crowd's answer arrived loud and clear: "Let him be crucified!" (Matt. 27:22). Pilate responded, "Why, what evil has he done?" but Barabbas heard only the loudly shouted response, "Let him be crucified!" (27:23). "Barabbas. . . . Let him be crucified! . . . Let him be crucified!" Imagine then, with those dreadful cries ringing in his ears, the sinking heart and trembling hands of the insurrectionist as the fall of heavy feet sound in the corridor, the soldiers approaching his room to inflict the punishment that Barabbas knows he deserves. He hears the sound of the keys, his terror mounting as the door swings open. Yet instead of receiving death, Barabbas is set free.

What does Barabbas find as he emerges into the dreary daylight of Jerusalem on that Passover day? A crowd follows a bloodied man carrying a cross. It is a man acquitted of all guilt, yet trudging in solitary condemnation. As he inquires further, the truth unfolds for Barabbas: Jesus is dying in his place. Hearing the hammer blows nailing Jesus to the cross, did Barabbas cry out in wonder, "Those blows were meant for me, but Jesus has taken my cross"?

Only Barabbas can say that Jesus took his physical place on the cross. But in terms of God's holy judgment, all who believe in Jesus Christ may say with Barabbas, "Jesus died in my place." Donald Grey Barnhouse, who imagined this scene, writes: "It was I who deserved to die. It was I who deserved that the wrath of God should be poured upon me. . . . He was delivered up for my offenses. He was handed over to judgment because of my sins. This is why we speak of the substitutionary atonement. Christ was my Substitute. He was satisfying the debt of divine justice and holiness."[10] Paul put it in memorable words: "For our sake [God] made him to be sin who knew no sin, so that in him we might become the righteousness of God" (2 Cor. 5:21). Jesus bore our sin that we might bear his righteousness in God's presence forever. Jesus died that we might live. Jesus was bound in the curse of sin so that we sinners might be set free.

Like Barabbas in his cell, hearing his name loudly called out, every one of us will be summoned by name to appear at the great tribunal of God's final judgment. On that great day he will be wearing his crown of glory, enthroned as Judge over all, and all who refused him will be condemned forever (Matt. 25:31–46). Will you have despised Jesus the bloody Savior, like those who cried, "Crucify him"? If, instead, you will call on Jesus to save you, your name will be called, like Barabbas, but the divine summons will arrive only to set you free.

Free for what? Charles Wesley answers in his captivating stanzas:

My chains fell off, my heart was free;
I rose, went forth, and followed thee.[11]

We follow Jesus through this world, with many crosses of our own to bear in his name, to an eternal glory secured by him for us. All who have lived in the gloomy dungeon of sin and unbelief may gain this freedom by believing his gospel: free to wear a salvation crown of glory to lay at Jesus' feet, and free to sing with gospel joy:

Amazing love! How can it be
That thou, my God, shouldst die for me?[12]

---

10. Donald Grey Barnhouse, *Addresses on the Gospel of John* (Neptune, NJ: Loizeaux, 1942), 822.
11. Charles Wesley, "And Can It Be That I Should Gain" (1738).
12. Ibid.

123

AUTHORITY TO JUDGE

John 19:6—12

*Jesus answered him, "You would have no authority over me at
all unless it had been given you from above."* (John 19:11)

he apostle John's account of the Roman trial of Jesus is laden with
dramatic irony. This is a writing strategy in which the reader
is aware that things are exactly opposite from the way they are
treated by the participants in the story. This irony is present in the reply
of the Jews to Pontius Pilate's desire to release Jesus. The Roman governor
presented a bloody, scourged Jesus to the people. They responded by crying
out, "Crucify him, crucify him!" Pilate answered, "Take him yourselves and
crucify him, for I find no guilt in him" (John 19:6). But the people replied,
"We have a law, and according to that law he ought to die because he has
made himself the Son of God" (19:7). The reader is aware of irony here on
at least two levels. First, there is an irony in the appeal of the Jews to the
Roman power, since they despised the Roman rule in Jerusalem. The greater
irony was that while they demanded Jesus' condemnation for identifying
himself as God's Son, Jesus really was what he claimed to be. The Jews did
not realize that it is not blasphemy to name yourself the Son of God if that is
who you are, a fact that Jesus has abundantly proved in the Gospel of John.

AUTHORITY FROM ABOVE

Pilate did not seem to grasp all this irony, but he did experience a sense of awe toward Jesus when it was alleged that Jesus claimed deity for himself. "When Pilate heard this statement, he was even more afraid" (John 19:8). To a typically superstitious Roman such as Pilate, the claim that Jesus was some sort of divine man was not so implausible as it was to the Jews. Gary Burge writes, "Pilate . . . undoubtedly is highly superstitious and the idea that in some fashion gods could appear in the world was not uncommon."[1] Moreover, the Jewish accusation confirmed Pilate's intense experience with Jesus. Alarmed at the possibility of truth in the Jewish claim, Pilate returned to ask Jesus, "Where are you from?" (19:9). This question was not a bare inquiry into Jesus' background but pertained to Christ's purportedly divine nature.

To Pilate's consternation, Jesus declined to answer his question. This refusal has spurred questions regarding Jesus' motive in remaining silent. Probably the best understanding is that there was simply no answer to give that would help Pilate fit Jesus into his pagan religious categories. Moreover, Pilate had already pronounced Jesus not guilty of all charges, and then subjected Jesus to the cruel Roman scourge. Pilate's experience reminds us that if we harden ourselves to Jesus' self-revelation, there may come a time when Jesus no longer speaks to us, the day for our salvation having passed. All four Gospels emphasize Jesus' silence before Pilate, seeing a fulfillment of Isaiah 53:7, "He was oppressed, and he was afflicted, yet he opened not his mouth."

Jesus' silence infuriated Pilate, who took it as an affront to his office. "You will not speak to me?" he demanded. "Do you not know that I have authority to release you and authority to crucify you?" (John 19:10). This statement raises important questions regarding the authority of human rulers such as Pilate, questions that have been in the background throughout this Roman trial.

Christians often wonder about their obligation to accept civil authority, especially when the civil power is wicked or incompetent. We ask whether the state has a legitimate right to demand obedience. Jesus answered that Pilate, as the official representative of the Roman Empire, did have authority over his temporal affairs. He said, "You would have no authority over me at

---

1. Gary M. Burge, *John*, NIV Application Commentary (Grand Rapids: Zondervan, 2000), 504.

all unless it had been given you from above" (John 19:11), a statement that acknowledges Pilate's secular authority.

It is important to note the distinction between *power* and *authority*. Power is the *ability* to enforce compliance; authority is the *right* to rule and govern. No one doubted Pilate's power, and so far as his rule extended over civil behavior, Jesus acknowledged that the governor also had authority, the legal right, as the legitimate civil official.

Jesus' acknowledgment points out that Christians are to obey and respect the civil authority of the land. According to the Bible, this obligation exists not only when we agree with its policies but also when we disagree. For instance, Christians might not agree with taxes or the purposes for which taxes are used. But when the question of paying taxes was put to Jesus, he answered by holding up a Roman coin, which had Caesar's likeness stamped on it. "Render to Caesar the things that are Caesar's," he said (Matt. 22:21). Then, as now, the emblems of the nation are emblazoned on its coins, and Jesus argues that this means that we have an obligation to pay our taxes to the nation. This does not seem to depend on the uses to which the government may put our money, since the coin that Jesus held up probably bore the image of Tiberius Caesar, a most cruel and depraved emperor who Jesus nonetheless said had an authority to demand taxes.

Paul stated the matter quite clearly in Romans 13:1, "Let every person be subject to the governing authorities." Paul justified this rule with the very explanation that Jesus gave to Pilate: "For there is no authority except from God, and those that exist have been instituted by God. Therefore whoever resists the authorities resists what God has appointed, and those who resist will incur judgment" (13:1–2). Secular rulers receive their authority by God's sovereign rule and are to be respected and obeyed as far as possible. James Montgomery Boice notes how this authority extended even to Pilate's trial of Jesus: "Pilate pronounced wrongly, as we know. But he had authority to make the pronouncement even if it was wrong. His authority was from God. Jesus did not suggest that it be wrested from him because he had made even so great an error as condemning the Son of God."[2] Using this same reasoning, Christians should be model citizens and should be scrupulous in the respectful tone of our speech and actions toward our elected officials. In a

2. James Montgomery Boice, *The Gospel of John*, 5 vols. (Grand Rapids: Baker, 1999), 5:1480.

democratic society, this does not preclude us from seeking to replace those in power or to repeal unjust laws. But we are obliged to obey the rulers and laws in place over us.

There are limits, however, to worldly authority and our obligation to obey it. These limits are just as implicit to Jesus' answer to Pilate as his admission of Pilate's secular authority. Jesus said, "You would have no authority over me at all unless it had been given you from above" (John 19:11). Therefore, since God is a higher authority than Pilate or any other human governing body, Christians must refuse to obey civil rulers when our obedience to God's Word is at stake.

One clear biblical example shows that Christians are not to heed government prohibitions against preaching or witnessing the gospel. Since Jesus has commanded his followers to spread the gospel (Matt. 28:18–20), we must be prepared to engage in civil disobedience if the government seeks to muzzle our witness. This was the example of Peter and John when the Sanhedrin forbade their preaching after Pentecost. The apostles answered, "Whether it is right in the sight of God to listen to you rather than to God, you must judge, for we cannot but speak of what we have seen and heard" (Acts 4:19–20). When they were later hauled in for this "offense," Peter and John plainly answered, "We must obey God rather than men" (5:29).

The second clear biblical instance requiring civil disobedience concerns the moral conduct of Christians. No government has the authority to countermand the laws of God, and Christians must violate the laws of men, even accepting punishment, rather than sin against God's Word. A classic example was the Nazi regime in Germany with its inhuman and wicked persecutions. One of its laws required citizens to have no dealings with Jews and to turn them in to be oppressed and even murdered. Many Christians obeyed these laws when they should have disobeyed, even at the risk of dreadful persecution against themselves.

One Christian who refused to comply with sinful Nazi edicts was Martin Niemoeller, a pastor who continued to preach the gospel and to speak out against government atrocities. A Christian friend once visited him in jail and urged him to stay silent about Nazi abuses. If Niemoeller would agree to this, his freedom could be secured. "So, why are you in jail?" he concluded. Niemoeller answered, "Why aren't you in jail?"[3] Likewise, Christians in

---

3. Quoted in ibid., 5:1481–82.

America have a moral obligation to righteously oppose the slaughter of unborn children, to speak out against racism, to oppose government and corporate corruption, and to stand against other evils, staunchly refusing to participate in such sins. Moreover, as our governments pass so-called hate-crime laws forbidding Christians to speak out against moral perversions such as homosexuality, Christians must continue to speak God's truth in love, accepting the unjust consequence of breaking such ungodly laws.

Jesus concluded his reply to Pilate with one additional note: "Therefore he who delivered me over to you has the greater sin" (John 19:11). Pilate's actions were sinful toward God, but not as sinful as those of the Jews who had betrayed Jesus into his hands. This statement proves that some sins are worse than others, indicating that those who sin against their knowledge of the truth commit a graver sin than those who sin in ignorance. It is most likely that Jesus has the high priest Caiaphas in mind as the one who "delivered" him over, but along with Caiaphas were all the other rulers and chief priests and indeed the whole mass of the people present. Since ultimate authority resides with God, and since the Jews possessed God's Word and had received compelling proofs of Jesus' authenticity as Messiah, their guilt in handing him over for death was more severe than even Pilate's. Pastors and other church leaders who use their sacred offices to deny or violate God's Word likewise commit sins that are particularly grievous and offensive to God, as do parents who use the Bible to harm their children or husbands who use biblical authority to abuse their wives.

PILATE'S FEARS

Throughout this account, Pilate is revealed as a moral coward who is tormented by the various sources of his fear. We have noted his fear of Jesus, stemming from the accusations against Jesus and his personal interactions with the Lord of glory. Pilate was unnerved by Jesus, and he greatly desired to get this prisoner off his hands. We see this fear working on Pilate in his repeated attempts to secure Jesus' release, so that when Jesus spoke about God's authority over Pilate, the governor "sought to release him" (John 19:12).

But Pilate also feared the Jews, and they steadfastly opposed his attempts to set Jesus free. When he again tried to release Jesus, "the Jews cried out, 'If you release this man, you are not Caesar's friend'" (John 19:12). For all his disdain of the Jewish people, Pilate obviously feared their united opposition to his judgments. This fear is the only explanation for his failure to release Jesus after acquitting him.

Finally, Pilate feared Caesar. The emperor at this time was the unstable Tiberius Caesar, who was especially suspicious of disloyalty in his servants. This made Pilate susceptible to the threat that the crowd now leveled: "the Jews cried out, 'If you release this man, you are not Caesar's friend. Everyone who makes himself a king opposes Caesar'" (John 19:12).

This was a serious threat that Pilate was bound to fear. We know that the Jews had sent complaints to Caesar in the past concerning Pilate.[4] But in this case, word would be sent to the paranoid emperor that Pilate was defending a seditious rebel who set himself up as king in opposition to Rome. Moreover, given what we know about the general corruption of Pilate's regime, he probably feared any scrutiny that might dig up problems in his government that would be awkward to explain. Some scholars think that the term "Caesar's friend" marks a special, official status that Pilate enjoyed. But even if this was only a general term, as is more likely, a report that Pilate was not serving the emperor's interest jeopardized not only his position but his life. Hearing this threat, Pilate made no more efforts to free Jesus. J. C. Ryle comments: "He would rather connive at a murder to please the Jews, than allow himself to be charged with neglect of Imperial interests and unfriendliness to Caesar."[5]

In contrast to Pilate and his fear of man, Jesus sets an example of the fear of God that enables his people to resist temptations to worldly compromise and sin. It is by fearing God that Christians are able to resist the fear of man, so that we do not shrink back from our witness to the gospel or compromise our conduct before the world.

The first thing that we can say about Jesus' attitude is his awareness of God's sovereignty over every detail of his life. Jesus alludes to God's sovereign control in his statement to Pilate that "you would have no authority over me at all unless it had been given you from above" (John 19:11). This states not only that Pilate is accountable to God but also that Pilate could do to Jesus only what God permitted. Jesus knew that God's will would be done, and

---

4. D. A. Carson, *The Gospel of John* (Grand Rapids: Eerdmans, 1991), 602.

5. J. C. Ryle, *Expository Thoughts on the Gospels: John*, 3 vols. (Edinburgh: Banner of Truth, 1999), 3:317.

so he trusted himself to his Father in heaven. Likewise, Christians can be delivered from the paralyzing fear of man by knowing that we are loved by a sovereign, omnipotent God who has promised to care for and protect us.

This is what the friends of the Old Testament hero Daniel did when they were carried into exile in Babylon. Daniel interpreted a dream for the Babylonian king, Nebuchadnezzar, in which he learned that "the God of heaven will set up a kingdom that shall never be destroyed, nor shall the kingdom be left to another people . . . , and it shall stand forever" (Dan. 2:44). Being thus informed of God's sovereignty over all history and human empires, Daniel's friends, Shadrach, Meshach, and Abednego, refused to bow to Nebuchadnezzar's golden statue. It was knowing God's sovereignty that freed them from the fear of even such a mighty ruler as the Babylonian conqueror. Like these and other bold believers who have left the mark of their witness on the world, we will oppose the unjust demands of secular rulers and refuse to buy into the sin culture of our times if we realize that the Lord we trust is more powerful than any worldly rulers and that he sovereignly reigns for our salvation.

The second way for us to avoid the fear of man is to become knowledge-able regarding the teaching of Scripture. Boice writes: "To want to do the right thing is not enough. We must know what the right thing is, and there is no way to know that apart from God's specific revelation of his standards in the Bible."[6] Jesus remained silent before Pilate because he knew God the Father's will that he would bear the cross. Perhaps this explains Jesus' refusal to answer Pilate's question about his origins, being concerned that Pilate might actually release him. Likewise, as his disciples, we need to know that Jesus has called us to be witnesses to his cross and to lead lives of holiness in obedience to God's Word.

Third, if we are to fear the Lord so as to be free from the fear of man, we must surrender our wills to the will of God. This is where Pilate was really undone. He had some belief in the power of gods, or else he would not have feared Jesus the way he did. And while he did not have the witness of the Bible, he knew perfectly well what was the right thing to do on this occasion. But his will was not yielded to truth. Meanwhile, Jesus had spent time in prayer before his arrest, and in that prayer he surrendered his will

6. Boice, *John*, 5:1486–87.

to the Father. "Father, if you are willing, remove this cup from me," Jesus had prayed. This shows that there is nothing wrong with asking God to remove the trials that we are facing. But Jesus concluded, "Nevertheless, not my will, but yours, be done" (Luke 22:42). We are likewise to surrender our wills to the Father, seeking to glorify him through lives of obedience to his Word, knowing that he is sovereign over all things and that "for those who love God all things work together for good" (Rom. 8:28).

FRIENDS OF THE KING

If we follow Jesus' example in fearing God rather than men, we will be made bold in all manner of situations. I mentioned Daniel in his captivity in the court of the Babylonian king. He realized in God's interpretation of Nebuchadnezzar's dream that God's kingdom is sovereign over all other kingdoms and alone will endure forever. He knew his duty from the Scriptures, and we know from later in his book how committed Daniel was to regular prayer, by which we can assume that he daily surrendered his will to God. It was for this reason that Daniel and his friends were able to refuse to worship the golden idol, giving a glorious testimony to faith in the only true God, so that even Nebuchadnezzar gave praise to the Lord (Dan. 3:28).

You may answer that Daniel and his friends were able to be faithful, but what did it get them? The Bible record shows that Daniel's friends were tossed into a furnace to be consumed and destroyed. That is true, just as it is true that Jesus' surrender to his Father's will caused him to be nailed to a cross to die. Is this what will happen to you and me, if we likewise surrender our will to obey God's Word? The answer is that suffering and death could very well be the result for us in this life. But we remember that after Jesus died, he rose from the grave on the third day and then ascended into heaven, where now he reigns in glory forever. "Worthy is the Lamb who was slain," the angels now sing with joy in his presence (Rev. 5:12). We, too, if we yield our hearts in surrender to God, through many trials here below, will spend an eternity in glory above with Jesus.

Moreover, if we commit ourselves to faith in Christ, not only will we secure an eternal destiny with him in heaven, but he will also walk with us here on earth. We remember that when Daniel's three friends were cast into the fire, they were not consumed. Nor were they alone, but a fourth man was seen walking in the midst of the fire with them. Nebuchadnezzar marveled, saying, "The appearance of the fourth is like a son of the gods" (Dan. 3:25). So it will be in the trials that would otherwise consume God's faithful people, that the glorious Son of God will walk with us to strengthen us by his grace. Just as Daniel and his friends were empowered not to bow to the false gods of their day, we will be given power for the witness that our generation needs, a witness that will be all the more powerful as Jesus' presence is evident with us in our sufferings and trials. In the end, through a faith that fears God and not man, the praise extolled in heaven will be spoken of us: "they have conquered by the blood of the Lamb and by the word of their testimony, for they loved not their lives even unto death" (Rev. 12:11).

I mentioned that John's account of Jesus' trial is soaked in irony. There is a final irony in the Jews' threatening words to Pontius Pilate. They told him that if he did not crucify Jesus, they would declare that he was not Caesar's friend. Pilate wanted so much to be a friend of Caesar, just as people today want so much to have the approval of the cultural elites. But Pilate had never really been Caesar's friend; it is probable that Caesar barely knew who he was and cared nothing for him as a person. In a few years, Caesar would turn against him and send Pilate into permanent exile in Gaul. In the end, Pilate's will was surrendered to a paranoid, brutal, cowardly man simply because he wore a laurel wreath on his head. Caesar was no savior to Pilate, despite the power and perks that Pilate derived from Caesar's approval. When Caesar had gotten all he wanted from Pilate, he would discard him and give his position to someone else.

Yet a different King stood before Pilate. To be sure, Jesus did not have a golden crown on his head but a crown of mocking thorns. Moreover, to affirm Jesus and embrace his kingdom meant receiving the scornful abuse of the world. Caesar would not like it, and Pilate might very well have to join Jesus on a cross. What, then, can recommend faith and allegiance to Jesus, whom the world crucified and crucifies still in malice and unbelief? What would make us desire, above all else, to be a friend of Jesus instead of Caesar? One answer is that Jesus truly is King, not of worldly empires but of the eternal reign of heaven. Having died on the cross, he rose from the grave and lives in glory forever. Jesus is God Almighty and King of kings, and his sovereign reign over earth and heaven will never end.

But there is another reason for us to be friends of Jesus: he will be a faithful friend to us. It is true that, like Caesar, Jesus demands our obedience and that as a King he might even call us to suffer death in his name. But Jesus calls us to that obedience only after he has suffered death for us in obedience to the Father's saving will. What Jesus demands of us he has himself endured for us, and he promises us the help of his Holy Spirit in our trials.

Are you a friend of Jesus Christ, trusting in him, surrendering your will to him as your King and Lord? If you have renounced the friendship of Caesar and become a friend of Jesus, you can know that he died for your sins. He promises that whatever fire you endure in this world for his sake, he will go through it with you, so that you will not be consumed (Isa. 43:2). And when your faith has achieved its triumph over the world (1 John 5:4), you will receive the crown of righteousness, which the sovereign Lord will award to his friends and disciples, for whose sins he died, and in the life to come you will reign with him in glory forever (2 Tim. 4:8; Rom. 8:17).

124

KING OF THE JEWS

John 19:13–22

*Pilate also wrote an inscription and put it on the cross. It read,
"Jesus of Nazareth, the King of the Jews." Many of the Jews read
this inscription, for the place where Jesus was crucified was near
the city, and it was written in Aramaic, in Latin, and in Greek.*
(John 19:19–20)

ohn's account of Jesus' arrest and trials differs in many respects
from that of the other Gospels. John seems to see no need to
repeat details recorded elsewhere, omitting such incidents as
Simon of Cyrene's help in carrying Jesus' cross (Matt. 27:32), Jesus' warning
to the weeping women (Luke 23:27–31), the Jews' mocking of Jesus (Mark
15:29–32), the darkness that fell on the land (Mark 15:33), Jesus' prayer
for his enemies (Luke 23:34), the crucified thief's request for salvation
(Luke 23:39–43), Jesus' cry of desolation (Mark 15:34), the tearing of the
curtain in the temple (Mark 15:38), and the centurion's confession of faith
(Mark 15:39). In the place of these, John adds some remarkable details,
including the Jews' objection to Pilate's inscription (John 19:19–22), Jesus'
quotations from Psalms 22 and 69 (19:24, 28–29), Jesus' committing his
mother into John's hands (19:25–27), his cry of triumph before death (19:30),

the failure of the soldiers to break his legs (19:31–33), and the piercing of Jesus' side with a spear (19:34). Not only did John want his eyewitness details to be recorded, but he inserts them to emphasize his message of God's sovereignty in the death of his Son and Christ's willingness to be a Sacrifice for our sins.

THE KING RENOUNCED

God's sovereignty and Christ's willing submission were the key features of Jesus' trial before Pontius Pilate. The Roman trial had fulfilled God's ancient prophecies (especially those of Isaiah 53) and displayed Jesus' meekness in suffering. It is impossible to obscure, however, the role of Pontius Pilate's corruption of Roman justice and the malice of the Jewish leaders toward their promised Messiah. Pilate had done everything he could, short of courageously performing his duty, to have Jesus released. The Jews, however, were adamant about Jesus' crucifixion, and when they threatened to accuse Pilate before Caesar, the governor gave in. He thus concluded the trial in dramatic fashion: "he brought Jesus out and sat down on the judgment seat at a place called The Stone Pavement, and in Aramaic Gabbatha. Now it was the day of Preparation of the Passover. It was about the sixth hour. He said to the Jews, 'Behold your King!'" (John 19:13–14).

John's citation regarding both the day and the hour has led to disputes among scholars. John places this event on "the day of Preparation of the Passover" (John 19:14). Some scholars have thought this to designate the day on which the Jews prepared for the Passover, which would have been a Thursday.[1] The attraction of this view is that, if true, Jesus the Lamb of God was crucified at the very time the Passover lambs were slaughtered in Jerusalem. There are two problems with this, however. The first is that the other Gospels specify that the Last Supper was the Passover meal (see Luke 22:7–8), which was Thursday night, so that Jesus was crucified on the Friday following. Additionally, the word for "preparation" means the day when preparations were performed in advance of the Sabbath day of rest (see John 19:31), which likewise places Jesus' crucifixion on a Friday.[2]

1. This view is developed in James Montgomery Boice, *The Gospel of John*, 5 vols. (Grand Rapids: Baker, 1999), 5:1490–92.
2. D. A. Carson, *The Gospel of John* (Grand Rapids: Eerdmans, 1991), 603–4.

Even more discussion has resulted from John's statement that Jesus' trial concluded at "about the sixth hour" (John 19:14). The problem here is that Mark specifies that "it was the third hour" when Jesus was crucified (Mark 15:25). The numerous attempts to reconcile this difference, including the idea that John used a Roman system of time in contrast to Mark's use of Hebrew time, are neither successful nor necessary. We remember that people in those days did not wear watches and did not keep track of minutes and seconds, but gave only approximations. Moreover, in Bible times the daytime was broken up into four three-hour segments starting at dawn and concluding at sundown. When Mark says that Jesus was crucified in the "third hour," this probably means sometime during the three-hour period begun at the third hour after dawn. John approximates the same period by saying that Jesus' trial concluded sometime before "the sixth hour." John's clarification helps us to see that Mark was referring more generally to late morning instead of specifying 9:00 A.M. as the time of Jesus' crucifixion. Since we know that darkness covered the land from noon until 3:00 P.M. (see Mark 15:33), this suggests that Jesus was scourged, led with his cross to Golgotha, and nailed to the cross sometime in the late morning. Instead of hanging on the cross for three hours before noon (as a reading of Mark alone might suggest), Jesus would have been on the cross a relatively short time before the noontime darkness began the three-hour torment of his spirit under the wrath of God.

While John notes the time when the trial concluded, he is more concerned with the dialogue between Pilate and the Jews. Having yielded to the crowd's wishes, Pilate brought Jesus to his seat of judgment, which was placed at an elevated area of specially paved stones. Normally, the judge would sit on the throne with the accused before him. But John uses a word that could be translated to say that Pilate sat Jesus on the throne before the people (John 19:13). Whether he did this or not, Pilate displayed Jesus, saying, "Behold your King!" (19:14). The irony in John's account is palpable.

Just as the faithless high priest Caiaphas unknowingly spoke the words confirming Jesus as the atoning Sacrifice for the nation—"It is better for you that one man should die for the people" (John 11:50)—so also the representative of worldly imperial rule acclaimed the bruised and bloodied Jesus in his office as King. God thus hailed his Son as Savior-King through the very lips of those who conspired unjustly to crucify him.

If Pilate's presentation of Jesus was ironic, the cry of the assembled Jews plumbed new depths of tragedy. "They cried out, 'Away with him, away with him, crucify him!'" If this were not enough madness, Pilate made one last appeal: "Shall I crucify your King?" To this, the chief priests answered, "We have no king but Caesar" (John 19:15). So intent were these false and self-serving shepherds on having a Messiah of their own making and a righteousness for their own boasting that they rejected the Savior-King whom God had sent. In despising Jesus, they renounced their sacred covenant with God, repudiating the principle at the heart of Israel's life from the beginning, namely, that God is himself King over his people. In God's place they pledged allegiance to a vile Gentile ruler. George Beasley-Murray comments that this renunciation of Jesus "is nothing less than the abandonment of the messianic hope of Israel[,] . . . their repudiation of the promise of the kingdom of God, with which the gift of the Messiah is inseparably bound in Jewish faith."[3]

We see in this horrific scene a warning to all who will not receive the crucified Jesus as Lord and King. The Jews show that in rejecting Jesus, one cannot avoid losing his or her soul. In earthly terms, those who hear but refuse Jesus' gospel, like these Jewish leaders who refused to humble themselves as sinners before God's throne of mercy, consign themselves to a life of increasing darkness. It might be the darkness of a Christless morality, a lifestyle of proud and graceless rebellion against God's gospel rule. Or, more frequently, it might be the darkness of an increasing descent into immoral wretchedness. In the case of the Jews, their rejection of Jesus led to the pride and folly that ultimately ended in the city's destruction at the pitiless hands of the Roman master that they had called on to rid them of Jesus.

Even worse are the eternal implications of renouncing the crucified Jesus as Savior and King. The Jews likely thought they were making a meaningless gesture by acclaiming their loyalty to Caesar, whom they actually despised. Yet their words were recorded in heaven. Paul would later explain that "being ignorant of the righteousness of God, and seeking to establish their own, they did not submit to God's righteousness" (Rom. 10:3). As a result, God's ancient people, to whom the Lord had held out his arms for salvation through

3. George R. Beasley-Murray, *John*, Word Biblical Commentary 36 (Waco, TX: Word, 1987), 343.

all the many centuries, put themselves in the position formerly occupied by the hated Gentiles: "strangers to the covenants of promise, having no hope and without God in the world" (Eph. 2:12).

How unreasonable was the Jews' rejection of Jesus, when their own Scriptures so plainly pointed forward to him! Yet it is equally unreasonable for people to refuse Jesus today, and with equally tragic results. How many people, thoughtlessly blaspheming the name of God's Son or flippantly casting aside the gospel offer of salvation, likewise consign their immortal souls to a just and eternal punishment? God has presented his crucified Son, only to find his grace contemptuously rejected. As the writer of Hebrews warned, "how shall we escape if we neglect such a great salvation?" (Heb. 2:3).

THE KING CRUCIFIED

John's account of what happened next is as brief and direct as the event is epochal: "So [Pilate] delivered him over to them to be crucified" (John 19:16). With this statement, John introduces the most important event in human history. Mark Johnston writes:

> It is for this moment that the whole of the Bible has been preparing us. From the time of the Fall, throughout the whole Old Testament revelation, God was leading his people towards that day when he would send a Saviour and through him bring about salvation for all time. Similarly, from the moment of the conception of Jesus in the womb of the virgin Mary, right through to the climax of his ministry in Jerusalem, the Gospels have been preparing us for this—his death, and everything that it would achieve.[4]

In approaching Jesus' crucifixion, we should observe that John gives little attention to the grisly details of Jesus' physical suffering. This contrasts with popular treatments of Christ's death, which often seek to stir up emotions with lurid details of what Jesus experienced. Neither John nor any of the other Gospels follow this approach. Admittedly, when the apostles mentioned the crucifixion, their original audiences understood a good deal of what this involved, many of them having witnessed such dreadful spectacles. This warrants our surveying the likely sequence of events in Jesus' crucifixion.

4. Mark G. Johnston, *Let's Study John* (Edinburgh: Banner of Truth, 2003), 246.

545

John writes that Pilate delivered Jesus "over to them," meaning that he consented to the people's wish. A squad of Roman soldiers would then have seized Jesus, and it is likely that he now received the *verberatio*, the savage scourging with the Roman whip that rent his flesh almost to the point of death. John continues: "they took Jesus, and he went out, bearing his own cross, to the place called The Place of a Skull, which in Aramaic is called Golgotha. There they crucified him, and with him two others, one on either side, and Jesus between them" (John 19:16–18).

A crucifixion was terrible to behold. William Barclay states that "the Romans themselves regarded it with a shudder of horror. Cicero declared that it was 'the most cruel and horrifying death.' Tacitus said that it was a 'despicable death.'"[5] For this reason, no Roman citizen could be crucified for any crime, this form of execution being typically reserved for slaves and rebels. Death by the cross was apparently invented by the Persians, imported to the Mediterranean by the Carthaginians, and perfected by the Romans. The basic point was to combine shame with physical anguish, as the sufferer hung in the air slowly and torturously to die.

The scourging that preceded the crucifixion was so brutal that many victims failed to survive it. It is apparently because of the loss of blood that Jesus suffered and the violence of his beating that the other Gospels record that he needed help carrying his cross. John, keen to emphasize Jesus' self-mastery, points out that Jesus began by hoisting his own cross. After his fairly long ordeal in traversing the so-called Via Dolorosa ("Way of Sorrows"), Jesus arrived at the place of crucifixion outside the city walls. Typically, the prisoner carried only his crossbeam, the vertical beam having been set in place in advance. John identifies the place of execution as "the place of a skull, which in Aramaic is called Golgotha." The Latin for "place of the skull" is *Calvary*. We do not know what accounts for this name, and though many have assumed that Jesus was crucified on a skull-shaped hill, neither Scripture nor early-church tradition validates this interpretation.

Once at Golgotha, Jesus' hands or wrists were nailed to the crossbeam, and when he was lifted up, his feet were nailed to the vertical post of the cross. Crucifixion victims often suffocated or slowly died of exposure and

5. William Barclay, *The Gospel of John*, 2 vols. (Philadelphia: Westminster, 1975), 2:291.

loss of blood, and the pressure on the nailed feet as the victim sought to raise his chest to breathe could only have been horrific.

Even this brief description shows that Jesus suffered unspeakable agony in dying for our sins. Yet his shocking physical suffering paled in comparison to the outpouring of God's wrath upon Jesus' soul. It was Jesus' spiritual horror that prompted his cry of desolation, summing up the anguish of his spiritual alienation from the Father: "My God, my God, why have you forsaken me?" (Matt. 27:46).

The details that John chose to highlight are undoubtedly significant to his message. First, Jesus was taken outside the city to die, just as the Israelites had for centuries cast away the remains of the sin offerings outside the walls. This was especially the case for the sin offering on the annual Day of Atonement. Leviticus 16:27 specifies that these carcasses be disposed of outside the camp, anticipating their fulfillment in the crucified blood of Jesus Christ outside the city.

The writer of Hebrews would later exhort Christ's followers to "go to him outside the camp and bear the reproach he endured" (Heb. 13:13), departing from the external rituals of Judaism in order to benefit from Christ's spiritual sacrifice. So it has been since the earliest days of our faith. History records the words of England's Archbishop Laud, the champion of lofty rituals and religious show, when he visited Scotland in 1633 and found no great cathedrals or other displays of religious grandeur. Laud scoffed that the poor people had "no religion at all that I could see—which grieved me much."[6] What Laud did not notice was that outside the camp of religious formalism the believing Scots had Christ and his atoning blood by faith alone. Christians continue to go to Christ's cross outside the camp, bearing the world's scorn for Jesus. We do not need today's staged worship experiences, dancing fountains, or any other machinery of religious salesmanship, but receive eternal life by the heart inclined to the cross through simple faith in God's Word.

Second, as Jesus carries the cross, John undoubtedly sees God's covenant curse for our sins resting on Christ's holy shoulders. From the early church, Christians have seen a comparison between Jesus carrying his cross and Abraham's son Isaac carrying the wood on his back for the

6. Quoted in F. F. Bruce, *Hebrews* (Grand Rapids: Eerdmans, 1990), 379.

sacrifice that was commanded to be offered in his blood. Isaac asked his father the question that summed up the longing of the entire Old Testament: "Behold, the fire and the wood, but where is the lamb for a burnt offering?" Abraham answered in true, saving faith: "God will provide for himself the lamb for a burnt offering, my son" (Gen. 22:7–8). When the two arrived atop Mount Moriah, on which God's temple would later be built, Abraham stretched his son upon the altar in obedience to God's command. Yet as Abraham prepared to strike down with the knife, an angel cried out to stop him. Stuck in a nearby thicket was a ram provided by God (22:12–13). That episode was now fulfilled as Jesus, taking not only Isaac's place but the place of every believer whose guilt would require him to be slain on the altar of God's holy justice. In the cross of Christ, God provides the Sacrifice to free us from our sins.

Third, not only was Jesus led outside the city walls carrying his cross, but once at the execution site he was crucified between two others. John writes: "There they crucified him, and with him two others, one on either side, and Jesus between them" (John 19:18). The other Gospels inform us that these others were dying as thieves, or perhaps more accurately as insurrectionists (possibly associates of Barabbas). John's point in noting these men is to emphasize the fulfillment of Isaiah 53:12, "he poured out his soul to death and was numbered with the transgressors." The Romans were probably meaning to shame Jesus further by placing him amid others dying for the crimes that Jesus had been acquitted of. But without doubt, John would have us see the glorious significance of Christ's atoning death. All through his ministry Jesus had been scoffed at for associating with sinners, yet he replied, "I came not to call the righteous, but sinners" (Mark 2:17). It was only appropriate, therefore, for Jesus to be crucified between guilty malefactors. Leon Morris writes:

> For the writers of the Gospels this was not an insult but the expression of an important truth. Jesus came to save sinners. He died to save them, and the fact that on the cross he hung between people who were obviously grievous sinners graphically illustrated that truth. His death was a death on behalf of sinners, and his position when he died brought that out for those who had eyes to see.[7]

7. Leon Morris, *Reflections on the Gospel of John* (Peabody, MA: Hendrickson, 1986), 658.

THE KING ACCLAIMED

John's account of the crucifixion emphasizes God's sovereignty and Jesus' mastery in submitting himself to death. So far, however, everything seems to have gone against Jesus. But John adds a detail that reminds us of God's control over every detail in this event and reveals Jesus' glory shining through his cross. We see this in the placard inscribed by Pontius Pilate, acclaiming Jesus' kingship even in the agony of his crucifixion. John recounts: "Pilate also wrote an inscription and put it on the cross. It read, 'Jesus of Nazareth, the King of the Jews'" (John 19:19).

Never wanting to miss the deterrent effect of a crucifixion, the Romans had a practice of writing out the criminal's offense on a tablet, called a *titlos*, that would be paraded in front as the victim carried his cross to the place of execution and was then affixed to the cross. So it was that Pilate, having personally examined the accused Jesus of Nazareth, directed that he be identified as the King of the Jews. In this action, we may be sure that the hand of God was ruling so that the honor of his Son would be made plainly known. Beasley-Murray writes, "Pilate, the judge and representative of the dominion that ruled the world, hereby declares that Jesus on his cross is King of his people."[8] A king conquers, provides, rules, and makes peace. Christ our King conquered our enemy the devil, provided forgiveness for our sins, rules in our hearts, and makes peace between sinners and God. All these kingly deeds Jesus achieved by dying on the cross for us, so it is proper for him to have been hailed as King there.

God in this way arranged that while his Son suffered crucifixion, all passersby would learn the reason for his death. John writes, "Many of the Jews read this inscription, for the place where Jesus was crucified was near the city, and it was written in Aramaic, in Latin, and in Greek" (John 19:20). Hebrew was the language of God's revelation,[9] Latin was the language of power, and Greek was the language of wisdom. Matthew Henry comments: "In each of these languages Christ is proclaimed King, in whom are hid all the treasures of revelation, wisdom, and power."[10]

8. Beasley-Murray, *John*, 346.
9. While many scholars believe that John 19:20 refers to Aramaic, the Greek text states that the sign was written in Hebrew, as well as Latin and Greek.
10. Matthew Henry, *Commentary on the Whole Bible*, 6 vols. (Peabody, MA: Hendrickson, 2009), 5:967.

A week earlier, Jesus had exclaimed, "The hour has come for the Son of Man to be glorified. . . . And I, when I am lifted up from the earth, will draw all people to myself" (John 12:23, 32). Now, just as he had said, Israel's King and the world's Savior was lifted up along the highway of Jerusalem and hailed before the eyes of all. By noting the three languages in which Jesus' kingship was declared, a detail that John alone notes, the apostle is stating that "Jesus is a King for everyone. He is not merely a Jewish Savior, though he is that. He is the Savior of the Greeks and of the Romans as well. He is the Savior of the world."[11]

Predictably, the Jewish leaders were incensed by Pilate's inscription as it was paraded before the cross and then affixed above the suffering form of Jesus. Their anger is easily understood, since the sign declared both the innocence of the man whom they had cruelly betrayed and their treason against God. Never lacking for cunning, they suggested only a small addition: "Do not write, 'The King of the Jews,' but rather, 'This man said, I am King of the Jews'" (John 19:21). This time, Pilate was obstinate: "What I have written I have written," he answered (19:22). It was God's will that truly would not be altered, and God's declaration of the righteousness, glory, and dominion of his Son can never be annulled by the indignant unbelief of rebel mankind. Thus was established the true cause of Jesus' death: He died because he was King of God's covenant nation and because only through his death could his beloved people be forgiven and enter eternal life. As John stated in the first verse of his account of Jesus' passion, "Having loved his own who were in the world, he loved them to the end" (13:1).

HAILING THE KING

As we reflect on the religious leaders' reaction to the sign hailing Jesus as King of the Jews, we see that the cross not only declares God's saving grace to the world but also reveals the state of human hearts. The chief priests' objection to Pilate's sign shows how hardened and dark their hearts had become since they would not humble themselves as sinners before God. As Paul later explained, to such people the cross exudes only the aroma of death. But there are others for whom the cross spreads "a fragrance from

11. Boice, *John*, 5:1502.

life to life" (2 Cor. 2:16). One such person was one of the men crucified with Jesus, whose salvation John probably intends for us to recall from the other Gospels. At first, both thieves reviled Jesus along with the others. But one of them, reflecting on his approaching death and perceiving Jesus' majesty as the King of the Jews, called out to Jesus for salvation. "Jesus," he pleaded, "remember me when you come into your kingdom." Jesus answered with a royal decree of grace from the cross, "Truly, I say to you, today you will be with me in Paradise" (Luke 23:42–43).

Can you give any justifiable reason why you should not do the same? Why should you not hail Jesus as the true King of glory, the sinless Savior who died out of love for you, gaining your forgiveness by bearing the curse of your sins on the cross? If you refuse to call on Jesus for salvation, you will be joining the Jewish leaders in preferring to be damned forever rather than humble yourself in submission to Jesus and his cross. Charles Spurgeon appeals to us all:

> He claims to be King, so stand at the foot of the cross, I pray you, and admit his claim. If you would have Jesus to be your Saviour, you must have him as your King; you must submit to his government, for he claims the right to rule over all who acknowledge him to be Jesus; yea more than that, he claims to rule all mankind, for all power is given unto him in heaven and in earth, and we are bidden to proclaim his kingdom throughout the whole world, and to say to all men, "Jesus of Nazareth is your King, bow down before him." . . . The claims of Christ . . . were published even from the tree on which he died; so do not resist them, but willingly yield yourselves up to Jesus now, and let him be King to you henceforth and for ever.[12]

12. Charles H. Spurgeon, *Metropolitan Tabernacle Pulpit*, 63 vols. (London: Passmore & Alabaster, 1908), 54:608.

125

BENEATH THE CROSS

John 19:23–27

This was to fulfill the Scripture which says, "They divided my garments among them, and for my clothing they cast lots."
(John 19:24)

O ne of the most important principles for interpreting the Bible is to recognize its Christ-centered character. This principle does not mean that every passage in the Bible must be forced to make a direct reference to Jesus, whether one is present or not. It does mean that the message of the Bible as a whole is directed to the person and work of Jesus Christ. Therefore, every passage in the Bible, whatever its content, should be interpreted within the context of the Bible's overall Christ-centered message. This is the interpretive principle taught by Jesus himself. In John 5, Jesus expressed dismay at the Jewish leaders' refusal to believe on him, since they were students of the Scriptures and, Jesus insisted, "it is they that bear witness about me" (John 5:39). In Jesus' famous conversation with the Emmaus road disciples on the day of the resurrection, Jesus opened the Scriptures and "beginning with Moses and all the Prophets, he interpreted to them in all the Scriptures the things concerning himself" (Luke 24:27).

The recognition of the Bible's central focus on salvation through Jesus Christ was a key principle of the Protestant Reformation. Martin Luther emphasized this point:

> He, *He*, Mary's Son, is the one who is able to give eternal life to all who come to Him and believe on Him. Therefore he that would correctly and profitably read Scripture should see to it that he finds Christ in it; then he finds life eternal without fail. On the other hand, if I do not so study and understand Moses and the prophets so as to find that Christ came from Heaven for the sake of my salvation, became man, suffered, died, was buried, rose, and ascended to Heaven so that through Him I enjoy reconciliation with God, forgiveness of all my sins, grace, righteousness, and life eternal, then my reading in Scripture is of no help whatsoever to my salvation.[1]

James Montgomery Boice comments of this:

> Luther's point is that the Scriptures are, both in their general outline and in specific details, God's Word to us about Jesus. It is undoubtedly this keen spiritual insight that made him the tower of strength and the winsome exegete that he was. Luther believed that the Bible was God's Word and that it was about Jesus. Consequently, whenever he approached the Bible, he knew from the start who was speaking in it and what its theme was.[2]

Lots for Christ's Clothing

One way in which the Old Testament pointed to Jesus was through the prophecies that were fulfilled at his cross. These prophecies served the dual purpose of proving that Jesus died according to God's foreordained plan and of providing the Bible's interpretation of Jesus' death as an atoning sacrifice for sin. The apostle John was keen to point out the fulfillment of prophecies in Jesus' death, explicitly noting four of them. Working backward from the last, John points out that Jesus' side was pierced by a spear in fulfillment of Zechariah 12:10 (John 19:37); Jesus' bones were left unbroken, as was foretold in Psalm 34:20 (John 19:36); before dying, Jesus gasped, "I thirst,"

1. Martin Luther, *What Luther Says*, comp. Ewald M. Plass, 3 vols. (St. Louis: Concordia, 1959), 1:69–70.
2. James Montgomery Boice, *The Gospel of John*, 5 vols. (Grand Rapids: Baker, 1999), 5:1508.

fulfilling Psalm 69:21 (John 19:28); and after crucifying Jesus, the Roman soldiers gambled for his clothes. John writes:

> When the soldiers had crucified Jesus, they took his garments and divided them into four parts, one part for each soldier; also his tunic. But the tunic was seamless, woven in one piece from top to bottom, so they said to one another, "Let us not tear it, but cast lots for it to see whose it shall be." This was to fulfill the Scripture which says, "They divided my garments among them, and for my clothing they cast lots." So the soldiers did these things. (John 19:23–24)

This dividing of Jesus' clothing and casting of lots for the final piece fulfilled Psalm 22:18: "they divide my garments among them, and for my clothing they cast lots."

It was apparently the standard Roman practice for the soldiers who performed an execution to take the victim's clothing. Scholars state that the average Jew of Jesus' time wore five articles of clothing: a loincloth, a tunic, shoes, a turban or scarf, and an outer robe. Since there were four soldiers, this permitted one article for each, with the outer garment left over. Normally, the robe would be torn apart at the seams and the pieces distributed, except that Jesus' robe was "seamless, woven in one piece from top to bottom." There was no point in tearing it up, so the soldiers decided to cast lots to see who would take the robe. This shows that while the soldiers had no notion of fulfilling ancient prophecy, God was exercising his sovereign control through their otherwise pointless actions. Just as Pontius Pilate had unknowingly published the truth about Jesus when he ordered that his placard declare him the "King of the Jews," so also the soldiers' unknowing action pointed Jesus out as the true David of Psalm 22 who suffers humiliation for God's people.

Many Bible interpreters have imagined an allegorical significance to Jesus' seamless robe beyond anything stated by the text. The early-church scholar Origen saw in it the wholeness of Christ's teaching, Cyprian saw it as depicting the unity of the church, and Cyril saw it as representing Christ's virgin birth.[3] Roman Catholic apologists touted Christ's seamless garment as symbolic of the church that should not be divided, accusing Luther

---

3. Leon Morris, *Reflections on the Gospel of John* (Peabody, MA: Hendrickson, 1986), 664.

and the other Reformers of "rending the seamless tunic" of Christ.[4] Some Reformed writers have also allegorized Christ's seamless garment, seeing it as a picture of Christ's perfect imputed righteousness. Noting the tendency for gross subjectivism in such allegories, we do better to avoid this kind of interpretation altogether when it is not specifically warranted by the text.

This does not mean, however, that there is no clear meaning to the dividing of Jesus' garments. This episode dramatized the certainty of Jesus' death once he was crucified, since it is dead men whose clothes are distributed. Moreover, the casting of lots for Jesus' clothing signified his humiliation in death, because Jesus' final possessions were carelessly handled by the men who had put him to death.

Perhaps most significant is the clear implication that Jesus was stripped naked in his crucifixion. Romans stripped their enemies and victims to shame them, and Jesus' nakedness in death was one way in which he offered himself as our Substitute. The shame of nakedness is part of the curse for our sin. Adam and Eve in the garden were naked and without shame because of their original righteousness (Gen. 2:25). But after they fell into sin, their nakedness was a source of shame, and they sought to cover themselves with fig leaves (3:7). Therefore, just as Jesus bore the thorns of sin's curse (3:18) in his mocking crown, he also bore the reproach of our nakedness in his death.

Christians should rejoice in this glorious gospel provision, especially those who are tormented in shame for their own sins or for sins of others committed against them. Jesus in his death bore not only the guilt but also the shame of sin. Isaiah foresaw Jesus dying with our reproach upon him, saying that "as one from whom men hide their faces he was despised" (Isa. 53:3). Therefore, none who come to God in Jesus' name need ever be ashamed, since Jesus has borne our shame and removed all disgrace from those he saves.

It is in this way that we rightly see the imputed righteousness of Christ in this scene. Jesus bore our sin not only to remove our guilt and shame but also to clothe us with his righteousness. Paul explained, "For our sake [God] made him to be sin who knew no sin, so that in him we might become the righteousness of God" (2 Cor. 5:21). John Calvin explains: "Christ was stripped of his garments, that he might clothe us with righteousness; his

---

4. Gordon J. Keddie, *A Study Commentary on John*, 2 vols. (Darlington, UK: Evangelical Press, 2001), 2:336.

naked body was exposed to the insults of men, that we may appear in glory before the judgment-seat of God."[5] Through faith in Christ, our sin is placed onto his cross and our nakedness is clothed in the white robes of his righteousness, that we sinners might stand unashamed before God.

Psalm 22 and the Torment of Christ

I pointed out that the fulfillment of Psalm 22:18 in the casting of lots for Jesus' clothing identifies him as the true David who suffers for God's people. There is good reason to believe that Psalm 22, which David wrote to lament his own sufferings as God's anointed shepherd, details the anguished experience of Jesus during the three hours that he suffered on the cross.

Mark's Gospel tells us that at the sixth hour, noon, a supernatural darkness fell on the land, obscuring the spiritual torment of Jesus as he bore our sins under God's wrath (Mark 15:33). This continued for three hours, until at the ninth hour Jesus surrendered his spirit and died. John's reference to the fulfillment of Psalm 22 identifies Jesus as the One who fulfills the suffering of David's psalm. Moreover, we should note that the first and the sixth of Jesus' seven sayings on the cross are taken from Psalm 22. Matthew tells us that when the time of darkness had almost expired, Jesus cried out, "My God, my God, why have you forsaken me?" (Matt. 27:46). This quotes the opening words of Psalm 22. Then, just before yielding his spirit into the Father's hands, Jesus quoted from the end of Psalm 22. David declares, "They shall come and proclaim his righteousness to a people yet unborn," and then concludes the psalm with "he has done it" (Ps. 22:31). This last statement can be translated in the way that Jesus states it in John 19:30, "It is finished."

Since Jesus responded to his sufferings on the cross by quoting the beginning and the end of Psalm 22, it is likely that the psalm as a whole depicts the flow of Jesus' experience during the crucifixion. We can outline this flow in three points: Jesus was forsaken, Jesus was crushed, and Jesus was executed.

First, Psalm 22 expresses the forsakenness of Christ by noting God's refusal to deliver him: "All who see me mock me; they make mouths at me; they wag their heads; 'He trusts in the LORD; let him deliver him;

---

5. John Calvin, *Calvin's Commentaries*, trans. William Pringle, 22 vols. (Grand Rapids: Baker, 2009), 18:230.

let him rescue him, for he delights in him!' " (Ps. 22:7–8). This was precisely the taunt thrown in Jesus' face during his crucifixion. Matthew records: "So also the chief priests, with the scribes and elders, mocked him, saying, 'He saved others; he cannot save himself. . . . He trusts in God; let God deliver him now, if he desires him. For he said, "I am the Son of God" ' " (Matt. 27:41–43). That God did not deliver Jesus from the cross, but abandoned his Son to suffer all the torment of his wrath on our sins, shows how Jesus suffered as one truly abandoned by God in his death.

Second, Psalm 22 speaks of Jesus' being crushed on the cross: "I am a worm and not a man, scorned by mankind and despised by the people" (Ps. 22:6). It might seem bizarre to us for Jesus to compare himself to a worm. But this expression in Jesus' time had come to refer to a certain kind of worm, the *tola*, from whose blood a valuable crimson dye was made. To release the dye, the animal was crushed, so that its blood would flow out. James Montgomery Boice comments: "This image throws light upon Christ's thoughts, for when Jesus thought of himself as the *tola*, he thought of himself as the worm who is *crushed* for God's people. His blood was shed for us that we might be clothed in bright raiment."[6] This perfectly accords with the prophecy of Isaiah 53:10: "it was the will of the LORD to crush him; he has put him to grief." In shedding his blood, therefore, Jesus submitted his soul to be crushed as he suffered under God's wrath on the cross for us.

Third, the bulk of Psalm 22 is devoted to David's grief over those who are determined to see him dead. Likewise, Jesus knows himself as One who is executed on the cross. "Many bulls encompass me; strong bulls of Bashan surround me" the psalm laments; "they open wide their mouths at me, like a ravening and roaring lion" (Ps. 22:12–13). Further threats include the sword, the mouth of the lion, and the horns of the wild oxen (22:20–21). The wild ox is especially significant as an animal on which victims were sometimes bound for execution. Jesus, following the pathos of this psalm, suffered by reflecting on the judicial aspect of his execution, knowing full well that he was judicially executed as he bore the sins that we committed.

6. Boice, *John*, 5:1511.

JESUS' FAMILY MATTERS

John does not dwell on Jesus' sufferings beyond referring us to Psalm 22, instead placing his focus beneath the cross. First, he told us of the soldiers who cast lots for his robe. In John 19:25–27, he then identifies four women who were present out of love for Jesus: "standing by the cross of Jesus were his mother and his mother's sister, Mary the wife of Clopas, and Mary Magdalene" (19:25).

It is not entirely clear how to understand this list of women. As some see it, John names two women only, first specifying them as Jesus' mother and her sister, and then giving their names as "Mary the wife of Clopas, and Mary Magdalene." There is no indication elsewhere, however, that Jesus' mother had remarried after the death of Joseph or that Mary Magdalene was her sister. Others see three women identified, with John saying that Mary's sister was "Mary the wife of Clopas." It is difficult to imagine two sisters with the same name, however, so it is probably best to take John as identifying four women. The first two are identified as Jesus' mother Mary and her sister, accompanied by Mary the wife of Clopas and Mary Magdalene. When we compare this list with that of Mark's Gospel, this indicates that Mary the wife of Clopas was the mother of Jesus' disciples "James the younger and of Joses" (Mark 15:40). More interesting still is that Mark names the fourth woman as Salome, and Matthew notes that she was "the mother of the sons of Zebedee" (Mark 15:40; Matt. 27:56), that is, the mother of the apostle John and his brother James. Since Mark specifies that there were other unnamed women in the vicinity of the cross, this identification of the fourth woman is far from certain. If this is true, however, it makes the apostle John the cousin of Jesus Christ according to the flesh. This might account in part for the close bond between them and also for Jesus' action in this passage.

Among these four women, it was Jesus' mother who drew his attention and should draw ours as well. Thirty years earlier, when she and her husband Joseph had presented Jesus at the temple, aged Simeon had blessed the child but spoken words of warning to the young mother, saying that "a sword will pierce through your own soul" (Luke 2:35). Did she think of those words as their reality struck with the force that only a mother watching her son dying can know? Standing steadfast by her Son, Mary continues the example of virtue for which her memory should be prized by all her brothers and sisters in Christ.

If Mary was faithful to her Son to the end, Jesus in response acted out of concern for her even in such an hour of darkness for himself. John records that a fifth friend of Jesus was present beneath the cross, namely, himself. To John, Jesus committed the care of his earthly mother: "When Jesus saw his mother and the disciple whom he loved standing nearby, he said to his mother, 'Woman, behold, your son!' Then he said to the disciple, 'Behold, your mother!' And from that hour the disciple took her to his own home" (John 19:26–27).

Jesus' concern for Mary's welfare is one more instance of his compassion and concern for all in need, even amid such physical and spiritual agony. Jesus had made provision for his murderers, praying for the Father to forgive them (Luke 23:34). Jesus had provided for the penitent thief who asked to be remembered in Jesus' kingdom, promising that he would be in Paradise that very day (23:43). Now Jesus attended to the needs of his mother, still ministering from the cross.

Jesus ministered to Mary in two important ways. First, he addressed her not as "Mother" but as "Woman." Some commentators have speculated that Jesus was seeking to spare Mary the grief of hearing her Son calling on her as his mother. But the clear and important significance of this way of speaking is that Jesus was alerting Mary to her need to relate to him not as a mother but as a member of that fallen race of Adam and Eve. The greatest mistake for even a spiritually minded person like Jesus' mother Mary is to seek a claim on Jesus through the merits of the flesh. J. C. Ryle comments: "Henceforth she must daily remember, that her first aim must be to live the life of faith as a believing woman, like all other Christian women. Her blessedness did not consist in being related to Christ according to the flesh, but in believing and keeping Christ's Word."[7]

Having called his mother to faith in him as Lord and Savior, Jesus then made provision for her temporal care after his departure. "Woman, behold, your son!" Jesus declared, directing Mary to the care of the disciple John. "Behold, your mother!" he said to John (John 19:26–27). John concludes,

---

7. Ryle, *Expository Thoughts on the Gospels: John*, 3 vols. (Edinburgh: Banner of Truth, 1999), 3:51–52.

"And from that hour the disciple took her to his own home" (19:27). Scripture does not record Mary's future life, but varying traditions state that Mary lived with John in Jerusalem for eleven more years until she died or, in an alternative version, that she traveled with John to Ephesus in later years and died there.[8]

Roman Catholic theologians have made this passage a centerpiece of their teaching of Mary as Co-Redemptrix along with her Son Jesus. Such a doctrine can be gleaned from this text only by turning Jesus' words on their head. Whereas Jesus plainly commits his mother to the care of his Beloved Disciple, Roman Catholics insist that Jesus was committing the apostles and the church into the care of his mother. Some of them go so far as to say that Jesus sees this installment of Mary over the church as his ultimate achievement on the cross. It is true that Jesus entrusted his church into the care of another, but his Farewell Discourse of the previous night made it clear that it was to the Holy Spirit that Jesus has committed his followers in his absence. "I will ask the Father, and he will give you another Helper," Jesus said, referring not to his earthly mother but to "the Spirit of truth," who will be "with you forever" (John 14:16–17).

Jesus' care for his mother does set an important example for us in our attentiveness to the needs of our parents in their elderly years. Jesus was faithful to fulfill the fifth commandment, which commands us to honor our father and mother (Ex. 20:12). But even as Jesus fulfills this commandment, he shows us that the spiritual family of believers is more significant than the blood relations of our earthly families. Mary had other sons, we know, but they had not yet believed on Jesus, so our Lord commits his mother not into their care but into the care of one who will have a spiritual, as well as material, interest in Mary's care. On the cross, Jesus was bringing together a new family by means of his atoning blood, and this spiritual family of God's born-again children is more important to Jesus than other earthly ties (see also Luke 8:21; 14:26). Jesus' concern for his mother did not deter him from fulfilling the redeeming work that God had given him to do, and while children are urged by his example to attend to the needs of their parents, we

8. Frédéric Louis Godet, *Commentary on the Gospel of John*, 3 vols. (Grand Rapids: Zondervan, 1893), 3:387.

should not be deterred from serving the Lord solely because of family considerations.

THE FAITHFUL SAVIOR

In recounting the crucifixion, John labors to highlight Jesus' faithfulness. Jesus was faithful to God in fulfilling the prophecies of Scripture to the letter, voluntarily undergoing abandonment, crushing violence, and a shameful execution so that God's saving plan might be fulfilled. Jesus was faithful to his mother, providing for her needs even while he suffered on the cross. Finally, Jesus was faithful to us as he bore our nakedness in sin, shed his crimson blood to cleanse us of our guilt, and provided the righteousness we need to stand in favor before God. The cross brings the message of the whole Bible into focus, showing that God has fulfilled his promised offer of salvation through the gift of his spotless Son to die on the cross for our sins, and then to rise from the dead in everlasting resurrection power. God the Father and God the Son have been faithful to their saving promises: will you have faith in them, thereby entering God's fatherly love through the gift of Christ's sin-atoning sacrifice?

The only conceivable reasons to refuse Jesus are those of the Jewish leaders and the Roman soldiers. The Jews wanted to be justified by their own righteousness, despite their obvious sins, so they reviled Jesus on the cross. The Romans were more interested in worldly riches, even the poor articles of Jesus' clothing, which they happily gathered while neglecting the righteousness he gives to those who believe. To the self-righteous, the Bible says, "God opposes the proud, but gives grace to the humble" (James 4:6). To the worldly and greedy, Jesus warns against the folly of seeking after riches but neglecting the higher matter of salvation. Jesus' cross declares that the great need of everyone living on earth—from a supposed saint such as Mary to the calloused Roman soldiers who crucified Jesus—is salvation from the sins that otherwise condemn us before God, a salvation available to all through faith in Christ.

We have seen that Psalm 22 seems to chronicle Jesus' experience during his torment on the cross. If that is true, then the conclusion to the psalm tells us that the salvation of sinners was the main thought in Jesus' mind as he looked on all those gathered beneath his cross. The psalm's final verse says: "They shall come and proclaim his righteousness to a people yet unborn, that he has done it" (Ps. 22:31). This righteousness of Christ that we proclaim today can be yours if you will stand beneath his cross, look to Jesus in faith, and yield to him the fidelity of your heart. Then the psalm of Jesus' cross will have been fulfilled in you when it declares that "those who seek him shall praise the LORD!" (22:26).

126

THE DEATH OF THE SAVIOR

John 19:28—30

After this, Jesus, knowing that all was now finished,
said (to fulfill the Scripture), "I thirst." (John 19:28)

Christianity is different from every other religion in its utter dependence on its founder. Jesus is uniquely linked to Christianity in the sense that there is no Christianity at all without him. This situation does not exist in any other religion. Buddhism and Confucianism rely on teachings that are ascribed to their founders but could have come from any other source. The men themselves are not necessary, but only their ideas. The same is true even of Islam in its relationship to Muhammad. While Muslims point to Muhammad as the recipient of the supposed revelation that came from the archangel Gabriel, the person and life of Muhammad himself are not necessary to the beliefs taught in the Qur'an.

In contrast, Christianity is a set of beliefs about Jesus himself. John Stott explained: "The person and work of Christ are the rock upon which the Christian religion is built. If he is not who he said he was, and if he did not do what he said he had come to do, the foundation is undermined and the whole superstructure will collapse. Take Christ from Christianity, and you disembowel it; there is practically nothing left. Christ is the center of Christianity; all else is circumference."[1]

Not only does Christianity require belief in the person and work of Christ, but our faith involves a personal relationship with Jesus as he continues to live and reign today. Jesus Christ is himself the substance of Christian faith and life.

When it comes to Jesus' saving work, the Christian faith centers on his sin-atoning death, to which we now come in John's Gospel. I intend to consider the death of Jesus in three studies, in which we will examine the fact of Jesus' death as a Substitute for sinners, the results of Jesus' death in atoning for our sin, and then the finality of Jesus' death, as seen in his triumphant cry, "It is finished" (John 19:30).

JESUS' CRY OF THIRST

When Christians believe in Jesus, we confess that he is both truly God and truly man. There is one person, Jesus Christ, with a divine and a human nature. Throughout church history, skeptics have sought to deny or limit the true deity of Jesus. Among those who want to revere Jesus, however, the tendency is to deny or at least downplay his true humanity. Yet it is essential that when Jesus was born of a virgin, the eternal Son of God took up a true human nature and became man. According to the Bible, in order for Jesus to pay the debt of man's sin, he must be a man. The writer of Hebrews stated: "he had to be made like his brothers in every respect . . . to make propitiation for the sins of the people" (Heb. 2:17).

In the early church, Gnostic philosophers taught that all matter is evil. Only spirit, they said, is noble and good. Under this view, it was inconceivable that God's Son truly suffered and died in a human body. Instead, they taught that Christ only seemed to be a man. This view is called *docetism*, based on the Greek word *dokeo*, which means "to seem": while it seemed that the Christ was a man, he was instead a kind of phantom. Or, in an alternative view, the divine Spirit occupied only a human shell that was the man Jesus. In any case, though Christ seemed to be a man, he really was not.

1. John R. W. Stott, *Basic Christianity* (Downers Grove, IL: InterVarsity Press, 1971), 21.

Any idea that Jesus was less than fully man is overthrown by his tormented words, "I thirst" (John 19:28). Charles Spurgeon writes: "Jesus was proved to be really man, because he suffered the pains which belong to manhood. Angels cannot suffer thirst. A phantom, as some have called him, could not suffer in this fashion: but Jesus really suffered, not only the more refined pains of delicate and sensitive minds, but the rougher and commoner pangs of flesh and blood."[2]

Death by crucifixion inevitably involved the torment of extreme thirst. Jesus had suffered a great loss of fluids from his scourging, and the shock to his entire system from the crucifixion would likely have caused a fever to rack his body. Then hanging on a cross under the Near Eastern sun, he felt the exquisite torture of severe dehydration.

John states that Jesus said, "I thirst," "knowing that all was now finished" (John 19:28). This statement indicates that Jesus was aware that his suffering of God's wrath had come to an end and it was now time for him to die. It is noteworthy that Jesus did not complain during earlier torments such as his two beatings by the Roman soldiers and the nailing of his body to the cross. Once the sixth hour came and Jesus began to suffer the infinite torment of God's wrath on his spirit, it is likely that the comparatively lighter pains of his bodily torture were hardly noticed. But now, Jesus' gasp, "I thirst," indicates that the spiritual torment had concluded and the end of his sacrificial sufferings was before him.

John states as well that Jesus cried in thirst "to fulfill the Scripture" (John 19:28). Commentators such as Donald Grey Barnhouse and A. W. Pink imagine that Jesus had been calmly perusing all the Old Testament prophecies of his death. Starting with Genesis, Jesus brought to mind all these detailed prophecies and made sure before he died that all were fulfilled. When Jesus got to Psalm 69:21, he realized that its prophecy of his being forced to drink vinegar had not yet come to pass, so he said, "I thirst," to provoke the soldiers to give him the sponge of sour wine to drink. With this last prophecy fulfilled, Jesus was then free to die.

It might be true that Jesus spoke in part to prompt the soldiers to fulfill the ancient prophecy, but that interpretation does not seem to account for the pathos of Jesus' gasping words from the cross. John does not depict Jesus as

2. Charles H. Spurgeon, *Majesty in Misery*, 3 vols. (Edinburgh: Banner of Truth, 2005), 3:186–87.

engaging in calm Bible scholarship, but rather shows Jesus suffering in the torment of his dying thirst. This episode fulfilled the Scripture, therefore, because Psalm 69 accurately foretold the physical and emotional suffering that Jesus would endure on the cross.[3]

Jesus' quotation from Psalm 69 gives a commentary on his experience of suffering as he neared his death. David wrote this prayer for salvation when he was surrounded by enemies. The immediate context of Jesus' reference includes grief over the malice of his tormentors: "Reproaches have broken my heart, so that I am in despair. I looked for pity, but there was none, and for comforters, but I found none. They gave me poison for food, and for my thirst they gave me sour wine to drink" (Ps. 69:20–21). Mark's Gospel confirms the lament of this psalm, combining both physical suffering and ridicule. When the ninth hour came at the end of Jesus' suffering, he cried aloud, "My God, my God, why have you forsaken me?" Thinking he had called to Elijah, the onlooking soldiers gave Jesus their sour wine to keep him alive long enough to make fun of him (Mark 15:34–36). As John tells it: "A jar full of sour wine stood there, so they put a sponge full of the sour wine on a hyssop branch and held it to his mouth. When Jesus had received the sour wine, he said, 'It is finished,' and he bowed his head and gave up his spirit" (John 19:29–30).

All through his account of the crucifixion, John has emphasized Jesus' sovereign mastery. It is therefore only at the end that Jesus bows his head, having apparently held it aloft all through his torment. The expression "bowed his head" is elsewhere used for the laying down of one's head on a pillow (Matt. 8:20), so that John sees Jesus peaceably placing his head into the Father's embrace. A normal crucifixion might continue for hours and sometimes even days. But having endured the torment of God's wrath on the sins of his people, Jesus laid down his own life at the time of his choosing. Matthew's Gospel tells us that so awesome and holy was the spectacle of Jesus as he yielded up his life that the centurion and the other soldiers supervising his cross exclaimed, "Truly this was the Son of God!" (27:54).

---

3. Taken this way, "to fulfill the Scripture" refers to what comes before it rather than to Jesus' saying, "I thirst." The meaning would be that Jesus knew that "all was now finished in order to fulfill the Scriptures," and then said, "I thirst." See J. C. Ryle, *Expository Thoughts on the Gospels: John*, 3 vols. (Edinburgh: Banner of Truth, 1999), 3:359–60.

HELL PREFIGURED AND PREVENTED

We should note a number of things about Jesus' cry of thirst and the response of the soldiers. First, we should realize the shocking irony of this event. John has noted many ironies throughout the account of Jesus' arrest, trial, and crucifixion. The greatest of these is the cry of thirst from the Savior, who is himself the fountain of life. Bruce Milne comments: "So the one who offered living water, which would mean never thirsting again, the one who cried on the last day of the feast, 'If anyone is thirsty, let him come to me and drink,' *he* now cries, *I am thirsty*."[4] Jesus suffered the bitter irony of this reversal not by some defect in himself, as if his own store of waters had run dry, but as a voluntary Sacrifice in our behalf.

We can understand the significance of Jesus' suffering when we realize what a poignant picture of hell he presented when he cried, "I thirst" (John 19:28). Sin often begins with a sensual appetite, as it did in the eating of fruit in the garden, and it leads to an everlasting sensual torment. Part of the sufferings of hell will be "the deprivation of every form of comfort. Man refused to obey his Creator—the time will come when the Creator will refuse to succor man."[5]

We remember the words Jesus spoke about the tycoon who died and went to hell in his parable of Lazarus and the rich man. That man had lived a selfish, greedy, and ungodly life, and in death he went to the realms of torment. Burning with thirst in hell, the former rich man begged for godly Lazarus to dip his finger in water and place just one cool drop on his tongue, for, he said, "I am in anguish in this flame" (Luke 16:24). The request was denied because of the impassable gulf between heaven and hell and because God himself has ordained the eternal torment of all those who perish in their sins. Jesus, enduring our hell, experienced this same unabated, fiery thirst so that we would be saved from it. Charles Spurgeon wrote: "If Jesus had not thirsted, every one of us would have thirsted for ever afar off from God, with an impassable gulf between us and heaven. Our sinful tongues, blistered by the fever of passion, must have burned for ever had not his tongue been tormented with thirst in

4. Bruce Milne, *The Message of John: Here Is Your King!* (Downers Grove, IL: InterVarsity Press, 1993), 281.

5. Charles H. Spurgeon, *Metropolitan Tabernacle Pulpit*, 63 vols. (Pasadena, TX: Pilgrim, 1969), 59:758.

our stead."[6] Psalm 22:15 described the torment of thirst that Jesus endured as the penalty for our sin: "my strength is dried up like a potsherd, and my tongue sticks to my jaws; you lay me in the dust of death."

The response to Jesus' cry provides an accompanying portrait of the wickedness of man's sinful nature that deserves the torments of hell. We hear much today about the goodness and nobility of man, and for this reason people resent the Bible's teaching of sin and divine judgment. But look at noble mankind as God incarnate cries for something to drink from the cross! When Jesus was to be born, man was unwilling to make room for him at the inn. Now as Jesus suffers the thirst of divine judgment, man has no soothing cup of water for him but shoves a vinegar-filled sponge into his bleeding mouth. The psalm that Jesus quotes declares, "I looked for pity, but there was none, and for comforters, but I found none. They gave me poison for food, and for my thirst they gave me sour wine to drink" (Ps. 69:20–21). The psalm goes on to plead for divine punishment on the cruelty of mankind: "Add to them punishment upon punishment; may they have no acquittal from you. Let them be blotted out of the book of the living" (69:27–28).

A final detail in this passage suggests Jesus' death as our only prevention from suffering the torments of hell. John writes that the soldiers put the sponge of sour wine "on a hyssop branch and held it to his mouth" (John 19:29). Hyssop was a bush that produced a spongelike blossom. Israel's priests used this plant for the brush with which to sprinkle the blood from the atoning sacrifices in the temple. David refers to it in Psalm 51:7, "Purge me with hyssop, and I shall be clean; wash me, and I shall be whiter than snow." Hyssop was also used during the first Passover in Egypt to daub the lambs' blood on the Israelite doorposts so that the angel of death would pass over (Ex. 12:22). When the hyssop was lifted up to Jesus' mouth, it was not to sprinkle blood for his cleansing, but for his blood to fall upon the hyssop, providing the true atoning blood to which David appealed when he sought to be cleansed of his sin.

JESUS' DEATH AS SUBSTITUTE AND SACRIFICE

John's record of Jesus' death points to the great reality that Jesus died as a Substitute and Sacrifice for sin. John recounts that Jesus, "knowing that

---

6. Spurgeon, *Majesty in Misery*, 3:191.

all was now finished" (John 19:28), cried out in thirst, drank the sour wine, bowed down his head, and "gave up his spirit" (19:30). In foretelling this event, the prophet Isaiah made known its meaning: "he was wounded for our transgressions; he was crushed for our iniquities; upon him was the chastisement that brought us peace, and with his stripes we are healed. All we like sheep have gone astray; we have turned—every one—to his own way; and the LORD has laid on him the iniquity of us all" (Isa. 53:5–6). The key ideas here are *substitute* and *sacrifice*. God sent his Son, Jesus, to die on the cross as a Substitute for sinners, offering his life as a Sacrifice to pay the debt of sin for all who trust in his blood.

The background for these ideas is the penalty of death for breaking God's law. According to the Bible, "None is righteous, no, not one" (Rom. 3:10), since we have all sinned by breaking God's commands. We have all therefore come under the just condemnation of death, as Ezekiel 18:4 states: "The soul who sins shall die." The penalty of death for sin was taught to our first parents, Adam and Eve, at the beginning of the Bible. God commanded them to obey under the threat of death (Gen. 2:16–17), which included both physical and spiritual death. Adam broke God's command, and as our covenant head, he thereby cast our whole race into sin (see Rom. 5:12–14). For this reason, and since we have all confirmed our condemnation by committing our own personal sins, we are all justly condemned to suffer both the physical death of our bodies and the everlasting death of our souls in hell. It was to save us from this penalty that the God of grace sent his Son, Jesus, to die in the place of his people. We deserve death as the consequence of our sins, but Jesus substituted himself in our place on the cross and offered himself as a Sacrifice to satisfy God's law against the debt of our sin.

One of the best illustrations of Jesus' death as a Substitute and Sacrifice is the one that God provided to Adam and Eve after they had sinned in the garden. God had threatened disobedience with death, saying, "Of the tree of the knowledge of good and evil you shall not eat, for in the day that you eat of it you shall surely die" (Gen. 2:17). But after sinning, Adam and Eve had not suffered their punishment. How would God's justice be served if Adam and Eve did not die for their sin? Genesis 3:21 answers that "the LORD God made for Adam and for his wife garments of skins and clothed them."

Imagine the dreadful wonder of our first parents, who had never envisioned the death of one of God's creatures. God caused a substitute to die in Adam and

Eve's place, the first death that anyone had ever seen! The sinless animals died as a sacrifice to pay the debt of the sin of the man and woman, and then they were covered in the sinless skins of the sacrificed animals. "So this is death!" Adam and Eve must have cried in horror. James Montgomery Boice comments: "Yet even as they recoiled from the sacrifice, they must have marveled as well, for what God was showing was that although they themselves deserved to die it was possible for another, in this case two animals, to die in their place."[7]

Adam and Eve would have realized that the death of animals could never take away the stain of human sin. The writer of Hebrews stated that even the animal sacrifices of the Old Testament were never understood actually to atone for human sin, but were a constant reminder of sin and of the need for a true atonement, since "it is impossible for the blood of bulls and goats to take away sins" (Heb. 10:4). This is why John the Baptist spoke as the last prophet of the Old Testament, pointing to Jesus as the true Substitute for sinners and the true Sacrifice for sin: "Behold, the Lamb of God, who takes away the sin of the world" (John 1:29). Jesus died as a Substitute and Sacrifice for those who confess their sins to God and look to Jesus in faith for salvation. John 3:16 says, "For God so loved the world, that he gave his only Son, that whoever believes in him should not perish but have eternal life."

This reminds us that when Jesus laid down his head upon the bosom of the Father and "gave up his spirit," he did not die as a victim but as a victor. "It is finished," he cried at the end, having completed the sacrifice that pays the debt of our sin in the courts of God's holy justice (John 19:30).

Hymns abound that sentimentalize the sacrificial death of Jesus for his people. Bernard of Clairvaux sang:

> What language shall I borrow to thank thee, dearest Friend,
> For this, thy dying sorrow, thy pity without end?
> O make me thine forever; and should I fainting be,
> Lord, let me never, never outlive my love to thee.[8]

The sacrifice of Christ is worthy of all such admiration and love. But we must be sure to do more than admire the sacrifice of Jesus on the cross. We must first sing:

---

7. James Montgomery Boice, *The Gospel of John*, 5 vols. (Grand Rapids: Baker, 1999), 5:1527.
8. Bernard of Clairvaux, "O Sacred Head, Now Wounded" (12th c.).

Bearing shame and scoffing rude, in my place condemned he stood,
Sealed my pardon with his blood: Hallelujah! what a Savior![9]

To be saved, we must personally take our own sins to the cross, confessing them to God and entrusting them to Christ our Savior, that he would bear them as our Substitute and offer himself as our Sacrifice to satisfy God's just wrath.

Jesus' Thirst for Salvation

Preachers of this text have long seen one last sense in Jesus' cry, "I thirst." Spurgeon writes:

> Christ is always thirsting after the salvation of precious souls, and that cry on the cross . . . was the outburst of the great heart of Jesus Christ as he saw the multitude and he cried unto his God, "I thirst." He thirsted to redeem mankind, he thirsted to accomplish the work of our salvation. This very day he thirsteth still in that respect, as he is still willing to receive those that come to him, still resolved that such as come shall never be cast out, and still desires that they may come.[10]

Whether or not this interpretation accurately assesses Jesus' cry of thirst from the cross, it certainly fits Jesus' constant burden for the salvation of others who are dying in sin. Jesus cried, "I thirst," so that we may never thirst; he died that we might have eternal life. Once at the feast, Jesus called out, "If anyone thirsts, let him come to me and drink" (John 7:37). Jesus told the woman of Samaria, "Whoever drinks of the water that I will give him will never be thirsty again" (4:14). Therefore, through faith in him, our souls are filled with the life of God that Jesus sends by the Holy Spirit. To drink from the troughs of this world—the fountain of sinful pleasure, the well of pride, the pool of worldly attainment—is to be ever thirsty, never satisfied and always left to cry, "I thirst." But with the cup of simple faith, we may drink and be filled from Christ's river of life: "I came that they may have life," Jesus said, "and have it abundantly" (10:10).

9. Philip P. Bliss, "Man of Sorrows! What a Name" (1875).
10. Spurgeon, *Metropolitan Tabernacle Pulpit*, 59:759.

According to the Bible, there are only two thirsts that Jesus would have his people continue to feel. The first is the inner longing for more of him in our hearts. Jesus would have our souls be yet thirsty until he is our all in this life and our glory in the life to come. The psalmist sang, "As a deer pants for flowing streams, so pants my soul for you, O God. My soul thirsts for God, for the living God" (Ps. 42:1–2). This is a thirst that will be filled: since Jesus took the wrathful cup of sour wine to his thirsty lips, believers may look for the cup of fellowship with God to be placed onto ours.

The second thirst that Jesus would have us to know is his own thirst for the saving of souls. He would have parents shed such tears for the salvation of their children that they rise up from prayer with a hunger and thirst after righteousness (Matt. 5:6). As Jesus once stopped for a drink at the well in Samaria (John 4:6–7), he would likewise have us know the thirst of weariness in our labors for the salvation of friends, family members, and even those far away in distant lands. The Savior who thirsted on the cross now beckons all who will come to drink from the life that he gives, and then bids us to share the invitation with others. In fact, it is with his invitation to drink that Jesus speaks for the last time in all the Bible: "The Spirit and the bride say, 'Come!' And let him who hears say, 'Come!' Whoever is thirsty, let him come; and whoever wishes, let him take the free gift of the water of life" (Rev. 22:17 NIV).

127

WHY DID JESUS DIE?

John 19:30

When Jesus had received the sour wine, he said, "It is finished,"
and he bowed his head and gave up his spirit. (John 19:30)

n the eleventh century A.D., Anselm of Canterbury (1033–1109) published one of the most important theology books ever written, a work that significantly aided the understanding of Christians on a vitally important doctrinal matter. The book was titled *Cur Deus Homo*, which in English means "Why the God-Man?" or "Why Did God Become Man?" The book arose from conversations Anselm had with a man named Boso, who was one of many people during that time who sought to be enlightened in the gospel. Responding to this earnest spiritual hunger for truth, Anselm applied his keen mind to the Bible's teaching of the incarnation and atonement of Christ. Later, Anselm published his conclusions, thinking them important for the good of the wider church.

Of all the important topics presented in *Cur Deus Homo*, probably the most significant was Anselm's teaching on the purpose and design of Christ's death. Up until his time, the leading theory of the atonement in the Western church was the ransom theory. This teaching followed Jesus' important statement that "the Son of Man came . . . to give his life as a ransom for

573

many" (Matt. 20:28). As the early church conceived this ransom, Christ died to offer a payment in his blood to the devil, who held mankind captive in sin. Even so great a theologian as Augustine of Hippo spoke of the cross as "the Devil's mousetrap."[1] Under this view, Satan had secured the right of possession over mankind because of sin, so that Christ had to offer his death to the devil. Satan thought he had secured his victory over Jesus, but the power of divine life that he "swallowed" at the cross overthrew his realm of evil and death.

Anselm correctly saw that this ransom theory gave too much credit to Satan, who never possessed a true right to mankind. Man's true debt is to God's holy justice and honor; it was the broken law, not Satan, that held sinful man in condemnation. This insight reveals man's predicament in sin. Anselm observed: "Sinful man owes God a debt for sin which he cannot repay, and at the same time he cannot be saved without repaying."[2] This problem, unsolvable from the position of the sinner, who possesses no coin with which to pay his debt of sin, provides the answer to the mystery of why God became man. It also answers a question raised by Jesus' cry from the cross. Hearing Jesus' victory peal, "It is finished" (John 19:30), we ask, "Why did Jesus die?"

THEORIES OF THE ATONEMENT

Like all other great theologians, Anselm was immediately opposed and severely criticized for his work. His chief opponent was his former student, the French theologian Peter Abelard (1079–1142). Abelard argued that Christ did not die to make any payment at all, but merely offered himself as an example of divine love and of human virtue. This theory is called the *subjective* theory of the atonement, since it grounds the purpose of the cross in the subjective experience of the Bible reader rather than in any objective achievement in Jesus' death. Philip Ryken explains that in this theory, "the death of Christ was not satisfactory, in the sense of providing atonement for sin, but exemplary, in the sense of showing the way to suffer and die with courage." Although Abelard's teaching was denounced as heresy in 1121,

---

1. Quoted in Stephen J. Nichols, *Pages from Church History: A Guided Tour of Christian Classics* (Phillipsburg, NJ: P&R Publishing, 2006), 101.
2. Ibid., 103–4.

his theory of Christ's death is standard teaching in liberal churches today. Ryken comments, "Whenever we hear Jesus presented more as an example than as a Savior, we are hearing the sons and daughters of Abelard."[3]

Thinking in terms of his medieval context, Anselm's satisfaction theory of the atonement emphasized sinful man's insult to God's *honor*. Later theologians added to this the Bible's emphasis on sin's violation of God's *justice*. The biblical description of sin as transgression, for instance, means a violation of God's law, to which God responds with a just wrath. James states that those who fail to keep God's law are accountable to divine justice, having "become a transgressor of the law" (James 2:11). Realizing this, evangelical Christians have emphasized that Jesus died to pay the penalty for the transgressions of his people. This view is called *penal substitutionary atonement*, meaning that Jesus atoned for our sins by bearing the penalty as our Substitute before God's unyielding justice.

Opponents have long derided this view of the cross. Episcopal bishop John Shelby Spong wrote, "I would choose to loathe rather than to worship a deity who required the sacrifice of his son."[4] This opinion was not surprising coming from a humanist who denies the veracity of the Bible. But more recently, similar attacks have arisen from within evangelical ranks. British "evangelical" Steve Chalke described the classic evangelical doctrine of the atonement as "a form of cosmic child abuse—a vengeful Father, punishing his Son for an offence he has not even committed."[5] Joel B. Green and Mark D. Baker wrote that in the traditional evangelical doctrine of the cross, "God takes on the role of the sadist inflicting punishment, while Jesus, in his role as masochist, readily embraces suffering."[6] These and similar assaults on the idea of Jesus' dying for our sins are issued in books printed by publishing houses long associated with evangelical Christianity.

In the place of penal substitutionary atonement, critics would have us embrace the liberal subjective view of the atonement or an updated version of the pre-Anselm view known as the *Christus Victor* theory. *Christus Victor*

3. Philip Graham Ryken, "The Medieval Achievement: Anselm on the Atonement," in *Precious Blood: The Atoning Work of Christ*, ed. Richard D. Phillips (Wheaton, IL: Crossway, 2009), 138.

4. John Shelby Spong, *Why Christianity Must Change or Die* (San Francisco: HarperCollins, 1999), 95.

5. Steve Chalke, *The Lost Message of Jesus* (Grand Rapids: Zondervan, 2003), 182.

6. Joel B. Green and Mark D. Baker, *Recovering the Scandal of the Cross: Atonement in New Testament and Contemporary Contexts* (Downers Grove, IL: InterVarsity Press, 2000), 30.

asserts that Jesus died to overthrow the cosmic powers of darkness. This is undoubtedly true, but the question remains as to *how* Jesus overthrew the power of Satan, evil, and death. The Bible's answer is that since "the sting of death is sin, and the power of sin is the law" (1 Cor. 15:56), Christ overthrew these powers by satisfying God's law. Jesus accomplished this through both his own perfect lifelong obedience and his death as our Substitute before the law's penalty for sin.

John tells us that before Jesus died, he cried out, "It is finished" (John 19:30), referring to a definite work that he had achieved. Peter identified this finished work by referring to penal substitutionary atonement: "he himself bore our sins in his body on the tree" (1 Peter 2:24). To hang on a tree was to bear God's curse (Deut. 21:23); Jesus died under this judgment because he "bore our sins." Paul went so far as to describe as "of first importance" the teaching that "Christ died for our sins in accordance with the Scriptures" (1 Cor. 15:3). In light of these definitive biblical statements, we see that while there are many facets of Christ's atonement, including Christ's victory over evil and his display of divine love, the key to them all is penal substitutionary atonement.

The Accomplishment of the Atonement

Another way to answer the question "Why did Jesus die?" is to consider what Christ accomplished on the cross. Penal substitutionary atonement tells us what Jesus did: he died to pay the penalty for our sins. But when Jesus cried out, "It is finished," what was the result and achievement of that payment? The answer is found in three words that every Christian should know and understand: *propitiation*, *redemption*, and *reconciliation*.

Propitiation is a concept that comes from the temple and the Old Testament sacrificial system. The Bible teaches that God's wrath burns against all sin, so in saving his people Jesus died to assuage God's wrath against the sinner. This teaching is classically stated in Romans 3:25, where Paul writes that "God put [Christ] forward as a propitiation by his blood, to be received by faith." Man's problem is stated in Romans 3:23: "all have sinned and fall short of the glory of God." Sinners can still, however, be "justified by [God's] grace as a gift, through the redemption that is in Christ Jesus" (Rom. 3:24). How can this happen? On what basis are sinners redeemed from sin and justified before God? Paul's answer is that God set forward his Son Jesus to die as a Sacrifice to pacify his wrath toward our sin.

The Greek word for *propitiation* is *hilasterion*, which translates the Hebrew word for the *mercy seat* that sat atop the ark of the covenant in the Most Holy Place, the inner sanctum of God's temple where his glory dwelt. Here, sacrificial blood was spread once a year for the sins of the people, on the Day of Atonement. The high priest came before the throne of God, where two golden cherubim gazed down on the tablets of God's broken law. The priest then poured the blood on the mercy seat atop the ark, averting God's wrath, since God now saw not the broken law but the sacrificial blood. Paul says that Jesus Christ was that Sacrifice, his the true blood of the mercy seat that propitiates God's wrath so that sinners may be accepted by God.

Some critics recoil at the idea of propitiation, considering it morally objectionable for God to require a sacrifice in order to forgive and pointing out the similarity of this doctrine to pagan rites of human sacrifice. The answer to this objection is that the pagan rites arose from a true recognition of man's need for a substitute to die for sin. The ancient Mayans, for instance, sacrificed vast thousands of lives in a quest for atonement. They failed to realize, however, that no multitude of sinful humans can offer an acceptable sacrifice to propitiate God's wrath; since each sinner receives his own punishment, he cannot die for others.[7] This is why Christianity does *not* teach that sinners must make a sacrifice to avert God's wrath, but rather that God himself provided the Sacrifice to avert his wrath against our sin. God sent his Son, the God-man Jesus Christ, to offer his infinitely precious life as the propitiation for our sins.

The last word in the Bible on propitiation—literally, its last reference—is given by the apostle John. In 1 John 4:10, the Beloved Disciple turns the complaints about propitiation onto their heads. What does it say about such a God, people bemoan, if he requires a sacrifice before he is willing to forgive? John replies, "In this is love, not that we have loved God but that he loved us and sent his Son to be the propitiation for our sins" (1 John 4:10). When we did not love God, he loved us by sending Jesus, his Son, to be the Sacrifice for our sin. The biblical doctrine of propitiation, therefore, declares God's saving love for sinners.

7. See Wendy Murray Zoba, "Maya Mysteries," *Books & Culture* 8, 1 (January–February 2002): 28.

The second great term for what Jesus accomplished on the cross is *redemption*. This is a term borrowed from the marketplace, involving the making of a purchase. Redemption presupposes some kind of bondage or captivity, circumstances that afflict us but from which we are not able to free ourselves. Redemption takes us from slavery to freedom, and from affliction to salvation. The greatest Old Testament example of redemption was God's deliverance of Israel from bondage in Egypt in the exodus. God told Moses: "I will deliver you from slavery to them, and I will redeem you with an outstretched arm and with great acts of judgment" (Ex. 6:6).

Redemption, therefore, speaks of God's saving us from a situation that we could never get ourselves out of, just as the Israelites would have remained in Egypt forever if God had not come to their aid. The New Testament takes this concept and applies it to the problem of our sin, which we could never solve by ourselves. We think of sins as a small matter, indulgences that do us little harm, but the Bible teaches that sin results in slavery and crushing misery out of which we are totally unable to escape on our own.

In the ancient world, there were three ways in which one could become a slave, and all three of them relate to our bondage to sin. First, a person might be born into slavery, and in the same way the Bible says that since Adam's fall, we are all born into sin, inheriting from Adam a sinful nature. David thus lamented: "Behold, I was brought forth in iniquity, and in sin did my mother conceive me" (Ps. 51:5). Second, a person might be enslaved as a result of military defeat. Likewise, we are mastered by sin's power over our flesh and overcome by temptations. Third, one might have debts that he could not pay and thus be sold into slavery. Similarly, our sin creates a debt before God's justice that we can never repay. In all these ways, our situation in sin is like that of a slave. Slaves lead lives of misery and bondage, and these are the very things that sin inflicts on us.

That is the bad news of our sin, as Jesus declared: "Everyone who commits sin is a slave to sin" (John 8:34). The good news of the gospel answers this predicament. Paul writes, "In [Christ] we have redemption through his blood, the forgiveness of our trespasses" (Eph. 1:7).

Perhaps the greatest Bible story teaching redemption is that of the prophet Hosea and his marriage to the sinful woman Gomer. Gomer faithlessly abandoned Hosea and pursued her many lovers, descending further and further into sin. All the while, God commanded Hosea to remain faithful to her, as a picture of his own faithfulness to sinful Israel. Ultimately, Gomer's sin caused her to be sold on the auction block as a slave, probably to pay debts that she had incurred. This pictures the degradation into which sin seeks to drag us all.

The men gathered to place bids on the body of this female slave. "Twelve pieces of silver," bid one. "Thirteen," called a voice from the back that Gomer might no longer have recognized. "Fourteen," came the reply. "Fifteen," said Hosea. "Fifteen silver pieces and a bushel of barley," came the counterbid. Stepping forward and reaching out to his wife, Hosea spoke, "Fifteen pieces of silver and a bushel and a half of barley." Everyone realized that he could not be outbid, and so the other men began to walk away. Gomer was rightly his already, but sin had torn her away. Now Hosea had bought her back with everything he had and draped her with his love: "So I bought her for fifteen shekels of silver and a homer and a lethech of barley. And I said to her, 'You must dwell as mine for many days. You shall not play the whore, or belong to another man; so I will also be to you'" (Hos. 3:2–3).

If we are in Christ, this is our story as well. James Montgomery Boice comments:

> We were created for intimate fellowship with God and for freedom, but we have disgraced ourselves by unfaithfulness. First we have flirted with and then committed adultery with this sinful world and its values. The world even bid for our soul, offering sex, money, fame, power and all the other items in which it traffics. But Jesus, our faithful bridegroom and lover, entered the market place to buy us back. He bid his own blood. There is no higher bid than that. And we became his. He reclothed us, not in the wretched rags of our old unrighteousness, but in his new robes of righteousness. He has said to us, "You must dwell as mine [and] . . . you shall not belong to another[;] . . . so will I also be to you."[8]

The final term that describes what Jesus accomplished on the cross is *reconciliation*. This idea comes from the realm of the family: we are reconciled to the Father's love through the blood of Christ.

Reconciliation assumes that by sin we were, as Paul writes, "alienated from the life of God" (Eph. 4:18). The good news of the cross is that God

8. James Montgomery Boice, *Foundations of the Christian Faith* (Downers Grove, IL: InterVarsity Press, 1986), 329–30.

has reconciled us to himself through the blood of Christ, making peace with those who were at war with his rule. We must never think that Jesus died to reconcile us to an otherwise unwilling Father. Rather, Paul insists, "All this is from God, who through Christ reconciled us to himself" (2 Cor. 5:18). Paul explains how God accomplished this reconciliation in one of the Bible's great verses: "For our sake [God] made him to be sin who knew no sin, so that in him we might become the righteousness of God" (5:21). God imputed our sin to Christ and Christ's perfect righteousness to us, so that we might be clothed in pure white to draw near to his holy love.

It was with these achievements in his triumphant heart that Jesus cried out, "It is finished" (John 19:30). Sin had ruined God's relationship with man, but Jesus overcame this barrier by propitiating God's wrath against our sin. The cross also delivered Christ's people from sin's power, redeeming us to salvation freedom with the coin of his blood. Having satisfied wrath on God's part and overthrown captivity on our part, Christ now grants sinners reconciliation with God through faith in his blood. Paul explained: "And you, who once were alienated and hostile in mind, doing evil deeds, he has now reconciled in his body of flesh by his death, in order to present you holy and blameless and above reproach before him" (Col. 1:21–22).

The Necessity of the Atonement

Why did Jesus die? We have answered by identifying Christ's death as a penal substitutionary atonement and by recognizing his achievement on the cross in terms of propitiation, redemption, and reconciliation. This leaves one important question about Jesus' death: why did Jesus *have* to die? Was the atonement truly necessary?

There are three ways in which we might answer this question. One answer is to say that it was not necessary for God to send his Son to die on the cross. God was not in any way obliged to save the sinful creatures who had rebelled against his rule. Man has no right to demand salvation, and no one could quarrel if God subjected us all to eternal punishment for our sins. The only necessity of salvation arises from God's own character. It is true that God's holy nature burns in just anger against all sin (Rom. 1:18). But it is also true that God's loving nature delights in mercy (Mic. 7:18). This loving mercy within God provided a necessity for salvation within himself; God's grace alone accounts for his ordaining to save a great company of people out of the human race (Rom. 9:15–16).

Since God's nature moves him to save his people, we then ask whether Christ's death was the necessary way for this to be achieved. Some have answered that the cross was not absolutely necessary and that there could have been other ways for God to save. Thomas Aquinas argued this view by stating that the atonement was only contingently necessary. He meant that God might have saved his people by some other means, but that once God chose to save by Christ's incarnation and atonement, then Jesus' death became necessary. While there were other possible ways in which a holy God could save sinners, this was the way that God chose as most advantageous to his own glory.

The problem with this view is that it is inconceivable that God should have required the sacrificial death of his Son if there had been any other way to redeem his people from sin. The cross was therefore not relatively or contingently necessary for our salvation, but as John Gerstner has put it, "the atonement must be antecedently, absolutely necessary, for there was no other way it could have been done . . . . It had to be and it was absolutely necessary that [Jesus] should take our nature upon himself. In that nature, the Lord Jesus Christ made a truly, infinitely, and satisfactory expiation of our guilt in the atonement in which we glory."[9]

Once man had fallen into sin, the problem of salvation involved the justification of those who deserve punishment. How can God uphold his perfect justice, remaining unstained in his holiness, and at the same time extend his mercy in a loving salvation of sinners? God's answer—the only possible answer—is that another must suffer the judgment in the place of those who are condemned. This raises the question: Who can offer this sacrifice? Who is both willing and able to die for sinners under God's wrath?

This was the question for which Anselm offered the Bible's answer in *Cur Deus Homo*. He pointed out that no sinner could offer the sacrifice, since a sinner already owed his life to pay for his own sins. Moreover, sin has so affected all mankind that we cannot even choose to please God and thus cannot make a true offering. Therefore, Anselm reasoned that only

---

9. John R. Gerstner, "The Atonement and the Purpose of God," in *Atonement*, ed. Gabriel N. E. Fluhrer (Phillipsburg, NJ: P&R Publishing, 2010), 62. See Gerstner's discussion of this issue on pages 61–63.

God himself possessed the moral purity and divine life to offer the needed sacrifice for sin. This posed another problem, since it is man who owes the debt to God's justice and therefore man who must make the sacrifice to pay for sin. The resolution of this problem was the final answer to the title of Anselm's book, *Why Did God Become Man?* He wrote:

> The debt was so great that, while man alone owed it, only God could pay it, so that the same person must be both man and God. Thus it was necessary for God to take manhood into the unity of his Person, so that he who in his own nature ought to pay and could not should be in a person who could. . . . The life of this one man was so sublime, so precious, that it can suffice to pay what is owing for the sins of the whole world, and infinitely more.[10]

Jesus' death for sin was absolutely necessary, since there was no other way for God to be both "just and the justifier of the one who has faith in Jesus" (Rom. 3:26). This is the necessity of which Jesus spoke to Nicodemus earlier in John's Gospel: "so must the Son of Man be lifted up, that whoever believes in him may have eternal life" (John 3:14–15).

The Exceeding Gravity of Sin

This leaves only one question: do you accept the necessity of Jesus' death for your salvation? Do you confess that only if God's Son paid the debt of your sin can you be saved from the holy justice of God? This is a necessity that many people reject. Some claim that they will make their own way to salvation. Others object to the idea that there is only one way to heaven and insist that many other roads lead to God. The Christian answer to these objections is one given by Anselm when addressing the same matter over nine hundred years ago. Replying to those who denied the need for an atonement to make satisfaction for man's guilt, Anselm wrote: "You have not yet considered the exceeding gravity of sin."[11] Sin is a personal affront to God's holy honor, and it must receive his personal, burning wrath. Sin is a rebellious transgression of God's law, and it must be punished for God's perfect justice to stand. So exceedingly great is the gravity of sin that you

---

10. Eugene R. Fairweather, ed., *A Scholastic Miscellany: Anselm to Ockham*, Library of Christian Classics 10 (Philadelphia: Westminster, 1956), 176.

11. Ryken, "The Medieval Achievement," 134.

owe God for your sins a debt that you cannot repay, and at the same time you cannot be saved unless that debt is paid. God's gracious provision, his saving gift to you, is the atoning death of Christ, which he now calls you to receive in faith, giving yourself to the Savior who gave himself for you.

The world yet insists that all roads lead to God, and the world is right. Of course all roads lead to God, for God is the Alpha and Omega of all things. But the horror that unbelievers will discover, if God's Word is true, is that the God to whom they arrive by any other way than the cross of Christ is an angry, offended, and awesomely holy God, whose perfect justice must consign them to an eternity of punishment in divine wrath. Yet the cross of Christ still stands before rebel mankind, pleading atoning mercy for all who will come to God by the one way of his Redeemer Son.

Jesus died to propitiate God's holy wrath, to redeem believers from the guilt and power of sin, and to reconcile all who will come to the adoring love of the Father. If you will come, then you will have a new answer for Anselm's question, "Why did God become man?" and also to the question raised by the cross, "Why did Jesus die?" You will answer, on the authority of God's Word: "Jesus became man and died for me, that I might be forgiven, redeemed from my sin, and together with all of Christ's people belong to him and enjoy God's love forever."

128

Finished!

John 19:30

"It is finished." (John 19:30)

My father had an expressive sense of humor that he often conveyed through his use of different languages. To express a sense of urgency, he would usually turn to the German language. He would bark out "schnell!" for "quickly" and "verstehen Sie?" to ask "do you understand?" with a tone of command. For more joyful expressions, my dad would move to Spanish or Italian. I especially remember his joyful cry when a difficult project or unpleasant chore was finished. "Fini!" he would cry, or "Finito!"

John tells us that when Jesus had completed his atoning work on the cross, before he gave up his spirit to the Father, he also cried out, "It is finished" (John 19:30). We do not know the tone of voice in which Jesus spoke this word (it is a single word in both Greek and Aramaic). It is hard to imagine, after all Jesus had gone through, that he spoke without a tone of exhaustion or pain. Yet it is certain that, as Leon Morris writes: "Jesus died with the cry of the Victor on his lips. This is not the moan of the defeated, nor the sigh of patient resignation. It is the triumphant recognition that he has now fully accomplished the work that he came to do."[1] For all who read John's Gospel with faith in Jesus' saving work, his cry "It is finished" is therefore a source of pure joy and spiritual blessing in any language.

CHRIST'S FINISHED WORK

Although the Greek for "It is finished" is only one word, that word expresses more than what comes through in the English translation. Charles Spurgeon stated, "It would need all the other words that were ever spoken, or ever can be spoken, to explain this one word. It is altogether immeasurable. It is high; I cannot attain to it. It is deep; I cannot fathom it."[2] There are important things we can say, however, about the Greek word *tetelestai*, which means, "It is finished." This word means more than that something has been completed. D. A. Carson comments, "The verb *teleo* from which this form derives denotes the carrying out of a task, and in religious contexts bears the overtone of fulfilling one's religious obligations."[3] This word, in other forms, has repeatedly appeared during the final days of Jesus' ministry. In his Farewell Prayer on the previous evening, Jesus anticipated this moment, saying to the Father, "I glorified you on earth, having *accomplished* the work that you gave me to do" (John 17:4; Greek *teleiosas*). The apostle John wrote of Jesus' ministry earlier that evening: "having loved his own who were in the world, he loved them *to the end*" (13:1; Greek *eis telos*). In this same vein, Jesus now announces the completion of his task on the cross: "It is finished."

As Jesus prepared to deliver his spirit into the Father's hands, what did he envision as having been completed and accomplished? First, he had completed the sufferings necessary to his atoning death for our sins. We know that this was at least part of Jesus' meaning, since his cry quotes the conclusion of Psalm 22, an Old Testament passage that chronicles his sufferings on the cross. No more would Jesus experience the terrible pain of scourging and crucifixion, endure the mocking ridicule of Roman soldiers and Jewish priests, and, worst of all, suffer the agony of divine wrath and separation from God's love. Mark Johnston comments on the sheer joy that

---

1. Leon Morris, *The Gospel according to John*, rev. ed., New International Commentary on the New Testament (Grand Rapids: Eerdmans, 1995), 720.

2. Charles H. Spurgeon, *Sermons on the Gospel of John* (Grand Rapids: Zondervan, 1966), 170.

3. D. A. Carson, *The Gospel of John* (Grand Rapids: Eerdmans, 1991), 621.

must have filled Jesus' heart as he spoke his last and dying words: "Father, into your hands I commit my spirit!" (Luke 23:46): "The only moment he had ever known when he could not call God 'Father' was over, and even as he prepares for death he is able . . . to take once more that term of intimate communion upon his lips (Luke 23:46)."[4] How glad we are that Jesus' sufferings are finished and that man's fury can never score him again.

> The head that once was crowned with thorns is crowned with glory now;
> A royal diadem adorns the mighty Victor's brow.[5]

Second, Jesus had now fulfilled all the prophecies of his life and death. How thorough the prophetic preview had been of what Jesus would endure for our sins! Virtually every important detail in the tragedy of Christ's cross was publicized in advance. His betrayal by a friend (Ps. 41:9), the disciples' forsaking him (Ps. 31:11), the false accusations and Jesus' silence before the judges (Ps. 35:11; Isa. 53:7), his formal acquittal (Isa. 53:9), his being numbered with transgressors (Isa. 53:12), his crucifixion (Ps. 22:16), the mocking of the onlookers (Ps. 109:25), the taunt about his failure to save himself (Ps. 22:7–8), the soldiers' gambling for his clothing (Ps. 22:18), his prayer for his enemies (Isa. 53:12), his being forsaken of God (Ps. 22:1), his thirsting cry (Ps. 69:21), his yielding up of his spirit into the Father's hands (Ps. 31:5), the preservation of his bones from being broken (Ps. 34:20), and his burial in a rich man's tomb (Isa. 53:9)—all were foretold in the prophetic witness. What an awe-inspiring proof of the divine inspiration of Scripture we have in the prophecies of Jesus' death! "How firm a foundation, ye saints of the Lord, is laid for your faith in His excellent Word!"[6] If there ever is to be a Messiah who fulfills the legions of prophecies given to authenticate his life and death, that Messiah could only be Jesus Christ, who fulfilled them all in a way that no one else could ever do.

Most importantly, we see in Jesus' cry the declaration of his finished work for our salvation. John Calvin observes that Jesus' cry from the cross points out the centrality of the atonement to the Christian faith, since it "shows that the whole accomplishment of our salvation, and all the parts of it, are

---

4. Mark G. Johnston, *Let's Study John* (Edinburgh: Banner of Truth, 2003), 248.
5. Thomas Kelly, "The Head That Once Was Crowned with Thorns" (1820).
6. Rippon's *Selection of Hymns* (1787).

contained in his death."[7] Mark Johnston adds, "His shout of accomplishment was the cry for which creation had been waiting since the fall of Adam."[8]

Earlier in his ministry, Jesus taught, "The Son of Man came not to be served but to serve, and to give his life as a ransom for many" (Matt. 20:28). That ransom payment had now been made and redemption achieved for the people who belong to Christ. There now remained nothing for Jesus to do in terms of his atoning work of satisfying God's wrath and redeeming his people from the bondage of sin. God the Son had been born of the virgin, had taken up a human nature, had lived a perfect life, and was dying a sacrificial death. All this was now accomplished! Jesus had asserted, "I am the good shepherd. The good shepherd lays down his life for the sheep" (John 10:11). That promise had been fulfilled, and Christ's sheep had now been saved by his blood. He came to do it, he had said he would do it, and now Jesus had finished his saving work perfectly.

When Christians say that they have faith in Jesus Christ, we mean that we are relying on the finished work that he completed on the cross. Skip Ryan writes: "When Buddha died, it is reported by tradition that his last words were, 'Strive without ceasing.' Jesus' last words were, 'I have done it.' Religion tells us to finish the work—to go out and do something and be something. Jesus says, 'Receive the finished work.'"[9] Resting in what Jesus has done, we need never fear the punishment of our sins, nor worry that God's law will condemn us in the end. We may rest on what he has completed, knowing that all that needed to be done for us to be saved has been done, finished on the cross. Many Christians live in needless self-loathing before God, thinking themselves unacceptable and despised because of their sinfulness and failure, when the truth is that Jesus has finished removing the whole of sin as an obstacle to our acceptance with God. With joy we may now take up Paul's challenge in Romans 8:34: "Who is to condemn? Christ Jesus is the one who died—more than that, who was raised—who is at the right hand of God, who indeed is interceding for us." Looking at our own works, we see everything not only as unfinished and imperfect, but as positively damning. But looking at Jesus' dying work on the cross, we know that our

7. John Calvin, *Calvin's Commentaries*, trans. William Pringle, 22 vols. (Grand Rapids: Baker, 2009), 18:234.

8. Johnston, *Let's Study John*, 248.

9. Joseph "Skip" Ryan, *That You May Believe* (Wheaton, IL: Crossway, 2003), 342.

salvation is finished by a perfect offering of the once-for-all Sacrifice that truly frees us from our sin.

Paid in Full

One way to fully appreciate the saving significance of Jesus' cry "It is finished" is to see that the Greek word *tetelestai* was used in commercial transactions to signify that a debt was paid in full. The word would be stamped on a purchase or written on a receipt to show that no more payment was needed and that the purchase was complete. When Jesus spoke this word, he was declaring that he had now paid every last penny of his people's sin debt to God's justice and that his redemption had been fully and eternally accomplished. This is why Peter wrote to the early Christians that "you were ransomed from the futile ways inherited from your forefathers, not with perishable things such as silver or gold, but with the precious blood of Christ, like that of a lamb without blemish or spot" (1 Peter 1:18–19).

Another place that we see this same truth regarding Jesus' finished sacrifice is Hebrews 1:3. The writer of Hebrews set forth the supremacy of Christ's ministry by writing: "After making purification for sins, he sat down at the right hand of the Majesty on high." Priests in the Old Testament never sat down in the temple, for there was no place for them to sit. The reason was that they were offering only a temporary sacrifice; there would always be more blood to be shed, so their work was never done. But when Jesus had offered his own blood for our sins, he sat down on his royal throne, for there was no more priestly work to be done. The writer of Hebrews expresses this point again later in his book, saying that "when Christ had offered for all time a single sacrifice for sins, he sat down at the right hand of God . . . . For by a single offering he has perfected for all time those who are being sanctified" (10:12–14). What can be plainer than this in declaring that Christ has fully paid for all the sins of his people, who believe on his name? John Murray wrote: "From whatever angle we look upon his sacrifice we find its uniqueness to be as inviolable as the uniqueness of his person, of his mission, and of his office. Who is God-man but he alone? Who is great high priest to offer such sacrifice but he alone? Who shed such vicarious blood but he alone? Who entered in once for all into the holy place, having obtained eternal redemption, but he alone?"[10] What is left for us to do but trust in Jesus' death for our sins and give him the glory of our hearts:

> Jesus paid it all,
> All to him I owe;
> Sin had left a crimson stain,
> He washed it white as snow.[11]

The finality of Christ's sacrificial death becomes important when considering the matter of present and future sins. Which of my sins did Jesus pay for on the cross? Did Jesus' death atone only for sins that I committed before being baptized (as the Roman Catholic Church teaches) or only those sins that I committed before I believed (as some unsound Protestant churches teach)? If either of these answers is true, then I must do something to pay for sins that I have recently committed, as well as for sins that I will commit in the future.

The Roman Catholic doctrines of penance and the Mass rely on an incomplete view of Christ's atonement. For Roman Catholics, the Mass provides an ongoing sacrifice of Christ's blood even today, so the atoning sufferings of Jesus are not finished. Moreover, Rome teaches that one must perform penance—punishments prescribed by a priest in order to be fully restored to God's favor from present sins—so that Christ's atoning death did not complete the work of forgiveness. Unsound Protestants will similarly say that we must ritually confess recent sins in order to be forgiven, and that if a believer in Christ dies with unconfessed sins, he or she will not be saved. The problem with these views is that Jesus exclaimed "It is finished" when his work was done on the cross. Jesus paid the debt of the sins of his people before the vast majority of them were even born. "I am the good shepherd," he said. "I know my own and my own know me, just as the Father knows me and I know the Father; and I lay down my life for the sheep" (John 10:14–15). When Jesus laid down his life for the sheep, he did not lose any of them or leave any of their sins unforgiven. Jesus died not for potential believers in general but for the specific, elect persons whom the Father had given to him from all history to be redeemed by his blood and enter into that salvation

10. John Murray, *Redemption Accomplished and Applied* (Grand Rapids: Eerdmans, 1955), 51.
11. Elvina M. Hall, "Jesus Paid It All" (1865).

through faith in him alone. Since Christ made a full and final atonement for all his people, those who believe in Christ may know that all their sins are forgiven. As John wrote in his first epistle, "the blood of Jesus . . . cleanses us from all sin" (1 John 1:7).

If we are to believe on Jesus' death for our forgiveness, then we must refuse to appeal anywhere else for any type of atonement. Calvin articulates this mandate, especially warning us against the Roman Mass or any other supposed means of atonement besides Christ:

> For he who was sent by the Heavenly Father to obtain for us a full acquittal, and to accomplish our redemption, knew well what belonged to his office, and did not fail in what he knew to be demanded of him. It was chiefly for the purpose of giving peace and tranquility to our consciences that he pronounced his word, *It is finished.* Let us stop here, therefore, if we do not choose to be deprived of the salvation which he has procured for us.[12]

FULL ATONEMENT: CAN IT BE?

Jesus' cry "It is finished" (John 19:30) prompts us finally to consider the efficacy of his atoning death to actually save his elect people. We may pose this question: Did Jesus effect my atonement with his death on the cross, or did his atoning work depend on my response in faith? Is it possible, in the latter instance, that having died on the cross for sins in general, and having cried out, "It is finished," Jesus still might not actually have saved anyone, and that his sacrifice was made of any value only when sinners later believed in his gospel? The answer to these questions can be gained by considering the biblical depiction of the design, intent, and actual achievement of Christ's death. The doctrinal distinction is set forth by the competing positions of the Arminian doctrine of *general redemption* versus the Reformed doctrine of *limited atonement* (also known as *particular redemption*).

The difference between these positions is not that one of them limits Christ's atoning work and the other does not. Both general redemption and limited atonement see a limit to Christ's saving death, or else they would embrace the liberal doctrine of universal salvation apart from faith. According to general redemption, Christ's atoning work was unlimited in scope but

12. Calvin, *New Testament Commentaries*, 18:236.

limited in efficacy. That is, Christ died equally for all persons but did not actually atone for the sins of anyone. Atonement was made effectual only when sinners actually believed. According to limited atonement, or particular redemption, Christ's atoning death was limited in scope, pertaining only to the elect, but unlimited in efficacy. Christ died for his own people, and his atoning death was utterly effectual in paying the debt of their sins, which is why the Holy Spirit was later sent to regenerate these same persons to a saving, personal faith.

The Bible should answer the debate, so we ask: What does the Bible say about the design and intent of Christ's atoning work? One answer was given by the angel who announced Christ's work to Joseph, Mary's betrothed. Joseph was to give the child the name *Jesus*, "for he will save *his people* from their sins" (Matt. 1:21). This is precisely as had been foretold through the prophet Isaiah: "He was cut off out of the land of the living, stricken for the transgression of *my people*" (Isa. 53:8). "The Son of Man came not to be served but to serve," Jesus said, "and to give his life as a ransom *for many*" (Matt. 20:28). "I am the good shepherd," Jesus preached. "The good shepherd lays down his life for *the sheep*" (John 10:11). John Murray observes:

> The very nature of Christ's mission and accomplishment is involved in this question. Did Christ come to make the salvation of all men possible, to remove obstacles that stood in the way of salvation, and merely to make provision for salvation? Or did he come to save his people? . . . Did he come to make men redeemable? Or did he come effectually and infallibly to redeem? The doctrine of the atonement must be radically revised if, as atonement, it applies to those who finally perish as well as to those who are the heirs of eternal life.[13]

In light of Jesus' triumphal cry from the cross, "It is finished," we must surely not believe that the salvation of his people was yet in doubt in any sense, even while we realize that there remained the need for the Holy Spirit to enter into time and bring each of those purchased with Christ's blood to a personal, saving faith. While a sinner can be saved only through faith alone, that faith rests on the once-for-all finished work of Jesus, when he paid in full the debt of our sins to God's justice and redeemed us into eternal life.

13. Murray, *Redemption Accomplished and Applied*, 63–64.

To deny the full efficacy of Christ's atoning death in saving all those who belong to him is to eradicate the only ground of assurance in salvation. We will never have the peace of assurance for our souls so long as we are looking to something in ourselves—something that we have done and something that we are doing—as that which finished our redemption. Instead, it is when you realize that even your faith is the outworking of Christ's finished work for you on the cross that you know the solid ground on which your salvation stands.

He Died for Me

Having emphasized the finished nature of Christ's work, we should conclude by noting that the results of his atoning death continue on throughout history. While Christ's work in dying for sins is finished, the work to which he calls us begins only when we look in faith to his cross. In this, too, understanding the finished nature of Christ's work will motivate us to respond in works of service to and witness for him.

Indeed, understanding Jesus' finished atonement for our salvation will profoundly influence the psychology of our devotion to him. There are some people who die for a principle, and we admire them for it. Socrates accepted the cup of hemlock for the principle of tacit consent to civic rule. For this act his influence has spread far and wide across the ages. There are others who die for a cause. If we share the cause, we may honor the martyr's name. Nathan Hale has gone down in American history as the revolutionary who declared, "My only regret is that I have but one life to give for my country." Schoolchildren are taught those words even today, and we remember Hale with respect. Logically, the doctrine of general redemption places Jesus in these categories, though as the most noble of persons who died for the greatest cause and highest principle possible.

But another category rises far above the rest. Some die for principle and others for a cause. But what about someone who died for me? This calls for a different kind of devotion altogether.

The movie *Saving Private Ryan* tells of a rescue operation immediately after the Allied invasion of Normandy, in June 1944. The War Department learns that three out of four boys in a family named Ryan died in battle on the same day. The Army's top general orders that the fourth son be rescued from behind German lines, where he parachuted on D-Day. An elite squad of Army Rangers is assigned to find Private Ryan. Their search leads to a bridge where German tanks are trying to break through Allied lines, and there the squad is destroyed as their quest finally succeeds. As the captain who saved Ryan lies dying on the bridge, surrounded by the bodies of the men from his squad, he draws Ryan close and gasps, "Earn this. Earn it." The movie concludes with Ryan, as an old man, returning to the cemetery where the men who died for him were buried. Falling to his knees at Captain Miller's grave, he says to the white plaster cross, "Every day I think about what you said to me that day on the bridge. I've tried to live my life the best I could. I hope that was enough. I hope that at least in your eyes, I earned what all of you have done for me." Turning to his wife, who comes up beside him, he stammers, "Tell me I have led a good life. Tell me I'm a good man."

Christians praise God that we are not required to earn what Christ has done for us, nor could we. Jesus did not say "Earn this" from the cross, but "It is finished." We receive his death by simple faith, as a gift of God's sovereign love and to the praise of his glorious grace, and we are thus liberated from a Christian life of bondage, trying always to earn our place in God's love.

Yet Jesus' cry "It is finished" becomes only the beginning for our faith, which we rest on his full atonement. As we serve Christ from the foundation of his finished work, we offer ourselves not merely for a principle, and not even for a great cause. We live for a person, the Savior Jesus Christ, whose finished work accomplished our eternal blessing. He died not merely for a principle or even for the greatest of causes. He died for us. So every Christian can, and surely must, say in response: "I live for him because he died for me."

129

ON HIM WHOM THEY PIERCED

John 19:31–37

For these things took place that the Scripture might be fulfilled:
"Not one of his bones will be broken." And again another
Scripture says, "They will look on him whom they have pierced."
(John 19:36–37)

hen Israel thirsted in the desert, Moses struck the rock of Horeb with his staff, and a stream of water sprang forth (Ex. 17:6). The wilderness was thus a land of death in which the water of life flowed for the refreshment of God's people. A noteworthy feature of that episode was that before God told Moses to strike the rock, he stated, "Behold, I will stand before you there on the rock of Horeb" (17:6). God offered himself to be struck in the place of his sinful people, with the result that the waters flowed to give them life. In John 19:34, the apostle John sees this symbolism fulfilled as the stricken and dead Jesus Christ is pierced with a soldier's spear "and at once there came out blood and water." For this reason Paul described the rock of Horeb as a "spiritual Rock," and specified that "the Rock was Christ" (1 Cor. 10:4).

It has been observed that if you squeeze the Gospel of John hard enough, water will pour out of it. In chapter 2, Jesus ordered the servants to fill the water basins with water and then turned the water into wine. Jesus was the source of joy at the wedding feast, giving power for water to become the wine that gladdens men's hearts (Ps. 104:15). In John 4, Jesus sat beside the Samaritan woman on Jacob's well. "Everyone who drinks of this water will be thirsty again," he said of the still well water, "but whoever drinks of the water that I will give him will never be thirsty again" (John 4:13–14). In this way, Jesus presented himself as the fountain of spiritual life for all who believe. Chapter 5 presents a paralyzed man who lies beside a pool. The pool of Bethesda supposedly had healing powers, only the man could not get into it. Jesus therefore took the place of the pool and granted the man healing. He then provided the river that Ezekiel had seen flowing from the temple of God, on the banks of which grew trees with "leaves for healing" (Ezek. 47:12). All these episodes led to Jesus' great gospel invitation at the Feast of Tabernacles: "If anyone thirsts, let him come to me and drink. Whoever believes in me, as the Scripture has said, 'Out of his heart will flow rivers of living water'" (John 7:37–38). John explained that Jesus referred to the gift of God's Spirit after Christ's resurrection, providing eternal life to those who believe. While John 7:37–38 may be seen as the high-water mark in John's Gospel, the water imagery continues with the blind man's washing in the pool of Siloam (9:6–7) and Jesus' washing the disciples' feet with water (13:3–10).

After this flood of Christ's life-giving water, how shocking was Jesus' cry "I thirst" from the cross (John 19:28). Here is the full expression of Jesus' bearing the curse of God for our sin: the fountain of life dried up in death, the spring of living water cut off at the source as the punishment for sin. Finally, Jesus cried, "It is finished," and gave up his spirit into the hands of the Father (19:30), having fully paid the punishment for our sins. What good news it is for Christ's people, then, when John tells us of the spear passing into Jesus' side, as Moses' staff struck the rock of old, and out of his crucified body the flow began again, not just of water but of blood and water together. Out of Jesus' death—by means of his blood—the living water flows once more, and beside this river will grow the Tree of Life, with fruit for the healing of the nations (Rev. 22:2).

NO BONES BROKEN

Jesus was crucified not only on a Friday but on the day of preparation before the Feast of Unleavened Bread. As the dark day drew on, not only was a Sabbath to begin at sundown, but this Sabbath would begin a holy week of sacred feasting. With this in mind, John writes: "Since it was the day of Preparation, and so that the bodies would not remain on the cross on the Sabbath (for that Sabbath was a high day), the Jews asked Pilate that their legs might be broken and that they might be taken away" (John 19:31). The reason for this request was the stricture of Deuteronomy, where the law declared that if an executed man was hung on a tree, "his body shall not remain all night on the tree, but you shall bury him the same day, for a hanged man is cursed by God" (Deut. 21:23). To leave a corpse exposed would defile the holy land, so the priests asked Pilate to hasten the deaths of those crucified, especially with such a holy Sabbath approaching. We see here yet another example of the Jews' hypocrisy. John Calvin notes: "In order to [keep] a strict observance of their Sabbath, they are careful to avoid outward pollution; and yet they do not consider how shocking a crime it is to take away the life of an innocent man."[1]

The Roman procedure for hastening the end of a crucifixion for which the Jews appealed, known as the *crurifragrium*, involved the smashing of the shin bones with a mallet or iron bar. As a result of this shockingly violent act of supposed mercy, the victim would experience shock and would no longer be able to push up and relieve the pressure on his abdomen. Within a short while, death would arrive by means of asphyxiation. To validate the biblical depiction, in 1968 the skeleton of a man crucified in the first century was found north of Jerusalem. One of the man's legs had been fractured and the other had been broken to pieces.[2]

According to John's eyewitness account, this horrific act was performed on the two men crucified with Jesus: "the soldiers came and broke the legs of the first, and of the other who had been crucified with him" (John 19:32). We know from Luke's Gospel that in this manner one of the two criminals experienced the release of his soul to join Jesus in glory, so that Christ's word was fulfilled: "Truly, I say to you, today you will be with me in Paradise" (Luke 23:43). This believing thief's suffering after his conversion and his horrible death remind us that the gospel does not preserve us from the temporal consequences of sins that we commit in this life. J. C. Ryle com-

1. John Calvin, *Calvin's Commentaries*, trans. William Pringle, 22 vols. (Grand Rapids: Baker, 2009), 18:238.

2. Andreas J. Kostenberger, *John* (Grand Rapids: Baker, 2004), 552.

ments: "The grace of God and the pardon of sin did not deliver him from the agony of having his legs broken."[3]

Having administered the *coup de grâce* to the two thieves, the soldiers approached the cross of Jesus. John relates: "But when they came to Jesus and saw that he was already dead, they did not break his legs" (John 19:33). With this information, John proves that Jesus had truly died on the cross.

By the time that John was writing his account, it was important to establish Jesus' death against two denials of the gospel. First, there were those who denied that Jesus was truly human and therefore that he actually suffered and died in a human nature and body. This is the heresy of *docetism*, a teaching common to the Gnostic heretics who considered spirit to be pure and all matter to be ignoble. Gnosticism properly dates from the mid-second century A.D., yet the ideas were incipient during John's ministry. Second, there were then, as now, those who denied the reality of Jesus' resurrection by means of the "swoon theory." Jesus was not raised, skeptics say, because he never died but only swooned on the cross. Jesus was supposedly secreted away from the cross and recovered from his wounds so that the early Christians might falsely claim a resurrection. To combat these denials, John cites the most reliable of morticians to bolster the gospel claim of Jesus' true death: Roman legionnaires who had seen corpses of every description and thus were expert judges of whether someone had died or not. So certain were these soldiers, led by a centurion, of Jesus' death that they thought it safe to ignore orders that had been given under pain of their own death. There simply was no point in breaking the legs of a man who in their certain judgment had undoubtedly already died.

In this providential arrangement, Christians can marvel at the wisdom of God. Our salvation relies so completely on the atonement of Christ that a credible claim against his death on the cross would thoroughly shake, if not destroy, our hope of glory. Gordon Keddie reminds us how easily "the death of a rock-star like Elvis Presley can become the subject of widespread denial, subsequently supported by supposed sightings by his devoted followers over the years."[4] With the evidence that John cites, however, neither

3. J. C. Ryle, *Expository Thoughts on the Gospels: John*, 3 vols. (Edinburgh: Banner of Truth, 1999), 3:368.
4. Gordon J. Keddie, *A Study Commentary on John*, 2 vols. (Darlington, UK: Evangelical Press, 2001), 2:348.

Christ's devoted followers nor his bitter enemies could ever say "that He did not really die, and that He was only in a swoon, or fainting fit, or state of insensibility. The Roman soldiers are witnesses that on the centre cross of the three they saw a dead man."[5]

THE DUAL FLOW OF GRACE

Perhaps to make sure of Jesus' death or simply as an act of callous disrespect, "one of the soldiers pierced his side with a spear" (John 19:34). We do not know for certain which side was pierced, although if the soldier was right-handed it would naturally be Jesus' left side that was penetrated. This is also suggested by the result, one that made doubly certain that Jesus was dead: "at once there came out blood and water" (19:34).

Numerous sober evangelical commentators consider this detail merely to provide one more proof of Jesus' death and urge that to seek a spiritual meaning in the blood and water is unjustified. This view does not account, however, for the importance that the apostle seems to place on this detail, going so far as to give it special notice in his first epistle. There, John states that Jesus "is he who came by water and blood—Jesus Christ; not by the water only but by the water and the blood" (1 John 5:6). Not only does the apostle clearly stress the significance of the blood and water, but these are symbols for which we do not lack clear explanations in the Bible. What insight, then, should we glean from this detail that John considered so important?

First, Christian physicians have sought to diagnose the cause of Jesus' death based on this evidence. Some have argued that Jesus must have died from a physically ruptured heart, with the result that the blood in the heart coagulated so that when the heart was pierced by the spearhead, a darker and a lighter stream of liquid flowed out. Whether or not this explanation is valid, we must remember that Jesus died on a note of triumph, not of a "broken heart," and that he voluntarily gave up his life by delivering his spirit into the Father's hands (John 19:30). Others have persuasively argued that the spear thrust probably penetrated Jesus' pericardium (the fluid sac surrounding the heart), so that blood from the heart flowed out along with water from the open wound.[6]

---

5. Ryle, *John*, 3:369.

6. See the discussion of these options in William Hendriksen, *Exposition of the Gospel according to John*, 2 vols., New Testament Commentary (Grand Rapids: Baker, 1953), 2:437–38.

Second, from the early church many have cited a mystical connection between the blood and water flowing from Christ's wound and the sacraments of baptism and the Eucharist. Augustine wrote, "Our sacraments have flowed out from Christ's side."[7] It is very doubtful, however, that John intended any such sacramental understanding of the blood and water of Jesus' wound, especially since there is no record in Scripture of the Lord's Supper and baptism being referred to by these labels.[8]

Third, evangelicals have seen the blood and water as signifying the chief blessings of Christ's sacrificial death. When it comes to the biblical imagery of *blood*, especially in John's writings, the clear and consistent usage pertains to *atonement* for sin, with the result of forgiveness and reconciliation with God (cf. John 6:53–54; 1 John 1:7). Likewise, the *water* rites of the Old Testament all pertain to spiritual *cleansing* from the defiling presence of sin (cf. John 3:5; 4:14; 7:38–39). Matthew Henry elaborates:

> Guilt contracted must be expiated by blood; stains contracted must be done away by the water of purification. These two must always go together. You are sanctified, you are justified (1 Cor. 6:11). Christ has joined them together and we must not think to put them asunder. They both flowed from the pierced side of our Redeemer. . . . Now was the rock smitten (1 Cor. 10:4), now was the fountain opened (Zech. 13:1), now were the wells of salvation digged (Isa. 12:3). Here is the river, the streams whereof make glad the city of our God.[9]

In emphasizing these two flows from Jesus' pierced side, John directs our faith to Christ's atoning death for both the forgiveness of our sins and the spiritual cleansing of the Holy Spirit, that is, for justification and sanctification. In this way, we see that Jesus died for our great dual problem in sin: our legal problem of guilt and our spiritual problem of corruption. These two problems (and their solutions) must always be distinguished, just as the blood and water flowing from Christ's side were not mingled, and they must always be kept together, since those whom God justifies in Christ he always sanctifies in Christ. Both result from and flow out of Jesus' sacrificial death for us. Through faith in his cross, we gain these two essential benefits, these

7. Quoted in Keddie, *John*, 2:350.
8. D. A. Carson, *The Gospel of John* (Grand Rapids: Eerdmans, 1991), 624.
9. Matthew Henry, *Commentary on the Whole Bible*, 6 vols. (Peabody, MA: Hendrickson, 2009), 5:972.

twin graces of our salvation, the yield of which is eternal life. This is why the apostle Paul constantly stated that a Christian's salvation is "in Christ," for from his crucified body flow both justification and sanctification, received by us through faith alone.

Because of the vital symbolism of the blood and water flowing from the body of Christ, it is no surprise that these have provided the themes for many a beloved Christian hymn. Fanny Crosby was inspired to write of this scene:

> Jesus, keep me near the cross:
> There a precious fountain,
> Free to all, a healing stream,
> Flows from Calv'ry's mountain.[10]

Even more familiar to most Christians are the words of Augustus Toplady's famous hymn "Rock of Ages," which so clearly relates both justification and sanctification to the crucified body of Jesus:

> Rock of Ages, cleft for me,
> Let me hide myself in thee;
> Let the water and the blood,
> From thy riven side which flowed,
> Be of sin the double cure,
> Cleanse me from its guilt and pow'r.[11]

To Fulfill the Scriptures

John's Gospel provides the only record of the piercing of Jesus' side and the flow of blood and water. Therefore, he takes pains to establish the credibility of his witness: "He who saw it has borne witness—his testimony is true, and he knows that he is telling the truth—that you also may believe. For these things took place that the Scripture might be fulfilled" (John 19:35–36). In this way, the apostle seems to seek to oblige the legal requirement for two witnesses (cf. Deut. 19:15), especially since in the late first century when he was writing, challenges to Jesus' death were already appearing. John asserts

10. Fanny J. Crosby, "Jesus, Keep Me near the Cross" (1869).
11. Augustus M. Toplady, "Rock of Ages, Cleft for Me" (1776).

that he is not alone in citing these events but is joined by the witness of the Old Testament prophets.

First, John points out that the Old Testament foresaw that "not one of his bones will be broken" (John 19:36). This could be a reference to Psalm 34:20: "He keeps all his bones; not one of them is broken." This verse serves as a more-than-adequate testimony to go along with John's account of Jesus' legs not being broken. He is probably thinking as well of the provision in Exodus 12:46 that the Passover lamb's bones must not be broken. In this way, John was not only establishing a witness to his record but also tying in its theological meaning. The fulfillment of the Passover lambs, the blood of which preserved Israelite homes from the angel of death on the eve of the exodus, occurred when Jesus offered his atoning blood for our sins on the cross. As Paul stated, "For Christ, our Passover lamb, has been sacrificed" (1 Cor. 5:7). When John says that he gives his testimony "that you also may believe" (John 19:35), he means that we should confess our need of Christ's blood and appeal to him for atonement and cleansing through faith in his cross.

Second, John notes the prophecy of Zechariah 12:10, "They will look on him whom they have pierced" (John 19:37). This establishes a biblical witness for the piercing of Jesus' side. But it also provides the theological grid for the meaning of Christ's death. Zechariah saw in Jerusalem's rejection of his own ministry the greater rejection of Israel's true Messiah. He prophesied not only Jesus' death but the preaching of his cross to bring repentance and saving faith to God's people. All this is included in the full statement of Zechariah 12:10: "I will pour out on the house of David and the inhabitants of Jerusalem a spirit of grace and pleas for mercy, so that, when they look on me, on him whom they have pierced, they shall mourn for him, as one mourns for an only child, and weep bitterly over him, as one weeps over a firstborn."

The prophet went on to speak of the saving grace that would flow from the preaching of Jesus' death: "On that day there shall be a fountain opened for the house of David and the inhabitants of Jerusalem, to cleanse them from sin and uncleanness" (Zech. 13:1). The ultimate result not only of Jesus' death, opening the fountain of his blood and water, but also of the preaching of his cross would be the fulfillment of God's ancient purpose in the covenant of grace: "They will call upon my name, and I will answer them.

I will say, 'They are my people'; and they will say, 'The LORD is my God'" (13:9). Just as John recorded the day when the blood and water flowed from Jesus' crucified body, and as Zechariah foretold the preaching of the cross for cleansing and salvation, today as the gospel is preached and believed, that fountain flows anew, so that all who look on him who was pierced, mourn for their sins, and call on him in faith will be forgiven, cleansed, and restored to God for eternal life.

Those who refuse to believe on Jesus' cross will nonetheless look on him whom they pierced when he returns in glory, and they will mourn over their own eternal destruction in the wrath of the triumphant Lamb who was slain but now reigns in glory and power. John wrote of this in the opening lines of the book of Revelation: "Behold, he is coming with the clouds, and every eye will see him, even those who pierced him, and all tribes of the earth will wail on account of him. Even so. Amen" (Rev. 1:7).

A FOUNTAIN FILLED WITH BLOOD

I mentioned earlier the names of two hymn-writers, Fanny Crosby and Augustus Toplady, who extolled the virtue of the blood and water flowing from Jesus' side. The hymn that is probably best known for celebrating this theme, "There Is a Fountain Filled with Blood," was written by the English poet William Cowper. By all accounts, Cowper possessed a sensitive, even fragile, disposition, and his mother's death when he was six years old left him mentally unstable. Frequently battling depression, he sought to protect himself by staying busy and keeping his mind diverted. A crisis came, however, when both his father and stepmother died, and then his closest friend was drowned. The result was a mental and emotional collapse, so that Cowper ended up in an insane asylum. At length, he was entrusted to the care of a Christian man, and it was during that time that Cowper came to grasp the meaning of the gospel and the knowledge that Christ had died for him.

Cowper's breakthrough reveals an awareness of the stream of grace that flows through all the Scriptures and comes to us by the wounds of Christ, which he grasped while reading Romans 3:24–25. Paul writes that sinners "are justified by [God's] grace as a gift, through the redemption that is in Christ Jesus, whom God put forward as a propitiation by his blood, to be received by faith." Cowper relates: "Immediately I received strength to believe it and the full beams of the Sun of Righteousness shone upon me. I saw the sufficiency of the atonement He had made, [and] my pardon was sealed in His blood. . . . I could only look up to heaven in silent fear, overwhelmed with love and wonder."[12]

Before long Cowper was able to leave the asylum, his heart cleansed by the fountain of Christ's blood. Throughout his life his mental struggles would continue, and he even attempted suicide at various times, yet it was this gospel that led him through a difficult life with light piercing the darkness of his soul. Many of his hymns remain popular still, with such titles as "God Moves in a Mysterious Way" and "O for a Closer Walk with God." But the hymn for which Cowper is best known gives his testimony to the cleansing blood of Christ, recounting how his burdened heart was set free "on that day" when the blood of Christ was shed for our sins:

There is a fountain filled with blood, drawn from Immanuel's veins;
And sinners, plunged beneath that flood, lose all their guilty stains.

The dying thief rejoiced to see that fountain in his day;
And there have I, as vile as he, washed all my sins away.

E'er since by faith I saw the stream your flowing wounds supply,
Redeeming love has been my theme, and shall be till I die. . . .

Dear dying Lamb, your precious blood shall never lose its pow'r;
Till all the ransomed church of God be saved to sin no more.[13]

---

12. Quoted in Elsie Houghton, *Christian Hymn-Writers* (Bryntirion, UK: Evangelical Press of Wales, 1982), 149.

13. William Cowper, "There Is a Fountain Filled with Blood" (1771).

130

SECRET DISCIPLES

John 19:38—39

*After these things Joseph of Arimathea, who was a disciple of
Jesus, but secretly for fear of the Jews, asked Pilate that he might
take away the body of Jesus, and Pilate gave him permission.*
(John 19:38)

ll through his Gospel, the apostle John's overriding purpose
has been for his readers to believe on Jesus Christ in saving
faith. In support of this aim, John has frequently set before us
examples of faith versus unbelief. These have included the twelve disciples,
the converted Samaritan woman, the man healed by the pool, and the two
sisters of Lazarus in the town of Bethany.

Therefore, John identifies saving faith as the explicit goal of his witness to Jesus' death, writing "that you also may believe" (John 19:35). We
should not be surprised to see yet another example of faith at the foot of the
cross. John has quoted Zechariah's prophecy of the cross, foretelling that
"when they look on me, on him whom they have pierced, they shall mourn
for him" (Zech. 12:10). The prophecy added, "On that day there shall be a
fountain opened for the house of David and the inhabitants of Jerusalem, to
cleanse them from sin and uncleanness" (13:1). John immediately provides

the example of two men who experienced this saving blessing, looking to the cross, responding in faith, and finding cleansing through Christ's atoning blood. These two men, Joseph of Arimathea and Nicodemus the Pharisee, who had previously been secret disciples, bear living testimony to the power of the cross to turn the hearts of sinners toward the Savior.

JOSEPH AND NICODEMUS

John recounts that after Jesus died, Joseph of Arimathea presented himself to the Roman governor and "asked Pilate that he might take away the body of Jesus" (John 19:38). Ordinarily, Romans left the corpses of crucified victims to decompose in public view, but in Judea the Jews were permitted to take down the bodies and bury them, with the bodies of executed criminals typically buried in mass graves.[1] Joseph was determined that Jesus' body would be honored in death, so he made his appeal to Pilate. According to Mark's Gospel, "Pilate was surprised to hear that [Jesus] should have already died." To make sure, Pilate sent for the attending centurion, who confirmed Jesus' death (Mark 15:44). Having learned this, Pilate granted Joseph the right to bury the body of Jesus.

Joseph of Arimathea is named only in the account of Jesus' burial, but the four Gospels give a combined description that includes a number of revealing details. Hailing from Arimathea, an otherwise unknown town in Judea (Luke 23:50), Joseph was both rich (Matt. 27:57) and powerful, being a member of the Sanhedrin, the Jewish ruling council. As such, he was held in great respect (Mark 15:43). Luke describes him as "a good and righteous man" (Luke 23:50), and Mark adds that he was "looking for the kingdom of God" (Mark 15:43), which suggests that he was living in expectation of the coming Messiah. Matthew and John state further that he was "a disciple of Jesus" (Matt. 27:57). John adds, however, that Joseph believed only "secretly for fear of the Jews" (John 19:38). Somewhere during Jesus' ministry, Joseph had come to believe in the Narazene as the long-awaited Messiah, yet he continued on the Sanhedrin in the company of those who opposed Jesus. Luke points out, however, that he "had not consented to their decision and action" in condemning and putting Jesus to death (Luke 23:51). We do

1. See discussion in George R. Beasley-Murray, *John*, Word Biblical Commentary 36 (Waco, TX: Word, 1987), 358.

not know whether Joseph absented himself from the Jewish trial of Jesus or remained silent during the proceedings. The key point is that while he believed on Jesus, he did so secretly, not divulging his faith to his peers.

John states that Joseph kept his faith secret "for fear of the Jews" (John 19:38). It was clear to Joseph that his fellow rulers would turn on him if he made known that he believed on Jesus. He knew that some people who professed faith in Jesus were being put out of the synagogue, becoming virtual outcasts from Jewish society (see 9:22). Moreover, Joseph knew of the plot to kill Jesus, a plot that also threatened the lives of his closest followers (see 12:10). There was little doubt that if Joseph openly professed faith in Jesus, the repercussions could have been severe.

In one way or another, every believer in Christ must face the fear of reprisals from the world. In many places, believers daily face the fear of arrest and bodily harm. True Christians everywhere face scorn from the world. Ironically, we live in a day when people are "coming out of the closet" boldly to proclaim every kind of sexual perversion and when virtually every human vice has been set free from scandal. Why, then, are people afraid to "come out" as believers in Jesus? The answer is the fear of what people will say and do in response.

The fear of man is an especially strong temptation for those who crave the praise of men. John mentioned secret disciples earlier in his Gospel, noting that "many even of the authorities believed in [Jesus], but for fear of the Pharisees they did not confess it, so that they would not be put out of the synagogue; for they loved the glory that comes from man more than the glory that comes from God" (John 12:42–43). We may presume that Joseph of Arimathea was one of the men noted there by John. Notice that their fear was twofold. Yes, they feared the reprisal of expulsion from society, but they also craved human praise.

Undoubtedly, a man such as Joseph had enjoyed worldly accolades for much of his life. The same would have been true of Nicodemus, the other secret disciple who joined him at the cross. The reason that they had pursued their careers was so as to be highly thought of by their contemporaries. The same thing occurs today: it is no surprise that more people desire high-status occupations than low ones. Young people labor and sweat through long years of schooling so as to attain to the kind of position in life that will not only provide wealth and ease but also inspire the high opinion of others.

How difficult it is to publicize their faith in Jesus Christ when they could lose the approval that they worked so hard to gain.

For this reason, the love of praise is just as deadly to Christian faith as the fear of man. If you find yourself craving and enjoying a fine reputation among worldly people, then you should realize that this desire poses a deadly peril to your soul, especially if it is already muting your witness. Charles Spurgeon warns that when a Christian "may begin to question rather, What will people say? than, What will God say? at the moment he falls into that mood he has introduced a weakening element into his life."[2]

Finally, we remember that Joseph of Arimathea was a rich man (Matt. 27:57). Jesus noted the hindrance that earthly riches pose to saving faith, saying that "it is easier for a camel to go through the eye of a needle than for a rich person to enter the kingdom of God" (19:24). The problem is not the wealth itself but the love of money, which Paul calls "a root of all kinds of evils" (1 Tim. 6:10). The ability to gain wealth is in itself an asset to a Christian, and the stewardship of wealth for the good of Christ's kingdom is a high and noble calling. Many faithful Christians enjoy riches with gratitude to God and give generously to the cause of the gospel. Yet wealth brings with it a host of worldly cares and temptations. In the case of Joseph of Arimathea, as with Nicodemus, earthly riches could only have magnified the fear of persecution and the desire for the praise of men.

Joseph stood apart from other secret believers by coming out boldly to speak for Jesus on the day of his crucifixion. When he and Nicodemus had overcome their fear, they probably realized how needless it had been all along. There is, in fact, no real danger for a Christian in the ridicule of the world. James Montgomery Boice writes, "In fact, the opposite is true. When we take a stand for righteousness, we are most secure. It is when we are silent that we are most in danger, not only in this life but in regard to the life that is to come."[3] The same is true of even more severe forms of persecution, as Christians have learned throughout the centuries. Those who lose their earthly wealth for Christ become rich in the things of the Spirit. Those who are secluded in prison for the gospel enjoy the close fellowship of Christ. And those who suffer death for their witness are immediately translated into realms of glory.

---

2. Charles H. Spurgeon, *Majesty in Misery*, 3 vols. (Edinburgh: Banner of Truth, 2005), 3:366–67.
3. James Montgomery Boice, *The Gospel of John*, 5 vols. (Grand Rapids: Baker, 1999), 5:1559.

THE COST OF SECRET DISCIPLESHIP

Lest we think too poorly of Joseph and Nicodemus for their secret discipleship, we should remember that when all the other disciples had scattered, except for John and the women, these two men came out publicly in allegiance to Jesus so as to give a fitting burial to his body. We are never told anything about them afterward, and it is possible that they were immediately persecuted. It is likely, however, that having come into the open, they were mostly grieved by what their cowardice had previously cost them.

Primary among their losses for failing to profess Jesus openly was the forfeited opportunity to fellowship with Jesus during his earthly ministry. For three years Jesus had been among the people of Israel, teaching, performing miracles, and setting hearts free. We do not know when Joseph first encountered Jesus, but Nicodemus had met with the Lord in the early days of his ministry. John reminds us that Nicodemus "earlier had come to Jesus by night" (John 19:39). The record of this earlier meeting in John chapter 3, which Nicodemus arranged in secret for fear of his fellow Jews, includes some of Jesus' most powerful statements. It was to Nicodemus that Jesus said, "You must be born again" (3:7). It was Nicodemus who heard perhaps the most beloved verse in the Bible from the lips of Jesus: "For God so loved the world, that he gave his only Son, that whoever believes in him should not perish but have eternal life" (3:16). Yet Nicodemus spurned the opportunity to be one of Jesus' close disciples during the three years that followed. How much spiritual growth must Nicodemus have forfeited by remaining in secret? The same was true in some measure of Joseph of Arimathea. Spurgeon writes:

> During that brief but golden period in which men walked and talked, and ate and drank with Jesus, Joseph was not with him. He was not among the twelve. . . . He lost many of those familiar talks with which the Lord indulged his own after the multitudes had been sent away. He missed that sacred training and strengthening which fitted men for the noble lives of primitive saints. How many opportunities he must have missed, too, of working for the Master and with the Master! Perhaps we hear no more of him because he had done no more.[4]

4. Spurgeon, *Majesty in Misery*, 3:368.

As Joseph and Nicodemus watched Jesus suffer the mocking hatred of mankind, did they grieve that they had failed to bow the knee to him, fearing man rather than worshiping God's Son? How bitter must their silence have tasted as they stood mutely observing the cross! A similar grief will come to those today who out of fear of the world deny Jesus the glory of their open profession, who blend in with the unbelieving world and shun the fellowship of suffering with Christ. Are you such a secret disciple? Do you believe in Jesus but say and do nothing openly for him? Then realize that the years of your earthly life are speeding by and soon you will never have the opportunity to give Jesus glory in a world that denies him. Meanwhile, how greatly you impoverish your soul as you forfeit the fellowship with Christ that comes by living boldly for him in this world!

Second, secret disciples forfeit the blessing of Christian fellowship. Boice writes:

> You also lose that blessed and valuable communion that you should and must have with other Christians. They are with Christ; if you are not with him, you are not with them either and you will suffer for it. An ember isolated from other embers soon burns out and is nothing but dead ashes. Place it near others and the flame soon grows and sets other wood burning. If you have never learned this before, put it down as a great and unalterable principle: *Christians need other Christians.* You need them. If you think you do not, you are either a fool or hopelessly proud or arrogant.[5]

Some will object that Christians do not always live up to their calling, and many have been hurt by sins in and of the church. This objection assumes that you are yourself superior to other Christians, a supposition that is contrary to belief in the gospel. If you realize that other Christians are sinners, then you should realize that you are also a sinner. You therefore need to be with other sinners who are growing in grace through their open profession of Christ. With this in mind, the writer of Hebrews urges: "Let us consider how to stir up one another to love and good works, not neglecting to meet together, as is the habit of some, but encouraging one another, and all the more as you see the Day drawing near" (Heb. 10:24–25). Boice adds to this:

5. Boice, *John*, 5:1561.

What company have you found that is superior? That of unbelievers? The world? If you are thinking along those lines, you are a great fool, for it is the world that, for all its supposed glamour and sophistication, crucified your Master. What makes you think it will treat you more kindly when once it finds that you belong to him?[6]

A third problem with secret discipleship is more than implied by the failure to commune with Jesus and fellowship with his people. Joseph and Nicodemus had also forfeited the assurance of their salvation during their secret discipleship. The question must be raised to all who refuse to own Jesus publicly out of fear of the world, the craving for praise, and the love of earthly riches: have you truly believed on Jesus? Do you really look upon him as the Son of God and trust him as your Savior? If so, how can you hide your allegiance to him? Jesus taught, "So everyone who acknowledges me before men, I also will acknowledge before my Father who is in heaven, but whoever denies me before men, I also will deny before my Father who is in heaven" (Matt. 10:32–33). How can you rest, secret disciple of Christ, while your cowardice keeps you under this dreadful ban?

In light of Jesus' requirement for an open and public profession of faith in him, we may state as a principle that ultimately there is no such thing as secret discipleship. It is true that under times of great persecution the church might be forced underground, so that a despondent Elijah may learn that there are yet seven thousand who have not bowed their knees to the idols (see 1 Kings 19:18). The example of Joseph and Nicodemus encourages us that there might be more believers around us than we had thought, believers who in time will stand forth boldly for Jesus. But we know of Joseph's and Nicodemus's faith and salvation only because *they no longer remained secret.* Mark tells us that Joseph "took courage and went to Pilate and asked for the body of Jesus" (Mark 15:43). Saving faith will give such courage, so that true disciples will no longer remain secret. In time of need and under the guiding presence of the Holy Spirit, they must and will become open with their faith in Jesus.

This provides the chief reason why a believer should always seize the opportunity to make his or her faith in Jesus known, especially when starting a new job, entering college, or similarly entering a new social setting: only an open and public Christianity will preserve us from worldly temptations and give us assurance of our salvation. How much better it would have been

6. Ibid.

for these two believers to have professed Christ earlier. How much better if your secret discipleship comes to an end today and you begin living openly for Jesus and giving him the glory of your life.

MOTIVES FOR A BOLD DISCIPLESHIP

I want to conclude with reasons why Joseph and Nicodemus finally came into the open with their faith in Jesus, which are also reasons why you should come out as a Christian, and if you are a Christian why you should live even more boldly and openly for him.

First, it is obvious that these two men were changed by what they saw at the cross. Their minds had previously accepted the truth about Jesus, but their reservations were conquered only by the majesty of his atoning death and the love of God that it revealed. So it is for everyone who comes to a full embrace of Christ and his gospel. Spurgeon comments:

> Is it not a remarkable thing that all the life of Christ did not draw out an open avowal from [Joseph]? Our Lord's miracles, his marvelous discourses, his poverty, and self-renunciation, his glorious life of holiness and benevolence, all may have helped to build Joseph in his secret faith, but it did not suffice to develop in him a bold avowal of faith. The shameful death of the cross had greater power over Joseph than all the beauty of Christ's life.[7]

This example reminds us why it is so important in our preaching and our witness not to fail to emphasize the death of God's Son to atone for our sins. The four Gospels have rightly been described as passion narratives with extended introductions, and our witness to Christ likewise must not stop at his sublime parables or compassionate acts of healing. We must proclaim the cross, and with it the biblical doctrines of sin, divine justice, and saving grace. Isaac Watts wrote words that every heart that has truly and boldly come to Jesus can endorse:

> When I survey the wondrous cross
> On which the Prince of glory died,
> My richest gain I count but loss,
> And pour contempt on all my pride.[8]

7. Spurgeon, *Majesty in Misery*, 3:369.
8. Isaac Watts, "When I Survey the Wondrous Cross" (1707, 1709).

Second, the public conversion of Joseph and Nicodemus was an instance of Christ's power to save as he reigns from the cross. Apart from the grace of his effectual calling, our sinful hearts are not able to believe, even seeing the love of God at the cross (see John 6:44; 1 Cor. 2:14). But through the cross Jesus has received power to gain his people for himself. This was Jesus' meaning when he stated, "And I, when I am lifted up from the earth, will draw all people to myself" (John 12:32). John Calvin writes: "here we have a striking proof that his death was more quickening than his life; and so great was the efficacy of that sweet savour which the death of Christ conveyed to the minds of those two men, that it quickly extinguished all the passions belonging to the flesh."[9] This truth should embolden us all the more in proclaiming the cross, since we know that the risen and enthroned Savior exerts his own mighty power to make the preaching of his cross effectual to save those "appointed to eternal life" (Acts 13:48).

Third, just as Joseph and Nicodemus seemed to have gained courage in the hour when most others had fallen away, we, too, should respond to the need today for open and bold disciples of Jesus. Do we not see the church beleaguered and besieged? Do we not see worldliness reigning in the lives of so many who profess to follow Christ? Do we not note how the prevailing winds of culture are all blowing against biblical doctrines and morality? How can we, in such a day as this—a day like that day in which Jesus died forsaken by almost all his friends—stand by in secret discipleship, blending in with the world even as it seeks to abolish the gospel and persecute the cross? It might be that some true men and women remain silent about Jesus when all is calm, but how can anyone be true and yet stand aloof while the battle rages with such ferocity as in our generation? If you have been secret or timid in your allegiance to Jesus, pray to God for the boldness that alone can make you useful to your generation, give you peace of conscience, and grant assurance to the reality of your salvation.

Fourth and last, Christians must be aware that souls around us are perishing in unbelief, many of them in want of a witness to Christ and his salvation. How can you say nothing to them as they draw near to the yawning gates of hell? Does not your conscience require you to come out for Jesus, or at least to pray to God for the courage to give the witness without which

9. John Calvin, *Calvin's Commentaries*, trans. William Pringle, 22 vols. (Grand Rapids: Baker, 2009), 18:244.

others cannot be saved? Paul lamented the idea that sinners should perish for want of a witness, and he reminded us of Isaiah's extolling verse: "How beautiful are the feet of those who preach the good news!" (Rom. 10:15, quoting Isa. 52:7).

In an earlier study, we learned of Judy Telchin, a traditional Jewish girl who was brought to faith in Jesus by the witness of a friend at college. She naturally feared the anger and sense of betrayal with which her family would respond. Despite her father's rage, however, Judy gave her simple and bold witness: "I believe that the Bible is the Word of God, and I believe that Jesus is the Messiah."[10] Judy's father, Stan, loved his daughter and therefore began studying the New Testament to disprove her new faith in Jesus. As he studied, his eyes were opened by the Lord and he saw for himself that Jesus is the Messiah. He went on to have a powerful evangelistic outreach to other Jews. Today, Stan Telchin and his book *Betrayed!* have been used to lead many Jews to Jesus. Because one young Jewish woman was bold to declare her faith in Jesus openly, Christ drew her family members and ultimately many others to himself through the cross.

When his daughter first declared her faith in Jesus, Stan Telchin initially felt betrayed by her. But when the Lord had opened his own eyes to Jesus, Stan realized that the true betrayal had come from those who had kept him from the truth of Jesus. Let us not betray the people in our life through a secret discipleship that holds back the only witness that can lead them to salvation. And like Joseph and Nicodemus, who could no longer stand by silently, but went boldly to ask Pilate for the right to honor his body, let us not betray Christ amid the darkness of this world. In the end, a secret discipleship finally betrays ourselves, since Jesus promised to bless those who boldly follow him, bearing the cross. "There is no one who has left house or wife or brothers or parents or children, for the sake of the kingdom of God," he said, "who will not receive many times more in this time, and in the age to come eternal life" (Luke 18:29–30).

---

10. Stan Telchin, *Betrayed!* (Grand Rapids: Chosen Books, 1981), 12.

131

A Garden Burial

John 19:38—42

*Now in the place where he was crucified there was a garden, and
in the garden a new tomb in which no one had yet been laid.*
(John 19:41)

*T*he apostle John opened his Gospel by presenting Jesus as the
Divine Word who spoke with power at the moment of creation:
"In the beginning was the Word" (John 1:1). Creation themes
continue throughout John's Gospel, including his reference to the water and
blood that flowed from Jesus' side, prompting us to recall the river of life
that "flowed out of Eden to water the garden" (Gen. 2:10). We inevitably see
as well a creation allusion in John's statement regarding the burial of Jesus'
body: "Now in the place where he was crucified there was a garden, and
in the garden a new tomb in which no one had yet been laid" (John 19:41).

The apostle does not make an explicit connection between Jesus' burial
and the events that took place in the original garden. Yet it is hard to imagine
that John, the author of the book of Revelation, with its many connections
between Old and New Testaments, would have failed to observe a parallel. In the garden, man came under the judgment of death for sin; Adam's
transgression delved into a tomb in fear of which his race has ever lived. Yet

through the long ages recorded in the Bible, God had left that tomb empty: mankind had not been destroyed but awaited its Deliverer, who would lie in that grave for the sins of his people. How fitting it was, then, that Jesus was laid in a garden tomb after his atoning death on the cross. F. B. Meyer writes: "In a garden man fell; in a garden he was redeemed!" Moreover, by Christ's death the garden's original design was achieved: "the death of Christ has sown our world with the flowers of peace and joy and blessedness."[1]

CRUCIFIED, DEAD, AND BURIED

These brief reflections help us to see that Jesus' burial was important to his saving work. The Apostles' Creed acknowledges this importance, reciting that Jesus "was crucified, dead, and buried." In John's record of Jesus' death, we have learned that every detail has great meaning, especially as the cross fulfills the Old Testament types and prophecies. What is true of his cross is true of Jesus' tomb: the laying of Jesus' body in the grave was an important part of his atoning work for our sins.

In 1671, the Puritan John Flavel published a series of forty-two sermons on the death of Jesus, titled *The Fountain of Life*.[2] In Flavel's sermon on the burial of Jesus' body, he listed five reasons why this was an important element of Jesus' saving achievement. The first purpose for Jesus' burial was *to prove the reality of his death*.

So vital is the death of Jesus to the Christian doctrine of salvation that this event has been an obvious target for those who would oppose the gospel. Writing late in the first century, John was familiar with denials of Jesus' true humanity and especially of his actual, physical death. Therefore, Flavel writes, "since our eternal life is wrapt up in Christ's death, it can never be too firmly established."[3] If it was not already certain that Jesus was dead after the Roman soldiers certified his death and drove a spearhead into his torso, Jesus' burial placed the matter beyond dispute. John tells us that Joseph of Arimathea and Nicodemus packed Jesus' body with spices and wrapped it in cloths (John 19:40; 20:7). John 20:7 speaks as well of a cloth

---

1. F. B. Meyer, *The Life of Love* (Old Tappan, NJ: Revell, 1987), 383.
2. In John Flavel, *The Works of John Flavel*, 6 vols. (1820; repr., Edinburgh: Banner of Truth, 1968), 1:17–561.
3. Ibid., 1:456.

that had been wrapped around the face. After Jesus' burial in this manner, there is no reasonable doubt as to the fact of his death.

Jesus' burial was also important *to certify the truth of his resurrection*, since it was necessary to establish that his body had been securely kept. This was surely one of God's aims in providing a previously unknown disciple to claim Jesus' body and place it in his own nearby tomb (see Matt. 27:60). Since Joseph's grave was a new tomb and had never been used, there was no possibility of confusion as to the body. Since the tomb was cut out of rock, there was no possibility for a secret entryway by which Jesus' followers might have stolen the body. Moreover, since Jesus' opponents asked Pilate to seal and set a guard on the grave, the security of his body was as safe as was conceivably possible (see 27:62–66). In their joint discussions regarding Jesus' burial, not only his disciples but also the Roman soldiers, Pontius Pilate, and the Jewish priests and Pharisees gave joint testimony to his death and to the security of his body in the grave.

A third reason for Jesus' burial was *to fulfill the types and prophecies* of the Old Testament. Just as Jonah was buried within the great fish, Jesus said that he would emerge from the grave on the third day with a gospel of salvation (Matt. 12:40). Jesus pointed out not merely that Jonah prefigured his death and resurrection, but also that Jonah's ministry of salvation to the wicked Gentiles of Nineveh prefigured Christ's resurrection power for the spread of the gospel to all nations. "The men of Nineveh will rise up at the judgment with this generation and condemn it," he preached, "for they repented at the preaching of Jonah, and behold, something greater than Jonah is here" (12:41).

An additional prophecy said that "they made his grave with the wicked and with a rich man in his death" (Isa. 53:9). This prophecy, so unlikely in view of the other circumstances of Jesus' execution, was fulfilled to the letter in the burial of his body in Joseph of Arimathea's grave. We are here reminded not only of the honor that God ascribed to his Son, not willing for his body to be callously disposed of, but also of the certain fulfillment of all of the Bible's prophecies and promises, especially those pertaining to Christ's second coming.

Fourth, Jesus was buried in the grave *to complete his humiliation*, the grave, writes Flavel, "being the lowest step he could possibly descend to in his abased state."[4] If the depth of Christ's love for us can be measured by the humiliation he endured for our salvation, then the grave bears the full testimony of our Savior's devotion to his people. Jesus was born to die for sin, and the Son of God who humbled himself to be fashioned as a baby in the womb of the virgin Mary humbled himself even further by submitting his body to be laid in the grave. "You lay me in the dust of death," says Psalm 22:15. John began his Gospel by proclaiming, "In him was life, and the life was the light of men" (John 1:4). How great is the love of Jesus, then, to endure the darkness of death so that we might be saved from it.

Fifth, Jesus was buried so as *to conquer death and the grave* for us. Flavel exults: "The great end and reason of his interment was *the conquering of death* in its own dominion and territories; which victory over the grave furnished the saints with that triumphant . . . song of deliverance, 'O death! Where is thy sting? O grave! Where is thy destruction?' "[5] Jesus entered the grave to break its power by his resurrection, opening the gates for his people who, like Jesus, will remain in their coffins not one minute longer than God appoints. Flavel concludes:

> Death is a dragon, the grave its den; a place of dread and terror; but Christ goes into its den, there grapples with it, and for ever overcomes it; disarms it of all its terror; and not only makes it to cease to be *inimical*, but to become exceeding *beneficial* to his saints; a bed of rest, and a perfumed bed; they do but go into Christ's bed, where he lay before them. For these ends he must be buried.[6]

THE BURIAL OF A KING

Having considered the purpose and design of Christ's grave, we should attend to the details of Jesus' burial. First, we should note that Jesus received a private, not a public, burial. Few people seem to have attended to the interment of God's Son. This accords with the general lack of honor granted to Jesus by the kingdom of this world. Isaiah said, "He was despised and rejected by men" (Isa. 53:3), and this continued in the disposing of Jesus' body. Jesus had told Pilate, "My kingdom is not of this world" (John 18:36), and

4. Ibid., 1:457.
5. Ibid.
6. Ibid.

accordingly the world ignored the King of heaven's funeral. Once the world had removed Jesus, it no longer had any concern for him, just as the world today permits no more than sentimental interest in Jesus. Israel's Messiah was therefore buried without pomp, but not without God's care for his body.

The Roman preference would have been for Jesus' body to remain on the cross to decompose and provide fodder for the carrion birds. Since this was contrary to Jewish law, the Romans permitted the Jews to bury the bodies of crucified victims. The Jews, however, did not permit the remains of criminals to desecrate their graveyards, so Jesus' body would probably have been disposed of in the burning dumpyard outside the city, the name of which, Gehenna, became symbolic for the fires of God's wrath in hell. The request of Joseph of Arimathea to bury Jesus body delivered him from this indignity.[7]

For all the public disinterest, John provides details that show that Jesus was buried in a manner fitting for a king: "Nicodemus also, who earlier had come to Jesus by night, came bringing a mixture of myrrh and aloes, about seventy-five pounds in weight. So they took the body of Jesus and bound it in linen cloths with the spices, as is the burial custom of the Jews" (John 19:39–40).

Myrrh was a fragrant resin used by the Egyptians and others in embalming the dead. The Jews mixed it with aloe, an aromatic powder. Their use was not to embalm the dead, since the Jews did not remove any organs in their burial preparations, but simply to combat the smell of the body's decomposition. Nicodemus brought an enormous amount of this spiced mixture, which scholars today consider to have exceeded sixty-five pounds. John describes the customary Jewish preparation of the body, with strips of cloth laden with myrrh and aloes wound around Jesus' body. More spice would have been packed around and under the body as well.

So staggering is the amount of spices cited by John, far exceeding that normally required, that some scholars have accused John of error or exaggeration. They fail to realize that John is continuing the royal theme that has pervaded his account of the cross. When Asa, one of the great kings of Judah, died, they buried him in a newly cut tomb "on a bier that had been filled with various kinds of spices prepared by the perfumer's art" (2 Chron. 16:14). Herod the Great's funeral procession included five hundred servants

7. R. C. Sproul, *John* (Orlando: Reformation Trust, 2009), 375.

bearing spices. Later in the first century, a ruler named Onkelos burned eighty pounds of spices at the funeral of the rabbi Gamaliel. When asked the reason, he answered, "Is not Rabbi Gamaliel far better than a hundred kings?" Joseph and Nicodemus were contemporaries of Onkelos and Gamaliel, and in their manner of burying Jesus they were declaring, "Is not Jesus far greater than all other kings?"[8]

Tombs were cut out of the solid sandstone that surrounded Jerusalem and typically included an inner chamber where the body (or bodies) would be laid in death. The doorway consisted of a groove into which a heavy stone had been fitted to block the entryway. Normally, the body would lie on its slab until it fully decomposed, at which point the bones would be placed into an ornate box called an ossuary. John notes that the time for Jesus' burial was short "because of the Jewish day of Preparation" (John 19:42). At sundown the holy Sabbath would arrive, leaving Joseph and Nicodemus little time to prepare. By God's providence, Joseph's own newly cut tomb was nearby, so this ruler who had been a secret disciple now had the honor of placing Jesus' body in his own grave. We praise our heroes today by burying them with honors in our national cemetery, and like the godly kings of old, Jesus was buried "with his fathers in the city of David" (2 Kings 15:7).

Jesus' humiliation called for him to die for the sins of others and be buried in another man's tomb. Having completed his work in death, Jesus thus began his exaltation to glory even in the grave. Since Jesus' body was preserved by God from suffering decay (Ps. 16:10), his tomb smelled only of sweet fragrance as it waited for the resurrection morning. F. W. Krummacher comments: "Who does not perceive that even in the circumstances of His interment, the overruling hand of God has interwoven for our consolation a gentle testimony, that His only-begotten Son had well accomplished the great task which He was commissioned to perform?"[9]

Comfort for Christians

The burial of Jesus is of great interest to Christians not only because of what it says about our Lord but because, unless Jesus first returns, each of us must also enter the grave.

---

8. George R. Beasley-Murray, *John*, Word Biblical Commentary 36 (Waco, TX: Word, 1987), 359.
9. F. W. Krummacher, *The Suffering Saviour* (1856; repr., Edinburgh: Banner of Truth, 2004), 443.

The burial of Jesus informs us of the biblical understanding of the body even in death and has thus shaped the burial practices of Christians from the earliest days of the church. According to the Bible, not only does a person inhabit the body, but the body is part of the person, even though death effects a separation of body and soul. The souls of believers depart in death for the presence of God in heaven (2 Cor. 5:8), and their bodies are placed in the grave to await the resurrection. Notice, in this respect, that while John 19:40 says that they bound "the body of Jesus," verse 42 states that "they laid Jesus" into the tomb. In other words, the body of Jesus was still Jesus. This shows that Jesus retained his full humanity even in death, and it argues that our bodies, even after the soul has departed, remain part of ourselves and ought to be treated with dignity and honor.

Because of the Bible's teaching on the body and on death, Christians have almost universally practiced the burial of the body rather than cremation.[10] Only recently has the practice of cremation spread among professing Christians. The primary reason seems to be financial, yet this trend testifies to the decline of biblical thinking among believers. In the Old Testament, the burning of bodies was considered a sign of divine judgment and a portent of the torments of hell, whereas the godly were buried with honor, as was the body of Christ (e.g., Josh. 7:25–26; 1 Kings 13:2; 16:18; 2 Kings 23:4).

It is true that with time a buried body will decay into much the same condition as those consumed in fire, but Christians have declined to treat the body as disposable remains, instead committing it to God's care with reverence. Cremation would seem to pose no barrier to God's ability to raise the dead, and we should note that the Bible never explicitly commands burial versus cremation. Yet our view of the afterlife will always influence how we handle the bodies of those who have died. Whereas cremation results from a pagan view of the body and the afterlife in which matter is released into spirit, Christian burial is shaped by the hope of a bodily resurrection. Paul writes: "The Lord himself will descend from heaven with a cry of command, with the voice of an archangel, and with the sound of the trumpet of God. And the dead in Christ will rise first"

---

10. For a thorough discussion of the biblical background pertaining to burial and cremation, see David W. Jones, "To Bury or Burn? Toward an Ethic of Cremation," *Journal of the Evangelical Theological Society* 53, 2 (June 2010): 335–47.

(1 Thess. 4:16). This description urges us to honor, preserve, and even dedicate real estate to the bodies of those who, having died in Christ, now await the resurrection of their bodies in the morning of the new creation. John Flavel summarizes: "There is a respect due to [Christian bodies], as they are the temples wherein God hath been served, and honoured by those holy souls that once dwelt in them; as also upon the account of their relation to Christ, even when they lie by the walls; and the glory that will one day put upon them, when they shall be changed, and made like unto Christ's glorious body."[11]

Second, the burial of Jesus provides Christians with great consolations against the fear of death. For not only did Jesus lie in Joseph's tomb, but he has entered the grave in advance of all his people. God told Jacob not to be afraid to go down to Egypt, since "I myself will go down with you to Egypt, and I will also bring you up again" (Gen. 46:3–4). Christians likewise should not fear the grave, since God will be with us there and has promised to raise us from it into glory.

Flavel lists several reasons why Christians face the grave without fear. First, "the grave *received*, but could not *destroy* Jesus Christ: death swallowed him, as the whale did Jonah his type, but could not digest him when it had swallowed him, but quickly delivered him up again."[12] Christ entered the grave not as a private person but as the covenant head of all his people. Just as his death exhausted the curse of sin against believers, so also his entering the grave has claimed it as the sleep chamber for those awaiting the resurrection. His resurrection is the ground of our certain hope to triumph over death and the grave. Paul exclaims, "Christ has been raised from the dead, the firstfruits of those who have fallen asleep" (1 Cor. 15:20).

Second, Christians gain consolation from knowing that just as our souls belong to Jesus through faith, our bodies are united to him even in death. "Precious in the sight of the LORD is the death of his saints" (Ps. 116:15), says the Bible, and our bodies are likewise precious to God even in the grave. Proverbs 14:32 says that "the righteous finds refuge in his death," and our refuge is the union of our bodies and souls to the Savior. In death, David sang, "I will fear no evil, for you are with me; your rod and your staff, they comfort me" (Ps. 23:4).

11. Flavel, *Works*, 1:461.
12. Ibid., 1:463.

Third, Christ has conquered death and the grave so that its curse is removed from his people. It is for this reason that David wrote of passing through "the valley of the shadow of death" (Ps. 23:4). Christians do not enter death as a final destination, but we pass through death into eternal glory, and even death itself has become in Christ no more than a shadow. Matthew Henry writes, "There is no substantial evil in it; the shadow of a serpent will not sting nor the shadow of a sword kill."[13]

Finally, Jesus reached the final depth of his humiliation in death and burial, yet his exaltation began even in the hurried minutes of his funeral. So also will the laying of our bodies in the grave begin our transition into glory. Charles Spurgeon writes:

> The grave—what is it? It is the bath in which the Christian puts on the clothes of his body to have them washed and cleansed. Death—what is it? It is the waiting room where we robe ourselves for immortality; it is the place where the body, like Esther, bathes itself in spices that it may be fit for the embrace of its Lord. Death is the gate of life; I will not fear to die, then.[14]

Isaiah's prophecy said that while Jesus died in the company of the wicked, he would be buried together with the rich (Isa. 53:9). So it is that riches and glory await all who die in Christ, since in him we have died to sin and risen through faith into never-ending life with God.

The Urgency of Trusting in Jesus

When man sinned in the garden, he dug a grave where either he or Jesus must die under God's judgment, and so it is for every sinner even today. Therefore, Christ concluded his earthly ministry by entering a garden and taking residence in the grave. There, he remedied the enmity with God brought on by Adam's sin and ours, and from his grave Jesus restores his people to fellowship and dominion with God. How urgent it is, therefore, that we should be in Christ through faith and that he should have entered that grave for us personally. Flavel notes:

13. Matthew Henry, *Commentary on the Whole Bible*, 6 vols. (Peabody, MA: Hendrickson, 2009), 3:259.

14. Charles H. Spurgeon, *Spurgeon's Sermons*, 10 vols. (1883; repr., Grand Rapids: Baker, 1987), 1:229.

The grave is a terrible place to them that are out of Christ; death is the Lord's sergeant to arrest them; the grave is the Lord's prison to secure them. . . . Death there reigns over them in its full power (Rom. 5:14). . . . But the case of the saints is not so; the grave (thanks be to our Lord Jesus Christ!) is a privileged place to them, whilst they sleep there; and when they awake, it will be with singing.[15]

What a great privilege it was for Joseph and Nicodemus, those two belated disciples, to bear Jesus' body into the grave where he would conquer death. What a privilege it is for us to bear his good news into a world held captive by fear of death. What an urgent matter it is for every soul to believe on Jesus Christ, placing our sins on his cross and our hopes in his resurrection life, taking up by faith the Christian song of rejoicing and praise:

O death, where is your victory?
   O death, where is your sting?

The sting of death is sin, and the power of sin is the law. But thanks be to God, who gives us the victory through our Lord Jesus Christ. (1 Cor. 15:55–57)

15. Flavel, *Works*, 1:464.

132

INSIDE THE EMPTY TOMB

John 20:1—10

> *Now on the first day of the week Mary Magdalene came to the*
> *tomb early, while it was still dark, and saw that the stone had*
> *been taken away from the tomb. So she ran and went to Simon*
> *Peter and the other disciple, the one whom Jesus loved, and said*
> *to them, "They have taken the Lord out of the tomb, and we do*
> *not know where they have laid him." (John 20:1–2)*

*I*n studies of the passion of Christ, Jesus' death is sometimes described as "tragic." The reason is that it was all so wrong: Jesus' arrest, suffering, and death were the result of hatred, deceit, and injustice. Jesus deserved none of all that was done to him, and what is more, he actually deserved the opposite. The people of Jerusalem hated him, the One who came to them with only love; they lied about the Author of truth; and they committed injustice against the most righteous man who ever lived. It was all so . . . well, tragic!

If we understand the literary category of tragedy, however, we will see that Jesus' suffering and death were anything but tragic. According to literary experts, a tragedy tells the story of a great person who is overthrown by a fatal flaw. The tragic plot has "the protagonist facing a dilemma that demands a choice.... The tragic hero makes a tragic choice that leads inevitably to catastrophe and suffering."[1] At the end of a tragedy, the hero is usually brought to repentance, receiving "some measure of moral perception as a result of his or her suffering."[2] A good example of a tragedy is William Shakespeare's play *King Lear*. The king is dividing his kingdom among his three daughters. Two of them seek to increase their shares by charming their father, but the third daughter, Cordelia, refuses to descend to flattery and is banished by an enraged King Lear. Only too late does the king realize that Cordelia is the only child who truly loves him. The play ends with a tragic King Lear weeping over his virtuous daughter's corpse, now aware of his mistake: "I might have saved her; now she's gone for ever! Cordelia, Cordelia!"[3]

Given this definition, you see why the death of Jesus Christ was *not* a tragedy. Jesus did not suffer because of a moral failing on his part. He did not make a tragic choice that led to his death. He did not cry out at the end, "What have I done?" but rather he triumphantly declared, "It is finished" (John 19:30). In the gospel story, we as sinners are the tragic figures who suffer misery because of our failings. Jesus died to free us from the tragic story of our sin-cursed lives.

What kind of story, then, is the gospel of Jesus and the cross told in John chapter 19? The answer is found in chapter 20, where the death of Jesus is seen not as a tragedy but as a comedy. This is not to demean the cross as though it told a humorous tale. Literarily speaking, comedy is "the story of the happy ending." According to Leland Ryken, a comedy "begins in prosperity, descends into tragedy, and rises again to end happily."[4] Given this definition, the greatest of all comedies is the story recounted in John chapter 20, the story of the resurrection of Jesus Christ and the victory he won over the greatest of our enemies—sin, judgment, sorrow, and death.

THE NOT-SO-EMPTY TOMB

Despite its happy ending, John 20 begins in joyless despair. Jesus died and was buried on Friday afternoon, and after resting on the Saturday Sabbath,

---

1. Leland Ryken, *How to Read the Bible as Literature* (Grand Rapids: Zondervan, 1984), 84.
2. Ibid.
3. William Shakespeare, *King Lear*, 5.3.
4. Ryken, *How to Read the Bible as Literature*, 81–82.

the women who had remained faithful to him returned to anoint his body with spices. John singles out one of the women, writing: "Now on the first day of the week Mary Magdalene came to the tomb early, while it was still dark, and saw that the stone had been taken away from the tomb" (John 20:1).

The account of the women at Jesus' tomb illustrates the significance of women in the Christian church and in the heart of our Lord. Female believers seem to have had a special and holy devotion to Jesus then, just as they often do now. Therefore, when all the male disciples except for John had gone into hiding with Jesus' arrest, a number of women remained close to him. If you are a woman, you should take inspiration from the pure-hearted devotion of these women for their Lord and Savior and also from the special place that they clearly occupied in Jesus' heart.

It is not altogether clear why John's account of the resurrection focuses on Mary Magdalene. Popular and irreverent literature, including the rock opera *Jesus Christ Superstar* and the best-selling book *The Da Vinci Code*, assumes an emotional or even sexual relationship between Jesus and this Mary. There is not a shred of evidence, biblical or otherwise, to support this line of thinking. Many writers assume that Mary Magdalene was a forgiven prostitute, associating her with the sinful woman of Luke 7, even though the Bible never identifies her as such. In fact, all that we know about Mary Magdalene comes from the records of her appearance at the cross and the empty tomb. The sole exception is the statement in Luke 8:2–3 that she had been formerly possessed by seven demons and that she gave financial support to Jesus out of her means. John seems to highlight her role not because this Mary had a unique relationship with Jesus but because she seems to have played a leading role among the faithful women, she was the first to meet the resurrected Jesus, and she bore the good news of Jesus' resurrection to the male disciples.

When Mary arrived at Jesus' grave, she was astonished to see that "the stone had been taken away from the tomb" (John 20:1). She noted the absence of Jesus' body: "They have taken the Lord out of the tomb, and we do not know where they have laid him" (20:2). Mary's exclamation shows that Jesus' followers did not arrange a fake resurrection since they did not even foresee the possibility, despite Christ's prior teaching that this would happen. The initial reaction of Jesus' disciples to the empty tomb was one of shock and bewilderment. The last thing Mary expected to find when she went to the tomb that Sunday morning was evidence of Jesus' resurrection.

When Mary came running with news that Jesus' body was missing, "Peter went out with the other disciple, and they were going toward the tomb" (John 20:3). John adds the detail that the two disciples raced to the tomb, most likely out of alarm over Mary's report. "Both of them were running together," John says, "but the other disciple outran Peter and reached the tomb first" (20:4).

Christians often speak of the "empty tomb" of Jesus' resurrection, but according to the Bible the tomb was not empty at all. Arriving first, John stooped to look: "he saw the linen cloths lying there, but he did not go in" (John 20:5). Simon Peter, always impetuous, arrived and went into the grave. "He saw the linen cloths lying there, and the face cloth, which had been on Jesus' head, not lying with the linen cloths but folded up in a place by itself" (20:6–7).

What John and Peter saw in the empty tomb was nothing less than evidence of a resurrection. Indeed, they saw the proof of the first resurrection ever. What happened here was different from the raising of Lazarus or any of the other raisings from the Old and New Testaments. When Lazarus came out of his tomb, he emerged with "his hands and feet bound with linen strips, and his face wrapped with a cloth" (John 11:44). For this reason, Jesus had to order those nearby to unbind him. Jesus' resurrection was different in kind; this was not a resuscitation but a resurrection into glory. Jesus did not wake up from death in his previous form of body, but, as John Stott explains, his body was "transmuted into something new and different and wonderful."[5] Because of what he saw in the not-so-empty tomb, John finally believed the truth about Jesus and his resurrection, and so should we.

SEEING AND BELIEVING

John relates that the disciples did not immediately jump to the conclusion that Jesus had risen from the dead. They believed in a future resurrection on the last day (see John 11:24), and they had seen Jesus' power to raise the dead, but the Gospels make it clear that after Jesus had died, none expected

5. John R. W. Stott, *Basic Christianity* (Downers Grove, IL: InterVarsity Press, 1959), 52.

to see him alive again. Their minds were changed by the persuasive evidence that was available to them and is available to us through the gospel's witness.

John describes the progression of faith in this episode by means of three different Greek words for *to see*: *blepo*, *theoreo*, and *horao*. The first of these, *blepo*, means simply "to look and see." This word appears in John 20:5, which states that when John first looked into the tomb, "he saw the linen cloths lying there." The second word, *theoreo*, appears in verse 6 to describe what happened with Peter: "Then Simon Peter came, following him, and went into the tomb. He saw the linen cloths lying there." This verb, which gives us our word *theorize*, means "to wonder regarding something's meaning." Peter looked on the graveclothes and thought about what he was seeing.

What Peter saw in the tomb was quite remarkable. When we studied Jesus' burial, we noted that the Jewish practice was to wrap a corpse in scented strips of linen that were bound around the body. In addition, a separate face cloth was wound around the head and chin to keep the head in position. These are the wrappings that John and Peter saw in Jesus' tomb. Apparently when Jesus was resurrected, his glorious body passed through the linen cloths wrapped around him so that they were not cast aside. Instead, when the body was removed, the weight of the spices caused the wrappings to collapse into a neat pile. John says that the strips of cloth that had been spiced and wrapped close around Jesus' body were "lying there" (John 20:6). The Greek word that John used for "lying there" (*keimena*) is used elsewhere of things that are carefully kept in order. In addition, "the face cloth, which had been on Jesus' head, [was] not lying with the linen cloths but folded up in a place by itself" (20:7). Evidently, since the face cloth was not packed with spices, it retained its circular shape after the body of Jesus passed through the material.

We can imagine Peter gazing on this scene, his mind whirling as he sought to make sense of the very suggestive evidence. If Jesus had been revived in a normal way, the graveclothes would be found disassembled and heaped beside the slab where his body had lain. But this is not what Peter saw. On the other hand, if Jesus' body had been removed by the kind of grave-robbers that Mary Magdalene feared had come, it is impossible to imagine why the graveclothes would be left at all, much less found in this position.

The evidence for Jesus' resurrection is so persuasive, including what Peter and John saw in the empty tomb, that it has been described as "the best attested fact in history."[6] Many legal scholars have scrutinized the evidence in the light of legal standards. One of them, the famous English jurist Sir Edward Clark, wrote, "As a lawyer I have made a prolonged study of the evidences for the first Easter day. To me the evidence is conclusive, and over and over again in the High Court I have secured the verdict on evidence not nearly so compelling."[7] Peter was the first of many who honestly considered the facts of Jesus' resurrection and responded by trusting him as their living Savior and Lord.

John tells of his belief in the resurrection by using a third word, *horao*, which can mean "to see with comprehension and understanding": "Then the other disciple, who had reached the tomb first, also went in, and he saw and believed" (John 20:8). Looking on the cloths lying so neatly and so remarkably undisturbed where Jesus' body had rested, John reached the only reasonable conclusion. Jesus' body must have been raised in glory so that it passed through the cloths, leaving the evidence for the resurrection behind. Stott comments, "A glance at these grave cloths proved the reality, and indicated the nature, of the resurrection."[8] Unlike Peter, who gazed on the scene wondering, John looked with faith, believing in the resurrection of Jesus in response to the evidence before him. We can imagine Peter standing over the graveclothes, saying, "I don't believe it!" John, prompted by the evidence, came to realize what the Bible had been saying about Jesus and believed. John would have answered, "Christ is risen!"

John follows with a statement that has puzzled commentators: "for as yet they did not understand the Scripture, that he must rise from the dead" (John 20:9). Scholars wonder whether this means that John's faith was not real or complete since his belief did not comprehend the Bible's teaching. The answer is that his faith was real, though not complete. The point is that Jesus provided evidences to lead his disciples into faith, just as he would soon appear to them personally to give an even more dramatic proof of his resurrection. For a true and fuller understanding of Jesus and his gospel, they would need to turn to the Scriptures with the new eyes that are born of faith. The same is true of us. Whatever witness was used

---

6. Matthew Arnold, quoted in James Montgomery Boice, *The Gospel of Matthew*, 2 vols. (Grand Rapids: Baker, 2001), 2:640.

7. Quoted in Stott, *Basic Christianity*, 47.

8. Ibid., 53.

to bring us to believe in Jesus, our faith must then be built up on the solid rock of God's Word.

Perhaps you have been led to believe in Jesus because of a change you have noticed in a friend who has become a Christian. Or perhaps you have come to recognize the absence of truth and love in the world and you see something different in the church. These are legitimate witnesses to Christ, just as the way that Jesus' resurrection changed the lives of the first disciples is a proof of his gospel. But living and enduring faith must always come from the truth and life that is in God's Word. "So faith comes from hearing," Paul wrote, "and hearing through the word of Christ" (Rom. 10:17). Peter and John had the enormous privilege of standing in the grave from which Jesus had risen, and yet, even after noting his coming to faith, John reminds us of our essential need to understand the Scripture if our seeing really is to be believing. If the future apostles Peter and John needed to ground and then feed their faith on the Bible, then so do you and I need to inform our faith with the Bible's teaching and feed daily on the life that is in the Word of God.

THE GOSPEL OF THE EMPTY TOMB

The Bible has much to say about the resurrection of Jesus Christ. John's record of his experience, however, includes the main points of what we might call the gospel of the empty tomb.

John's first important remark about the resurrection occurs in the opening words of the passage: "Now on the first day of the week" (John 20:1). We would be wrong to discount this statement as merely marking time; for John, the chronological is always theological. In this case, a more natural way of marking time would be to say that it was the morning of the third day since the crucifixion. So why does John speak of "the first day of the week"?

One answer can be found in the feasts of Old Testament Israel, remembering the way in which John has used the feast weeks to structure his record of Jesus' ministry. The feasts culminated not on the last day of the week but on the eighth day, the beginning of the new week. It had been on the eighth and "last day of the feast" of Tabernacles that Jesus stood up and cried, "If anyone thirsts, let him come to me and drink. Whoever believes in me, as the Scripture has said, 'Out of his heart will flow rivers of living water'" (John 7:37–38). John explained that Jesus was speaking of the Holy

Spirit, who would come after he was resurrected. Jesus was resurrected on the eighth day of the Passover week, the day after the Sabbath. The book of Acts records that the Spirit came upon the church on Pentecost, which was the day after the seventh Sabbath from the Passover—the eighth day of the seventh week (Lev. 23:15–16). The symbolism of these feast weeks agrees with John's emphasis on the first day of the new week: the hope of the ancient Scriptures and of the people of God is not found in the old week of the law but in the new week of the gospel, beginning with the first day of the new creation in the resurrection of Jesus Christ.

So great is the significance of the "first day of the week" in Christ's resurrection that the apostolic church shifted its day of worship from Saturday to Sunday, to mark the first day of the new creation in Christ (see Acts 20:7). The church was acknowledging one of the central and joyous truths of the Christian gospel, namely, that coming to Christ begins a new and eternal life, based on the definitive act of Jesus' death for our sins that has put away the old life and his resurrection that has begun the new. Paul explained that "if anyone is in Christ, he is a new creation. The old has passed away; behold, the new has come" (2 Cor. 5:17).

John organized his Gospel not only around the feast weeks, but also with the seven miracles that he records as signs to inspire faith in Jesus as the Savior. John sees the miracle of Christ's resurrection as the final and definitive sign. One commentator explains: "Now, on the eighth day, comes the eighth sign; the 'signs' performed during the ministry led the disciples to the beginning of faith (2.11), but they made no impact upon most of the onlookers (12.37). Now, with the resurrection itself, the ultimate 'sign' which will explain what Jesus has been doing . . . , the new day has opened. People of all sorts are hereby summoned to believe (20:30–31)."[9]

John indicates not only that Christ's resurrection inaugurates a new era of history, but also that the resurrection provides a new power for godly living. As we earlier noted, this resurrection was not like the earlier raisings. Lazarus came forth from the grave in his old body and in the power of his old life. In time, Lazarus would die again. Jesus, however, emerged from his tomb in a glorified body that will never die. James Montgomery Boice comments: "Today we need not think of Jesus as the vulnerable Jesus

---

9. N. T. Wright, *The Resurrection of the Son of God* (Minneapolis: Fortress Press, 2003), 669.

of history. Jesus died, but he died once for all. He was buffeted and spat upon and cursed, but that will not be repeated. We pray today to a powerful Lord, to an exalted Lord. This Lord will return one day to take his own to be with him in glory."[10]

The disciples would learn the full biblical significance of the resurrection under Jesus' teaching of the Scriptures during the days that followed. Then they would learn that Jesus' resurrection was merely the first of a great multitude. Christ was raised as "the firstfruits of those who have fallen asleep" (1 Cor. 15:20). The firstfruits were the initial crop that came out of the field during the first of the two annual harvests. The Feast of Firstfruits gave thanks to God for the harvest to come when the first crops came in. Christ's resurrection constituted the firstfruits of God's true harvest, in which the believers of all ages will be gathered. Therefore, when a believer is born again, that spiritual resurrection guarantees his or her participation in the future glorious, bodily resurrection of all who belong to Christ. Paul explained what every believer has to look forward to, by comparing our present bodies with our future resurrected bodies that are modeled on the glorious body of the resurrected Jesus: "What is sown is perishable; what is raised is imperishable. It is sown in dishonor; it is raised in glory. It is sown in weakness; it is raised in power. It is sown a natural body; it is raised a spiritual body. . . . Just as we have borne the image of the man of dust, we shall also bear the image of the man of heaven" (15:42–49).

Furthermore, note that John refers not merely to the Bible's teaching of Jesus' resurrection, but to the Scripture's witness to the *necessity* of the resurrection: "they did not understand the Scripture, that he *must* rise from the dead" (John 20:9). It was necessary on Jesus' part that he should rise from the grave, so that he might triumph over his and our enemies, that his gospel claims might be vindicated, and that the Father's acceptance of his atoning blood should be proved. Paul says that Jesus "was delivered up for our trespasses and raised for our justification" (Rom. 4:25). This means that, having died for our sins, Jesus was resurrected to present the atonement in his blood to the Father in order that our sins might be forgiven.

It was also necessary for the disciples that Jesus should be raised, so that they would receive power to believe and then to spread the gospel.

---

10. James Montgomery Boice, *The Gospel of John*, 5 vols. (Grand Rapids: Baker, 1999), 5:1568.

John concludes the passage by saying that "the disciples went back to their homes" (John 20:10). Because of the resurrection, however, their lives would never be the same. D. A. Carson explains the immediate significance for their faith: "Their Master was not in God's eyes a condemned criminal; the resurrection proved that he was vindicated by God, and therefore none less than the Messiah, the Son of God he claimed to be."[11] There was more to come in Jesus' postresurrection appearances and his ongoing relationship as their living Lord. For all this, it was necessary that he should be raised, so that his people would be not only those who are forgiven in his blood, but also those who live and witness in the power of his resurrection life.

Finally, it is necessary for us that Jesus should be raised, and it is necessary that we should believe and rely on his resurrection power. Paul lists faith in the resurrection as one of the central and necessary doctrines for Christian salvation (1 Cor. 15:3–4). Christian faith is never belief in the dead letters of mere doctrines, much less a reliance on dead legalism or self-righteousness. Saving faith is a relationship to a living Lord and Savior and the experience of heavenly power for righteousness, peace, and joy in the Holy Spirit (Rom. 14:17). Because of the resurrection, "the kingdom of God does not consist in talk but in power" (1 Cor. 4:20).

LAUGHTER AND LIFE

Based on what we have seen in the empty tomb, we grasp why the gospel of Jesus is not a tragedy but a comedy. We learned earlier that a comedy is not so much a funny story but one with a happy and glorious ending, a tale in which tragic sorrow is replaced with laughter. Christ's resurrection is the source of the purest mirth and wonder-filled delight. The resurrection promises that God is making everything right that has ever been wrong and that history is moving to a happier ending than we ever imagined was possible. By entering through the stone that was removed and looking in faith on Jesus' resurrection, we begin the happy story of eternal life that is described in the book of Revelation: "death shall be no more, neither shall there be mourning, nor crying, nor pain anymore, for the former things

11. D. A. Carson, *The Gospel of John* (Grand Rapids: Eerdmans, 1991), 632.

have passed away" (Rev. 21:4). In this way, life in Christ really becomes like a movie that ends with a wedding, a kiss, and a happily-ever-after life.

Isn't it true, however, that Christians can expect trials and sorrows in this life? The answer is Yes. But D. L. Moody tells a story that shows the difference it makes to know the happy ending of Jesus and all his people. A bright teenage girl was suddenly afflicted with a grave disease, so that she was paralyzed and nearly blind. Her hearing, however, was unimpaired, so she could understand the conversation taking place between the doctor and her parents. The doctor remarked sympathetically, "She has seen her best days, poor child." At this, the girl, a believer in the crucified and resurrected Jesus, suddenly spoke: "No, doctor, my best days are yet to come, when I shall see the King in his beauty."[12] Knowing this great gospel truth, she had laughter in her heart even on the threshold of death. If we will likewise trust in the gospel of Jesus' resurrection, he not only will assure us of our own better days to come, despite all the trials of life, but will give us power to live for his glory in this dying world.

---

12. Quoted in Boice, *John*, 5:1568.

133

TO MY FATHER AND YOUR FATHER

John 20:11—18

*Jesus said to her, "Do not cling to me, for I have not yet
ascended to the Father; but go to my brothers and say to
them, 'I am ascending to my Father and your Father, to my
God and your God.'"* (John 20:17)

So now faith, hope, and love abide, these three; but the greatest of these is love" (1 Cor. 13:13). If we were to seek an illustration of Paul's great accolade for love, we could do little better than Mary Magdalene at the tomb of Jesus Christ. As she approached the empty tomb on the resurrection morning, love is all that Mary had left: her faith in Jesus, and the hope that went with that faith, had died on the cross the previous Friday. With her faith and hope gone, only love drew Mary with affection and concern for the body of Jesus. Because of her love, Mary would be the first to see the resurrected Lord, and it would be through her rekindled faith that Jesus would send news of his triumphant resurrection from the grave.

LOVE THE GREATEST

Despite superficial differences between the record of the four Gospels, it is possible to reconstruct a probable sequence of events on that Sunday morning. Around dawn, Jesus was raised from the dead, accompanied by an earthquake and the coming of angels, so that Pilate's guards fled in terror (Matt. 28:2–4). Later, a group of faithful women set out for the tomb. Seeing the stone rolled away, Mary Magdalene fled for the male disciples while the other women entered the tomb and heard the angels' news of the resurrection (John 20:1–2; Mark 16:2–5; Matt. 28:5–6). Summoned by Mary Magdalene, John and Peter raced to the open tomb. Entering in, they saw the graveclothes left behind and returned to their houses (John 20:3–10). Mary Magdalene returned to the grave after the men had departed. There, "Mary stood weeping outside the tomb" (20:11).

The picture that John paints of this scene is among the most lovely and moving in all of Scripture. Mary's love has drawn her back alone to the tomb. No doubt terribly fatigued by grief and labor, she reaches the end of her emotional capacity and breaks down, weeping. Her mind has apparently fixated on the missing body. Jews "regarded with abhorrence any disrespect paid to a corpse,"[1] and Mary is distressed over the possibilities involved with the empty tomb.

Drawn by love, Mary "stooped to look into the tomb" (John 20:11). There, "she saw two angels in white, sitting where the body of Jesus had lain" (20:12). It might seem strange that the angels did not reveal themselves to John and Peter during their visit to the tomb, until we remember the teaching of Hebrews 1:14: "Are [angels] not all ministering spirits sent out to serve for the sake of those who are to inherit salvation?" Apparently, John and Peter did not need the angels' ministry, whereas Mary's grief prompted their reappearance.

It is probable that the angels, in all the holiness of their dazzling-white raiment, intended to lift Mary's heart from her fretful preoccupation over the fate of Jesus' body. Presenting a living image of the ark of the covenant, the angels were perched on either side of the slab where Jesus' body had lain as the true Sacrifice for sin, sitting "one at the head and one at the feet" (John 20:12). Geerhardus Vos comments: "Placed like the cherubim on the mercy-seat, they covered between themselves the spot where the Lord had reposed, and flooded it with celestial glory."[2] The angels asked Mary, "Woman,

---

1. Leon Morris, *The Gospel according to John*, rev. ed., New International Commentary on the New Testament (Grand Rapids: Eerdmans, 1995), 740.

2. Geerhardus Vos, *Grace and Glory* (Edinburgh: Banner of Truth, 1994), 73.

why are you weeping?" It is a testimony to the power of grief over a dearly loved one, and perhaps also to the tenderness of the holy female heart, that Mary seems not to have reacted to the glorious sight of the heavenly visitors. Looking through tear-filled eyes and gripped only with concern over Jesus' body, Mary answered, "They have taken away my Lord, and I do not know where they have laid him" (20:13).

The presence of such mighty divine servants should have clued Mary in that nothing could have been going amiss. We remember that angels were present to serve Jesus at every turning point of his earthly life, starting with his conception and birth, and continuing through the cross and empty tomb. The angels provide a tangible reminder of God's almighty presence to fulfill his promised acts of salvation. When Christ returns in glory to judge the living and the dead and to gather his saints from the four corners of the earth for the final resurrection, his innumerable angels will again attend that mighty work.

Still preoccupied over Jesus' body, Mary turned from the tomb. She shows that even so glorious a spiritual experience as seeing angels is no comfort if we have not found Christ. Turning around, Mary encountered the sight for which her heart had longed, but in a way that she never expected: "She turned around and saw Jesus standing, but she did not know that it was Jesus" (John 20:14). Mary is not the only disciple who will fail to recognize Jesus that resurrection day: Luke says that the Emmaus road disciples' "eyes were kept from recognizing him" (Luke 24:16), and it is possible that the same was true of Mary Magdalene. John's symbolism is suggestive, however. Mary needed to realize that she was looking in the wrong place, seeing Jesus only after she had turned around. Likewise, she had been looking for the dead Jesus of the past rather than the living Jesus who was now before her in the garden. In a passage of great touching beauty, John tells us what happened next: "Jesus said to her, 'Woman, why are you weeping? Whom are you seeking?' Supposing him to be the gardener, she said to him, 'Sir, if you have carried him away, tell me where you have laid him, and I will take him away.' Jesus said to her, 'Mary'" (John 20:15–16).

Jesus' appearance to Mary includes both a gentle reproof and a tender ministry of compassion. The reproof came in the question, "Woman, why are you weeping?" These words were aimed not at the grief that poured from Mary's love but at the unbelief that was operating within the grief. Jesus revealed his resurrection life as the answer and antidote to Mary's fear and sorrow. His resurrection had transformed the scene of grief so that love would no longer be devoid of faith and hope. Paul wrote to the Thessalonians with a similar message, urging them not to "grieve as others do who have no hope" (1 Thess. 4:13). To be sure, Christians grieve the sorrows of life, but with the resurrected Jesus standing before our faith, we gain a joy and a peace that bear testimony to his victory. In our grieving, let us never forget the resurrected Jesus and the hope that he gives.

Even more poignant is the compassionate care that Jesus gave to grieving Mary. How striking it is that on the morning of his victory over cosmic powers of evil, Jesus has full attention for the hurts of a precious disciple. Mark Johnston comments, "His people are not mere numbers in a book, they are individual people with individual needs, and he knows them through and through."[3] In the garden outside his empty tomb, Jesus fulfilled the promise of Psalm 34:18, just as he will fulfill it in our need: "The LORD is near to the brokenhearted and saves the crushed in spirit."

Notice as well that Jesus opened Mary's eyes by calling her name. Christ draws his people to himself personally and by name, the Good Shepherd calling his sheep so that they recognize his voice (John 10:16, 27). John Calvin comments: "Thus in Mary we have a lively image of our calling; for the only way in which we are admitted to the true knowledge of Christ is . . . by that voice with which he especially calls the sheep which the Father has given to him."[4] Have you heard the voice of Jesus calling you through his witness in the gospel? If you have, you will open your heart and respond with an answering faith.

Paul said that "faith, hope, and love abide, these three; but the greatest of these is love" (1 Cor. 13:13). In Christ's ministry, love is truly seen as the greatest of all the graces, his love bringing our faith and hope to life. Like grieving Mary, we find that the place for us to renew our faith and hope is in the love of the One who died for our sins—a love that by his resurrection power is as "strong as death" (Song 8:6).

3. Mark G. Johnston, *Let's Study John* (Edinburgh: Banner of Truth, 2003), 254.
4. John Calvin, *Calvin's Commentaries*, trans. William Pringle, 22 vols. (Grand Rapids: Baker, 2009), 18:258.

Not Yet Ascended

When Mary first turned and saw Jesus, her eyes blinded by tears and unbelief, she thought him to be the gardener and asked him about the missing body. But when Jesus spoke, she recognized him in the tone of that beloved voice. Mary cried out, "Rabboni," which means "Teacher" (John 20:16). This title of reverence had apparently been used by Mary previously to express her discipleship to Jesus, just as all who follow the Lord are to be taught from his Word.

Seeing Jesus, Mary raced forward to him. Probably her actions were similar to those of the other women when they saw the Lord: "they came up and took hold of his feet and worshiped him" (Matt. 28:9). Jesus' reaction has puzzled commentators: "Jesus said to her, 'Do not cling to me, for I have not yet ascended to the Father'" (John 20:17).

Two approaches to this riddle can be discarded rather easily. Some liberal commentators have argued that Jesus' warning proves that he was not resurrected in a true body, but the fact that Jesus later told Thomas to place his fingers in his wounds shows this view to be false. Others have suggested that Jesus needed immediately to ascend to heaven and present his atonement before the Father's throne. Yet the Bible records Jesus as ascending later (see Acts 1:9–10), and an ascension on the day of resurrection is hard to imagine, given the Scripture's silence about what would have been a pivotal event.[5]

There are two other ways to understand Jesus' warning to Mary that not only make sense of it but also help us to grasp the meaning. First, Jesus seems to have been informing her that his ascension was not yet to take place, so that she had no need to hold on to him as if she would lose him again.

Second, Jesus was pointing out that his death and resurrection had forever transformed his relationship to Mary and the other disciples. Because she thought she had lost the physical nearness of Jesus, we can imagine her excitement at seeing him restored to bodily life. But Jesus would not have her hold onto the past and the former mode of relationship. He was not stifling her desire for a relationship, but merely pointing her to the higher mode that would ensue with his ascension and the sending of the Holy Spirit. Vos explains that "the desire for a real communion of life would soon be met in

5. While Hebrews 9:11ff. validates the importance of the ascension in completing the atonement, it tells us nothing about the timing of this event.

a new and far higher way than was possible under the conditions of local earthly nearness."[6] Christians today, living on the other side of Christ's ascension and the coming of the Spirit at Pentecost, enjoy a higher form of communion with Jesus even than the disciples who knew him in the flesh. We have spiritual communion with the living Savior through the Spirit who indwells us. As Paul expressed it: "Christ . . . lives in me" (Gal. 2:20).

Wearied or discouraged Christians will sometimes lament that Christ seems far distant. But he is not! Having ascended into glory, Jesus is now intimately close to each of the great multitude of his disciples on earth. Paul therefore urges us not to think we must engage in some mechanism to draw Jesus close to us: "'Do not say in your heart, "Who will ascend into heaven?"' (that is, to bring Christ down) or '"Who will descend into the abyss?"' (that is, to bring Christ up from the dead). But what does it say? 'The word is near you, in your mouth and in your heart' (that is, the word of faith that we proclaim)" (Rom. 10:6–8). Jesus lives in us by the Holy Spirit's inward ministry of God's living Word.

This situation, however, had not yet fully come when Mary met Jesus outside the tomb before his ascension, so Jesus wanted to point her forward, not backward, for her hope of communion with him. "There can be no holding Jesus back. In future Jesus is to be present with her by his Spirit."[7]

RESTORED TO THE FATHER'S LOVE

Not only did the resurrection cause a new kind of relationship with Jesus on earth, but he sent Mary to deliver the good news of a new relationship with God in heaven. Jesus told Mary not to cling to him but instead to "go to my brothers and say to them, 'I am ascending to my Father and your Father, to my God and your God'" (John 20:17). Jesus looks to the great end for which he had come into the world, suffered, and died: the restoration of God's people to his fatherly love, to the praise of the glory of God's grace.

In his incarnation, Jesus made solidarity with mankind, so as to call his disciples "brothers" (see Heb. 2:10–11). Now he fulfills the promise of Psalm 22:22: "I will tell of your name to my brothers." Jesus declares that through faith, his people gain entry into the family of God's love. This is the blessing of which

---

6. Vos, *Grace and Glory*, 79.

7. Paul Beasley-Murray, *The Message of the Resurrection*, The Bible Speaks Today (Downers Grove, IL: InterVarsity Press, 2000), 90.

John wrote in the first chapter of his Gospel: "to all who did receive him, who believed in his name, he gave the right to become children of God" (John 1:12).

Through union with Christ in faith, the relationship that Jesus has eternally with the Father is conveyed to us by adoption. Not only now is his God "your God," but God relates to us in the same relationship as to Jesus: he ascends to "my Father and your Father." By different means—Christ by eternal origin and we by adoption—Christ's people now stand before God in the same familial position occupied by Jesus. Jesus is now our elder brother, bringing us into his relationship of love with the Father.

We can see the wonder of what Jesus was saying to Mary by comparing him with others who experienced a sudden elevation. One example is that of England's King Henry V. In his youth, Prince Harry was known for drinking, gambling, and enjoying the company of loose women along with his friends of ill repute. When Harry was elevated to the throne, his friends expected to move their escapades into the palace. Instead, King Henry turned his back on his immoral friends and began to act in a manner appropriate to his royal office, to the great benefit of the nation.

Jesus is different from this precisely in that he came to earth to draw sinners to himself and take them with him into his kingdom. Of course, Jesus never defiled himself with sin. Yet "when he entered into glory through his death, resurrection, and ascension, he did not turn his back on his companions but rather ushered them into relationships that were uniquely his own. Now God becomes their Father as well as his, and they are given family privileges."[8]

In ministering to Mary's brokenhearted love, what better words could Jesus have uttered than this promise of adoption into the Father's love with him! The good news was not that Jesus was returning to the old relationship, but rather that he is bringing his friends and disciples with him into the glorious embrace of God's fatherly love. News of this royal elevation should lift us out of sin into royal lives of holy joy.

THE DOCTRINE OF ADOPTION

The doctrine of adoption is one of the great saving truths of the gospel. Obviously, all people are God's creatures and in some sense are his "offspring"

8. James Montgomery Boice, *The Gospel of John*, 5 vols. (Grand Rapids: Baker, 1999), 5:1576.

(Acts 17:29). But the liberal teaching that all are children of God's love irrespective of our relationship to Jesus Christ is false. So great is the breach of sin between God and man that Paul proclaims us "by nature children of wrath" (Eph. 2:3). Jesus went so far as to offend the Jews by describing them as children of the devil because of their wicked deeds (John 8:44). According to the Bible, only those who are born again to faith in Christ are children of God and are blessed with adoption into his love (see 1:12).

The gospel doctrine of justification through faith alone is itself a great marvel. God accepts guilty sinners as just in his sight, acquitting them by virtue of his Son our Redeemer. Jesus justifies us by paying the debt of our sin and imputing his perfect righteousness to our account, so that robed in his white garments we stand righteous before God. Justification is by grace alone, a free gift to his people, since God had no obligation to forgive our sins. But the glory of God's grace is such that he goes beyond justification to adoption. God sent his Son to cleanse us in his blood, to bring us justified into his presence, and then to enter us into his own family with the status of dearly beloved sons. Just as Christians are all brides of Christ, we are also all—men and women—adopted as sons, since sonship involves the idea of heirship in glory together with the eternal Son, Jesus Christ.

Adoption in Christ brings several great privileges. We have the privilege of receiving God's loving care and provision for our lives. No father allows his children to go hungry or defenseless, and God is the best and most faithful of all fathers. Moreover, we enjoy the privilege of familial access to God in prayer. Christians wonder what makes prayer "work": the answer is adoption by grace. When we come to God through Christ, we may be certain of God's answering our prayers according to his holy and wise will for our good and his glory.

A third great privilege of sonship is the loving discipline by which the Father trains his children for holiness. Some will doubt that divine discipline and chastisement are much of a blessing. Hebrews 12:6–7 reminds them: "'For the Lord disciplines the one he loves, and chastises every son whom he receives.' It is for discipline that you have to endure. God is treating you as sons."

The greatest of all our blessings as God's children is our access into his presence so that we might walk with him in a personal relationship of love. Sinclair Ferguson points out what a privilege it is to be invited by someone you greatly admire into an intimate friendship. He takes you aside and says: "Don't call me Mr. anymore, but use my first name." "But that privilege pales into insignificance by comparison with what we have here. Christ is giving us access to the presence of his Father, and saying to us: 'You may now speak to him as I speak to him; with the same right of access, with the same sense of intimacy, with the same assurance that he loves you.'"[9] Jesus sent this message to all his brothers, in all generations, saying, "I am ascending to my Father and your Father, to my God and your God" (John 20:17). As a result, it is no longer presumption for a believer to expect God's acceptance; rather, the presumptuous Christian is the one who doubts God's acceptance, love, and care.

Some Christians struggle to open their hearts to God as Father because of their disappointment in or even the abuse of their earthly fathers. But God is the true Father that all our hearts have yearned for, the Father who nurtures us in unbreakable covenant love. God's fatherly love gives a heritage, a godly identity, and a sure hope for the future to all his children through faith in Christ.

We noted that the Bible speaks of "faith, hope, and love," and that "the greatest of these is love" (1 Cor. 13:13). The greatest love in all eternity is the covenant, fatherly love of God for his people in Christ. Jesus was speaking of this divine love when he said, "Greater love has no one than this, that someone lay down his life for his friends" (John 15:13). Do not turn your heart away from the Father in heaven, but come to him through faith in the perfect, redeeming love of Christ, opening your heart to God through prayer in Jesus' name.

The Family Business

Hearing Jesus' message, we now realize why Jesus did not want Mary Magdalene to cling and linger outside the empty tomb. For along with the privileges of sonship there is the obligation to work in the family business. Sonship calls us to bear God's holy name in honor and pursue the family characteristic of holiness. It also requires us to take the gospel message—news of forgiveness of sin, justification through faith, and adoption by grace—to

9. Sinclair B. Ferguson, *Children of the Living God* (Edinburgh: Banner of Truth, 1989), 33.

all those whom Jesus will call as his brothers and ours. God is gathering his family by Christ's witness through his people. Salvation by grace is the family business, and we are to work joyfully and hard for the harvest.

There would be time for Mary simply to bask in the relief and delight of the privileges that Christ was granting through his death, resurrection, and ascension into heaven. But there is also a time for gospel labor, and the morning of the resurrection was one of those times. "Do not cling to me," Jesus told her, "but go to my brothers and say to them, 'I am ascending to my Father and your Father, to my God and your God'" (John 20:17). Mary thus became the apostle to the apostles: she "went and announced to the disciples, 'I have seen the Lord'—and that he had said these things to her" (20:18).

Our family obligation is nothing less: to take the good news of Christ and deliver it to the world, telling everyone that we have seen the Lord. If you are outside the family bond of God's love in Christ, if you still walk in the guilt of your sins, and if you have no way of access into the Father's loving presence and no hope for a future glory in heaven, then hear the call of Christ in his gospel. May his life-giving Spirit grant you faith to claim for yourself God's offer of forgiveness and adoption. Place your own name in Jesus' promise—"I am ascending to my Father and your Father"—to know the precious gift of salvation, with eternal access to the fatherly love of your God in heaven.

134

THE GREATEST NEWS EVER HEARD

John 20:18

*Mary Magdalene went and announced to the disciples,
"I have seen the Lord"—and that he had said these things
to her. (John 20:18)*

*D*uring England's war with Napoleon Bonaparte, the people of London anxiously awaited news from the battlefields of Europe. On one occasion, a British admiral attempted to convey news of a victory by the Duke of Wellington during his Peninsula campaign. Using a semaphore system, the admiral transmitted his first word: "Wellington." The next word soon followed: "defeated." At this moment, fog enshrouded the signals so that no more could be seen. In this form, the news reached London: "Wellington defeated!" It took several hours for the fog to lift, allowing the rest of the signal to be sent. There on the mast could now be seen the final letters of its message from the war: "the enemy." How this changed everything: "Wellington defeated the enemy!" When this new message was quickly spread, the nation's gloom was replaced with a great joy.[1]

---

1. Supplement to *Encyclopedia Britannica* (London: Archibald, Constable & Co., 1824), 6:650.

The news of Wellington's victory at the battle of Waterloo, when it finally came, was all the more wonderful in that it was so unexpected. England had been led to believe that all was lost, so the news of victory brought great rejoicing. Something similar happened with the resurrection of Jesus Christ. When Jesus died on the cross and was buried, a fog fell upon the hearts of his disciples so that their faith virtually died. But when the tomb was found empty on Sunday morning, with angels announcing that "he has risen" (Matt. 28:6), the joy of the believers was all the greater. Even better was the news brought by Mary Magdalene, who reported, "I have seen the Lord" (John 20:18). This was the greatest news ever heard, not only because it was so unexpected but because it is true, because of what it proves about God, and because of what it signifies to us and offers to all.

GREAT NEWS THAT IS TRUE

We live in an age when readers are jaded by reported news that turns out not to be true. News of a great sale at your favorite store turns out to be a cheap ploy to get customers in the door. News passed along by friends turns out to have been distorted or mistaken. Even news reported in the papers and on television often turns out to have been skewed by ideology or agenda. But the greatest news ever heard—the report of Jesus' resurrection from the dead—is news that can be verified as accurate and true. This is why the Christian church has delighted to repeat the words first spoken by the angel in the empty tomb: "Come, see" (Matt. 28:6). We invite the world to examine the proofs for Jesus' resurrection, asserting with the apostle Paul that God has publicly proved the claims of Christ, giving "assurance to all by raising him from the dead" (Acts 17:31).

So compelling is the evidence for Christ's resurrection that it has been described as "the best attested fact in history."[2] Let me develop this evidence. First are the New Testament documents, which come to us with far more reliable attestation than any other such ancient testimony. All four Gospels attest to the resurrection. Some people are troubled by the minor variations in the different Gospel accounts, but that is consistent with what we would expect of an honest recounting from different perspectives. Furthermore,

2. Matthew Arnold, quoted in James Montgomery Boice, *The Gospel of Matthew*, 2 vols. (Grand Rapids: Baker, 2001), 2:640.

telltale signs of tampering are absent. For instance, in the Jewish culture of the apostles' time, women had such low standing that their testimony was rejected in the courts. Yet the Gospels present women as the first eyewitnesses, hardly a strategy that one would employ to commend a faked story. The Gospel records present themselves as credible testimony to the resurrection.

Second, there is the matter of the empty tomb and the missing body. Matthew states that the authorities drummed up a false story that the disciples came at night and stole Jesus' corpse (Matt. 27:62–66). This proves that the Jewish leaders did not have the body, for with it they could easily have discredited the resurrection. Moreover, are we to believe that the disciples overcame the Roman guards, broke the seals without being noticed, and made off with Jesus' body from a rock tomb? None of the disciples were men of power or wealth, and they all had scattered in fear. Furthermore, it is quite clear from all the Gospels that despite Jesus' advance warning, the disciples were not expecting him to rise from the dead but were as surprised as anybody else. Therefore, the stolen-body theory fails as simply ludicrous, and the missing body speaks eloquently for the resurrection.

This leads, third, to Jesus' postresurrection appearances. The Gospels record a great many of these. Matthew tells us that the group of women ran into the resurrected Jesus outside the tomb. John adds that later that day, Jesus appeared and talked to the gathered disciples (John 20:19–20). Many subsequent appearances of Jesus are also recorded in the Gospels, including Jesus' ministry to overcome Thomas's unbelief (John 20:26–28) and Luke's record of Jesus' ministry to the Emmaus road disciples (Luke 24:13–35). The book of Acts tells us, "He presented himself alive to [the disciples] after his suffering by many proofs, appearing to them during forty days and speaking about the kingdom of God" (Acts 1:3). Finally, Paul recounts his own record of Christ's postresurrection appearances, culminating with his conversion on the Damascus road. Paul writes:

> He was raised on the third day in accordance with the Scriptures, and . . . he appeared to Cephas, then to the twelve. Then he appeared to more than five hundred brothers at one time, most of whom are still alive, though some have fallen asleep. Then he appeared to James, then to all the apostles. Last of all, as to one untimely born, he appeared also to me. (1 Cor. 15:4–8)

Notice Paul's claim that at the time of his writing most of the witnesses to Christ's postresurrection appearances were still living. He was happy to include that detail, inviting investigation. If the Gospel records were a fraud, there were plenty of living witnesses to expose it. Nor can these visitations be written off as delusions, for so great a number of people on different occasions can hardly conspire to have the same hallucination.

That leads to a fourth piece of evidence. The first is the Gospel records themselves, then the empty tomb and missing body, and then the postresurrection appearances. There may be no better attestation to Christ's resurrection, however, than the resulting transformation of the disciples. Somehow we have to account for the energizing of a dispirited group of fugitives into the fearless band of apostles who boldly proclaimed the gospel of Christ in Jerusalem so soon after Christ's execution and then intrepidly took that same message across the ancient world to the seat of power in Rome itself.

Let us delve deeper here. Perhaps the resurrection was a hoax. If it was, then Peter and John certainly knew that it was, for not only were they the leading disciples but the Gospels make it clear that they were witnesses of the empty tomb. Whatever they saw powerfully motivated them, Peter especially. The Gospels, in their astonishing honesty, admit that on the night of Jesus' arrest, Peter three times denied knowing Jesus. This was before Jesus was even tried or executed. How is it, then, that after seeing the instructive example of Jesus' torturous death, this same Peter stood before the Jewish leaders just a few weeks later and passionately preached the first Christian sermon? Peter declared to the same violent leaders who had crucified his Lord: "You, with the help of wicked men, put him to death by nailing him to the cross. But God raised him from the dead" (Acts 2:23–24 NIV). What can explain this turn of events except the resurrection itself?

Predictably, Peter was threatened and beaten by the authorities. Yet Peter and John did not relent in their preaching of the risen Jesus. Luke tells us how they responded: "Then they left the presence of the council, rejoicing that they were counted worthy to suffer dishonor for the name. And every day, in the temple and from house to house, they did not cease teaching and preaching Jesus as the Christ" (Acts 5:41–42).

You might explain this transformation as the power of a delusion or the determination to play a losing hand all the way to the end, but the only credible explanation is that Peter and John saw the empty tomb, met the risen

Lord Jesus, and knew that the resurrection was a fact. They were personal witnesses, and their lives were transformed with power. Along with all the other disciples, they cheerfully faced years of hardship and persecution for the gospel, all but one of them suffering death for a message that they refused to betray. G. Campbell Morgan concludes:

> It may be that in the history of the race, individual men have been found, who, swept by some fanaticism, have been willing to die for fraud. . . . But this is not a case of isolated individuals, but a whole company and society of men and women and children, ever increasing in number, all of them more or less having to suffer in those early centuries; and the central fact, for the declaration of which they endured all things, was this story of the resurrection.[3]

The fifth and last evidence is the Christian church. The New Testament says that in the power of the Holy Spirit, secured for the disciples by the risen Lord Jesus, the gospel message would demolish strongholds of enemy thought, bringing men and women from all over the world to a saving knowledge of God through Jesus Christ, creating in him a new society of holiness and love. This is precisely what has happened, and we gather today to add our ongoing testimony to the reality of Christ's resurrection power in the world.

"I have seen the Lord," Mary Magdalene said (John 20:18), and her message of Christ's resurrection is set before the watching eyes of the world. The great Princeton theologian Charles Hodge evaluated these proofs for Christ's resurrection against accepted standards of legal veracity. He pointed out that for a fact to be proved, it must be of such a nature as to be capable of verification and certain knowledge by the witnesses. The witnesses themselves must be of sound mind and integrity. Hodge concludes, "If these conditions be fulfilled, human testimony establishes the truth of a fact beyond a reasonable doubt. If, however, in addition to these grounds of confidence, the witnesses give their testimony at the expense of great personal sacrifice, or confirm it with their blood . . . then it is insanity and wickedness to doubt it. All these considerations concur in proof of the resurrection of Christ, and render it the best authenticated event in the history of the world."[4] According

---

3. G. Campbell Morgan, *The Crises of the Christ* (1903; repr., Grand Rapids: Kregel, 1989), 380–81.

4. Charles Hodge, *A Commentary on the First Epistle to the Corinthians* (London: Banner of Truth, 1964), 314.

to Peter, preaching in Jerusalem just weeks after Christ's crucifixion, so sure are the proofs of Jesus' resurrection that they enable us to "know for certain that God has made him both Lord and Christ" (Acts 2:36), morally obliging us before God to accept the evidence and believe on Jesus as the resurrected Savior.

GREAT NEWS ABOUT GOD

Seeing that the Gospel record of Jesus' resurrection is proved to be true, Mary's message of seeing the Lord is also great news because of what it tells us about the God of the Bible.

First, Christ's resurrection proves that the God of the Bible is the true and living God. Reuben A. Torrey explained: "Every effect must have an adequate cause . . . and the only cause adequate to account for the resurrection of Christ is God, the God of the Bible." After all, Jesus spent his years of ministry teaching about the Bible's God, the God of Abraham, Isaac, and Jacob, the God of Israel, and the God and Father of Jesus himself. Before his arrest, Jesus made the claim that when he had been crucified, God would raise him from the dead. Torrey writes: "This was . . . an apparently impossible claim. For centuries men had come and men had gone, men had lived and men had died, and so far as human knowledge . . . was concerned, that was the end of them. But this man Jesus does not hesitate to claim that his experience will be directly contrary to the uniform experience of long, long centuries. . . . That was certainly an acid test of the existence of the God he preached, and God stood the test."[5]

The fact that Christ's resurrection proves the God of the Bible is good news, because the Scriptures proclaim a God of glory and grace. True, the God of the Bible is sovereign, righteous, and holy so as to judge all sin with the curse of death. But the Bible also reveals him as a God of compassion and mercy for sinners. Most notably, the Bible says that God "so loved the world, that he gave his only Son, that whoever believes in him should not perish but have eternal life" (John 3:16).

Speaking of God's Son, the resurrection also proves the deity of Jesus Christ. It cannot credibly be denied that during his time on earth, Jesus

---

5. Reuben A. Torrey, *The Uplifted Christ* (Grand Rapids: Zondervan, 1965), 70–71.

claimed to be equal to God and taught that God would prove Christ's deity by raising him from the dead on the third day. One of the accusations at Jesus' trial had been that he claimed that Jerusalem's temple was a symbol for him, the One in whom God dwells with his people (Matt. 26:61). When asked for a sign to prove his divine claims, Jesus pointed to Herod's temple, which had taken forty-six years to build, and compared it to himself: "Destroy this temple, and in three days I will raise it up" (John 2:19). John explains that Jesus was referring to his own death and resurrection, a proof of Christ's deity that the disciples remembered after Jesus had risen from the grave (2:21–22).

Harry Houdini became famous as the world's greatest escape artist by having himself chained inside a nailed crate and thrown into a river, emerging alive just in time to survive. But not even Houdini could do what Jesus claimed that he would do and then did. Jesus was publicly tortured and put to death at the orders of a Roman governor, his death overseen and assured by a battle-hardened Roman centurion. When Jesus had been publicly certified as dead, his body was provided to a rich believer, who performed the accepted burial rites on Jesus' body. The body, wound with spice-laden strips of cloth, was placed in a tomb, the door of which was shut, sealed, and then guarded by Roman sentries who watched over the grave on pain of death. Virtually nothing more could possibly have been done to prove that Jesus really was, as the Apostles' Creed puts it, "crucified, dead, and buried." Yet Jesus still rose from the grave, providing such clear proof of his resurrection that only rebellious obstinacy can account for its denial. As the apostles would go on to preach, the resurrection set God's seal on Jesus' claim to deity. Paul wrote to the Romans, for instance, that Jesus "was declared to be the Son of God in power according to the Spirit of holiness by his resurrection from the dead" (Rom. 1:4).

A third great claim that Jesus proved by his resurrection was his promise that his death would atone for the sins of believers. Jesus said that he came "to give his life as a ransom for many" (Matt. 20:28). He died, but how can we know that his death was acceptable to God as a Sacrifice for our sins? Perhaps Jesus had somehow sinned, so that his death would not be acceptable as a Sacrifice for others. Perhaps his claims were overblown: it was a great claim, after all, that he would pay in his suffering and death the penalty for all the sins of all the people who believe in him. How can we know that by trusting in him, we really are forgiven and justified before God?

The answer and proof of Christ's atonement and our justification in him is Jesus' resurrection from the grave. Paul says that Jesus "was delivered up for our trespasses and raised for our justification" (Rom. 4:25). Torrey writes: "When Jesus died, he died as my representative, and I died with him; when he arose, he rose as my representative, and I arose in him; . . . I look at the cross of Christ, and I know that atonement has been made for my sins; I look at the open sepulcher and the risen and ascended Lord, and I know the atonement has been accepted. There no longer remains a single sin on me, no matter how many or how great my sins may have been."[6]

GREAT NEWS FOR US

Because it proves Christ's atonement for our sins, Mary Magdalene's report, "I have seen the Lord," is the greatest of all the news that we have ever heard. But there are other reasons why the resurrection of Jesus is great news for us. The resurrection proves that the Savior we trust is a living and exalted Lord. It was marvelous news for the Old Testament Jacob when he learned that Joseph, the son he had presumed dead, was in fact alive (Gen. 45:26). How great was Jacob's joy when he traveled to Egypt and resumed living contact with his well-beloved child. Similarly, those who read the Gospel accounts of Jesus Christ and see in him the greatest, most sublime, most beloved Teacher, Lord, and Savior are filled with the same joy as Mary Magdalene experienced when we learn that Jesus is not dead but lives in heaven. We can now look forward to an eternity of communion with him.

Not only did Jacob rejoice to learn that Joseph was alive, but moreover, Joseph was seated on the throne of Egypt and empowered to dispense the riches of that mighty realm. How much greater is Mary Magdalene's report to us, since we find that Jesus has now ascended to the throne of heaven. There, Paul writes, Jesus is seated at God's right hand, "far above all rule and authority and power and dominion, and above every name that is named, not only in this age but also in the one to come. And [God] put all things under his feet and gave him as head over all things to the church" (Eph.

---

6. Reuben A. Torrey, *The Bible and Its Christ* (New York: Revell, 1906), 107–8.

1:21–22). What can harm us now or hinder the cause of Christ's kingdom, since our Lord has taken the seat of divine, eternal power in heaven? Paul reasons: "I am sure that neither death nor life, nor angels nor rulers, nor things present nor things to come, nor powers, nor height nor depth, nor anything else in all creation, will be able to separate us from the love of God in Christ Jesus our Lord" (Rom. 8:38–39).

News of Christ's resurrection thus assures us of power for our present struggles in life. Paul prayed that our hearts would be enlightened, to know "what is the immeasurable greatness of his power toward us who believe, according to the working of his great might that he worked in Christ when he raised him from the dead" (Eph. 1:17–20). This says that in sending his Spirit to empower us for life and godliness, Christ has given us the same power by which he was raised from the dead so that we might prevail in faith through the many trials of our lives.

Christ's resurrection not only testifies to the power available to believers in the present, but also assures Christians of our own place in heaven and of a future glorious resurrection of our bodies. Jesus had said, "In my Father's house are many rooms. . . . And if I go and prepare a place for you, I will come again and will take you to myself, that where I am you may be also" (John 14:2–3). He also said: "I am the resurrection and the life. Whoever believes in me, though he die, yet shall he live" (11:25). Can we trust Jesus for these claims—that he will give us present spiritual power to prevail in faith and a resurrection into glory when he returns? We can believe him, since he proved his claims by his resurrection from the grave.

Great News for All

The final reason why Mary's report, "I have seen the Lord" (John 20:18), is the greatest news ever heard is that it is good news for all. Some news is good, but not for everyone. The news of Wellington's victory at Waterloo was good for the English but bad for the French. Almost all earthly good news is like that: one benefits, but another loses. The good news of Jesus' resurrection is different because he is the only One who paid the price for the blessings that he now offers to all. Only one thing is required: we must respond to the evidence of Jesus' atoning death and glorious resurrection with saving faith. We must trust Jesus, based on the Gospel record, to be our

Savior and surrender our hearts to him as our Lord. Have you done that? If not, what will you say in your defense when God demands a reason why you rejected the greatest good news, news that glorifies him as the God of grace and truth and conveys his mercy for sinners? Because the resurrection is true, the Bible urges all: "Believe in the Lord Jesus, and you will be saved" (Acts 16:31).

Finally, having believed, and having come to know the living Lord Jesus for ourselves and having felt his saving power in our lives, let us take the place of Mary Magdalene so that others may hear, believe, and be saved. "I have seen the Lord," she declared. If God's Spirit has shined the gospel truth in your heart, then you have also seen the Lord in the living Word of the Bible. Now Jesus calls you to take up the calling that he first gave to Mary: to go and tell others the greatest news ever heard, the news that Jesus Christ, who died for our sins, is alive to reign forever and grant eternal life to all who will believe.

135

THE CRUCIFIED CHRIST
PREACHING

John 20:19–21

When he had said this, he showed them his hands and his side.
Then the disciples were glad when they saw the Lord.
(John 20:20)

reachers have long celebrated the seven sayings of Jesus spoken on the cross, sometimes referring to these as the last words of our Lord. That description is misleading, however, since Jesus had much to say after he rose from the grave. For this reason, some commentators speak of the "real last words of Christ," the statements recorded by John during Jesus' postresurrection appearances in chapters 20 and 21. These sayings include Jesus' benediction of peace (John 20:19–21), John's version of the Great Commission (20:21), Jesus' command for Thomas to believe (20:27), Christ's benediction on those who will believe without having seen him (20:29), his command for the disciples to "feed my sheep" (21:17), and his final exhortation to "follow me" (21:19). These are all vitally important sayings of the Lord, all the more so because of their having been spoken in the period after Christ's resurrection.

Important as the postresurrection sayings are, Jesus' own emphasis was expressed not in words but actions: "he showed them his hands and his side" (John 20:20; see also 20:27). A similar emphasis on the cross is seen in Luke's record of Jesus' ministry to the downcast Emmaus road disciples. Jesus urged them: "Was it not necessary that the Christ should suffer these things and enter into his glory?" (Luke 24:26).

By noting Jesus' emphasis, we are helped to understand the relationship of the resurrection to the crucifixion. It is the resurrected and living Christ who comes with power to bring us to faith. That faith is to be focused on his atoning death, which Jesus presents as the source of every blessing to those who believe. This priority is found throughout the New Testament. Paul summed up the apostles' ministry, saying, "We preach Christ crucified" (1 Cor. 1:23). How appropriate, then, that in his record of Jesus' postresurrection ministry, John presents our Lord as the crucified Christ preaching.

Christ in the Midst

Having focused in the previous passage on the events of the resurrection morning, John now advances to the evening of that most pivotal of days. "On the evening of that day, the first day of the week" (John 20:19), John tells us about Jesus' appearance to the gathered disciples and the cross-centered message that Jesus brought.

Speaking of the resurrection Sunday, the disciples unwittingly began a practice that Christians observe today: meeting together on the first day—the resurrection day—of the week. Luke's parallel account informs us that included in this gathering were "the eleven and those who were with them gathered together," presumably including the faithful women. Also included were the two Emmaus road disciples, who had returned to Jerusalem after conversing with Jesus on the road. They reported: "'The Lord has risen indeed, and has appeared to Simon!' Then they told what had happened on the road, and how he was known to them in the breaking of the bread" (Luke 24:33–35).

We can imagine the amazed wonder and confusion that marked this gathering. John's eyewitness record specifies that the doors were "locked . . . for fear of the Jews" (John 20:19). So violent were the impressions of the crucifixion that even this gathering to hear reports from those who had seen Jesus alive was marked with fear and dread. Might they be arrested—especially now that Jesus' body was missing from the tomb—and might they suffer a similar fate as their Lord? Still, merely gathering as Jesus' disciples was an act of faith. John Calvin comments: "This example is worthy of notice; for, though they are less courageous than they ought to have been still they do not give way to their weakness . . . but they gather courage so as to remain together."[1] Many Christians today, living under government persecution, continue to meet secretly and in fear. They, like the disciples gathered on the resurrection Sunday, will find that Christ cannot be kept from joining his people in their need.

It is not hard to imagine these disciples casting anxious glances at the locked door, perhaps starting at passing footfalls in the street. A knock at the door announced the Emmaus road disciples, who then gave their remarkable account of conversing with Jesus and hearing his scriptural explanation for the cross and resurrection. Luke says that it was while this report was being made that the most amazing visitor of all arrived. John writes: "Jesus came and stood among them and said to them, 'Peace be with you'" (John 20:19).

The clear impression given by John's account is that Jesus appeared to the disciples without entering the door. This would be impossible for a normal human body, but Jesus now possessed a gloriously resurrected body. This same body, having earlier passed through the graveclothes in the tomb, appeared among the disciples seemingly out of thin air. F. B. Meyer summarizes the facts: "He was not subject to all the laws that govern our physical life. He could pass freely through unopened doors, and at will He could manifest Himself, speak, stand, and walk, or subject Himself to physical sense."[2]

Luke's Gospel specifies that Jesus' resurrected form was a true, though marvelously transformed, physical body. He notes that the disciples "were startled and frightened and thought they saw a spirit" (Luke 24:37), so Jesus showed them his hands and feet to prove that this was the same body that had been crucified. "Touch me, and see," he said. "For a spirit does not have flesh and bones as you see that I have" (24:39). Jesus even ate a piece of broiled fish to prove that his body was real. This being the case, any theory of Christ's resurrection body that considers it to have lost

1. John Calvin, *Calvin's Commentaries*, trans. William Pringle, 22 vols. (Grand Rapids: Baker, 2009), 18:263–64.
2. F. B. Meyer, *The Life of Love* (Old Tappan, NJ: Revell, 1987), 389.

a finite, human form is disproved. The Gospels' evidence rules out, for instance, the Roman Catholic idea that Jesus' body took on such divine attributes as infinity, which is necessary to the Catholic doctrine of transubstantiation, whereby millions of people may eat Jesus' literal flesh in the ritual of the Mass.

Furthermore, there is an organic connection between Christ's postresurrection body and the bodies that we will possess after Christ returns. In his first letter, John says that in our resurrection, "we shall be like him, because we shall see him as he is" (1 John 3:2). Paul states that our raised bodies, having borne the curse of sin in Adam, will in Christ bear resurrection glory: "Just as we have borne the image of the man of dust, we shall also bear the image of the man of heaven" (1 Cor. 15:49). Believers do not receive new bodies in the resurrection, but rather our old, corrupt, and mortal bodies are gloriously renewed, Paul describing them with words such as "imperishable . . . glory . . . power . . . a spiritual body . . . [and] immortal" (1 Cor. 15:42–45, 53).

Jesus appeared not only to prove that he was raised and living, but also to deliver a message: "Peace be with you" (John 20:19). The traditional Hebrew greeting, *shalom*, offered the blessing of God's rich peace. Coming from Jesus' lips on this occasion, the blessing of peace brought relief to the disciples. Since their last gathering, perhaps in this same room, the disciples had failed Jesus miserably. Peter had denied him, and the others had forsaken him. Would Jesus now reject them or subject them to bitter reproach? A. W. Pink writes: "Well might He have said, '*Shame* upon you!' But, instead He says, '*Peace* be unto you.' He would remove from their hearts all fear which His sudden and unannounced appearance might have occasioned. . . . Having put away their sins He could now remove their fears."[3]

Having appeared and spoken his benediction of peace, Jesus "showed them his hands and his side" (John 20:20). Showing his wounds proved that this glorious visitor was the very Lord they had known and seen crucified. George Beasley-Murray comments that "the Crucified is *the risen Lord*, in the fullest sense of the term, and the risen Lord is *the Crucified*, the flesh and blood Redeemer, whose real death and real resurrection accomplished salvation."[4]

---

3. Arthur W. Pink, *Exposition of the Gospel of John* (Grand Rapids: Zondervan, 1975), 1096.
4. George R. Beasley-Murray, *John*, Word Biblical Commentary 36 (Waco, TX: Word, 1987), 379.

THE SOURCE OF PEACE

It is noteworthy that Jesus' resurrection did not remove the marks of crucifixion from his body. Jesus considered these wounds to be a vital part of his resurrection glory and essential for his saving ministry for his people. George Hutcheson comments: "Christ, even in his exaltation, looks upon his sufferings for his people as his crown and glory; therefore did he rise again with his pierced hands and side . . . and retained these prints . . . in his state of exaltation."[5] Having presented these wounds to his followers, Jesus pointed out three glorious realities that flow to his people through his atoning death.

First, Jesus announced the blessing of peace for those who believe in him. "Peace be with you," he said in greeting the disciples. Jesus then "showed them his hands and his side" and repeated his words of blessing, "Peace be with you" (John 20:19–21). Before departing for the cross, Jesus had promised, "Peace I leave with you; my peace I give to you" (14:27). Now Jesus shows what he has done to provide that peace. Jesus' "Peace be with you" on Easter evening is the counterpart to his words, "It is finished," spoken on the cross.[6]

Through his sacrificial death in our place, Jesus provides peace *with God* through the forgiveness of our sins. The marks on Christ's body proclaimed that God's just wrath against our sins has been satisfied by Jesus' death. In biblical terms, Jesus offered a propitiation on our behalf: that is, the cross exhausted the fury of God's holy anger toward our sins, receiving the full punishment that we deserved by our violations of God's law. Paul expressed these truths in the pivotal statement of his letter to the Romans: "all have sinned and fall short of the glory of God, and are justified by his grace as a gift, through the redemption that is in Christ Jesus, whom God put forward as a propitiation by his blood, to be received by faith" (Rom. 3:23–25).

The book of Revelation, in which John opened a window for us to see the worship of heaven, presents Christ's saving death as the defining act by which God's saving reign of peace is forever established. John describes the hushed awe of mighty angels as Jesus appears in glory as "a Lamb standing,

5. George Hutcheson, *Exposition of the Gospel of John* (Lafayette, IN: Sovereign Grace Publishers, 2001), 421.
6. Beasley-Murray, *John*, 379.

as though it had been slain" (Rev. 5:6). Falling on their faces, the heavenly congregation sings rapturously before the Lamb of God: "Worthy are you to take the scroll and to open its seals, for you were slain, and by your blood you ransomed people for God from every tribe and language and people and nation" (5:9). Heaven had wept at the breaking of God's peace through sin, but now heaven rejoices because there is peace with God for sinners through the atoning blood of his holy Son. Here on earth we have equal reasons to rejoice in the wounds that Jesus displayed to his disciples. Paul explained that since we are justified through faith in God's Son, "we have peace with God through our Lord Jesus Christ" (Rom. 5:1).

In addition to affording us peace *with God*, Jesus' death offers believers the peace *of God* to dwell in our hearts. This is what Jesus had in mind when he promised his disciples, "My peace I give to you" (John 14:27). This is God's own peace dwelling in our souls. Paul wrote of this blessing as belonging to believers who turn to God in prayer: "The peace of God, which surpasses all understanding, will guard your hearts and your minds in Christ Jesus" (Phil. 4:7). Jesus' peace is not like that of the world—"Not as the world gives do I give to you," he said (John 14:27). To the world, peace is merely the temporary cessation of hostility. A fragile truce is the only kind of peace known to the nations of our world, and often even our closest personal relationships are corrupted by sin. In contrast, Jesus offers a divine peace that comes from knowing that our acceptance in God's love has been secured by Jesus' sacrifice and that God's blessing of spiritual provision has been secured through our union with Christ in faith.

Do you know the peace that flows from Christ's wounds on the cross? If you have not looked to Jesus in faith, trusting his blood to cleanse your sins, then you have no legitimate hope for peace with God and no access to the peace that God gives through the ministry of his Word and in prayer. "Peace be with you," Jesus declared to his disciples, showing forth the wounds of his cross. Having died for sin, Jesus offers everyone his peace through faith in his atoning blood.

The Source of Joy

Verse 20 speaks of a second blessing that flows from Jesus' wounds and results from the peace that he gives: the blessing of joy. John recounts: "He showed them his hands and his side. Then the disciples were glad when they saw the Lord." The disciples rejoiced both in the proof that Jesus was alive through his resurrection and in the display of the wounds that had redeemed them from their sins.

It is important for Christians to live with godly joy. We are to embrace all of God's saving gifts and give God glory through our rejoicing in his grace. Paul wrote that we can even "rejoice in our sufferings," since we know that in Christ our suffering leads to endurance, "and endurance produces character, and character produces hope," all "because God's love has been poured into our hearts through the Holy Spirit who has been given to us" (Rom. 5:3–5).

It is Christ's intention that those who know their sins forgiven by his cross should live with great joy in the Lord. The situation for most Christians today, however, is illustrated by a king who commanded his subjects to come to his palace and bring their best bags. His subjects were confused and alarmed, wondering why the king wanted their bags. Many of them, resenting the command, brought their smallest bags or even bags filled with large holes. When they arrived at the palace, however, the king did not take their bags from them but invited them to enter his treasury and fill their bags with gold to take home. Those who had brought their largest bags to offer the king went home with an abundance of treasure, while those who came resentfully went home with little from the king.[7] This is how it works for Christians coming to God and his gift of peace and joy. Those who withhold themselves from God gain little of his treasures, while those who open wide their lives for the praise and service of God end up greatly enriched with an abundance of rejoicing.

John's brief statement shows how we can find the joy that Jesus offers. Jesus had offered peace and showed his followers the wounds of his cross. "Then," John says, "the disciples were glad when they saw the Lord" (John 20:20). The Puritan Thomas Goodwin writes that "when a believer, though but by faith, seeth the Lord Jesus Christ . . . it begets a joy which is unspeakable. . . . All the joys in this world are mean things, things that men shall be ashamed of, but this . . . is a magnific joy . . . full of glory."[8] It was the

7. Illustration from James Montgomery Boice, *The Gospel of John*, 5 vols. (Grand Rapids: Baker, 1999), 5:1591–92.

8. Thomas Goodwin, *Works*, 10 vols. (Grand Rapids: Reformation Heritage Books, 2006), 4:330–31.

sight, by faith, of Christ and his peace-winning wounds that sent Charles Wesley's heart soaring in song:

> Arise, my soul, arise, shake off your guilty fears;
> The bleeding Sacrifice in my behalf appears:
> Before the throne my Surety stands, before the throne my Surety stands,
> My name is written on his hands.[9]

THE SOURCE OF MISSION

The third consequence of Christ's atoning death is the commissioning of his disciples to the missionary work of his gospel. "Jesus said to them again, 'Peace be with you. As the Father has sent me, even so I am sending you'" (John 20:21). We should see this as a natural progression of Christ's saving work in a sinner's life. His atonement grants peace, and that peace fills a Christian with supernatural joy. It is out of that joy that we go to the world, bearing the news of Christ's peace to everyone that we can.

The question is sometimes raised: what gives Christians the right to go about proclaiming their Savior's message and calling others to reject their former beliefs so as to trust in Jesus? The answer is that Christ has commissioned his followers to proclaim his gospel to the world, calling all to faith in him. As he was sent by the Father, now believers are sent by Jesus to proclaim his gospel to the world. Leon Morris writes: "The church . . . is a group of people who have been saved by Christ's saving death and resurrection and who, on the basis of that death and resurrection have been commissioned to bring the message of salvation to sinners everywhere."[10]

Some think that since John says that believers are sent by Jesus "as the Father has sent me" (John 20:21), then Christians are to model our ministry on the kinds of miracles that Jesus performed, or at least on social activism that is designed to implement his ethics. It is true, of course, that good deeds and works of mercy should commend our witness, yet the Gospels place their emphasis on our proclaiming the message of Jesus and his salvation. Luke's version of the commission that Jesus gave elaborates on what he did and what we now are to do: "Thus it is written, that the Christ should suffer

---

9. Charles Wesley, "Arise, My Soul, Arise" (1742).

10. Leon Morris, *Reflections on the Gospel of John* (Peabody, MA: Hendrickson, 1986), 709.

and on the third day rise from the dead, and that repentance and forgiveness of sins should be proclaimed in his name to all nations, beginning from Jerusalem" (Luke 24:46–47). Atoning death and life-giving resurrection are Christ's chief works. Our chief work is to proclaim the forgiveness and renewal that Christ offers to all who believe.

There is, however, an important consideration for us in the word *sent*. Jesus was sent into the world, and now he has sent believers into the world. We therefore dare not stand aloof from the world or be unconcerned for its troubles. Christians are to be involved in the world as life-preserving *salt*, and we are to shine in the midst of the world with the saving *light* of Jesus' gospel (see Matt. 5:13–16). By his incarnation, Jesus identified with the world into which he came, without entering into its sin. Then, by his atonement, Jesus proclaimed his gospel of salvation. We are likewise to identify with the world and be involved in its life, without participating in sin. Having loved the lost, we are then to proclaim Jesus as the only true hope of peace and joy, offering a dying world life in his name.

How does God make missionaries out of the kind of self-centered and spiritually hesitant people who come to salvation through faith? The answer is found in our passage. As peace and joy result from Christ's atoning death, so also does grateful rejoicing in the cross motivate Christians and make us effective as gospel witnesses.

An illustration of how God makes true witnesses is seen in the book of Jonah. Jonah's book begins with God's commissioning of the prophet in a way similar to Jesus' commissioning of his disciples. "Arise," God said, "go to Nineveh, that great city, and call out against it" (Jonah 1:2). Nineveh was the most wicked city of that age, and Jonah so resented God's command to preach there that he rebelled and fled. God pursued Jonah and struck the ship on which he was fleeing with a great storm. The prophet ended up being thrown overboard into the sea to drown. God, who was orchestrating all this, arranged for Jonah to be swallowed by a great fish so that he would not die. There in the darkness of that hellish watery sepulcher, Jonah realized his sin and turned to the Lord in faith. "Salvation belongs to the LORD!" he cried in praise (Jonah 2:9). God then had the great fish spit Jonah out onto dry land, so that his experience served as an example of saving death and resurrection.

Having experienced God's grace for himself, Jonah was now willing to obey God. God gave him the same instructions as before, but with one small and vitally important modification. Whereas the Lord had previously commanded Jonah to go to the great and wicked city of Nineveh and call out "against" it, now God called him to the same place, yet this time to preach "to" it.[11] Jonah shows that anyone can preach *against* sin, but only those who have rejoiced over the wounds of Christ's death can preach *to* sinners in the power of God's grace. We will likewise proclaim Christ's salvation to our world, as he proclaimed it to us, if our hearts are gripped with wonder for the marvel of God's grace and if we are made glad by seeing the Lord and the marks that show how he died for our sins.

This informs us, finally, of the message that Christians are to bear to the world on Christ's behalf. John's record presents the crucified Christ preaching, and the apostle Paul declares in response: "we preach Christ crucified" (1 Cor. 1:23). This means that in the same manner that Jesus presented himself to the fearful disciples, we bear to the world a message of divine peace and joy through atoning mercy. "Peace be with you," Jesus said to his disciples, holding forth his hands and pointing to the wound in his side. To an unbelieving world, we lovingly offer a peace that it has never known: peace with God through the forgiveness of sins achieved by Christ's death and the peace of God as Christ's Spirit lives within the hearts of all who believe, who thus were made glad "when they saw the Lord."

---

11. See Richard D. Phillips, *Jonah & Micah*, Reformed Expository Commentary (Phillipsburg, NJ: P&R Publishing, 2010), 96.

136

POWER AND AUTHORITY

John 20:22–23

"If you forgive the sins of any, they are forgiven them; if you withhold forgiveness from any, it is withheld." (John 20:23)

hen Christians describe the ministry of Jesus during his first coming, they usually focus on his virgin birth, his ministry of good works and teaching, his atoning death on the cross, his resurrection from the grave, and finally his ascension to the throne of heaven. Some version of this outline is found in the great creeds of the church. What, however, is missing from this list? One answer is the vital but easily overlooked ministry of Jesus to the disciples after his resurrection and before his ascension into heaven.

During the important forty days of Jesus' postresurrection ministry, the risen Lord focused on preparing the men who would serve as his apostles. Scholars are virtually united in asserting that behind the New Testament office of apostle is the Jewish office of *shaliach*. A *shaliach* was an agent and steward who carried out the legal, financial, or personal affairs of his master. To deal with a man's *shaliach* was to deal with the man himself. In order to fulfill this role, the *shaliach* required two things: power and authority. He must have the power to execute transactions, and he must have the authority to do so. As Jesus met with his disciples on the evening of his resurrection, he granted both of these: power through the Holy Spirit and authority to proclaim the forgiveness of sins.

POWER THROUGH THE HOLY SPIRIT

Among the four Gospel writers, Luke gives the most attention to this period of Christ's ministry, but he does so in the opening paragraph of the book of Acts. Luke says that Jesus "presented himself alive to them after his suffering by many proofs, appearing to them during forty days and speaking about the kingdom of God" (Acts 1:3). Careful study of Acts will show the importance of this training as the themes that Luke mentions are unfolded in the preaching of the apostles throughout the book of Acts. While John emphasizes Jesus' providing proofs to establish the disciples' faith in his resurrection, he is agreed with Luke in highlighting Jesus' gift of the Holy Spirit to his church and to the apostles. As John tells it, Jesus showed the disciples his hands and wounded side, declared peace to them, and commissioned them to be his witnesses in the world. John continues, "And when he had said this, he breathed on them and said to them, 'Receive the Holy Spirit'" (John 20:22).

When John says that Christ breathed out the Holy Spirit, this continues his ongoing emphasis on the new creation that Jesus brings through his death and resurrection. John began his Gospel by describing Jesus' coming as a renewal of the original work of creation. Jesus is the divine "Word" who was "in the beginning with God" and through whom "all things were made" (John 1:1–3). On the day of the first creation, the Word went forth from God and brought all things into being, with the Spirit hovering over the primordial cosmos (Gen. 1:1–2). Now, at the dawn of the new creation, the risen Lord breathes out the Holy Spirit anew upon the primordial church.

Earlier, Jesus had told Nicodemus that "unless one is born again he cannot see the kingdom of God" (John 3:3). He explained the new birth as the work of the Holy Spirit and compared the Spirit to the blowing wind. The Greek word for *spirit* is the same as the word for *breath*, so Jesus may be taken to have said that one is born again by receiving the holy breath of God. We think as well of Genesis 2:7 when God breathed his own life into Adam so that the first man became "a living creature." Now Jesus breathes his life into his believers so that they might be born again to a new and living relationship with God. A. W. Pink writes: "Who can fail to see that here in John 20, on the day of the Saviour's resurrection, the *new creation* had begun, begun by the Head of the new creation, the last Adam acting as 'a quickening spirit' (1 Cor. 15:45)!"[1] Henceforth, it is in the church that God's life will be known and through the church that God's work will continue in the world.

We should note two things about the giving of the Holy Spirit in this passage. The first is that the Spirit is Christ's provision to his church. In his Farewell Discourse, Jesus had foretold that he would send the Spirit from the Father and further explained that the Spirit "will bear witness about me" (John 15:26). "He will glorify me, for he will take what is mine and declare it to you" (16:14). This means that the Spirit's presence results from a living relationship with Jesus. Some people today seek the Spirit's power by means of spiritual techniques or euphoria-inducing worship, and others associate the Holy Spirit with bizarre and exciting spiritual manifestations. Yet Jesus associates the Spirit with a faith that glorifies his person and work.

We see why John links the giving of the Spirit to Christ's Great Commission to his church: it was "when he had said" that he was sending his people into the world that he then breathed the Spirit upon them. This tells us a second thing about Christ's gift of the Holy Spirit: the Spirit is provided to empower the church in the ministry to which it is called in the world. At the heart of this ministry is the proclamation of the gospel with the aim of gathering men and women in discipleship to Christ.

According to the New Testament, the Spirit's power is absolutely essential to the work of the church in the world. Sin's reign in our lives is so overwhelming that no one can turn in faith to Christ without God's supernatural working (see 1 Cor. 2:14; Eph. 2:1–5). Therefore, without the Spirit, churches may do many things, some of them worthwhile, but they cannot bring anyone into Christ's new creation through a living faith. For sinners to believe, the Holy Spirit must attend the ministry of God's Word with power (see 1 Peter 1:23; John 3:5). This highlights the importance of a regenerate ministry, going forth in a spirit of faith and prayer, relying on Christ to be faithful in sending the Holy Spirit to empower his trusting servants.

1. Arthur W. Pink, *Exposition of the Gospel of John* (Grand Rapids: Zondervan, 1975), 1100.

The great Old Testament illustration of what would happen when Christ sent the Spirit into a spiritually dead world is found in Ezekiel 37. In an era of judgment and despair, God summoned the prophet to a dry valley filled with bones. This was the ultimate picture of a dead church; it was a society extended to the utmost point of depravity, depicting the utter inability of fallen mankind to respond to God's Word. There, God asked the prophet, "Son of man, can these bones live?" Ezekiel answered wisely: "O Lord GOD, you know." God commanded him, "Prophesy over these bones, and say to them, O dry bones, hear the word of the LORD." Then turning to the valley, the Lord spoke to the dry bones: "Behold, I will cause breath to enter you, and you shall live" (Ezek. 37:3–5). Ezekiel preached, and as God's Word went forth in the power of the Spirit, the bones began moving, came together, and rose up to be a great congregation in service to God.

What God prefigured to Ezekiel, Jesus was now setting in motion by breathing the Holy Spirit to empower the witness of his gospel. This is our confidence in ministering salvation to a dead, unbelieving world, and it is for this empowering in our ministry and witness that we should pray. Luke records Jesus as saying to the disciples: "You will receive power when the Holy Spirit has come upon you, and you will be my witnesses in Jerusalem and in all Judea and Samaria, and to the end of the earth" (Acts 1:8).

AUTHORITY TO FORGIVE?

In order to represent his master, a *shaliach* required not only power to conduct his work but also the authority to dispose of his master's goods. Jesus therefore added his own grant of authority to his church: "If you forgive the sins of any, they are forgiven them; if you withhold forgiveness from any, it is withheld" (John 20:23).

Before we consider the nature of this authority, we should note that here Jesus identifies the forgiveness of sins as the essential provision of the salvation that he came to offer. There are always those who criticize an emphasis on "getting people into heaven," and would have us downplay the biblical themes of sin, judgment, and forgiveness. "We need to emphasize a this-worldly Christianity," they say, "focused on what Christ does to change our present world." Verse 23 shows, however, that Christ's own emphasis was on the forgiveness of sins through faith in the gospel message. John Calvin thus refers to forgiveness as "the sum of the Gospel." He states: "The principal design of preaching the Gospel is, that men may be reconciled to God, and this is accomplished by the unconditional pardon of sins."[2]

There is a question, however, concerning exactly *what* authority is being given by Christ in John 20:23 and *to whom*. The interpretation of this verse accounts for a great deal of the difference between Protestant Christians and Roman Catholics. In considering this difference, we should first acknowledge the great deal of common ground between Protestants and Catholics. Both believe in the Trinity and the deity of Christ. Both uphold the virgin birth, Christ's death for our sins, his bodily resurrection from the grave, and Christ's gift of the Holy Spirit to empower his church. Protestants and Catholics alike affirm the divine origin of Holy Scripture and agree on the authority of Scripture's moral commands. We might therefore assume, as many have done, that differences between the two groups are superficial. Their differing views of this verse, however, reveal a deep disagreement about the Bible's teaching on salvation, showing that when it comes to the way that sinners are saved, Protestants and Roman Catholics really affirm two fundamentally different religions.

Jesus told the gathered believers, "If you forgive the sins of any, they are forgiven them" (John 20:23). Roman Catholicism sees this statement as establishing a special priesthood possessing the authority to pronounce the absolution of sins. Claiming warrant from this verse, Roman Catholic priests hear confessions, prescribe penance, and remit sins. Opposing this doctrine is the Protestant teaching that God alone has authority to forgive sins, that God has not committed this special authority to the church and its clergy, and that what the church receives here is the authority to proclaim the forgiveness of sins through faith in Christ and his gospel.

Which view correctly interprets this text? By carefully considering this statement in the light of the Scripture's whole teaching, we can see five reasons why the Roman Catholic priesthood is in error and why the Protestant doctrine correctly interprets Christ's teaching.

First, the Bible clearly teaches that God alone has authority to forgive sins. Jesus affirmed this truth while teaching in Capernaum. A paralytic was lowered to Jesus' feet through a hole that his friends had made in the

2. John Calvin, *Calvin's Commentaries*, trans. William Pringle, 22 vols. (Grand Rapids: Baker, 2009), 18:270–71.

roof. Seeing the man's faith, Jesus said, "Son, your sins are forgiven" (Mark 2:5). Some scribes heard this and objected, saying, "He is blaspheming! Who can forgive sins but God alone?" (2:7). Jesus did not challenge this assertion, but rather proved his deity, and his right to forgive, by telling the paralyzed man, "Rise, pick up your bed, and go home" (2:11). Jesus' response makes no sense if it was not true that only God has authority to forgive.

Second, the Roman Catholic doctrine fails to note that Jesus was speaking to a mixed gathering of believers, including Clopas and probably a number of the believing women. For this reason, there is no warrant for taking John 20:23 as specially addressing the church's clergy. Instead, we must see Christ as addressing believers in general and the church as a whole. This being the case, the authority granted here by Jesus is given to every believer and to the whole church. This is why Protestants deny the Roman Catholic doctrine of a special priesthood and counter it with the Reformation doctrine of the priesthood of all believers. Christ has fulfilled once for all the sacrificial ministry of the Old Testament priesthood, offering his own life as a sufficient atonement for sin. Now the whole church is entered into the remaining priestly ministries of worship and prayer. This is why in Revelation 1:5–6 John rejoiced that Christ "has freed us from our sins by his blood and made us a kingdom, priests to his God and Father."

The Protestant denial of a special priesthood authorized to remit sins is confirmed, third, when we realize that no apostle ever claimed such authority and that there are no instances in the New Testament of an apostle's granting the forgiveness of sins. This evidence counters the idea that while previously only God could forgive sins, this divine authority was now delegated to the apostles. If, so, then why do we never read of their remitting sins on their own authority? An example is Peter's ministry to the centurion Cornelius, in which the apostle did not absolve sins but rather preached Christ and his gospel: "he commanded us to preach to the people and to testify that he is the one appointed by God to be judge of the living and the dead. To him all the prophets bear witness that everyone who believes in him receives forgiveness of sins through his name" (Acts 10:42–43). That is not the priestly absolution of sins but the apostolic preaching of the gospel of forgiveness through faith in Jesus.

Fourth, a careful study of John 20:23 helps us to understand what Jesus meant in his grant of authority to the church. In the Greek text, the verbs *are forgiven* and *is withheld* are in the perfect tense, so that they are more accurately translated as "have been forgiven" and "have been withheld." The perfect tense describes a present state based on a past action. The church is authorized, therefore, not to remit sin but to tell sinners the terms on which they may know that their sins have been forgiven or, conversely, that forgiveness is withheld. In other words, the church is not authorized to say, "Your sins are forgiven," but rather, "Your sins have been forgiven."

Fifth, the objects in this verse are plural, not singular. The Greek text does not speak of the forgiveness of a person's sins but persons' sins; the King James Version correctly, if archaically, refers to "whose soever sins." The significance of this distinction is that Jesus was granting the church the authority not to forgive individuals but rather to make distinctions between types or categories of persons with respect to the forgiveness of sins. William Barclay summarizes the proper interpretation of this verse: "One thing is quite certain—no man can forgive any other man's sins. But another thing is equally certain—it is the great privilege of the Church to convey the message and the announcement and the fact of God's forgiveness to men."[3]

The Church's Declarative Authority

So far, we have contrasted Roman Catholic and Protestant views of forgiveness. There is also, however, a difference of opinion on this verse among Protestants, some of whom see Christ as authorizing only the preaching of forgiveness, while others see Christ as granting to the church a declarative authority concerning forgiveness of sins.

Roman Catholics rightly complain that many Protestants do not take seriously what Jesus actually says in this verse. The fact is that Jesus is stating far more than that the believers are to preach forgiveness. Some kind of authority concerning forgiveness is established here, involving an *if-then* relationship. If the believers and the church rightly declare forgiveness, then the sins have been forgiven. Likewise, if forgiveness is rightly withheld by the church, forgiveness really is withheld.

What this requires is a proper connection of the Bible's clear teaching on forgiveness only through personal faith in Jesus and the Bible's high view

3. William Barclay, *The Gospel of John*, 2 vols. (Philadelphia: Westminster, 1975), 2:318.

of the church. Seeking this link, Reformed theology understands that Jesus granted a declarative authority concerning the forgiveness of sins. Of course, the church may not grant forgiveness on any basis of its own choosing. Rather, Christians and the church are to preach forgiveness through faith in Christ's blood, and having done so have authority to declare forgiveness through faith in Christ in such a way that we may know that those sins really are forgiven. The sins are not forgiven *because* the church has said so, yet on the basis of the divinely established way of salvation, the church may declare forgiveness with real and divinely granted authority.

This is the same authority referred to by Jesus in Matthew 16:19. Peter had just made his Great Confession of faith, and Jesus responded with his famous declaration: "I will give you the keys of the kingdom of heaven, and whatever you bind on earth shall be bound in heaven, and whatever you loose on earth shall be loosed in heaven." In Jewish teaching, the authority to bind and loose pertained to the admission of persons to the fellowship of the church. This declarative authority was granted to Peter as a believer in Christ, was later granted to the apostles together in Matthew 18:18, and was granted to the church as a whole here in John 20:23.

When it comes to the church's declarative authority, there are important things to note. The first is that as the church is faithfully setting forth the Bible's teaching on forgiveness and salvation, its declarations are to be received by men as though Christ himself were speaking. The Puritan Thomas Watson wrote of faithful preaching: "Know, that in every sermon preached, God calls to you; and to refuse the message we bring, is to refuse God himself."[4] Thus Paul's answer, "Believe in the Lord Jesus, and you will be saved," represented an authoritative answer to the Philippian jailer's question, "What must I do to be saved?" (Acts 16:30–31).

Second, while we must emphasize that Christ grants both power and authority to believers in general and to his church as a whole, it is also true that Jesus has established officers who will often exercise this authority on behalf of the church. We see, for instance, the apostle Peter exercising Christ's declarative authority to Simon Magus, when that charlatan tried to purchase salvation: "You have neither part nor lot in this matter, for your heart is not right before God" (Acts 8:21). In another example, the question

---

4. Thomas Watson, *A Body of Divinity* (Edinburgh: Banner of Truth, 1958), 221.

regarding the status of Gentile converts resulted in the Jerusalem Council. This vital issue regarding salvation was not decided by a meeting of the whole church, but "the apostles and the elders were gathered together to consider this matter" (15:6).

This declarative authority is exercised in various ways today. In many churches, the worship service includes a corporate confession of sin and a declaration of pardon. This declaration is to be sharply distinguished from the kind of priestly absolution uttered in Roman Catholic churches. No Protestant minister should ever declare, especially to a mixed gathering that has merely recited a prayer, "I absolve you." Rather, ministers declare the pardon offered by Christ in the Bible, and those who have truly confessed and believed should hear these words as though spoken by Christ himself. Similarly, when a pastor utters a benediction at the end of the worship service, following the apostolic example in the New Testament, these are not priestly invocations of divine blessing but prophetic prayer-exhortations beseeching God to glorify himself through his Son and provide the blessings of salvation to his people.

Another important exercise of spiritual authority takes place when the elders of the church receive new members on the basis of a profession of faith in Christ. This is one of the most important duties of elders and should never be taken lightly. When the elders admit someone into the church or administer baptism to a believer, they are declaring on behalf of Christ that the person should anticipate entry into heaven, and such persons should derive assurance of their salvation from this declaration. The same significance pertains to the admission of persons to participate in the sacrament of the Lord's Supper.

On a negative note, Jesus' teaching relates to the exercise of church discipline, especially when it comes to the censure of excommunication. He added to the disciples, "If you withhold forgiveness from any, it is withheld" (John 20:23). This corresponds to Jesus' clear teaching on church discipline in Matthew 18:17–18. If a sinner "refuses to listen even to the church," Jesus directed, "let him be to you as a Gentile and a tax collector. Truly, I say to you, whatever you bind on earth shall be bound in heaven, and whatever you loose on earth shall be loosed in heaven" (Matt. 18:17–18). This means that when the elders of Christ's church faithfully exercise church discipline in accordance with God's Word, and find themselves obliged to remove a member from the church fellowship, that person should tremble before the prospect of eternal divine judgment unless he repents, since Christ declared that what is faithfully bound and loosed by his church on earth reflects the divine authority of heaven itself.

AMBASSADORS FOR CHRIST

The third note we should make about the church's declarative authority is that it obliges every church, and every Christian, to sound forth the gospel offer of forgiveness through faith in Jesus. Paul reflected this obligation when he wrote: "In Christ God was reconciling the world to himself, not counting their trespasses against them, and entrusting to us the message of reconciliation. Therefore, we are ambassadors for Christ, God making his appeal through us" (2 Cor. 5:19–20).

This being the case, the final note we should make on Christ's grant of power and authority to the church for proclaiming the forgiveness of sin is the application that Paul himself made: "We implore you on behalf of Christ, be reconciled to God. . . . Behold, now is the favorable time; behold, now is the day of salvation" (2 Cor. 5:20–6:2).

137

THOMAS BELIEVING

John 20:24–29

Then he said to Thomas, "Put your finger here, and see my
hands; and put out your hand, and place it in my side. Do not
disbelieve, but believe." (John 20:27)

he Bible might be called God's book of blessings. This is not
to say that the Scriptures contain only blessings. There are
commands, warnings, and even curses as well. But the Bible
predominates in blessings. The purpose of the Bible is to lead us into God's
blessings so that God might be blessed in blessing his people.

The Bible begins with blessings, as God created all things and called
them "good." The Bible also ends with a blessing: "The grace of the Lord
Jesus be with all. Amen" (Rev. 22:21). In between, we find blessing upon
blessing. After making man, "God blessed them. And God said to them, 'Be
fruitful and multiply and fill the earth and subdue it'" (Gen. 1:28). When
God led Israel out of bondage, he put a benediction into the mouth of his
priest, Aaron: "The LORD bless you and keep you; the LORD make his face
to shine upon you and be gracious to you; the LORD lift up his countenance
upon you and give you peace" (Num. 6:24–26).

When God's Son, Jesus, came to earth, he spoke remarkable blessings. His Beatitudes begin, "Blessed are the poor in spirit, for theirs is the kingdom of heaven" (Matt. 5:3). Jesus blessed children (Mark 10:16), faithful servants (Matt. 24:46), and those who keep his Word (Luke 11:28). In the Gospel of John, Jesus spoke his last blessing when the disciple Thomas had believed, an especially significant blessing since it refers directly to us: "Blessed are those who have not seen and yet have believed" (John 20:29). Since salvation is received through faith, this blessing provides a key to them all: Jesus promises us, even if we have not seen him with our eyes, that if we believe his Word, we will be blessed with all the blessings that have ever been blessed by God.

THOMAS DISBELIEVING

In the last of his records of Christ's appearances to his disciples in Jerusalem, John turns to an event recorded nowhere else in Scripture: Jesus' ministry to the disbelief of the disciple Thomas.

We do not know as much about Thomas as the more prominent disciples. What we learn of him in John's Gospel, however, presents a consistent picture of dogged, loyal pessimism. In chapter 11, Thomas reacted to the news that Jesus was going back within the reach of the menacing religious leaders by saying, "Let us also go, that we may die with him" (John 11:16). Later, when Jesus began his Farewell Discourse by saying that he was going to heaven to prepare a place for the disciples, Thomas complained, "Lord, we do not know where you are going. How can we know the way?" (14:5). This small amount of evidence suggests that Thomas was loyal to Jesus and even courageous, but that he was also fatalistic and dour. This picture is confirmed by his refusal to believe the reports of Jesus' resurrection. When Jesus died, Thomas's gloomy mind saw the extinction of all hope. A. W. Pink observes, "He reminds us very much of John Bunyan's 'Fearing,' 'Despondency' and 'Much Afraid,' in his Pilgrim's Progress—types of a large class of Christians who are successors of doubting Thomas."[1]

It is with this Thomas that John concludes his account of Jesus' death and resurrection: "Now Thomas, one of the Twelve, called the Twin, was not with them when Jesus came. So the other disciples told him, 'We have

---

1. Arthur W. Pink, *Exposition of the Gospel of John* (Grand Rapids: Zondervan, 1975), 1105.

seen the Lord.' But he said to them, 'Unless I see in his hands the mark of the nails, and place my finger into the mark of the nails, and place my hand into his side, I will never believe'" (John 20:24–25). It is for saying these words that Thomas has been known to history as "doubting Thomas." We should not disparage him, however, as if he were the only disciple to doubt: all the disciples failed to believe on Christ's resurrection at some point.

When it comes to people with sincere doubts, the Bible is remarkably gracious and accommodating. Consider the Queen of Sheba, who had heard the incredible stories about the wisdom and glory of King Solomon, so that she traveled to Jerusalem "to test him with hard questions" (1 Kings 10:1). Her behavior revealed her as a skeptic of the best kind: she did not believe everything she heard, but she was open to believing the truth. So she inquired personally, posing Solomon riddles and asking to see the evidences for the claims that she had heard. The Bible records, "When she came to Solomon, she told him all that was on her mind. And Solomon answered all her questions" (10:2–3). After seeing the truth for herself, the Queen of Sheba exclaimed, "I did not believe the reports until I came and my own eyes had seen it. And behold, the half was not told me" (10:7).

This kind of doubt—a genuine quest for the truth and a willingness to believe it—is often blessed by God and should be honored by all his servants. If you find it hard to believe what you have heard about Christianity and want to know the truth, you should turn to the Bible with an open mind and heart. You should feel free to ask your questions of pastors and other Christians. As long as you are truly seeking truth and are sincerely open to believing if you are persuaded, then Jesus' promise applies to you: "everyone who asks receives, and the one who seeks finds" (Luke 11:10). If you are sincerely wondering about Jesus, your quest is likely to end with the Queen of Sheba's ringing affirmation: "Behold, the half was not told me!"[2]

The problem with doubting Thomas, however, was that he really was not a doubter at all. Instead, Thomas was a determined disbeliever. He set forth conditions, demands that expressed not his willingness but his unwillingness to believe: "Unless I see in his hands the mark of the nails, and place my finger into the mark of the nails, and place my hand into his side, I will never believe" (John 20:25). Thomas was not unsure or puzzled,

2. For a thorough treatment of the Queen of Sheba's virtuous skepticism, see Philip Graham Ryken, *1 Kings*, Reformed Expository Commentary (Phillipsburg, NJ: P&R Publishing, 2011), 262–64.

but stubbornly rejected the news of Jesus' resurrection. Leon Morris writes: "He would not be persuaded by the combined testimony of all the rest of the apostolic band. . . . He could not understand why all the apostles, sensible men whom he knew well, had accepted it. And no matter how stupid they had been, he was not going to follow their example."[3]

It is interesting that Jesus appeared to the disciples on Resurrection Sunday and then did not appear to them again until the next Sunday (when John says that Jesus returned "eight days later," he is counting inclusively, as was the Jewish pattern). It is possible that Jesus was emphasizing the gathering of his people for worship on the Lord's Day. Thomas, alone of the remaining eleven disciples, had not been present in the previous week's gathering when Jesus first appeared. It is not surprising, then, that while the other disciples were strengthened in their faith, Thomas drifted into a hardened state of unbelief. His absence from the fellowship contributed to his unbelief.

This reminds us why all believers need to be regular and consistent in attending the worship of the church. This principle is especially true for those who are wavering in their faith or godliness. Alexander Maclaren urges: "The worst thing that a man can do when disbelief, or doubt, or coldness shrouds his sky, and blots out the stars, is to go away alone and shut himself up with his own, perhaps morbid, or, at all events, disturbing thoughts. The best thing that he can do is to go amongst his fellows. If the sermon does not do him any good, the prayers and the praises and the sense of brotherhood will help him."[4] Of all the blessings that we miss when we fail to attend church, the most certain is the strengthening of our faith through the ministry of God's Word. Because he was absent when Christ first appeared to the disciples, Thomas missed the joy of Christ's presence and the Lord's ministry of peace. It is no wonder that he spent a week in despondency when he might have been rejoicing in the resurrection.

Thomas benefited, nonetheless, by the faithful Christian friendship of his fellow disciples. They might have reasoned, being aware of God's sovereignty in salvation, that there was nothing for them to do about Thomas's absence. But that is not what they did. Even though they could not persuade Thomas about what they had seen, their witness seems to have accounted for his presence on this second Sunday, so that Thomas was present when the Lord

---

3. Leon Morris, *Reflections on the Gospel of John* (Peabody, MA: Hendrickson, 1986), 714.

4. Alexander Maclaren, *Expositions of Holy Scripture*, 17 vols. (Grand Rapids: Baker, 1982), 11:320.

appeared again. Likewise, believers today should be alert to those who have drifted away from the church and should provide the encouragement and witness they need in order to return to the fold of Christ.

SEE MY HANDS

Despite his unbelief, Thomas was brought to faith by Jesus' second appearance in the midst of his disciples. John writes: "Eight days later, his disciples were inside again, and Thomas was with them. Although the doors were locked, Jesus came and stood among them and said, 'Peace be with you'" (John 20:26). If this sounds familiar, the reason is that this is a virtual replay of the previous week's appearance. In his resurrected body, Jesus was able to appear right before his disciples without coming through the door. This time, he spoke directly to the remaining unbeliever: "Then he said to Thomas, 'Put your finger here, and see my hands; and put out your hand, and place it in my side. Do not disbelieve, but believe'" (20:27).

There are three points for us to note about Jesus' ministry in calling Thomas to faith. The first is that Jesus did not mind repeating his earlier ministry. Jesus was born in this world to offer peace with God to men and women lost in sin, so it was no burden for him to repeat this message a second time. Indeed, Jesus delights today to present himself over and over again to sinners whom he is calling to salvation, speaking to their hearts, "Peace be with you." If you have been saved, it is because Jesus came to you through his Word and declared peace. He told you that his atoning death had put an end to God's wrath against your sins and summoned you to lay down your arms in surrendering faith. If you recognize that Jesus offers peace with God and eternal life, then it is Jesus himself who has come before you and speaks to your soul through the Bible, calling you to faith.

Second, Jesus also presented the cause of our restoration to God. Just as in his earlier appearance, he displayed the marks of his sacrifice for our sins upon the cross. Jesus constantly sets the cross before us to stir up our faith and grant us peace. If you find yourself doubting God's love, remember the cross, where God's Son freely gave his life for you. If you feel that you could not possibly have peace with God, remember the wounds of Christ and see the price that satisfied God's justice toward you. If you close your eyes at night and fear that you might die and be sent to hell, remember 1 John 1:7: "the blood of Jesus [God's] Son cleanses us from all sin."

It is because of this focus on the cross that Jesus instituted the sacrament of the Lord's Supper to provide a perpetual memorial of the peace he won through his atoning death. Receiving the emblems of Christ's body and blood, broken and shed for our sins, every believer should be assured not only that God will receive his or her soul into heaven in the future but also that God's blessing has been secured for us right now. A. W. Pink writes: "When we have gone astray, what is it that recalls us? Not occupation with the intricacies of prophecy or the finer points of doctrine (important and valuable as these are in their place) but the great foundational truth of the Atonement. It was the sight of the Saviour's *wounds* which scattered all Thomas' doubts, overcame his self-will, and brought him to the feet of Christ as an adoring worshiper."[5]

Third, notice the pastoral care with which Jesus ministered to Thomas's disbelief: "Then he said to Thomas, 'Put your finger here, and see my hands; and put out your hand, and place it in my side. Do not disbelieve, but believe'" (John 20:27). On the one hand, Jesus was graciously answering Thomas's demand, not ridiculing or rebuking Thomas but ministering to his unbelief. J. C. Ryle comments: "It is hard to imagine anything more tiresome and provoking than the conduct of Thomas . . . . But it is impossible to imagine anything more patient and compassionate, than our Lord's treatment of this weak disciple. . . . He deals with him according to his weakness, like a gentle nurse dealing with a froward child."[6] On the other hand, Jesus in this way revealed to Thomas the truth of his deity. How could Jesus know what Thomas had said, unless he was the Lord of resurrection life, the God who knows all secrets? When Thomas finally believed, it was not ultimately because of the testimony of his friends, valuable as that was, but because Jesus had revealed himself personally in such a way that Thomas could no longer disbelieve.

William Hendriksen points out how thoroughly Jesus responded to Thomas's objections with a gracious answer designed to win his faith. Thomas had insisted, "Unless I see in his hands the mark of the nails," and Jesus told

5. Pink, *John*, 1110–11.
6. J. C. Ryle, *Expository Thoughts on the Gospels: John*, 3 vols. (Edinburgh: Banner of Truth, 1999), 3:455–56.

him, "See my hands." Thomas demanded to "place my finger into the mark of the nails," and Jesus invited him, "Put your finger here." Thomas added that he must "place my hand into his side," so Jesus answered, "Place it in my side." "I will never believe," Thomas insisted, but Jesus commanded in sovereign grace, "Do not disbelieve, but believe" (John 20:25–27).[7] In every conversion, Jesus personally ministers to the unbelief of the individual sinner and sovereignly calls the individual soul, "Do not disbelieve, but believe." If Jesus is calling to you, you should listen and respond. When Jesus comes before you through his Word, you should put away your unbelief and follow the example that Thomas gave before you.

DOUBT REPLACED WITH FAITH

The first thing we notice about Thomas's conversion is that he does not seem actually to have placed his fingers into the wounds of Jesus' hands and side. Once Jesus had revealed himself to Thomas, the disciple no longer placed any demands before his faith; instead, his faith compelled him to drop all his objections and immediately profess Jesus as Savior and Lord. It was not because his demands had been met that Thomas decided that he was willing to believe. Instead, Christ's personal self-disclosure overwhelmed the unbelief and drew Thomas to Christ as a servant and worshiper.

In this way, Thomas moved from being the last holdout to Jesus among the disciples to the one who offered the highest profession of faith in Christ. It was just as Paul would later declare: "Where sin increased, grace abounded all the more" (Rom. 5:20). In John's Gospel, indeed in all four of the Gospels, there is no greater profession of faith than the one given by the once-disbelieving Thomas: "Thomas answered him, 'My Lord and my God!'" (John 20:28).

Thomas professed Jesus in two vital terms that every Christian must likewise embrace. First, he named Jesus his Lord, committing himself wholly to Jesus for salvation, worship, and obedience. Thomas thus gave the confession of Psalm 16:2: "I say to the LORD, 'You are my Lord; I have no good apart from you.'" Some Christians are taught that we may look to Jesus as Savior while withholding commitment to him as our Master. Thomas belies

---

7. William Hendriksen, *Exposition of the Gospel according to John*, 2 vols., New Testament Commentary (Grand Rapids: Baker, 1953), 2:465.

this notion, showing that faith in Christ demands a self-surrender to him as our sovereign Lord.

Second, Thomas professed the deity of Christ, worshiping him as "my God." J. C. Ryle calls this "a distinct testimony to our blessed Lord's divinity. It was a clear, unmistakable declaration that Thomas believed him, whom he saw and touched that day, to be not only man, but God. Above all, it was a testimony which our Lord received and did not prohibit, and a declaration which He did not say one word to rebuke."[8]

In order for Jesus to offer the salvation presented in the Bible, it is necessary for him to be God. His eternal priestly mediation, his sufficient atonement for sin, and his perfect redemption, along with the effectual, sovereign call by which he summons sinners to believe, all require that Jesus be very God of very God. Ryle comments:

> Forever let us bless God that the Deity of our Lord is taught everywhere in the Scriptures, and stands on evidence that can never be overthrown. Above all, let us daily repose our sinful selves on Christ with undoubting confidence, as one that is perfect God as well as perfect man. He is man, and therefore can be touched with the feeling of our infirmities. He is God, and therefore "is able to save unto the uttermost them that come unto God by him."[9]

Thomas worshiped Jesus and confessed him as the Lord, the sovereign, covenant Savior of the Bible, and as the one true and living God, incarnate in the flesh for our salvation. Do you confess these things to be true of Jesus? If you do, be sure to add another word that Thomas inserted. He confessed Jesus not only as Lord and God but as "*my* Lord and *my* God!" (John 20:28). Jesus offers himself to you, so do not fail to receive him in worshiping faith. And then offer yourself to him in surrendering adoration, acclaiming him as "my Lord and my God." If you do, like Thomas, you will be saved.

BLESSED ARE THE BELIEVERS

With Thomas's glorious confession, the apostle John brings the record of his Gospel to its climax. He began with an assertion to the deity of Jesus. "In

8. Ryle, *John*, 3:457.
9. Ibid., 3:458.

the beginning was the Word," he wrote, "and the Word was with God, and the Word was God" (John 1:1). Over twenty chapters, John has told of the remarkable ministry of Jesus, centered on the seven great signs of his deity, and then focusing on Christ's departing ministry, his saving crucifixion, and his glorious resurrection. For John, the fitting climax to this whole Gospel record is a determined unbeliever who was confronted by the sovereign grace of Jesus and confessed the titanic truth declared all through this Gospel: "My Lord and my God!" To John, the gospel is not merely true but saving truth; he wrote his Gospel so that, like Thomas, "by believing you may have life in his name" (20:31).

It is with the evangelistic purpose of this Gospel in mind that John concludes Jesus' ministry to Thomas with words spoken by Christ about disciples who would come afterward. Jesus said to Thomas, "Have you believed because you have seen me? Blessed are those who have not seen and yet have believed" (John 20:29).

Do you have conditions and demands—things that you must see—before you will consider believing in Jesus? Jesus might or might not answer them in the way that you desire, but he will reveal himself to you personally if you will seek him through his Word. Jesus was reminding Thomas that there would be legions of disbelievers saved without a physical demonstration of Christ's resurrection body, but with an equally effectual revelation of Christ in the written record of the apostles. It is through his Word that Jesus stands before us today, calling us to faith with a self-disclosure that is just as real and powerful as that which brought Thomas to his knees and with a special blessing for those of us who believe.

Jesus insisted to Thomas that if you believe without having seen him, you will be blessed. What are these blessings? They include the blessings received by anyone who has ever believed: your sins will be forgiven, you will receive the free gift of eternal life, you will be accepted into God's embrace as a dearly beloved child, you will be delivered from the judgment that is to come, you will be raised in a glorious body like the resurrected body of Christ, you will have power to lead a holy and spiritually peaceful life, and you will be blessed to be used by God as a witness for the salvation of others. These blessings and more will be yours by making Thomas's confession your own, acclaiming Jesus as "my Lord and my God!" If you have done this, then you can marvel at the truth that Jesus' final gospel blessing was a benediction spoken over you: "Blessed are those who have not seen and yet have believed" (John 20:29).

138

THAT YOU MAY BELIEVE

John 20:30—31

These are written so that you may believe that Jesus is the
Christ, the Son of God, and that by believing you may have life
in his name. (John 20:31)

hen a loved one has died, we sometimes comfort ourselves by noting what a full life he or she has lived. But no one ever lived a more full life than Jesus during just the three years of his public ministry. In the final verse of his Gospel, the apostle John writes that if everything Jesus did was recorded, "I suppose that the world itself could not contain the books that would be written" (John 21:25). Not only did Jesus do many lives' worth of deeds, but their chief beneficiary was not him but others. Charles Spurgeon exults, "Our Lord's life was as ample as his own festivals; it feeds thousands, and with the fragments that remain many baskets might be filled."[1] For this reason, John did not even attempt to give a full account of Jesus' life. Instead, he selected material that would give testimony to the person and work of Jesus, with one clear purpose: "so

1. Charles H. Spurgeon, *Metropolitan Tabernacle Pulpit*, 63 vols. (Pasadena, TX: Pilgrim, 1973), 27:653.

that you may believe that Jesus is the Christ, the Son of God, and that by believing you may have life in his name."

JOHN AND HIS GOSPEL

In the final verses of chapter 20, we come to the finale of the Gospel of John. There remains another chapter, which is a sort of epilogue concerning Jesus' calling of the disciples to their future service as apostles. But with Thomas's confession of faith, John's Gospel account of Jesus has reached its completion. He began by asserting the deity of Christ: "In the beginning was the Word, and the Word was with God, and the Word was God" (John 1:1). Now John's long record of Jesus' ministry has culminated in Thomas's affirmation, "My Lord and my God!" (20:28).

John points out that "Jesus did many other signs in the presence of the disciples, which are not written in this book" (John 20:30). Scholars suggest that his reference to "this book" indicates John's awareness of the other biblical Gospels, which record details that John has left out. John has selected his material, much of it found nowhere else, to present a persuasive witness to the person and work of Christ.

In particular, John focused his book on Jesus' "signs." The signs were public miracles that attested to the truth of Jesus' deity. These were the turning of water into wine at the wedding of Cana (John 2:7–11), the healing of the official's son (4:46–54), the healing of the paralytic by the pool (5:2–9), the miraculous feeding of the five thousand (6:2–14), Jesus' walking on water (6:16–21), his giving of sight to the man born blind (9:1–7), and the raising of Lazarus from the grave (11:38–44). Some commentators believe that John was also referring to the postresurrection appearances of Jesus as signs and perhaps even to his death and resurrection as the greatest of all signs to Jesus' saving deity. The miracles are called *signs* because of what they *signify*: they are *sign*ificant in pointing the reader to God's offer of salvation in Christ. John has not recorded all the signs that he could have written down, but what he has recorded is sufficient to call us to confess Jesus, together with Thomas, as "Lord and God."

John reminds us that the object of saving faith is Jesus Christ himself. We are not saved by believing that certain doctrines are true. We are not saved by trusting the church to take care of our souls. We are saved only by responding in personal faith to the biblical testimony to Jesus, trusting and yielding our lives to him as our Lord. In this respect, what John says of his own Gospel is true of every single book in the Bible and of the Bible as a whole: its purpose is to lead us to "believe that Jesus is the Christ, the Son of God, and that by believing you may have life in his name" (John 20:31).

John also sets a good example for us in keeping the focus of his witness on Jesus himself. Spurgeon points out that many of the prominent episodes recorded in the other Gospels but left out of John are events in which the evangelist himself was a leading participant. "He omits, as if of set purpose, those places of the history in which he would have shone." Examples are the raising of Jairus's daughter, Jesus' transfiguration on the mount, and Jesus' request for his three closest disciples to pray with him in the garden of Gethsemane. Spurgeon observes: "He leaves out that which would have brought John into the front, in order that he may fill up the whole foreground of his canvas with the portrait of his Lord. Everything is subordinated to the one grand end 'that ye should believe that Jesus is the Christ.'"[2] In this way, John lives out the words he records spoken by John the Baptist, "He must increase, but I must decrease" (John 3:30), and reminds us that the goal of our witness is always to glorify Jesus and never to advance ourselves.

JESUS IS GOD'S SON

John says that he recorded details about Jesus not based on how interesting they were or how they might satisfy our curiosity. He presented those signs that would lead us to faith in Jesus. According to John, what we are to believe concerns both the person and the work of Jesus. Speaking of his person, John marshaled his testimony to persuade us that Jesus is "the Son of God" (John 20:31).

The miracles that John records bear testimony to Jesus' deity, since they cannot be accounted for in any other way. The One who could turn water into wine must be the Lord of the harvest. Jesus said that the man born blind had lived in that state so "that the works of God might be displayed in him" (John 9:3), and it was Jesus' works that were glorified when the man was given sight. Most impressively, Jesus claimed deity for himself when he told

2. Ibid., 27:655–56.

686

grieving Martha, "I am the resurrection and the life" (11:25). It might be easy to make such a claim, but only God could then stand before the tomb where dead Lazarus had lain for four days, call out his name, and see him emerge alive from the grave. John revealed these and all the other signs of his Gospel so that we might be persuaded that Jesus is the Son of God.

In John's time, just as in ours, the issue of the deity of Christ was far more than merely a theological matter. It was also a political matter, in which the believer declared his ultimate loyalty and worship. It is not incidental that John likely wrote his Gospel while ministering in Ephesus, the great city of the province of Asia, which also was a center for the worship of the Roman emperor. The streets of John's city frequently witnessed processions in which the loyal devotees to the imperial cult professed, "Caesar is Lord, Caesar is God!" It is against such deluded paganism that John records Thomas's profession to Jesus, "My Lord and my God!" (John 20:28). John's point in declaring Jesus' deity is therefore not merely our need to affirm a point of doctrine. Rather, to believe on Jesus is to commit yourself to the worship of him alone, to the exclusion of all others. Moreover, while we embrace our proper secular duties, a Christian commits to the glory and advancement of Christ's kingdom instead of the glory of the kingdoms of this world. Bruce Milne observes the relevance to us:

> Caesar worship is not dead—the false deities are still chanted in our streets, the gods of state and nation, and all the other traditional religions or their amalgam, of New Age and Satanism, and selfism in its multiple forms. In the face of these false claimants we exalt in our worship the one who alone is worthy, "our Lord, our God"—Jesus Christ![3]

JESUS IS THE CHRIST

John had a second interest as he selected the material to present in this Gospel. In addition to seeking to persuade us that Jesus is uniquely the Son of God in his person, John sought for us to believe on Jesus' saving work: "These are written," he explains, "so that you may believe that Jesus is the Christ" (John 20:31).

---

3. Bruce Milne, *The Message of John: Here Is Your King!* (Downers Grove, IL: InterVarsity Press, 1993), 307.

In referring to Jesus as "the Christ," John reminds us that *Christ* is not part of Jesus' name but rather the title and office that he fulfills. *Christos* is the Greek translation of the Hebrew word *Messiah*, which means "the Anointed One." Jesus is the long-awaited Messiah, fulfilling the saving expectation of God's Old Testament people. This is how Jesus identified himself when he launched his ministry in the synagogue of Nazareth: "The Spirit of the Lord is upon me, because he has anointed me to proclaim good news to the poor. He has sent me to proclaim liberty to the captives and recovering of sight to the blind, to set at liberty those who are oppressed, to proclaim the year of the Lord's favor" (Luke 4:18–19). That prophecy from Isaiah 61:1–2 shows that the God-anointed Messiah would come as the Savior who would grant liberty, understanding, and divine favor. John presents Jesus as this Christ and summons us to believe on him for salvation.

We can further understand the biblical meaning of the word *Christ* by noting that there were three anointed offices in the Old Testament that pointed forward to Jesus and that he perfectly fulfilled. These are the offices of prophet, priest, and king. The purpose of the prophets was to reveal God and his ways to mankind. The priests served to bring the people into God's presence for worship and service. The kings ruled God's people on the Lord's behalf. These three anointed offices find their fulfillment in Jesus, who perfectly and eternally fills these roles for the salvation of believers. John's Gospel provides witnesses who compel us to faith in Jesus as the Savior who meets these three needs: our need to know God, our need to be reconciled with God, and our need to be ruled by God.

First, John's Gospel identifies Jesus as the true Prophet who reveals God to his people. He began by referring to Jesus as the God-revealing "Word" (John 1:1). In John 3, Jesus instructed a Pharisee who was supposed to be a teacher of Scripture but who did not even know that one must be born again (3:3–8). When Nicodemus marveled, "How can these things be?" (3:9), Jesus taught him with words of sublime gospel truth: "For God so loved the world, that he gave his only Son, that whoever believes in him should not perish but have eternal life" (3:16). In John 4, Jesus offered God's gift of eternal life to the Samaritan woman at the well. When she replied that a prophet would someday come to explain these things, Jesus replied, "I who speak to you am he" (4:26). Jesus revealed the prophetic truth of God not only in his words but also in his person, so that the woman went back to her village witnessing: "Can this be the Christ?" (4:29).

On the night of his arrest, Jesus summed up his prophetic office by telling the disciples, "Whoever has seen me has seen the Father" (John 14:9). Jesus meant that as the Son of God, he revealed God to the world by his words, works, and ministry. His teaching expressed God's offer of salvation to sinners. To see Jesus, the great and final Prophet, is to see and know God, and to believe in Jesus as Savior is to come to God in truth. This is the question that John poses to us: Do you believe in Jesus as the Savior who uniquely reveals the truth of God?

John also provides witnesses to Jesus in his anointed office as saving Priest for his people. The Old Testament priests brought the people into the holiness of God's presence by offering sacrifices to atone for sin. John records that John the Baptist identified Jesus as the true and final Sacrifice for our sins: "Behold, the Lamb of God, who takes away the sin of the world!" (John 1:29). It was as the true Priest that Jesus cleansed the temple, driving out all the profiteers who sought to make money off the people's need for forgiveness (2:13–17). When a woman caught in adultery was brought for judgment, Jesus stood against her condemnation as a true Priest of God's mercy and grace. Driving away the accusers of the law and granting her forgiveness of sin, Jesus sent her away as one restored to God and called to holy living (7:53–8:11). In presenting Jesus as the anointed Priest of God's mercy, John calls on us to confess our need for saving grace and to believe on Jesus' atoning death for the forgiveness of our sins.

Third, John's Gospel bears testimony to Jesus' royal office as the anointed King over God's people. Jesus' miracles reveal this royal sovereignty over sickness, blindness, and even death. Jesus came as a King with power from heaven as he spoke and the ruler's son was healed, as he opened up his storehouse and fed the five thousand with just a few fish and loaves, as his command granted the paralytic strength to stand, and especially as his sovereign voice called dead Lazarus from the grave. Jesus was not, however, the kind of king that the Jewish people were seeking: the kind of military conqueror they called for when Jesus entered Jerusalem on Palm Sunday. Instead, Jesus would gather his kingdom by being lifted up on the throne of his cross, by which he cast down every spiritual oppressor and established his reign of grace over the earth. As John records, Jesus was crucified under a placard inscribed by

Pontius Pilate, which read, "Jesus of Nazareth, the King of the Jews" (John 19:19). John's Gospel challenges you: have you sought Christ's royal grace and submitted your grateful heart to his saving rule? If you have received him as sovereign Ruler, as well as prophetic Revealer of God and sin-atoning Priest, then you may know that you have gained the right to eternal life.

BELIEVING IN JESUS

Given all that John records concerning Jesus, it is astonishing that people are reluctant to claim him as Savior and Christ. Jonathan Edwards asked: "What are you afraid of, that you dare not venture your soul upon Christ? Are you afraid that He cannot save you, that He is not strong enough to conquer the enemies of your soul? . . . Are you afraid that He will not be willing to stoop so low as to take any gracious notice of you?" If you are hesitant to trust your salvation to Jesus, then John's witness to his miraculous signs and his many acts of mercy should persuade you that Jesus is all that you could desire in a Savior and more. Edwards answers: "What is there that you can desire should be in a Savior that is not in Christ? . . . What excellency is there wanting? What is there that is great or good? What is adorable or endearing; or, what can you think of that would be encouraging which is not to be found in the person of Christ?"[4]

Consider the virtues that we might seek in a Messiah. Are you looking for a Savior who is high and lifted up? Edwards asks: is not the Son of God "a person honorable enough to be worthy that you should be dependent on Him? Is He not a person high enough to be appointed to so honorable a work as your salvation?" Or you might ask that a Savior has suffered and gained a fellow feeling with those who are afflicted. Then "has not Christ been made low enough for you? And has He not suffered enough," having borne the wrath of God against our sins? Or, Edwards asks, perhaps you realize that you must have a Savior who is near to God and so able to mediate successfully on your behalf. "Can you desire Him to be nearer to God than Christ is, who is His only-begotten Son?" Again, you might desire the Savior to be near and accessible to you. "Would you have Him nearer to you than to be in the same nature, united to you by a spiritual union, so close as to be fitly

4. Jonathan Edwards, *Altogether Lovely: Jonathan Edwards on the Glory and Excellency of Christ* (Morgan, PA: Soli Deo Gloria, 1997), 44–45.

represented by the union of the wife to the husband, of the branch to the vine, of the member to the head?"[5]

Finally, you might demand a Savior to have "given some great and extraordinary testimony of mercy and love to sinners by something that He has done." "Can you think or conceive," Edwards answers, "of greater things than Christ has done? Was it not a great thing for Him who was God to take upon Himself human nature, to be not only God, but man thenceforward to all eternity? But would you look upon suffering for sinners to be a yet greater testimony of love to sinners . . . ? And would you desire that a Savior should suffer more than Christ has suffered for sinners? What is there wanting, or what would you add if you could, to make Him more fit to be your Savior?"[6] The answer is that given all that John has revealed about Jesus as Son of God and Savior for all who believe, there is nothing more we could ask or desire than what we find in God's Son. Therefore, let us believe in him, committing our salvation wholly into his mighty, pierced hands, knowing that "whoever believes in the Son has eternal life . . . . He does not come into judgment, but has passed from death to life" (John 3:36; 5:24).

LIFE IN HIS NAME

According to John, the subject of his Gospel is Jesus. His aim is that we would believe on Jesus as God's Son and as the Christ. Finally, the ultimate purpose for this evangelistic book concerns the reader: "that by believing you may have life in his name" (John 20:31).

Eternal life is the standard definition given to salvation in this Gospel, occurring seventeen times and referred to many more times simply as "life." This salvation first involves the gift of *judicial life* in Christ. Consider a lawbreaker who faces the penalty of death but receives an unexpected pardon. That person received life and rejoiced greatly for it. So it is for us, sinners condemned to eternal death under God's holy law (Rom. 6:23). Through faith in his name, Jesus by his death served the penalty due to us. This is why John's Gospel teaches, "Whoever believes in the Son has eternal life; whoever does not obey the Son shall not see life, but the wrath of God remains on him" (John 3:36).

5. Ibid., 45–46.
6. Ibid., 46.

A memorable illustration of a man seeking judicial life comes from the first chapter of John Bunyan's *The Pilgrim's Progress*. Bunyan's Christian learns from the Bible that he and his city are doomed to the just penalty of death. Fleeing for safety to the cross, Christian cries out, "Life! Life! Eternal life!"[7] John the apostle would have us flee to Jesus, the Son of God and the Christ, that in his name we might be forgiven through his shed blood, acquitted because of his satisfaction of the law's demands, and declared just in his perfect righteousness. Justification through faith in Christ is eternal life, free from the deadly penalty due to our sins.

Second, eternal life is the spiritual power imparted to our souls by the Holy Spirit. Jesus offered this gift to the people of Jerusalem, crying out: "If anyone thirsts, let him come to me and drink. Whoever believes in me, as the Scripture has said, 'Out of his heart will flow rivers of living water'" (John 7:37–38). That offer refers to the Spirit's regenerating power in our lives. Spurgeon writes: "God the Holy Spirit is with believers, breathing into them a new, holy, heavenly life. They are dead to the world . . . , and buried with Christ, but they live unto God, never more to be slain by sin."[8] Unlike Christ's gift of judicial life, which can never be improved, the spiritual life that he gives continues to grow eternally. Eternal life therefore secures us the legal right to heaven through forgiveness, and begins in our souls the godly life that will continue incorruptible forever.

If we understand what kind of life is offered to us by this Gospel, and if we feel our need for this salvation, then surely we will urgently seek the means by which we might have eternal life for ourselves. The answer, John insists, is that eternal life comes through faith in Jesus, by believing in his name. You cannot buy it with any great quantity of earthly wealth. You need not earn it, nor can you, but Jesus has secured it by his perfect life, atoning death, and glorious resurrection.

The God of grace offers you eternal life through his Son. Will you receive it? If you have received it, will you strengthen your faith by renewing your belief in John's testimony to God's Son, Jesus Christ? The whole of John's Gospel, this sacred book set before you by the merciful grace of God, pleads with you to believe on Jesus. Submit yourself wholly to him, resolving to worship him alone as Lord and God. Trust him and call on Jesus to be your Savior, and through faith in his name you will have eternal life.

7. John Bunyan, *The Pilgrim's Progress* (Nashville: Thomas Nelson, 1999), 13.
8. Spurgeon, *Metropolitan Tabernacle Pulpit*, 27:661.

139

Back to Galilee

John 21:1—14

*The disciple whom Jesus loved therefore said to Peter,
"It is the Lord!"* (John 21:7)

There is something powerful about going home. At home, we remember not only where we came from but who we are. At our spiritual home we recall how we first met Jesus, experienced the power of God's grace, and took our first steps of faith. Home may be the church in which we were nurtured in saving faith, the dining table where our fathers and mothers prayed and opened God's Word, the campground where we opened our youthful hearts to Jesus, or the college campus where a friendly witness led us to Christ.

If we have a place we call home, then we can understand why Jesus instructed the disciples to return to Galilee after his resurrection to await him. Before his crucifixion, Jesus instructed them, "After I am raised up, I will go before you to Galilee" (Mark 14:28), a directive reinforced by the angel's report to the women in the empty tomb (16:7). Galilee was the region where Jesus had proclaimed his kingdom in holy words and mighty deeds, gathering his new Israel before returning to Jerusalem to bear the cross. After the resurrection, it is probably here that Jesus "appeared to more than five hundred brothers at one time," as Paul records (1 Cor. 15:6). After this first appearance, Jesus climbed a mount where he gave his Great Commission and then ascended into heaven (Matt. 28:16–20).

It was on a Galilean hill that Jesus had spoken his Sermon on the Mount. It was in towns such as Capernaum, Cana, and Nain that Jesus performed his notable miracles of healing, deliverance, and raising from the dead. On one shore of the Sea of Galilee, Jesus delivered a man from the legions of demons that he sent into a herd of swine to perish in the waters. On the other shore Jesus performed his great miracle of feeding the five thousand, after which he gave his Bread of Life Discourse. It was in these waters that Jesus called Peter, James, and John to leave behind their fishing nets and become "fishers of men" (Matt. 4:19). It is not surprising, therefore, that Jesus regathered his disciples in Galilee, recalling their hearts to the kingdom and gospel they had learned from him in their native land, before finally leaving them. J. C. Ryle comments: "He knew well the influence which scenery and places exercise over the mind of man. He would recall to the memory of His disciples all that they had witnessed in the early days of His ministry. . . . Where he had begun with them, there He would have one of His last interviews with them, before leaving the world."[1]

THE CHURCH TOGETHER

John chapter 21 does not recount the whole of Jesus' final ministry in Galilee, but only a last encounter beside the familiar lake of that name. The evangelist says that after his appearances in Jerusalem, "Jesus revealed himself again to the disciples by the Sea of Tiberias" (John 21:1). It is not surprising that having been told only to report to the region of Galilee, Peter and the other disciples returned to the lake where they had formerly worked and where Jesus had called them to their ministry. John relates, "Simon Peter, Thomas (called the Twin), Nathanael of Cana in Galilee, the sons of Zebedee, and two others of his disciples were together" (21:2). This accounts for seven of the eleven remaining disciples, of which all of those named hailed from Galilee, including John himself and his brother James, who are identified by the name of their father, Zebedee.

1. J. C. Ryle, *Expository Thoughts on the Gospels: John*, 3 vols. (Edinburgh: Banner of Truth, 1999), 3:482.

The very fact of the disciples' regathering in Galilee should be a cause for rejoicing in the gospel. Jesus' crucifixion had fulfilled the ancient prophecy, "Strike the shepherd, and the sheep will be scattered" (Zech. 13:7; Matt. 26:31). But now the disciples had gathered in open allegiance to Jesus, presenting themselves in the region of Jesus' most public and notorious works. No longer did Peter think of denying his Lord; no longer were the other disciples scurrying for a place of cover. What can account for this renewal of courage and faith other than the fact of Jesus' resurrection, of which they had now become witnesses?

Moreover, in this list of names we are reminded of the character of Christ's church. As it was then, so has the church always consisted of those who have been spiritual failures and nonentities. This list of names is headed by one who denied his Lord and another who was determined in disbelief. Included are an apparently quiet figure, Nathanael; combative personalities, the sons of Zebedee; and two others who are such background figures that their names are not even mentioned. James Montgomery Boice observes: "These are the ones who do Christian work—normal people, with all the failings we are heir to, not fictitious characters of superhuman faith and fortitude."[2] They were now gathered and unified as sinners cleansed of their sins by Christ's atoning death and renewed by faith in their resurrected Lord.

We were first introduced to these names in John chapter 1. In between the first and the twenty-first chapters were many challenges and adventures that might easily have overwhelmed them and separated them from Jesus. But Jesus had taught them, beside these very waters: "All that the Father gives me will come to me, and whoever comes to me I will never cast out. . . . For this is the will of my Father, that everyone who looks on the Son and believes in him should have eternal life, and I will raise him up on the last day" (John 6:37, 40). Therein lies the secret of their perseverance in faith and discipleship. The presence of these names in John 21 bears testimony to God's sustaining grace and Christ's persevering mercy. Those whom Jesus had called to salvation then were not lost, and we who are called to saving faith today will likewise never be lost but will persevere to the end of our own gospel stories.

2. James Montgomery Boice, *The Gospel of John*, 5 vols. (Grand Rapids: Baker, 1999), 5:1625.

A LESSON IN MINISTRY

It is not hard to imagine how Peter and his friends ended up on boats in the lake. When we return to our homes, we tend to walk down the memory lane of our prior activities. Moreover, the disciples probably needed to provide for their material needs while they waited for Jesus to appear. It is therefore not surprising to read: "Simon Peter said to them, 'I am going fishing.' They said to him, 'We will go with you.' They went out and got into the boat, but that night they caught nothing" (John 21:3). It seems that Jesus was waiting for this to happen before he revealed himself to them again, since this fishing expedition would facilitate Jesus' final lesson on angling for the salvation of men.

The disciples' night of fishing on the boat has a symbolic meaning that is obvious to those who are familiar with the Gospel episodes that occurred on this lake. In the Bible, the sea stands for the chaos of the world; since Galilee was a region famous for Gentiles, those fishing on this sea are naturally considered examples of the church's call to bear a gospel witness to the world. The fact that they were fishing at night is not necessarily symbolic; many fishermen prefer the nighttime for their labors, and in the ancient world the darkness kept the fish from seeing the heavy ropes of their nets.

The first of four lessons taught here on the subject of service to Christ is *the futility of laboring according to our own wisdom.* Some commentators believe that the disciples' failure to catch fish indicates that they were disobeying Jesus' call to ministry by returning to this labor. There is no reason, however, to suggest that they were abandoning their call to serve the gospel just because they were fishing for their food. What is evident, however, is that they were laboring according to their own wisdom, skill, and power. We are used to accomplishing things by the kind of diligence and hard labor that Peter and the others showed by fishing all night. But in the realm of the spiritual work of Christ's kingdom, the rule is the one that Jesus gave the disciples on the night of his arrest: "Apart from me you can do nothing" (John 15:5). This is true of service to Christ in general, but especially of evangelism.

How confident we often are in our plans for reaching the world around us. Just as Peter was certain that he knew how to fish on the Sea of Galilee, we are sure that we understand the demands of our generation. Consequently, we devote little time to prayer and often fail to evaluate our methods in light of Christ's Word. It is no surprise that for all the noise and earthly results we achieve, when it comes to actually being used to bring others to saving faith, our programs can seem as empty as Peter's nets. Bruce Milne points out that "the church in the western world has never had such an array of helps, resources and methodologies as at present," many of them provided by psychology and sociological theories, and dependent on technological gadgetry.[3] Yet the spiritual harvest of churches in the West pales compared to churches in the Global South and in Asia. These churches, lacking our material resources and knowing nothing of contemporary "success" methodologies, produce a harvest of souls that far outstrips anything known in the West.

In many impoverished portions of the world, the growth of the church seems almost out of control. Why? Milne comments: "In their poverty and weakness they have to rely on prayer for the power of God and the simple direct sharing of the gospel."[4] In North America, prayer has ebbed to a low tide, so that it is virtually impossible to get church members to make a commitment to concerted prayer. Just as Peter labored through the night in his own strength to find his nets empty in the morning, our widespread self-reliance and emphasis on worldly methods has left the church in the West spiritually poor and empty-netted.

A second and related lesson taught in these verses is that *those who labor in obedience to Christ's Word will enjoy Christ's power and provision*. John continues: "Just as day was breaking, Jesus stood on the shore; yet the disciples did not know that it was Jesus. Jesus said to them, 'Children, do you have any fish?' They answered him, 'No.' He said to them, 'Cast the net on the right side of the boat, and you will find some.' So they cast it, and now they were not able to haul it in, because of the quantity of fish" (John 21:4–6).

Jesus called out to the disciples, using a word that might be rendered as "Fellows." As of yet, the disciples did not recognize Jesus. But just as fishermen are generally eager to cast their lines where someone suggests that there will be success, the disciples immediately followed his counsel. Their

3. Bruce Milne, *The Message of John: Here Is Your King!* (Downers Grove, IL: InterVarsity Press, 1993), 312.
4. Ibid.

net landed in the midst of a great school of fish so that they could not even manage to haul it aboard.

Commentators debate whether Jesus merely knew where the fish were or whether he performed a miracle in placing the fish into the net. Such a debate misses the point, which is that Christ has the power to grant success to those who minister in obedience to his Word. Throughout the Gospels, the disciples never catch any fish on their own, but when they heed Christ's word, their nets are full to bursting. After a night without one catch, a single cast at Christ's command garners more fish than they can handle. A. W. Pink translates the lesson to Christian ministry: "He tells the servants that success in their ministry is due not to their eloquence, their power of persuasion, or *their* any thing, but due alone to *His* sovereign drawing-power. . . . Our Lord's object was to show the disciples that the secret of success was to work at His command, and to act with implicit obedience to His Word."[5] Evangelism must therefore prayerfully rely on Christ's leading and blessing, and must involve a careful resolve to obey God's Word in everything. In spiritual ministry, the Bible's saying is true: "in keeping [his commandments] there is great reward" (Ps. 19:11).

Analyzing this situation more carefully, we note that Jesus spoke four times. First, he queried them as to the success of their labors according to the flesh: "Children, do you have any fish?" (John 21:5). His purpose was not to berate them for failure but to have them pronounce with their own lips, "No, we have no fish." They had to see and admit that their methods were failing. Second, Jesus then gave them a command: "Cast the net on the right side of the boat." This was attached with, third, his promise of blessing: "you will find some" (21:6). The point was not *where* they were to fish but *how*: in careful attendance on his Word.

Fourth, once the disciples had brought the net to the shore, Jesus directed them to present their haul at his feet: "Jesus said to them, 'Bring some of the fish that you have just caught.' So Simon Peter went aboard and hauled the net ashore, full of large fish, 153 of them" (John 21:10–11). Commentators throughout the centuries have racked their brains seeking ever more clever symbolic meanings for the number 153. The point, however, seems

5. Arthur W. Pink, *Exposition of the Gospel of John* (Grand Rapids: Zondervan, 1975), 1124, 1127.

simply to be the great size of the haul and the fact that each was counted and known before the Lord.

Concluding Jesus' four statements to the disciples, we see the third lesson for ministry and service: *the work performed at Christ's command and achieved by Christ's power will be accepted by Christ at the end of the age.* If we seek to serve Christ by human inventions, we will have nothing to present to him when his return tests the work of each of his servants (see 1 Cor. 3:11–15), but by obeying his commands we will have a profit to return to our Master.

The language of this passage strongly suggests Christ's future return in glory. First, this appearance is described as Jesus' revealing or unveiling of himself (John 21:1). Moreover, the nets are brought out of the sea to where Jesus is standing on the land, and after a long night the harvest takes place "just as day was breaking" (21:4). Just as the net was brought to Jesus and the fish counted before him, so also will all the gospel labor that we perform at his command be laid out and accepted by our Lord with approval and delight. We may even anticipate the words that Jesus will say, taken from his parable of the talents: "Well done, good and faithful servant" (Matt. 25:23). How great will be the joy of that day, for which the 153 fish symbolized a great harvest that seemed to overflow the net, yet it was not broken and not a single fish was lost.

COME AND DINE

The final lesson from this episode shows *the priority of personal fellowship with Christ.* This was a lesson that Peter had learned and put vigorously into practice. It was John who first recognized Jesus on the shore. When Jesus commanded them to cast the net, John, identified as "that disciple whom Jesus loved," cried out, "It is the Lord!" (John 21:7). This shows the value of Christians' working together, some of whom will be stronger in perception and others in action, as were John and Peter, respectively. John also shows us where the praise is due for all our success in ministry: when Christ's blessing causes our net to fill, let us cry out and give praise to him, saying, "It is the Lord!"

The fishing boat was a hundred yards from the shore (John 21:8), so we can understand why Peter failed to identify Jesus in the murky predawn light. As soon as John spoke and the identity of the stranger registered in Peter's mind, "he put on his outer garment, for he was stripped for work, and threw himself into the sea" (21:7). With all the power that his strong arms could muster, Peter propelled himself to Jesus.

At this point we should consider the similarities and differences between this scenario and an earlier encounter between Peter and Jesus in a boat on this same lake some years earlier, perhaps at this same spot. Jesus had been teaching alongside the water, and the crowd became so great that Jesus called Peter to take him out in the boat where he could preach. When Jesus had finished teaching, he directed Peter to a spot where he should lower his nets. When Peter reluctantly obeyed, a catch of fish so large filled his nets that they were unable to hold them without breaking. What is noteworthy is that on that prior occasion, when Peter recognized the deity of Christ, he fell to his knees and begged Jesus to leave him: "Depart from me, for I am a sinful man, O Lord," he said (Luke 5:8). Recognizing the presence of the holiness of God, Peter did the reasonable thing in confessing his sin and unworthiness.

Now, in John 21, Peter has a similar experience of Jesus and receives an identical proof of Christ's deity, yet Peter responds in a completely different manner. Whereas earlier he begged for Jesus to leave him, now he dives into the water and swims as hard as he can to gain Jesus' presence. What has changed in Peter's life? Has he come to realize over the intervening months that he really is not so great a sinner? Quite the opposite: Peter has recently committed the greatest sin of his life and seen himself to be a bigger failure than he ever imagined, denying Jesus three times on the night of his arrest. So what has changed? The answer is that Peter has learned the grace of God for sinners in the death and resurrection of Jesus. In particular, the resurrected Jesus had appeared to Peter and the other disciples, not greeting them with terrifying words of judgment or stinging words of rebuke, but blessing them with mercy and love. "Peace be with you," Jesus had said, and then directed their attention to the wounds in his hands and side (John 20:19–20).

Jesus likewise invites us to draw near to him and seek intimate spiritual fellowship *through his saving grace for those who believe.* The first proof of this invitation is seen in his reception of Peter. If Jesus offered peace through his sin-atoning blood to the disciple who denied him, then Jesus offers saving grace to all who will come through faith in his gospel Word.

A second incentive for us to draw near to Jesus is seen in *his compassionate care for his own*. Following Peter, the other disciples came to shore in the boat. They arrived to find that Jesus had anticipated their hunger and made provision for their needs: "When they got out on land, they saw a charcoal fire in place, with fish laid out on it, and bread" (John 21:9). Pink comments: "Even in His resurrection-glory He was not unmindful of their physical needs. Ever thoughtful, ever compassionate for His own, the Saviour here showed His toiling disciples that He cared for their bodies as well as their souls."[6]

This combination of fish and bread was no doubt meant to remind the disciples of the miracle of multiplying the fishes and loaves to feed the five thousand who had gathered beside this very lake. They remind us that Jesus has a supernatural abundance of provision and a compassionate heart to meet the needs of all who trust in him. Paul writes: "My God will supply every need of yours according to his riches in glory in Christ Jesus" (Phil. 4:19). Even more blessed than meeting our material needs, Christ provides the spiritual refreshment and satisfaction for which our hearts long, when we make a priority of coming to him in regular communion and prayer.

A final reason for us to draw near in fellowship to Christ is *his personal invitation for us to come*. John writes, "Jesus said to them, 'Come and have breakfast'" (John 21:12). It is interesting that John adds that "none of the disciples dared ask him, 'Who are you?' They knew it was the Lord" (21:12). This probably indicates the awe that was natural to them in the presence of the resurrected Lord of glory, just as an awareness of Christ's presence in the Holy Spirit communicates holy awe to us as well. Noting the reticence of these men who had been so close to him, "Jesus came and took the bread and gave it to them, and so with the fish" (21:13). Jesus likewise has bid sinners today to come into his presence to dine on his saving fare, and he sends the Holy Spirit to empower us in the spiritual encouragement we need. "Behold, I stand at the door and knock," he says. "If anyone hears my voice and opens the door, I will come in to him and eat with him, and he with me" (Rev. 3:20).

6. Ibid., 1126.

Come, You Blessed

John marks this encounter as the third of the appearances of Jesus to the disciples gathered together after the resurrection (John 21:14). Jesus continues to invite sinners into the blessing of his presence and provision. Consider the invitations that he sets before you in the Bible. Jesus invites you into a transforming relationship of discipleship and blessing. "Come to me, all who labor and are heavy laden, and I will give you rest," he offers. "Take my yoke upon you, and learn from me, for I am gentle and lowly in heart, and you will find rest for your souls" (Matt. 11:28–29). Jesus invites you to bring your barrenness to him and be filled with his renewing spring of life: "If anyone thirsts, let him come to me and drink. Whoever believes in me, as the Scripture has said, 'Out of his heart will flow rivers of living water'" (John 7:37–38). Then, if you will live in trusting fellowship with him, serving at his command and by his power, at the end of the age Jesus will invite you to share in his eternal glory. "Come, you who are blessed by my Father," he will say, "inherit the kingdom prepared for you from the foundation of the world" (Matt. 25:34). All these marvels start now through a personal relationship of faith in Jesus, who invites you, saying, "Come, and dine" (John 21:12).

Let us not only accept these invitations from Jesus for communion and blessing, but, like Peter, place our highest priority on fellowship with Christ. Peter shows us that going home is really going to Jesus. He reminds us that more important than what we do for Jesus and what he accomplishes through us is the relationship of joy, adoration, and refreshment that we gain in his presence. Let us become familiar enough, like John, that we identify Jesus' presence in our lives, frequently crying out in delight, "It is the Lord!" (John 21:7). Just as he came to these fishermen in their workplace, Jesus desires us to see him in all the settings of our lives: at work, in play, in prosperity, under trials, in failure, and in success: "It is the Lord!" So also, like Peter, let us cultivate an instinct of spiritual longing for Jesus that will lead us to fly joyfully to the nourishment of his Word, to communion with him in prayer, and to the praise of him in worship together with others to whom he has revealed himself in saving grace.

140

PETER RESTORED

John 21:15–17

When they had finished breakfast, Jesus said to Simon Peter,
"Simon, son of John, do you love me more than these?" He said
to him, "Yes, Lord; you know that I love you." He said to him,
"Feed my lambs." (John 21:15)

art of what makes the gospel such good news is that sinners can not only be forgiven but also be restored. This idea is so hateful to the devil that he seeks to counter the gospel with deceptive lies. Satan might reluctantly admit that Christians may be forgiven our sins and delivered from judgment. But when it comes to leading a happy and useful Christian life, and especially to being used by the Lord in some important way, Satan whispers to us that our sin has disqualified us forever. This is especially the devil's message to those who have sinned greatly after becoming Christians. Christians who have sinned, he urges, might as well continue sinning, or at least accept the fact that their failure has bound them to a low plane of Christian existence and service.

The antidote to Satan's lies is always the Word of God. The antidote to this particular lie is found at the end of the Gospel of John, where we learn of Peter's restoration not just to salvation but to apostolic service. We would be hard-pressed to commit a sin as grievous as Peter did when he denied Jesus three times on the night of his arrest. Therefore, Peter's restoration encourages us that we may be restored not only to salvation but also to usefulness to Christ.

THREE QUESTIONS FOR PETER

In the first half of John 21, Jesus met the disciples along the shore of the Sea of Galilee after filling their net with fish. Jesus awaited them beside a charcoal fire where a meal was cooking (John 21:9). Learning that it was Jesus, Peter flung himself into the waters and eagerly propelled himself into the Lord's presence. We can imagine that after the meal began, however, Peter might have become uneasy. He would have looked at the charcoal fire, his mind suddenly turning to another charcoal fire that had burned outside the high priest's residence on the night of Jesus' arrest. Peter had huddled there together with some of the temple guard. On the way into the courtyard, the door-maiden asked whether he was one of Jesus' disciples, and Peter denied it. Then by the fire, one of the guards recognized Peter and said to him, "You also are one of them." Peter replied, "I am not." Then a servant to the high priest suggested that Peter had been with Jesus earlier that night. Peter again denied Jesus, at which moment, according to Luke, Jesus "turned and looked at Peter" (Luke 22:58–61). At that look, the unfaithful disciple went away, weeping bitterly for his failure.

It seems likely that Jesus had arranged for this similar fire to await Peter beside the Sea of Galilee. Taking his own place where the temple guards had sat, Jesus looked at Peter once more, asking three times whether he loved him, one question for each of Peter's denials.

It is frequently taught that the key to understanding Jesus' questions and Peter's answers is found in the different Greek words used in this passage for *love*. In the first two of Jesus' questions, he asked for Peter's love using a verb form of the word *agape*. This is said to refer to the highest form of love, a divine love that involves the whole will. Peter answered by using the word *phileo*, which refers to a lower form of love, involving affection and friendship. Under this view, taught by many able teachers of Scripture, Peter was too abashed by his failure on the night of Jesus' arrest to claim anything but the lower form of love for Jesus. His chastened spirit could no longer assert any claim to a higher love. In his third question, Jesus lowered his demand from *agape* to *phileo*, accepting the love that Peter could assert and being willing to work in his disciple to produce the greater love in due time.

The problem with this approach is that the apostle John seems to use these two words for *love*, *agape* and *phileo*, more or less interchangeably. The concepts identified by the two words are valid: there is a divine love of the will, normally identified as *agape*, and a lower, human love of attraction and affection, associated with *phileo*. The problem is that John does not tend to use the words *agape* and *phileo* in such a technical sense. For instance, in referring to himself as "the disciple whom the Lord loved," John uses *agape* in one instance and *phileo* in another (John 20:2; 21:7). Moreover, John tends to vary his vocabulary for stylistic reasons. In this passage, recounting a conversation that probably occurred in Aramaic, not Greek, John uses two different words for *love*, two different words for *knowing*, and two different words for the idea of tending Jesus' sheep. Therefore, most scholars today doubt that the key to understanding Jesus' questions lies in the difference between *agape* and *phileo* in John's use.[1]

How, then, do we understand Jesus' questions? First, we should note that Jesus began not only by asking whether Peter loved him, but by specifying, "Simon, son of John, do you love me more than these?" (John 21:15). We remember that earlier on the night of Peter's denials, Jesus had warned that all the disciples would fall away after his arrest, but that the disciples should await him in Galilee after his resurrection (Matt. 26:31–32). Peter insisted that he would remain true even if the other disciples did not: "Though they all fall away because of you, I will never fall away" (26:33). Now, here they were in Galilee, and Peter had fallen away. "Do you still think that you love me more than the others do?" Jesus inquired. Peter's answer revealed his chastened spirit: "Yes, Lord; you know that I love you" (John 21:15). Jesus then asked Peter twice more: "Simon, son of John, do you love me?" (21:16–17). Peter repeated his first answer: "Yes, Lord; you know that I love you" (21:16). For his third answer, he said, "Lord, you know everything; you know that I love you" (21:17).

1. For a detailed exegetical consideration of this matter, see Leon Morris, *The Gospel according to John*, rev. ed., New International Commentary on the New Testament (Grand Rapids: Eerdmans, 1995), 768–70.

By inquiring about Peter's love three times, Jesus was not rubbing salt in his wounds but doing the serious work of bringing his disciple to a true repentance. We can be sure that this was painful for Peter. We can imagine that with each question, his mind would have remembered each of the three times he had denied his Lord. John notes that "Peter was grieved because he said to him the third time, 'Do you love me?'" (John 21:17). This grief was a necessary part of the Lord's work of prompting repentance for the sake of true restoration. With Jesus homing in on the full extent of his betrayal, Peter could answer only by appealing to the Lord's omniscience. If Peter loved the Lord, then Jesus would know it because the Lord had himself instilled the love that Peter needed: "Lord, you know everything; you know that I love you" (21:17). Peter shows that only a genuine believer can take solace in the Lord's true knowledge of our hearts.

We can see Jesus' purpose in bringing Peter to repentance not only in matching his three questions to Peter's three denials, but also in Jesus' form of address. In John's Gospel, ever since this disciple's calling to follow Jesus, he had been known as *Peter*, which means "the Rock" (John 1:42). This name refers to Peter's confession of faith, which was an example of the Great Confession on which Jesus would build his church (see Matt. 16:16–18). Now, Jesus reverts to Peter's former name, referring to him as "Simon, son of John" (John 21:15). This amounts to a temporary deposing of Peter from his office. Before there could be thought of restoring Peter to his calling as an apostle, they must first retrace the steps by which Peter could be considered even a Christian. So it is for us all: more basic than our calling to service is our calling to salvation through a loving faith in Christ.

Repentance and Restoration

Jesus had already forgiven Peter his sin, promising peace to Peter and the others on the night of his resurrection. So why did Jesus need to drive Peter to so painful a repentance? There are three answers, the first of which was *for the sake of Peter's own conscience.* Until Jesus had addressed Peter's great sin, the matter must continually hang over the disciple's spirit. Alexander Maclaren explains: "The threefold denial needed to be obliterated by the threefold confession; . . . every black mark that had been scored deep on the page by that denial needed to be covered over with the gilding or bright colouring of the triple acknowledgment. And so Peter thrice having said, 'I know him not!' Jesus with a gracious violence forced him to say thrice, 'Thou knowest that I love thee.' "[2]

Was it cruel of Jesus to require Peter to recall each shameful stage of his betrayal, dragging him, as it were, by the scruff of the neck to turn his face to the very details of his sin? No, it was true kindness to insist on Peter's repentance: "The Lord wounds only that He may heal."[3] Unlike the false prophets of Israel who sought to heal the wounds of sin lightly (cf. Jer. 6:14), Jesus demands a thorough healing so as to gain a true peace.

Jesus' kindness is seen in that at each of Peter's steps of recalling his denial, Jesus assured him not only of forgiveness but of full restoration. It would have been cruel had Jesus left Peter in doubt as to his acceptance, but Jesus did not leave any doubt. In the light of Christ's super-abounding grace, Peter was not cast down by his sin but lifted up in the amazing divine love that saved him. This example encourages Christians to seriously examine our sins before God's presence in prayer. In this way, we will grow in grace through repentance and by recalling the unfailing love that freely suffered death for our redemption. Only against the true depth of our guilt may we measure the height of God's love for us and glory in the cross of Christ as we ought.

The second reason that Peter needed to be brought to a detailed repentance was *to ensure that he learned the lesson from his failure.* Beneath Peter's sin in denying Jesus was a dangerous self-confidence. Peter had boasted of laying down his life for Jesus (John 13:37), when Peter really needed Jesus to lay down his life for him. Indeed, it is evident that the reason Jesus permitted Peter to fall, praying for his faith to be restored but handing him over to his sin (Luke 22:31–34), was the benefit to Peter upon his repentance. A. W Pink explains: "That fall was necessary in order to reveal to Peter the condition of his heart, to show him the worthlessness of self-confidence, and to humble his proud spirit."[4] We will be blessed if we learn that lesson from Peter's repentance, not needing to be allowed to fall or to suffer the pain of our own sin and repentance.

2. Alexander Maclaren, *Expositions of Holy Scripture*, 17 vols. (Grand Rapids: Baker, 1982), 11:373–74.
3. Arthur W. Pink, *Exposition of the Gospel of John* (Grand Rapids: Zondervan, 1975), 1138.
4. Ibid., 1133.

The third reason why Peter needed to repent thoroughly was *for the sake of his future calling as an apostle.* What authority could Peter wield in the matter of faith in Christ if his failure on the night of Jesus' arrest remained hanging over his head? His betrayal must have "cast a great shadow over his usefulness and, indeed, his credibility in the church and before the world."[5] This explains why Peter's repentance must take place in the presence of several other future apostles. His sin pertained to his public office in the church and thus demanded a public repentance and a public restoration by Christ.

This episode speaks directly to the question whether church leaders who fall into sin today can be restored to their office. Most commonly, we learn of pastors who fall to sexual sin and are required to quit the pulpit. In other cases, church leaders may be removed for financial fraud or abuse of spiritual authority. The question is raised whether such a fallen leader can ever be restored to his former position. We know that everyone can be restored to salvation through faith and repentance, but is it possible for a pastor or elder to be restored to office after committing a gross and scandalous sin?

In light of Jesus' treatment of Peter here, the answer must be Yes. Sins of a sexual or financial nature cannot be considered more grievous than Peter's denial of Jesus. Jesus shows us, however, that there must be a serious and determined work of repentance and not merely glib confessions or facile apologies. Since it will be harder for us to establish a true change of heart than it was for Jesus, the work of repentance and restoration today is likely to involve a lengthy period of time and a thorough process of confirmation.[6]

Following Jesus' example in refusing to use Peter's apostolic name, leaders who grievously sin should first be deposed from office to preserve the honor of Christ and the well-being of his people. Paul says that elders "who persist in sin" must be rebuked publicly before the church (1 Tim. 5:20). From this, we should conclude that the repentance of a fallen church leader should also be expressed publicly before the church. Noting the importance of a deep, thorough, and public process of repentance, however, we should also note that when true repentance has been established—including a genuine repudiation of the sin itself—we should be willing to restore fallen spiritual

5. Gordon J. Keddie, *A Study Commentary on John*, 2 vols. (Darlington, UK: Evangelical Press, 2001), 2:327.

6. Obviously, the difficulty of restoration will be related to the severity of the sin. In some extreme cases, there might be civil punishments to be served, and there might be other reasons why the loss of public reputation makes restoration to office imprudent.

leaders to their positions of service in the church. Experience might show that such restoration is rare in practice. The reason is not that restoration is impossible but rather that fallen leaders are so seldom willing to humble themselves to make an honest confession and enable the church to establish a credible and true repentance.

It may be objected that a pastor or elder who has greatly sinned cannot be trusted not to sin again. By this logic, however, no one is eligible to serve as a leader in the church, since even the holiest Christians have often sinned and even the strongest spiritual leaders can be led into sin if they are not wary regarding their lives. If we believe in the power of God's Spirit and if we can have confidence in the grace that God gives in repentance, there is no reason for us to lack confidence in a restored leader's ability to serve in a godly and effective way. Peter's example after he was restored, recorded in the book of Acts and reflected in his letters, proves the power of Christ's restoring grace. For Christians who repent and look anew to Christ, failure is never final.

THE PASTORAL CALLING

As Jesus secured Peter's repentance with three demands to affirm his love, he also restored Peter with three commissions to the pastoral office. When Peter first answered, "Yes, Lord; you know that I love you," Jesus answered, "Feed my lambs" (John 21:15). When Peter affirmed his love a second time, Jesus said, "Tend my sheep" (21:16). Finally, when Peter answered Jesus' question by asserting Christ's knowledge of his love, Jesus concluded, "Feed my sheep" (21:17). In his abounding grace, Jesus did not say, "All right, Peter, you are forgiven. But of course, I can never use you in a place of leadership again." That might be the way we would reason about Peter, but it is not how Jesus responded. Instead, Jesus publicly restored Peter to his calling as a shepherd over the flock of God.

Observing Peter's restoration, we can note three important things about the pastoral office to which Peter and the other apostles were called. The first is that those called to spiritual leadership are shepherds over the flock that belongs to Jesus and is precious to the Lord. Notice that Jesus told Peter to serve "my lambs" and "my sheep" (John 21:15–17). Pastors should therefore not be surprised when believers are weak and immature, since Christ calls them "lambs," nor that the "sheep" are prone to wander and are in need of constant care, proper feeding, and leading. Most importantly, a pastor is to remember that the church is composed of lambs that Jesus says are "mine." James Montgomery Boice comments: "There is nothing that will make us more diligent in Christ's service than the firm recognition that we are only undershepherds of that Chief Shepherd to whom the flock belongs and to whom we are responsible."[7] Similarly, since Christ has no possession more dear to him than the souls of those for whom he shed his precious blood, his confidence in the restored Peter is seen in his committing of these sheep to Peter's care.

Second, we have in Peter's restoration a helpful description of the pastoral calling. To what work is a pastor called by Christ? First, Jesus said, "Feed my lambs." Next, he told Peter, "Tend my sheep." Finally, Jesus returned to the initial theme, saying, "Feed my sheep."

Here we see the two dimensions of the pastoral calling. Like the apostles before them, pastors today are called to the work of feeding the flock of God with the spiritual nourishment of God's Word and also of shepherding and leading the flock through pastoral care.

There is no warrant for the Roman Catholic dogma that here the church is placed under Peter's sole authority as the single potentate who rules in the absence of Christ. The book of Acts shows that Peter never claimed or exercised such a lordly rule over the church. Matthew Henry comments: "This charge given to Peter to preach the gospel is by a strange artifice made to support the usurpation of his pretended successors, that fleece the sheep, and, instead of feeding them, feed upon them."[8]

Paul's description agrees with that of Jesus in speaking not of princes over the church, but of Christ's providing "shepherds and teachers" to serve the church (Eph. 4:11). Paul's description perfectly matches Jesus' calling to Peter to feed the sheep and tend the flock. Ministers of the gospel are not called to be fund-raisers, program organizers, building custodians, or committee chairmen, but teachers of God's Word and pastors of Christ's flock.

Since Jesus places his sheep under the care and feeding of his undershepherds, this makes membership in a faithful church a matter of urgent

7. James Montgomery Boice, *The Gospel of John*, 5 vols. (Grand Rapids: Baker, 1999), 5:1642.

8. Matthew Henry, *Commentary on the Whole Bible*, 6 vols. (Peabody, MA: Hendrickson, 2009), 5:995.

concern for every follower of Christ. Decades later, Peter would himself pen the classic description of the kind of faithful shepherd the church needs: "Shepherd the flock of God that is among you, exercising oversight, not under compulsion, but willingly, as God would have you; not for shameful gain, but eagerly; not domineering over those in your charge, but being examples to the flock. And when the chief Shepherd appears, you will receive the unfading crown of glory" (1 Peter 5:2–4).

We must never slight the pastor's calling to lead the flock, but we should note that Jesus emphasizes the teaching function of his shepherds. Jesus specified the feeding of his sheep first and last to Peter. This tells us that a pastor's primary responsibility is to feed the flock of Christ. How are Christ's sheep to be fed? The Bible's answer: by teaching and preaching the Word of God. To be called by Christ to the pastoral office is therefore to be gifted and prepared to preach and teach the Scriptures with fidelity and power. Called to this work, a faithful pastor must devote a significant portion of his working time to the prayerful preparation of his teaching so as to most wholesomely feed the beloved sheep who belong to Jesus.

Boice suggests five principles for a successful ministry of God's Word. First, the Bible should be taught on a regular schedule, primarily in "the preaching that goes on Sunday by Sunday in a faithful, Bible-teaching church." Second, the Bible should be taught in a systematic manner, ideally in the sequential exposition of whole books of Scripture. In this way, the church is fed with a balanced diet of the whole counsel of God. Third, the Bible should be taught as comprehensively as possible. This means that Christians are not to be focused only on prophecy or Pauline theology or creation studies but should be taught from all the kinds of biblical literature. Fourth, pastors must preach and churches must receive God's Word prayerfully. With David, we must ask the Lord: "Open my eyes, that I may behold wondrous things out of your law" (Ps. 119:18). Finally, the Bible must be taught obediently. Boice comments: "When God speaks, he speaks for a purpose. He expects us to obey him. Do we obey him? If we do, our lives and the lives of those for whom we are responsible will be changed."[9]

9. Boice, *John*, 5:1643–44.

A final point seen in Jesus' restoration of Peter is the primacy of love for those who lead Christ's flock. Indeed, the fact that Jesus confronted Peter over the matter of his love shows the importance of love for the whole of the Christian life. R. Kent Hughes comments:

> The abiding principle is that before all things, even service to him, we must love him with all our hearts. That is the highest priority in life. It is the first question for every theologian. It is the essential question for the pastor. It is the supreme question for every missionary. It is the number one question for every one of us who wants to please God. Loving God is the highest priority of our lives.[10]

Love for Christ is preeminently necessary for the shepherds of Christ's flock. Ligon Duncan tells of an aged saintly woman of the Scottish kirk who said, "The older I grow, the more I love the Lord's people." "Isn't that sweet," thought the man to whom she spoke. She continued, however, "The older I grow, the more I love the Lord's people and the less I trust them." Duncan comments: "The Lord's people will hurt you. You will seek to serve the Lord's people; they will let you down. When that happens, you are being given the privilege of reflecting your Savior, because he washed the feet of the disciples who abandoned him."[11]

It is only love for Christ and his church that empowers us to continue serving Christ's flock when the church fails us. A. W. Pink observes: "The work is so laborious, the appreciation is often so small, the response so discouraging, the criticisms so harsh, the attacks of Satan so fierce, that only the 'love of Christ'—His for us and ours for Him—can 'constrain' to such work. 'Hirelings' will feed the goats, but only those who love Christ can feed His sheep."[12] Love for Christ's flock will give a pastor persuasiveness with his congregation, patience for their failings, and an eloquence that mere learning can never supply. When it comes to shepherding the flock of Christ, "other qualities may be desirable, but love is completely indispensable."[13]

---

10. R. Kent Hughes, *John: That You May Believe* (Wheaton, IL: Crossway, 1999), 473.

11. J. Ligon Duncan, "One People," in *Only One Way? Reaffirming the Exclusive Truth Claims of Christianity*, ed. Richard D. Phillips (Wheaton, IL: Crossway, 2006), 121.

12. Pink, *John*, 1139–40.

13. Morris, *The Gospel according to John*, 772.

To Love Thee More

We should not conclude our study of this passage without asking Jesus' question to Peter of ourselves. "Do you love me?" Jesus asks. It is essential that we be able to answer this question, apart from which no further advance can be made.

Thankfully, Jesus did not say, "Do you love me perfectly?" or "Do you love me as I deserve?"—in which case we must all be turned away, abashed. He simply asks for our love. If we belong to Jesus, then like Peter, even filled with self-doubt and shame, we may answer, "Lord, you know." "You know all my failings, all my weaknesses, and all my needs. But you also know that, Yes, I do love you." Implied in that answer, of course, is a desire to love Jesus better and more completely, a longing to love him as he deserves to be adored by his redeemed people. The way to love Jesus more fully is to spend time with him, since we long to be with those we love. So let us be eager to open up Christ's Word and fervent in opening our hearts in prayer. William Cowper supplies words that will help us to answer Jesus' plea when we pray:

> Lord, it is my chief complaint
> That my love is weak and faint;
> Yet I love Thee and adore,—
> Oh! for grace to love Thee more![14]

---

14. William Cowper, "Hark, My Soul, It Is the Lord!" (1768).

141

THE ORIGINAL AND
ETERNAL CALL

John 21:18–25

*Jesus said to him, "If it is my will that he remain until I come,
what is that to you? You follow me!"* (John 21:22)

he final words in John's Gospel speak of the immensity of the
glory of Jesus: "Now there are also many other things that Jesus
did. Were every one of them to be written, I suppose that the
world itself could not contain the books that would be written" (John 21:25).
These words, according to J. C. Ryle, "bring to an end the most precious book
in the Bible." He compares our reading of John's final verse to "listening to
the parting words of a friend."[1] Anyone who has devoted a great deal of time
to studying this great Gospel record is bound to regret its end and wish that
John might have told us more of the "many other things" to which he refers.

John's conclusion does not focus on the actual final words that Jesus spoke
before his ascension into heaven, words known to us as the Great Commission: "Go therefore and make disciples of all nations" (Matt. 28:19). Instead,

---

1. J. C. Ryle, *Expository Thoughts on the Gospels: John*, 3 vols. (Edinburgh: Banner of Truth,
1999), 3:510.

John concludes his Gospel with the meeting of Jesus with his disciples beside the Sea of Galilee, which reaches back to when he first called his disciples. "Follow me," Jesus had invited them (John 1:43). In the twenty-one chapters of John's Gospel since that calling, the disciples had received quite an education in following Jesus. They had been present for his staggering miracles, both public and private, such as the feeding of the five thousand and the raising of Lazarus from the grave. They had received Jesus' teaching and seen displays of his divine majesty. They had witnessed the mounting opposition and ultimately the rejection of Jesus, followed by his tortured death on the cross. The despair that followed was countered by the astonished joy of his resurrection. Because of these dramatic experiences, the disciples were no longer the men they had been when Jesus first called them to follow. Yet here at the end of his ministry, Jesus renews that original call. John has told us that the purpose of his Gospel is to lead us to faith in Jesus as "the Christ, the Son of God" (20:31). Now, in concluding his Gospel, John provides Jesus' own definition of saving faith: "Follow me" (21:19). James Montgomery Boice observes that these words "are a reminder that Christianity is Christ, not just believing in some abstract sense, but believing in him to the point of turning our back on all else to follow him."[2]

Different Experiences in Life and Death

A common mistake that Christians and sometimes churches make is to expect everyone's experience in following Christ to be exactly the same. This meeting with his disciples by the lake, however, shows something of the great variety that there is in the Christian experience. We can see these differences simply by comparing Peter with John. Peter is consistently portrayed as an impetuous man of action: he was the first to enter the empty tomb and was the one who dived off the fishing boat in order to race into Jesus' presence. John was more reflective and perceptive. In Jesus' empty tomb, it was John who understood the meaning. Here on the lake, it was John who alerted the others, "It is the Lord!" (John 21:7). There are strengths and weaknesses to different kinds of personalities, so no Christian should feel pressure to adopt a personality different from the one that God gave to

2. James Montgomery Boice, *The Gospel of John*, 5 vols. (Grand Rapids: Baker, 1999), 5:1654.

him or her. Instead, God places us into churches where different kinds of Christians can work together in partnership, just as Peter and John served so effectively together in the early days of the church.

Jesus gave a prophecy to Peter that speaks to a difference between the experience of the young and the old: "Truly, truly, I say to you, when you were young, you used to dress yourself and walk wherever you wanted, but when you are old, you will stretch out your hands, and another will dress you and carry you where you do not want to go" (John 21:18). In Peter's young days, he was free to do what he wanted. But in his old age, he would have to learn to handle limitations. The young are eager to make a mark on the world, unbounded in their confidence of changing things for the better. Lacking experience, however, young Christians will sometimes make foolish choices. Aged Christians have usually learned what to do, but often lack the ability to do it. The church needs both impetuous youth and veteran realism, and both life settings have much to offer the church while requiring their own kinds of grace from the Lord.

Jesus' parting ministry especially highlighted the different deaths by which Peter and John would glorify him. Peter, we learn, would get the wish he expressed on the night of Jesus' arrest: "Lord, why can I not follow you now? I will lay down my life for you" (John 13:37). On that occasion, Jesus replied by prophesying Peter's denials. Yet Jesus added that while Peter could not follow Jesus to the cross then, "you will follow afterward" (13:36). Now, Jesus foretells Peter's crucifixion, saying that "when you are old, you will stretch out your hands, and another will dress you and carry you where you do not want to go" (21:18). The expression "stretch out your hands" was used specifically to speak of those who were laid out on a cross for execution.[3] Just as Jesus was given his cross and then taken to the place of torment and death, Peter would be put to the cross and taken to the place of his execution, which Jesus refers to as "where you do not want to go."

It was the uniform testimony of the early church that Jesus' prophecy was fulfilled in the early days of the Roman emperor Nero's persecution, around A.D. 64. Eusebius's *Church History* from the fourth century A.D. states that Peter was crucified head downward by his own request, perhaps to make restitution for his earlier denials.[4] This seems unlikely, since a mature Peter

3. See C. K. Barrett, *The Gospel according to John* (London: SPCK, 1956), 585.
4. Eusebius, *The Ecclesiastical History*, 3.1.

716

would have known better than to seek atonement by any other means than Christ's suffering for our sins. Moreover, earlier sources, such as Clement of Rome in A.D. 96 and Tertullian in A.D. 212, affirm Peter's martyrdom in a way that fulfilled Jesus' prophecy, but make no mention of Peter's being crucified upside down.[5] On his own cross, Peter would be given grace to "glorify God" in his death (John 21:19), having previously failed Christ because of his fear of death.

John, on the other hand, is reputed to have been the only apostle who did not suffer a martyr's death, though he was much persecuted. When Peter inquired about John's death, Jesus answered: "If it is my will that he remain until I come, what is that to you?" (John 21:22). John points out that this saying gave rise to the spurious rumor that he would not die until Jesus returned, a tradition that John was keen to correct in verse 23. This false report reminds us that not all traditions from the early church are true. As Jesus suggests, John's death was different from Peter's, the Beloved Disciple dying in bed instead of suffering on a cross. The point is that Christians will face different death situations by which we may glorify God.

Those who are persecuted for Jesus are granted an especially powerful platform to witness by means of their courage and faith. Some of the most famous examples were given by the English Reformers. These were men who preached to considerable effect during the days when a pro-gospel party was in power over the nation. After six years of freedom to preach, however, Queen Mary I, the Roman Catholic zealot known to history as "Bloody Mary," came to the throne in 1553. She immediately outlawed gospel preaching and soon sent the Reformed preachers to be burned alive at the stake. This terrible ordeal gave the gospel heralds their most potent platform for glorifying God, and the spiritual power they displayed in death indelibly engraved their witness to Christ upon the nation's heart.

One of the English martyrs was Rowland Taylor. The people who attended his parting watched him say good-bye to his family. "Farewell, my dear wife," he began: "be of good comfort, for I am quiet in my conscience. God shall raise up a father for my children." To one daughter, Taylor then said, "God bless thee, and make thee His servant." Kissing his older daughter, he said, "God bless thee. I pray you all stand strong and steadfast to Christ and his

5. Tertullian, *Antidote for the Scorpion's Sting*, 15.

Word, and keep you from idolatry." Taking his place at the stake, Taylor spoke out: "Good people, I have taught you nothing but God's Holy Word, and those lessons that I have taken out of God's blessed Book—the Holy Bible; and I am come hither this day to seal it with my blood." When the flames were lit, Taylor held up his hands and called upon God: "Merciful Father of heaven, for Jesus Christ my Saviour's sake, receive my soul into Thy hands." There he stood in the flames without crying out or moving, until one of the guards struck his head and ended his life.[6]

Few Christians will be granted the opportunity of sealing their life's witness in so dramatic a dying witness. But in all the varieties of life and death, we should aim to exhibit our faith to Christ's glory. J. C. Ryle states: "Let us pray, while we live in health, that we may glorify God in our end. Let us leave it to God to choose the where, and when, and how, and all the manner of our departing. Let us only ask that it may 'glorify God.'"[7]

TAKING UP THE CROSS

The experience of one Christian may vary considerably from that of another, but all Christians share a common calling, which Jesus spoke to Peter: "Follow me" (John 21:19). According to the New Testament, following Jesus includes two dimensions: a lifestyle of learning from Jesus through his Word, and a willing embrace of cross-bearing self-denial.

First, to follow Jesus is to abide in his Word so as to grow in our knowledge of his teaching and experience of his life. "If you abide in my word," Jesus said, "you are truly my disciples, and you will know the truth, and the truth will set you free" (John 8:31–32). Studying John's Gospel, believers are drawn into the truth and life of Jesus. "I am the light of the world," he said. "Whoever follows me will not walk in darkness, but will have the light of life" (8:12). In Matthew's Gospel, Jesus said, "Take my yoke upon you, and learn from me, for I am gentle and lowly in heart, and you will find rest for your souls" (Matt. 11:29). A life of following Jesus is therefore one of daily, prayerful devotion to his Word, as his Spirit shines in our hearts to illumine the pages of Holy Scripture.

6. J. C. Ryle, *Light from Old Times* (1890; repr., Moscow, ID: Charles Noland, 2000), 129–32.
7. Ryle, *John*, 3:513.

Second, following Jesus requires a Christian to deny himself and take up his cross. This was Jesus' clearest explanation of discipleship: "If anyone would come after me, let him deny himself and take up his cross daily and follow me. For whoever would save his life will lose it, but whoever loses his life for my sake will save it" (Luke 9:23–24).

Christian self-denial begins with the renunciation of any righteousness of our own before God. Christians renounce our pride and humble ourselves before God, seeking his saving mercy through the grace of Christ. Christian self-denial also requires us to renounce all sin. This is not to say that Christians cease sinning completely, which is impossible because of our ongoing struggle with a sinful nature (cf. 1 John 1:8). But Christians do turn from sin and earnestly seek God's grace to live a new and holy life that pleases God. John Stott writes: "We cannot follow Christ without forsaking sin. . . . It is not sufficient to feel pangs of remorse or to make some kind of apology to God. Fundamentally, repentance . . . is an inward change of mind and attitude towards sin which leads to a change of behavior."[8]

Many Christians find it hard to imagine leaving certain sinful habits behind. But those who follow Jesus renounce such sins by appealing to the Savior to provide the power we need to repent. An old Puritan prayer asks the Lord: "Give me to die with You that I may rise to new life, for I wish to be as dead and buried to sin, to selfishness, and to the world, that I might not hear the voice of the tempter and might be delivered from his lusts."[9] That is the petition of the sin-renouncing follower of Christ.

Self-denial further requires us to be willing to accept any calling of Christ or any change that is God's will for our lives. "Whoever loses his life for my sake," Jesus said, "will find it" (Matt. 10:39). God might call a Christian woman to the mission field in a way that seems to imperil her chances for marriage. If she is to follow Christ, she will deny herself and go where the Lord calls. Following Christ might require a man to abandon his career in order to preach the gospel. Christian self-denial might cause a family to move into a poor neighborhood as part of a

---

8. John Stott, *Basic Christianity* (1958; repr., Downers Grove, IL: InterVarsity Press, 2006), 138–39.

9. Arthur Bennett, ed., *The Valley of Vision: A Collection of Puritan Prayers and Devotions* (Edinburgh: Banner of Truth, 1975), 172.

Christian witness to the city. Likewise, following Christ might require a believer to remain right where he or she is, learning to be content and offering his or her best service to the Lord in the church and in his or her worldly setting.

Finally, Christian self-denial will require followers of Jesus to actively embrace crosses that will be painful and cause suffering. Jesus said that to follow him is to "take up [your] cross daily" (Luke 9:23). By this, Jesus does not mean some unavoidable circumstances that we consider to be "carrying our cross." True cross-bearing, like Christ's, is voluntary and intentional, freely accepting worldly scorn and even persecution for the sake of Christ.

It is perhaps because so few Christians really take up the cross that the church in the West today is not persecuted so much as ignored. The Christians who are made to suffer for Christ are those who refuse to compromise with the world and therefore are most useful to it. Stott comments:

> If we were to hold fast the old-fashioned Gospel of Christ crucified for sinners, and of salvation as an absolutely free and undeserved gift, then the Cross would again become a stumbling block to the proud. If we were to maintain the high moral standards of Jesus—of uncorruptible honesty and integrity, of chastity before marriage and fidelity in it, and of costly, self-sacrificial love, then there would be a public outcry that the church had returned to Puritanism. If we were to dare once more to talk plainly about the alternatives of life and death, salvation and judgment, heaven and hell, then the world would rise up in anger against such "old-fashioned rubbish."[10]

Do self-denial and cross-bearing seem unappealing? Yet those who take up the cross are drawn into an ever-deepening fellowship with Jesus, a holy communion that is worth more than all the treasures of the world. It is the cross-bearing Christian, the believer who actively embraces a countercultural, Christ-following lifestyle, who learns the reality of Psalm 16:11: "You make known to me the path of life; in your presence there is fullness of joy; at your right hand are pleasures forevermore."

10. John Stott, quoted in R. Kent Hughes, *John: That You May Believe* (Wheaton, IL: Crossway, 1999), 481.

A SAVIOR TO FOLLOW

In these final verses of John's Gospel, we encounter several additional compelling reasons to follow Jesus. The first is that Jesus is a sovereign Savior, *who rules with divine foreknowledge over our lives.* Jesus proved his foreknowledge by accurately prophesying the circumstances of both Peter's and John's deaths. What a comfort it is, and a cause for anticipation, for believers to realize that our Savior has appointed all that lies ahead of us. Following Jesus means an unfolding of God's will for our service and ministry in his kingdom. Moreover, while we discover much of Christ's will as it happens, we have certain knowledge of where following Jesus will lead us. Jesus said, "For this is the will of my Father, that everyone who looks on the Son and believes in him should have eternal life, and I will raise him up on the last day" (John 6:40).

Second, we follow a Savior *who has left a sure witness to his gospel.* This is emphasized in John's next-to-last verse: "This is the disciple who is bearing witness about these things, and who has written these things" (John 21:24). "This . . . disciple" refers back to verse 20, which identifies the author as the apostle John: "the disciple whom Jesus loved . . . , the one who had been reclining at table close to him and had said, 'Lord, who is it that is going to betray you?'" (21:20). Just as Jesus was well suited to reveal God, being the One "in the bosom of the Father" (1:18 KJV), John is ideally suited to give his eyewitness testimony to Jesus, being "the disciple whom Jesus loved."

Scholars debate the significance of the statement "and we know that his testimony is true" (John 21:24). Does the first-person plural suggest that some group of people—perhaps the elders from John's church in Ephesus—added their certification as to the truthfulness of John's account? This is possible, and if so, the statement would add one more attestation to both John's authorship of this Gospel and the truthfulness of its testimony. It seems more likely, however, that John himself speaks in the first-person plural, addressing himself with special formality because he is aware of making a solemn declaration in the sight of heaven. Moreover, there are many examples in John's writings in which the apostle used the plural "we" for emphasis (John 3:2, 11; 20:2; 1 John 1:2, 4–7; 3 John 12). John's insistence that "we know that his testimony is true" (John 21:24) amounts to a solemn oath testifying that Jesus has left us an accurate, inspired testimony in this Gospel so that we may confidently follow Christ through his Word.

Third, in Jesus believers follow a Savior *who goes before us*. As we take up our cross and follow Jesus, we look up and see the cross he bore for us. The path of discipleship that believers tread is worn with the footsteps of Jesus himself: our Lord has faced and conquered the threats that we face, and Jesus laid down his life to open the passage for his sheep.

This is why Jesus stresses to Peter the importance of the disciple's keeping his eyes on his Master. When Jesus had told Peter about the manner of his death, Peter saw John walking up behind and asked, "Lord, what about this man?" There is nothing wrong with a gracious interest in the Lord's will for others, but Peter was taking his eye off Jesus and concerning himself with the affairs of another believer. Therefore, Jesus rebuked him, saying, "If it is my will that he remain until I come, what is that to you? You follow me!" (John 21:21–22). The point of this reproof was not to teach that John would live forever, but rather to remind Peter to keep his eyes fixed on his Lord. Once earlier, Peter had walked on the water of this very lake when Jesus called him. While Peter looked on Jesus, he walked on the waves. But when Peter looked away from Jesus to see the danger around him, he sank into the waters. Now, Peter was taking his eyes off Jesus in order to compare his situation with that of other believers.

The temptation to look not at Jesus but at the circumstances of fellow believers is a serious one. Matthew Henry warns: "So apt are we to be busy in other men's matters, but negligent in the concerns of our own souls—quick-sighted abroad, but dim-sighted at home—judging others, and prognosticating what they will do, when we have enough to do to prove our own work and understand our own way."[11]

In his *Narnia* novel *A Horse and His Boy*, C. S. Lewis depicts this principle through a conversation between Aslan, the Christ-figure lion, and the boy Shasta, recounting the ways in which Aslan had been present during the events of the boy's life. He was the one who drove the jackals away while Shasta slept and propelled the boat that carried Shasta to the shore to receive help. The boy listens and begins to understand that his life has

---

11. Matthew Henry, *Commentary on the Whole Bible*, 6 vols. (Peabody, MA: Hendrickson, 2009), 5:998.

been shaped by the grace of a Savior. He then asks, "Then it was you who wounded Aravis?" "It was I," Aslan answers. "But what for?" Shasta asks. "Child," the lion replies, "I am telling your story, not hers. I tell no one any story but his own."[12]

Fourth, in following Jesus we look to a Savior *who has promised to come again*. In his comments about John, Jesus spoke of his remaining "until I come" (John 21:22). This provides all the more reason for us to follow by keeping our eyes on Jesus. For we know that if we do, the day will come when Jesus "will 'turn around' and look at us, and we will see him face to face."[13] We will then ask Jesus where he has been leading us, and he will remind us of his prayer to the Father: "I desire that they also, whom you have given me, may be with me where I am, to see my glory" (17:24).

The Glory of Unending Discipleship

John concludes his Gospel with words that seem almost fanciful, but convey an earnest message: "Now there are also many other things that Jesus did. Were every one of them to be written, I suppose that the world itself could not contain the books that would be written" (John 21:25). This reminds us of the sufficiency of the written testimony of the Scriptures. The apostles could have written more, but they provided what is needed to bring us to saving faith in Jesus. "In the beginning was the Word, and the Word was with God, and the Word was God," John began (1:1). "In him was life, and the life was the light of men" (1:4). "To all who did receive him, who believed in his name, he gave the right to become children of God" (1:12). "And the Word became flesh and dwelt among us, and we have seen his glory, glory as of the only Son from the Father, full of grace and truth" (1:14). These are the themes that John was commissioned in the Spirit to record for us, along with the great testimony, "Behold, the Lamb of God, who takes away the sin of the world!" (1:29). Of this ample and sufficient testimony, Jesus said: "Truly, truly, I say to you, whoever hears my word and believes him who sent me has eternal life. He does not come into judgment, but has passed from death to life" (5:24).

12. Quoted in Hughes, *John*, 482.
13. Bruce Milne, *The Message of John: Here Is Your King!* (Downers Grove, IL: InterVarsity Press, 1993), 320.

Given all the glories unfolded for us in the Gospel of John, what a marvel it is to learn that there is so much more yet to learn and experience of Jesus. Following Jesus is eternally immense; ours is a massively glorious calling! If the world could not contain everything there is to say about our Lord, those who follow him into glory will take infinite delight in the eternal exploration of his grace and truth.

Jesus says, "Follow me," at the commencement of our newborn spiritual life. He repeats, "Follow me," at every step of our Christian journey through this world. But Jesus will also be summoning us to follow him for unbroken eons in the eternal glory to come. Following Jesus now is only the beginning. The cross we bear in this world we will exchange for a crown of glory in heaven. "Whoever has seen me has seen the Father," he told the disciples (John 14:9), and there will be more and more of us to see and know and glory in God forever and ever as we follow his Son with adoring eyes.

"Follow me," Jesus says at the beginning, and the way of the cross seems immeasurably hard. But if we fix our eyes on him, "the founder and perfecter of our faith" (Heb. 12:2), we find that his grace changes everything and changes us. Isn't that what we have witnessed in the Gospel of John? The further we go in following Jesus, and the further into glory he leads us in the ages yet to come, we will trace our experience in lines of worship and song:

> Jesus, lover of my soul, let me to Thy bosom fly . . . .
> Other refuge have I none, hangs my helpless soul on Thee. . . .
> Thou, O Christ, art all I want; more than all in Thee I find . . . .
> Spring Thou up within my heart; rise to all eternity.[14]

14. Charles Wesley, "Jesus, Lover of My Soul" (1740).

Select Bibliography of Commentaries Cited or Consulted

Augustine. *Homilies on the Gospel of John*. In *Nicene and Post-Nicene Fathers*, edited by Philip Schaff. 13 vols. Peabody, MA: Hendrickson, 1999.

Barclay, William. *The Gospel of John*. 2 vols. Philadelphia: Westminster, 1975.

Barnhouse, Donald Grey. *Illustrating the Gospel of John*. Grand Rapids: Revell, 1973.

Barrett, C. K. *The Gospel according to John*. London: SPCK, 1956.

Beasley-Murray, George R. *John*. Word Biblical Commentary 36. Waco, TX: Word, 1987.

Boice, James Montgomery. *The Gospel of John*. 5 vols. Grand Rapids: Baker, 1999.

Borchert, Gerald L. *John 12–21*. Nashville: Broadman & Holman, 2002.

Bruce, F. F. *The Gospel of John*. Grand Rapids: Eerdmans, 1983.

Burge, Gary M. *John*. NIV Application Commentary. Grand Rapids: Zondervan, 2000.

Calvin, John. *Calvin's Commentaries*. Translated by William Pringle. 22 vols. Grand Rapids: Baker, 2009.

———. *New Testament Commentaries*. Translated by T. H. L. Parker. 12 vols. Grand Rapids: Eerdmans, 1959.

Carson, D. A. *The Gospel of John*. Grand Rapids: Eerdmans, 1991.

Dodd, C. H. *Historical Tradition in the Fourth Gospel*. Cambridge: Cambridge University Press, 1963.

Flavel, John. *The Works of John Flavel*. 6 vols. 1820. Reprint, Edinburgh: Banner of Truth, 1968.

Godet, Frédéric Louis. *Commentary on the Gospel of John*. 2 vols. Grand Rapids: Zondervan, 1893.

Hendriksen, William. *Exposition of the Gospel according to John*. New Testament Commentary. Grand Rapids: Baker, 1953.

Henry, Matthew. *Commentary on the Whole Bible*. 6 vols. Peabody, MA: Hendrickson, 2009.

Hughes, R. Kent. *John: That You May Believe*. Wheaton, IL: Crossway, 1999.

Hutcheson, George. *Exposition of the Gospel of John*. Lafayette, IN: Sovereign Grace Publishers, 2001.

Johnson, Mark. *Let's Study John*. Edinburgh: Banner of Truth, 2003.

Keddie, Gordon J. *A Study Commentary on John*. 2 vols. Darlington, UK: Evangelical Press, 2001.

Kostenberger, Andreas J. *John*. Grand Rapids: Baker, 2004.

Krummacher, F. W. *The Suffering Saviour*. 1856. Reprint, Edinburgh: Banner of Truth, 2004.

Luther, Martin. *Luther's Works*. Vol. 22, *Sermons on the Gospel of St. John, Chapters 1–4*. St. Louis: Concordia, 1957.

Maclaren, Alexander. *Expositions of Holy Scripture*. 17 vols. Grand Rapids: Baker, 1982.

Meyer, F. B. *The Life of Love*. Old Tappan, NJ: Revell, 1987.

Milne, Bruce. *The Message of John: Here Is Your King!* Downers Grove, IL: InterVarsity Press, 1993.

Morris, Leon. *The Gospel according to John*. Rev. ed. New International Commentary on the New Testament. Grand Rapids: Eerdmans, 1995.

———. *Reflections on the Gospel of John*. Peabody, MA: Hendrickson, 1986.

Palmer, B. M. *Sermons*. 2 vols. 1875. Reprint, Harrisonburg, VA: Sprinkle, 2002.

Pink, Arthur W. *Exposition of the Gospel of John*. Grand Rapids: Zondervan, 1975.

Ridderbos, Herman. *John: A Theological Commentary*. Grand Rapids: Zondervan, 1997.

Ryan, Joseph "Skip." *That You May Believe*. Wheaton, IL: Crossway, 2003.

Ryle, J. C. *Expository Thoughts on the Gospels: John.* 3 vols. Edinburgh: Banner of Truth, 1999.

Sproul, R. C. *John.* Orlando: Reformation Trust, 2009.

Spurgeon, Charles H. *Majesty in Misery.* 2 vols. Edinburgh: Banner of Truth, 2005.

———. *Metropolitan Tabernacle Pulpit.* No. 1212. Pasadena, TX: Pilgrim, 1969.

Index of Scripture

Genesis
1—**1:**75, 305
1:1—**1:**7, 167; **2:**417
1:1–2—**2:**666
1:3—**1:**8, 18, 20
1:26—**1:**8, 11, 55, 465;
   2:137, 466
1:27—**1:**293; **2:**401
1:28—**2:**675
1:31—**1:**549
2:2–3—**1:**304
2:7—**2:**666
2:10—**2:**614
2:15–25—**1:**304
2:16–17—**2:**207, 569
2:17—**1:**60, 181; **2:**27, 569
2:25—**2:**555
3—**1:**143; **2:**197
3:1—**2:**207
3:1–7—**1:**560
3:4–5—**2:**105
3:5—**1:**203
3:7—**2:**555
3:7–8—**1:**239
3:14—**2:**298
3:15—**2:**36, 175, 527
3:18—**2:**526, 555
3:21—**2:**293, 569
3:24—**2:**206
4:2—**1:**643
4:12—**1:**511; **2:**197

4:23—**1:**511
6:5—**1:**163
8:11—**1:**91
11:1–9—**2:**197
12:3—**1:**572; **2:**457
14:18—**1:**572
14:22—**2:**417
15:5—**1:**572
16:13—**2:**417
17:1—**2:**417
18:3—**1:**559
18:10—**1:**559
18:13—**1:**559
18:17—**1:**559
18:17–18—**2:**305
18:19—**1:**559
18:20—**1:**559
18:25—**1:**182, 238
21:10—**1:**551
22:7–8—**1:**86; **2:**548
22:12—**2:**50
22:12–13—**2:**548
22:14—**1:**573; **2:**418
24—**1:**395
28:12—**1:**119
28:17—**1:**119
28:19—**1:**119
30—**1:**395
45:26—**2:**652
46:3–4—**2:**621
50:20—**2:**11

Exodus
3:1–2—**1:**643
3:14—**1:**260, 385, 512, 574;
   2:418, 493
6:6—**2:**578
12—**1:**86
12:5—**2:**521
12:11—**1:**352
12:13—**2:**36
12:22—**2:**568
12:32—**2:**366
12:46—**2:**601
13:21—**1:**514
16—**1:**305
16:1–8—**1:**351
16:4—**1:**388
17:6—**2:**594
19:5—**1:**39
20:3—**1:**257
20:5—**1:**578
20:8–10—**1:**302, 466, 598
20:8–11—**1:**304
20:10—**1:**596
20:12—**2:**560
25:22—**1:**261
29:38–39—**1:**86
31:12–17—**1:**304
32:5—**1:**258
32:22—**1:**259
33:13—**2:**266
33:18—**1:**61; **2:**213

33:18-20—**1**:70
33:19—**2**:213, 480
33:20—**1**:61
34:30—**2**:401
40:13—**2**:447

Leviticus
8:30—**2**:448
16—**1**:344
16:10—**1**:344
16:21-22—**2**:523
16:27—**2**:547
17:10-14—**1**:424
19:18—**2**:178
20—**1**:500
23:5-8—**2**:499
23:15-16—**1**:454; **2**:631
23:36—**1**:480

Numbers
1:46—**1**:53n1
2:17—**1**:56
3:4—**1**:258
6:24-26—**2**:675
11:13—**1**:412
11:15—**2**:439
12:3—**1**:204
21—**1**:162
21:4-6—**1**:162
21:4-9—**1**:407
21:8-9—**1**:163
24:17—**1**:341
27:16-17—**1**:630

Deuteronomy
6:4—**1**:310
7:7-8—**1**:170
13:1-5—**1**:519, 597
16:1-8—**1**:451
16:9-12—**1**:451
16:13-15—**1**:451
16:16—**1**:451

17:6—**1**:519
17:7—**1**:503
18:15—**1**:353, 490
18:15-16—**1**:116
18:18—**1**:77; **2**:163, 528
18:21-22—**1**:519
19:15—**1**:519; **2**:600
21:23—**1**:435; **2**:576, 596
22:22—**1**:500
27:4—**1**:244
27:4-5—**1**:244
27:26—**1**:435
28:2-6—**1**:243
28:15-19—**1**:244
28:15-68—**1**:249
31:6—**1**:542; **2**:261
31:16—**2**:15
34:5—**2**:305

Joshua
1:5—**2**:261
7:25-26—**2**:620
24:15—**2**:305

Judges
2:10—**1**:99; **2**:399

Ruth
2:14—**2**:168
3:18—**2**:471

1 Samuel
1:3—**2**:418
2:9—**1**:511
3:9—**1**:566
13:14—**1**:204
16:7—**1**:141
18:1—**1**:201
18:4—**1**:201

2 Samuel
7:12-13—**2**:109

7:13—**2**:528
7:13-14—**1**:248
11:2-4—**2**:185
11:27—**1**:236-37
15:31—**2**:165
17:23—**2**:165
23:4—**1**:20

1 Kings
1:33-38—**2**:523
8:10—**2**:413
8:12—**1**:70
10:1—**2**:677
10:2-3—**2**:677
10:7—**1**:287; **2**:677
13:2—**2**:620
13:6—**2**:366
16:18—**2**:620
17:17-24—**1**:313, 444
18:35—**1**:417
18:38-39—**1**:417
19:4—**2**:439
19:11—**2**:214
19:11-12—**2**:218
19:18—**2**:610

2 Kings
1:8—**1**:77
4:32-37—**1**:313
4:42-44—**1**:351
5:5—**1**:434
5:7—**1**:313
5:10—**1**:434
5:12—**1**:434
15:7—**2**:619
17:24—**1**:220
20:20—**1**:589
23:4—**2**:620

2 Chronicles
16:14—**2**:618
32:30—**1**:589

Nehemiah
8:10—**2:**421

Job
11:7-8—**1:**160
19:25-26—**2:**29
19:25-27—**2:**359
35:16—**2:**35
40:4—**2:**35
42:4—**2:**35
42:6—**2:**469

Psalms
1:1—**2:**502
1:2-3—**1:**17; **2:**422
1:3—**1:**485, 541; **2:**128
1:5—**1:**293
1:14-15—**1:**368
2:2-4—**2:**70
3:4—**2:**510
6:8—**2:**44
9:12—**2:**44
16:2—**2:**681
16:10-11—**2:**29
16:11—**1:**232; **2:**698
19:7-8—**2:**443
19:10—**1:**544; **2:**619
19:13—**1:**145
22—**1:**117; **2:**541, 554,
    556-58, 561, 585
22:1—**1:**117; **2:**586
22:6—**2:**557
22:7-8—**2:**557, 586
22:12-13—**2:**557
22:15—**1:**343; **2:**568, 617
22:16—**1:**343; **2:**586
22:18—**2:**554, 556, 586
22:20-21—**2:**557
22:22—**2:**417, 640
22:26—**2:**562
22:27—**2:**407
22:31—**2:**556, 562

23—**1:**148, 635-36, 640-41;
    2:16
23:1—**1:**635-36, 639; **2:**138
23:2—**1:**639
23:2-3—**2:**138
23:3—**1:**20, 32, 622, 639, 657
23:4—**1:**640; **2:**621-22
23:5—**1:**640, 641; **2:**498
23:6—**1:**641, 657
24:3-5—**2:**207
24:5—**2:**207
24:10—**2:**411
25:4-5—**1:**346
25:5—**1:**432
27:1—**1:**443, 510; **2:**112
27:4—**2:**421
27:10—**1:**612
30:5—**2:**357
31:5—**2:**586
31:11—**2:**586
31:14-15—**1:**471
33:6—**1:**8
34:4—**1:**374
34:8—**1:**374
34:15—**2:**45
34:18—**2:**45, 638
34:20—**1:**343; **2:**553, 586,
    601
35:11—**2:**586
35:19—**2:**320
36:9—**1:**227
37:4—**1:**354
40:7—**1:**447
40:7-8—**2:**406
40:8—**1:**404; **2:**293, 407
41:9—**1:**447; **2:**164, 586
42:1—**1:**230
42:1-2—**2:**572
42:11—**2:**195
46:1—**2:**8
46:4—**1:**428
51:5—**1:**550; **2:**578

51:7—**2:**568
51:11-12—**2:**299
69—**2:**541, 566
69:1—**1:**368
69:4—**2:**320
69:9—**1:**133
69:20-21—**2:**566, 568
69:21—**1:**343; **2:**554, 565, 586
69:27-28—**2:**568
72:17—**2:**407
73:23-24—**2:**29
75:8—**2:**498
76:10—**2:**320
79:13—**1:**615
80:8-9—**2:**282
82—**1:**669
82:5—**1:**510, 586
82:6—**1:**668
82:6-7—**1:**668
85:10—**1:**506-7
89:20—**2:**305
90:8—**1:**237
103:12—**2:**375
103:13—**1:**48
103:14—**1:**505
104:1-2—**2:**413
104:15—**1:**123, 641; **2:**283,
    595
107:20—**1:**8
109:25—**2:**586
113-118—**1:**480
116:8—**2:**51
116:15—**2:**621
118:25-26—**2:**82-83
119:18—**1:**346; **2:**711
119:67—**2:**287
119:71—**2:**333
119:105—**1:**20, 193, 543; **2:**21
121:1-2—**2:**55
126:5—**2:**51
139:1-3—**1:**164
143:3—**1:**511

Proverbs
1:16—**1:**294
2:13—**1:**510
3:5—**1:**432, 463
4:19—**1:**510
4:23—**2:**185
6:16-17—**2:**243
9:17—**1:**142
14:32—**2:**621
16:18—**2:**187
17:17—**2:**5
18:10—**2:**417, 433
19:21—**2:**65
21:4—**1:**294

Ecclesiastes
3:11—**1:**320
12:7—**1:**321

Song of Solomon
5:16—**1:**392
8:6—**2:**638

Isaiah
1:6—**1:**143, 294, 549
1:15—**1:**294
1:18—**1:**270; **2:**196
5:5-6—**2:**283
5:7—**2:**282
6:1—**2:**111, 119
6:3—**1:**144; **2:**119
6:4—**2:**119
6:5—**1:**144
6:9-10—**2:**115
6:10—**1:**294
7:14—**1:**343
8:22—**1:**511
9:2—**1:**18, 510, 587
9:6—**1:**284
9:7—**2:**109
11:2—**1:**212
11:6—**2:**271

11:9—**2:**398
12:3—**1:**480; **2:**599
25:6—**1:**129
29:18—**1:**606
35:1-2—**2:**434
35:5-6—**1:**476
40:11—**1:**622, 643
41:8—**2:**305
42:1—**2:**85
42:3—**1:**91
42:6—**1:**247
43:2—**2:**540
43:2-3—**1:**372
44:3—**1:**227
44:7-8—**2:**163-64
46:9-10—**1:**406
50:6—**1:**343
51:17—**2:**497
52:7—**2:**613
52:13—**2:**114
52:13-14—**2:**109
53—**1:**87, 117; **2:**114, 542
53:1—**2:**114
53:2—**2:**282
53:3—**2:**527, 555, 617
53:3-5—**1:**117
53:5—**1:**343; **2:**37, 175, 409, 509, 526
53:5-6—**1:**248; **2:**66, 569
53:6—**1:**86
53:7—**1:**92; **2:**506, 532, 586
53:8—**2:**500, 591
53:9—**1:**343; **2:**586, 616, 622
53:10—**1:**395; **2:**109, 557
53:10-12—**2:**406-7
53:11—**2:**411
53:12—**2:**409, 448, 524, 548, 586
54:10—**1:**170
54:13—**1:**418
55:1—**1:**227, 270

55:1-3—**1:**356
55:6—**1:**478
55:6-7—**1:**498
55:8—**1:**432
55:9—**1:**170; **2:**43, 302
55:10-11—**2:**443
57:20-21—**1:**125
58:11—**1:**486
58:13-14—**1:**305-6, 598
59:9—**1:**511
61:1—**1:**343
61:1-2—**1:**476; **2:**688
62:5—**2:**293
64:6—**1:**69, 382
64:8—**2:**418

Jeremiah
1:5—**2:**448
2:13—**1:**227
2:21—**2:**282
6:14—**2:**274, 707
7:23—**1:**224
9:23-24—**2:**396
17:9—**1:**141, 294; **2:**242, 508
17:13—**1:**503
25:15-28—**2:**497
31—**1:**117
31:3—**1:**170
31:33-34—**1:**418
31:34—**2:**398

Ezekiel
2:1—**1:**162
2:3—**1:**162
11:5—**1:**236
15:1-6—**2:**295
15:3—**2:**295
15:6—**2:**295
18:4—**2:**569
20:10-20—**1:**304
34:2-3—**1:**616
34:23—**1:**619

36—**1:**420
36:25–27—**1:**153
36:26—**1:**418
36:27—**1:**156
37—**1:**420
37:3–5—**2:**668
37:4—**1:**420; **2:**444
37:10—**1:**420; **2:**444
37:25—**2:**109
47:1–12—**1:**487
47:2—**2:**396
47:3—**2:**396
47:4—**2:**396
47:5—**2:**397
47:7—**2:**397
47:12—**2:**397, 595

Daniel
1:8–16—**2:**441
2:22—**1:**236
2:44—**2:**537
3:1–30—**2:**442
3:25—**2:**539
3:28—**2:**538
6:1–28—**2:**442
7:13–14—**1:**118, 162, 324;
 2:93
9:26—**2:**81, 109

Hosea
3:2–3—**2:**579
4:6—**2:**399

Joel
2:28—**2:**350

Amos
5:21—**1:**256

Jonah
1:2—**2:**663
2:9—**2:**663

4:3—**2:**439
4:8—**2:**439

Micah
3:6—**1:**510
4:2—**1:**270
5:1—**2:**506
5:2—**1:**343
7:18—**2:**580

Zephaniah
1:15—**1:**511

Zechariah
3:1—**1:**501
3:3–4—**1:**507
6:12–13—**2:**528
7:5—**1:**256
9:9—**2:**84
9:9–10—**2:**89
9:10—**2:**84
11:12—**1:**343
12:2—**2:**497
12:10—**1:**343; **2:**106, 553,
 601, 604
13:1—**1:**79; **2:**599, 601, 604
13:7—**2:**695
13:9—**2:**602
14:8—**1:**486
14:21—**1:**134

Malachi
2:10—**1:**563
3:1–3—**1:**133
4:5—**1:**76

Matthew
1:20—**2:**254
1:21—**1:**240, 646; **2:**103,
 336, 365, 370, 428, 591
2:1–18—**1:**38
2:2—**2:**389

3:12—**2:**295
3:14–15—**2:**447
3:15—**1:**405
3:16—**2:**255
3:17—**1:**93, 119, 213, 335;
 2:103, 282, 494, 521
4:1–11—**1:**280
4:4—**1:**391
4:10—**1:**453
4:19—**2:**694
5–7—**1:**348
5:3—**1:**609; **2:**676
5:3–10—**2:**162
5:6—**1:**96, 379; **2:**572
5:13—**1:**96; **2:**228
5:13–16—**2:**663
5:14—**1:**517, 584
5:16—**1:**20, 195, 465, 584
5:17–18—**2:**407
5:18—**2:**33
5:22—**2:**44, 295
5:48—**1:**69; **2:**95
6:9—**1:**49; **2:**364, 367, 418
6:9–13—**2:**386
6:10—**1:**404; **2:**367
6:11—**1:**391; **2:**367
6:12—**1:**504; **2:**367
6:12–13—**2:**150
6:13—**2:**187; **2:**367
6:19–20—**1:**638
6:21—**1:**638
6:24—**1:**192
6:25–34—**1:**377
6:26—**1:**49
6:33—**1:**379; **2:**201
7:19—**2:**295
7:20—**2:**285
7:21—**2:**249, 306, 447
7:23—**2:**249, 447
7:24–27—**1:**98
7:28–29—**1:**208
8–9—**1:**348

8:20—**1**:56; **2**:566
8:23-26—**2**:44
8:26—**2**:54, 217
9:9—**1**:298, 418, 620; **2**:137
9:11-13—**1**:241
9:12—**2**:155
9:12-13—**1**:577
9:24—**2**:16
9:29—**1**:362
9:36—**1**:505
9:37—**1**:365
9:37-38—**2**:227
10—**1**:349
10:2—**1**:105
10:19-20—**2**:259
10:28—**1**:238
10:30—**1**:49
10:32-33—**1**:264; **2**:315, 610
10:34—**1**:489
10:39—**2**:719
11:3—**2**:220
11:4-5—**1**:476
11:4-6—**2**:220
11:11—**1**:197
11:14—**1**:78
11:17—**1**:397
11:21-22—**2**:126
11:28—**1**:111, 270; **2**:217,
    257, 283, 319
11:28-29—**1**:130, 204, 308;
    2:702
11:29—**2**:718
12:1-8—**1**:308
12:8—**1**:308
12:40—**2**:93, 616
12:41—**2**:616
13—**1**:349
13:5-6—**1**:540
13:21—**1**:540
13:22—**1**:540
13:23—**1**:541; **2**:290
13:39-42—**2**:295

13:41—**2**:93
13:42—**1**:327
13:55—**1**:452
14:19—**1**:391
14:22—**1**:367
14:23—**1**:371; **2**:227
14:24—**1**:369
14:25—**1**:372
16:13—**1**:384
16:13-18—**1**:46
16:14—**1**:384
16:15—**1**:384
16:15-16—**1**:441
16:16—**1**:384; **2**:34, 233
16:16-17—**1**:445
16:16-18—**2**:706
16:17—**1**:93, 418
16:18—**1**:101, 442, 471;
    2:459
16:27-28—**2**:93
17:2—**2**:473
17:5—**2**:103, 469
17:9—**2**:473
17:10-13—**1**:78
17:12—**2**:93
18:8-9—**2**:44
18:17-18—**2**:673
18:18—**2**:459
19:14—**2**:217
19:21—**1**:151
19:24—**2**:607
19:28—**2**:93
20:18-19—**2**:88
20:28—**1**:241, 407, 633;
    2:93, 147, 152, 161, 206,
    318, 360, 374, 428, 587,
    591, 651
20:38—**2**:573-74
21:2—**2**:83
21:8—**2**:82
21:21—**1**:362
21:33-39—**1**:40

22:13—**1**:511
22:21—**2**:533
22:37-39—**1**:303; **2**:243
22:37-40—**2**:178
23:37—**1**:475
24:27—**2**:93
24:35—**2**:209
24:46—**2**:676
25:21—**2**:270
25:23—**2**:699
25:31-32—**1**:195; **2**:125
25:31-34—**1**:497-98
25:31-46—**2**:530
25:34—**2**:702
25:40—**2**:484
25:41—**1**:497-98
25:46—**1**:497-98
26:2—**2**:93
26:15—**2**:145
26:22—**2**:167
26:24—**2**:169
26:25—**2**:168
26:26—**1**:425
26:26-28—**1**:646
26:26-29—**2**:493
26:31—**2**:695
26:31-32—**2**:705
26:33—**2**:705
26:39—**2**:227
26:41—**2**:497
26:45—**2**:93
26:48—**2**:493
26:56—**2**:377
26:57-65—**2**:355
26:57-66—**2**:499
26:61—**2**:505, 651
26:63—**2**:499
26:64—**2**:93
26:73—**2**:507
26:75—**2**:508
27:4—**1**:447; **2**:522
27:15-23—**2**:355

27:16—**2:**523
27:17—**2:**516
27:19—**2:**515
27:22—**2:**529
27:23—**2:**529
27:29–30—**2:**174
27:32—**2:**541
27:40–42—**2:**356
27:41–43—**2:**557
27:46—**2:**13, 105, 122, 355, 378, 403, 547, 556
27:50—**2:**122
27:54—**1:**670; **2:**566
27:56—**2:**558
27:57—**2:**605, 607
27:60—**2:**616
27:62–66—**2:**616, 647
28:2–4—**2:**636
28:5–6—**2:**636
28:6—**2:**646
28:9—**2:**358, 473, 639
28:16–20—**2:**694
28:18—**2:**225, 407, 414
28:18–19—**2:**201
28:18–20—**2:**534
28:19—**2:**309, 714
28:19–20—**1:**405; **2:**440
28:20—**1:**542

Mark
1:4–5—**1:**76
1:6—**1:**77
1:15—**2:**353
1:24—**1:**444
1:38—**1:**210, 633
1:39—**1:**210
2:5—**2:**670
2:7—**2:**670
2:11—**2:**670
2:17—**2:**548
2:27—**1:**305
3:16–18—**1:**105

3:17—**1:**106
3:18—**2:**268
3:31–35—**1:**452
4:35–41—**1:**38
4:39—**1:**485; **2:**272
6:20—**2:**437
6:45–51—**2:**431
6:46—**1:**371
6:51—**1:**373
7:3—**1:**124
8:36—**1:**610
8:38—**2:**118
9:47—**2:**295
9:48—**1:**327
10:16—**2:**676
10:17—**1:**381
10:21—**1:**270
10:30—**2:**353
11:17—**1:**132
11:30–32—**1:**330
14:1–9—**2:**72n1
14:8—**2:**79
14:19—**2:**190
14:22—**1:**425
14:22–25—**2:**493
14:28—**2:**693
14:29—**2:**187, 502
14:31—**2:**502
14:50—**2:**377
14:51—**2:**495
14:61–63—**2:**511
14:71—**2:**507
15:10—**2:**523
15:11—**2:**523
15:25—**2:**543
15:29–32—**2:**541
15:33—**2:**541, 543, 556
15:34—**2:**122, 541
15:34–36—**2:**566
15:38—**2:**541
15:39—**2:**541
15:40—**2:**558

15:43—**2:**605, 610
15:44—**2:**605
16:2–5—**2:**636
16:7—**2:**693
16:15—**2:**248

Luke
1:15—**1:**63
1:17—**1:**78
1:32–33—**1:**118
1:35—**2:**327, 407
1:42—**1:**122
1:78–79—**1:**512
1:79—**1:**587
2:14—**2:**103
2:35—**2:**558
3:16—**1:**202; **2:**74
3:22—**2:**327
4:14—**1:**281
4:16–21—**1:**461
4:18—**1:**213, 544; **2:**327
4:18–19—**1:**213; **2:**688
4:29–30—**1:**22
4:30—**1:**528
5:8—**1:**239; **2:**700
5:10—**2:**138, 309
5:13—**1:**493; **2:**217
5:20—**1:**493
5:21—**1:**213
5:23–24—**1:**213
5:23–25—**1:**493
6:14—**1:**105
6:16—**2:**268
6:20—**1:**638
6:26—**1:**457
7—**2:**626
8:2–3—**2:**626
8:21—**2:**560
8:35—**1:**591
9:10—**1:**360
9:11—**1:**353
9:12—**1:**352, 358

9:13—**1**:359
9:14—**1**:352
9:16—**1**:362
9:17—**1**:354
9:20—**1**:350
9:22—**2**:360
9:23—**1**:114, 356, 515, 638;
    2:240, 302, 361, 720
9:23–24—**1**:96; **2**:89, 719
9:24—**1**:114, 517
10—**2**:7, 39
10:1–19—**2**:152
10:19–20—**2**:224
10:38–42—**2**:25
10:39—**2**:7
10:40—**2**:41
11:10—**2**:677
11:13—**2**:260
11:28—**2**:676
12:15—**1**:638
12:19–21—**1**:380
12:43—**2**:201
14:26—**2**:560
15:6—**1**:116
16:24—**1**:321; **2**:567
17:5—**1**:185
17:21—**2**:354
18:13—**1**:145
18:14—**1**:495
18:29–30—**2**:613
18:31–33—**2**:186
18:38—**1**:360
18:40—**1**:360
19:5—**1**:620
19:8—**1**:591
19:10—**1**:111, 254, 407, 633;
    2:206
19:37–40—**2**:87
19:42—**2**:83
19:43–44—**2**:83
20:25—**2**:515
22:7–8—**2**:542

22:14–23—**2**:493
22:19—**1**:425
22:20—**2**:186
22:22—**2**:185
22:23—**2**:167–68
22:24—**2**:168, 187
22:30—**2**:471
22:31—**2**:188, 278
22:31–32—**2**:190–91
22:31–34—**2**:707
22:40—**2**:188
22:42—**2**:102, 240, 538
22:51—**2**:497
22:54—**2**:377, 503
22:58–61—**2**:704
22:60—**2**:191
22:61–62—**2**:191
23:1–49—**2**:500
23:2—**2**:514
23:18–23—**2**:313
23:19—**2**:523
23:27–31—**2**:541
23:34—**2**:32, 217, 319, 541,
    559
23:39–43—**2**:541
23:42–43—**1**:22; **2**:551
23:43—**1**:321; **2**:17, 559, 596
23:46—**2**:13, 586
23:50—**2**:605
23:51—**2**:605
24:13–35—**2**:647
24:16—**2**:637
24:20–21—**2**:262
24:21—**2**:356, 468
24:26—**2**:656
24:27—**1**:343; **2**:519, 552
24:32—**1**:316; **2**:120, 218,
    359
24:33–35—**2**:656
24:37—**2**:657
24:39—**2**:657
24:39–43—**2**:263

24:45—**2**:369
24:46–47—**1**:271–72; **2**:663

John
1—**1**:604
1–2—**1**:479
1–4—**1**:292; **2**:489
1–11—**1**:xv
1:1—**1**:7, 9, 116, 165, 208,
    236, 460, 573; **2**:163,
    255, 614, 683, 685, 688,
    723
1:1–2—**2**:412
1:1–3—**1**:5, 16, 322; **2**:56,
    137, 666
1:1–18—**1**:15, 36
1:3—**1**:25
1:4—**1**:15, 16, 80, 165, 188,
    514, 641; **2**:30, 172, 209,
    617, 723
1:4–5—**1**:15, 18, 23, 27
1:5—**1**:20, 22, 25, 42, 43,
    604
1:6–7—**1**:27
1:6–9—**1**:25
1:7—**1**:27, 28–29, 31, 271
1:8—**1**:30, 331
1:9—**1**:31, 36–37, 80, 116,
    188, 512
1:9–10—**1**:36
1:9–11—**1**:35–36
1:10—**1**:36–38, 40
1:10–11—**1**:604
1:11—**1**:39–41, 80, 281;
    2:122, 522
1:12—**1**:44, 45, 48, 50, 551;
    2:233, 641–42, 723
1:12–13—**1**:44, 152, 566
1:13—**1**:50, 51
1:14—**1**:11–13, 53–54, 137,
    208, 352, 459, 525;
    2:137, 388, 403, 518, 723

1:15—**1:**63
1:15–18—**1:**62
1:16—**1:**64, 71
1:17—**1:**67, 80, 124
1:18—**1:**9, 70, 336; **2:**215
1:19—**1:**76, 129, 292
1:19–20—**1:**76
1:19–28—**1:**76
1:19–36—**1:**520
1:19–42—**1:**280
1:19–51—**2:**71
1:19–4:54—**1:**576
1:21—**1:**76
1:22–23—**1:**79
1:23—**1:**75, 78, 82, 83; 330
1:25—**1:**79
1:26—**1:**79, 80
1:26–27—**1:**30, 81
1:29—**1:**xv, 29, 47, 68, 81,
    85, 87, 93, 116, 182, 202,
    271, 330, 425, 479, 590,
    601, 671; **2:**345, 570,
    689, 723
1:29–34—**1:**85
1:31—**1:**89, 619
1:32—**1:**29, 91
1:33—**1:**89, 92
1:33–34—**1:**213
1:34—**1:**30, 92–93, 116, 271
1:35–36—**1:**104
1:35–37—**1:**95
1:35–42—**1:**94, 103–4
1:36—**1:**113
1:38—**1:**95, 97, 109, 116
1:38–39—**1:**94, 103
1:39—**1:**99–100, 109; **2:**137
1:41—**1:**57, 106, 113, 115–
    16, 271–72; **2:**92
1:41–42—**1:**101
1:42—**1:**109; **2:**706
1:43—**1:**112; **2:**715
1:43–51—**1:**112, 280

1:44—**1:**115
1:45—**1:**115–16
1:46—**1:**114–15
1:47—**1:**115, 119
1:48—**1:**116
1:48–49—**1:**115
1:49—**1:**9, 118
1:50—**1:**118
1:51—**1:**112, 118–20, 389
2—**1:**131; **2:**594
2–3—**1:**450
2:1—**1:**129
2:1–11—**1:**334
2:1–12—**1:**121, 236, 280,
    285
2:3—**1:**123
2:3–5—**1:**122
2:4—**1:**122, 453; **2:**92, 360
2:5—**1:**123
2:6—**1:**124
2:7–9—**1:**126
2:7–11—**2:**685
2:10—**1:**121, 123, 127
2:11—**1:**57, 123, 128–29,
    140; **2:**631
2:12—**1:**122
2:13—**1:**131
2:13–16—**2:**44, 121
2:13–17—**2:**689
2:13–22—**1:**130, 280
2:14—**1:**131
2:15–16—**1:**132
2:16—**1:**132
2:16–17—**1:**130
2:17—**1:**133
2:18—**1:**134, 140
2:19—**1:**135, 137, 248; **2:**651
2:20—**1:**131
2:20–21—**1:**135
2:21–22—**2:**651
2:22—**1:**135; **2:**276
2:23—**1:**140, 476

2:23–24—**1:**538
2:23–25—**1:**140, 149, 282,
    432
2:24—**1:**147
2:24–25—**1:**140
2:25—**1:**141
3—**1:**214, 216, 220, 605;
    2:608
3:1—**1:**149, 150
3:1–8—**1:**149
3:1–21—**1:**280
3:2—**1:**150, 158–59, 333,
    339, 520; **2:**319, 721
3:3—**1:**37, 127, 147, 149,
    151, 154, 159, 179, 184,
    228, 264, 586, 605, 657;
    2:209, 257, 264, 666
3:3–8—**2:**688
3:4—**1:**152, 155, 159
3:5—**1:**152, 154; **2:**209, 599,
    667
3:6—**1:**152, 153, 155
3:7—**1:**151, 152–53, 157,
    163, 190, 203, 209, 257,
    285, 497; **2:**608
3:8—**1:**155, 166, 184, 263,
    428
3:9—**1:**158, 159; **2:**688
3:9–10—**1:**158
3:9–21—**1:**158
3:10—**1:**160
3:10–12—**1:**159
3:11—**1:**159, 161; **2:**721
3:12—**1:**161
3:13—**1:**159; **2:**93
3:14—**1:**162, 163, 181, 184,
    203, 209, 257, 389; **2:**93,
    391
3:14–15—**1:**166, 173, 407,
    611; **2:**582
3:15—**1:**12, 163; **2:**391

3:16—**1**:13, 16, 27, 36, 45,
  88, 96, 163–64, 167–77,
  179–81, 183–87, 209,
  231, 247, 285, 436, 590;
  2:9, 195, 266, 321, 390,
  409, 570, 608, 650, 688
3:16–18—**1**:177
3:17—**1**:183, 297, 314
3:18—**1**:27, 45, 88, 182, 229,
  279; **2**:107
3:19—**1**:21, 38; 187–90, 195,
  211, 228, 457, 510, 549;
  2:126, 174, 337, 526
3:19–21—**1**:165, 187–88
3:20—**1**:189, 191–92
3:21—**1**:193, 194
3:22—**1**:198
3:22–30—**1**:197
3:22–36—**1**:280
3:23—**1**:277
3:23–24—**1**:198
3:25–26—**1**:198
3:27—**1**:199
3:28—**1**:79, 200
3:29—**1**:200
3:29–30—**1**:197
3:30—**1**:202–4; **2**:686
3:31—**1**:152, 207–9
3:31–36—**1**:207
3:32—**1**:208, 210–12
3:33—**1**:211
3:34—**1**:212, 336
3:35—**1**:213
3:36—**1**:16, 33, 45, 71, 157,
  184, 214–15, 458, 508,
  590, 611, 626; **2**:18, 42,
  210, 280, 390, 691
4—**1**:217, 264; **2**:595
4:1–10—**1**:216
4:1–42—**1**:281
4:3—**1**:217
4:6—**1**:218, 235

4:6–7—**2**:572
4:7—**1**:221
4:7–9—**1**:219
4:9—**1**:220, 223
4:10—**1**:151, 216, 223, 226–
  29, 235, 296; **2**:108
4:10–14—**1**:225
4:11—**1**:228
4:12—**1**:228
4:13—**1**:65, 631
4:13–14—**1**:225, 226
4:13–15—**2**:595
4:14—**1**:65, 231, 232, 266,
  281, 285, 589, 631; **2**:391,
  397, 571, 599
4:15—**1**:233, 235
4:15–19—**1**:234
4:16—**1**:241, 245, 269
4:16–18—**1**:234–35
4:16–21—**1**:281
4:17—**1**:241
4:17–18—**1**:241
4:19—**1**:242
4:19–20—**1**:245
4:19–22—**1**:243
4:20—**1**:244
4:21—**1**:248
4:22—**1**:243, 245–47, 249,
  252, 281
4:23—**1**:253, 254
4:23–24—**1**:254
4:23–26—**1**:253
4:24—**1**:257
4:25—**1**:260
4:26—**1**:260, 655; **2**:688
4:27—**1**:262
4:27–30—**1**:262
4:27–42—**1**:271
4:28—**1**:265
4:28–29—**1**:260, 262, 264,
  268, 272
4:29—**1**:28, 269; **2**:163, 689

4:30—**1**:269
4:31–34—**1**:273
4:34—**1**:274, 275; **2**:406
4:35—**1**:275
4:36—**1**:277
4:37—**1**:277
4:37–38—**1**:277
4:38—**1**:277
4:39–41—**1**:275
4:42—**1**:37, 271, 278
4:43—**1**:269
4:43–54—**1**:280
4:44—**1**:281, 414
4:45—**1**:282
4:46—**1**:281
4:46–54—**1**:334; **2**:685
4:47—**1**:282
4:49—**1**:283
4:49–50—**1**:280
4:50—**1**:284, 285–86; **2**:26
4:52—**1**:284, 286
4:53—**1**:287, 288
4:54—**1**:282
5—**1**:266, 292, 319, 450,
  466, 520, 589; **2**:552, 595
5–8—**2**:489
5:1—**1**:292
5:1–9—**1**:291
5:1–15—**1**:341
5:1–8:59—**1**:576
5:2—**1**:292
5:2–9—**2**:685
5:3—**1**:292, 294
5:3–5—**1**:291
5:4—**1**:294–95
5:5–7—**1**:294
5:6—**1**:297
5:7—**1**:294
5:8—**1**:297, 299
5:8–9—**1**:291, 297
5:9–10—**1**:300–301
5:9–18—**1**:300

5:10—**1:**302

5:11—**1:**303

5:14—**1:**307

5:17—**1:**308, 310

5:18—**1:**308, 310, 470

5:19—**1:**310–11

5:19–24—**1:**309

5:20—**1:**311–12, 322

5:21—**1:**297, 313–14, 317

5:22–23—**1:**314, 320

5:23—**1:**315

5:24—**1:**34, 309, 316–17, 326, 328, 337, 553; **2:**37, 210, 340, 390, 403, 458, 691, 723

5:25—**1:**320, 322, 327

5:25–26—**1:**655

5:25–30—**1:**319

5:26—**1:**16, 322, 390, 428

5:26–27—**1:**322

5:27—**1:**323, 655; **2:**93

5:28–29—**1:**322

5:29—**1:**325–26

5:30—**1:**324, 523

5:31—**1:**330

5:31–38—**1:**329

5:32—**1:**330

5:34—**1:**332

5:35—**1:**28, 31, 331–32

5:36—**1:**329, 332, 664; **2:**219, 223

5:37—**1:**335

5:37–38—**1:**335

5:38—**1:**335–36

5:39—**1:**28, 339–40, 342, 345; **2:**552

5:39–40—**1:**338, 347

5:39–47—**1:**338

5:40—**1:**342, 345

5:41—**1:**342

5:42—**1:**341

5:43—**1:**341

5:44—**1:**342

5:45–47—**1:**344

5:46—**1:**353, 513, 525, 606

6—**1:**131, 386, 412, 416, 418, 422, 438, 445, 449–50, 452, 457, 461, 654; **2:**29

6–8—**1:**351

6:1–13—**1:**357

6:1–15—**1:**334, 348

6:2—**1:**349, 350

6:2–14—**2:**685

6:3—**1:**353

6:4—**1:**352, 425

6:5—**1:**350

6:5–6—**1:**357–58

6:7—**1:**350, 361

6:8–9—**1:**106, 361

6:10—**1:**352, 361

6:10–11—**1:**348

6:11—**1:**362

6:11–13—**1:**364

6:11–14—**1:**353–54

6:12—**1:**354

6:14—**1:**350, 355

6:15—**1:**355, 367, 370

6:16–17—**1:**367

6:16–21—**1:**334, 366

6:17—**1:**367, 370

6:18—**1:**367

6:19—**1:**369, 371–72

6:19–20—**1:**366

6:20—**1:**372, 373

6:20–21—**1:**372

6:22—**1:**376

6:22–29—**1:**375

6:24–25—**1:**376

6:26—**1:**377

6:26–27—**1:**355

6:27—**1:**378, 379–80, 382–83, 385

6:28—**1:**381

6:28–29—**1:**375; **2:**128

6:29—**1:**175, 382–83, 385, 404, 425

6:30—**1:**386

6:30–31—**1:**413

6:30–36—**1:**384

6:31—**1:**387

6:32—**1:**387–88, 433

6:32–33—**1:**405

6:33—**1:**378, 388, 390

6:34—**1:**388, 412

6:35—**1:**68, 98, 334, 351, 354, 362, 384–85, 388, 392, 394, 423, 425, 443, 481, 512, 519, 525, 625, 655; **2:**203, 493

6:36—**1:**386, 394, 405

6:36–40—**1:**620

6:37—**1:**393, 394–95, 398, 400, 403, 405, 413, 445, 628; **2:**68, 135, 695

6:37–39—**2:**390

6:37–40—**1:**393

6:38—**1:**402, 403, 405, 407

6:38–40—**1:**402–3, 405

6:39—**1:**373, 395, 402, 411, 445; **2:**68, 135, 284, 495

6:39–40—**1:**405, 408; **2:**190

6:40—**1:**402, 403, 406–7, 409, 411, 425, 447, 449; **2:**391, 695, 721

6:41—**1:**432

6:41–47—**1:**412

6:42—**1:**413

6:43—**1:**414

6:44—**1:**397, 412, 415, 417, 419, 437, 445; **2:**108, 171, 612

6:45—**1:**346, 418–19

6:45–46—**1:**419

6:47—**1:**419, 421, 425

6:48—**1:**423, 655

6:48–50—**1:**423
6:48–59—**1:**422
6:51—**1:**423, 425–26, 429
6:52—**1:**424, 432
6:53—**1:**424, 430, 655; **2:**93
6:53–54—**1:**426; **2:**599
6:54—**1:**422, 427–28
6:55—**1:**427
6:56—**1:**428–29
6:57—**1:**428; **2:**264
6:58—**1:**429–30, 433, 655
6:59—**1:**429
6:60—**1:**432; **2:**422
6:60–65—**1:**431
6:60–66—**1:**188
6:61—**1:**433, 436; **2:**313
6:62—**1:**436, 655
6:63—**1:**425, 431, 437–38,
 440, 445
6:64—**1:**431, 432
6:65—**1:**437, 445
6:66—**1:**442; **2:**313
6:66–71—**1:**441
6:67—**1:**442, 448
6:68—**1:**11, 392, 443, 445,
 449
6:68–69—**1:**xvi, 57, 441,
 468
6:69—**1:**444–45, 536, 655
6:69–70—**1:**446
6:70—**1:**445–46
6:71—**1:**446
7—**1:**166, 351, 451, 453, 500
7–9—**1:**479
7:1—**1:**451
7:1–13—**1:**450
7:3–4—**1:**452
7:5—**1:**452; **2:**92
7:6—**1:**453, 457–58
7:6–7—**1:**450
7:7—**1:**457
7:8—**1:**455

7:9—**1:**455
7:10—**1:**455
7:12—**1:**456
7:13—**1:**456, 466
7:14—**1:**459
7:14–24—**1:**459
7:15—**1:**460
7:16—**1:**459–60, 462
7:17—**1:**463–64
7:18—**1:**465, 525
7:19—**1:**465
7:20—**1:**466, 468
7:21—**1:**466
7:22–23—**1:**466
7:24—**1:**467
7:25–26—**1:**469–70
7:25–36—**1:**469
7:26—**1:**470
7:27—**1:**472
7:28—**1:**473
7:28–29—**1:**473
7:29—**1:**473
7:30—**1:**122, 471; **2:**360
7:31—**1:**475
7:32—**1:**470
7:33—**1:**474, 477
7:33–34—**1:**474
7:35–36—**1:**474
7:37—**1:**352, 479–81, 490,
 498, 514, 525, 590, 620;
 2:121–22, 571
7:37–38—**1:**111; **2:**319, 595,
 630, 692, 702
7:37–39—**1:**479
7:38—**1:**484–86
7:38–39—**2:**599
7:39—**1:**484
7:40—**1:**490
7:40–41—**1:**489
7:40–43—**1:**490
7:40–52—**1:**489
7:41—**1:**491

7:43–44—**1:**492
7:44—**1:**491, 494
7:45–46—**1:**22, 493
7:46—**1:**xv
7:47–48—**1:**493
7:49—**1:**494
7:50–51—**1:**495
7:52—**1:**496
7:53–8:11—**1:**499; **2:**689
8—**1:**451, 499n1, 519, 528,
 532, 537, 547–48, 557,
 567, 604–5
8:4–5—**1:**501
8:6—**1:**501
8:6–8—**1:**503
8:7—**1:**503
8:9—**1:**504
8:10–11—**1:**499, 505
8:11—**1:**508
8:12—**1:**20, 37, 98, 196, 352,
 385, 481, 499n1, 509–19,
 522, 525, 527, 529–30,
 536, 542, 590, 625, 655;
 2:29, 172, 203, 233, 493,
 718
8:13—**1:**519
8:13–20—**1:**518
8:14—**1:**27, 520, 522
8:15—**1:**520–21, 524
8:16—**1:**523, 589
8:17–18—**1:**518, 524
8:18—**1:**27, 589
8:19—**1:**526, 536
8:20—**1:**122; **2:**92, 360
8:21—**1:**528–31
8:21–30—**1:**528
8:22—**1:**530
8:23—**1:**530
8:24—**1:**14, 39, 148, 215,
 527, 530, 551, 553, 575;
 2:18, 69
8:25–26—**1:**532

8:26—**1:**532, 589
8:27—**1:**534
8:28—**1:**534–35, 655
8:28–29—**2:**407
8:29—**1:**589
8:30—**1:**536, 538
8:31—**1:**538–40
8:31–32—**1:**14, 46, 99, 537,
   542, 544, 548, 557, 561,
   566, 570; **2:**138, 209,
   289, 520, 718
8:32—**1:**259, 336, 548, 601
8:33—**1:**548–49, 558
8:33–36—**1:**547
8:34—**1:**416, 446, 549–50;
   2:578
8:35—**1:**551
8:36—**1:**70, 91, 421, 547,
   550–51, 554
8:37—**1:**558–59
8:37–47—**1:**557
8:38—**1:**559
8:38–39—**1:**559
8:39—**1:**9, 560
8:39–40—**1:**559
8:41—**1:**562
8:42—**1:**563, 589, 655
8:43—**1:**563
8:44—**1:**48, 147, 501, 532,
   557, 560–63, 566–67;
   2:208, 642
8:45—**1:**564
8:46—**1:**562, 564, 668
8:47—**1:**564, 566
8:48—**1:**568
8:48–59—**1:**567
8:49—**1:**568
8:50—**1:**568–69
8:51—**1:**570
8:52—**1:**570
8:53—**1:**570
8:54—**1:**569

8:54–55—**1:**570
8:55—**1:**571
8:56—**1:**572
8:57—**1:**572
8:58—**1:**573, 655
8:59—**1:**539, 574–76, 586
9—**1:**576–77, 589, 595, 604,
   615, 627; **2:**49, 117
9–12—**2:**489
9:1—**1:**576, 586
9:1–2—**1:**577
9:1–5—**1:**576
9:1–7—**2:**685
9:1–41—**1:**335
9:1–11:57—**1:**576
9:2—**1:**579
9:3—**1:**580, 586; **2:**686
9:4—**1:**581, 583, 587; **2:**409
9:4–5—**1:**576
9:5—**1:**584, 587
9:6–7—**1:**585, 588; **2:**595
9:6–12—**1:**585
9:7—**1:**590
9:8–9—**1:**591
9:10–11—**1:**592
9:11—**1:**602
9:12—**1:**592
9:13—**1:**595
9:13–23—**1:**594
9:14—**1:**596
9:15—**1:**597
9:16—**1:**594
9:17—**1:**597, 602
9:18—**1:**601
9:21—**1:**600
9:22—**1:**599, 601; **2:**606
9:24—**1:**605
9:24–25—**2:**319
9:24–41—**1:**604
9:25—**1:**28, 609
9:26—**1:**606
9:27—**1:**606

9:28–39—**1:**606
9:29—**1:**605
9:30—**1:**609
9:30–33—**1:**607
9:33—**1:**602
9:34—**1:**607, 616
9:35—**1:**604, 610, 627; **2:**329
9:35–38—**1:**602
9:36—**1:**611
9:37—**1:**611, 655
9:38—**1:**611, 627
9:39—**1:**608, 611
9:40–41—**1:**608
10—**1:**479, 628, 653–54,
   663; **2:**7
10:1—**1:**616, 618
10:1–3—**1:**615
10:1–5—**1:**614, 624
10:2—**1:**614
10:2–3—**1:**619
10:3—**1:**620
10:3–4—**1:**622; **2:**423
10:5—**1:**617
10:6—**1:**624
10:6–9—**1:**624
10:7—**1:**385, 624, 626; **2:**203
10:8—**1:**627
10:9—**1:**512, 620, 624, 627,
   629, 630–31, 634, 641;
   2:29
10:9–10—**1:**631
10:10—**1:**17, 127, 224, 233,
   285, 430, 633–34, 642;
   2:206, 209, 283, 571
10:11—**1:**385, 426, 512, 625,
   643, 645–46; **2:**29, 50,
   203, 587, 591
10:11–21—**1:**643
10:12—**1:**644
10:13—**1:**644
10:14—**1:**407, 648, 649;
   2:234, 423

10:14–15—**1:**98; **2:**457, 589
10:14–16—**1:**649
10:15—**1:**426, 646
10:16—**1:**622, 649–50;
 2:407, 457, 638
10:17—**1:**650; **2:**635
10:17–18—**2:**375
10:18—**1:**646–47
10:19–21—**1:**652
10:22–29—**1:**653
10:23–24—**1:**655
10:24—**1:**655
10:25—**1:**27, 655–56
10:26—**1:**656
10:27—**1:**407, 656, 658;
 2:57, 638
10:27–28—**1:**47, 657–58
10:28—**1:**631, 657–59, 664,
 666; **2:**190, 284, 329, 382
10:28–29—**1:**648, 653;
 2:408, 432
10:29—**1:**628, 657, 660, 664
10:30—**1:**13; 664–65; **2:**275
10:30–42—**1:**663
10:32—**1:**663–64, 667
10:33—**1:**664–65, 668
10:34–36—**1:**668
10:35—**1:**669
10:36—**1:**663–64, 669
10:37—**1:**664
10:37–38—**1:**669
10:38—**1:**665
10:40—**2:**7
10:40–42—**1:**83, 671
10:41—**1:**671
11—**2:**6, 15, 19, 33
11:1–6—**2:**5
11:3—**2:**7, 9
11:4—**1:**319; **2:**5, 10, 12
11:5–6—**2:**11
11:6—**2:**26
11:7—**2:**19

11:7–16—**2:**14
11:8—**2:**19
11:9—**2:**19–20
11:9–10—**2:**14
11:11—**2:**15, 18
11:12—**2:**16
11:14–15—**2:**18, 54
11:15—**2:**18
11:16—**2:**22, 676
11:17–19—**2:**24
11:17–26—**2:**24
11:20—**2:**25
11:21—**2:**25, 34
11:22—**2:**27, 34
11:23—**2:**28, 30, 53
11:24—**2:**28, 627
11:25—**1:**335, 385, 429,
 512, 570, 626; **2:**15, 23,
 30–31, 34, 54, 203, 653,
 687
11:25–26—**1:**11, 184, 314;
 2:24, 29
11:26—**2:**23, 30–31, 37
11:27—**1:**444; **2:**33–34,
 36, 42
11:27–32—**2:**33
11:28—**2:**41
11:28–29—**2:**38
11:31—**2:**41
11:32—**2:**7, 39
11:33—**2:**39, 43–44
11:33–37—**2:**43
11:34—**2:**45–46
11:35—**2:**44, 46, 49, 53, 217
11:36—**2:**49
11:37—**2:**49
11:38—**2:**53
11:38–44—**2:**52, 685
11:39—**2:**27, 53
11:40—**2:**54
11:41–42—**2:**55
11:42—**2:**56

11:43—**1:**620; **2:**56, 59, 122
11:43–44—**1:**298, 314, 319,
 444, 493; **2:**52, 203, 210
11:44—**1:**621; **2:**56, 59–60,
 627
11:44–46—**2:**319
11:45—**2:**12
11:45–46—**2:**62
11:45–51—**2:**61
11:45–53—**1:**189
11:47—**2:**62, 69
11:47–48—**2:**62
11:48—**2:**62–63
11:49–50—**2:**61, 65
11:50—**1:**426; **2:**66, 78, 334,
 543
11:51—**2:**65
11:52—**2:**67
11:53—**2:**65
11:54—**2:**68
11:55–56—**2:**68
11:57—**2:**69, 72, 81
12—**2:**39, 114, 121, 194
12:1–11—**2:**71, 72n1
12:2—**2:**41, 72
12:3—**2:**71–72
12:4–5—**2:**76
12:5—**2:**79
12:6—**1:**661; **2:**76, 169
12:7–8—**2:**77
12:9—**2:**77, 82
12:9–19—**2:**492
12:10—**2:**78, 606
12:10–11—**2:**77
12:11—**1:**333; **2:**6, 79
12:12–13—**2:**82
12:12–19—**2:**80
12:13—**2:**82, 492
12:14–15—**2:**80, 84
12:16—**2:**88, 276
12:19—**2:**89, 93
12:20–22—**1:**106; **2:**92

12:20–26—**2:**91
12:23—**1:**60, 122, 484, 534;
   2:91–93, 360, 388, 550
12:24—**2:**94
12:25—**2:**96–97
12:26—**2:**99
12:27—**1:**122; **2:**102, 109,
   194
12:27–28—**2:**102
12:27–33—**2:**493
12:27–34—**2:**101
12:28—**2:**103, 110, 129
12:29—**2:**104
12:31—**2:**104, 342
12:32—**2:**101, 104, 106, 186,
   388, 550, 612
12:33—**2:**186
12:34—**2:**109
12:35—**2:**112, 116
12:35–36—**2:**111–12
12:35–43—**2:**111
12:36—**2:**112–13, 122
12:37—**2:**114, 631
12:38—**2:**114
12:39—**2:**115, 117
12:39–40—**2:**115
12:41—**1:**144; **2:**112, 119
12:42—**2:**118
12:42–43—**2:**606
12:43—**2:**118–19
12:44—**2:**122
12:44–46—**2:**122
12:44–50—**2:**121
12:45—**2:**123
12:46—**1:**19, 24, 297; **2:**124
12:47—**2:**125, 421
12:48—**2:**125
12:49–50—**2:**121, 127
12:50—**2:**127–28
13—**2:**121, 134
13–17—**2:**134, 489
13–21—**1:**131

13:1—**1:**122, 248; **2:**133–34,
   137, 140, 144, 155–56,
   482, 550, 585
13:2—**2:**145, 169
13:2–11—**2:**143
13:3—**2:**143, 145, 155
13:3–10—**2:**595
13:4–5—**2:**143–44
13:6—**2:**146
13:6–9—**2:**144
13:7—**2:**146
13:8—**2:**147, 149, 154
13:9—**2:**149
13:10—**2:**149, 151, 158, 164
13:11—**2:**151
13:12—**2:**154
13:12–14—**2:**154
13:12–17—**2:**144, 153
13:13—**2:**157
13:13–14—**2:**153, 248
13:14—**2:**157
13:15—**2:**154, 157
13:16—**2:**161–62
13:17—**2:**160–61
13:18—**2:**164
13:18–19—**2:**163–64
13:18–30—**2:**163
13:20—**2:**170
13:21—**2:**165–66, 194
13:22–25—**2:**166
13:23—**2:**72, 166, 168
13:23–25—**2:**500
13:24—**2:**167
13:25—**2:**167
13:26—**2:**168
13:27—**2:**169, 170, 174, 491
13:29—**2:**171
13:30—**2:**172
13:31—**1:**484; **2:**94, 173–76,
   182
13:31–35—**2:**173
13:32—**2:**176

13:33—**2:**177, 204
13:34—**2:**173, 178, 180, 183,
   247
13:34–35—**2:**478
13:35—**2:**181
13:36—**2:**183, 186, 189, 204,
   716
13:36–37—**2:**356
13:36–38—**2:**183
13:37—**2:**184, 186, 204, 501,
   707, 716
13:38—**2:**183–84, 186, 188,
   191, 502, 508
14—**2:**241, 281, 322
14–16—**2:**177, 213, 283
14:1—**2:**194, 200
14:1–3—**2:**189, 193, 204
14:2—**1:**640; **2:**193, 196–99
14:2–3—**2:**196, 380, 653
14:3—**2:**199, 233, 241, 263
14:4–6—**2:**202
14:5—**2:**204, 676
14:6—**1:**111, 119, 385, 443,
   512, 543, 626; **2:**202–5,
   207, 209, 211, 402, 493,
   520
14:7—**2:**213, 241
14:7–11—**2:**212
14:8—**2:**204, 212–14, 217
14:9—**1:**13, 18, 137, 336,
   351, 666; **2:**43, 146, 212,
   214–17, 219–21, 255,
   318, 403, 689, 724
14:9–10—**2:**216
14:10—**1:**664; **2:**219
14:11—**2:**219
14:12—**2:**222–23, 225–26,
   231, 233–34, 259
14:12–15—**2:**253
14:13—**2:**227, 233, 235–36,
   239–40
14:13–14—**2:**232, 296, 309

14:14—**2:**236, 239, 241
14:15—**2:**228, 241–42,
   244–45, 249, 260, 265,
   421
14:16—**2:**247, 253, 257, 324,
   344
14:16–17—**2:**251, 260–61,
   276, 560
14:17—**2:**251, 254–55,
   257–58
14:18—**2:**262–63
14:18–24—**2:**261–62
14:19—**2:**30, 262–64,
   269–70
14:20—**2:**264–65
14:21—**2:**246, 265–66
14:21–24—**2:**267
14:22—**2:**204, 268
14:23—**2:**246, 268
14:24—**2:**246, 270, 421
14:25–31—**2:**271
14:26—**2:**218, 257, 276–77,
   344, 519
14:27—**2:**271–72, 274, 280,
   379, 659–60
14:28—**2:**275
14:29—**2:**279
14:30—**2:**278–79
14:31—**2:**279, 385
15—**1:**296, 313, 323, 539
15:1—**1:**385, 626; **2:**234,
   281–82, 493
15:1–2—**2:**281
15:1–4—**1:**539
15:1–5—**2:**281
15:1–11—**2:**386
15:2—**2:**284, 286, 296
15:3—**2:**288
15:4—**1:**100; **2:**234, 289, 291
15:4–5—**2:**290
15:5—**1:**102, 512; **2:**284,
   289–90, 502, 696

15:6—**2:**294
15:6–11—**2:**291
15:7—**2:**296, 309
15:7–8—**1:**102; **2:**291
15:8—**1:**539; **2:**298
15:9—**2:**292–93
15:10—**1:**100; **2:**293
15:11—**2:**299–300
15:12—**2:**248, 302, 306
15:12–13—**2:**248
15:12–17—**2:**301
15:13—**2:**50, 139, 179, 274,
   302–4, 643
15:13–14—**2:**301
15:14—**2:**302, 306
15:14–15—**2:**304
15:15—**2:**305
15:16—**1:**219; **2:**135, 307–9,
   316
15:17—**2:**306, 310
15:18—**1:**568; **2:**311–13
15:18–25—**2:**311
15:19—**1:**458; **2:**315–16
15:20—**1:**568; **2:**276, 314
15:21—**2:**317, 318
15:22–23—**2:**318
15:24—**2:**319
15:25—**2:**315, 320
15:26—**1:**28; **2:**324–25, 327,
   344, 667
15:26–27—**2:**322
15:26–16:4—**2:**322
15:27—**1:**28; **2:**324, 326
16—**2:**323
16:1—**2:**323, 329
16:2—**2:**329–30
16:3—**2:**330, 334
16:4—**2:**330, 334
16:4–11—**2:**333
16:6—**2:**334
16:7—**2:**334, 352
16:8—**2:**334, 338, 341, 380

16:8–9—**2:**336
16:8–10—**2:**339
16:8–11—**2:**344
16:9—**2:**337
16:10—**2:**340
16:11—**2:**341
16:12—**2:**344
16:12–13—**2:**344
16:12–15—**2:**343
16:13—**2:**258, 343–44,
   346–50, 460–61
16:13–14—**1:**165
16:13–15—**1:**98
16:14—**2:**258, 347, 350, 380,
   667
16:14–15—**2:**407
16:15—**2:**352
16:16—**2:**353–54, 357
16:16–22—**2:**353
16:17—**2:**354
16:18—**2:**354
16:18–25—**2:**437
16:19–20—**2:**354, 357
16:20—**2:**354, 356–57
16:21—**2:**360
16:21–22—**2:**360
16:22—**2:**361–62
16:23—**2:**363–64, 368, 370,
   380, 425, 435
16:23–27—**2:**363
16:24—**2:**369–70, 435
16:25—**2:**365, 368–69, 373
16:26—**2:**365–66
16:27—**2:**365, 370, 372
16:28—**2:**373–75, 381
16:28–33—**2:**373
16:29–30—**2:**376
16:30—**2:**374
16:31—**2:**376
16:32—**1:**248; **2:**376–78
16:33—**1:**475; **2:**27, 362,
   373, 378–81, 386

17—**2:**134, 385–86, 388, 416, 436, 446, 456
17:1—**1:**122, 248, 454; **2:**239, 385–86, 388, 411
17:1-2—**2:**385, 388, 392
17:1-5—**2:**386–88, 437, 456
17:2—**2:**389, 390–91
17:3—**1:**71, 259, 347, 543; **2:**395–396, 399, 402–3
17:4—**1:**58, 395; **2:**365, 403, 405–6, 409, 411, 453, 585
17:4-5—**2:**405
17:5—**1:**335; **2:**275, 408, 411–13
17:6—**2:**135, 416–17, 419–21, 446
17:6-8—**2:**416–17
17:6-19—**2:**386, 456
17:7—**2:**423
17:7-8—**2:**422
17:8—**1:**336; **2:**423–24
17:9—**1:**648; **2:**427, 458
17:9-10—**2:**428
17:9-13—**2:**426–27
17:10—**2:**429
17:11—**2:**426, 430–31, 433, 437, 439, 451
17:11-17—**2:**140
17:12—**2:**295, 433, 495
17:13—**2:**434–35, 437
17:14—**2:**437, 442
17:14-16—**2:**457
17:14-17—**2:**436–37
17:15—**2:**437, 439
17:16—**2:**441, 446
17:17—**1:**9, 46, 99, 545; **2:**436, 442–44, 446, 449, 457, 481, 520
17:18—**1:**29; **2:**450–52, 455
17:18-19—**2:**446
17:19—**2:**446–50

17:20—**2:**456–58, 460
17:20-21—**2:**456
17:20-23—**2:**456
17:20-26—**2:**386, 456
17:21—**2:**458–59, 463–64
17:22—**2:**463
17:23—**2:**460, 464
17:24—**2:**466–68, 470–74, 723
17:25—**2:**480
17:25-26—**2:**477–78
17:26—**2:**477, 481, 485
18—**2:**489, 522
18:1—**2:**491
18:1-11—**2:**489
18:2—**2:**491
18:3—**2:**491–92
18:4-5—**2:**489, 493
18:4-6—**1:**494
18:6—**1:**504; **2:**493
18:7—**2:**495
18:9—**2:**495
18:10—**1:**417
18:10-11—**2:**497
18:11—**2:**497
18:12-14—**2:**500
18:12-27—**2:**499
18:15—**2:**377, 500
18:15-16—**2:**501
18:16—**2:**501
18:17—**2:**501
18:18—**2:**502
18:19—**2:**503
18:20-21—**2:**504
18:22—**2:**505
18:23—**2:**505
18:24—**2:**505
18:25—**2:**507
18:25-27—**2:**507
18:26-27—**2:**499
18:28—**2:**517
18:28-38—**2:**510

18:29—**2:**512
18:30—**2:**512
18:31—**2:**512
18:32—**2:**512
18:33—**2:**512–13
18:34—**2:**512
18:35—**2:**512
18:36—**2:**513, 617
18:36-37—**2:**510
18:37—**1:**98, 212; **2:**516, 518–20
18:38—**2:**515–16, 519, 522
18:38-19:6—**2:**521
18:39—**2:**523
18:40—**2:**523
19—**2:**625
19:1—**2:**524
19:1-3—**2:**355
19:1-5—**2:**516
19:2-3—**2:**525
19:4—**2:**517, 522, 526
19:5—**2:**526
19:5-6—**2:**521
19:6—**1:**38; **2:**522, 527, 531
19:6-12—**2:**531
19:7—**2:**515, 531
19:8—**2:**532
19:9—**2:**532
19:10—**2:**532
19:11—**2:**531, 533–36
19:12—**2:**515, 535–36
19:13—**2:**543
19:13-14—**2:**542
19:13-22—**2:**541
19:14—**2:**542, 543
19:14-16—**2:**516
19:15—**1:**21, 86; **2:**544
19:16—**2:**517, 545
19:16-18—**2:**546
19:18—**2:**548
19:19—**2:**549, 690
19:19-20—**2:**541

19:19–22—**1:**527; **2:**541
19:20—**2:**549
19:21—**2:**550
19:22—**2:**550
19:23–24—**2:**554
19:23–27—**2:**552
19:24—**2:**541, 552
19:25—**2:**558
19:25–27—**2:**541, 558
19:26–27—**2:**501, 559
19:27—**2:**560
19:28—**2:**554, 563, 565, 567,
    569, 595
19:28–29—**2:**541
19:28–30—**2:**563
19:29—**2:**568
19:29–30—**2:**566
19:30—**2:**410, 490, 556, 564,
    569–70, 573–74, 576, 580,
    584, 590, 595, 598, 625
19:31—**2:**542, 596
19:31–33—**2:**542
19:31–37—**2:**594
19:32—**2:**596
19:33—**2:**597
19:34—**1:**485; **2:**542, 594, 598
19:35—**2:**601, 604
19:35–36—**2:**600
19:36—**2:**553, 601
19:36–37—**2:**594
19:37—**2:**553, 601
19:38—**2:**604–6
19:38–39—**1:**166; **2:**604
19:38–41—**1:**496
19:38–42—**2:**614
19:39—**1:**264; **2:**608
19:39–40—**2:**618
19:40—**2:**615, 620
19:41—**2:**614
19:42—**2:**619–20
20—**2:**625, 667, 685
20–21—**2:**655

20:1—**2:**626, 630
20:1–2—**2:**624, 636
20:1–10—**2:**624
20:2—**2:**626, 705
20:3—**2:**627
20:3–10—**2:**636
20:4—**2:**627
20:5—**2:**214, 627–28
20:6—**2:**214, 628
20:6–7—**2:**627
20:7—**2:**615, 628
20:8—**2:**629
20:9—**2:**629, 632
20:10—**2:**633
20:11—**2:**636
20:11–18—**2:**635
20:12—**2:**636
20:13—**2:**637
20:14—**2:**637
20:15–16—**2:**637
20:16—**1:**621; **2:**639
20:17—**2:**418, 639–40,
    643–44
20:18—**2:**644–46, 649, 653
20:19—**2:**656–58
20:19–20—**2:**647, 700
20:19–21—**2:**659
20:20—**2:**215, 655–56, 658,
    660–62
20:21—**1:**224
20:22—**2:**666
20:22–23—**2:**665
20:23—**2:**665, 668–70,
    672–73
20:24–25—**2:**677
20:24–29—**2:**675
20:25—**2:**215, 677
20:25–27—**2:**681
20:26—**2:**679
20:26–28—**2:**647
20:27—**2:**264, 655–56, 675,
    679, 680

20:28—**1:**9; **2:**264, 404, 474,
    681–82, 685, 687
20:29—**2:**655, 676, 683
20:30—**2:**685
20:30–31—**1:**585; **2:**631, 684
20:31—**1:**xv, 7, 10, 14, 24,
    26, 45, 98, 178, 236,
    315, 627; **2:**35, 279, 327,
    462, 683–84, 686–87,
    691, 715
21—**1:**417; **2:**694, 695, 700
21:1—**2:**694, 699
21:1–14—**2:**693
21:2—**1:**114; **2:**694, 721
21:3—**2:**696
21:4—**2:**699
21:4–6—**2:**697
21:5—**2:**698
21:6—**2:**698
21:7—**2:**693, 699–700, 702,
    705, 715
21:8—**2:**699
21:9—**2:**701, 704
21:10–11—**2:**698
21:12—**2:**701–2
21:13—**2:**701
21:14—**2:**702
21:15—**2:**703, 705–6, 709
21:15–17—**2:**703, 709
21:15–19—**2:**189
21:16—**2:**246, 705, 709
21:16–17—**2:**705
21:17—**2:**655, 705–6, 709
21:18—**2:**716
21:18–19—**2:**190
21:18–25—**2:**714
21:19—**2:**715, 717–18
21:20—**2:**721
21:21–22—**2:**722
21:22—**2:**714, 717, 723
21:23—**2:**717
21:24—**1:**6; **2:**167, 721

21:25—**2:**684, 714, 723
21:29—**2:**655

Acts
1:1–2—**2:**225
1:3—**2:**647, 666
1:8—**1:**90; **2:**328, 668
1:9–10—**2:**639
1:14—**1:**452
1:15—**2:**224
2:1–41—**1:**454
2:23—**1:**647; **2:**116, 320, 335
2:23–24—**1:**90; **2:**264, 648
2:27—**2:**522
2:36—**2:**650
2:37—**2:**335
2:38—**2:**328
2:41—**2:**224
2:42—**1:**99; **2:**331
2:42–47—**2:**159
2:47—**2:**159, 314
3:13–15—**2:**358
3:14—**2:**523
4:12—**2:**127, 211
4:18—**2:**314
4:19–20—**2:**534
4:29—**2:**318, 331–32
4:33—**1:**66; **2:**328
5:29—**2:**534
5:40—**2:**314
5:41—**2:**317, 331
5:41–42—**2:**648
6:7—**2:**320, 359
7:56—**1:**119
7:58—**2:**314
7:60—**2:**15
8—**1:**277
8:9–24—**2:**252
8:12—**1:**554
8:20—**2:**252
8:21—**2:**672
8:24—**2:**366

9:4—**2:**330
9:11—**1:**155; **2:**227
10:38—**1:**667
10:42–43—**2:**670
11:15—**2:**400
12:7f—**2:**437
13:2—**2:**252
13:48—**2:**612
14:22—**1:**367, 579
15:6—**2:**673
15:8—**1:**141
15:14—**2:**92
16:7–8—**2:**333
16:14—**1:**418
16:19—**1:**417
16:25—**1:**255
16:26—**1:**256
16:30—**1:**381
16:30–31—**1:**383; **2:**672
16:31—**1:**613; **2:**128, 654
17:11–12—**2:**423
17:16—**2:**399
17:22—**1:**531
17:23—**2:**399
17:26—**2:**19
17:29—**2:**642
17:30—**2:**128
17:31—**2:**200, 646
18:9–10—**2:**230
19:2—**2:**252
19:9—**2:**210
19:23—**2:**210
20:7—**1:**305; **2:**631
20:27—**2:**349
26:9—**2:**330

Romans
1:1—**2:**304
1:4—**1:**213, 526; **2:**410, 651
1:16—**1:**229, 316, 536, 545;
　2:41, 58, 229, 464

1:18—**1:**239, 564; **2:**67, 336,
　580
1:20—**2:**398
1:21—**1:**141, 170; **2:**398
2:5—**1:**552; **2:**337
2:12—**2:**337
3:10—**2:**337, 569
3:10–12—**1:**550
3:10–18—**1:**142–43
3:11—**1:**253
3:13—**1:**294
3:23—**1:**45, 105, 382, 555,
　601; **2:**195, 205, 576
3:23–24—**1:**137; **2:**206
3:23–25—**1:**261, 658; **2:**659
3:24—**1:**145; **2:**21, 576
3:24–25—**2:**602
3:25—**1:**137–38, 145; **2:**175,
　576
3:26—**2:**582
4:5—**1:**145
4:11—**1:**558
4:25—**2:**410, 632, 652
5:1—**1:**96; **2:**273, 660
5:2—**1:**49
5:3–4—**1:**580
5:3–5—**2:**661
5:6—**1:**240, 291, 647
5:8—**1:**105, 171, 240, 647;
　2:303, 479
5:12—**1:**579; **2:**27
5:12–14—**2:**569
5:14—**2:**623
5:18—**2:**174
5:19—**2:**409
5:20—**2:**681
6:5—**2:**448
6:11–12—**2:**420, 449
6:11–13—**2:**98
6:14—**1:**552, 553

6:23—**1**:60, 105, 182, 239,
   326, 407, 552; **2**:209,
   259, 691
7:4—**2**:283
8—**2**:475
8:1—**1**:507; **2**:410
8:2—**1**:552
8:4—**1**:404; **2**:244
8:7—**1**:386; **2**:250
8:7-8—**1**:293, 416
8:15—**2**:257
8:15-16—**2**:366
8:17—**1**:49; **2**:472, 540
8:21—**1**:554
8:26—**2**:252, 364
8:26-27—**2**:260
8:27—**1**:141
8:28—**2**:10, 27, 538
8:30—**2**:416, 429
8:31—**2**:129
8:32—**1**:174
8:34—**1**:508; **2**:191, 256,
   366, 375, 427, 587
8:35—**1**:169, 660
8:35-39—**1**:409; **2**:141
8:38-39—**1**:169, 661; **2**:653
9:6-7—**1**:558
9:15-16—**2**:581
9:16—**2**:455
9:18—**1**:446
9:25-16—**1**:446
10:3—**2**:544
10:6-8—**2**:640
10:9—**1**:105, 139
10:13—**1**:105, 284
10:14—**1**:147; **2**:455
10:14-17—**1**:650
10:15—**2**:455, 613
10:17—**1**:51, 259, 298, 316,
   336, 439; **2**:630
11:11-12—**1**:250
11:20-21—**1**:252

11:25-26—**1**:250
11:29—**1**:659; **2**:274
11:36—**2**:395, 401
12:2—**1**:259, 542, 545, 618;
   2:40, 59, 98, 258, 372,
   445
13:1—**2**:533
13:1-2—**2**:533
13:11-12—**2**:201
13:13-14—**1**:18
14:17—**1**:17, 22, 184, 194,
   428, 639; **2**:286, 420,
   633
15:24—**1**:57

1 Corinthians
1:10-17—**1**:198
1:22-24—**2**:108
1:23—**1**:434; **2**:94, 656, 664
1:24—**2**:94
1:24-25—**2**:170
1:26-29—**1**:494-95
1:30—**2**:450
2:1—**2**:326
2:2—**1**:535, 646; **2**:357
2:4—**2**:326
2:8—**2**:318, 527
2:10-11—**2**:350
2:14—**1**:154, 228, 264, 293,
   386; **2**:258, 612, 667
2:16—**2**:305
3:11—**2**:211
3:11-15—**2**:699
3:13-15—**2**:290
4:7—**1**:199
4:20—**1**:297; **2**:633
5:7—**2**:521, 601
6:11—**2**:599
6:19—**1**:138; **2**:269
6:19-20—**1**:138, 515; **2**:135
7:31—**2**:126, 441
7:39—**2**:229

8:1—**2**:479
10:4—**2**:594, 599
10:13—**2**:238
11:23-24—**1**:391
11:24—**1**:425
12:11—**2**:252
12:12—**2**:460
12:21—**2**:460
12:26-27—**2**:460
12:27—**1**:138
13:3—**2**:245
13:4-7—**2**:180
13:13—**1**:631; **2**:478, 635,
   638, 643
15:2-3—**1**:436
15:3—**2**:462, 576
15:3-4—**2**:633
15:4—**2**:462
15:4-8—**2**:647
15:6—**1**:333; **2**:224, 694
15:9—**1**:237
15:18—**2**:15
15:20—**2**:621, 632
15:42-44—**2**:10
15:42-45—**2**:658
15:42-49—**1**:224; **2**:632
15:43-44—**2**:17
15:45—**2**:255, 667
15:49—**2**:658
15:53—**2**:658
15:55-57—**2**:623
15:56—**2**:576
15:58—**1**:398

2 Corinthians
1:20—**2**:176
2:11—**2**:306
2:16—**1**:652; **2**:551
3:17-18—**1**:91
3:18—**1**:203; **2**:401
4:2—**1**:439, 534, 571; **2**:504
4:4—**1**:561; **2**:145

4:6—**1:**61, 165, 336, 530, 571; **2:**256, 402, 415
4:7—**2:**360
4:17—**1:**569; **2:**22, 474
5:8—**1:**321, 429; **2:**17, 620
5:10—**1:**325
5:17—**1:**552; **2:**397, 631
5:18—**2:**580
5:19-20—**2:**674
5:20-6:2—**2:**674
5:21—**1:**92; **2:**150, 293, 530, 555, 580
6:2—**1:**139, 328; **2:**117, 259
6:14—**2:**441
10:3-5—**2:**441
10:4-5—**2:**519
10:5—**2:**218
12:9—**1:**581; **2:**188, 235, 360

Galatians
1:4—**2:**353, 441
2:6—**2:**411
2:11f—**2:**459
2:20—**2:**267, 289, 640
3:2—**2:**260
3:13—**1:**435
4:4—**1:**405, 454
4:4-5—**2:**407
5:6—**1:**600; **2:**180
5:13—**2:**138
5:16—**2:**349
5:22-23—**2:**238, 283, 285
5:25—**2:**349
6:1—**2:**158
6:7—**1:**237
6:9—**1:**370
6:10—**2:**156
6:14—**1:**61, 646; **2:**358

Ephesians
1—**2:**227

1:4—**1:**170, 628; **2:**135, 308, 416, 421, 429
1:4-5—**1:**51; **2:**390
1:4-6—**1:**170
1:5—**2:**460
1:5-6—**2:**393
1:7—**2:**21, 578
1:11—**1:**406
1:17-20—**2:**653
1:18—**2:**138, 208
1:20-22—**1:**229; **2:**407, 414
1:20-23—**2:**473
1:21-22—**2:**652-53
1:23—**1:**138
2:1—**1:**154, 416, 655, 657; **2:**32, 58
2:1-2—**1:**285
2:1-3—**1:**228; **2:**209, 392
2:1-5—**2:**667
2:2—**2:**524
2:2-3—**1:**563
2:3—**2:**342, 642
2:4—**1:**164
2:4-5—**1:**168, 285; **2:**32, 59
2:5—**1:**154; **2:**265
2:8—**1:**284, 403
2:8-9—**1:**437, 656-57; **2:**308, 392, 424
2:10—**2:**308
2:12—**2:**545
2:13-14—**2:**179
2:14—**2:**379
2:14-16—**1:**12
2:18—**1:**260
2:20-22—**2:**346
2:21-22—**2:**269
3:8—**1:**237
3:14—**2:**366
3:18-19—**1:**168
3:19—**2:**302

3:20—**2:**236
4:2-3—**2:**157
4:3—**2:**460
4:7-11—**2:**346
4:11—**2:**710
4:18—**1:**161, 246, 294; **2:**208, 579
4:22-24—**1:**552; **2:**59, 420, 448
4:23-24—**1:**428
4:24—**1:**155; **2:**342
4:30—**2:**252
5:1—**1:**48; **2:**302
5:15-16—**2:**14
5:22—**1:**405; **2:**247
6:1—**1:**405
6:5—**1:**405
6:12—**1:**511

Philippians
1:6—**1:**156; **2:**433, 2:496
1:11—**2:**283
1:21—**1:**321; **2:**17, 289
1:23—**2:**17, 454
1:29—**2:**317
2:3-4—**2:**145, 156
2:4-5—**1:**360
2:5—**2:**156
2:6—**2:**147
2:6-8—**2:**407
2:7—**2:**148
2:9—**2:**358
2:9-11—**2:**407
2:11—**2:**69, 358
3:8-11—**2:**361
3:10—**1:**347
3:20—**2:**420
4:1—**2:**429
4:4—**2:**434
4:6-7—**2:**379
4:7—**2:**273, 277, 280, 660
4:11—**1:**66

4:13—**1:**66, 299
4:19—**1:**545, 638–39; **2:**55, 109, 701

Colossians
1:10—**2:**283
1:13–14—**1:**495
1:15—**1:**563; **2:**43, 123
1:21–22—**2:**580
1:27—**2:**486
2:3—**2:**209
2:9—**1:**54
2:15—**2:**341
3:17—**2:**235

1 Thessalonians
1:9—**2:**399, 449
4:3—**1:**404; **2:**21, 308
4:13—**2:**638
4:13–14—**2:**28
4:16—**2:**59, 621
5:16–17—**2:**369
5:17—**2:**503

2 Thessalonians
1:7–10—**1:**139
1:9—**1:**182

1 Timothy
1:5—**1:**341; **2:**310, 479
1:15—**1:**237
2:2—**1:**405
2:5—**1:**47
3:16—**1:**55
4:1—**2:**252
5:20—**2:**708
6:10—**2:**607
6:17—**2:**238

2 Timothy
1:8—**2:**240
1:12—**2:**496

2:13—**2:**378
3:12—**2:**312
3:15—**1:**462; **2:**98
3:16—**2:**288
3:16–17—**2:**260, 445
4:1—**2:**125
4:2—**2:**444
4:3–4—**1:**433
4:8—**2:**540
4:9—**1:**541

Titus
1:1—**2:**304
2:12–13—**2:**288
2:13—**2:**200
2:14—**2:**269, 429
3:3—**1:**549
3:5—**1:**508, 555

Hebrews
1:1–2—**2:**208
1:1–3—**1:**13; **2:**403
1:2—**2:**346, 485
1:3—**1:**57, 137, 563; **2:**148, 588
1:8–9—**2:**95
1:10–12—**2:**265
1:14—**2:**437, 484, 636
2:3—**1:**175; **2:**545
2:3–4—**2:**328
2:4—**1:**332; **2:**223
2:10–11—**2:**640
2:10–13—**2:**407
2:10–15—**2:**407
2:12—**2:**417
2:13—**2:**450
2:14–15—**2:**279
2:17—**1:**172; **2:**564
3:13—**2:**483
4:12—**1:**115, 439, 497, 545; **2:**116, 288, 376
4:13—**1:**141, 236

4:15—**1:**92; **2:**51, 407
6:20—**2:**200
7:24–25—**1:**659
7:25—**2:**407, 427
8:10—**1:**259, 261
8:12—**1:**261
9:11–14—**2:**450
9:12—**2:**199
9:14—**2:**256
9:22—**2:**498
9:27—**1:**325, 531, 555, 577; **2:**27
10:4—**2:**570
10:5—**2:**407
10:7—**1:**404, 447; **2:**293, 447
10:12–14—**2:**588
10:24–25—**1:**131; **2:**609
11:3—**1:**444
11:6—**2:**226
11:10—**2:**198
11:16—**1:**60
11:37–38—**1:**59
12:2—**2:**103, 200, 300, 358, 435, 470, 724
12:6—**1:**49, 139, 237, 579
12:6–7—**2:**642
12:10—**2:**287
12:11—**1:**579; **2:**283
12:28–29—**1:**257
13:1—**2:**483
13:2—**2:**484
13:2–3—**2:**484
13:3—**2:**483
13:5—**1:**542; **2:**55, 261
13:5–6—**2:**20
13:13—**2:**547
13:15—**2:**283
13:17—**1:**405
13:20—**2:**469

James
1:2–3—**1:**637–38; **2:**287, 393

1:17—**2:**47
1:18—**1:**51, 439
2:5—**1:**145
2:10—**1:**302
2:11—**2:**575
2:17—**1:**326; **2:**295
2:23—**2:**305
3:1—**1:**669
4:2—**2:**370
4:6—**2:**561
4:7—**2:**169
4:8—**2:**378

1 Peter
1:5—**2:**431, 496
1:6-7—**2:**287
1:7—**1:**368
1:12—**2:**298
1:15—**2:**299
1:16—**1:**382
1:18-19—**1:**552; **2:**588
1:19—**2:**358, 508, 522
1:20—**2:**406
1:23—**1:**52, 105, 127, 165,
    190, 387, 420, 439; **2:**57,
    320, 375, 458, 667
1:24-25—**1:**152
2:5—**1:**101, 112
2:9—**1:**101; **2:**435
2:12—**1:**52, 77
2:13-14—**1:**405
2:24—**1:**87; **2:**576
2:24-25—**2:**509
3:15—**1:**110
3:18—**1:**372
5:2-4—**2:**711
5:5—**1:**203
5:7—**2:**26, 380
5:8—**2:**278

2 Peter
1:1—**2:**304

1:3—**2:**349
1:4—**1:**52, 428
1:10—**2:**416
1:16—**2:**326
1:16-18—**1:**523;
1:17-18—**2:**219
1:19—**1:**523; **2:**120, 219
1:21—**1:**160; **2:**255, 325
2:14—**1:**549
3:10—**2:**441
3:18—**1:**71; **2:**40

1 John
1:1—**2:**326
1:2—**2:**721
1:3—**2:**326
1:4-7—**2:**721
1:5—**2:**66
1:6-2:2—**1:**299
1:7—**1:**23, 193; **2:**293, 471,
    590, 599, 680
1:7-9—**2:**151
1:7-2:2—**1:**138
1:8—**1:**91; **2:**247
2:1—**2:**256
2:1-2—**1:**196
2:2—**1:**648
2:3—**2:**249
2:5—**2:**249
2:15-17—**2:**420, 451,
    517
2:17—**1:**38
2:19—**1:**399, 661
2:20—**1:**617
2:22—**2:**462
3:2—**1:**328, 553; **2:**200, 359,
    658
3:3—**1:**328; **2:**482
3:5—**1:**90
3:8—**1:**90, 444
4:7-8—**2:**479
4:8—**2:**307, 479

4:9—**2:**294
4:9-10—**1:**174; **2:**50
4:10—**2:**365, 577
4:11—**1:**176
4:14-15—**1:**46
4:16—**2:**292
4:19—**2:**9, 245, 266, 294,
    365
5:4—**2:**382, 540
5:6—**2:**598
5:9—**1:**525
5:11-12—**1:**555
5:19—**1:**26; **2:**353, 437
5:20—**2:**397, 399
5:21—**2:**399

3 John
12—**2:**721

Jude
24—**2:**496

Revelation
1:5-6—**2:**670
1:7—**2:**602
1:13-18—**2:**413
1:16—**2:**116
2:5—**2:**446
2:17—**1:**102
2:28—**1:**102
3:20—**2:**701
3:21—**2:**471
5:6—**2:**474, 660
5:9—**2:**39, 358, 660
5:9-10—**1:**88
5:9-12—**2:**414
5:12—**2:**474, 538
6:16-17—**2:**469
12:11—**2:**539
13:8—**2:**416
14:8—**2:**125-26
14:13—**2:**16

19:9—**1:**129
19:17—**1:**270
20:9—**1:**655
20:10—**1:**182
20:11-13—**1:**325
20:11-15—**1:**629
20:12—**1:**238, 315; **2:**125
20:12-15—**1:**410

20:14—**2:**396
20:15—**1:**182, 326; **2:**416
21:2-3—**1:**129
21:3—**2:**269
21:3-4—**2:**51
21:4—**2:**361, 634
21:8—**2:**396
21:27—**1:**325

22:1—**1:**227; **2:**397
22:2—**2:**595
22:3-5—**2:**402
22:5—**2:**17, 397
22:7—**2:**90
22:14—**1:**325
22:17—**1:**270; **2:**572
22:21—**2:**675

Index of Subjects and Names

Aaron, blessing of, **2**:675
abiding in the Word, **1**:539–44, 546, 548, 566, 571; **2**:718
abiding with Christ, **1**:99–100, 428; **2**:289, 292–300
abortion, **1**:505; **2**:48, 127, 535
Abraham, **1**:336, 395, 551, 570; **2**:175, 198
    as friend of God, **2**:305
    faith of, **1**:559
    and Lot, **2**:484
    offspring of, **1**:558–59, 560
    rejoiced to see Jesus's day, **1**:572–73
    sacrifice of Isaac, **1**:86–87, 572; **2**:547–48
Absalom, **2**:165
absolution, **2**:673
abundant life, **1**:127, 634–42; **2**:31
academic institutions, **2**:439–40
Achan, **1**:236, 377, 605
ACTS (acronym for prayer), **2**:366
Acts of the Apostles, as acts of ascended Christ, **2**:225
actual sins, **1**:550
Adam (and Eve), **2**:175, 197
    creation of, **2**:666
    expelled from garden, **2**:527
    shame in nakedness, **2**:555
    sin of, **1**:239, 586; **2**:174, 526, 569
    temptation of, **1**:56–61, 181; **2**:278, 491
Adams, George, **1**:636
adonai, **2**:418
adoption, **2**:257, 372

adultery, **1**:500–501
affliction, **2**:12, 109–10, 287, 333, 376–77
affluence, **1**:11
afterlife, **1**:320–22, 328; **2**:620
agape, **1**:171; **2**:704–5
agathos, **1**:645
age to come, **2**:353
aging, **1**:422
agnosticism, **1**:19
Ahithophel, **2**:165
AIDS, **1**:358, 517, 578, 600
alcohol, **2**:421
Alexander the Great, **2**:104, 236
alienation from God, **1**:12, 26; **2**:259
allegorical interpretation, **1**:295–96
allegory, **1**:615; **2**:554–55
aloe, **2**:618
altar calls, **1**:258
"Amazing Grace" (hymn), **1**:268, 587
ambition, godly and ungodly, **1**:199
Ambrose, **1**:17
amen, **1**:179
American Civil Liberties Union, **2**:313–14
American Civil War, **1**:175; **2**:367
American evangelicals, **1**:431
American Revolution, **1**:94, 469, 531, 648; **2**:592
Amish, **2**:439
amusement parks, **1**:367
Ananias and Sapphira, **1**:377
Ancient of Days, **1**:162, 324

Andrew, **1:**95, 100–102, 104–11, 113, 271–72, 360–61; **2:**92
angel of death, **1:**86, 425
angels, **1:**120; **2:**484
animal sacrifices, **1:**86; **2:**570
Annas (high priest), **2:**499–500, 503–6
annihilationism, **1:**327
Anointed One, **1:**46, 107; **2:**35, 255, 370, 688. *See also* Messiah
anointing with oil, **1:**640–41
Anselm, **2:**573–74, 581–83
anthropology, theology as, **1:**143–44
antinomianism, **2:**243
Antiochus Epiphanes, **1:**654
apatheia, **2:**46
apostello, **2:**451
Apostles' Creed, **1:**29; **2:**526, 615
apostles, **2:**308, 451, 665
   as servants, **2:**304–5
   witness of, **2:**326–32
   ministry, **2:**223
apostolic revelation, as foundation for church, **2:**346
apostolicity, of the church, **2:**331
apprenticeship, **1:**311–12
Arimathea, **2:**605
Aristotle, **1:**513
Arius, **1:**7, 9
ark of the covenant, **1:**53, 56, 137, 260, 344; **2:**577
ark, **1:**91, 629
Arminians, **1:**415; **2:**284, 590
aroma of death, **2:**550
assent, as element of saving faith, **1:**178, 193
assurance of salvation, **2:**248–50, 285, 467–70, 474–75, 610
atheism, **1:**13, 30, 68–69; **2:**399, 452
atonement, **1:**60, 86, 248, 344, 436, 534, 645–48, 653; **2:**95–96, 174, 553, 564, 573–83, 585–90, 597, 599
   full efficacy of, **2:**591–92

attitude, **2:**154–56
Augustine, **1:**17–18, 23, 67, 76, 91, 230, 322, 397, 415–17, 455, 463, 575, 649, 653; **2:**197–98, 306, 324, 354, 409, 510, 516, 574, 599
Augustus Caesar, **2:**274
authority, **2:**532–35
   over all flesh, **2:**389, 391–92
   to forgive, **2:**668–71

Babel, **1:**119
Babylonian captivity, **2:**84, 441–42, 537
backsliding into sin, **1:**192
Baker, Mark D., **2:**575
baptism, **2:**589, 599, 673
   disputes over, **2:**462–63
   with Holy Spirit, **1:**90–92
   of John the Baptist, **1:**79–80, 82–83, 89
Baptist, Elijah, **1:**329
Barabbas, **1:**38; **2:**516, 523–24, 529–30, 548
Barclay, William, **1:**65, 124, 220, 295, 332, 341, 378, 424, 457, 515, 520, 544–45, 591; **2:**25–26, 28, 56, 65, 82, 114, 177, 216, 345, 396, 410, 546
Barnes, Alfred, **1:**311
Barnhouse, Donald Grey, **1:**99, 142, 191–92, 218, 286, 340, 373, 493, 496, 578, 628; **2:**34, 54, 96, 105, 237, 374, 444, 565, 629–30
Baron, David, **2:**85
Barth, Karl, **1:**426
bearing Christ's name, **2:**317
Beasley–Murray, George, **2:**274–75, 544, 658
Beatitudes, **2:**162, 676
behold, **2:**8
belief, **2:**31–32, 34, 54, 195, 219, 339
   true and false, **1:**538–42
Beloved Disciple, **2:**166–67, 717
   as witness to the gospel, **2:**721
benediction, as prophetic not priestly, **2:**673

Benes, Andy, **2:**232–33, 237
Bereans, **2:**423
Berkhof, Louis, **2:**407
Bernard of Clairvaux, **2:**570
Bethel, **1:**119
Bethesda, **1:**292–93
Bethlehem, **1:**392, 413
Bethsaida, **2:**92
Bible
    as Christ-centered, **2:**552–53
    content of, **2:**346–48
    inspiration and inerrancy of, **2:**462
    as one grand story of, **1:**574
    relevance of, **1:**670
    study of, **1:**98–99
biblical proclamation, **1:**104–5, 107
Black Beauty (film), **1:**146
blasphemy, charge against Jesus, **1:**316,
        330, 575, 664, 668–69; **2:**499, 505–6,
        511
blessing, **1:**194, 243–44; **2:**160, 499, 682–83,
        702
    of belonging to Jesus, **2:**471
    in the Bible, **2:**675
    of church unity, **2:**463, 465
    from obedience, **2:**266
    of Sabbath, **1:**304, 306–7
blind man, healing of, **1:**335, 577, 580, 584,
        586–93, 595, 601–3, 608–11; **2:**117
blindness, **1:**571, 588, 605–13; **2:**115
blood and water, **1:**484–85; **2:**598–99,
        601–2
blood of bull and goats, **2:**570
blood of Christ, **1:**429–30, 485, 552; **2:**680
blood sprinkled with hyssop, **2:**568
Boaz, **2:**471
body, church as, **2:**459–60
Boice, James Montgomery, **1:**18, 30, 56,
        128, 135, 170, 179, 201, 212, 217, 234,
        255, 264, 266, 332–33, 381, 393, 412–
        13, 431, 444, 476–77, 504, 515, 542,
        565, 579, 598–99, 610, 628, 639, 653,

657, 665; **2:**6, 9, 34, 47, 60, 64–66,
        69, 91, 93, 99, 103, 112, 115, 128, 134,
        137, 160, 169, 174, 210, 239–40, 248,
        250, 252, 267–68, 274, 339, 345–46,
        356, 366, 371, 379, 387, 438–39, 452,
        459, 474, 481, 491, 502, 514, 518, 522,
        533, 553, 557, 570, 579, 607, 609–11,
        695, 710–11, 715
boldness, **1:**358, 364–65
bondage, **1:**510–11
bondage of the will, **1:**415–16
bones of Jesus, not broken, **2:**553, 597, 601
Bonhoeffer, Dietrich, **1:**114
Bono, **1:**161
Book of Life, **1:**325–26
Book of Signs, **1:**57, 236, 334; **2:**52, 68, 121,
        127
Book of the Passion, **2:**121–22, 134
booths, **1:**451, 459
born again, **1:**127, 151–57, 184, 262
born from above, **1:**152, 154
born of God, **1:**50–52
bowing of the head, **2:**566
Bread of Life Discourse, **1:**223; **2:**694. *See
        also* Jesus, as bread of life
breath, **2:**666
bride, prepared for groom, **1:**205–6
bridegroom, **1:**200, 205
Bridges, Jerry, **2:**434
Brontë, Charlotte, **1:**595
brothers of Jesus, **1:**451–53
Brown, Dan, **1:**9
Bruce, F. F., **1:**266, 403, 442, 464, 486;
        2:115, 179
Brunner, Constantine, **1:**251
Buddha, **1:**209, 611
Buddhism, **1:**42, 209, 610–11; **2:**563
Bultmann, Rudolf, **2:**526–27
Bunyan, John, **1:**185–86; **2:**338, 692
burden-bearing, **2:**453, 483
Burge, Gary, **2:**57, 532

burning bush, **1:**260–61, 373, 385, 512, 522; **2:**493
Burr, Aaron, **1:**558
Burroughs, Jeremiah, **1:**173; **2:**106, 227, 316

Caesar, **2:**370
    rendering to, **2:**511, 515
    worship of, **2:**687
Caesarea Philippi, **1:**441, 443
"Caesar's friend," **2:**535–36, 539–40
Caiaphas, **1:**426; **2:**64–69, 78, 334, 499–500, 505–6, 535, 543
Cain, **1:**236, 511; **2:**197
calling
    in Christian ministry, **1:**358, 360–62
    into the world, **2:**451–52
Calvary, **2:**546
Calvin, John, **1:**202, 268, 426, 443, 472, 494, 502, 504; **2:**46, 118
    on ascension of Christ, **2:**354
    on atonement, **2:**586–87, 590
    on authority of Christ, **2:**389
    on bondage to sin, **1:**549
    on death of Christ, **2:**612
    on deity of Christ, **2:**275–76
    on dirty feet, **2:**151
    on doctrines of grace, **1:**653–54
    on election, **1:**406, 419
    on enlightenment, **1:**542
    on forgiveness of sins, **2:**668–69
    on glory of the cross, **2:**175
    on "greater works" of disciples, **2:**225
    on healing of blind man, **1:**588–89
    on holiness of Christ, **2:**450
    on Holy Spirit, **2:**258, 277, 325, 351–52
    on Jesus as Good Shepherd, **2:**495
    on Sabbath, **2:**596
    on suffering for Christ, **2:**331–32
    on Satan, **1:**560
    on Peter, **2:**189, 501
    on prayer, **2:**8

    on preaching, **1:**532
    on resurrection, **2:**30
    on resurrection Sunday, **2:**657
    on righteousness of Christ, **2:**555–56
    on worship, **1:**258
Calvinism, **1:**393–94, 653–54
Camp, Walter, **1:**94
Campbell, Archibald, **1:**42
Camus, Albert, **2:**15
Cana, **1:**281, 282
    miracle at, **1:**75, 122–29, 236, 265, 281, 334, 453
Capernaum, **1:**397, 429, 432
Capernaum official's son, **1:**282–88, 292, **1:**334
Capernaum paralytic, **2:**669–70 (Mark)
capital punishment, **2:**512
capitalism, **1:**520
Carey, George, **2:**461
Carey, William, **1:**654
Carmichael, Amy, **1:**582–83
Carson, D. A., **1:** 336, 398, 460, 499n1, 589, 634–35, 656; **2:**27, 94, 144, 208, 275, 388, 464, 585
Carter, Leon, **1:**329
casting of lots, for Jesus' clothing, **2:**554–56
centurion, at crucifixion, **1:**670; **2:**566
ceremonial law, **1:**67–68, 344
ceremonial washing, **1:**124, 265
Chalke, Steve, **1:**436; **2:**575
Chalmers, Thomas, **1:**266, 608
Charing Cross (London), **1:**535
children of God, **1:**49
Christian
    definition of, **2:**233
    sees glory of God in Christ, **1:**57, 61
Christianity
    antithesis with other religions, **1:**209–10
    exclusivity of, **2:**202–11
    as heart-religion, **1:**259

origins of, **1:**94
uniqueness of, **2:**563
Christian life, **1:**193, 203, 356, 368
exuberance of, **1:**631
as fruit-bearing, **2:**289
as increasing enlightenment in the truth, **1:**542
looks to Jesus, **2:**221
and obedience, **1:**404–5
works in, **1:**382–83
Christian Sabbath, **1:**304–8
Christians
disharmony among, **2:**431–32
keep God's Word, **2:**421–24
legalistic spirit of, **1:**303–4
as realists, **1:**95, 234; **2:**193, 195, 200
as salt and light, **2:**663
scattering of, **2:**377–78
separated from the world, **2:**419–21
"Christless Christianity," **1:**95
Christless religion, **1:**124–25
Christlikeness, **1:**156, 357, 360
Christmas, **1:**15
Christology, **1:**6, 443, 625
Christus Victor theory of the atonement, **2:**575–76
Chrysostom, John, **1:**411
church, **2:**457–58
as apostolic, **2:**332
authority to declare forgiveness of sins, **2:**670–74
as body, **2:**459–60
as body of Christ, **1:**138
as bride of Christ, **1:**396
as community not club, **2:**155–56, 178
discipline, **1:**607; **2:**673–74, 708
diversity in, **1:**112
holiness of, **2:**437, 446, 457
as lambs, **2:**709–10
love for, **2:**156–57
love of, **2:**477–78, 481–84
marks of, **2:**387

materialism in, **1:**377–78
membership, **1:**582
mission of, **2:**450–55
size of, **1:**375
unity of, **1:**112, 648–51; **2:**431–32, 458–65
weakness of, **1:**391
and the world, **2:**438–42
church growth, **1:**133, 534; **2:**156, 159
Churchill, Winston, **2:**17
Cicero, **2:**546
circumcision, **1:**466–67
cities of refuge, **1:**629–30
citizens of heaven, **2:**420
City of Man, **2:**516
civil authority, obedience to, **2:**532–35
civil disobedience, **2:**534
clay, **1:**588, 596
cleanliness, **1:**124, 291
cleansing, **1:**82, 89; **2:**146–52, 288, 599, 602–3
Clement of Alexandria, **2:**386
Clement of Rome, **2:**717
Clopas, **2:**670
cloud, **1:**514–15; **2:**413
cold hearts, of Pharisees, **1:**599–600
colonnade of Solomon, **1:**655
Colony of Mercy, **2:**238
Columbus, Don Diego, **1:**225
comfort, **1:**640; **2:**28–29, 39, 619–22
comforter, **2:**253
coming to Jesus, **1:**392, 400–401
commitment, **1:**178, 193; **2:**166
communion with God, **2:**268–70
Communism, **1:**664
community, vs. club, **2:**155–56, 178
compassion, **1:**303, 354, 359–60, 364–65; **2:**158
complacency, **2:**266
comprehending the light, **1:**22
condemnation, **1:**16, 182, 324–27, 508, 626; **2:**124–26, 569

condemnation of world, **1:**188–89;
  2:318–19
confession of faith, **1:**263–64; **2:**429–30
confidence in God, **2:**55–56
confidence in prayer, **2:**240
confidence in the gospel, **2:**226
conflict, inevitability of, **1:**601–2
Confucianism, **2:**563
Confucius, **1:**209
conquest, **1:**344
conscience, **1:**496; **2:**706
consecration, **2:**447–50
Constantine, **1:**470
consumerism, **1:**514; **2:**438, 440
consuming passion for Jesus, **1:**204–6
contentment, **1:**199
Continental Divide, **1:**489, 498, 612
conversion, **1:**314, 318
conviction, of sin, **1:**241–42, 245
Cornelius, **2:**399–400, 404, 670
corruption, moral and spiritual, **2:**437
Council of Nicaea, **1:**7, 9
counselor, Holy Spirit as, **2:**253
counterculture (1960s movement), **1:**44
counterculture, Christian faith as, **1:**44–45
courage, **2:**610, 612
Court of the Gentiles, **1:**131–32
Court of Women, **1:**526
courtroom, **1:**338–39
courtroom of heaven, **1:**187–88
covenant of grace, **2:**457
covenant of redemption, **1:**395; **2:**390,
  406–8
Cowper, William, **1:**261; **2:**602–3, 713
Cranmer, Thomas, **2:**330
creation, **1:**75, 305, 308, 310, 479; **2:**137, 666
  curse on, **2:**526
  in Gospel of John, **2:**614
cremation, **2:**620
Crosby, Fanny, **2:**600, 602
cross, **1:**425, 534–35; **2:**88–89, 95–96, 103,
  355, 403

centrality of, **1:**646
condemns all worldly religions, **1:**457
faith in, **1:**427
glory of, **1:**60–61; **2:**98–99, 103–7,
  174–77
humiliation of, **2:**147–48
as offense and stumbling block,
  1:433–36; **2:**94
preaching of, **2:**108
shame of, **1:**60
as symbol, **2:**477
weakness of, **2:**86
cross–bearing, **1:**515; **2:**109–10, 141, 190,
  394, 530, 718–20, 724
crossing cultural barriers, **1:**219–21, 228
crowd
  attracted to Jesus' personality, **1:**432
  demand for sign, **1:**413
  division among, **1:**490–92
  failed to read signs, **1:**377, 383, 385–87
  murmuring of, **1:**414–15, 432–33
  unbelief of, **1:**452, 465–67
crown of glory, **2:**530, 724
crown of thorns, **1:**241; **2:**89, 525–26, 528,
  539
crucifixion, **2:**106, 355, 512, 565, 596
  and resurrection, **2:**656
  wounds from, **2:**659
crurifragrium, **2:**596
cultural influence, **2:**441
culture war, **2:**86
cup of blessing, **2:**498
cup of God's judgment and wrath,
  2:497–98
cup of sour wine, **2:**572
curses, **1:**243–44; **2:**675
cursing of barren tree, **2:**71
cynicism, of Sanhedrin, **2:**62–64
Cyprian, **2:**554

Da Vinci, Leonardo, **2:**168
Damascus road, **1:**397–98

Daniel, 1:369; 2:441–42, 537–39

darkness, 1:15, 20–24, 40, 42, 188, 190, 196, 367, 509–12, 516–17, 529–30, 548–49, 550, 554, 571, 586–87, 593, 605, 611; 2:112–13, 124, 126, 172

   at crucifixion, 2:543, 556

   of cosmic powers, 2:576

   of Jewish leaders, 2:544

   opposes Jesus, 1:604

   of world, 1:611–12

Darwin, Charles, 1:17

Dathenus, Petrus, 1:144–45

David, 2:164–65, 528

   and Jonathan, 1:201–2

   as man after God's own heart, 1:204

   offspring of, 1:248

   as shepherd, 1:643

   as type of Christ, 1:344

   repentance of, 2:299

   sin with Bathsheba, 1:142, 236–37, 242; 2:185

Dawkins, Richard, 2:399

Day of Atonement, 1:137, 260–61, 344; 2:523, 547, 577

day of judgment, 1:238, 320, 409–10

Dead Sea, 1:66, 487

death, 1:11, 182–83, 374, 510–11, 640; 2:13–18, 22–23, 30–31, 34, 57, 193

   cannot end eternal life, 1:429

   cause for sorrow, 2:47

   as consequence of sin, 2:569

   conquering of, 1:285, 660–61; 2:174, 381, 617, 621–22

   as outrage, 2:46

declaration of pardon, 2:673

decree, 1:406, 454

definitive sanctification, 2:448

Demas, 1:541

demon, cry of, 1:444

denominations, 1:651; 2:463–64

depravity, 1:38–39

depression, 1:378

desert, 1:352, 355–56

devil, spiritual offspring of, 1:560–63

devotion to Jesus, 2:38–39, 72–75, 79

Diet of Worms, 1:461

diligence, in searching Scriptures, 1:345–46

dirty feet, 2:150–51

discernment, 1:359

disciple, as learner, 1:544

disciple, experienced, 1:542–44

disciples, 1:432; 2:166–68

   belief of, 2:376

   as branches, 2:283–84, 288–89

   calling of, 2:137–38, 715

   commissioning of, 2:662–64

   education of, 2:715

   failure of, 1:41

   gathered on resurrection Sunday, 2:657

   ignorance of, 2:87–88

   indifference of, 1:358–59

   regathering in Galilee, 2:694–95

   in secret, 2:606–11

   as servants, 2:304–5

   true and false, 1:442

   as witness, 1:28; 2:326

   unworthiness of, 2:136

discipleship, 1:97–102, 272; 2:321, 695, 702, 722

   as costly, 1:516

   as privilege, 2:234

   blessed, 1:538, 544–45

   boldness in, 2:611–13

   cost of, 2:311

   experienced, 1:538

   in secret, 2:613–14

   proved, 1:538–42

   proving, 2:298–99

discipline, 1:49; 2:94

disobedience, 2:299

dispensationalism, 2:243

Dispersion, 1:474

Dobson, James, 1:164

docetism, **2:**564, 597
doctrine, **2:**460–62
   and love, **2:**478–80
   in New Testament, **2:**347–48
doctrines of grace, **1:**393–94, 400, 654–58
Dodd, C. H., **1:**179, 312, 604–5
Dollar, Creflo, **1:**637
donkey, **2:**83–86, 523
Donne, John, **1:**88–89
door, **1:**619, 625–30, 632
doubt, **1:**408, 464, 546; **2:**677–78, 681
dove, **1:**91
drawing of God, **1:**417–21, 445
"drawn" to Jesus, **2:**107–8
drug culture, **2:**242
Duncan, Ligon, **1:**258; **2:**712
dying to sin, **2:**97–98

earthly agendas, **1:**521
earthly kings, **2:**86
earthly needs, **1:**379
earthly prosperity, **1:**355
East–West schism of the church, **2:**324–25
Ecce homo, **2:**527–29
ecology, **2:**440
economic Trinity, **2:**325
ecumenism, **2:**458–59, 464
Eden, **2:**491, 527
Edwards, Jonathan, **1:**125, 143, 284, 558,
   583, 654; **2:**690–91
effectual call, **1:**418–19, 620
effectual grace, **2:**138
Ehrman, Bart, **1:**9
eighth day, **1:**480–81
Einstein, Albert, **1:**522
election, **1:**222, 394–96, 406, 413, 445–46,
   621, 628, 653, 657; **2:**135, 308–9,
   316–17, 390, 392, 416–17
El-Elyon, **2:**417
Elijah, **1:**28, 70, 76–79, 87, 313, 336, 384,
   444, 525; **2:**213, 218, 220, 439, 457,
   610

Elisha, **1:**313, 351, 434; **2:**457
Elliot, Jim, **1:**331–32
Elohim, **2:**417
El–Roi, **2:**417
El–Shaddai, **2:**417
Emancipation Proclamation, **1:**545
Emmaus road, **1:**316, 343; **2:**120, 519, 552,
   656
enlightenment
   from Christ, **1:**36–37, 43
   from God's Word, **1:**542–44
Enlightenment (Western humanism), **1:**513
entertainment, **1:**230, 490, 618; **2:**438, 440
envy, **1:**199–200
Ephesus, **1:**474; **2:**687
Erasmus, **1:**415
eros, **1:**171
Esau, **1:**119
escapism, **2:**273
eschatology, **2:**353–54
eternal death, **1:**327–28
eternal life, **1:**11, 37, 71, 163, 165, 174–77,
   183–86, 214–15, 227, 232–33, 285,
   316–18, 327, 337, 355, 378, 382, 419,
   427–29, 443, 445, 484, 612, 628, 634,
   657, 659, 666; **2:**31, 42, 96, 128, 149,
   209, 265, 390–92, 393–404, 425, 615,
   683, 691–92
eternal rest, **1:**305
eternal security, **1:**630, 653, 659–62
eternity, **2:**201
Eucharist, **1:**424; **2:**599
Eusebius, **2:**716
evangelism, **1:**104, 106, 224; **2:**108, 696–98
   as crossing barriers, **1:**218–21
   of Jews, **1:**250–52
evil, **1:**507, 510
evolution, **1:**17, 513; **2:**345
excommunication, **1:**607, 610; **2:**329–30, 673
exegete, **1:**71
exodus, **1:**53, 304, 351–56, 407, 423, 425,
   451, 459, 480, 514, 519; **2:**80

expository preaching, 1:461
extravagance, 2:74–75
eyewitnesses, 1:136, 210; 2:326, 328, 504, 721
Ezekiel, 1:616, 619; 2:396–97, 444, 668

faith, 1:155, 177–81, 211, 214–15, 231–32, 317; 2:32–42, 117, 220
    boldness of, 1:358, 364–65
    challenge of, 2:118–19
    comes to Jesus seeking salvation, 1:285–86
    content of, 2:35–37
    does not save by itself, 1:286
    of the ear, 1:658
    and eternal life, 2:391–92
    of the foot, 1:658
    as gift, 1:437, 656; 2:424–25
    as great distinction, 1:45–47, 50, 52
    and great works, 2:226
    growth of, 2:40–41
    of the hands, 1:658
    kept secret, 2:606
    as living practice and habit, 1:33
    looks upward to God, 2:55
    and love, 2:180
    necessity of, 1:427
    not blind, 1:330
    and peace, 2:279
    as personal, 1:427
    salvation through, 1:658
    as seeing, 1:179–80, 608–9
    strengthening of, 1:287
    as weak and failing, 2:378
    without works, 2:295
faithfulness, of minister, 1:364
fall, 1:574
"falling away," 2:329
false faith, 1:538–39
false gods, 2:687
false lights, 1:513–14
false messiahs, 1:520

false prophet, 1:617
false religion, 1:245–47, 296
false righteousness, 2:339
false shepherds, 1:615–18, 621, 643–44
false spirituality, 1:530–31
false teaching, 1:246, 543, 617
family, church as, 2:460
Farewell Discourse, 2:177, 183, 253, 257
    and departure of Christ, 2:333, 354
    encouragement in, 2:311
    figures of speech in, 2:368
    on Holy Spirit, 2:344, 560, 667
    on martyrdom, 2:322–23
    on obedience, 2:265–66, 306
    peace in, 2:379
    promises in, 2:261–62, 309
Father, 2:418, 432
    accepted Jesus's saving work, 2:340, 405, 415
    care of, 1:49
    drawing of, 1:417–21, 445; 2:107–8
    election of, 2:135
    glorifying, 2:298–99
    as God, 1:309–10
    love for the Son, 1:311–12; 2:292–93, 469
    love of, 1:48, 172; 2:464
    patience of, 1:169
    prayer to, 2:364–68
    as pruner, 2:286–87
    revealed in Jesus Christ, 2:215–17
    sending of the Son, 1:213–14, 460; 2:453–54
    unity with the Son, 1:664–67
    as vinedresser, 2:283, 291
    will of, 1:405–10
    as witness, 1:27, 335–36, 525
fear, 1:510
    of death, 1:553; 2:621
    of God, 2:320, 536–38
    of man, 2:536–38, 606–7, 609

Feast of Booths (Tabernacles), 1:450–51, 454–59, 471, 486, 512–13; 2:80, 82, 122
Feast of Dedication, 1:655–56
Feast of Unleavened Bread, 1:454, *See also* Passover
Feast of Weeks, 1:451. *See also* Pentecost
feeding on Christ, 1:391, 428
feeding on flesh of Christ, 1:426, 429–30
feeding on Word of God, 1:393
feeding the five thousand, 1:188, 223, 334, 349–56, 357–58, 361, 376, 380–81, 441–42, 450; 2:701
fellowship with Christ, 2:699–701–2
fellowship, 2:166, 483, 609–11
Ferguson, Sinclair, 1:48, 49, 156; 2:327, 420
fiducia, 1:178
fifth commandment, 2:560
fig tree, 1:115
filioque clause (Nicene Creed), 2:324–25
final judgment, 1:315, 322, 325–27; 2:125, 348, 530
financial fraud, 2:708
finding Jesus, 1:115–16
firstfruits, 1:451, 456
fish symbol, 2:477
fishers of men, 2:694
fishing, 2:696–99
fixing eyes on Jesus, 2:722–24
flagellatio, 2:524
Flavel, John, 1:172, 174–75, 553; 2:408, 615–17, 621–23
flesh, 1:54, 425, 437–38, 520; 2:389, 391–92
Fletcher, Joseph, 2:242
flogging of Jesus, 2:524–25
flood, 1:91, 629
floodlights, 2:351
following Jesus, 1:355–56, 448–49, 515, 623, 658; 2:503, 715–24
folly, 1:510–11, 530
food that endures to eternal life, 1:378–79, 381, 383

food that perishes, 1:378–79, 383
football, 1:94
foot-washing, 2:74, 144–47, 154, 248, 482
Ford, Henry, 1:12
"Forever People," Christians as, 1:428
forgiveness, 1:96, 504–6, 508, 556, 666; 2:340, 372, 668–74
fountain of life, 1:481–87, 497
"Fountain of Youth," 1:226, 230, 233
fountain, of Christ's blood, 2:602
fragrance from life to life, 2:550–51
fragrant aroma, 2:79
Franklin, Benjamin, 2:14
free will, 1:396, 415–17
freedom, 1:446, 547
  from fear, 1:544–45
  salvation as, 1:544–45
  from self, 1:545
  from sin, 1:545, 553–56; 2:578
  from wickedness of world, 1:545
freethinkers, 1:548
French Revolution, 1:471
friend of the bridegroom, 1:200
friends of Jesus, 2:539–40
friendship, 2:5
Fromm, Erich, 1:11–12
fruitlessness, 2:283–86, 295
fruit of faith, 1:485, 539–42, 546; 2:249, 2:283–91, 295–96, 298, 308–9
fruit of the Spirit, 2:283
fullness of time, 1:454
fustigatio, 2:524

Galilee, 1:281, 282, 2:693–94, 696
Gamaliel, 2:619
garden of Eden, 2:614–15
gardening, 1:102
gatekeeper, 1:619, 621
Gehenna, 2:618
gender roles, 2:440
general call of the gospel, 1:420, 620
general redemption, 2:590

Gentiles, **1:**88, 220, 249, 263, 434–35, 474; **2:**616

geography, shapes theology, **1:**614

Gethsemane, **2:**101–2, 386, 489–96

Girardeau, John L., **1:**23–24; **2:**94

giving, **1:**380

glorification, **2:**21–22

glory, **1:**58–60, 530; **2:**93–94, 98–100, 388

glory cloud, **2:**413

glory–seeking, **2:**466–67

Gnosticism, **1:**6; **2:**564, 597

God, compassion of, **1:**351

    accepted Jesus's saving work, **2:**340, 405, 415

    cares about our sorrows, **2:**44

    compassion of, **2:**266

    as eternal, **1:**170

    faithfulness of, **2:**175

    feelings of, **2:**46–48

    glory of, **1:**194, 324, 568–69, 581, 584; **2:**12–13, 103–4, 109–10, 182, 239–40, 298, 392, 412

    holiness of, **1:**169; **2:**43, 149, 403

    as infinite, **1:**170

    as judge, **1:**238

    justice of, **2:**175, 205, 479, 575, 582

    knowledge of our sin, **1:**235–37

    loathes all sin, **1:**182

    love of, **1:**163–64, 168–77, 351; **2:**106, 294, 310

    love of complacency, **2:**266

    mercy of, **1:**357

    power of, **1:**351

    promise of, **2:**175–76

    righteousness of, **2:**478–79

    seeking sinners, **1:**254

    sovereignty of, **1:**170, 180, 222; **2:**329, 454–55, 536–38

        in crucifixion of Jesus, **2:**542, 549, 554

        in grace of, **1:**398, 417

        in salvation, **1:**402–3, 445, 620

Godet, Frédéric, **1:**222, 442; **2:**389, 406

godliness, **2:**442

golden calf, **1:**258–59, 355

Golgotha, **2:**546

Gomer, **2:**578–79

good, **1:**645

Good Shepherd, **1:**617; **2:**50, 60

good works, **1:**193, 246–47, 326, 381–83, 664, 667–70; **2:**181, 269, 295–96, 429

Goodwin, Thomas, **2:**661

gospel, **1:**25–26, 161, 224, 316, 472, 506

    offense of, **2:**205

    to the nations, **2:**616

    rejection of, **2:**172

    spread of, **2:**224

    as two–edged sword, **2:**113, 116

    urgency of Christ, **2:**155

grace, **1:**61, 64–66, 68–70, 161, 283–85, 396–98, 402, 505, 508; **2:**388, 454, 602

    conquers death, **1:**285

    under trials, **1:**602

    and truth, **1:**60–61

"grace upon grace," **1:**64–66

Graham, Billy, **1:**555

gratitude, and obedience, **2:**293

grave

    conquered by death of Christ, **2:**617

    conquered by resurrection of Christ, **2:**621–22

Great Awakening, **2:**441

great commandment, **2:**243

Great Commission, **1:**271–72; **2:**225, 309, 412, 694, 714

    in Gospel of John, **2:**655, 662–64, 667

Great Confession, **1:**384, 441–43, 445

greater works, **2:**223–28, 230

Greek philosophy, **1:**10

Greeks, in Jerusalem, **2:**92, 100

Green, Joel B., **2:**575

Greenleaf, Simon, **1:**136, 333–34

grief, **2:**25–27, 706
growth, **1:**485
guilt, **1:**21, 68, 144, 147, 552

Hale, Nathan, **1:**648; **2:**592
Hallel, **1:**480
Hallelujah" (Boice hymn), **2:**474–75
Hamilton, Alexander, **1:**558
Handel, George Frideric, **2:**345
Hanging Gardens of Babylon, **2:**104
Hanukkah, **1:**655
happiness, **2:**159–62
hard teaching, **1:**432–33
hardened hearts, **1:**134, 283, 526, 656
hardened unbelievers, **1:**574–75
Hardy, Thomas, **1:**414
Harnack, Adolf von, **1:**76
harvest, **1:**275–77, 279, 454, 456, 458, 480
hate, **2:**313
Hawthorne, Nathaniel, **2:**401
healing, **1:**57, 64, 294, 313–14, 334, 476
    on the Sabbath, **1:**308, 310, 333, 466–67
health–and–wealth gospel, **1:**475, 617
heart
    as deceitful, **1:**141–42, 294; **2:**242, 508
    God's knowledge of, **1:**141
    hardening of, **2:**113, 115–18
heaven, **2:**206–7, 468
    glory in, **2:**472–74
    hope of, **2:**196–99, 201
    opened, **1:**119–20
    as "with Christ," **2:**471–72
hedonism, **2:**481
hell, **1:**327; **2:**567–68, 618
helper, Holy Spirit as, **2:**254
Hemingway, Ernest, **1:**125–26
Hendriksen, William, **1:**128–29, 191, 194,
    590, 597; **2:**76, 102, 106, 117–18, 124,
    200, 328, 374, 504–5, 598n6, 680
Henry of Navarre, **1:**541
Henry, Matthew, **1:**522, 596, 599; **2:**9, 16,
    38, 78, 273, 322–24, 349, 365, 381,

    412–13, 433, 470, 485, 504, 549, 599,
    622, 710, 722
Heraclitus, **1:**10–11
Herbert, George, **2:**165–66
heresy, **1:**6, 369; **2:**374
Herod, **1:**38, 63, 188, 499; **2:**618
heroes, in Scripture, **1:**59–60
heterodox, **2:**411
Hicks, Edward, **2:**271–72, 274, 280
high priest, **1:**260
High Priestly Prayer, **2:**467–68, 395,
    426–35
history, in New Testament, **2:**347
Hitler, Adolf, **2:**104
holiness, **1:**138, 156, 169, 355–56, 670;
    2:99, 267, 308, 403, 419, 421, 429,
    450, 482
    of Lord's Day, **2:**305–7
    as missional, **2:**452–53
Hollywood, **1:**618
"Holy One of God," **1:**444
Holy Spirit, **2:**135
    and application of salvation, **2:**335
    baptism of, **1:**90–92
    at baptism of Jesus, **2:**255
    as comforter, **2:**380
    coming on Pentecost, **1:**480
    convicting work of, **2:**334–42
    deity of, **2:**252
    glorifies Christ, **2:**350–52
    as guide, **2:**349–50
    as helper, **2:**218, 251–54, 276–77, 324,
        344, 560
    illuminating work of, **1:**165; **2:**254–57,
        277, 349, 368, 485, 519–20
    inspiration of, **2:**349
    as living water, **1:**484
    and new birth, **1:**155, 160, 437–38
    outpouring of, **1:**90
    as person, **2:**252, 260
    power from, **2:**180, 666–68
    power of, **2:**180, 225, 259–60, 666–68

and prayer, 2:364
procession of, 2:324
promise of, 2:225, 230–31, 263
rested upon Jesus, 1:212–13
and revelation, 2:344–50
sending of, 1:98
as Spirit of truth, 2:257–58
strengthens faith, 1:185
as witness, 1:28; 2:323–27
home, 2:197–98, 693
homogeneous unit principle, 2:156
homosexuality, 1:505, 600; 2:48, 127,
    535
hope, 2:28–29, 200, 486, 490, 508–9
    for glory, 2:467
    of heaven, 2:196–99, 201
    of resurrection, 2:46, 620, 623
    in this age and age to come, 2:353
hora, 454
Hosanna, 2:82–83
Hosea, 2:578–79
hospitality, 2:483–84
"hour," 1:248, 454
Hughes, Kent, 1:66, 132, 198, 257, 259, 314,
    318, 342, 369–70, 621, 638; 2:13, 77,
    107, 712
human responsibility, and divine sover-
    eignty, 1:403
human traditions, 1:596
humanism, 1:520; 2:438, 452
humble servanthood, 2:154, 157–59
humiliation, of the cross, 2:147–48
humility, 1:202–4, 237–38, 346, 465, 523;
    2:74, 84–87, 146–47, 156, 158
Hunter, A. M., 2:99
hurricanes, 1:580
Hutcheson, George, 1:211, 232, 368, 396,
    414, 522; 2:38–39, 49, 216, 471, 659
Huxley, Aldous, 1:190
"hyper," 1:426
hypocrisy, 1:194, 448, 516; 2:76, 517
hyssop, 2:568

"I am," 1:260–61, 373, 385, 512, 574, 624;
    2:29, 418
"I am" sayings of Jesus, 1:98, 102, 105,
    384–85, 390–91, 481, 493, 499n1,
    512, 525, 573–74, 625–26; 2:203,
    233–34, 281, 283, 493–94, 509
idols, idolatry, 1:239, 258, 295, 442; 2:115,
    283, 399
ignorance, 1:159, 249, 315, 491, 496,
    510–11, 530, 605; 2:185–87, 192
illumination, 1:165
image of God, 1:11, 102, 293, 600; 2:123,
    137, 466
imitation of Christ, 2:95, 301–2
imperialism, 2:482
imputation, of righteousness of Christ,
    1:507; 2:150, 293, 555–56
"in Christ," 2:600
"in spirit and truth," 1:254
incarnation, 1:7, 54–55, 371, 403–4, 424;
    2:101, 137, 374, 494
indicative and imperative, 2:195
individual, and the group, 1:11–12
inheritance, 1:411; 2:147
injustice, 2:158, 283, 517
inscription, at the cross, 2:549, 554
Internet, 1:492
invalid, healing of. See paralytic, healing
    of
invitation of Jesus Christ, 1:269–70
invitation, 1:481–85, 487, 620, 628–29
Irenaeus, 1:6
Ironside, Harry, 1:19–20, 30, 96–97, 100,
    491; 2:464, 522
irony, 1:605
    of Jesus' cry of thirst, 2:567
    in trial of Jesus, 2:531–32, 539, 543
irresistible grace, 1:396–98, 401
Isaac, 1:551, 572; 2:547–48
Isaiah, 1:144; 2:111–12, 114–15, 119–20,
    163–64, 175
Ishii, Tokichi, 2:32

Ishmael, 1:551
Islam, 1:209, 611
Israel
    as false and wild vine, 2:282–83
    false shepherds of, 1:616, 619
    as flock of God, 1:616
    rejection of Jesus, 1:39–41
    in the wilderness, 1:352, 412
"it is finished," 2:584, 590

Jackson, Stonewall, 1:544; 2:19–20
Jacob, 1:115
Jacob's ladder, 1:119–20, 388–89
Jacob's well, 1:226, 228–29, 266
James, brother of Jesus, 1:452
Jane Eyre (novel), 1:594–95
Jane Grey, Lady, 2:98
jealousy, 1:199
Jehovah (name), 1:260, 385, 574; 2:418
Jehovah's Witnesses, 1:9; 2:275
Jerusalem, 1:469, 528–29
    fall of, 1:6; 2:295
    Jesus' lament over, 1:475
    Jesus' triumphal entry into, 2:71, 80–90
Jerusalem Council, 2:673
Jesus (name), 1:240
    Jesus Christ
    abandoned by disciples, 2:506–8
    accomplishment of salvation, 2:335
    arrest of, 2:492, 495–97
    artistic renderings of, 1:130
    ascension of, 1:98, 474, 593; 2:275–76, 340, 413
    authority of, 1:460–62, 493, 522–24, 667, 2:56
    baptism of, 1:119, 335; 2:103, 255, 327, 494
    as better tabernacle, 1:61
    birth of, 2:103
    as blameless, 2:522, 524
    blood of, 1:241; 2:568
    as bread of life, 1:98, 334, 351, 354–55, 362, 388–93, 423, 426, 525, 624; 2:203

brothers of, 1:451–53
burial of, 2:596, 605, 608, 615–23
care for lost, 1:217–19
come down from heaven, 1:413–14
commissioned by Father, 1:213–14
compassion of, 1:360, 363, 364–65, 376, 505, 587; 2:39–40, 701
conquered death, 2:381
at creation, 2:614
crucifixion of, 2:545–49, 553–62, 565–66
cry of thirst, 2:564–66, 571–72, 595
death of, 1:148, 622; 2:13, 22, 426, 597–98, 605
decisive impact on history of world, 1:477
deity of, 1:7–10, 46, 128–29, 141, 235–36, 319, 323–24, 337, 350, 372, 388, 437, 665–67; 2:67, 101, 124, 137, 195, 275–76, 370, 374, 412, 462, 564, 682, 685–87
departure of, 2:333–34, 354, 364, 374–75
discipling the Twelve, 2:140
as divider, 1:490–98
as the door, 1:625–29, 630, 632, 634; 2:203
emotions of, 2:45
endowed with Holy Spirit, 1:212–13
enters Jerusalem, 2:689
as example, 1:114; 2:55–56, 154–59
faithfulness of, 2:561
as final prophet, 2:163–64
finished work of, 2:584–93
foreknowledge of, 2:188, 721
forsaken at cross, 2:547, 556–57
as fountain of life, 1:481–84
friendship of, 2:5, 302–4, 540
fulfillment of Old Testament, 1:250, 476, 507
fullness of grace, 1:64–66
as giver of life, 1:313–14, 443

glory of, 1:57–59, 128, 569; 2:93, 119–20, 174–77, 387–88, 411–15, 429, 472–74, 714

as Good Shepherd, 1:98, 114, 116, 426, 615, 619–23, 635–42, 643–52; 2:50, 138, 190, 203, 284, 475, 495, 587, 589, 591

good works of, 1:664, 667–70

grew tired and thirsty, 1:218

healing of, 1:476

as Holy One of God, 1:444

humanity of, 1:54, 218, 221, 414; 2:47, 67, 124, 137, 195, 275–76, 370, 374, 412, 564, 620; 2:101

humiliation of, 1:404; 2:454, 555, 616–17, 619, 622

humility of, 1:57, 98, 241, 283; 2:85–87, 144, 154, 318

innocence of, 2:515

intercession of, 2:140, 190–91, 373, 375, 385–86, 426, 467–68, 477

intimate affection of, 2:72

as judge, 1:139, 195, 314–15, 320, 322–24

as king, 1:47; 2:257, 259, 370, 513, 539, 549–51, 688–90

knowledge of man, 1:140–43, 147–48

as Lamb of God, 2:345

as life, 1:16–18

lifted eyes to heaven, 1:362

lifted up, 1:163; 2:14, 104–6

as light, 1:18–24, 31–32, 98, 116, 196, 510, 517, 525, 584, 590; 2:112, 172, 203

as Lord, 1:443; 2:160, 370, 389, 391, 681–89

as Lord of the Sabbath, 1:308

love of, 1:648; 2:49–50, 2:294

love for his disciples, 2:177

love for his own, 2:134–36, 138–42, 156, 292–93, 302, 470–71

love for the world, 2:134

miracles of, 1:188, 475–76, 668–70; 2:52, 62, 68, 114, 219–20, 492

as new Moses, 1:353, 357, 423

obedience of, 1:92, 382, 404–5, 447; 2:406–10

as object of faith, 2:56–60

in Old Testament, 1:342–45

omniscience of, 1:222

one with the Father, 1:664–67

overcame the world, 2:381–82

passion for lost, 1:273, 279

postresurrection appearances of, 2:214–15, 263–65, 473; 2:655–65, 702

power of, 1:372; 2:58; 2:697–98

prayer during storm, 1:371

prayer in Gethsemane, 2:101–2

preaching of, 1:531, 532

as priest, 1:46–47; 2:51, 256, 259, 370, 427, 447, 467–69, 688–89

promises of, 2:261–70, 368–70

as prophet, 1:46, 490; 2:255–56, 259, 370, 688–89

as Redeemer, 1:353

rejected by his own, 1:39–41, 281; 2:522–24

removed himself from public sphere, 1:576, 592–93

resurrection of, 1:135, 480, 535; 2:50, 264, 340, 357, 462, 468, 616

as resurrection and the life, 1:184, 314, 570; 2:29–31, 34, 54, 57, 203, 687

return of, 1:497; 2:90, 125, 199–200, 348, 699, 723

as revelation of God, 1:12–13, 18, 70–71, 666; 2:43–44, 123, 215–17, 375, 402–4

righteousness of, 2:85, 340, 555–56

as rock, 2:594

sacrifice of, 2:302–4, 568–71, 589

sanctification of, 2:449–50

as Savior, 1:10, 64, 240, 242–43; 2:220

self–defense, **1:**568

self–satisfaction on the cross, **2:**405, 411

as servant, **2:**160

silence before Pilate, **2:**532

silences wind and stills waves, **1:**95

as Son, **1:**46, 62–63, 310

sovereignty of, **2:**170

submission of, **2:**496–99, 500, 542, 549

as substitute, **2:**568–71

suffering of, **1:**371–72, 584; **2:**109, 121–22, 528, 547, 565–66, 585

as Teacher, **1:**97–99, 101, 113, 210–11, 432–36

trial of, **2:**505–6, 511–18, 531–36, 539, 541–43

triumph in passion, **2:**489–90

triumphal entry, **2:**71, 80–90

troubled in heart, **2:**194

as true David, **2:**556

as true temple, **1:**135, 137

uniqueness of, **1:**64–71, 208–9

vindication of, **2:**127–29

as the vine, **2:**281–90, 291

walked on water, **1:**334

as the way, the truth, and the life, **1:**543; **2:**202–11

weeping of, **2:**45–50, 53

as witness, **1:**27, 109–10, 210–12, 271, 330, 525, 527

as the Word, **1:**7–10, 12, 17, 71, 116

works of, **2:**226

zeal of, **1:**136, 351, 587

Jewish crowd, at trial of Jesus, **2:**512, 515–16, 523, 527, 531, 543, 544

Jewish exclusivism, **1:**88

Jewish leaders, **1:**340–42, 470

incensed at Pilate's inscription, **2:**550

opposition to Jesus, **1:**41; **2:**92

rejection of Jesus, **2:**561

as religious elites, **1:**301

unbelief of, **2:**507

Jews

hostility toward Samaritans, **1:**248

legalism of, **1:**303

offense at the cross, **1:**434–35

rejection of Messiah, **1:**249; **2:**544–45

Jezebel, **1:**500

Job, **2:**35, 469

John Paul II, Pope, **2:**461

John, **1:**100

as "Beloved Disciple," **1:**6–7; **2:**166–67

compared with Peter, **2:**715–16

at denial of Peter, **2:**500–501

as eyewitness, **1:**265; **2:**490

Mary's care committed to, **2:**559–60

before Sanhedrin, **2:**331

persecution of, **2:**717

John, Gospel of

authorship of, **1:**5–6; **2:**721

conclusion of, **2:**714–15

dating of, **1:**6

epilogue of, **2:**685

gaps in, **1:**450

as gospel of belief, **2:**31

Great Commission in, **2:**655, 662–64, 667

miracles in, **1:**585

on glory, **2:**388

on water, **1:**589

prologue of, **1:**15, 25, 27, 36, 44, 604

purpose of, **2:**604, 684–86

selectivity of material, **2:**685

as "spiritual gospel," **1:**6

John the Baptist, **1:**25, 63, 384; **2:**74, 390

call to repentance, **1:**82–83

character of, **1:**197–204

death of, **1:**349, 350

doubt of, **2:**219–20

Elijah–like role of, **1:**77–78

as gatekeeper, **1:**619

as prophet, **1:**208

as "the voice," 79

as witness, **1:**28, 29–32, 75–83, 85, 92–93, 104–5, 271, 330–32, 525, 671

Johnston, Mark, 1:7, 13–14, 70–71, 283, 454, 564–65, 591; 2:28, 287, 387, 526, 545, 585–87

Jonah, 1:236, 368; 2:439, 616, 663–64

Jonathan, 1:201–2

Jones, Douglas, 2:157

Jordan, Michael, 1:522

Joseph (husband of Mary), 1:311, 413, 453

Joseph (son of Jacob), 1:580

Joseph of Arimathea, 1:166; 2:605–13, 619, 623

Josephus, 2:81, 282

Joshua, 1:605

Joshua (high priest), 1:501, 507; 2:528

joy, 1:123, 127–28, 146, 200–202, 374; 2:197, 299–300, 362, 434–35, 482, 660–62
    through life of prayer, 2:369
    of new life, 2:360–62
    in the resurrection, 2:357–60, 362

Judaism, 1:209, 513

Judas (not Iscariot), 2:204, 268

Judas Iscariot, 1:399, 446–48; 2:190, 522
    betrayal of Christ, 1:662; 2:184–85, 386, 489, 491–93
    challenged devotion of Mary, 2:75–77
    contrast with Peter, 1:661–62
    departure of, 2:173, 174
    as false professor, 2:295
    hanged himself, 2:165
    lessons from, 2:170–71
    relationship with Jesus, 2:168–69
    and Satan, 2:145, 169
    as son of destruction, 2:433
    as uncleansed, 2:151–52

Judas Maccabaeus, 1:654–55

Jude (brother of Jesus), 1:452

judgment, 1:26, 188, 195, 238, 337, 374, 511, 524; 2:116
    conviction of, 2:341–42
    deliverance from, 2:294–95
    of this world, 2:104–5

judgment day, 1:139, 325–27; 2:125–26

judicial life in Christ, 2:691–92

justice, 1:504, 506

justification, 1:96, 324, 657; 2:21–22, 273, 372, 419, 462, 581, 599–600, 692

Justin Martyr, 1:435, 439, 472

kairos, 1:454

kalos, 1:645

karma, 1:246, 577

Keddie, Gordon, 1:523, 607; 2:77, 116, 164, 183, 289, 298–99, 349, 371–72, 597

Keillor, Garrison, 2:316

Keiper, Ralph, 2:110, 238

Keller, Phillip, 1:635–36, 644

Kenya, 1:509, 516–17

keys of the kingdom, 2:672–74

Kidron brook, 2:393, 427, 489–90, 491

Kimball, Edward, 1:108, 111

king of peace, 2:83–87

"King of the Jews," 2:523, 549–50, 554

king, 1:47; 2:688

King, Martin Luther, Jr., 1:547

kingdom of God
    advancement of, 2:201, 430
    not of this world, 2:513–14
    and truth, 2:518–19

kingdoms of this world, 2:510–12

knowledge
    of Christ, 1:347; 2:265–68
    of God, 2:213, 395–404, 418, 478–81
    as element of saving faith, 1:178, 193
    of self, 1:143–46
    of sin, 1:237–38
    of Word of God, 2:180, 537

Knox, John, 1:654

Kochba, Simon Bar, 1:341

Korea, 1:35, 42

Krummacher, F. W., 2:133–34, 137, 139, 145, 494, 502–3, 619

Kusmic, Peter, 2:312

Lamb of God, **1:**85–89, 92–93, 96, 116, 137, 182, 353, 425; **2:**345, 689
lame man. *See* paralytic man, healing of
lamp, John the Baptist as, **1:**31
last day, **2:**125
Last Supper, **1:**362; **2:**143, 482, 542
Last Supper (Da Vinci portrait), **2:**168
Latimer, Hugh, **1:**103–4, 111, 331
Laud, William, **2:**547
law
    and grace, **1:**68; **2:**243
    required witnesses, **1:**503
    weakness of, **1:**67
Lawrence, T. E., **1:**414
Lazarus, **2:**6–12
    call of, **1:**620
    death of, **2:**10, 18–19, 24–25, 45
    raising of, **1:**188–89, 298, 314, 319, 333, 335, 670; **2:**7, 12, 44, 50, 52, 58–59, 61, 114, 210
    as witness, **2:**72, 77–78, 82
Lazarus and rich man, parable of, **2:**567
leaves for healing, **2:**595
Lebanon, **1:**439–40
Lee, Robert E., **2:**94–95
legalism, **1:**21, 302–3
Lehman, Frederick M., **1:**169
leprosy, **1:**234
Levitical priests, **1:**344
Lewis, C. S., **1:**55, 192, 274, 323, 483, 523–24, 649; **2:**198, 278–79, 722–23
Lewis, Peter, **2:**234–35
liberal theology, **1:**608; **2:**243
    on atonement, **1:**436
    on miracles, **1:**333, 349–50
    on way of salvation, **1:**626
life, **1:**16–19, 20
life after death, **1:**320–22, 328
light, **1:**8, 15, 18–24, 31, 196, 509–10, 517; **2:**112–13, 124, 126, 172
    Christians as, **2:**663
    and darkness, **2:**494, 518

    double function of, **1:**604
    of God's Word, **1:**193–94
    as unquenchable, **1:**41–43
limited atonement, **2:**302, 428, 590–91
Lincoln, Abraham, **1:**545
lion, **2:**557
"Little Bilney" (monk), **1:**103–4, 106, 111
living faith, **1:**265
living water, **1:**223–24, 226–28, 231–33, 285, 484–88, 497; **2:**567, 571–72, 595
Livingstone, David, **1:**654
Lloyd-Jones, Martyn, **1:**29, 77, 153–54, 189, 239–40, 283–85, 379, 407, 434, 543, 550, 654; **2:**125–26, 313, 347, 393–94, 397, 400, 422, 442, 458, 461–62
logos, **1:**10–11, 335
London, **1:**535
loneliness, **1:**33
Lord of the Rings, **1:**58
Lord's Day, **1:**305–8, 467; **2:**678
Lord's Prayer, **1:**146; **2:**364, 367, 386
Lord's Supper, **1:**391, 424–25; **2:**186, 680
lordship salvation, **2:**97
love, **1:**171, 670; **2:**155, 157–59, 294, 310, 421, 704–5
    for Christ, **2:**245–48, 250, 713
    for the church, **2:**156–57, 712
    and doctrine, **2:**478–80
    for enemies, **2:**152
    for God, **1:**600–601; **2:**243, 268–69, 310
    for Jews as God's ancient people, **1:**249–50
    and the law, **2:**242–44
    for the lost, **1:**268–69
    as mark of the church, **2:**477–78, 481–84
    as new commandment, **2:**177, 178–82, 477
    for neighbor, **1:**600–601; **2:**243, 310
    for one another, **2:**201, 306, 483
    and propitiation, **2:**577
    of self, **2:**516

Lovelace, Richard, 1:145

Luther, Martin, 1:5, 10, 66, 98, 103, 168, 193, 286, 288, 346, 396–97, 399–400, 415–16, 419, 455, 461–62, 508, 529, 532, 536, 538, 609–10, 653; 2:234, 330, 387, 553

MacArthur, John, 1:106, 107–8

Maccabaeus, Simon, 2:82

Machen, J. Gresham, 1:433–34, 435; 2:67

Maclaren, Alexander, 1:95, 106, 127, 282, 666; 2:52–53, 112–13, 178, 435, 494, 678, 706–7

makeup, 1:148

Malchus, 2:497, 507

man born blind, healing of. See blind man, healing of

man by the pool, healing of. See paralytic, healing of

manna, 1:304–5, 350–53, 387–89, 412, 430, 461

mansions, in heaven, 2:198

Manton, Thomas, 2:474

marriage, 1:179, 598

marriage supper of the Lamb, 1:129

Martha, 1:444; 2:6–8, 12, 25–27, 29, 33–37, 40–41, 53, 72

Martyn, Henry, 1:654

martyrdom, 2:322–23, 330

Mary (mother of Jesus), 1:38, 453; 2:326
    at the crucifixion, 2:490, 558–60
    perpetual virginity of, 1:122, 452
    as Co-Redemptrix, 1:122; 2:560
    veneration of, 1:295, 296
    at wedding in Cana, 1:122–24, 126, 128

Mary (wife of Clopas), 2:558

Mary I, Queen, 2:717

Mary Magdalene, 1:621; 2:558

Mary of Bethany, 1:41; 2:6–8, 12, 25, 33, 37–41, 72–79, 145

material blessings, 1:96

material needs, 1:229; 2:158–59

materialism, 1:377–78, 475; 2:438

Matthew, calling of, 1:418

Maugham, Robin, 1:389

Maugham, William Somerset, 1:389–90

Mayans, 2:577

McComiskey, Thomas, 2:85

M'Cheyne, Robert Murray, 2:336, 340

McIlvaine, Charles, 1:427

meaning, 1:11

meaninglessness, 1:190

means of grace, 1:420

Melchizedek, 1:572

mercy, 1:357, 360, 506

mercy seat, 1:137, 260–61, 344; 2:577

merit, 2:371

Messiah, 1:10, 107, 116, 269, 574, 619, 655; 2:35–36, 64, 255, 370, 505, 512, 688
    crucifixion of, 1:435
    death of, 2:105
    false ideas about, 1:472–74
    from the Jews, 1:248
    humiliation of, 2:84–86
    ignorance about, 1:491
    as lifted up, 2:109
    worship of, 1:260

Meyer, F. B., 1:199–200, 569; 2: 73–74, 297, 337, 339, 615, 657

Michelangelo, 1:101–2

Middle Ages, 2:459

military, change of command in, 2:363–64

Miller, Ward C., 1:565

Milne, Bruce, 1:133, 168, 302; 2:157–58, 200, 212, 464, 567, 687, 697

Milton, John, 1:386

ministry, 1:358–65
    of mercy, 1:357
    of Word of God, 2:277, 711

miracles, 1:57, 64, 119, 188, 349–50, 352, 475–76, 597–98, 656; 2:52, 62, 68, 114, 223–24
    as signs, 1:282; 2:685
    as witness to Christ, 1:332–35

misery, **1:**510–11
mission, **2:**450–55, 482, 662–64
modern missionary movement, **1:**654
monasticism, **2:**267, 438–39
money, **1:**380
Monica (mother of Augustine), **1:**17, 397
Moody, Dwight L., **1:**108–9, 666
Morgan, G. Campbell, **1:**16, 200
Morley, Christopher, **2:**484
Mormons, **1:**668; **2:**345
Morris, Leon, **1:**8, 22, 27, 58–59, 123, 151,
        170–71, 173, 178–79, 183, 202, 232,
        245, 257, 277, 314, 377, 397, 451,
        467, 631, 660; **2:**15, 116, 149, 237,
        299–300, 309, 379, 391, 401, 417,
        548, 584–85, 662, 678
mortality, **1:**190
Moses, **1:**63, 67, 77, 87, 260–61, 336, 351,
        385, 387–88, 423, 519, 522, 525,
        630–31; **2:**213, 439
    asked to see glory of God, **1:**70
    at burning bush, **2:**493
    drew water from rock, **1:**490; **2:**594–95
    and the exodus, **1:**352–53
    lifted bronze serpent, **1:**163, 173, 181,
        184–85, 389, 407
    as mediator, **1:**117
    meekness of, **1:**204
    on miracles, **1:**597–98
    prophet like, **2:**528
    reflected God's glory, **2:**401
    as shepherd, **1:**643
    as type of Christ, **1:**344
    witness of, **1:**344–45
Most Holy Place, **1:**344
motives, **1:**375
Mount Ebal, **1:**243–44, 247, 249–50
Mount Gerizim, **1:**243–45, 249–50, 254
Mount Moriah, **2:**548
Mount of Olives, **2:**83, 281–82, 290
Mount of Transfiguration, **1:**335, 523;
        2:219

Mount Sinai, **1:**336, 353
Mount Zion, **1:**250, 254, 256
movies, **2:**421
Mueller, George, **1:**362–63, 583; **2:**97
Muggeridge, Malcolm, **1:**142, 231, 579–80
Muhammad, **1:**209, 611; **2:**563
Murray, John, **1:**394, 396; **2:**588, 591
Musculus, Wolfgang, **2:**177
Muslims, **1:**611; **2:**48, 58, 563
myrrh, **2:**618

Naaman, **1:**434
Nadab and Abihu, **1:**258
Nairobi, Kenya, **1:**509, 516
nakedness, shame of, **2:**555
name of God, **2:**417–19, 479
name of Jesus, prayer in, **2:**370–72
Napoleon, **1:**50, 410; **2:**20, 217
Nathan, **1:**242
Nathanael, **1:**114–18, 120; **2:**694–95
nationalism, **1:**521
Nazareth, **1:**114, 281, 528, 536
Nazi Germany, **2:**534
Nebuchadnezzar, **2:**295, 441, 537–38
Nederhood, Joel, **1:**464; **2:**98
needs, **1:**359
Nero, **1:**470, 664; **2:**20, 716
New Age, **1:**296
new birth, **1:**50, 152–57, 160, 162–66, 180,
        188, 232; **2:**59, 170–71, 485, 666
    effects of, **1:**263–69
    and witness, **1:**272–79
new commandment, **2:**177–80, 477
new covenant, **1:**117; **2:**178
new creation, **1:**75, 552; **2:**666–67
new exodus, **1:**351–56
New Hebrides islands, **1:**276
new life, **1:**155–56, 184, 298–99; **2:**59, 264,
        360–62
"new morality," **2:**242–43
new self, **2:**448
new sight, **1:**611

New Testament
    contents of, **2:**346–48
    quotations of Old Testament, **1:**117
Newton, Isaac, **1:**521
Newton, John, **1:**265, 268, 345–46, 397,
    587; **2:**236, 241
Nicene Creed, **2:**324, 331
Nicodemus, **1:**37, 149–55, 158–66, 188,
    216–17, 224, 228, 257, 264, 271, 292,
    333, 424, 428, 496–97, 516, 605;
    2:209, 319, 391, 582
    at burial of Christ, **2:**605–13, 618–19,
    623
    conversion at the cross, **2:**490
Niebuhr, Reinhold, **1:**562
Niemoller, Martin, **2:**534
Nightingale, Florence, **1:**583
Nineveh, **2:**616
Noah, **1:**91, 336, 629
noblesse oblige, **1:**52
notitia, **1:**178

obedience, **1:**404–5, 515; **2:**228–29, 242–48,
    265–66, 285, 306–7, 394, 422
    and assurance, **2:**248–50
    and gratitude, **2:**293
offense, **1:**433
offspring of the woman, **2:**527
Oh In Ho, **1:**42–43
ointment, **2:**73, 76
old covenant, **1:**265
Old Testament, **1:**247–48
    Christ in, **1:**296, 342–45
    fulfilled in Christ, **1:**250, 476; **2:**565,
    615–16
    law, **1:**524
    offices of, **1:**46; **2:**688
    promises of, **2:**36–37
    quoted by New Testament, **1:**117
    salvation by faith in, **1:**573
    types in, **1:**344, 345, 388–89, 572
Olivet Discourse, **2:**71

"one–anothering," **2:**157–59
Onkelos, **2:**619
ontological Trinity, **2:**325
opposition to Jesus, **1:**43, 191, 456–58, 518,
    572; **2:**63, 69
Origen, **2:**554
original sin, **1:**293, 550
orphans, **1:** 362–63, 583; **2:**262, 269
orthodox, **2:**411
Osteen, Joel, **1:**147, 636
outside the camp, **2:**547
Oval Office, **2:**206
overconfidence, **2:**187–88, 192, 502
Owen, John, **1:**169, 586; **2:**16, 123, 254, 426

Packer, J. I., **1:**169; **2:**252, 351, 396
paganism, **1:**246
Paine, Thomas, **1:**531
Palestine, shepherding in, **1:**614, 625
Palm Sunday, **2:**82, 86
Palmer, Benjamin Morgan, **2:**255–57,
    424–25, 467–68, 472
Papania, Tom, **1:**156–57
Paradise Lost (Milton), **1:**386
paraklete, **2:**254, 255–56, 276, 324, 344
paralytic, healing of, **1:**291, 292–99,
    300–301, 308, 313, 319, 334, 589
parents, **1:**312; **2:**560
    parents, of man born blind, **1:**599–600,
    603
    sins of, **1:**577–78
Parker, Joseph, **1:**205
particular redemption, **1:**647–48; **2:**428,
    590–91
Pascal, Blaise, **1:**328
"passion of Christ," **2:**121
Passover, **1:**131, 352, 423, 425, 480; **2:**72,
    80, 144, 175, 521
Passover Feast, **1:**450; **2:**542
Passover lamb, **1:**86, 456; **2:**542
pastoral office, **2:**709–10
Paton, John G., **1:**120, 276, 277–78, 654

Paul
  in Athens, **2:**399
  benediction of, **2:**395
  conversion of, **2:**330
  on Damascus road, **1:**397–98
  gospel in book of Romans, **1:**105
  on ingathering of the Jews, **1:**250
  on love, **2:**478
  on prayer, **2:**227, 235
  thorn in the flesh, **1:**581; 235
Pavarotti, Luciano, **1:**522
Pax Romana, **2:**274
peace movement, **2:**440
peace, **1:**96, 374, 485; **2:**83–84, 195,
    272–80, 378–80, 658–60, 664
  of God, **2:**660
  with God, **2:**273, 660, 679. *See also*
    reconciliation
  of the world, **2:**274
Peanuts (cartoon), **1:**366
Pelagius, **1:**415
penal substitution, **2:**575–76, 580
penance, **2:**589
Pentecost, **1:**451, 454, 456; **2:**80, 224, 263,
    328, 335, 481
Penteteuch, **1:**344
pericardium, **2:**598
perishing, **1:**181–84
Perry Mason (television program), **1:**187
persecution, **1:**470–71, 540, 664; **2:**20,
    311–12, 314–18, 320–22, 329–32,
    377–78, 534, 610, 717–18
  of John, **2:**717
  of Peter, **2:**716–17
perseverance, **1:**369, 398–400, 408–9, 541,
    546; **2:**229–30, 329, 432, 695
personal invitation from Jesus, **1:**109–11
personal obedience, **2:**244
personal testimony, **1:**107–11, 113
Peter, **1:**101–2, 106, 360–61; **2:**92, 204, 694
  accepted Jesus's saving work, **2:**340,
    405, 415
  cleansing of, **2:**149, 152
  compared with John, **2:**715–16
  contrast with Judas, **1:**661–62
  Great Confession of, **1:**384, 441–43,
    445, 661; **2:**672, 706
  crucifixion of, **2:**190, 716–17
  denied Jesus, **1:**662; **2:**184–91, 194, 278,
    377, 500–503, 507–9, 704–5, 708
  differences from Judas, **2:**184–85
  inconsistency of, **2:**147
  ignorance of, **2:**185–87
  overconfidence of, **2:**502
  relationship with Jesus, **2:**167
  repentance of, **2:**191, 508
  restoration of, **2:**246, 508, 703–9,
    712–13
  salvation of, **2:**189–90
  before Sanhedrin, **2:**331
  sermon at Pentecost, **1:**108; **2:**335
  struck servant with sword, **2:**497, 507
  transformation of, **1:**90
  walked on water, **2:**722
  witness of, **1:**110
Peter Abelard, **2:**574
Pharaoh, **1:**499
Pharisees, **2:**28, 62–63, 69, 118
  abuse of law, **1:**505, 618
  anger of, **1:**316
  attacks on Jesus, **1:**241, 523–24, 567
  blindness of, **1:**586, 605–13
  on cleanliness, **1:**124
  cold hearts of, **1:**599–600
  darkness of, **2:**113
  distorted truth, **1:**598, 670
  division among, **1:**495–97
  as false shepherds, **1:**616, 643–44
  good works of, **1:**194
  hypocrisy of, **1:**516
  legalism of, **1:**21, 467
  motives of, **1:**342
  not offspring of Abraham, **1:**559–60,
    562–63

opposition to Jesus, **1:**518, 536, 551

persecution by, **2:**320

plot to murder Jesus, **1:**474

pride of, **1:**191, 493–95

questioned John the Baptist, **1:**79

rejection of Jesus, **1:**524–26, 528–29

respectability of, **1:**150

ritualistic religion of, **1:**296

on the Sabbath, **1:**301–4, 306–7, 310, 333, 595–98, 600

on Scriptures, **1:**340–41

self-righteousness of, **2:**480–81

sought to silence Jesus, **1:**470–72, 532–33

on traditions, **2:**423

at triumphal entry, **2:**89

unbelief of, **1:**519–22, 525–26, 530, 570, 574, 601, 610; **2:**114–15, 122–23

on woman caught in adultery, **1:**505–7

worldly interests of, **1:**341–42

wrongful excommunication by, **2:**329

phileo, **2:**704–5

Philip, **1:**112–14, 116, 277, 350, 360–61; **2:**92, 204, 212–21

philos, **1:**171

philosophy, **1:**150

physical death, **1:**314, 570; **2:**30–31

physical life, **1:**16

physical lineage, **1:**557–58

piercing, of Jesus' side, **2:**490, 598–600–602

pilgrim, Jesus as, **1:**56

Pilgrim's Progress (Bunyan), **1:**185–86; **2:**338, 692

pillar of fire, **1:**352, 514

Pink, A. W., **1:**10, 56, 67, 99, 161, 203, 211, 230, 236, 240, 256, 361–62, 370, 380, 390–91, 398–99, 416, 418, 423, 432, 438, 447–48, 455, 471, 502–3, 548–49, 554, 564, 569, 572, 588, 619, 648; **2:**16, 56–57, 60, 87, 102, 115, 118–19, 126, 150, 186, 195, 208–9,

223, 234, 246, 283–84, 296, 317, 327, 381, 454, 565, 658, 667, 680, 698, 701, 707, 712

Pipa, Joseph, **1:**305

Pipper, Rebecca, **2:**439

Place of the Skull, **2:**546

Plato, **1:**11, 513; **2:**262

pleasure, **1:**306, 530

Polycarp, **1:**541–42; **2:**294

Ponce de Leon, Juan, **1:**225–26, 230, 233

Pontius Pilate, **1:**38; **2:**490, 493, 499–500, 511–20, 522–29

and burial of Jesus, **2:**605, 616

condemnation and judgment of, **2:**520

cowardice of, **2:**535–36, 539, 542

declared Jesus innocent, **1:**241; **2:**355, 512, 515, 524–25, 531–32

inscribes Jesus as King of the Jews, **2:**549–50, 554

as superstitious, **2:**532

yields to crowd's demands, **2:**543, 544

pool of Bethesda, **2:**595

pool of Siloam, **1:**588–90, 595

Pool of St. Anne, **1:**292

possessions, **2:**73

postmodern culture, **1:**413, 608, 664; **2:**128, 516

poverty, **1:**33; **2:**158

power, **1:**96, 485

vs. authority, **2:**533

for preaching, **1:**365

in weakness, **2:**359–60

"power of positive thinking," **2:**195

Praetorium, **2:**522, 529

pragmatism, **1:**124; **2:**65, 515–18

praise, **1:**256

prayer, **1:**100; **2:**7–9, 141, 188, 192, 309–10

evangelistic, **1:**420

to the Father, **2:**364–68

of George Mueller, **1:**363

goal of, **2:**239–40

and great works, **2:**227

in name of Jesus, **2:**233–39, 370–72
neglect of, **2:**502–3
power in, **2:**296–98
as privilege, **2:**380
reliance on, **2:**697
of repentance, **2:**707
and searching Scriptures, **1:**346
as time in the "garden," **2:**235
preaching, **1:**108, 283, 461, 487, 529–36
predestination, **1:**402, 446, 628; **2:**114, 316, 448
pre–evangelism, **1:**223
Prentiss, Elizabeth, **2:**287
present evil age, **2:**353, 362
President of the United States, **2:**206
Presley, Elvis, death of, **2:**597
prestige, **1:**96
pride, **1:**40, 192–93, 315, 494, 545; **2:**146, 187, 377
priest, **1:**46–47; **2:**62, 688
priesthood of all believers, **2:**435
profession of faith, as open and public, **2:**610
progress, **1:**513
progressive revelation, **2:**344–45
progressive sanctification, **2:**448
Promised Land, **1:**243–44, 351, 354; **2:**282
proofs, of resurrection of Jesus,, **2:**666
prophecy, **1:**343, **2:**163–64, 348
prophet, **1:**46, 77; **2:**688
propitiation, **1:**427; **2:**576–77, 580, 583, 602, 659
prosperity gospel, **1:**96, 377, 617, 636–38
provision, **1:**358, 362–64, 636, 638
Prudentius, **1:**403
pruning, **2:**286–87
psychology, **2:**96
Ptolemaic system of astronomy, **2:**160, 162
Puritans, on the Lord's Day, **1:**307
purity, **1:**485
purple robe, **2:**525, 528

Quakers, **2:**271–72
quality of life, **1:**127

Rabbi, **1:**113, 116
Jesus as, **1:**97–99
Rabbi Eliezer, **1:**220
Rabbi Hillel, **1:**340
rabbis, **1:**460
racism, **1:**520–21; **2:**535
Rainsford, Marcus, **2:**431
ransom, **1:**552; **2:**587
ransom theory of the atonement, **2:**573–74
rationalism, **2:**218
Raws, William, **2:**240
reaping, **1:**277
rebellion, **1:**44; **2:**316
reconciliation, **2:**204–7, 372, 579–80
redemption, **1:**308, 310, 574; **2:**471, 579–80, 587
of culture, **2:**441
as particular, **1:**647–48; **2:**590–91
Reed, John, **1:**75
Reformation, **2:**461, 553
Reformed theology, **1:**393
regeneration, **1:**160, 180, 419; **2:**209–10. See *also* new birth
Reiu, D. E. V., **1:**339
rejoicing, **1:**332; **2:**369, 434
in sufferings, **2:**661
relationship with God, **2:**400
relationship with Jesus, **1:**13, 95, 100
relativism, **1:**435, 626; **2:**438, 516–18
religious formalism, **1:**296
religious leaders
anger of, **1:**316
rejection of Jesus, **1:**577
repentance, **1:**82–83, 138, 155, 185, 521; **2:**706, 719
reprobation, **2:**117
restoration, of sinners, **2:**679, 703
resurrection, **1:**320, 322, 525–26; **2:**12, 28–32
of judgment, **1:**325–27
relation to crucifixion, **2:**656
resurrection bodies, **2:**658
resurrection life, **1:**184, 410–11

resurrection Sunday, 2:657–78
revelation, 2:344–50
　　of truth, 2:207–9
Revelation (book), 2:474, 659–60
reward, 1:202, 277
rhema, 2:125
rich fool, parable of, 1:379
rich young ruler, 1:381
Ridderbos, Herman, 1:38, 307–8; 2:45, 53,
　　253, 377–78
Ridley, Nicholas, 1:331
righteousness, 1:379, 382; 2:85
righteousness, conviction of, 2:339–40
river, everlasting life as, 2:396–97
rivers, of living water, 1:485–86
robbers, 1:615–16
robe of Christ, as seamless, 2:554–55
"Rock of Ages," 1:47, 91–92, 552; 2:600
rock of Horeb, 2:594
rock, Peter as, 2:706
Roman Catholics, 1:209; 2:277
　　on baptism, 2:589
　　on body of Jesus, 2:658
　　on Christian unity, 2:459
　　on extrabiblical teaching, 2:345
　　on forgiveness of sins, 2:669–71
　　on Lord's Supper, 1:424
　　on Mary as Co-Redemptrix, 1:122;
　　　　2:560
　　on the Mass, 2:589–90
　　on Peter, 2:167, 710
　　on tradition, 1:606
Roman empire, 1:548; 2:312, 315, 511
Roman soldiers
　　at arrest of Jesus, 2:492, 494
　　at crucifixion of Jesus, 2:561
　　mockery of Jesus, 2:524–26
Romans Road, 1:105, 391
Rome, decay of, 1:378
Rosetta Stone, 2:217
Rubin, Jerry, 2:242
Ruth, 2:471

Rutherford, Samuel, 2:471
Ryan, Skip, 1:155, 180; 2:74, 161, 206, 341
Ryken, Philip, 2:203, 574–75
Ryle, J. C., 1:86, 87, 123, 152, 172, 215, 222,
　　245, 266, 287, 310, 315, 317, 368,
　　375–76, 380–81, 390, 395, 410, 426,
　　453, 465, 471, 482, 515, 532, 559, 568,
　　573, 616–17, 644, 668; 2:8–9, 29–31,
　　47, 78, 81, 88, 95, 99, 105, 115–16,
　　119–20, 124, 136, 169, 171, 176, 178,
　　187, 197–99, 292, 299, 302, 307, 317,
　　376, 389, 409, 412, 432, 506, 523, 559,
　　596–97, 680, 682, 694, 714, 718

Sabbath, 1:129, 301–8, 310, 333, 466–67,
　　596–98, 600; 2:596
　　as sign of God's eternal rest, 1:305
sacraments, flowed from Christ's side,
　　2:599
sacrifice, 1:60, 68, 344; 2:568–71
　　of Son of Man, 1:162–63
sacrificial animals, 2:344–45
sacrificial lamb, 1:86–88, 92, 137, 425
Sadducees, 2:28, 62, 118
safety, 1:630–31
Sagan, Carl, 2:399
saliva, 1:588
Salome (mother of sons of Zebedee), 2:558
salt, 2:663
salvation, 1:180–81, 374; 2:106, 290, 602
　　by grace, 1:402, 417, 437, 656–58
　　eternal life as, 2:396
　　as freedom, 1:544–45
　　and glory of God, 2:392–94
　　by grace, 1:402, 417, 437, 656–58
　　from the Jews, 1:247–48
　　one way of, 1:626–27
　　preservation of, 2:496
　　Sabbath as, 1:307–8
　　as universal and particular, 1:217
　　as work of God, 1:382
　　by works, 1:381–82; 2:306

Samaria, Samaritans, **1:**218–21, 222, 244, 248–50, 276–77, 281–82, 568
Samaritan woman, **1:**65, 216–17, 221–24, 226, 228–29, 233, 238, 244–49, 254, 260, 292, 516, 589; **2:**108, 163, 391, 571, 595
  new birth of, **1:**262–70
  sin of, **1:**235–36, 241–42
  witness of, **1:**272–78
Samuel, **1:**336, 566
sanctification, **1:**657; **2:**21–22, 308, 318, 419–21, 437, 447–50, 599–600
  in truth, **2:**442–45, 446–47, 449
sandals, strap of, **1:**81, 202
Sanhedrin, **1:**189; **2:**62–64, 69, 81, 314, 493, 499, 505, 605
Satan, **1:**560–62
  attacks of, **2:**278–79
  encourages self-righteousness, **1:**501–2
  as the evil one, **2:**437
  falseness of, **2:**208
  influence on Judas, **2:**145, 169
  lies of, **2:**703
  resisting of, **2:**169
  temptation of Jesus, **1:**453
satisfaction, **1:**31, 274–75, 530
  in earthly pleasures, **1:**230–31
  of the Father, **2:**410
satisfaction theory of the atonement, **2:**575
saving faith, **1:**178–79, 193, 285–86, 426–27, 658; **2:**34, 201, 423, 604, 685–86, 715, 723
Saving Private Ryan (film), **2:**139, 592–93
Savior, **1:**10
scapegoat, **1:**344; **2:**523
Schaeffer, Francis, **2:**181–82, 438, 462
Schulz, Charles, **2:**153–54, 161–62
scourging, **2:**524, 546, 565
scribes, **1:**21, 295, 339–41, 345, 347, 460, 473, 505, 596; **2:**356, 360
Scripture
  authority of, **2:**127
  searching of, **1:**345–47

study of, **2:**445
sufficiency of, **2:**723
as witness, **1:**27–28, 339–47
sculpting, **1:**101–2
Sea of Galilee, **1:**66, 367, 487; **2:**272, 694, 704
sea, as symbol of world in sin, **1:**367–68
secular humanism, **1:**17, 124, 221
secularism, **2:**439–40, 443
seeing and believing, **1:**385–87; **2:**54, 214–15
seeker, **1:**253–54
self-centeredness, **1:**274
self-confidence, **2:**376, 707
self-deceit, **1:**144
self-defense, **1:**567–68
self-denial, **2:**94–95, 97, 99–100, 718–20
self-help, **1:**124, 296, 490
selfishness, **1:**199, 545; **2:**160
self-love, **2:**516
self-righteousness, **1:**194, 502, 595; **2:**480–81
sensualism, **2:**438
sent, **2:**161, 662–63
separation, of church and state, **2:**314
Septuagint, **2:**266
Sermon on the Mount, **1:**98, 147, 208, 379, 391; **2:**95, 162, 249, 364, 694
serpent lifted in the wilderness, **1:**162–63, 173, 181–85, 389, 407
serpent, temptation of Adam and Eve, **1:**181; **2:**278
servanthood, **2:**144–46, 147, 160–62
servants, **2:**304–5, 314
service, **1:**357; **2:**88–89, 154, 248
"set apart," **2:**309
sexual liberation, **1:**44
sexual perversion, **2:**606, 708
sexual purity, **1:**500
sexuality, **2:**439–40
shadow of death, **1:**640
Shadrach, Meshach, and Abednego, **2:**441–42, 537–39

shaliach, 2:665, 668
shalom, 2:658
shame, 2:555
sharing, 2:248
sheep, helplessness of, 1:622–23, 631, 639,
    657, 658; 2:709–10
shekinah glory, 1:56–57; 2:413
shepherds, shepherding, 1:114, 116, 614–
    23, 625, 630–31, 635–36; 2:709–12
shopping malls, 1:367
Sibbes, Richard, 1:184
signs, 1:64, 127, 475–76; 2:52
    demand for, 1:385–87
    miracles as, 1:585
signs and wonders, 1:282
Simeon, 2:558
Simeon, Charles, 1:343, 345–46; 2:199
Simon. *See* Peter
Simon Magus, 2:252, 672
Simon of Cyrene, 2:489
sin, 1:12, 32, 147, 182; 2:169
    awfulness of, 1:447; 2:105
    bondage to, 1:89, 548–51, 563–65; 2:578
    conviction of, 2:336–37
    as darkness, 1:511
    deceitfulness of, 2:483
    defeat of, 1:660–61
    gravity of, 2:582–83
    pollution of, 2:150–51
    power of, 1:552–54
    prosperity gospel on, 1:637
    renouncing of, 2:719
    separates us from God, 1:238–39
    state or condition of, 1:531
    struggles with, 2:247
    and suffering, 1:579
    toying with, 2:171
    worthy of judgment, 1:238
sincerity, in searching Scriptures, 1:345
situational ethics, 2:242
sixth hour, 2:543
sleep, death as, 2:15–17

Smith, George Adam, 1:614, 625
Smith, Joseph, 2:345
socialism, 1:520
Socrates, 2:102, 262
Sodom and Gomorrah, 1:559
soils, parable of, 1:540
sola Scriptura, 1:462; 2:461
soldiers, division among, 1:492–95
Solomon, 1:344, 377
Son of God, 1:46, 116, 118, 208–9, 323, 525;
    2:36, 505, 511, 539, 686–87
Son of Man, 1:118–20, 322, 324
    belief in, 1:610–13
    glorification of, 2:93–94
    lifted up, 1:165–66, 173, 407, 534; 2:109,
        388, 550
    sacrifice of, 1:162–63
"Sons of Thunder," 1:106
sons of Zebedee, 2:558, 694–95
sonship, 1:559; 2:257
sorrow, 2:354–56, 362
soul, 1:320–21, 390
sovereign grace, 1:284, 445–46, 654,
    656–58
Spencer, Ichabod, 1:267
spices, at burial of Christ, 2:618
spiritual blessings, 1:96
spiritual celebrities, 1:64
spiritual deadness, 1:38–39, 285
spiritual death, 1:314, 327; 2:30
spiritual gifts, 1:268
spiritual inability, 1:293, 386, 655–56
spiritual life, 1:16; 2:692
spiritual lineage, 1:557–60
spiritual maturity, 1:237
spiritual needs, 1:229; 2:158–59
spiritual recreation, on Lord's Day, 1:306
spiritual resources, 2:188–89, 192
spiritual resurrection, 2:59, 264
spiritual transformation, 1:19
spiritual war, 2:495
spirituality, 1:194

Spong, John Shelby, **1:**436; **2:**575

Sproul, R. C., **1:**78, 181

Spurgeon, Charles, **1:**40, 45, 51, 97,
154–56, 199, 205–6, 359, 408, 465,
481–82, 485–86, 493, 630, 654; **2:**8,
135–36, 140, 286, 355, 358, 400,
428, 430, 453–54, 524, 551, 565,
567, 571, 585, 607–8, 611, 622, 684,
686, 692

St. Augustine, Florida, **1:**226

Steinmetz, Charlie, **1:**12

Stephen, death of, **2:**314, 330

Sternberg, Brian, **1:**300–301

stewardship, **1:**582

still, small voice, **1:**70

stoicism, **2:**193

Stoics, **2:**102

stoning, **1:**574, 663, 668

storge, **1:**171

storm, on the sea, **1:**367; **2:**272

Stott, John, **2:**563, 719

strife, among Christians, **1:**199

stumbling block, cross as, **1:**434–35

subjective theory of the atonement,
2:574

substitute, **1:**425; **2:**568–71, 575–76

substitutionary atonement, **1:**427, 433, 436;
2:462, 530, 575–76

"suffered under Pontius Pilate," **2:**526

suffering Savior, **1:**86

Suffering Servant, **1:**395; **2:**114

suffering, **1:**373, 577–84; **2:**99, 102, 158,
190, 240, 317, 330–31

suffering, joy of, **2:**321

suicide, **1:**126, 378

Sunday, **1:**454, 480; **2:**656

supernatural, **1:**349

superstition, **1:**294–95, 297, 510–11

Suzanna (apocryphal book), **1:**501

swoon theory, **2:**597–98

syllogism, **1:**597

Synoptic Gospels, **1:**348, 441–42

tabernacle, **1:**53, 55–57, 60–61, 137, 344,
352–53

Tacitus, **2:**274

Taylor, Hudson, **1:**59

Taylor, Rowland, **2:**717–18

Telchin, Judy, **1:**109–11, 114, 117; **2:**613

Telchin, Stan, **1:**109–11, 114, 117–18, 250;
2:613

telomerase, **1:**422, 428

temple, **2:**133–34

cleansing of, **1:**131–39

destruction of, 6

Temple Mount, **1:**589–90

temptation, **1:**33, 146, 550; **2:**141, 240, 377

ten Boom, Corrie, **2:**297–98

Ten Commandments, **1:**61, 67, 116–17, 147,
239, 304, 353, 391, 404, 433, 598;
2:243–44, 307

tent of meeting. *See* tabernacle

Tertullian, **2:**182, 322–23, 717

testimony, **1:**30. *See also* witness

tetragrammaton, **2:**418

Thaddeus, **2:**268

thanksgiving, **1:**256

theology, **2:**479

theophanies, of Old Testament, **2:**213

theoreo, **2:**123

thieves, **1:**615–16

thieves at the cross, **1:**321; **2:**548, 551,
596–97

thirst, **1:**481–84, 487–88, 497, 590, 620;
2:391, 571–72

for satisfaction, **1:**228–31

Thomas Aquinas, **2:**581

Thomas, **2:**22, 204, 205, 210–11, 404, 694

bleessing to, **2:**676

called to faith, **2:**679–82

confession of faith, **2:**681–82, 685

doubt of, **1:**9; **2:**474, 676–79

Thomas, Robert J., **1:**35, 42–43

Tiberius Caesar, **2:**511, 533, 536

time, **1:**454, 583

time, in the Bible, **2:**543
Titanic (ocean liner), **1:**183
tithing, **1:**380
Titus (Emperor), **1:**89
tola, **2:**557
tolerance, **1:**513
Tolkien, J. R. R., **1:**58
tombs, **2:**619
Toplady, Augustus, **1:**91–92, 552; **2:**600,
    602
Torah, **1:**344
Torrey, R. A., **2:**227–28, 236–37, 371
total depravity, **1:**143, 293–94, 394, 396,
    398, 413, 653
Tournier, Paul, **2:**197
Tower of Babel, **1:**119; **2:**197
Tozer, A. W., **1:**203–4; **2:**432
tradition, **1:**296, 524, 606
tragedy, **1:**605
transfiguration, **1:**57, 335, 523; **2:**103, 219,
    473
transubstantiation, **1:**424; **2:**658
Tree of the Knowledge of Good and Evil,
    1:181
trials, **1:**367–73, 485, 540, 554, 579–81, 602;
    2:10–11, 12, 49, 54, 108–10, 272–73,
    296, 376–77, 381–82, 393
    prosperity gospel on, **1:**637
    as pruning, **2:**287
tribulation, **1:**475; **2:**27, 362, 381–82, 393
Trinity, **1:**8, 159, 665; **2:**67, 101, 176, 325,
    352, 459
triumphal entry, **1:**60
troubled hearts, **2:**194–95
true light, **1:**31–32, 43
true religion, **1:**244–47
true spirituality, **2:**218–19
trust, as element of saving faith, **1:**178
trusting in Jesus, **2:**622–23
truth, **1:**68, 147–48, 543–45; **2:**207–9, 344,
    518–20
    calling to, **1:**670

and church unity, **2:**460–62
distortion of, **1:**598
embracing of, **1:**463–64
and sanctification, **2:**442–44, 446–47,
    449
as relative, **2:**516
TULIP, **1:**394
Twelve, **2:**138
two cities, **2:**510–11
two–age eschatology, **2:**353–54
types, in Old Testament, **1:**344, 345,
    388–89
tyranny, **2:**482

Uganda, **1:**363
unbelief, **1:**30, 38, 45, 214–15, 217, 315,
    385–87, 413, 415, 442, 464, 490,
    496, 498, 525–26, 530, 562–65, 601,
    605, 656; **2:**26, 62, 115, 117, 122, 169,
    171–72, 338
    cause of, **1:**189–93, 220–21, 228
    condemning of, **2:**124–26
    of Jesus's brothers, **1:**452–53
    in Nazareth, **1:**528
    perishing in, **2:**612–13
    stubbornness of, **1:**519–22
unconditional election, **1:**394–96, 653
ungodly, **1:**37
unhappiness, **1:**274–75
union with Christ, **1:**312–13; **2:**450, 496
    in death, **2:**621–22
Unitarians, **2:**275
United States Army, **1:**309
upbringing, **1:**557, 565
upstaging, **1:**197
utilitarianism, **2:**515–17
Uzziah, **2:**111

Valley of Dry Bones, **2:**444, 668
Van Til, Cornelius, **1:**386
Venn, John, **2:**18
verberatio, **2:**524, 546

Via Dolorosa, **2:**546

vicarious sacrifice, **1:**647; **2:**66

Victory Boys' Camp, **1:**556

video clips, in worship, **1:**259

vine, **1:**539; **2:**281–83, 288

vineyard and tenants, parable of, **1:**40

virgin birth, **1:**7, 413, 452, 473; **2:**374, 554

voice, John the Baptist as, **1:**79

voice of God, **1:**336, 566

    in low whisper to Elijah, **2:**218, 220

voice of Jesus, **1:**620–21, 657; **2:**58–59

Voltaire, **1:**471

Warfield, Benjamin B., **1:**135–36; **2:**31, 45–46

water

    in Gospel of John, **1:**266, 589; **2:**594–95

    flowing from rock, **1:**480

    necessity of, **1:**226–27

    as sign of Holy Spirit, **1:**484–85

water and the Spirit, **1:**152–53

water jar, **1:**265–66, 268

Watson, Thomas, **1:**321; **2:**261, 672

Watts, Isaac, **1:**531; **2:**611, 389

Way, **2:**210

weak faith, **1:**287, 408, 541

weakness, **1:**33, 222; **2:**141

wealth, **1:**96, 380, 637–38; **2:**73, 607

weddings, **1:**121

weeds, parable of, **2:**294–95

week, as unit of time, **1:**479

weeping, **2:**47–48

Wesley, Charles, **1:**404; **2:**402, 530, 662

West, moral collapse of, **2:**452

Westminster Confession of Faith, **1:**54, 321; **2:**17–18, 326

Westminster Shorter Catechism, **1:**465; **2:**257, 298, 466

Whitefield, George, **1:**77, 654

whoever–statements, **1:**392

wickedness, **1:**144–48

wild ox, **2:**557

will, bondage of, **1:**415–16

will of God, **1:**463–64, 468, 582; **2:**453

will of man, **1:**51

will of the flesh, **1:**51

wine, as symbol of joy, **1:**123

Winner, Lauren, **1:**146

"with Christ," **2:**471–72

witness, **1:**27–31, 34, 76–84, 93, 104, 110, 271, 277, 288, 329–31, 338–39, 365, 518, 671; **2:**56, 78, 191–92, 201, 220, 225, 322–23, 327–32, 662–63

    and church unity, **2:**464

    as objective and subjective, **2:**325

wolves, **1:**630

woman at the well. *See* Samaritan woman

woman caught in adultery, **1:**500–508; **2:**689

women

    at the crucifixion, **2:**558

    in the ministry of Jesus, **1:**220; **2:**670

Word

    became flesh, **1:**12, 54, 61

    eternity of, **1:**7–8

    tabernacled among us, **1:**55–56

Word and Spirit, **1:**438–39

Word of God, **1:**160, 336, 374; **2:**127–28, 277

    confidence in, **1:**533

    divides, **1:**497

    and faith, **1:**286–87

    feeds the flock, **2:**711

    as living and active, **1:**115

    produces cleansing, **2:**288

    sanctification from, **2:**442–45

    sufficiency of, **2:**219

    treasuring of, **2:**422

work, **1:**306

works of Christ, as witness, **1:**27

works righteousness, **1:**301–4, 598, 618

works, salvation by, **2:**97

world

    blending with, **2:**119

calling into, 2:451–52
condemnation of, 2:318–19
conviction of, 2:335–42
danger of, 2:431
darkness of, 1:611–12
does not know God, 1:37–38; 2:479
as divided, 1:652
glory of, 2:413
hatred of, 1:457; 2:311–21, 329–31, 437
in high priestly prayer, 2:140–41
John's use of, 1:36, 170–71
love of, 2:98
peace of, 2:274
rejection of Jesus, 1:36, 44, 478
separation from, 2:480
setting agenda for the church, 2:440
sin of, 1:88, 545
as unbelieving, 1:37–38
values of, 2:514–17
world hunger, 1:26; 2:440
world religions, reliance upon law, 1:68–69
World War I, 1:173
World War II, 1:274, 555, 659–60
worldliness, 1:37, 356, 369, 432; 2:377, 457, 612
worldly approval, 1:569
worldly glory, 2:104
wordly pleasures, 1:306
wordly princes, 2:511
worldly success, 1:637
worm, 2:557
worship, 1:14; 2:39, 474
    attendance at, 2:678

in Christ, 1:260–61
with fervent and sincere gratitude, 1:146
on Lord's Day, 2:678
as seeker-sensitive, 1:253–54
in spirit, 1:254–57
in truth, 1:257–59
zeal for, 1:131–34, 136
wounds of Christ, 2:659, 679–80
wrath of God, 1:12, 22, 173, 183, 215, 239, 511, 552, 578; 2:105, 108, 176, 304, 336, 382, 403, 497–98
fell on Christ, 2:547, 566, 576–77, 580, 583

Yahweh, 1:260, 373, 385, 574; 2:370, 417–18
Yahweh Sabaoth, 2:418
Yahweh-Yireh, 2:418
Yancey, Philip, 2:156
Yastrzemski, Carl, 1:62
Yong, Amos, 1:419
Young, E. J., 2:398
Young, Egerton, 1:651

Zacchaeus, 1:591, 620
Zacharias, Ravi, 1:142, 439–40; 2:15
Zamperini, Louis, 1:554–56
Zealots, 2:83, 523
Zechariah (father of John the Baptist), 1:512, 587
Zechariah (prophet), 1:256; 2:84, 89, 528, 601, 604
Zweig, Ferdynand, 1:251

AVAILABLE IN THE REFORMED EXPOSITORY COMMENTARY SERIES

1 Samuel, by Richard D. Phillips
1 Kings, by Philip Graham Ryken
Esther & Ruth, by Iain M. Duguid
Daniel, by Iain M. Duguid
Jonah & Micah, by Richard D. Phillips
Zechariah, by Richard D. Phillips
The Incarnation in the Gospels, by Daniel M. Doriani,
Philip Graham Ryken, and Richard D. Phillips
Matthew, by Daniel M. Doriani
Luke, by Philip Graham Ryken
John, by Richard D. Phillips
Acts, by Derek W. H. Thomas
Galatians, by Philip Graham Ryken
Ephesians, by Bryan Chapell
Philippians, by Dennis E. Johnson
1 Timothy, by Philip Graham Ryken
Hebrews, by Richard D. Phillips
James, by Daniel M. Doriani

FORTHCOMING

Ecclesiastes, by Douglas Sean O'Donnell
1 Peter, by Daniel M. Doriani